$6 ⁹⁵

S-1

Keenan

D1444674

The Family

Robert O. Blood, Jr.

THE FREE PRESS
A DIVISION OF MACMILLAN PUBLISHING CO., INC.
New York

COLLIER MACMILLAN PUBLISHERS
London

THE FREE PRESS
A Division of Macmillan Publishing Co., Inc.
866 Third Avenue, New York, New York 10022

Collier–Macmillan Canada Ltd., Toronto, Ontario

Library of Congress Catalog Card Number: 71–171039

Printed in the United States of America

printing number
3   4   5   6   7   8   9   10

ACKNOWLEDGMENTS

The author and publisher gratefully thank the following for permission to
quote from their works:

Phillippe Aries. *Centuries of Childhood: A Social History of Family Life*, translated
by Robert Baldick. Copyright © 1962 by Jonathan Cape Ltd. Reprinted by permission of Alfred A. Knopf, Inc., and Jonathan Cape Ltd.

Judith Blake. *Family Structure in Jamaica: The Social Context of Reproduction.*
© 1961 by The Free Press. Reprinted by permission of The Macmillan Company.

J. K. Campbell. *Honour, Family and Patronage: A Study of Institutions and Moral
Values in a Greek Mountain Community*, 1964. Reprinted by permission of The
Clarendon Press, Oxford.

Elizabeth Colson. *Marriage and the Family Among the Plateau Tonga*, 1958.
Reprinted by permission of the author and Manchester University Press for the
Rhodes–Livingstone Institute.

E. E. Evans–Pritchard. *Kinship and Marriage Among the Nuer*, 1951. Reprinted
by permission of The Clarendon Press, Oxford.

Hildred Geertz. *The Javanese Family.* © 1961 by The Free Press. Reprinted by
permission of The Macmillan Company.

William J. Goode. *World Revolutions and Family Patterns.* © 1963 by The Free
Press of Glencoe, a Division of The Macmillan Company. Reprinted by permission
of The Macmillan Company.

Alexander J. Humphreys. *New Dubliners: Urbanization and the Irish Family.*
Copyright © 1966 by Alexander J. Humphreys. Reprinted by permission of the
author, Fordham University Press, and Routledge & Kegan Paul, Ltd.

Mirra Komarovsky. *Blue-Collar Marriage.* Copyright 1964. Reprinted by permission of Random House, Inc.

David Landy. *Tropical Childhood: Cultural Transmission and Learning in a Rural
Puerto Rican Village*, 1959. Reprinted by permission of The University of North
Carolina Press.

Theodore Lidz, Alice R. Cornelison, Stephen Fleck, and Dorothy Terry. "The Intrafamilial Environment of Schizophrenic Patients: II. Marital Schism and Marital Skew," *The American Journal of Psychiatry,* vol. 114, 1957. Copyright 1957, the American Psychiatric Association. Reprinted by permission of Theodore Lidz and the American Psychiatric Association.

Elliot Liebow. *Tally's Corner: A Study of Negro Streetcorner Men.* Copyright © 1967 by Little, Brown and Company, Inc. Reprinted by permission of Little, Brown and Company (Inc.).

Leigh Miniturn and William W. Lambert. *Mothers of Six Cultures: Antecedents of Child Rearing,* 1964. Reprinted by permission of John Wiley & Sons, Inc.

A. R. Radcliffe–Brown and Daryll Forde, editors. *African Systems of Kinship and Marriage,* 1950. Reprinted by permission of the International African Institute.

Peter Townsend. *The Family Life of Old People: An Inquiry in East London,* 1957. Reprinted by permission of Humanities Press, Inc. and Routledge & Kegan Paul, Ltd.

Beatrice B. Whiting. *Six Cultures: Studies of Child Rearing* (New York: Wiley), 1963. Reprinted by permission of the author.

Peter Wilmott and Michael Young. *Family and Class in a London Suburb,* 1960. Reprinted by permission of Humanities Press, Inc. and Routledge & Kegan Paul, Ltd.

CONTENTS

PREFACE

This book is an outgrowth of two decades of teaching courses on the sociology of the family to students at William Penn College, the Merrill-Palmer Institute, the University of Michigan, and International Christian University (in Japan). Although I used many different textbooks during those years, I never found one which was comprehensive, systematic, and analytical enough to satisfy me. I wanted to understand (and help my students understand) why the family is the way it is under varying social conditions and to make sense out of the internal structures and processes involved in family life. To achieve this understanding required bringing together scattered materials from a widely diverse literature, much of it written in a language too technical for the average undergraduate to understand, and in any case written from diverse viewpoints. Writing this book has been an exciting experience in making sense out of that literature and integrating it into a systematic whole which I believe will stimulate the thinking not only of students but of their teachers as well.

I hasten to add that even though I have attempted a comprehensive review of the scientific literature, I am well aware that I have not been able to read all of the wealth of significant research which has been published. There comes a point in writing a textbook when the author must resolutely forego the temptation to read any more books and devote himself to writing his own. I regret this necessity, but that is one aspect of the finiteness of human existence. Fortunately, I can look forward to including more of the present literature (as well as future writings) in subsequent revisions of this text. In the meantime, I dare to offer this first edition as a contribution to your understanding of the family.

Pendle Hill
Wallingford, Pennsylvania

ROBERT O. BLOOD, JR.

THE FAMILY AND ITS SOCIAL ENVIRONMENT

Family patterns vary enormously in different parts of the world, at different times in human history, and even within a given society at a particular time. The task of Part One of this book is to answer the question: Why? Why do families behave as they do? Does sheer chance govern the forms they take, or do external forces shape them?

The social sciences are based on the assumption that human behavior can be understood as the result of social forces. Behavior is not simply random, either for individuals or for groups. Generalizations can be made about tendencies for people to react in certain ways to particular stimuli. The task of social scientists is to look for such generalizations which make human behavior understandable.

In the case of families, the task is the same. Although the title of this book is "the family" (singular), this concept applies only to the family as a social institution, in contrast to the economy or the political system or the educational system. Only at a high level of abstraction is it possible to talk about *the family* in general. Because the concrete world is composed of diverse family patterns, we must either speak of families in the plural or refer to particular family types, such as the blue-collar family, the medieval family, or the Chinese family.

It is easy to *describe* family types. But reading such descriptions makes one no more a social scientist than touring a foreign country makes one a comparative sociologist. To see Venice and Paris is to learn *what* is there, but not *why*. Only as one begins to *compare* one culture to another (and especially large numbers of cultures to each other) can generalizations emerge. Then differences between Catholic countries and Protestant countries may indicate some effects of religion. Or differences between big cities and small towns may reveal effects of urbanization. And as soon as one starts thinking about effects, one begins to understand why.

In the first half of this book, I will attempt to explain why family life takes varying forms. Each chapter of Part One will seek to explain the external sources of such facets of family life as the formation, growth, and differentiation of families. These internal aspects are treated as dependent variables affected by forces outside the family.

Conversely, the external forces are treated as independent variables whose variance causes family life to assume particular patterns. To talk about causes is to be bold—some would say even foolhardy—in the present state of the social sciences. How certain I can be about those causes varies greatly—but mostly on the thin side. In searching for links between variables, I will try to find solid evidence. But when the evidence peters out, I will hazard a guess. To write this way is to stick my neck out, risking that future research may chop it off. But, in the meantime, perhaps the generalizations and the explanations which I propose here will stimulate others to test and prove them so that the sociology of the family may advance toward greater precision and certainty.

THE EFFECT OF EXTERNAL SYSTEMS ON THE FAMILY

I will explore the impact of the social environment on the family in two stages. First I will examine the effect of other social institutions on the family under conditions of equilibrium. After that, I will turn to the impact of social change and mobility on the family.

If the effect of other social institutions is to be understood, those institutions must be thought of as variables. One kind of variability is the *presence or absence* of the institutions themselves. For example, in primitive societies the school does not exist as a separate institution. This makes it possible to compare families in societies with and without school systems. A more important kind of variability involves the *form* that an institution takes. Governments may be weak or powerful, economies agrarian or industrial, religion Buddhist or Hindu. By comparing families under such varying social circumstances, one can assess the impact of those institutions on family life.

Influence between social institutions is reciprocal. The family influences other social institutions as well as being influenced by them. For example, William J. Goode (1963)* believes that certain family systems facilitate industrialization as much as the latter affects family systems. However, in this book I am primarily concerned with the effect of society on the family and will largely ignore the reverse effect. This is not to decry the value of the latter, but to circumscribe my task. My concern, then, is how each social institution makes the family what it is.

chapter one
THE ECONOMIC SYSTEM AND THE FAMILY

The choice of which system to begin with is partly arbitrary, but the economic system is a good place to start. Especially in simple societies on the margin of starvation, economic sustenance is related to the very survival of the family. Hence the tasks of staying alive command extraordinary attention. Even for societies under more secure economic conditions, economic

* Parenthetical dates refer to the date of publication of references listed in the References section, pp. 630–648.

roles consume more time than any other activities outside the home in all cases except that of the privileged leisure class.

The importance of economic forces is more than just a question of time. I have already suggested that in primitive societies, the economics of family life is a matter of life and death. In advanced societies, one may be able to take for granted that there is enough food and shelter for survival. But even there, economic factors powerfully intrude upon the family. For example, the location of the husband's work determines whether he sees his family constantly or only briefly between dawn and dusk. The economic system similarly determines whether wives must work for their husbands, may work for someone else, or may not work at all. Such drastic alternatives in the allocation of the partner's working hours profoundly affect the life of the family.

One need not be a Marxist in order to conclude that the economic system is important for the family. So it may be a correspondingly appropriate social institution with which to begin.

THE MEANS OF SUBSISTENCE

Among the economies the world has known, I will focus on three: hunting and gathering economies, agrarian economies, and industrial economies. I will treat these economies as pure types or "ideal types." Before discussing the effect of these economic systems on the family, some brief explanations are in order.

Hunting and gathering economies are the most primitive of the three. They depend parasitically on whatever nature has to offer. If the number of people is small and the number of animals large, a hunting and gathering economy may offer a lavish and dependable food supply. But only temporarily. The human population tends to increase until the hunters and gatherers deplete the food supply. The per capita share decreases until starvation sets in. In the long run, a crude equilibrium may emerge between the number of people and the amount of food, but the location of that equilibrium is likely to be on the precarious edge of starvation. Characteristic of most hunting and gathering societies, therefore, is an undependable food supply. When the hunter is lucky, there is food to spare and people gorge themselves. But when luck fails, they starve.

Agriculture is a major step forward. No longer does the community depend merely on what nature has to offer. The farmer improves on nature, increasing the food which can be derived from a particular area of land. The larger the number of people, the more hands there are to work the land, so production and population increase hand in hand—up to a point. The threat of famine is further reduced by the ability to store some of the new crops. Whereas the flesh of game animals soon spoils in the hot and moist climates where many primitive peoples live, the grains and cereals which are the staple crops of agrarian societies are more easily stored and shipped to guard against temporary or localized crop failures. Agrarian societies thereby acquire an economic stability unknown to most hunting and gathering societies.

The chief characteristic of industrial societies is change. Technological innovation accelerates in the later stages of industrialization. The standard of living provided by machines and other inventions rises indefinitely. Change and rising affluence create a very different setting for family life.

Having classified the three major types of economies, I can now examine their impact on particular facets of family structure and functioning.

Family Formation

In primitive societies, the means of subsistence are so ineffective that population clusters are small. If population grows very large in one locality, the food supply which could be gathered within a day's journey from home base would be too sparse to sustain life. Not only must such communities remain small but they must be homogeneous. If the food supply is precarious, every man must join in the hunt. If every man is a hunter, there can be no specialization of occupational roles among males. And without a division of labor, there is no basis for stratification of rich and poor or for any other social differentiation among heads of families.

In small, homogeneous communities, children and young people tend to be given free rein by their parents. On the one hand, parents know that their children will remain under the supervision of their friends, because no one is a stranger in such a community. On the other hand, parents know that there is no danger of their children becoming involved with the "wrong" people. If everyone is the same, there are no "bad" people (just as there are no "good" people).

Before marriage, this social homogeneity promotes a permissive attitude toward sexual experimentation. Adolescent boys and girls in most primitive societies are free to engage in sexual intercourse. This sexual freedom is closely related to a subsequent freedom to choose one's own marriage partner. If the community is essentially homogeneous, parents don't care whom one marries. If all young people are socially equal, there can be no such thing as a "bad" marriage. Therefore parents don't have to worry about protecting children from marrying the "wrong" person. Family formation can be viewed relatively nonchalantly and entrusted to young people themselves.

By contrast, most agrarian societies place family formation under the strict control of the elders. This stems from the dependence of agrarian families on the ownership of land. Unlike hunters, whose fortune depends mostly on luck, the fortune of a farming family depends on hard work and careful husbanding of tangible resources. Gradually over the generations, some families become large landholders and others sink into tenancy or serfdom. This creates a rigid form of social stratification because the handing down of land from generation to generation so largely determines the economic status of the heirs. Stratification divides the population into social classes which prefer not to intermarry (or in the case of castes are prohibited from intermarrying). In a stratified society, a high status family would risk losing prestige and economic security if a child were to marry beneath himself. To protect the integrity of the family wealth, agrarian parents carefully control their children before marriage and at the time of mate selection. Before marriage, lovemaking and sex play are typically prohibited, especially for girls from high status families. Selection of marriage partners is taken away from young people and exercised by parents in negotiation between families either directly or through a matchmaker. In such ways, elders insure that the next generation will carry on family traditions and maintain family wealth intact.

Preserving the family wealth is most difficult not for the biggest land-owners but for the smallest. Population growth under equal inheritance splits the land again and again until further subdivision would make the average family's plot so small that it would not keep a family alive. At that point, inheritance patterns tend to shift from equality to unilateral inheritance (usu-ally by the first-born son, *i.e.,* "primogeniture"). This prevents the land from being further subdivided.

Primogeniture directly affects family formation. Either the son must bring his bride into his parents' household or must not marry until his father has died or retired. In rural Ireland, sons traditionally worked for their fathers until they were well into their thirties, by which time the father was ready to retire and the inheriting son could marry and take over the farm (Humphreys, 1966). In agrarian societies generally, the problem of safe-guarding the family land tends to take the process of family formation out of the hands of young people and to concentrate it in the hands of those who own and control that land. This concentration of power has less effect on residual sons who will not inherit the land. In some agrarian societies they go off to the city or go abroad to seek their fortune, which gives them correspondingly more freedom in premarital behavior and mate selection.

The less such alternative economic opportunities are available, the more parents must try to provide all their children with the economic pre-requisites for marriage. Sometimes this takes the form of a dowry which the bride carries into marriage; sometimes, of a bride price paid by the man's family. The larger the economic transaction involved, the more young people must depend on their parents to be able to marry. In settled agrarian socie-ties, the economic alternatives are apt to be few. If the land is monopolized by the elders, the next generation must depend on the generosity of those elders to be able to marry at all.

A special problem arises for families with no son to take over the farm. Farmers whose ancestors struggled to acquire and improve the family land are reluctant to see control of that land pass to a stranger even if he is the husband of a daughter. To minimize this sense of loss and to maximize control over the land, sonless parents in many agrarian societies adopt a husband for the eldest daughter. Adoption changes the young man from being a mere in-law to being a member of the family subject to the full authority of the parents. In this way, continuity of the family line and the family name from generation to generation is guaranteed.

In industrial societies, young people no longer depend on their parents for economic opportunity. Money to support a new family is secured not by working on one's father's farm but by working for an independent em-ployer. This enables the son to marry whenever he is old enough to find a job and gives him an independent economic base from which to defy his parents' wishes in deciding both when to marry and whom to marry. In industrial societies, therefore, parents lose the economic leverage which they previously held over family formation (Goode, 1963). Parental investment in children's marriages diminishes and children may marry without any working capital. Rather they marry in the expectation that an employer will pay them wages with which they can support a wife and children.

The ability of young people in industrial societies to marry independently of their parents destroys the power of parents over family formation. Self-selection of marriage partners returns to the human scene after having been eclipsed in the feudal era. However, self-selection in modern societies is more complicated than in primitive societies. The innovativeness of technological societies produces an increasingly specialized division of labor. Stratification does not disappear, but it does become less rigid. If occupations are no longer inherited with the family estate, social mobility becomes possible. Young men by their own efforts may rise above their fathers' stations. And a young woman who makes a "good" marriage is elevated to her husband's station rather than dragging him down to hers and social ostracism (as happened in feudal India when a Brahmin married an untouchable).

Even within social strata, there is little uniformity. Occupations of similar ranks and prestige may differ sharply in the type of work involved. A given social class is no longer homogeneous in its values and attitudes. The individual person emerges from the solidarity of the primitive band or the feudal caste to acquire a distinctive personality. Personality differences complicate the task of mate selection so that even if parents were given the power to decide, they could no longer be trusted to find compatible partners for their children. These complexities of modern technology force the individual to do his own selecting.

If the individual is to shop around for his own partner, he must have a great deal of premarital freedom. He must be able to date potential marriage partners to test their suitability for marriage. He must be able to get to know members of the opposite sex as individuals. This necessary freedom of premarital association makes possible considerable freedom in sexual behavior.

In summary, then, the characteristic living and working conditions of hunting, agrarian, and industrial economies produce patterns of family formation which are respectively permissive, restrictive, and permissive. However, the similarity of hunting and industrial societies masks a contrast between the relatively standardized personalities of eligible partners in primitive societies which makes permissiveness possible, and the diversity of personalities in industrial societies which makes permissiveness necessary.

Family Growth

Once families are formed under these three economic systems, they also differ in their patterns of bearing and rearing children.

Child-Bearing The number of children born in both primitive and feudal societies tends to be close to the physiological capacity of human beings because effective means of birth control are not generally available. The chief difference between the two economies lies in the ability of the average family to support children once they are born. In hunting societies, the birth of a son provides another potential hunter but the birth of a daughter increases the number of non-hunters. If the pressure of population on food resources is critical, a tribe may turn to female infanticide. Cruel though the deliberate extermination of baby girls is, the alternative may be just as cruel: starvation for the whole community. Without deliberate intervention in population growth, starvation and disease will restore a Malthusian balance. Infant girls are not necessarily killed; they may simply be allowed to die unattended in the wilderness. In any case, the larger the ratio of males to females, the more easily the family will survive.

An additional value in altering the sex ratio at birth is the hazardousness of male occupations. In primitive societies, men spend much of their time from adolescence onward in fighting. Either they fight animals in the hunt for food or men from other tribes who encroach on their territory. In the first instance, it is not always the animal who becomes food for the hunter. Primitive weapons may prove no match for animal fangs and teeth, especially if the animal is larger and stronger than the man. In the defense of territory against invasion, the primitiveness of weapons may reduce the death toll below the body counts of modern warfare. Nevertheless, even bare-handed men can kill one another. So the occupational injury and death rate for men in primitive societies is high, reinforcing the value of an unbalanced infant sex ratio.

In agrarian societies, the family's ability to support extra mouths is more predictable. Up to a point, at least, extra children can be counted on to support themselves by their own work. From early childhood, boys and girls are expected to care for small animals and to weed and cultivate the fields. By the time they reach adolescence, they may not only support themselves but contribute a surplus to the family wealth. The larger a farm family, the more prosperous it tends to become.

Having at least one son to inherit the land is essential. Since infant and child mortality due to disease are almost as high in agrarian societies as in primitive societies, extra sons provide "spare parts" to fill gaps in the line of succession.

A third reason for wanting children is their ability to support parents in old age. In an economic system focused on the responsibility of each family to care for its own, children are the security on which the aged depend once they retire from active life. By contrast, in primitive societies, the shortage of food may require the sacrifice or self-sacrifice of the aged as another means of reducing the burden on the food supply.

Only with the rise of industry do children become economic liabilities. To be sure, in the early years of the industrial revolution, parents sent their children to work in the cotton mills of England and New England (Aries, 1962). But as that revolution proceeded, the increasing productivity of industry freed working men from depending on children for family survival. As wages went up, new laws prohibited parents from exploiting their children. These laws converted children from assets into liabilities.

Modern science provided knowledge of the process of conception and technical means of preventing conception. Most industrial societies responded to the opportunity by slashing their birth rates. In many, the ideal number of children became two: one boy and one girl. Within industrialized societies, only families who continued to gain their subsistence from the land continued to prefer larger numbers of children. For example, farm wives in Jamaica typically described families as "large" when they had ten children, whereas non-farm families on the same island thought families became large when they reached seven. Similarly, nonfarm women became seriously interested in practicing birth control as soon as they had two or three children whereas farm wives did not become interested until they had four or more (Stycos and Back, 1964:30,57). Thus the impact of the whole system of subsistence on family growth patterns is echoed in consistent differences within a society as well.

In the later stages of industrialization when industry became so productive that workers could afford television and a new car and multiple children besides, the birth rate rose again. Even then, however, the new ideal of three children fell far short of the large-family ideal of agrarian societies. However, as long as agrarian societies were untouched by modern medicine, their number of children who survived to maturity was not much greater than that of affluent societies whose children could more dependably be counted on to survive.

Childbirth Rituals   In underdeveloped countries, the hazardousness of life creates anxiety about whether pregnant women will survive and their babies be safely born. Lacking scientific understanding and medical skill for coping with these life-and-death crises, such peoples develop rituals which they believe will safeguard mother and child, invoking magical and supernatural protection against evil forces (Stephens, 1963). Some of these practices may have practical utility. For instance, a post-partum sex taboo prevents mothers from becoming pregnant again too soon. Men with pregnant wives were forbidden by one Melanesian culture to hunt or fish, making them available to provide the physical and emotional security which pregnant women cherish (Powdermaker, 1933). However, the official reason why such men should not hunt and fish was not that they were needed at home but that they were sure to have bad luck if they tried to snare game under these circumstances. The same tribe extended the concept of post-partum sex taboos to the owner of pigs: For a month after a sow had given birth, the owner and his wife must not have intercourse or else the piglets would sicken and die. Magical practices thus applied to the welfare of animals as well as of wives and children. In general, the more precarious the existence, the more elaborate the rituals to offset the insecurity of their economic conditions.

Conversely, in developed societies, modern medicine has reduced the need for magical practices. The more developed the economy, the fewer the anxiety-allaying practices required. Nevertheless, Read (1944) described how anxiety about the pain of childbirth could be relieved by prenatal classes and exercise. And more recently American husbands have enrolled in childbirth-preparation classes reminiscent of the *couvade* (a custom in primitive societies where the husband imitates some of the childbirth behavior of his wife). Hence economic development has not terminated childbirth rituals completely but decreased their number and made their content more instrumental in nature.

Child-Rearing   Once a child is born, his up-bringing is affected by economic conditions. In many primitive societies, the same anxiety which produces ritual safeguards before birth results in extraordinary attention to survival needs after birth. Stephens noted (1963) that 17 primitive societies gave extravagant attention to their newborn infants, whereas only four gave little nurturance (one of which was the Rajputs of agrarian India, hardly a precarious economy). The practical implications of this constant attention can be seen in Lewis' observation (1951) that after weaning finally occurs in Tepoztlan and children are largely neglected, they are apt to sicken and die.

By contrast, in more secure societies, children are weaned earlier or given animal milk from the very beginning. Modern health and sanitation practices have greatly reduced infant mortality. But the lesser attention given young children by their mothers and their away-all-day fathers in such societies may deprive today's children of body contact and other nurturant acts which they could benefit from. (Harlow and Harlow [1966] found that contact with a warm-bodied, soft mother is prized by infant monkeys.)

In primitive societies, the mother has no choice. Either she must nurse the child or it will die. Modern technology gives mothers a choice and most American mothers choose the easy way, substituting the bottle for the breast. It is possible, however, that as the United States becomes even more affluent, mothers may become more nurturant toward their children. Maternal leisure and the consumption orientation of contemporary America predispose parents to more indulgent and permissive attitudes toward small children.

These permissive attitudes recall the permissiveness of hunting and gathering societies toward premarital association and mate-selection. I suggested earlier that the smallness and homogeneity of the primitive community made it possible for parents to entrust their children to the care of neighboring adults and of their peers. In those societies, this trust develops long before the child reaches adolescence and eligibility for marriage. From the time he is old enough to wander away from home, the mother feels confident that he will be watched over by her friends and relatives (Mead, 1949). Since in primitive societies there is rarely a delinquent subculture among young people, the mother need not fear the influence of alien peers. So tightly knit is the primitive community and so uniform its culture that the mother can afford to be relaxed about her children's socialization. In such a homogeneous community, there are no alternative cultural patterns which the child might learn. With only one pattern of behavior available, socialization into that pattern is an almost inevitable outcome of mere residence in the community. In general, then, post-infants in primitive tribes are not closely tied to the mother's "apron-strings" but are free to play about the community until the time comes to begin productive work.

This does not mean that the child has nothing to learn or that it does not matter what he learns. The precariousness of life "on the frontier" forces the family and the tribe at large to depend on every son's learning the arts of hunting and warfare. But each family can share this teaching responsibility with the whole community because the undifferentiated community agrees unanimously on what every child should learn.

The content of that teaching has been studied by Barry *et al.* (1959). Hunting and fishing societies train for achievement, self-reliance and independence. These values reflect the need for the hunter to dare to go out into the jungle and fight his adversary to the death. Conversely, such societies place little stress on training for responsibility and obedience. In an unstratified society, there is no one to obey (except a chief who is usually little more than the best hunter) and no one to assume responsibility for. For the hunter and the primitive warrior, it's every man for himself.

So great are the hazards of these primitive occupational roles that such societies must be sure that their apprentices are fully trained before they are turned loose in the jungle. The transition from childhood to adulthood is generally marked by initiation ceremonies which make fraternity hazing look like child's play. Some kind of ordeal, frequently an extensive sojourn alone in the wilderness or painful torture impresses upon the novitiate the seriousness of his new role as a man on whom the community will rely for survival.

The independence training in primitive societies should not be confused with an encouragement of creativity. Primitive societies are illiterate. They must depend on their old people, on those with the longest memories, for knowledge about how things have been done before. This dependence deprives a society of information about the remote past when life might have been different. It reduces close to zero any awareness of social change. Moreover, primitive societies lack means of transportation or communication which would bring them into contact with different cultures. Social isolation reinforces their sense that the remembered way of doing things is the only way. Faced with a perennial fear of defeat by hostile forces, primitive men cling fiercely to traditional ways and sacramentalize them. They produce a sacred society, subject neither to criticism nor to change.

Under such tradition-directed circumstances, the independence inculcated in children is a personal independence, an ability to function independently in the traditional manner, not an independence from the culture itself.

Agrarian societies are almost as tradition-bound as primitive tribes, but not so desperately so. The beginnings of literacy among the upper strata enable the development of political and social philosophy and of special careers for independent spirits. In medieval Europe, for example, men and women who wished to escape from the normal pattern of life could join the more idealistic life of monastic orders.

But one of the vows which monks and nuns must take is obedience—which is precisely the key value in feudal societies. Barry and his colleagues found that agrarian societies stress two values in raising children: training in obedience and training for responsibility. These are two sides of the same coin: Obedience is what one owes his superiors and responsibility is what one owes his dependents. A feudal child begins life owing obedience to almost everyone and gradually acquires responsibility.

What is it about an agrarian economy which makes obedience and responsibility so important? The landed basis of agriculture stratifies a feudal society into frozen castes and feudal families into superior and inferior generations. The dense population of settled farm land leaves little room for the lonely vigils of the jungle hunter. The members of a feudal society are bound together by inherited, unchangeable social relationships between those who owe obedience and those who carry the burden of responsibility. In the family, faithful obedience guarantees that one will inherit the family property without which life would be impoverished, and exercising responsibility guarantees that there will be something for one's progeny to inherit.

Barry did not include industrial societies in his study, but Pearlin and Kohn (1966) made a cross-national comparison of quasi-feudal Italy with the ultra-modern United States. Their Italian families still emphasized obedience, even though their sample was drawn from Torino, a North Italian industrial city. Presumably, however, that emphasis was not as strong as it would have been in Southern Italy (the most feudal part). By contrast, Pearlin and Kohn's American parents emphasized self-control. This suggests that industrialization undermines belief in the virtue of sheer obedience and replaces it with a valuation of more independent behavior.

The self-control taught by modern parents resembles the self-reliance taught by primitive parents. Perhaps the primitive desire for bravery in the face of physical danger is analogous to the modern desire for aggressiveness in taking advantage of economic opportunities. However, a different note is introduced by the complexity of industrial society. The payoff of self-control for modern children is to enable them to be upwardly mobile. This means that they are capable of learning a new way of life rather than simply imitating the ways of their parents. In this sense, industrial parents teach their children to be psychologically even more self-reliant than do primitive parents.

If children in industrial societies are to learn things which their parents do not know, someone else must teach them. That someone is the school teacher. In Chapter 5 I will examine the effects of the educational system in detail. Suffice it to note here that only in industrial societies do rank and file parents surrender the custody of their children to outside experts.

One other feature of an industrial economy is relevant: Industrial technology is constantly changing. This means that even a child who does not rise above his parents' station in life must live in a different world from theirs. Social change is an intrinsic feature of industrial societies, unlike the desperate sacredness of tribal customs and the frozen structure of feudal kingdoms. The modern child must be taught to be self-reliant not only to better his life but simply to keep up with changing times. Parents at best can launch their children into such a world, not lead them through it.

Family growth, then, in primitive and feudal societies, is a matter of urgent personal and social concern, whereas in modern societies, it can be approached with greater confidence and with greater freedom of choice. For modern parents, children are a consumption good to be enjoyed rather than a source of economic survival or security. Thanks to technology, children can be born at will and inducted into a brave new world where they soon become relatively independent of their increasingly obsolete parents.

Family Structure

Hunting, agrarian, and industrial societies differ also in their family structure. Patterns which are present in rudimentary form in primitive societies are elaborated and institutionalized in feudal societies but largely abandoned in the modern era. In each case it seems possible to attribute much of the difference in family structure to the means of subsistence.

Sex Roles   In hunting and gathering societies, the only division of labor is by sex. In any given society, all men do the same things (hunting and warring) and all women do the same things. There is some variation between societies, but Murdock (1937) discovered a strong tendency for men to dominate in hunting large animals, fishing at sea, and making weapons. Women monopolized such domestic tasks as fire-tending, cooking, and weaving. Many of the masculine tasks took men far from home while the feminine tasks could be performed either in the hut or nearby.

Biological factors play important roles in determining this division of labor. In the struggle with man and beast, the larger physique and stronger musculature of men is an asset. Women conversely have a finer musculature which enables them to excel over clumsy-fingered men at such tasks as sewing and basket-weaving.

The fact that women get pregnant and nurse children is another determinant. Pregnant or nursing women are handicapped in traveling. Hence they tend to do the sedentary and localized tasks at home or near home. Even after an older child is weaned, his younger siblings tend to hobble his mother so that, as a side-effect, she can also conveniently care for older children. These limits on women's mobility confine them to lagoon fishing instead of deep-sea fishing, to rudimentary gardening, and to gathering berries and nuts in the nearby woods.

Insofar as all men perform the same tasks and those tasks are different from women's, sex roles in primitive societies are sharply segregated. This segregation is accentuated by male initiation ceremonies which admit boys to the sacred mysteries of the magic with which males placate the supernatural powers before embarking on hazardous expeditions. These secrets must be kept from women whose uncleanliness (manifested in menstrual bleeding and bleeding in childbirth) would contaminate and sap the power of the magic rites. Initiation ceremonies not only separate the men from the women but create intense solidarity among boys who are initiated together. Going through the same ordeal makes them feel peculiarly close for the rest of their lives.

Against this background it is understandable that men spend most of their leisure time together (and women likewise). With such contrasting roles in life, the two sexes have little in common and feel more comfortable among their own kind. To be sure, sexual intercourse is one of the forms of recreation in a primitive community and brings the sexes together physically. But we should beware of assuming that intercourse denotes psychological intimacy. That is largely reserved for persons of the same sex.

The segregation of the sexes does not in this instance mean that women have an especially low status. With the men away from home so much, women in primitive societies must be almost as self-reliant as men. Indeed, Barry *et al.* (1959) found a remarkably similar pattern in the child-rearing practices for girls to that which I have already described for boys. If men are to be able to go off on the hunt, their wives must be prepared to stay home alone. So girls as well as boys are taught to be self-reliant, independent, and achievement-oriented.

Self-reliant women are by definition not likely to be very submissive when their husbands return. Moreover, the division of labor by sex means that roles not performed by men must be performed by women. Insofar as a primitive tribe lives on the verge of starvation, the two sexes must collaborate to avoid that fate. Women's roles, then, are crucial as well as independent.

These two features make women economically important and roughly equal to men. They don't have complete equality, because the greater hazardousness of male roles gives men a prestige edge. But there is far more equality of the sexes in a typical hunting and gathering society than we will see in feudal societies.

One prerequisite for success in hunting and warfare is intimate knowledge of the terrain. A hunter must know the habits of his prey, where to find his elusive quarry at various seasons of the year and various times of the day. A warrior must know how to conceal himself from his foe, to cut him off in flight, to ambush him, to steal upon him in the day. Only those who have lived their whole lives in a particular hunting ground can have such intimate knowledge. Such factors mean that hunters tend either to marry local girls or to bring their brides into their home communities. For the man to move to the woman's village would be too risky. Hence matrilocality is rarely practiced among tribes dependent on hunting for their sustenance.

Peasant women in agrarian societies have important roles like their primitive forebears. The typical peasant woman works in the rice paddies or the fields alongside her husband. Her reproductive capacity provides the labor force for increasing the family wealth. So in peasant families, a man needs a hard-working and vigorous wife who can cooperate with him in cultivating the soil and bearing children. However, women need husbands even more. Feudal societies offer peasant women no alternative to marriage. (Religious roles are an option chiefly for high status women, and even then only for the exceptional few). So women depend on men more than vice versa, a factor which tends to lower their status.

However, the crucial difference between a hunting and an agrarian society is the fact that the peasant husband and wife work together. No longer is the husband away for hours or days at a time. Because he is home all the time, his wife need no longer be self-reliant. Although her work is important, it is more the contribution of an employee than of a partner. The man is the supervisor who tells his wife what to do.

Thus the settling of families on land tends to lower the status of women. This subordination can be seen in Barry's study where the emphasis on self-reliance drops more sharply for girls than for boys when agrarian societies are compared with hunting and fishing societies. The stabilization of the feudal family on the land subordinates the man to his elders and the woman to both her elders and her husband.

Where the means of subsistence involves raising animals, the roles of the sexes are intermediate between those in hunting and in agricultural societies. In a Greek mountain community, for example, Campbell (1964) found that the men were away much of the time tending their sheep in mountain pastures. This absence may explain why Barry and his associates found that girls in animal-raising societies were trained to be more self-reliant than in agricultural societies (though not as much as in hunting and fishing societies). In the Greek case, the stay-at-home women had auxiliary assignments with the animals. If a sick sheep needed nursing care, the shepherd brought it home for his wife to care for. If a feeding problem arose, the wife taught a bereaved ewe to suckle the extra lamb of a ewe with twins.

Industrialization gives women economic opportunities which are not dependent on their husbands. If a modern woman chooses to work, it will not be alongside her husband or working cooperatively on his behalf. Rather she ordinarily works for someone else. Independent employment raises the status of women.

Although external employment enables the modern woman to become self-reliant like her primitive predecessors, in other ways industrial society makes her even more her husband's equal and companion. Substituting machines for muscle power largely nullifies the prestige advantage and the role monopolization of men under primitive conditions. In a technological economy, women can do almost anything men can do (except for combat, which is still a jungle art). As the vocational roles of men and women lose their distinctiveness, their statuses and prestige tend to merge and they become able to understand and mingle with each other. The leisure-time segregation of the sexes disappears as their working-hours segregation disappears.

Although machines blur the consequences of the muscular differences between men and women, they do not affect the monopoly of women over childbearing and therefore over child-rearing. This continuing biological difference propels women into child-associated jobs such as school teaching. But the invention of birth control frees women from lifelong child-bearing and therefore diminishes the segregative impact of this biological factor.

Modern technology has developed labor-saving machinery and prepared foods, shrinking the number of hours required for keeping house and enabling women to combine the roles of housewife and working wife more easily. This too contributes to the convergence of the roles and statuses of the sexes in modern society.

Age Roles Both hunting and agrarian societies are conservative and resist change. The sacredness of custom and the lack of literacy make older men the repositories of wisdom. However, the precariousness of life undermines the prestige of those who have passed their prime physically. Hence it is mature adults, rather than the aged, who wield the most power.

In agrarian societies the position of the aged is enhanced by the security of existence and by their control of the land. It is no longer necessary to be physically agile in order to retain power, only to be mentally alert. Only with senility must the reins of power be surrendered. In agrarian societies, therefore, the position of the aged is powerful and secure. In feudal China, Confucianism codified the superiority of the aged in the doctrine of filial piety under which obedience was owed to one's elders while they lived and honor was due them after death. The power of the aged was institutionalized in the idealized family structure of agrarian societies—the multiple-generation family which *extended* through time over as many generations as were alive at the same time (and which is therefore called the "extended family" system). The priority given to the aged in agrarian societies gives rise to extended families and is in turn supported by that kind of family structure.

In contrast to both hunting and agrarian societies, industrial societies are not conservative. The continual and accelerating process of technological invention and scientific discovery produces corresponding changes in every facet of life. The faster life changes, the more rapidly parental education becomes obsolete. Even adults who enroll in refresher courses fall behind the oncoming generation who enjoy a fullblown modern education and do not have to unlearn old ways of doing things. These adult handicaps are compounded by the fact that it becomes more difficult to learn new ways the older one gets.

Industrial societies tend to be split therefore between bright young men with the latest training and the greatest creativity versus older men whose experiential advantage is undermined by the obsolescence of their knowledge. This unsettles the normal pattern of age grades. At the very least it lowers the older generation and raises the oncoming generation until age-grading becomes less rigid. In some cases, age grades may even be reversed, with younger men telling their elders what to do.

Generally speaking, then, age grades become less important in modern societies. In the family, the authority of parents is weakened. No longer can they expect unquestioning obedience. They may even discover that their children have something to teach them. Life in modern families becomes more of a give-and-take affair in which the generations treat each other increasingly as equals as the children approach maturity.

The effects of the economic system on the role of the aged can also be seen by examining the descent groups which exist in different societies. Such groups do not even exist in industrial societies, which trace their descent through ancestors on both the husband's and the wife's side but whose living antecedents do not form social groups which function as formal organizations. By contrast, in societies where the aged are important, the elders on one or both sides of the family tend to form powerful organizations through which they control the economic and domestic activities of their offspring.

TABLE 1-1 Descent Groups by Subsistence Activity

| | SUBSISTENCE ACTIVITY | | |
DESCENT GROUP	Hunting and Gathering or Fishing	Agriculture (Without Animals), Especially Slash and Burn*	Animal Husbandry
None	68%	37%	28%
Matrilineal and patrilineal	9	3	3
Matrilineal	7	24	6
Patrilineal	16	36	63
Total	100%	100%	100%
Number of Societies	82	129	176
Women do most of the work	1%	33%	9%

Adapted from d'Andrade, 1966:183.
* Slash-and-burn agriculture involves cutting down and burning forest growth in order to provide garden plots which are temporarily enriched by the ashes of the burned wood. This "fertilizer" is quickly dissipated, so the yield from this type of agriculture is low.

Table 1-1 shows that most hunting and gathering or fishing tribes do not have descent groups either. Two reasons may be suggested. The lack of any form of capital which could be transmitted to subsequent generations through inheritance gives a descent group no economic reason for existence. Secondly the life span in primitive societies is so short and unpredictable that there is a relatively weak personnel base on which to form organizations led by old people.

Table 1-1 shows that the greater the development of wealth, the greater the development of lineages. If that wealth is in the form of animals herded by men, men tend to dominate the lineage (*i.e.,* it is a patrilineal descent group). Matrilineal groups are relatively uncommon, but under the primitive conditions of slash-and-burn agriculture, women play relatively important occupational roles and correspondingly more often dominate the descent groups.

There is a considerable correlation between the economic roles of the sexes and the kinship roles which they play. But our primary concern here is not with sex roles but with age roles. Table 1-1 most dramatically shows the rise of kinship organizations dominated by the aged with the development of more advanced forms of agriculture. If we were to add a column for industrial societies, descent groups would presumably vanish with the disappearing power of the aged in such societies.

Household Complexity   Members of descent groups do not necessarily live together. However, the same age roles which lead to the formation of lineages through which parents control the lives of children also frequently lead them to retain their children at home even after marriage. Consequently there is also a correlation between the type of economy and the tendency of the structure of the immediate family to become multigenerational.

TABLE 1-2   Household Composition by Subsistence Activity

	SUBSISTENCE ACTIVITY		
HOUSEHOLD COMPOSITION	Hunting and Gathering Only	Agriculture Only	Animal Husbandry Plus Agriculture*
Nuclear families only	83%	46%	11%
Extended families	17	54	89
Total	100%	100%	100%
Number of Societies	24	160	18

Adapted from Nimkoff and Middleton (1960):217.
* Societies in which animal husbandry is at least as important as agriculture.

Table 1-2 shows a sharp divergence in household complexity in differing economic systems. Nuclear families (consisting of husband, wife, and children, but no other relatives) overwhelmingly predominate in tribes which rely exclusively on hunting and gathering as means of subsistence. At the other extreme, societies which depend as much on raising animals as on growing crops are even more likely to prefer extended (multiple-generation) families. The difference between agricultural societies with and without animals suggests that the possession of herds of animals predisposes families to become extended in form, *i.e.,* to keep at least one son at home even after he marries. I suggested earlier that one force tending toward family extension is the desire of landowning families to insure continuity in the ownership of their land. Another result of the rise of agriculture is presumably an increased economic ability to survive for longer years and to support a larger and more complex household. Now animal husbandry appears as a third factor in producing extended family systems. In most cases the animals involved are cattle or sheep. Even with sheep (but more especially with cattle, since they are so large), it becomes almost impossible for a man to provide the necessary care and protection if he has no sons to help him. Herding animals is a distinctively masculine responsibility; hence wives are little help except in caring for newborn or sick animals. If animals are not kept in enclosures and fed hay and grain but pastured on natural grasses, herders must become seminomadic, traveling far from home in the search for grass. If there are more than a few animals, one man can hardly control their movements on these journeys. Moreover, even a man who could ordinarily handle his herd needs occasional relief from 24-hour duty and needs emergency assistance to protect his animals from predatory animals and thieves. These practical concerns force a herder to rely on other men for assistance if he is to prosper and raise more than a few animals. In a money economy, additional assistance can be hired if one offers to pay enough. In simpler societies, a free labor market is rarely available and seldom dependable. The only dependable source of labor is within one's own household. Hence a man with a flock of sheep or a herd of cattle needs to keep at least one son with him in the household economy. The more sons he can secure, the larger his herd can grow, and the more efficiently and flexibly it can be cared for. Animal husbandry, in short, is a corporate, collective, cooperative activity, unlike intensive agriculture which can be handled successfully by one man with the help of his wife. Animal husbandry thus generates strong pressures for a patrilocal pattern of residence, requiring sons to remain at home after marriage.

Within agricultural societies, the ratio of men to land is not constant nor is the productivity of land uniform. As long as ample land is available, the formation of extended families is inhibited because sons may start their own farms on new land. When the supply of new land first becomes exhausted, conditions are ideal for the creation of an extended family system because farms tend to be large enough to support large households. In some parts of Japan, for example, farmhouses were traditionally large enough to house not only the older couple but multiple sons and their wives and children. As long as individual farms remain large, the ideal tends to be for extended families to be very large, embracing all sons and their families, who share equally in the family inheritance.

Such a large family system is not likely to endure indefinitely on a fixed land base. If a household containing two sons were to double in size in each succeeding generation, before long both house and land would become overtaxed. Ultimately such a large family system faces the threat either of collapsing into poverty, which would threaten the loss of the entire estate, or adopting some estate-preserving mechanism. A frequent solution to this centrifugal tendency is to adopt a more conservative inheritance policy. To replace equal inheritance which they can no longer afford, the family resorts to inheritance by only one son, sometimes the first (primogeniture), sometimes the last (ultimogeniture). In any case, continuity from generation to generation is maintained through only one son who becomes the stem through which the land is maintained intact. (Hence the name "stem family system" for this custom.) Once a stem system arises, it requires residual sons to establish independent families which remain nuclear in form for at least the first generation but which hopefully become stem families themselves in later generations if they acquire the economic base to do so.

If economic conditions are even more severe or if the physical isolation of a community prevents the emigration of non-stem sons, the family system may be altered even further. In one mountain area of Japan (Shirakawa-mura), the adaptation took the form of allowing only the eldest son to marry. All other sons and all daughters remained in the household but were not allowed to marry. Extra-legal sexual relationships provided nonmarrying daughters with children ineligible for inheritance. Thus the integrity of a relatively unproductive mountain landholding was safeguarded without enforcing complete celibacy on the residual population (Tamaki, 1959).

So far I have proceeded as though the chief way of complicating household composition were by adding generations. However, it is also possible to add extra marriage partners, especially extra wives. Polygyny (as this is called) is just as rare in hunting and gathering societies as vertically extended families, for many of the same reasons. To erect a complex family structure of any kind requires economic security and wealth. However, Osmond (1965) found that multiple wives were most characteristic of simple agriculture in which there was no use of the plow, whereas monogamy was more characteristic of intensive agriculture in which the ground was broken by the use of plows. It is not entirely clear what the causal factor is here, but it may be the role of women in the economy. Under simple agriculture, women may make a major economic contribution by growing their own crops using hoes and other simple tools. But plows are difficult for women to use, so an economy which relies on plowing reduces the economic importance of women and makes extra wives less self-supporting. When the evolution of agriculture passes beyond the hoe stage, families do not become less complex so much as shift their complexity from the horizontal to the vertical.

Perhaps this shift in the direction of extension provides another clue to the causal forces at work. Since simple agriculture normally produces less wealth than intensive agriculture, the lesser wealth is more apt to be entirely consumed in the present. By contrast, the greater wealth produced by advanced agricultural techniques offers more possibility for building up an estate to be handed down at death. And once the possibility of intergenerational transmission of property arises, there is a corresponding tendency to form an intergenerational household.

In any case, we should modify our general conception of the relation of the economic system to household complexity by suggesting that the nuclear families of hunting and gathering economies tend to be succeeded by the transitory complexity of polygyny in the early stages of agricultural technology, only to be succeeded in turn by the more permanent complexity of monogamous extended families under intensive agriculture.

Nimkoff and Middleton (1960) failed to include industrial societies in their study, but I assume that in most modern societies the nuclear family is the normative pattern. Goode (1963) concluded that the "fit" between the nuclear family system and the modern industrial system was basically close. Indeed the relationship between the two works both ways. A backward society which happens to have a nuclear family system can more easily become industrialized because (1) nuclear families can more easily move in response to shifting labor demands and (2) independent husbands are free to accumulate wealth which can be invested in economic enterprises (Habakkuk, 1955). Conversely, when a backward society with an extended family system is industrialized, the family system tends to be destroyed. Japan is sometimes cited (*e.g.,* by Greenfield, 1961) as an industrialized society where an extended family system has survived, but the facts belie this. For instance, the percentage of extended households was 52 percent in five rural prefectures in 1920, but in 1951 it was only 14 percent in a Tokyo ward (Dore, 1958). And even in rural Japan, farm boys have trouble finding wives because few modern girls are willing to live with their mothers-in-law. So the preference for neolocal residence bred in urban Japan has penetrated the countryside as well.

How does industrialization undermine extended family systems? The processes involved are the converse of the ways in which a nuclear family system aids industrialization. (1) Industrial jobs lure young men away from the farm by providing alternative employment (whereas in many feudal societies a son has no place to go and must stay home if he wants to survive). (2) Industrial jobs pay relatively high wages in comparison to subsistence agriculture. For such reasons, industrial jobs deprive rural families of the adult children necessary for the ongoing life of an extended family. (3) With the exception of family businesses, industrial employment seldom offers an economic basis for extended-family solidarity, since even if all the members of the family moved to a factory town, they would be employed as individuals, subject to uncoordinated hiring and firing by an alien employer (in contrast to the cooperative solidarity of an extended family working its own farm). (4) The very fact that family members are employed separately means that their fortunes tend to vary. Although the norms of extended family systems require that wealth be shared with one's kin, independently employed workers become increasingly reluctant to pool their money with lazier or unluckier relatives. Differential financial progress alienates kin from one another and further weakens the solidarity of the kin group. Such strains undermine whatever remnants of the extended family system may remain. Although exceptional extended families may be found in industrial societies, especially in their early stages, the ideal pattern shifts from this collective emphasis to the independence of a nuclear family system.

THE HUSBAND'S OCCUPATION AND HIS FAMILY BEHAVIOR

Most of the rest of this chapter will be concerned with the impact of particular aspects of industrial economies on family life. Within a complicated modern economy, the kind of work a man may do differs enormously from job to job. The nature of that job affects the man's attitude toward life, strengthening certain qualities and discouraging others. By a process of adult socialization, the job changes the man and makes him a different husband and a different father than he would otherwise be.

The Man as Husband

One way jobs differ is in the extent to which they exhaust a man physically. If he comes home dead tired, he can hardly play the role of husband at all.

Slater and Woodside, for example (1951), found that tired English laborers were rarely interested in having sexual relations with their wives. Only on Saturday nights and weekends generally did their respite from work leave them with enough energy to be sexually active. Similarly, Rosser and Harris (1965) commented that the physical exertions required by most jobs in past generations depleted energy which might otherwise have gone into domestic activities. However, the mechanization of work has left the average man less tired than in earlier eras. So family life has become more important. Increased leisure time and increased energy have enabled the average working man (in this case in Wales) to spend more time doing things with his family and fixing up his house.

Whereas some jobs threaten family life by depleting the husband's energy, others contribute to marriage by providing the husband and wife with something to talk about. Komarovsky (1964) found that jobs vary along at least two dimensions in their conversational possibilities:

(1) Some are interesting and others monotonous. If a man finds his work challenging and stimulating, his wife is likely to share his enthusiasm. But a man who always turns the same nut on an assembly line or files papers in the same pigeon-holes will seldom have anything to report. One of Komarovsky's blue-collar employees was asked if his wife took an interest in his job. His answer was, "I don't take much interest in it myself, so I wouldn't expect her to if I couldn't."

(2) Some jobs are less technical than others. A man may find his work fascinating but if it is highly technical he may not be able to communicate very much with his wife about it, no matter how hard he tries. Presumably this problem especially troubles men engaged in mechanical and scientific work. By contrast teachers, ministers, and social workers deal with human relations issues which any wife would be interested in hearing about and able to comprehend.

Relatively rare but particularly profound in its impact on husband–wife relations is an official ban on communication with the wife. For some men in military occupations, the wife is not supposed to be told anything, not even the nature of the tasks in which he is engaged. If communication is taboo, the wife inevitably feels cut off from the husband's work. Only knowing that he can't help withholding information prevents her from resenting him. But even that does not prevent the non-communication from leaving a vacuum where there otherwise might be a link between the partners.

The Man as Father

I have already suggested that jobs which require little physical exertion leave men fresher to interact with their families. The kind of work a man does and the setting in which he does it also affect the way he treats his children and the things he expects of them. Generally speaking, whatever behavior pays off in his work he will unconsciously try to teach his children. If he is required to take orders at work, he will teach his children to be obedient. If his occupation requires independent creativity, he will encourage his children to be independent.

Table 1-3 shows that fathers in an Italian city encouraged their children

TABLE 1-3 Fathers' Valuation of Obedience and Self-Control
by Closeness of Job Supervision and by Major Component of Work

FATHER VALUES IN CHILD	CLOSENESS OF JOB SUPERVISION			
	Close Supervision	Intermediate Supervision	Loose Supervision	Self-Employed
Obedience	54%	34%	26%	23%
Neither	17	25	30	26
Self-control	29	42	44	51
Total	100%	101%	100%	100%
Number of fathers	48	65	119	77

	MAJOR COMPONENT OF WORK		
	Things	People	Ideas
Obedience	44%	28%	14%
Neither	32	23	23
Self-control	24	49	63
Total	100%	100%	100%
Number of fathers	118	104	84

Adapted from Pearlin and Kohn (1966):474–475. Source: Fathers of fifth-grade children in
Torino, the fourth largest city in Italy.

to develop qualities that would fit them for work similar to that of their
fathers. All the differences portrayed in the double-table held both within the
middle class and within the working class. Regardless of class, the more closely
the father was supervised on the job, the more he expected obedience of his
children. In another analysis, the same researchers found that men expected to
be self-reliant at work expected self-control from their children, whereas men
with little opportunity to be self-reliant gave their children little chance for
self-control at home. In short, obedient fathers expected obedient children,
whereas men who worked independently not only allowed their children similar freedom but encouraged them to exercise self-control.

   The bottom half of Table 1-3 shows that fathers raised their children
differently according to the major component of their work. Those who
worked mostly with things expected their children to be relatively obedient but
men who worked mainly with ideas emphasized self-control (with people-
manipulators in between). Men who work with ideas frequently must produce
new ideas. To be creative a man must be independent of the status quo and
able to abandon existing ideas in the search for new ones. By contrast, most
men who work with things must produce standardized products to fit precise
specifications. In many cases those products must fit neatly in combination
with products made by other men in a complexly interdependent whole. Obedience, then, is prerequisite to the successful production of industrial products.
People on the other hand can neither be "created" as freely as ideas nor
stamped out as uniformly as metal products. So the give and take required in
working with people creates an intermediate attitude toward self-control/
obedience in children.

   In sum, then, a man's involvement in the occupational system alters
his behavior as both husband and father.

ECONOMIC ORGANIZATION AND FAMILY ORGANIZATION

Most of the men discussed in the preceding section were employed by corporations. Relatively few ran their own businesses. But, historically, economic organization and family organization have often been combined in family enterprises, and even now family businesses exist alongside separate economic organizations in free enterprise societies. This condition—whether a family has its own enterprise or the husband works for an alien employer—has many repercussions for family life.

Family Enterprise or Separate Economic Organization

The family farm is one form of family business. In the United States, the farm home is normally located in the midst of the farm plot so that work place and residence are combined. In other countries, the family may live in a rural village from which the farmer (and perhaps his wife) commutes to work in outlying fields. Even so, the separation between home and work is relatively slight in comparison to most non-farm families, especially if the wife works with her husband.

Family Farms   Several studies in the United States have shown how families involved in operating their own agricultural enterprise differ from urban families split between homes and outside employment.

One effect of being close to their work is that farmers are able to work whenever they feel like it, day or night, weekdays or weekends. They tend to be involved in their work longer hours and spend correspondingly less time in their own homes. For example, Thorpe and Gross (1955) found that farm husbands spent 21 percent less time at home on weekends and 13 percent less time on weekdays. The latter difference might be wiped out in larger communities where the journey to work is more time consuming than in the small Michigan towns studied. The basic point, however, is that separation of work place from residence does not automatically cut the husband off from his family. Instead it may guarantee that his leisure time will be available to his family. In a sense the farm husband is "near and yet so far." Physically he may be only a few yards away, but if he is preoccupied with his work he may be less available for family activities than a town husband who leaves his work behind when he punches the time clock at 5:00 P.M.

One consequence of a farmer's preoccupation with his work is that he is less available to help his wife with household tasks. As a result, farm wives often do all the work around the house, unassisted by their husbands. For example, I found (1958) that more Michigan farm than city wives did all the grocery shopping, cooked the husband's breakfast, did the evening dishes, straightened up the living-room in preparation for company, mowed the lawn, and repaired things around the house. The only exceptions were shoveling the walks (which may lead to the farmer's work place) and keeping track of the money and bills (which often are mingled with the farm accounts). When all these tasks were put together, 58 percent of the farm wives, but only 30 percent of the Detroit wives, did nearly all the housework unassisted.

Nor is this just a reallocation of the same work load, since farm wives tend to produce more homemade things than city wives. For instance, farm wives labor longer in their kitchens and sewing rooms: 55 percent of the Michigan farm wives but only 1 percent of the Detroit wives produced more than half of the baked goods, canned or frozen foods, fresh vegetables, and dresses their families consumed. This suggests that farm wives not only do a larger *proportion* of the work required to keep their households operating, but that they extend themselves more than their city cousins to save money by greater total home *production* of goods that would otherwise have to be purchased.

A third consequence of living on a farm is that wives are drawn directly into the farm work itself. In the Michigan case, 70 percent of the farm wives, but only 8 per cent of the city wives, participated directly in their husband's productive activities. To some extent, this discrepancy was offset by a greater tendency of city wives (19 percent) than of farm wives (9 percent) to earn money through outside employment. Be that as it may, the urgent pull of farm tasks involves both husbands and wives in the work of their family enterprise whereas for urban husbands and wives, the chief area of collaboration is inside the home.

The lesser participation of the male members of farm families in household tasks and their greater occupational involvement extends to sons as well as fathers. In a study of Wisconsin high school boys, Straus (1962) found that 16 percent of the farm boys but only 7 percent of the town boys avoided housework completely. But most of the farm boys were heavily involved in farm chores, 61 percent to the extent of twenty hours a week or more. Although the town boys more often held outside jobs than the farm boys, town income went mostly for personal expenses whereas farm work contributed to the whole family's prosperity. Thus husbands, wives, and sons (and presumably daughters, too) all collaborate in the work of family farms.

Family Businesses   Urban families who own businesses, especially those who live on the business premises, have much the same experience as farm families. Again the husband gets involved day and night in the business operations and other family members come to his assistance, leaving little time for leisure. If the business is a retail store, a restaurant, or other public service enterprise, there is a tendency to stay open as long as the customers are interested, so the whole life of the family may be devoted to the customers' needs. One Japanese girl in a class of mine remembered her childhood with misgivings:

> In my family, both my parents and grandparents worked from early morning to late at night in the family store. Because the store was located next to the house, the problem of not seeing anyone was a minor one. The biggest problem was being in constant contact without having too much to do with each other. Consequently there weren't too many family-centered activities. The family store received top priority and it was usually a great effort to have even one parent attend any school activity. The only times both parents and my grandfather were present were at my high school graduation and my grandmother's funeral.
>
> My childhood and adolescent years were somewhat lonely, even with the presence of the family. This is not to say there wasn't any interaction

with my parents but that it wasn't a profound relationship which I experienced. Because everyone was working all the time, no one had time for each other. However, those rare moments of family activities were tremendously exciting because they were novel in a family like mine.

In urban Dublin, Humphreys (1966) found that entrepreneurial families were much like Irish country families, even when the family lived away from the business. No matter where the business was located, it provided a focal point for family members, in contrast to the dispersal of activities which characterizes most urban families.

In Dublin, the ownership of a family business gave parents (especially fathers) greater control of their children (especially sons). Each family selected at least one son to learn the father's business or profession (in familistic countries like Ireland or Japan, fathers hope to hand on their professional clientele along with their law office or clinic). The chosen son began serving his apprenticeship in his spare time from an early age. His training and education were dictated by the family's needs, not by his own interests. When the son finished this training, he was taken into the business as a junior or full-fledged partner. Eventually he inherited the whole business or at least a controlling interest in it (to avoid the danger of splitting it up through equal inheritance). The problem was not primarily one of money: daughters received good dowries at marriage and residual sons were given the best of training and even capital with which to launch their own careers. But managerial control was vested in a single son to maintain the integrity of the business.

In order to insure the future welfare of the business, entrepreneurial families were also interested in controlling the marriage of the inheriting son. A spendthrift wife could waste the family's capital. An incompetent mother could ill-prepare her sons to carry on the business in the next generation. So these Dublin families vigilantly supervised their sons to prevent involvement with lower-class girls. By vetoing matches with unsuitable partners, they delayed the average age at which their sons married.

Although family formation may be delayed by concern to find the right partner, once a new match is contracted, business families tend to bear many children just like farm families because in both cases children tend to be commandeered for the family enterprise at an early age. In the early phases of the Industrial Revolution in England, cottage industries provided work for young family members in their own homes—weaving or spinning cloth for textile brokers (Goode, 1963). Under such circumstances, children were sometimes an economic asset or at least partially self-supporting, so family size remained large as it had been in rural areas. The same tendency exists to this day in situations wherever children help with family enterprises.

Once a substantial business had been in an Irish family for several generations, a network of kin ties developed by marriage and reproduction—one centered around the kin group's common economic interests. This made a whole host of kin interested in the activities of the inheriting son. Especially for him but for others as well, the business became a focus for social interaction and mutual social control among the economically involved kin.

It is hardly necessary to note that each of these features of Dublin entrepreneurial families resembles that of Irish farm families: (1) geographical concentration of activity, (2) occupational training, (3) occupational succession, (4) unilateral inheritance, (5) parental control of children's heterosexual association and marriage, (6) delayed marriage, and (7) close-knit kin ties. And for the same reason—the dependence of the family on physical property for its livelihood.

Although kin dependent on a common enterprise may have close business contacts, this does not necessarily mean that they will wish to spend their leisure time together. Sometimes economic interdependence prevents the free flow of affection in "pure" friendships. Just as friendship may be spoiled by the tensions arising out of economic transactions (as when a friend fails to repay a loan), so friendly relations among kin may be cooled by involvement in a family business. Adams cited a young American engineer who worked in the same firm with his father and brother: "We do very little except in a business way. We see enough of each other there . . . I don't want to be really close to them because of business; business really keeps us apart" (1968: 132). In this case, business kept kin apart socially and perhaps affectionally, but kept them together vocationally. So distinctions must be drawn between the types of relationships which family enterprises foster and those which they hinder.

Family Homes   One does not ordinarily think of home ownership as a profit-making enterprise. Nevertheless for profit-minded homeowners, it may be as much of an investment as a business. And quite apart from its resale value, a home may become the focal point of family activities in much the same way as a farm or store. The one difference is that whereas a family enterprise preempts the whole of life, a home occupies only the spare time of a man employed elsewhere.

In a London suburb, Willmott and Young (1960:26) felt that homeowners were "the husbandmen of England . . . back in a new form," so much did they behave like farmers: (1) The house became the geographical focus of the leisure time of men who otherwise would have frequented the pubs to which non-homeowning Englishmen are devoted. (2) The home (like the farm) offered unlimited opportunities for work. Especially older houses needed constant repair, renewal and modernization, to say nothing of routine seasonal tasks. (3) The harder the husband worked on his house, the greater the benefit to the family fortune. The payoff would not show until the house was sold, but an improved home meant a greater inheritance in the future. More immediately, a man's own labor saved the expense of hiring an outsider. So both by saving expense and by increasing the ultimate income from the home, the man's efforts paid off. Indeed so great was the potential gain from working at home that one suburban husband took an eight-month holiday between jobs to remodel his house:

> He knocked walls down to make larger rooms, he rebuilt and re-equipped the kitchen with a steel sink unit, built-in cupboards and Marley tiles, he erected a garage and a conservatory screened by pink venetian blinds. Looking on it purely as a commercial proposition, let alone any-

thing else, he was very well satisfied with the results. "I made these vast improvements and now I hope to make at least £1,000 on the property if it's sold." (Willmott and Young, 1960:26)

As with farmers and entrepreneurs, the work of maintaining a home also provided activities in which other family members could join. Wives and children (especially sons) were co-opted into Willmott and Young's suburban home-maintenance whenever a man needed an assistant. And more remote relatives were imported to assist or teach the homeowner. Even though these relatives had no direct economic stake in the value of the house, home ownership nevertheless provided a basis for interaction among relatives. Particularly, we may assume, it promoted interaction among male relatives who otherwise seldom would have associated with each other. In this sense, owning a home is like owning a business—it gives the man a far greater interest in the economic aspects of family life which for other urban families are largely left in feminine hands.

In urban Bethnal Green, Willmott and Young noted that living in some-one else's property prevented working class men from taking an interest in their dilapidated tenements. To these renters, repairs were the landlord's responsibility, and who wants to do someone else's work for him? Renting especially deters homework when its economic benefits go to an absentee owner. There may even be a danger that the rent might be raised if the owner were to discover his tenants luxuriating in improved quarters. This means that men alienated not only from their work but from their home as well have no place to turn for productive use of leisure and devote it instead to away-from-home pursuits which create further alienation. To the outside employer and the outside landlord must be added the outside bar-keeper, leaving men with no economic–ecological basis for involvement with wives and children. The alienation of modern man from his family is then complete.

Separate Organizations   Alien landlords and alien amusements are minor influences on family life in comparison to the effect of removing economic production from the family. In contrast to the integration of work and family in family farms and businesses, the splitting of the two is characteristic of the industrial era. The scale and complexity of modern enterprise are too great to be confined to a family tree.

When a man goes to work for a separate employer he is removed from home for all his working hours. This simultaneously dethrones him as boss of the family enterprise and sequesters him out of sight of the rest of the family. The subordinate members of the family are thereby freed from the husband's control and supervision during the time he is away. No longer are they subject to his direct orders and oversight. Consequently their status rises, at least during his absence. The wife becomes the daytime head of the household. This upsets the age-old relationship of the sexes in which women were routinely subordinate to their husbands.

For example, Miner and DeVos (1960) found that when Algerian families moved to the capital from a rural oasis, the cloistering of women collapsed. In the oasis, men were always present so they could go shopping to supplement the food the family produced for itself. In Algiers, men were away all day long so their wives had to do the shopping. (For poor families in backward countries, the lack of food storage equipment such as refrigerators means that shopping must be done every day or even for every meal.) Once Algerian women were liberated from the home, they gained new respect from their husbands.

Not only is the man's traditional role as guardian of his wife undermined by outside employment, but he can no longer function full-time as father to his children. Sons and daughters lose much of their contact with their father and lose all opportunity to observe him at work and therefore to be trained by him. The father surrenders to his wife the custody of his children while they are young and to the educational system the responsibility for their occupational training. This abdication gives the wife a second boost. Not only is she emancipated from her husband's control but she gains new responsibility for the children. This consolidates the wife's new position as a more or less equal partner to her husband, in contrast to her earlier position as an employee.

Humphreys (1966) noted that this shift in the position of the man and woman altered their relationship to their children. Whereas the Irish countryman's authority over his children commanded respect but prevented intimacy, the alienated urban father was more approachable, more friend than boss. Conversely, the woman's earlier position as mediator between father and children was lost. One consequence of her new responsibility for the children was that they no longer found her quite so lovable. Indeed the more she exercised discipline, the more she came to be resented, enabling the man to become the new mediator between parental authority and childish rebelliousness.

It would be wrong to conclude that the departure of the husband simply reverses the roles of the parents without undermining their collective authority. External employment offers not only men but women and children economic alternatives to family dependence. Wives can get jobs which will boost their status. Children, when they grow up, no longer depend on their family to furnish them with a dowry for marriage or the means of subsistence. The availability of outside economic opportunities weakens the authority of the parents because it robs them of much of their economic persuasiveness.

In tropical Africa, Goode found (1963) that young men became more independent of their parents when they could earn the bride price themselves instead of depending on their parents to furnish it. In Dublin, jobs not only made men independent of their parents but enabled them to marry earlier than their country cousins (Humphreys, 1966). Nor was it only men whose employment facilitated early marriage; girls no longer depended on a parent-bestowed dowry and made their own contribution to financial eligibility for earlier marriage.

In both Africa and Ireland, the authors noted an even greater challenge to parental authority. As long as young men work for their fathers, the latter remain in control. But when sons work for someone else, they sometimes become more successful than their fathers. Whenever this happens, the traditional respect of young people for their elders loses its functional basis. Humphreys noted that among Dubliners there was "considerably less veneration and glorification of the aged than among the country people" (p. 36). In impoverished Africa, the roles of father and son were sometimes reversed. Whenever a father depended on his son's wages for support, there was an economic basis for reversing age grades as well. So in modern societies where the fortunes of fathers and sons are largely independent and unpredictable, the relationship of the generations becomes confused.

Nor are parents the only elders who lose status. In both Africa and Ireland, the economic basis for the superiority of the inheriting son is also destroyed. In the early stages of this transformation, the eldest son may still inherit the family property, but if his younger siblings can leave to seek their fortune elsewhere, his authority over them is weakened. (Thus Goode described the Bantu Kavirondo of South Africa.) Once the whole family becomes dependent on alien employment, the entire basis for distinctions among children disappears and inheritance patterns tend to change (as in Dublin) to equality.

In short, the dispersion of employment among outside employers breaks down both the age-grading and the sex-grading of the feudal family system. The better the opportunities for external employment, the more the family structure is leveled and family ties are weakened. This does not mean that the family unit is necessarily destroyed but that the basis for its unity must shift from hierarchical authority and functional economic interdependence to a more voluntary relationship among peers. Unhappy wives can leave home to get divorced and unhappy children can leave early to get married. No longer are the individual members of the family in the grip of the patriarch who was at once head of the family and boss of the business.

Corporate Intervention in Family Life

So far I have considered employers far-away beings who lure men, women, and children away from home. But employers are not always so aloof. Sometimes they attempt to control not only their employees, but also their employees' families. They seek to capture control of the latter and to use their influence to their own advantage at the expense of the immediate interests of the family.

Before detailing the forms of this corporate intervention in family life it is important to recognize two qualifications. (1) Intervention is not characteristic of all employers but only some. The difference between those who do and those who do not meddle in their employees' domestic affairs seems to be a matter of company philosophy attributable to personal leadership of the company management rather than predictable on the basis of institutional characteristics of these corporations. In others words there does not seem to be any evidence that interventionism increases with corporate size or with company prosperity or in companies whose main concern is with services to people (to venture some plausible hypotheses). All I can say is that some companies care and some don't about the private lives of their employees.

(2) It is possible to say, however, that companies who care at all care far more about some employees than others. Generally speaking, they couldn't care less about their ordinary, rank-and-file employees. The masses

are not important enough to worry about. The employees who really matter are the company's executives. So corporate intervention is characteristic of only some corporations and affects only their higher status employees.

Commandeering Executive Loyalty   Regardless of company policy, every corporate executive faces a conflict of loyalty between the claims of his work and the claims of his family. In a sense this is true for every employee, regardless of status. But we become so accustomed to the average man's 40 hours at work that we fail to see them as encroaching on his "normal" family life. In the case of executives, however, there is no time-clock to say when work is done. Many executives work overtime at the office, and most of those who don't take office problems home with them, in briefcase or in their heads to be pondered at home. The greater an executive's responsibility, the harder it is to forget those responsibilities and give himself to wife and children. Yet wives and children normally feel entitled to substantial shares of attention and lay claims to more when they don't feel that they get enough.

So far I have simply described the executive's behavior. Why does he act that way? Partly it is the inevitable claim that unsolved problems make on the human brain. Until problems are solved it is difficult to forget about them, even if one tries. But an executive does not have only his brain to deal with. In competitive businesses there is the threat that one's company will fall behind if those problems are not solved fast enough. And in the competition between junior executives for advancement, there is the threat that one's advancement will fall behind. Finally there is the explicit pressure of superiors to get work done, no matter what. And no-matter-what means specifically that the corporation asks its executives to subordinate the claims of their families to the claims of the company.

I am not primarily concerned here with the pressures which the corporation puts directly on its executives. Insofar as this pressure succeeds, it affects the family indirectly by keeping the husband away from home. My interest here is rather in ways the corporation seeks to intervene in family life directly in order to capture and retain the institutional loyalty of its executives.

William H. Whyte, Jr., (1952) graphically portrayed various ways in which some companies sought to win their executives to their side at the expense of their families.

(1) In order to minimize the husband's sense of being deprived of the comforts of home, some corporations provide similar comforts to top executives who stay at the office too late to go home or who are away from home on company business. Plush dining rooms and bedroom suites may be provided at the plant. Lavish expense accounts enable businessmen to live more luxuriously away from home than at home. Even alternative sexual facilities in the form of call girls are supplied at some business conventions. Insofar as such facilities meet the domestic needs of the executive, the lure of home is dimmed.

(2) Other tactics seek not to replace the wife but to neutralize her. Propaganda campaigns directed at both partners carry the message that "What's good for General Motors is good for executive families." Translated this might mean that families who supply their man's services to the corpo-

ration can expect to be paid off handsomely in enhanced prestige and higher income as he advances in the corporate hierarchy. Less directly, companies seek to win wives and children to their side by integrating them into "the company family." Company facilities for women's and children's recreation and company sponsored trips and outings for dependents make the latter depend less for their good times on the man of the family and depend more on the corporation. Once the family members come to see the corporation as a bountiful giver, it's harder to resist the family man's transformation into a company man. Better yet, some companies buy the loyalty of employee children more directly by giving them first preference for summer employment. In such ways, the whole family gradually comes to be a company family.

(3) Beyond mere neutralization of family claims, some corporations seek to use the family (especially the wife) as an instrument for safeguarding and promoting executive efficiency. Such companies act on the assumption that behind every successful man there stands a woman. What services can the wife perform? She can encourage him to work hard. She can assist him by skillfully entertaining his customers and colleagues. She can make useful contacts for him in the community by getting to know key men and women through respectable civic activities. And when his morale falters, she can provide unilateral psychotherapy (at the same time safeguarding him from having to hear about her own or the children's troubles). All these are services which many middle class wives provide for their husbands anyway. But some corporations, not content to leave such matters to chance, go out of their way to teach wives how to help their husbands (and, incidentally, the corporation) get ahead.

Safeguarding Social Relations   Wives are a threat to corporations in other ways besides the claims they place on their husbands' time. Women are typically social creatures and in their social activities they can upset the company's delicately balanced internal and external relationships.

Within the company, the problem is to preserve the complex hierarchy of managerial relationships. Whyte noted that just as the company executives are ordered in a carefully ranked hierarchy of statuses with correspondingly ordered status symbols such as size of office, size of desk, and presence or absence of a carpet, so wives need to be correspondingly ordered in their appearance and behavior. For a wife to act either above or below the status determined by the husband's company position is to create jealousies or resentments among other wives and strain the corporate structure. For a wife to behave differently than would be expected from her husband's position creates a status-incongruence which strains the delicately ordered system, leading to open competition between women (especially where the wife acts "above" her station), triggering a cycle of oneupmanship competition. Such feminine competition threatens the corporation's control of the promotion-selection process. Since advancement within the company is precarious at best, no company wants to suffer such feminine aggressiveness any more than an extended family wants to surrender its mate-selection powers to young lovers unconcerned about how their choices may affect the family system.

In order to prevent unrestrained competition among wives, a company may establish norms about such status symbols as the family car, home, and country club and seek to enforce family conformity to these company norms. If the family conforms, the wife has lost some of her freedom of choice but is protected from emotional strains she might otherwise encounter. Since that strain would probably strain the husband–wife relationship, the family as a unit may gain more than it loses from this particular intervention.

Another place where the wife may threaten the company is in the community. I have already mentioned the positive role which the corporation hopes she will play by respectable civic activities. Conversely, a wife may damage her husband's prospects for advancement while he is young and damage the company's image when he is older and more conspicuously identified with the company's management by any form of deviant behavior. What is deviant is usually determined by the community rather than by the company. The company simply adopts the policy that executive wives should avoid offending potential customers or existing customers who might be lost by sufficiently flagrant offenses.

Two major forms of deviant behavior are to be avoided. One is personal delinquency such as public drunkenness, promiscuity, thievery, or other unseemly behavior. The other is anything viewed as controversial by the community. In many places this applies to civil rights activities, particularly to public demonstrations, and to political activity on behalf of minority political parties and radical candidates. In general this means that companies expect wives to be conservative in their behavior and to remain inconspicuous except in the most respectable and prestige-filled activities. Their husbands, too, are subject to the same norms, of course, so here too perhaps the result of joint conformity to company norms is increased family solidarity. The sacrifice in this case is not of family unity (as in the case of the loyalty conflict between corporation and family) but the surrender of personal freedom and personal values. The relevance to family life is that this is another area where the corporation intrudes in the life of not just the husband but his wife (and even his children).

ECONOMIC CONDITIONS

In Chapter 2, I will be concerned with various effects of differential wealth within the same society. But here my concern is with differences between societies or differences within the same society at different times. In other words, my focus is on the general economic condition of the society.

Conditions change in two ways. In the developed countries there is a *long-term trend* toward increased affluence. In industrial economies there also are *short-range fluctuations* between periods of prosperity and depression. In both cases the purpose of this chapter is to make static comparisons between societies at different points on these economic scales, not to trace the process of change from one point to another. The dynamic emphasis on the consequences of processes of economic change will be reserved for the chapter on social change (Chapter 9).

Societal Affluence

Does family life differ with the level of affluence of the society? In a sense I have already answered that in dealing with the contrast between the precarious subsistence of hunting societies and the greater security of agrarian societies. However, my concern here is with differences in level of affluence between modern societies. Since the contemporary United States is the most affluent society which has ever existed, it can be compared either with earlier periods of American history or with other contemporary societies such as Japan which have a similar industrial economy but where the per capita income is lower. Family life may also be studied under differing degrees of affluence in agrarian societies (as measured, for example, by the availability of agricultural land).

Family Formation The more abundant the resources for family living, the easier the process of family formation. Specifically, the age of marriage tends to be lower in affluent societies or affluent regions. For example, rural young people in frontier regions of Japan married much earlier than those in thickly settled farming areas where land was difficult to obtain prior to parental retirement (Goode, 1963). The most extreme delay was rural Ireland where the average farmer did not marry until he was thirty-six years old (Humphreys, 1966). Similarly age of marriage tends to be lower in affluent urban societies than where marriage must be delayed as people struggle to accumulate enough money to pay for wedding expenses and to secure housing. In contemporary urban Japan, for example, starting salaries are too low to support a wife and children, so men delay marriage until their late twenties whereas American men marry in their early twenties. The latter pattern is several years earlier than a generation or two before in American history when American young men felt it wise to have money in the bank before risking marriage.

If young men can marry easily, this has secondary repercussions. (1) Parental control over marriage lessens because parents no longer need to supply land, housing, or capital. (2) Whereas men marrying late frequently marry young brides, early-marrying men choose wives closer to their own age, making their marriages more equalitarian (Goode, 1963). (3) Societal taboos on premarital heterosexual association and on premarital sexual intercourse weaken. If young people happen to fall in love or a girl happens to get pregnant, it is less disastrous in an affluent society. Whereas early marriage in a tight economy wrecks the young man's chances for completing his education and for occupational success, increasing numbers of young people in affluent societies have found it possible to combine education and marriage. This is not to suggest that there may not be strain between the two roles, but that the severity of the conflict weakens as it becomes easier for young men to secure scholarships and for their wives to secure jobs which will pay the husband's way through school. In general, then, young people in affluent societies begin dating earlier and become more intimately involved than do those for whom early involvement is more costly.

Family Growth Once families are formed, affluence promotes family growth. In post-war America, middle-class families preferred an average of three children in contrast with the two-child ideal for less-affluent Japan. Goode (1963) noted that a severe housing shortage in the Eastern European Communist nations after World War II severely depressed the birthrate because of the lack of room for additional family members. Presumably as such industrializing nations achieve affluence in the future, their family size preferences will increase—just as most American families became dissatisfied with having only one or two children when they could afford to have more at the same time that they could afford cars and television sets.

Status of Women   Given any particular number of children, wives in affluent societies are less tied down at home than those with fewer economic resources. Labor-saving devices enable contemporary American women to get their housework done faster. Baby-sitters can be afforded to emancipate them from their child-rearing responsibilities. And automobiles enable them to make a fast get-away from home to go shopping or to the movies or to play golf. By contrast, Landy (1959) found wives in rural Puerto Rico saddled with endless housekeeping chores because they could not afford efficient equipment: "Water must be brought long distances; clothes washed in the stream; fuel gathered; ironing done with heavy charcoal-burning irons . . . (1959:79–80). For affluent women emancipated from such drudgery, domestic roles are less burdensome even when they marry young and have relatively many children.

Fewer burdens of domestic responsibilities enable affluent women to leave home for work as well as for play, if they so desire. Within a given society, the most affluent women are least apt to work because they need the money the least. But between societies, only those which provide resources for child care through social facilities or through personal assistance are able to release women to pursue careers during their child-rearing years.

Child-Rearing   Freedom to earn money when combined with the higher incomes of affluent husbands creates such a comparative abundance of money that parental attention shifts from the problems of making money to the problems of spending it; from a production-orientation to a consumption-orientation; from valuing deferred gratification of impulses for the sake of future rewards to valuing immediate gratification because "you can't take it with you."

When parents find life easy, they develop a more relaxed attitude toward their children. When economic conditions are so abundant that almost anyone can hope to achieve a good life, parents need not train their children so rigorously to compete for economic success. As America moved from the scarcity of the nineteenth century to the abundance of the twentieth, parents shifted from emphasizing the traditional virtues of thrift and hard work to encouraging popularity and sociability. Symbolizing the new concerns of affluent parents were Margaret Ribble's plea for "the rights of infants" (1943) and Doctor Spock's post-war encouragement of more permissive child-rearing practices. David Riesman noted the shift from the tough-minded conscientiousness of "inner-directedness" to the more flexible approach of "other-directedness" (1954). And in the 1960's, religionists and philosophers responded with a more flexible "new morality." All these trends may be traced to economic affluence.

Family Stability   The same affluence-born freedoms which lighten the burden of family life also make it easier to leave the family altogether. Children in an affluent society expect to find separate housing after their education is completed, rather than being cloistered with their parents until marriage. And husbands and wives in affluent societies can afford to be critical about the quality of their marriages. If they don't like what they find, they can afford the expenses of getting a divorce and of establishing two domiciles instead of one. Such reasoning suggests that the long-term rise in the American divorce rate is at least partly due to the rising standard of living.

To Farber (1964) the rising divorce rate suggested that affluent Americans were coming to think of themselves as "permanently available" for marriage and remarriage, regardless of their current marital status. In other words, the new American was becoming a comparison shopper, always on the look-out for a better partner than his current one.

For the future, I predict an emphasis on more meaningful relationships in marriage and at the same time a growing uncertainty as to the duration of any particular relationship. We will see later that high-intensity relationships are difficult to maintain over a lifetime, so the citizens of super-affluent societies may change partners in somewhat the same fashion that they will change their automobiles and perhaps even their houses for new and better models or at least for different models as they tire of the old one.

Economic Fluctuations

Short-run fluctuations in economic conditions affect family behavior in many of the same ways as long-range differences. For example, Pinard (1966) found both family formation and family dissolution impeded by economic recessions when people could afford neither to get married nor to get divorced. Although a recession may cause couples to postpone getting married, they can less easily curb the impulse to intimacy. Hence, some of the children who might otherwise have been born legitimately under prosperity are born illegitimately or at least conceived premaritally instead. Christensen and Meissner (1953) found that children born in the early years of the Great Depression were more apt to be conceived premaritally than in more prosperous years before or since. Presumably the economic reverses and unemployment suffered by young people between 1929 and 1931 caused some to postpone marriage until they were "forced" to get married by the discovery of pregnancy. The same economic conditions presumably encouraged heavier reliance on efforts to prevent pregnancy altogether, but since contraception methods were relatively unreliable in those days, premarital pregnancies were common.

Less clearly a product of the Depression but plausibly linked to it was the high level of parent–youth conflict which observers like Kingsley Davis (1940) and Talcott Parsons (1942) noted in American youth in the 1930's. By contrast Elkin and Westley, writing in more prosperous times (1955), labelled their article "The Myth of Adolescent Culture" because they found so little evidence of a rebellious, deviant culture during the prosperous early post-war years.

If adolescents finishing high school find it impossible to get a job, and therefore must give up or postpone hopes of going to college or getting married, no wonder they may vent their anger and frustration on their parents.

This suggests that Parsons' irresponsible youth culture results from the frustration of "responsible" goals, rather than being an intrinsically adolescent phenomenon. Worsening economic conditions tend to produce conflict between parents and teen-agers whereas improving conditions enable young people to rely on their parents as models for their own lives. In any case, intergenerational relations cannot be understood just in terms of biological factors such as age, but must be seen against the backdrop of the resources available to both generations from the economy at large.

chapter two

THE STRATIFICATION SYSTEM AND THE FAMILY

It has been impossible to discuss the effect of the economic system on the family without encroaching on the subject of stratification. My treatment of the consequences of agrarian subsistence, for example, necessarily touched upon the consequences of large landholdings versus small. In this chapter we will find many parallels to the previous one. Generally speaking, the consequences of differential wealth within a society are similar to the consequences of economic differences between societies. Nevertheless, the level of analysis is different. Whereas Chapter 1 was basically concerned with differences between total economies or with differences in the level of functioning of a given economy over time, Chapter 2 will focus on differences among families within a given society at a particular time. Nor will I be concerned exclusively with economic differences. Rather I will examine the whole range of hierarchically ordered differences in social status due to differences not only in wealth but in occupational prestige, education, and ethnicity. The general question will be: What are the consequences for family life of occupying a high or low position in the social structure? In most cases, it will be the husband's occupation, education, etc., which will concern me because in most societies the wife and children are assigned their social status on the basis of the husband–father's social position.

ECONOMIC RESOURCES

Within a given society, some families struggle to survive in the face of poverty. At the opposite extreme, other families make up a leisure class based on wealth handed down from their ancestors. Between these extremes is an enormous gulf filled with widely varying economic circumstances. Those circumstances affect almost every facet of family living from beginning to end.

Family Formation

The family in most societies is the unit of consumption. Without something to consume, the whole basis for family life breaks down. Hence the formation of families has economic prerequisites.

Money Enough To Get Married   To form a new family costs money both initially and for its continuing sustenance. In some societies a sum of money must be paid from one family to another before the match can be contracted. In almost all societies there are ritual expenses for the wedding ceremony. And unless money to support the family is in sight before marriage, the marriage will seem impossible (or at least unwise).

Longmore (1959) found that low-paid Bantu laborers in South Africa often found it difficult to accumulate the money necessary to pay the "bride price" to the bride's family. Sometimes such men married anyway, incurring the wrath of the bride's family. More often, however, official marriage was postponed indefinitely until the financial demands of the parents could be met. Yet this did not mean the relationship itself was severed. Rather the woman was likely to become pregnant outside of wedlock, to bear and raise illegitimate children, and perhaps even to establish a common residence with her man. But legal, official, publicly-recognized marriage was financially impossible.

In the Caribbean islands, there is no bride price custom, yet the poorest islanders still can't afford to marry. Studies in Jamaica by Blake (1961) and by Stycos and Back (1964) reported the expenses of the wedding as a barrier to marriage. Custom required that the bride and groom wear special clothes, and people would rather not have a wedding at all than have one in ordinary working clothes. Paradoxically the postponed wedding becomes increasingly difficult to finance as the expenses of bearing and rearing children fall on couples living together or merely visiting one another.

Even if a couple could afford the wedding itself, it might still be postponed if they could not afford the other expenses which custom required of married people. Jamaican culture demanded that couples have their own house and a minimum of furniture. The man's income was expected to be good enough to relieve his wife of the necessity of working. If these economic resources were lacking, it would be presumptuous to get married. One should not marry legally unless one were able to play the economic roles expected of married people. If one were too poor for that, it would be better to remain at home with one's parents, maintaining only a "visiting" relationship. Or, if one had just a bit more money, one might be able to establish a common domicile supported by the labor of both partners or a home not really adequate to meet the standards expected of respectable married folk. So a common-law union often seemed the most practical adaptation to poverty.

In these cases, the poverty-stricken segment of the society has worked out a way of allowing family formation to occur on a non-legal basis under circumstances which make socially respectable, legal processes unavailable. Family formation is not so much postponed as diluted. If the best one can do is to achieve a common-law marriage, that's not the same as having a "real" one. Lack of social, ecclesiastical, and legal support for such a marriage weakens it. Indeed, Rodman (1961) argued that one of the advantages of such informal relationships in Trinidad was that the man could easily desert his "wife" and children whenever unemployment forced him to leave in search of a new job. Perhaps then we should say that under conditions of poverty, men and women form "quasi-families"—the best they can do under the circumstances, but qualitatively impaired nevertheless.

If we add to the insecurity of the marriage bond the shortage of money to live on from day to day, we see that the weakest marriages face the most difficult stresses. Hardly a fair arrangement, but reminiscent of the Biblical phrase that "from those that have not will be taken away even that which they have."

Parental Control of Marriage   I have already noted that in South Africa poverty made it difficult for young couples to meet the financial requirements set by parents (in that case the woman's parents). The inability of poor parents to control the marrying of their sons and daughters involves more than just the bride-price problem.

Poor families are less able to provide their children with the upbringing necessary to prepare them for marriage. For instance, Latin American girls are supposed to be chaperoned from the time they reached puberty until they are safely married. But poor families can neither afford to pay a governess the way aristocratic families do nor to assign the mother to chaperoning duties in view of the large number of other children she has to raise and the fact that she may have to be away from home working to make ends meet (Blake, 1961). Indeed, Blake found not only that poor Jamaican girls lacked supervision to safeguard their virginity, but that the family often pushed them into external situations where they were liable to be seduced into premarital involvements. For instance, children of both sexes were asked to run errands for the family and encouraged to get jobs to ease the perennial shortage of money. As a result, girls frequently became involved in early sexual affairs, premarital pregnancies, and eventually in quasi-familial relationships. Under these circumstances, poverty weakened parental control over the mating process, enabling young people to drift more rapidly into heterosexual involvements at the same time that it delayed completion of the process of forming a legal tie. In other words, poverty promotes an extended period of quasi-family relationships which begins relatively early and continues relatively late. By contrast, in wealthy families such half-formed relationships are carefully prevented by stringent parental prohibition of early liaisons and by generous assistance in the formation of solid families at the appropriate time.

The problem for wealthy families is not simply one of timing. Unlike poor families who have nothing to lose by entering into relationships, rich families fear the potential involvement of their children with persons less well-to-do than themselves. The greater their wealth, the more they censor the involvement with less well-to-do partners and promote liaisons with others of similar wealth. And where inherited wealth is at stake, the threat of disownment for a bad marriage gives parents a powerful weapon in controlling the mate-selection of their child.

Family Growth

Theoretically one might expect a scarcity of economic resources to impede not only family formation, but also family growth. Couples whose income is so low that they have postponed marriage might be expected to postpone child-bearing also and to curtail the number of children born.

However, I have already suggested that poor people who postpone formal wedding ceremonies are far less apt to postpone sexual intercourse.

The remaining question is whether they will sever the link between intercourse and conception by using contraceptives effectively. The answer is epitomized in the saying: "The rich get richer and the poor get children."

Some of the reasons why the poor get children involve associated factors such as inadequate education. But some result directly from inadequate finances. Slater and Woodside (1951) pointed out that British working class couples were handicapped by lack of facilities such as bathrooms, hot water, and privacy in their crowded, deteriorated living quarters. Under such circumstances, certain methods of contraception were not easily employed. Save where public medical services make contraceptive materials available without charge, the cost may seem prohibitive (even though the cost of an unprevented child is even higher).

The last point needs to be qualified, however, for children are sometimes self-supporting or a source of potential income for their parents. For the poorest Indians in a remote Mexican village, children were economic assets (Romney and Romney, 1963). They dropped out of school at an early age to begin economic productivity in the age-old patterns of peasant children in agrarian societies. And when their parents grew feeble, children became a source of "social security" for those who lacked the means to save for retirement in a society with inadequate old age pensions. To have many children was not only to broaden one's retirement base but to save any one child from too much of a burden to support.

But large numbers of children are desired by poor people only under special economic circumstances. In modern industrial societies, the poor generally prefer fewer children because they realize that the larger the number of mouths to feed, the less food there will be for each. But since poor people practice contraception less effectively, their actual family size tends to be large. In other words, the fewer the number of children the family can afford, the more they actually have.

How many children a family can afford is not purely a matter of money. It also depends on the family's standards. Parents who feel that every child should go to college can "afford" fewer children on the same income than those who expect their children to drop out of school. Freedman (1963) determined this by comparing a family's income with the amount that might ordinarily be expected for a man of the husband's occupation, education, and age. In a national sample interviewed in 1955, he found that this "relative income" influenced child-bearing more than the absolute income when the analysis was restricted to couples who had successfully planned their family size. Indeed, when the effects of several economic variables were disentangled from one another, only unexpectedly low income led poor families to have fewer children.

Nevertheless, the discouraging effect of poverty on child-bearing clearly becomes apparent when families successfully plan their child-bearing. Goldberg's 1960 reanalysis of fertility data from Indianapolis found that although the poorest families generally had the most children, the more successfully they planned their families, the more this child-bearing pattern tended to be reversed. Poor families who controlled the number but not the spacing of their children had slightly fewer children, but those who controlled both the number and the spacing had appreciably fewer children. So the more successfully couples plan their families, the more their family growth tends to be geared to their economic resources.

When resources become available by inheritance from earlier generations, they are particularly secure and therefore foster especially large family norms. One example may be found in Baltzell's 1953 study of high income Philadelphia families. The older Philadelphia families, especially those whose economic security was symbolized in family ancestors in the Social Register as far back as 1900, had the largest number of children, more than families whose wealth had been more recently achieved. For families whose economic resources are not only ample but have long been so, additional children are accommodated easily without threat to that economic base.

Child Development   Once children arrive, the family's resources determine their ability to provide them with the goods and services necessary for their development. In the poorest American families, children are mentally impoverished partly because there aren't enough toys or physical objects in the home for them to play with. Conversely, more well-to-do parents are able to buy not only toys as such, but expensive "educational" toys designed to give the child opportunities for choice and creativity in their manipulation.

Under acute poverty, however, the problem is not simply that the home is unequipped but rather that it does not suffice to shelter the family as a group. This problem will be discussed in more detail later in this chapter under the heading of "family autonomy."

Even if the house can shelter the family from the weather, it may not provide the necessary equipment for basic family functions. For example, in poor Puerto Rican homes Landy (1959) found that family meals were impossible. With no table big enough to hold food for the whole family and not enough chairs for all to sit down at once, families could not eat together. They had either to eat serially or to disperse themselves throughout the tiny house, sitting on the edges of beds or on the floor, squatting on their haunches or standing up. In many poor homes, each family member eats at his own convenience rather than all gathering at a common time. The effect of either pattern is to deprive the family of an opportunity for group interaction and therefore of an opportunity to create family feeling and family unity. One reason why poor families are so weak is that the physical environment does not allow the growth of social solidarity.

Landy also noted that the methods of discipline parents used were affected by their resources. One technique was impossible: physical isolation. If a home is small enough, the child cannot be segregated from the rest of the family. Meagre resources also deprive parents of the opportunity of offering economic rewards as an incentive for good behavior.

Finally, economic resources affect a family's ability to allow their children the privilege of advanced education. As has been mentioned, the tendency of poor families is to put all children to work as early as possible. Even if a family can spare the child from the necessity of contributing to its collective support, it may still be unable to assist the child with the expenses of an education. In the seventeenth century, as Aries (1962) pointed out, urban working class families could contribute little to the support of their children away from home. Yet to go to school in those days most children had to pay not only tuition but room and board in a town away from home. The net result for children of all but the well-to-do was to delay their education until they were old enough to work their way through school.

By contrast, even the average family in the contemporary United States is able to assist its children with not only secondary but higher education. Indeed, Goode (1963) pointed out that middle-income families are beginning to offer their children a luxury formerly reserved only to the children of the rich: the privilege of marrying before becoming completely self-supporting. An increasing number of parents subsidize their children's education and thus enable them to marry early without impairing the completion of that higher education. When economic resources rise this high, the hard choices of earlier days are no longer necessary. Such families allow their children to enjoy both prolonged preparation for life and to enjoy adult life itself at the same time (just as the same families can afford to have both many children and a high standard of living, simultaneously). Under such circumstances economic resources are no longer a source of anxiety, but a source of security and support for an abundant life.

Family Structure

If poverty produces an unorganized, loose structure in families who do not eat together, wealth makes possible interaction patterns which set apart the status of male from female and of old from young. This is partly a question of sheer physical space within the household.

Sexual Segregation   In many agrarian societies, the ideal family pattern is the segregation of the sexes from each other and the sequestering of women behind closed doors. But to separate the sexes requires at least two rooms. Therefore the poorest families cannot afford the luxury of fulfilling that norm. Goode (1963) pointed out that both in India and in the Islamic Arab countries only families above the poverty level could afford the luxury of sex segregation. Indeed, the wealthier the family, the sharper the segregation.

This is not just a question of subdividing the household. Segregation ideally meant the cloistering of women within the household to protect them from contact with strange men in the outside world. This means that women could not work outside the home even in their husbands' fields, much less work for anyone else. Nor could they even shop for their consumption needs. To be able to withdraw the woman from such useful functions, the man had to be able to earn enough to support a non-working wife and the household needed servants to do the shopping.

On the one hand this style of life had economic prerequisites. On the other, the invisibility of the wife testified to the family's affluence. The cloistered wife thus became a status symbol of the family's wealth. Symbols in other cultures included the bound feet of the Chinese gentry wife which prevented her from doing useful work and the "lily white hands" which testified that their owner had not darkened her skin by working outdoors or reddened her skin by washing the family dishes. In short, the family structure of wealthy families tends to give women a special position which poorer families cannot afford.

Age Grading   Wealth similarly creates or widens age differentials within the family. When poor families force their children to contribute to their support, the whole family's dependence on them gives them substantial equality. If children can threaten to withhold their contribution, they can bargain with their parents. Conversely, I have noted how parental control of inheritable wealth gives those parents power over their children. And since power tends to be respected, this means a correspondingly wider psychological gap between the generations.

In agrarian societies, the power of the elders often extends over multiple generations into the formation of extended families. The wealthier the family, the more easily it can support additional generations in the same household. Indeed, economic resources contribute to the growth of the family structure just as they contribute to growth through extensive child-bearing. Only wealthy families can feed so many mouths and house so many bodies. And wealthy families can afford segregated living quarters for the several generations. For example, in Chinese gentry homes, the family elders had special quarters which symbolized their special status within the extended family.

Just as wealth makes extended families possible, it also makes polygyny possible. In societies which permit polygyny, the wealthiest man has the most wives while a poor man must content himself with one or none. Nor is it just a question of a man's ability to support wives (since they may be at least partly self-supporting). Rather the more important the man, the more wives he needs to assist with his many responsibilities. Colson reported that among the Zambian Tonga:

> Men remarked that Europeans had servants who worked whether a wife was there or not, and this they regarded as a reasonable if somewhat expensive substitute for polygyny. Those who have many visitors desire more wives to help with the cooking and to provide the food necessary to feed the throng. It is a matter of pride . . . to feed all who come, and under village conditions it is usually impossible for one woman to cope with all who visit an important man. Chiefs, councillors, and headmen are therefore likely to be polygynists. So are many men who are trying to cultivate extensive acreages and produce large surpluses for sale. . . . Wives are a source of labour more dependable than the hired hand. They also produce children who play an important role in productive activities. (1958:121–122)

The greater a family's wealth, the larger and more complex the family tends to become. Structurally this often involves sharper segregation between the sexes and between the generations. Conversely, the poorest families tend to have relatively undifferentiated structures as men and women, parents and children, struggle collectively to maintain their precarious toehold on life.

If wealth makes complex families possible, differential wealth within the community tends to make them necessary. One example is the complex family system which arose in highly stratified areas of medieval and early modern Japan. Specifically, Ariga (1967) found that the isolated mountain community of Ishigami in northern Japan was dominated by one family which had been the first to settle there and which owned most of the land. Families which entered the community later were able to settle there only by entering into adoptive relationships with the wealthy Saito family. The land-monopoly of the original family and the landlessness of the immigrant families produced a complex network of relationships between families which included not only the usual extended family system of lineal descendants but one involving adopted non-relatives. In 1935, the main house of the Saito family contained 13 blood-related persons in the main-family line and 13 others belonging to four different non-related family units stemming from adopted children who had been brought into the household to increase the family labor force and enable them to exploit their land more fully.

This enormous complexity of a well-to-do household in a highly stratified community (from which there was no economic escape because of the village's isolation) contrasts with the lack of complex households in more equalitarian communities. For instance, a village (Kawairi Mura) in the more prosperous Western part of Japan provided quite different conditions (Fukutake, 1952). Most of the families in the village were landowners, but none held an un-usually large tract. Moreover, landless families could move into industrial employment in nearby Okayama City. The result of this lack of inordinate wealth on the one hand and of hopeless poverty on the other was a simple family structure involving an older couple and at most one married child. In not a single case did the economic situation allow the addition of non-related family members to the household as in Ishigami.

In short, economic conditions affect not only the internal structure of the nuclear family but also the agglomeration of nuclear families into complex households composed of several generations or even of adopted adults.

TABLE 2-1　Family Structure, by Degree of Social Stratification

FAMILY STRUCTURE	DEGREE OF SOCIAL STRATIFICATION		
	Little or None	Moderate*	Considerable**
Nuclear families only	63%	46%	36%
Extended families	37	54	64
Total	100%	100%	100%
Number of societies	173	44	295

*No slavery but important distinctions based on ownership of property, short of hereditary social classes.
** Slavery and/or relatively great stratification among free men. Adapted from Nimkoff and Middleton (1960):220.

Table 2-1 indicates that the Japanese case is simply one illustration of a general tendency for complex family systems to develop in countries which are highly stratified. The tighter the stratification, the greater the tendency of an extended family system to develop. In most cases, extended families do not include nonrelated persons. But the more stratified the society, the larger the number of slaves or other landless men whose hard work enables the landed gentry to live in leisure in their complicated households. Without a landless proletariat, it is difficult for families in agrarian societies to become rich enough to afford a complex household and to perpetuate it over enough generations for it to become the normative family system for that society. A high degree of stratification may not make complex families inevitable, but it makes them feasible.

Family Autonomy

The very existence of the family as a separate social group requires a minimum of economic resources. Aries (1962) suggested that not until the eighteenth century did the poor people of Europe have houses big enough to sustain family life. Before that, the hovels of the poor were so tiny and so crowded with animals as well as people that they offered no space within which family activities might take place. To be sure, they offered shelter from the rain while people slept, but a family asleep is hardly a family interacting. In short, their shelter was so inadequate that "home" was not a place to stay, but a place to flee during one's waking hours. Under such dispersed circumstances, the very concept of a "family" hardly took shape.

Thus, Aries maintained, only in the houses of the medieval rich could the family as a social unit come into being, set apart from the teeming life of the neighborhood. This segregation of the family from other social units did not happen automatically with the erection of larger buildings. At first there were no other buildings for the transaction of business and so the family business intruded on the life of the family. Customers and clients came to do their business, and friends, too, entered uninvited and stayed as long as they wished. Even the sleeping quarters of these big houses were a melange of humanity. The idea of a separate bedroom for a married couple had not yet developed. Several couples or groups of boys and girls slept together in the same room, interspersed with servants of various sorts. These early houses did not afford the luxury of halls as passageways; rather one had to pass through one bedroom in order to reach another. The result was a complete lack of privacy and autonomy for the marital dyad, much less for the nuclear family unit.

Aries found that only with the eighteenth century "the family began to hold society at a distance, to push it back beyond a steadily extending zone of private life" (p. 398). The houses of the rich developed specialized areas for the private existence of family members. On that physical foundation, the family established its first base in modern civilization. With such a belated development of a physical foundation for family life among the rich, we can imagine how much later this sense of family autonomy reached down into the masses. Even today in many societies, the poorest families lack adequate shelter to make family life possible.

Resources tend to fluctuate over the family life cycle. When a new family is first formed it may start with few or no resources unless it has been amply endowed by the older generation. Especially if a new family has been formed prematurely (in the sense that the couple have married at an earlier than usual age), its resources are liable to be inadequate. At the same time, the couple's parents have been married long enough to have accumulated resources. This creates an intergenerational imbalance of resources. When this imbalance takes the particular form of a lack of housing for the young couple and a housing surplus for one or both sets of parents, the young couple are likely to establish their domicile with their elders.

In the United States, inadequate finances often forced teenage married couples and more especially high-school-aged couples to double-up with either the boy's or the girl's parents (Glick, 1957). Usually this was a relatively brief interval of a few years until the couple's finances enabled them to move out into an apartment of their own.

But what if a housing shortage means that even couples with modest resources cannot secure a place to live? This was the situation in a Welsh city studied by Rosser and Harris (1965). So few public housing projects had been built during World War II that couples typically had to wait ten years after marriage until their name came to the top of the waiting list. Under these circumstances there was no alternative to living doubled up with one set of parents or the other. Fortunately, most parents had such large houses that doubling up was relatively easily accommodated, and almost universally practiced.

At the other end of the life cycle, retirement from productive work may deplete a couple's income so that independent living again becomes difficult to pay for. This is one reason (along with physical infirmity and loneliness after bereavement) why old people tend to double up with their adult children. However, as with young couples, doubling up depends not only on one party's need for housing but on another's ability to supply it. In Vienna, Rosenmayr and Köckeis (1963) found joint living most frequent in the middle class, since at that moderate income level supply and demand were most evenly balanced. Among lower income old people, the need was greater but their children's houses provided less opportunity. On the other hand, well-to-do professional and big business families had the means to live independently even in old age.

Family autonomy thus tends to be lost in old age when financial resources are inadequate to sustain independent living provided that other units in the kin network have space to accommodate their impoverished aged dependents. Presumably if those other units could offer not only space but money, they would transfer payments to the old couple to enable them to continue their separate existence.

In a modern welfare state, old people whose own resources are insufficient for independent living may be rescued by the government from having to depend on their children. Townsend (1957) studied British respondents old enough to remember when there had been no such thing as old age pensions. Said one old woman: "It's a wonderful thing since they came in. . . . When you're old you don't have to be a burden on your children" (p. 164). Old men particularly appreciated the ability to maintain their financial autonomy *vis-à-vis* their children—having earned their own way all their lives, they would find it particularly difficult to have to beg for money or shelter from their children. To have to make such claims would be painful not only for the supplicant but for the supplier as well. If the latter's resources were only marginal, the parents' claims might strain not only the family finances but the inter-family relationship. Townsend found that under modern conditions inter-family relationships flourished best when government-furnished economic resources were sufficient not only to enable the older family to preserve its physical autonomy but to demonstrate its financial autonomy by continuing to give birthday gifts to the grandchildren and otherwise functioning in a normal independent way.

The critical juncture for the loss of family autonomy in old age is when resourceless couples belong to kin networks which are endowed with extra space but lack extra money.

TABLE 2-2 Living Arrangements of Unmarried and Married Persons Aged 65 and Over, by Size of Dwelling

MARITAL STATUS AND LIVING ARRANGEMENTS	NUMBER OF ROOMS		
	1–3	4	5+
Unmarried			
Living alone	69%	49%	25%
With married child	5	16	28
With unmarried child	15	21	20
With others	11	14	27
Total	100%	100%	100%
Married			
Living with spouse only	82%	69%	59%
With married child	1	2	8
With unmarried child	13	23	27
With others	4	6	6
Total	100%	100%	100%
Number of Cases			
Unmarried	379	287	618
Married	337	295	577

Adapted from Shanas, Townsend, Wedderburn, Friis, Milhoj, and Stehouwer, 1968:190. Source: British national sample of old people, 1962. Note that these data fail to differentiate between cases where the old person moved in with someone else and those where the other person is living in the old person's home.

The crucial effect of space on doubling up in old age can be seen in Table 2-2. The larger the number of rooms in the house, the larger the proportion of old people living jointly with married or unmarried children. A general tendency to minimize encroachments on family autonomy was visible: two married couples seldom lived together; rather, an aged couple usually lived with an unmarried child or a widowed parent with a married child. Particularly rare was double-couple living if the house was small. However, the larger the house, the greater the possibility that two couples might share the same roof without having to share rooms. Larger houses offer more possibilities of at least limited segregation of family units within a complex household.

Given adequate resources, most families prefer to live separately. But if poverty is severe, doubling up may be necessary to physical survival even though it may exert a heavy toll on the survival of the family unit. When poverty forces families in already crowded quarters to take in outsiders, the family's ecological base is undermined. If the outsiders are not close relatives but complete strangers, the invasion is doubly disastrous. On the one hand, strangers bring with them strange ways, in contrast to the relatively easy accommodation of parents and children who have lived together before and shared the same family ways. On the other hand, strangers are not protected from sexual competition by the incest taboo governing relatives, so the marital dyad's sexual monopoly is liable to be replaced by sexual competition.

Such, at least, was the experience of many Polish peasant families who migrated to American cities in the early 1900's (Thomas and Znaniecki, 1958). Because of poverty, men could seldom afford to take their wives with them when they emigrated from Poland. Because of poverty in the new land, separated men and single men could not afford to live in hotels or other profit-making institutions but needed the cut-rate accommodations provided by immigrant families. Because of the latter's poverty, they could not afford to turn down the opportunity to increase their income by taking in boarders.

As a result of these complementary economic forces, a large proportion of immigrant families provided shelter for solitary male immigrants. The social consequence was that family autonomy was shattered and that in a large number of cases the wife entered into sexual relations with one or more of those boarders. The point is not that poverty forced her into prostitution. Indeed Thomas and Znaniecki do not suggest economic motives for the sexual relationship. Rather, once the family's autonomy was breached by the poverty-motivated taking in of boarders, the way was open for non-economic motives to produce extramarital involvements which further weakened the already precarious solidarity of the immigrant family.

More recently, the poverty of Negro families in American cities combined with the housing pressures of prejudice-walled ghettoes invaded by migration from the rural South produced the same infringement of family autonomy with the same disorganizing results. Conversely it takes both adequate finances and adequate housing to provide a secure base for family living.

Family Disorganization

I have already suggested that poverty makes it difficult for a family to achieve or maintain its autonomy and that when the home is invaded by outsiders the family tends to be disorganized. Outside invasion is not the only way in which poverty disorganizes family life. It undermines family solidarity directly, between husbands and wives and between parents and children.

Role Failure   In modern societies, the husband is expected to be the chief support for his family. If he fails in this responsibility, he loses not only the respect of his dependents but even his own self-respect. This demoralizes the whole family. This demoralization is a stratified phenomenon, most pervasive among families at the bottom of the social heap.

Liebow (1967), for example, noted that few impoverished Negro men in Washington, D. C., were able to support their families for very long. This failure was a source of almost chronic disappointment to their wives. Perhaps the wives were naive to expect otherwise, but it is difficult not to in a society where the cultural norms call for the husband to support his family. When that expectation is disappointed, the whole system of reciprocal role expectations in marriage is thrown out of kilter.

Failure in economic roles is particularly widespread among black Americans, but wherever it occurs it has the same disorganizing effect. Komarovsky's blue-collar whites were just as upset by the husband's financial inadequacies as were Liebow's blue-collar blacks. Indeed, insofar as poverty is a relative matter, the smaller the proportion of families in one's social group who suffer from unemployment or from low wages, the sharper the contrast between expectations and reality.

In any case, poor families in rich societies, regardless of color, suffer the repercussions of not having enough money. When every unusual expense produces a major crisis, conflict over money is endemic. When life is soured by inadequate food, clothing, and shelter, family members take their frustrations out on each other in quarrels. Couples who try to avoid fighting by avoiding each other are correspondingly alienated from each other. When few discretionary resources are available, neither parents nor children can plan for the future, and children tend to turn elsewhere for any hope of escape from their bleak existence.

Marriage Failure   It would be surprising indeed if men and women faced with such basic role failure did not find their marriages impaired both subjectively and objectively. When poor couples are asked how they feel about their marriages, they often confess that they are unhappy. For instance, among Komarovsky's blue-collar couples, almost half of those earning less than $3,500 were unhappy in contrast to barely one third of those earning more. Moreover, Komarovsky felt that even the so-called "happy" marriages suffered visibly from their economic inadequacy in such subjective forms as "anxiety about the future, the sense of defeat, concern about the failure to give one's children a good start in life" and a general lack of enthusiasm about the success of their marriage (p. 290). In general, then, poverty undermines the psychological satisfactoriness of marriage.

It does not necessarily follow, however, that riches unambiguously add to marital happiness. That depends on the ease with which the money is obtained. Money earned the hard way, by long hours at work, may still be better than poverty but interferes with the husband's ability to be a companion to his wife (perhaps the crucial role on which her marital happiness depends).

Table 2-3 shows that in both the United States and Japan, the wife's marital satisfaction declined at the highest income levels. Other data from the same studies suggest that companionship is indeed impaired when men work more than fifty or sixty hours a week. The tendency of marital satisfaction in Japan to decline at a relatively lower income level than in the U. S. presumably reflects the fact that Japanese working hours are typically longer (fifty hours instead of the standard American forty hours) and that hardworking Japanese businessmen are conspicuously absent from home. The relativity of income is also apparent in the table since Tokyo wives found that they could live satisfactorily by their standards and within their cost-of-living environment on incomes which would have been below the poverty threshold in the United States.

So economic resources cannot be provided to the family at too great a

TABLE 2-3 Wife's Marital Satisfaction, by Husband's Income

	HUSBAND'S INCOME				
	*Very Low**	*Low*	*Moderate*	*High*	*Very High*
Wife's marital satisfaction					
Detroit	4.4	4.8	5.1	5.2	5.0
Tokyo	—	5.4	5.5	4.5	4.5
Number of wives					
Detroit	64	148	119	43	25
Tokyo	—	210	161	43	27
*Annual income					
Detroit	< $3,000	$3,000+	$5,000+	$7,000+	$10,000+
Tokyo	—	< $1,000	$1,000+	$1,333+	$1,667+

Adapted from Blood (1967):166. The Detroit families were a cross-section sample of the entire range of 1954 incomes in the city but none of the Tokyo families were poverty-stricken by 1958 Japanese standards.

cost in time without diminishing marital happiness. Presumably this means that inherited wealth is a particularly satisfactory basis for family life and that working men whose hourly wages are high but who resist the temptation to work as many hours as possible have an alternative way for combining occupational roles and family roles without detriment to either.

If we disregard the complicating factor of the cost of earning income and focus only on income itself, it seems safe to assume that there is a straight-forward relationship between income and family happiness. If poverty-induced unhappiness is sufficiently severe it tends to destroy the entire marriage. Insofar as the economic basis of marriage is inadequate, the rate of failure rises correspondingly.

Figure 2-1 presents an indirect test of this hypothesis. Ideally we should have information about the economic resources during the period of marriage which preceded the subsequent marital dissolution. We can only assume that most of the men with low incomes portrayed in this figure also had relatively low incomes while they were still married. One other problem is that low-income men are doubly handicapped: Not only are their first marriages more apt to end in failure, but their ability to enter into second marriages is impaired as well. Therefore they are more apt to be stranded in a currently post-married state than prosperous men who can move swiftly from one marriage to the next. Given these twin interferences with family success and with family re-formation, no wonder poor men are more apt to be discovered by census takers as currently separated or divorced.

From beginning to end, poor people fight a losing battle with respect to marriage and family life. They can hardly afford to get married in the first place, to have as many children as they would like, or to keep their grown children with them in societies which cherish extended families. On the other hand, they find it difficult to resist external encroachments on their autonomy and the internal corrosion which comes with personal disappointment and with disillusionment in the man's income-producing role. No wonder, then, their families are unstable. They lack the economic prerequisites for stability.

FIGURE 2-1.   *Separated and Divorced Men, by Current Income*

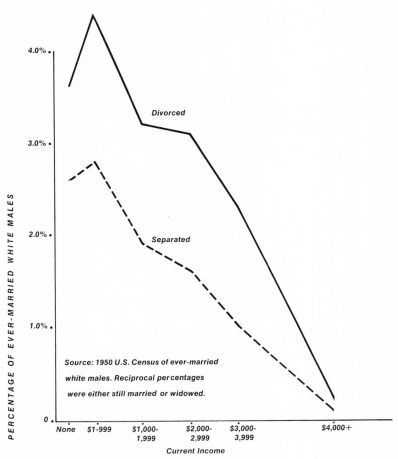

Adapted from Hillman (1960):41.

OCCUPATIONAL STATUS

Occupation and income are closely related to each other. Generally, professionals and managers are paid more than unskilled laborers. So there is a good deal of overlapping between these two types of stratification. But whereas I examined the economic resources available to married couples in the previous section, I will now pay closer attention to the people themselves and more especially to the man. In interpreting the consequences of the man's occupational status for his family, I will be especially interested in the way the occupation has affected him. My hypothesis is that blue-collar work offers little opportunity for learning human relations skills, but that white-collar work often involves such skills. I assume that to play such contrasting occupational roles forty or more hours a week, year after year, has a socializing effect on the man which carries over into his behavior as husband and father and indirectly affects his wife's behavior in her family roles.

In any case, our independent (causal) variable here is the man's occupation, arrayed from high-status professional and managerial work to low-status unskilled labor, from white-collar to blue-collar work. I will also include in my studies references to middle-class versus lower-class or working-class families since the white-collar–blue-collar distinction is usually the chief component in this classification scheme. In these "class" studies, the independent variable may not always be exclusively occupational. But I believe they will illustrate my basic thesis that the higher the social status, the greater the ability to perform marital and parental roles.

Premarital Behavior

In the U.S.A., economic resources are generally so high that even the lowest groups are not delayed in getting married. Indeed, lower class people generally marry and become more sexually involved earlier than higher status peers.

Kinsey (1948) found that low-status boys were more apt to engage in premarital intercourse by the time they reached their late teens. Almost 80 percent of unskilled workers but less than 40 percent of white collar workers had engaged in premarital intercourse at that age. Moreover, this difference in the proportion of boys ever engaging in intercourse was compounded by differences in the frequency of intercourse. Semi-skilled workers had typically engaged in premarital intercourse more than once a week whereas those middle-class men who had ever had intercourse at all typically did so only every four or five weeks. Indeed, so common was premarital intercourse in the semi-skilled group that it accounted for more than half of their entire sexual climaxes from all sources, compared to less than 10 percent for the entire middle-class group. By contrast, the latter derived most of their sexual "outlets" from masturbation.

Status differentials in the sexual behavior of American girls were less clear-cut since even working class girls often preferred to remain virgin until marriage. However, the active sexuality of lower-class boys required the co-operation of at least some girls. Hence the lower class was sharply divided between an extraordinarily promiscuous minority and a more restrained majority. Relatively little is known about this promiscuous minority though it seems probable that they were concentrated in the lower reaches of the work-

TABLE 2-4 Premarital Sexual Behavior of 16–20-Year-Old Boys, by Adult Occupational Status

Premarital Sexual Behavior	Unskilled	Semi-Skilled	Skilled	Lower White Collar	Upper White Collar	Professional	High/Low Ratio***
Ever experienced premarital intercourse between ages 16–20.*	79%	77%	66%	39%	39%	35%	0.44X
Median weekly frequency of premarital intercourse for those ever experiencing it.	0.9	1.1	0.6	0.3	0.2	0.2	0.22
Sources of sexual climax of all boys (with or without premarital intercourse)** {Premarital intercourse	40%	51%	37%	9%	9%	8%	0.25X
Masturbation	38	29	44	64	67	70	1.84
Other	22	20	19	27	24	22	
Total climaxes	100%	100%	100%	100%	100%	100%	
Number of Boys	198	318	104	516	1021	416	

Adapted from Kinsey (1948):422–423 and 430–431. Source: American boys who subsequently entered the same occupation as their fathers.

* Reciprocal percentages never engaged in premarital intercourse during the five-year period.

** Percentage of all sexual climaxes experienced during the five-year period derived respectively from intercourse, masturbation, or such other sources as nocturnal emission and petting to climax.

*** The High/Low Ratio is the ratio of the highest status (far right column) to lowest status (far left column). For instance, 0.44X means that 0.44 times as many professionals as unskilled men had premarital intercourse between ages 16 and 20; 1.84X means that 84% more of the professional group's climaxes derived from masturbation compared to the proportion for unskilled men.

ing class. In studying an impoverished Polish–American village in Connecticut during the Depression, Green (1941) noted that the girls were vulnerable to sexual exploitation because they lacked attractive occupational opportunities. Since the only jobs available were in "sweat-shops" or domestic service, the girls were desperately eager to get married and often succumbed to boys' sexual overtures in the hope that they might thereby hasten their escape into marriage. Perhaps the strategy worked. At least early marriage was the common pattern for those lower-class young people.

One consequence of the greater premarital sexual involvement of some working-class girls is a higher proportion of premarital pregnancies. Christensen and Meissner (1953) found that 16 percent of the brides of unskilled laborers but only 5 percent of the brides of professional men in Tippecanoe County, Indiana, bore their first child within seven months after marriage. To some extent this status differential may also have reflected a greater middle-class tendency to secure an abortion when confronted with a premarital pregnancy. But the general tendency of low-status people to practice contraception less faithfully after marriage seems likely to occur premaritally as well. Rainwater (1966:104) reported a general tendency for lower-class girls to report that "they were completely unprepared for sexual relations in marriage or for their first premarital experiences, that no one had ever told them much about sex and that they had only a vague idea of what was involved." This ignorance of the facts of life provided no basis for contraceptive precautions and left the lower-class girl who engaged in sexual relations vulnerable to conception.

If premarital sexual relations result from ignorance on the girl's part and impulsive behavior on the boy's, it follows that mate-selection will also be chancy. From their study of British working-class couples, Slater and Woodside (1951) were impressed with the extent to which marriages resulted from chance encounters on neighborhood street-corners and in public gathering-places such as dance halls, cafes, and pubs. This informality in working-class mate-selection may be contrasted with the tendency of middle-class people to marry those they met in such organized settings as colleges, churches, and clubs.

Once working-class couples began going together, they moved more rapidly into marriage. Kanin (1960) found in a study of married students at a midwestern university that girls from working-class backgrounds married after only 13 months of going steady whereas those from upper-middle-class backgrounds went steady two years before getting married. Since the husbands of all these girls were attending the same university, we cannot attribute the difference to the interference of education in the middle-class case. Rather, the middle-class girls seem to have approached marriage more deliberately.

We may summarize the premarital behavior of low-status young people as less restrained, less planned, and more precipitate. Conversely the higher the occupational status of young people and their families, the more restrained their premarital behavior seems to be.

Marital Interaction Patterns

Having blundered at an early age into premarital sexual relations, working-class couples fall into patterns of sexual interaction which prove relatively unsatisfactory after marriage. One measure of this differential satisfaction is the physiological response of the wife to orgasm in intercourse. Kinsey (1953) found that the higher the wife's father's occupational status, the higher the percentage of her marital intercourse which resulted in orgasm. He failed to report comparable figures for the *husband's* occupational status, but the wife's orgasm capacity was even more closely related to her own educational level. It seems, therefore, that wives of men in higher occupational statuses also experience more orgasms.

TABLE 2-5 Interest in and Enjoyment of Marital Sexual Relations by Husbands and Wives, by Social Class

	SOCIAL CLASS		HIGH/ LOW RATIO
	Lower Class	Middle Class	
Husbands			
Great interest and enjoyment	59%	78%	1.32X
Mild interest and enjoyment	41	22	0.54
Slightly negative toward sex	0	0	
Reject sexual relations	0	0	
Total	100%	100%	
Number of husbands	115	56	
Wives			
Great interest and enjoyment	37%	50%	1.35X
Mild interest and enjoyment	21	36	1.71
Slightly negative toward sex	30	11	0.37
Reject sexual relations	12	3	0.25
Total	100%	100%	
Number of wives	137	58	

Adapted from Rainwater (1966):98. Source: White and Negro married individuals in Chicago, Cincinnati, and Oklahoma City.

A more direct way of assessing the satisfactoriness of marital intercourse is to ask people how they feel about their experience. Table 2-5 shows the results of one such inquiry. Although men generally reported enjoying intercourse more than women, middle-class individuals of both sexes reported more positive feelings than lower-class individuals. Negative reactions were heavily concentrated among the lower-class women whereas relatively few middle-class women felt negative about their sexual experience. More detailed data presented by Rainwater showed that when lower-class men and women were further subdivided, the upper-lower class was intermediate in its feelings but the lower-lower class was especially negative. For example, fully 20 percent of the lower-lower-class women rejected sexual relations.

This shows that the lower the husband's occupational status, the less satisfactory marital intercourse is for both him and his wife. And this lesser satisfaction seems to be not only psychological but, at least in the case of the wife, physiological as well.

What makes lower-class people have less meaningful sexual experience? Slater and Woodside suggested that working-class intercourse in Britain was relatively monotonous. They described the men they studied as "complacent" and noted that marital intercourse had become simply habitual. For the wives, the most common attitude was one of boredom, expressed in such comments as:

> "I'm not keen." "I don't think there's anything in it." "Sometimes it bores me." "I'm not really interested." "It's something that's got to be done, and the quicker the better." "My heart's not in it." "It's the one part of marriage I could do without." (1951:167)

TABLE 2-6 Value Derived from Marital Sexual Relations by Husbands and Wives, by Social Class

	SOCIAL CLASS		HIGH/ LOW
Sexual Relations Provide	*Lower Class*	*Middle Class*	*RATIO*
Husbands			
Socio-emotional closeness and exchange	37%	75%	2.03X
Psychophysiological pleasure and relief only	63	25	0.40
Total	100%	100%	
Number of husbands	71	56	
Wives			
Socio-emotional closeness and exchange	56%	89%	1.59X
Psychophysiological pleasure and relief only	44	11	0.25
Total	100%	100%	
Number of wives	55	46	

Adapted from Rainwater (1966):102.

Why do working-class husbands and wives find sex much more boring than their middle-class peers do? Table 2–6 offers one explanation. For both sexes, but more especially for men, Rainwater found that working-class couples emphasized sheer physiological pleasure and relief of tension. This self-regarding attitude means that the partner is being exploited for one's own benefit without much concern for the partner's own response, to say nothing of concern for any emotional closeness. Middle-class couples by contrast are concerned for the partner and for the relationship, which may be interpreted as indicating their fuller socialization for the role of husband and of wife. Middle-class people are as concerned for their interpersonal relations in bed as for good human relations in the office. Such concern for the partner's feelings and for the couple's mutual relationship makes middle-class sexual intercourse more satisfying to both partners.

When working-class men are married to wives who dislike (or at least often refuse) sexual intercourse, these men become sexually frustrated. One consequence is a greater tendency of lower-class men to engage in extramarital intercourse during the early years of marriage when their sexual drive is still powerful. Kinsey (1948) found that unskilled men engaged in 17 times as much extramarital intercourse between the ages of 21 and 25 as professional men of the same age. This promiscuous sexuality after marriage resembles the more promiscuous pattern of working-class men before marriage—involvement with multiple partners is a lower-class male habit.

After children are born, the same inadequacies in working-class marriages provide poorly socialized men with another potential sexual object—their daughters. Although incest is relatively rare in the United States, it is concentrated primarily among men at the bottom of the social scale. Nor are the men alone responsible for this deviant solution to their sexual problem. Kaufman, Peck, and Tagiuri (1954) found in a study of incestuous men (all of them from poverty-stricken homes) that their wives tacitly found in the incestuous relationship a "solution" to their own sexual problem: If the husband could have sexual relations with a daughter, the wife would not have to be bothered by his sexual demands. For incest to occur, frequently requires socialization inadequacies on the part of both parents, a situation which is normally found only in the more disorganized segments of the lower class.

Segregation of the Sexes Underlying the sexual difficulties of lower-class families is a pattern of segregation between men and women. Rainwater (1964) noted in a review of the literature on "cultures of poverty" in the United States, Britain, Puerto Rico, and Mexico, that the roles of husbands and wives were sharply segregated in all four. And in his 1966 study, Rainwater found that marriages split by such role segregation had substantially less sexual satisfaction than marriages in which husbands and wives shared more of their marital activities with each other.

What causes the sexes to shun each other within working-class marriages? Partly it reflects a broader social segregation of the sexes. In Puerto Rico, Landy (1959) described lower-class rural patterns as "extremely prudish, in theory and practice, with regard to the insulation and protection of the female." He found that middle-class families often attended social functions in town "where the sexes mix freely, an unheard-of occurrence for lower-class families where sex separation lines cross every area of life."

The segregated social life of lower-class men and women in turn results from their greater dependence on propinquity as a basis for social relations. Insofar as a lower-class boy grew up in a certain neighborhood, he is likely to have been a member of a locality-based male gang. Girls likewise have strong peer groups. Since lower-class marriages also are more apt to be based on propinquity, both partners will have continuing ties after marriage with their premarital buddies. The man's leisure is apt to be spent at the corner pub with his old pals, and the wife's in neighborhood kaffee-klatsches or with her mother and other female relatives. As a result, husband and wife spend relatively little time together, either by themselves or with other couples.

By contrast, middle-class couples are more apt to marry across neighborhood lines or even across community boundaries. Their specialized leisure interests and their organizational memberships throw them together with people from a distance. Even if one partner settles down in his old neighborhood, the other is likely to be a stranger to that neighborhood (which forces him to depend on the spouse more than if both were at home in the neighborhood). Actually, middle-class couples are less likely to settle in either partner's neighborhood. The specialized interests which encouraged marriage across geographical space also pull the couple away from their home bases into new residential locations. Then both partners will be in new communities where the only persons they initially know are each other. Such social isolation forces them into greater interdependence (Bott, 1957).

In addition to greater sex role differentiation in the working class, there also tends to be less communication between partners and less joint activity of husband and wife. For instance in both Detroit and Tokyo, Blood (1967) found less "informative companionship" between husband and wife. When a working-class husband returned home from work, he was less apt to tell his wife about things that had happened during the day (perhaps because his job was less interesting), but she too was less apt to communicate her day's events. And in the crucial form of husband–wife companionship—going out together just for a good time—blue-collar Tokyo couples "dated" each other barely half as often as white-collar couples.

In a study of German men, Rainwater (1962) found that lower-class husbands gave less affection and emotional support to their wives, labelling them "frills" which they could not afford. The cost in this case was not economic but emotional. These men found the world so difficult and unrewarding that they did not have enough emotional resources to be able to give to their wives. Rather, they tried to get from their wives some of the solace which their role in the outside world did not provide.

That the wives were not happy with this situation is implied by Rainwater's report that the men often complained that their wives were "too sensitive" and "too emotional." In any case, the men found their wives difficult to understand and felt that they had never been able to bridge the gulf between the sexes.

In general, then, sex-role segregation seems to be more characteristic of working-class than of middle-class couples in industrial societies. At first glance this seems strange in contrast to our earlier discussion of the greater sex-segregation of wealthy families in agrarian societies. Perhaps the seeming contradiction can be resolved by saying that economic resources make rigid segregation possible but not inevitable. The degree of segregation in modern working-class families is far less intense than in feudal elite families. Modern middle-class families have the economic resources to segregate the sexes if they so desired, but for the reasons suggested here, they prefer togetherness.

Marital Power Structure   Whereas the segregation of working-class marriages is a comparatively clear-cut phenomenon, the power structure of those marriages is less easy to assess. One might expect on the basis of the greater demandingness of the German working-class husbands that working-class marriages would be more patriarchal.

A study by Rainwater, Coleman, and Handel (1959) suggested that such was indeed the case. The authors reported that workingmen's wives saw their husbands as "dominant and controlling" and as the "personified representatives of the external world" (p. 70). However, it is important to note that their sample was restricted to wives who were especially apt to have that point of view because (1) none of them was employed outside the home (yet external employment is generally more common in the working class than in the middle class) and (2) all of them had small children. These wives were therefore cut off from meaningful involvement in the outside world and forced to depend on their husbands as the families' representatives in that world. These conditions were two of the most powerful sources of husband-dominance found by Blood and Wolfe (1960) in our study of Detroit marriages. It seems likely, therefore, that if Rainwater, Coleman, and Handel had studied a cross-section sample of the entire working class, they would have found less husband-dominance than in their restricted segment of that class.

Even so, it is important to note the particular forms which that "dominance" took. For example, the working-class wives were "afraid to act openly in a fashion contrary to their husband's wishes" but this seems to have reflected the weakness of the marriage bond more than the husband's power (p. 69). Or, to put it another way, the husband's power stems from the marginality of his position in the family, not from his centrality.

Waller (1938) pointed out many years ago that there is a kind of power which accrues to the person who has the "least interest" in a relationship. By threatening to sever the relationship altogether, that person can coerce the more interested party into making concessions. But that is a precarious basis for power. It seems to be the characteristic workingman's basis. Rainwater reported that "men go their own ways . . . are quite independent and can easily leave" their families altogether (p. 71). So working-class men seem to exert a type of power based on their marginal position in the family, a marginality which gives them leverage over the wife when they want to use it.

But if the lower-class man's position is marginal, who occupies the central place in his family? By default the answer must necessarily be his wife. Much as the lower-class woman might like to depend on her husband, she finds that she cannot. For the day-to-day management of the family affairs, she is stuck—reluctantly to be sure, but stuck nevertheless—with the burden of responsibility. She has to make decisions unaided, despite her lack of self-confidence compared to better-educated middle-class wives. She has to control the family purse strings for fear her husband will gamble away or drink up the little money they have. Much as the working-class man and woman both might like to think of the husband as powerful, in actuality he is strong only erratically. Mostly he isn't that interested in the ordinary decisions of family life and is happy to dump them on his wife's shoulders.

By contrast, white-collar men and especially executive and professional men are more responsible in their marriages (Blood and Wolfe, 1960). The higher the man's occupational status, the greater his power tends to be at home. Whether this is power *over* the wife may be debated. The chief difference from the working class is that men who exercise responsibility at work tend to be more responsible in domestic affairs as well. Their wives apparently welcome this greater involvement, and on major financial issues defer to their husbands because they see them as having expert knowledge derived from their experience at work. This seems to be a voluntary deference by the wives more than a coercive dominance by the husbands.

In power structure, then, modern stratification resembles the pattern in feudal societies. Goode (1963) noted that in feudal Japan "descriptions of lower class and especially peasant behavior . . . suggest that the wife was somewhat more of a partner and less of an obsequious supporting servant than in upper-strata families" (p. 346). So the higher the man's position in the class system, the higher his position within the family.

Family Crises

If working-class families tend to be hastily formed, the husband and wife have a distant relationship, and the husband's position tends to be marginal, it follows that such marriages should be unstable. Various data support this inference.

In both Tokyo and Detroit, I found (1967) that blue-collar marriages were less satisfactory than white-collar ones. In the Detroit case, the data were gathered from wives only, but in Tokyo information from both sexes showed that blue-collar marriages were evaluated as less satisfactory by the participants.

Such subjective dissatisfaction in low-status marriages which are still intact is paralleled by correspondingly more frequent marital dissolution.

TABLE 2-7 Desertion and Divorce Rates, by Husband's Occupation

ACTUAL VS. EXPECTED NUMBER OF BROKEN MARRIAGES	HUSBAND'S OCCUPATION						HIGH/ LOW RATIO
	Labor and Service	Semi-Skilled	Skilled	Clerical and Sales	Mana-gerial	Profes-sional	
Desertions	127%*	126%	61%	58%	58%	30%	0.24X
Divorces	84%	146%	95%	106%	47%	61%	0.73X

Adapted from Kephart (1955):459, 461. Source: Philadelphia desertion cases in the Municipal Court in 1950 compared to the 1950 census of occupations in Philadelphia; and Philadelphia divorce cases 1937–1950 compared to an average of the 1940 and 1950 censuses of occupations. *This figure means that there were 27 percent more desertion cases involving men in labor and service occupations than would be expected from the number of such men in the local population.

Table 2-7 shows that both desertion cases and divorce cases were more common in low-status families. The difference by occupational status was especially prominent for desertion cases which reflect the abandonment by the husband of financial responsibility for his wife and children. The irregularity in divorce rates may reflect the fact that a legal divorce is not strictly speaking necessary unless a man wants to remarry or unless there is a dispute over the property settlement or custody of the children. Thus the number of legal divorces secured by laborers and by service workers is probably depressed by reluctance to pay the legal fees required in the absence of compelling reason to do so. Indeed, it seems probable from my earlier discussion of the difficulties of family formation for impoverished men that a certain proportion of cases in this lowest category drift into subsequent common-law unions in order to avoid the costs of legalizing the failure of the old marriage. It may also be that more desertion cases would be brought to court if low-status wives hoped they could get more support from their impoverished husbands. In other words, the true rates of marital dissolution among laborers and service workers were probably higher than indicated by either the desertion or divorce cases. If we could discover the actual rates of abandonment of families by their husbands, they would be even more closely linked to occupational status than these court statistics show.

Just as when economic resources are low, so when occupational status is low, marriages tend to work less well in the sense of being unsatisfactory to the participants and of ending up in failure.

Families also differ by class status in the kinds of crises which they experience. Koos (1950) found lower-class families plagued by physical crises such as unemployment and conflict with other families living in the same crowded tenement. Such crises were especially common in the disorganized lower-lower class but eased somewhat with the relative economic stability and better housing achieved by the upper-lower class. Middle-class families seldom faced these physical problems. They could take family security and family autonomy for granted. Their physical security made it possible for them to define crises as the interpersonal psychological tensions which arose between husband and wife or between parents and children. Lower-class families experienced the same tensions but were so preoccupied with physical problems that they could not afford to worry about their psychological ones. They considered quarreling, for example, a chronic state rather than a crisis. Interpersonal conflicts were less frequent in middle-class families which gave those families a normally harmonious base-line against which quarrels became crises. The tendency to so define what would have been treated as normal in a working-class family also reflected the higher ideals of middle-class families. They hoped to achieve chronic harmony and felt threatened by occasional breaches of the peace. So they defined such breaches as crises and mobilized their resources to meet them.

The contrast between the physical problems of the lower class and the psychological problems of the middle class is paralleled by their contrasting patterns of extramarital behavior. We have already seen that working-class men engage in more extramarital intercourse than middle-class men during the early years of marriage. I have suggested that this working-class behavior is largely a response to sexual frustration in the face of a strong biological drive. By contrast, Kinsey reported (1948) that the proportion of middle-class men engaging in extramarital intercourse rose as they grew older (reaching a peak during their forties, in contrast to a declining frequency among working-class men. This means that for middle-class men, extramarital intercourse increases as their biological drive decreases. To explain this paradox it is necessary to note that marital satisfaction declines with length of marriage. This suggests that for middle-class men the main cause of extramarital adventures is not biological but psychological. This is not to ignore the biological component in their sexual experience, but to suggest that they are searching primarily for love, affection, and understanding rather than for biological satisfaction. If extramarital affairs are crises for both classes, this means that the same event has a biological meaning for one class but a psychological meaning for the other.

Koos found that two thirds of middle-class crises involved parent–child relationships while the remaining third were husband–wife conflicts. Although middle-class families are more apt to define parent–child conflicts as crises, working-class parents are also concerned with their children. But the focus of the concern is different. Again, the difference might be summarized in the contrast between physical and psychological problems.

Kohn (1963) found working-class families preoccupied with securing behavioral conformity from their children whereas middle-class families focused on more subtle, psychological phenomena. This difference reflects contrasting actual circumstances. Because their methods of socialization are less effective, working-class parents encounter more defiant and unsocialized behavior from their children. They worry about whether their children will be caught stealing and must cope with rebellious behavior at home. Middle-class parents can count on greater conformity from their children and can therefore turn their attention to more subtle psychological questions.

In general, then, working-class families not only face more frequent tensions but the kinds of problems they encounter are more concrete than middle-class crises.

Response to Crises   The fact that middle-class crises are subtle does not mean that they are taken lightly. Koos' middle-class families reacted to their crises more seriously than his working-class families, perhaps because their troubles were less chronic, but also because they were more subject to their control. Most of the crises faced by working-class families originate outside the family in economic conditions and neighborhood conditions beyond their control, so there is little such families can do except learn to live with their problems. As a result, most of his lower-class families were moderately disorganized with little hope of improvement.

Koos' middle-class families, by contrast, mobilized all their resources to cope with their occasional crises. They took them extremely seriously, often dropping everything else to focus on the cause of the trouble. All those involved in the conflict were asked to sit down together, discuss the problem, and arrive at a mutually satisfactory solution. Although the crisis caused severe disorganization at the moment (in the sense that all other activities were suspended for the time being), in the long run confronting the crisis produced greater understanding and raised the quality of family functioning above its pre-crisis level. In other words, middle-class families not only solved their problems more successfully, but learned from them. Later, they could look back and say, "I'm glad we went through that crisis because we learned to understand each other better as a result of it."

In trying to solve tough external problems, Koos' working-class families often turned to social agencies. More than half had gone to a private or governmental agency at one time or another, especially to ask for money. By contrast less than one tenth of his middle-class families had ever sought outside help. Presumably, this difference in external reliance reflected both the difference in problems faced and in the family's ability to cope with those problems.

We have already seen that problems of working-class families were externally derived and could not be resolved by the families themselves. Only if outside agencies helped could the families hope to weather their crises and return to normal. The middle-class families, on the other hand, faced problems which were strictly internal and could draw upon richer personal resources (such as superior education and experience in solving problems in human relations). Hence they had less need to seek outside help. Where they did seek outside assistance, it was not money, but mediation that they wanted. Only if family members could not find their own way to compromise solutions did they call in a detached third party. Normally, they tried to solve their problems by using their own resources, turning to outside agencies only in those rare cases where their own resources proved inadequate.

Another resource utilized almost exclusively by lower-status families is advice columns in newspapers and magazines. The writers of letters to one women's magazine were mostly waitresses, factory workers, sales clerks, typists and beauty operators (Hillman, 1954). They had typically dropped out of school after only one year of high school and married before their peers were old enough to graduate. Although not yet 21 years old on the average by the time they wrote the columnist, 29 percent had already been married more than once and another 22 percent were separated or divorced. They asked for information about sex and birth control, reflecting their involvement in abortions, illegitimate births, venereal disease, and nonmarital intercourse.

We have seen that middle-class families rarely turn to social agencies or advice columns for help in trouble. However, wives at all social levels have informal confidantes with whom they share their troubles and from whom they seek advice. In this sense, middle-class wives are no more self-reliant than working-class wives. However, Mayer (1966a) found that the particular confidantes chosen by wives of upper-middle class executives and professional men in New York City differed from those chosen by wives of blue-collar men.

Figure 2-2 shows that both lower-class and middle-class women's closest confidantes were apt to be relatives. Middle-class wives, however, were considerably more likely than lower-class women to have friends as confidantes. Indeed if all confidantes were taken together (an average of five per wife in this study), a majority of the middle-class confidantes were friends whereas a majority of the lower-class confidantes were relatives. Similarly lower-class women found relatives more satisfactory audiences for their troubles, disclosing substantially more information about their marital difficulties to kin confidantes than to friend confidantes (whereas middle-class wives disclosed almost as much to friends as to relatives). In general, then, relatives were the first recourse for wives of both social classes and were extraordinarily important to lower-class wives since their pattern of life was more narrowly confined to a circle of relatives.

These confidantes were almost entirely feminine (hence I use the feminine spelling of the word) and the kin utilized were almost entirely primary kin (parents, siblings, and children). Both Mayer and Komarovsky found that in the rare instances where wives' confidantes were masculine, they were always primary kin (fathers or brothers). Surprisingly, however, the primary kin were not always the wife's; in some cases they were her husband's.

Mayer's working-class women rarely crossed family lines (only two cases out of 23). But his middle-class wives were almost as apt to turn to the mother-in-law or a sister-in-law as to their own mother or sister. Those who did so expressed their sense of closeness to their in-laws, and this in turn reflected the bilateral solidarity of both partners with each other's families. By contrast, the narrow range of sociability which cuts lower-class wives off from outside friendship makes it difficult for them to feel close to their in-laws, too. In both social classes, kin are the most important resources for this form of psychotherapy. But whereas working-class women acquire most of their

FIGURE 2-2. Proportion of Relatives among Closest Confidantes, by Social Class

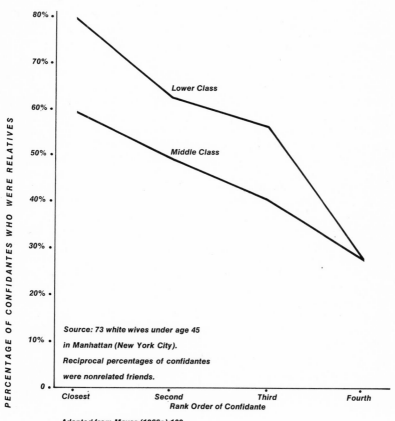

Source: 73 white wives under age 45
in Manhattan (New York City).
Reciprocal percentages of confidantes
were nonrelated friends.

Adapted from Mayer (1966a):109.

kin at birth, middle-class women add a new set at marriage. Only for the middle-class could the old saying "We have not lost a daughter but gained a son" be transposed to read "I have not lost my mother but gained another."

Middle-class wives not only relied more often on unrelated friends (perhaps because they lived farther away from relatives) but utilized a larger circle of friends (perhaps for the same reason). Within that larger circle, however, they were more selective than lower-class wives who tended to tell their troubles indiscriminately to all of the fewer friends available to them. Middle-class wives selected a smaller number of confidantes to whom they revealed a more complete picture of their complaints about their husbands. This reliance on one or two best friends was especially marked during the first decade of marriage when they were trying to work out a satisfactory relationship with their husbands.

The extraordinary openness of middle-class wives with these selected confidantes was not carried on behind the husband's back, for these wives were extraordinarily open at home, too. Confident that their problems could be solved, they worked on them directly with the husband, using friends and relatives for supplementary advice. For lower-class wives, by contrast, to confront the husband was to risk alienating him. Some working-class wives complained to the husband about his behavior, hoping to coerce him into changing his behavior, but with little two-way communication or mutual problem-solving. Many, however, kept their mouths shut at home, opening them only in the safety of their childhood family circle where sympathy with their hopeless plight could be counted on.

Mayer's picture complements Koos'. Even where the lower-class wife is concerned with a marital problem rather than the usual external problems, her approach tends to be external in the sense of going outside the household rather than confronting the husband directly. And since she seldom takes a corrective approach to her marital problems, she is forced to live as perennially with her interpersonal problems as the whole family does with its physical problems.

Lower-class family crises, then, tend to be more destructive in their long-range effects because they are less easily resolved even with the help of outside agencies. For such reasons, crises cause lower-class families to fall apart whereas, once surmounted, such crises may even strengthen a middle-class family and enrich its subsequent life together.

Family Growth

Class differences in reproductive behavior fluctuate widely under varying historical circumstances. The British Royal Commission on Population pointed out in 1949 that the Victorian middle classes (managers and professional men) were the first to begin limiting their families. As a result the middle-class birth rate fell sharply while the working-class birth rate remained high, producing a widening gap between their rates of child-bearing. However, one or two generations later, the working classes followed the example of their superiors and began limiting their family size, too. This narrowed the class differences which had opened in the earlier transitional period. As the economic and social conditions of the working class improved, their aspirations for their style of life also rose. So in an atmosphere of increasing optimism, they limited their children to the number whom they could endow with a satisfactory start in life.

The gradual disappearance of class differences in the number of children intentionally produced tends to mask qualitative differences in the fate of children at different class levels. These are revealed in contrasting patterns of adoption. Jeffery (1962) found sharp differences between occupational groups in Arizona in the circumstances under which children were adopted. Big business and professional men adopted children only when they were unable to bear children of their own. Social agencies supplied them with illegitimate children of unrelated persons. Lower-middle class adoptions more commonly involved adoption by the husband of children born to his wife in a previous marriage which had ended in divorce. This occurs more often in the lower-middle class because their divorce rate is higher than that of the upper-middle class.

At the bottom of the social scale, unskilled workers, farm laborers, and unemployed men frequently adopted children who were distantly related to them but whose parents were unable to care for them. Grandchildren, nieces, or nephews were legally adopted when both parents had died, had abandoned their children by mutually "deserting" the family, or had abused their children until a court had declared them unfit to retain custody of their children. Such cases reveal the instability of the lower-lower-class nuclear family and the importance of the kin network in rescuing dependent children. One other form of adoption was concentrated in the lower-lower class, namely adoption by a man of an illegitimate child born to his wife by another man prior to their marriage. Illegitimacy is relatively common among low-status girls (whereas high-status girls who become premaritally pregnant tend to rid themselves of the child by securing an abortion or placing the child for adoption). The greater tolerance of illegitimate related children by lower-class people is one reason for their greater willingness to adopt such children.

High-status families, then, adopt children of anonymous origin as a next-best substitute for bearing their own children. Lower-status families are less able to be serviced by social agencies for such purposes and more apt to be confronted with problem children of their own or of near relatives. Adoption is intended to meet the needs of children deprived of one or both parents (rather than of adults deprived of children). But in the lowest-status families it is not only the children who benefit from adoption procedures. Legal adoption may benefit the family economically by making it eligible for public assistance benefits to support the dependent child. Low-status families turn to the adoption court as a means of access to funds through other government agencies. They resemble Koos' lower-class families who sought financial help for tangible problems from social agencies.

Adoption, then, for low-status families is typically a response to a crisis in their own family or in a related family. For middle-status families it is also a response to crisis but the crisis is less apt to be externally imposed. For high-status families, on the other hand, adoption is an alternative way of achieving family growth. It therefore expresses deliberate family initiative in the same way that high-status families deliberately plan their reproduction.

Child-Rearing Methods

Once children are born or adopted, stratification affects the methods by which they are raised. Low-status families rely heavily on physical coercion; high-status families, on psychological methods.

Among the lower-lower class families of rural Puerto Rico, Landy found a severity of punishment that verged on brutality:

> Mothers punish with hands, switches, sticks, and straps. Of all instruments the last is probably the most effective because it is the symbol of paternal authority. Most men have two belts, one to wear and one to leave home. The one at home hangs on a nail in plain view of the children and the mother is authorized to use it whenever she feels the need. Nearly all mothers are convinced that spanking performs a useful function. . . . They put the child "in his place," "humble him," and "make him respect." "To teach, a parent has to hit," says one mother. And another says: ". . . the only thing that I have to do is look at them and they know if they do not do as I want they have the strap for sure." (1959:134–135)

Conversely, mothers rarely employed reasoning, and when they did so it was more a warning of what-will-happen-to-you-if-you-do-that than a discussion between parent and child. Indeed, reported Landy, "listening to the child's side and reasoning out a reply which would consider the child's testimony as possibly valid rarely occur" (p. 131). Even if the child had been in a fight, the parent would not listen to the child's report of what happened because to do so would be to surrender, however temporarily, the superior, authoritative position. Could it be that the ruthless assertiveness of these parents was at least partly due to the very precariousness of their authority? It seems that these parents reacted both out of the impoverishment of their child-rearing techniques (lacking skill in the subtleties of reasoning) and out of the threat to their authority posed by unruly children. When parental authority is spontaneously respected because children look up to their parents as role models and love them for having given much, it is not necessary to make an issue of authority. Only when authority is challenged or rests on a makeshift foundation does it become an issue.

TABLE 2-8   Fathers' Valuation of Obedience and Self-Control by Social Class

FATHER VALUES IN CHILD	UNITED STATES		ITALY	
	Working Class	Middle Class	Working Class	Middle Class
Obedience	39%	13%	45%	31%
Self-control	6%	20%	11%	23%
Number of fathers	36	46	148	160

Adapted from Pearlin and Kohn (1966). Source: Washington, D.C. and Torino, Italy. Reciprocal percentages did not select the particular value as one of the three most important for their children.

Table 2-8 shows the emphasis on obedience by working-class parents in two more cultures, the continental United States and Italy. Self-control, by

contrast, was considered a virtue almost exclusively by middle-class parents.*
Self-control, after all, is the opposite of parent-control (which is what obedience means). Working-class parents unsure of their own authority can hardly
afford to tolerate children who develop the capacity for self-control. That
would threaten the parents too much—and with good reason. The relationship
between parents and children in the working class is less secure, so children
allowed to control themselves would be less apt to follow in their parents'
footsteps. On the other hand, middle-class parents who grant their children
the right to control themselves can more confidently assume that they will
govern themselves wisely (*i.e.,* in harmony with the parents' own values).

TABLE 2-9   Child-Rearing Methods, by Social Class

Child-Rearing Method	Lower-Lower (Puerto Rico)	Upper-Lower (U.S.)	Upper-Middle (U.S.)	High/Low Ratio
Maternal rejection	100%	40%	24%	0.24X
Obedience demanded instantly	83	30	27	0.33
Aggression toward peers restricted	94	46	33	0.35
Aggression toward parents severely punished	100	51	37	0.37
Child pressured to do well in school	89	45	35	0.39
Severe toilet training	100	53	40	0.40
Masturbation severely punished	94	62	39	0.41
Frequent keeping track of child	89	53	42	0.47
Interrupting adults restricted	100	65	60	0.60
Pressure for neatness and orderliness	72	58	45	0.63
Child expected to go far in school	22	52	63	2.86
Reasoning used	0	63	71	infinity

Adapted from Landy (1959):201–213. Source: Rural Puerto Rican families with incomes
under $800/year. U.S. data from a study by Maccoby *et al.* which has been reported elsewhere
in different form (1954). Source: Greater Boston. Their upper-lower group included some
fathers with lower-white-collar occupations.

Table 2-9 suggests that the differences between social classes in valuing
obedience tend to be carried out in practice. The lower the social status, the
more parents insisted on instant obedience and cracked down on their children
for aggression toward them or even for interruptions. In the judgment of the
researchers, such actions were part of a larger pattern of emotional rejection
of the child by low-status mothers.

* Some, but not all, of the difference in values between social classes can be
attributed to differences in occupations. For example in Italy 26 percent of the
working class, but only 12 percent of the middle class, were closely supervised;
64 percent of the working class, but only 42 percent of the middle class, had jobs
requiring relatively little self-reliance; and 63 percent of the working class, but
only 14 percent of the middle class, worked mainly with things. All these characteristics of working-class jobs reinforced the emphasis on obedience rather than
on self-control.

Rejection, however, did not mean unconcern with the child's behavior. On the contrary, the lower the social status, the more the mother concerned herself with the whereabouts and the activities of the child, presumably because she had learned from experience that her child was apt to get in trouble. One form of trouble was fighting with other children, which lower-lower-class mothers tried harder to prevent.

Low-status mothers were concerned with their children's behavior inside as well as outside the home. Heavy pressure was exerted for neatness and orderliness (not easy achievements in crowded lower-class homes). Severe toilet training and a taboo on masturbation reflected the sexual inhibitions of lower-class women.

The fact that lower-class children tend to drop out of school is reflected in the pessimism of these mothers, few of whom expected their children to go far in school. Presumably their very anxiety about school leads the low-status mothers to push their children to do well there. However, Landy noted that doing well often meant "being good," "acting right," or "staying out of trouble" for the Puerto Rican mothers whereas for middle-class mothers its meaning was more apt to be academic. One reason why low-status children do poorly in school is that their homes offer them little intellectual stimulation. The complete absence of reasoning in the Puerto Rican homes deprived the children of a mental exercise that the higher status American children more often enjoyed.

In general, Table 2-9 suggests a quality of desperation in low-status homes, with the mothers trying to save their children from the fate which they know all too well is likely to befall them in a cruel world. The middle-class parents, by contrast, were generally more tolerant with their children, reflecting greater confidence that their children would become well-socialized adults.

In Europe, it was high-status families which first "invented" childhood. Aries (1962) noted that medieval society thought of children simply as little men. Only among the aristocracy in the early modern period were children set apart as an innocent, playful group dressed in distinctive costume. Long after a separate status for childhood arose among the aristocracy, children were still treated as little men in the working class.

Perhaps Table 2-9 can be interpreted the same way. For the lower-lower class, children were expected to be toilet-trained and modest from an early age. (Modesty training for little girls began at 2.0 years in Puerto Rico, but not until age 3.4 among the upper-middle-class Boston families.) They were expected to conform to adults by instant obedience and neat and orderly behavior. By contrast, higher-status families had a more relaxed approach to children, an easier acceptance of childish peccadilloes, an ability to wait patiently for children to grow up which allowed children to be viewed as temporarily separate from the adult world.

This general picture of greater permissiveness in high-status families does not apply to all aspects of life. White-collar families are concerned about some issues more than blue-collar families—for example, television. I found (1961) that children in low-status families watched television longer hours and were more apt to be allowed any program they wished. Conversely, upper-middle-class families controlled both the amount and the content of their children's television-consumption. For middle-class parents, television must not be allowed to monopolize the child's time because a child needs to engage in other activities if he is to grow in a well-rounded fashion. They also felt that television was an important educational instrument—for good or ill. They allowed their children to stay up past their usual bedtime to watch special programs of an educational nature, but at the same time they censored programs which they thought were harmful, especially violent programs.

Another way of distinguishing between lower-class and middle-class child-rearing would be to say that low-status parents seem concerned to raise their children in such a way as to minimize interference with the parents' lives whereas high-status parents focus on what they judge to be the welfare of the child himself. This difference may lie behind the erratic fluctuations in the behavior of low-status parents. Part of the time they ignore their children and are extremely *laissez-faire*. At other times they intervene in their children's lives more abruptly than middle-class parents. For example, in the same study of television, I found low-status fathers more apt to intervene directly in their children's viewing, not because they wanted to censor program content but because they wanted to watch a different program themselves. The child, therefore, was normally allowed to watch anything he wanted, but might be interrupted in the middle of a program without warning and for no child-oriented reason.

The working-class emphasis on toilet-training is paralleled by an eagerness of low-status American mothers to wean the child from breast to bottle. In both cases, a trained child is less of a nuisance to his mother. Middle-class mothers, by contrast, are more willing to put up with toilet "accidents" and with nursing if they think their child will be benefited psychologically. These differences in parental orientation are related to other stratification variables —messes can be tolerated more easily in less hectic and crowded living quarters.

Low-status families have been less adequately socialized in their childhood upbringing and by their occupational experience with the result that they are more preoccupied with their personal problems, whereas middle-class parents have been more successfully socialized into concern for the welfare of others. That concern produces greater willingness to put up with interference from their children, and greater interest in their children's activities. Middle-class parents generally are more consistent, rational, and deliberately motivated in their child-rearing methods, whereas lower-class parents are more moody, inconsistent, and irrational.

Table 2-10 pictures the control policies of a large sample of middle-class and lower-class American families. Lower-class fathers and mothers were more often autocratic, not even allowing a teenage child to express his views before telling him what to do or not to do. At the opposite extreme, lower-class parents were also more apt to ignore the child or give him free rein to do as he pleased. This bifurcation of the lower-class families as a group is reminiscent of the fluctuating and inconsistent behavior of lower-class parents as individuals.

Middle-class families were more apt to be either democratic or equalitarian. This corresponds to the middle-class willingness to reason with children and seems appropriate for children who are approaching adulthood.

TABLE 2-10 Paternal and Maternal Control of Children, by Social Class

| PARENTAL CONTROL SYSTEM | SEX AND SOCIAL CLASS OF PARENT | | | |
| | FATHERS | | MOTHERS | |
	Lower	Middle	Lower	Middle
Autocratic	22%	14%	11%	7%
Authoritarian	17	18	14	12
Democratic	28	35	34	38
Equalitarian	14	15	17	19
Permissive	18	17	24	24
Laissez-faire, ignoring	2	2	1	1
Total	100%	100%	100%	100%
Number of cases	3883	3477	3883	3477

Adapted from Elder (1962):247. Source: Seventh– to twelfth-grade children in Ohio and North Carolina schools. The control categories form a series from nonlistening parental control to noncommunicating child control. "Democratic" was defined as requiring that the final decision either be formulated by the parents or at least meet their approval after extensive parent–child discussion.

Child-Rearing Outcomes

Different methods of child-rearing should produce different kinds of children. Goode (1964) suggested that high-status parents supply more resources to their children—not just economic resources, but social and psychological benefits. One gift is a high status in society. Generally speaking, a family gives its children the father's status as their own starting point in life. That status may be improved upon by the child's efforts or lost by his failures. For children from high-status families, it provides a head start in life.

As a result of such benefits, children from high-status families are more apt to feel indebted to their parents and dependent upon them. Insofar as they (as well as society at large) look up to their parents, they will take their parents as role models for their own behavior. They more often discuss with their parents such crucial decisions as selecting a marriage partner, a college, and a vocation. Moreover, parents and children are more apt to agree. This contrasts with lower-class families where parents are as often resented as appreciated and rebelled against as followed. The higher the social status of the parents, the more successfully children should be socialized.

So much for a general theoretical introduction. What is the evidence? First of all, many data show that children in high-status families do look up to their elders. In Java, Geertz (1961) noted that grandparents and other senior relatives were addressed in highly respectful language by children in aristocratic families whereas ordinary children did not use deferential language. In the United States, Schneider and Homans (1955) observed that terms of address for the father tend to reflect his social status. Upper-class men tend to be addressed as "father," a term of respect for his authority and his high position in family and society. Middle-class men are addressed more familiarly as "Dad" (or "Daddy" by their daughters), terms of familiarity and equalitarianism, the latter a coquettish term of affection reflecting a quasi-flirting relationship. In the working-class the term of address is apt to be "Pa," the term of reference "my old man." The latter is a term of disrespect which sometimes borders on contempt. In general, the child's respect for his father seems to correspond to the society's respect for him.

Corresponding to the equalitarian familiarity with the father expressed in the middle-class term "Dad" is a greater emotional closeness in that class. In Greensboro, North Carolina, Adams (1967) found that 65 percent of white-collar men felt close to their fathers, compared to only 42 percent of blue-collar males. The class difference widened when Adams asked whether sons would like to "be the kind of person" the father was. Only 11 percent of the blue-collar but almost five times as many (53 percent) of the white-collar males said "yes."

To summarize, parents in the highest-status families are highly respected (and probably seen as somewhat distant). Parents in middle-status families are seen as close and treated familiarly and are also taken as role models. But in the lower class, parents are neither respected nor loved as much and are rejected as life models. Ignoring the aristocratic minority, we should expect the positive relations of middle-class families to produce more positive outcomes in the children themselves.

A subjective outcome is the memories teenagers have of their childhood. Thirteen-year-old boys and girls in New York City had strikingly different memories according to social class (Epstein, 1963). Lower-class children remembered angry feelings, aggressive behavior, and sexual behavior more often than middle-class children. Middle-class children remembered their childhood as so happy the researcher called it "euphoric" and more often referred to their parents in their memories. The middle-class findings suggest a happier childhood in which the child's relationship to his parents played a central role. The lower-class memories suggest a childhood which may have been filled with more behavior problems or else (to cite the researcher's interpretation) a childhood which did not socialize the child sufficiently to cause him to repress his memories of problematic behavior. Either way, the lower-class children's memories suggest socialization inadequacies, if the task of socialization is to teach behavior-controlling norms.

High-status fathers have by definition achieved more in the occupational system than low-status fathers. Although part of that achievement may have been due to their own head start a generation earlier, some may have been due to greater achievement motivation. Hence it should be no surprise that middle-class boys have more of that same motivation than lower-class boys. Rosen (1961), for example, found that middle-class boys in the Northeastern United States had consistently higher achievement motivation scores than working-class boys.

To Albert Cohen (1955), one of the main reasons why boys from low-status families join delinquent gangs is that their parents give them such a poor start in life that they feel they don't stand a chance to achieve the goals of American society. Faced with a sense of frustration, they become an easy prey to the delinquent culture of the neighborhood gang, given the weak counter-influence of their parents. In Flint, Michigan, Gold (1963) found that lower-class fathers were less able to control their sons because their sons respected them less. Boys from low-status homes have both more reason to rebel against the social code and less restraint from their parents against doing so.

This rebelliousness of lower-status youth contrasts with the picture Elkin and Westley encountered (1955) when they studied a middle-class suburb of Montreal. In that community, adolescents were generally unrebellious and conformed to their parents' values. So great was the solidarity between parents and their teenage children that the parents felt little anxiety about their children's behavior away from home. They felt confident that their children had successfully incorporated their value system and could be trusted to behave in ways of which they would approve.

To summarize the entire pattern of class differences in family relationships, a general theme of trouble runs through the experience of low-status families. Premaritally young people drift into ill-conceived relationships which are not firmly established. Their shaky marriages involve limited integration of the roles of the sexes and tend to fall apart after enduring stubbornly insoluble, tangible problems like unemployment and crowded housing. Parent–child relationships are equally trouble-laden. Children more often arrive unplanned as a result of uncontrolled reproductive behavior or as a result of disasters in other related families. The children are managed only with difficulty and the parent–child relationship breaks under the weight of frustration in much the same way that the husband–wife relationship breaks. All in all, life confronts low-status families with troubles which are often too difficult for their limited resources to cope with. The result is a series of failures in many aspects of family life. This is not to blame those families for their failures. But the seriousness of the problems and the tragedy of the failures in the lowest-status families represent hard facts which are consequences of being at the bottom of the stratification system.

EDUCATION

The effect of the husband's or wife's education on their family life in many respects parallels the effect of economic resources and occupational status. It would be redundant to reiterate those parallel effects. Rather, I will concentrate on such distinctive effects of education as the skills which educated people derive from their education. Among these are skills in sexual relations specifically and in interpersonal relations within the family generally, skill in solving conflicts, and skill in maintaining marital vitality.

Sexual Skills

Kinsey (1953) found that college-educated men and women used a wider variety of techniques of foreplay in marital intercourse than did high-school educated people. College-educated women were also more apt to have intercourse in the nude whereas a larger minority of less well-educated women were inhibited in this regard.

These differences in sexual technique produced differences in the wife's responsiveness to orgasm. For instance, during the tenth year of marriage, only 35 percent of Kinsey's high school-educated subjects had an orgasm as much as 90 percent of the time, compared to 41 percent of college graduates and 53 percent of those who had gone to graduate school. If response to orgasm is an index of success in sexual intercourse, education seems to have produced a higher level of sexual skill.

Knowledge of methods of birth control rises with education. Figure 2-3 shows how such knowledge increased with education among working-class people in relatively underdeveloped Puerto Rico. The increase was especially marked for those living in cities where family planning clinics were more available than in the countryside. Yet for rural adults, also, education reduced their isolation from knowledge about this technical aspect of family living.

If reproductive behavior is to be brought under control, it is necessary not only to know about possible methods, but also to want to use them and to be able to do so effectively. Education affects all three aspects of family planning. In a later chapter I will look at the effect of education in emancipating people from old-fashioned attitudes. Of primary interest here is the effect of education on technical skillfulness in using contraceptive methods.

Table 2-11 shows that the better-educated an American woman was, the greater the likelihood that she had successfully planned both the number of children born and the timing of their births. Conversely, wives who failed to limit the number of children born to the desired maximum were heavily concentrated among poorly educated women. Indeed, not only were there a larger proportion of poorly educated women who had more children than they wanted, but the number of unwanted children born to such women was greater. Thus college-educated women with excessive children had only 0.8 surplus children on the average whereas grade-school-educated women with more than they wanted had 1.5 extra children. Or, to convert the surplus to percentages, the college women who failed had only 30 percent more children than they wanted but the grade-school women had 55 percent more than they wanted.

Communication with the Opposite Sex

I have referred before to the difficulties of low status men and women in communicating with each other. Lack of education is one handicap which renders such people inarticulate. Conversely, the more education people acquire, the more fluent they become in communicating ideas and messages to bridge the gap between the sexes. Moreover, successful communication requires not simply fluent expression but attentive listening. Indeed, the ability to receive messages in marriage may be rarer (and more in need of educational training) than the ability to transmit them.

The basic pattern portrayed in Table 2-12 is duplicated in my Detroit research (Blood and Wolfe, 1960), but I have omitted the American data here in order to simplify the table. In both Detroit and Tokyo, education increased the frequency of communication by wives more than by husbands. There are two possible reasons: (1) education emancipates women from their traditional reticence, and (2) education leads women to marry husbands at least as well educated as themselves (whereas an educated man may marry an uneducated woman if he chooses). Hence marriages containing an edu-

FIGURE 2-3.   Number of Methods of Birth Control Known by Urban and Rural
              Residents, by Education

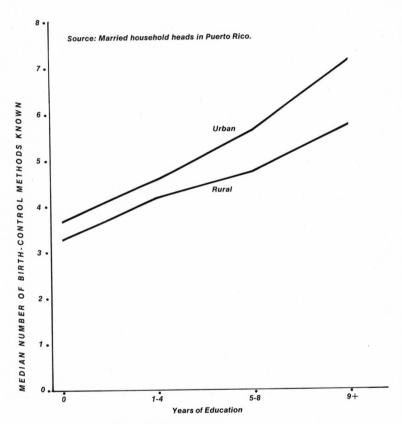

Adapted from Hill, Stycos, and Back (1959):109.

TABLE 2-11 Effectiveness of Family Planning, by Wife's Education

| | WIFE'S EDUCATION | | | | |
| | GRADE SCHOOL | HIGH SCHOOL | | COLLEGE | HIGH/LOW RATIO |
EFFECTIVENESS		1–3	4 years		
No accidental pregnancies	30%	42%	50%	53%	1.77X
Number planned but spacing accidents	38	37	37	36	0.95
Excess (unwanted) children	32	21	14	11	0.34
Total	100%	100%	100%	100%	
Number of wives	255	579	1153	427	

Adapted from Whelpton, Campbell, and Patterson (1966):247. Source: National sample of white wives aged 18–39 in 1960, U.S.A.

TABLE 2-12 Marital Communication Skills, by Husband's and Wife's Education

| | EDUCATION | | | | |
| | HIGH SCHOOL | | COLLEGE | | HIGH/LOW RATIO |
	1–3	4 years	1–3	4 years	
Intellectual companionship (discuss the news per year)					
By husband's education	157	160	176	177	1.13X
By wife's education	130	170	182	198	1.52
Informative companionship					
Husband tells events (per year)					
By husband's education	177	156	178	177	1.00
Wife listens					
By wife's education	122	171	178	209	1.71
Therapeutic communication					
Husband tells troubles					
By husband's education	1.60	2.06	2.27	2.38	1.49
Wife listens					
By wife's education	1.71	2.27	2.26	2.73	1.60
Wife tells troubles					
By wife's education	2.66	3.00	3.07	3.30	1.24
Husband listens					
By husband's education	2.80	2.91	2.82	3.14	1.12
Number of husbands	10	66	93	275	
Number of wives	21	279	96	48	

Adapted from Blood (1967):151. Source: Tokyo couples under age 40 in 1959. Therapeutic communication is weighted 4 for always, 3 usually, 2 half the time, 1 seldom, 0 never.

cated wife usually benefit from the twin education of both partners, whereas this is not the case if only the husband has been highly educated.

Table 2-12 shows that the frequency with which Tokyo husbands and wives discussed the day's news rose steadily with the education of each partner. In addition to communication skills, this may reflect skill in gathering information about the news, since better-educated persons may read more newspapers and listen to more news programs. This would give them a greater store of information to share with each other and to comment upon.

This point was made by Komarovsky (1964) in noting the "impoverishment of life" among blue-collar American families. She found that some couples wanted to talk to each other but did not have anything to say. One high school alumnus said "I wish we had more things to talk about, but when I try to think of something I don't know anything to talk to her about." And another man explicitly saw his lack of education as the cause of his mental poverty: "If my wife and I had a little more education, maybe we'd have what you call it—more interests? Maybe we could come together better, maybe life would be more interesting for us" (p. 156). Table 2-12 suggests that his hunch was probably correct.

Informative companionship refers especially to the husband's report of events which happened to him and around him during the day while he was away from home. The correlation between the wife's frequency of listening and her education suggests that husbands are more apt to explain the intricacies of their daily life to wives they judge capable of understanding what they are talking about. Educated wives make better audiences than women whose horizons have not been broadened by education.

However, one should not rule out the husband's education as a source of communication just because there is relatively little difference in Table 2-12 at that point. My Detroit data showed an impact of the husband's education on his frequency of telling his wife about the day's events which did not appear in this Tokyo data, and Komarovsky also found a difference: 39 percent of her high-school graduates but only 15 percent of the drop-outs discussed their jobs with their wives "quite a lot." So we can assume that education generally promotes both a man's willingness to talk about his work and his perception of his wife as a meaningful audience.

The bottom half of Table 2-12 involves a more emotional type of communication. The question is, how often after one partner has a bad day does he tell his troubles to his spouse? Komarovsky described the blue-collar men in her sample as crippled by a "trained incapacity to share" their feelings. This was due not only to their lack of formal education, but also to their informal socialization into an ideal of masculinity which held that to express one's feelings would be sissified. Whatever the reason, her high school drop-outs were consistently less expressive than husbands who had finished high school. While my Tokyo men, too, were less expressive than the women, the effect of education was to liberate both sexes into greater reliance on one another in time of trouble.

Without being told the partner's troubles, it is impossible for a married person to give any empathy in return. The fact that the wife tells her troubles only makes empathy possible; it doesn't guarantee it. Nevertheless, Table 2-13 shows a marked effect of education on the husband's understanding of the wife's problems. Thus education improves both the ability of husbands and wives to communicate their troubles to each other and also their ability to respond empathically.

Who do poorly educated men and women talk to if they don't talk to each other? To some extent the answer is "no one." However, if they talk to anyone, it is more apt to be a friend of the same sex than anyone of the opposite sex, even the spouse. The deeper and more personal the subject matter, the more difficult it is to talk to a stranger from another world, and the more natural it seems to turn to a member of one's own world. In Komarovsky's sample, almost half the drop-out wives, compared with less than a fifth of those who finished high school, shared more of themselves with female confidantes than with their husbands. Conversely, only the better educated wives generally lived up to the American ideal that "one's husband should be also one's most intimate friend" (1964:210).

TABLE 2-13 Husband's Understanding of Wife, by Husband's Education

RESEARCHER'S ASSESSMENT OF HUSBAND'S UNDERSTANDING OF WIFE	HUSBAND'S EDUCATION		HIGH/LOW RATIO
	Under 12 years	12 years	
High empathy	22%	53%	2.41X
Average empathy	35	29	0.83
Low empathy	43	18	0.42
Total	100%	100%	
Number of husbands	40	18	

Adapted from Komarovsky (1964):361. Source: White, native-born husbands in an American city of 50,000.

Communication with the Older Generation

The generation gap is another communication problem in family life which yields to the skills gained from education. Since women tend to specialize in interpersonal relations anyway, the ones especially affected by education are the men whose normal diffidence is thus overcome.

Table 2-14 shows how even a relatively modest increment of education improved the relationships between parents and children who had lived together in the same family. This was less true of relationships with the mother-in-law. That relationship compounds the generation gap and the marriage gap. To feel close to one's mother-in-law means to be able to establish a strong tie with the spouse and then to leap from the spouse to the spouse's parent. Probably only college-educated men and women can bridge such a double gap very successfully. For the men and women in Komarovsky's blue-collar sample, finishing high school helped a bit, but not very much under those difficult circumstances.

Conflict Resolution

The most difficult topic of communication is a marriage problem. Without education, men and women find it so hard to talk about their problems that they give way to sheer emotional outbursts and even to physical abuse. With education, there is more hope for a rational approach or at least for a more restrained conflict between the partners.

TABLE 2-14 Closeness of Working-Class Husbands and Wives
to Their Fathers, Mothers, and Mothers-in-Law, by Education

	HUSBANDS		WIVES	
	Under		Under	
RELATIONSHIP WITH	12 years	12 years	12 years	12 years
Father				
Close or very close	14%	54%	24%	50%
Intermediate	56	31	56	36
Hostile or estranged	29	15	20	14
Total	99%	100%	100%	100%
Mother				
Close or very close	32%	68%	50%	80%
Intermediate	58	24	27	15
Hostile or estranged	10	8	23	5
Total	100%	100%	100%	100%
Mother-in-law				
Good	24%	25%	27%	33%
Average	39	58	41	33
Strained or no contact	36	17	32	33
Total	99%	100%	100%	99%
Minimum number of cases	28	12	21	14

Adapted from Komarovsky (1964):366, 367. Relationships to mothers-in-law are limited to
those living within two hours' distance.

TABLE 2-15 Modes of Conflict Used by Working-Class Husbands and Wives, by Education

	HUSBANDS		WIVES	
	Under		Under	
MODE OF CONFLICT	12 years	12 years	12 years	12 years
Drinking	14%	0%	4%	0%
Violent quarrels, occasionally beating,				
breaking things	25	14	41	5
Withdrawal and repression	38	36	33	23
Moderate "flare-ups"	11	23	7	36
Talking out	11	27	15	36
Total	99%	100%	100%	100%
Number of cases	41	18	33	25

Adapted from Komarovsky (1964): 363. Percentages represent the proportion of all modes of
conflict which involved the specified mode.

Table 2-15 shows that drinking was confined exclusively to the high
school drop-outs in Komarovsky's sample. Indeed, together with withdrawal
and repression (which were also slightly more common among drop-outs),
these methods represent ways of "dropping out" of conflict. Of the two,
drinking is a more physical form of escape and perhaps more characteristic
of the lowest educated men and women. The violent quarrels, which are also
heavily concentrated among the poorly educated people might be labelled

a physical form of attack, especially when verbal belligerency breaks over into physical attack on the spouse or on dishes and other smashables.

By contrast, the better-educated men and women reported that they engaged either in more restrained emotional outbursts or that they were able to talk out their problems. Even in the few cases where drop-outs claimed that they talked about their problems, Komarovsky reported that the meaning was often different. The less their education, the more their talking out became simply a verbal way of achieving personal catharsis rather than a method of resolving conflicts. Only with increased education did talking increase understanding, reveal motives, or correct misperceptions between the partners. This suggests how difficult conflict-resolution is and how much it depends on the mental and verbal skills which come with education.

Dropouts from School and Marriage

By now it should not surprise the reader to learn that marriages are generally happier and more stable for well-educated persons than for those with little education. Family success is a stratified phenomenon in relation to education as much as to income or occupational status. The greater skillfulness of educated men and women in interacting and communicating with each other produces marriages which are generally more satisfactory to the participants and more durable.

Both the husbands and the wives in Komarovsky's blue-collar sample described their marriages as happier if they were high-school graduates than if they had not graduated. I found that Detroit wives' marital satisfaction was consistently higher the higher the husband's education (Blood and Wolfe). In Tokyo I found (1967) that both partners were more satisfied with their marriages the higher the wife's education. More than half the college-educated wives' marriages satisfied both partners whereas less than one fifth of the marriages of the high school drop-outs were mutually satisfactory.

Curiously, however, the straightforward relationship between education and the subjective evaluation of marriage is complicated by irregularities in relation to the objective stability of marriage. In general, stability tends to increase with each increment of education. However, the exceptions to this rule form an interesting pattern. In both the 1950 and 1960 U. S. censuses divorce rates tended to be higher for high school and college drop-outs than for those who had completed a lower level of education (to say nothing of those who had completed a higher level—Hillman, 1960; Udry, 1966). Moreover a special report from the National Office of Vital Statistics in 1957 showed that college drop-outs not only had more first divorces but also had more multiple divorces than men who had graduated from high school and never gone to college.

Apparently men and women who start an educational program and do not finish it are very apt to do the same with marriage, even though their marriages may not be unusually unhappy. A mild degree of unhappiness seems more apt to dissolve the marriage of a person who quit school in the midst of a degree program than for someone who completed a lesser program.

In general, education is associated with marital success, but this generalization is particularly firm for completed units of education, whereas incompleted bits may be symptomatic of a tendency to contract out of one's undertakings before they are finished.

Another complication in Udry's data was the tendency of divorce rates to shoot up for women who had been to graduate school, whereas they fell for men who went to graduate school. Although no breakdown was given by completion of graduate degree programs, the divorce rate for the graduate women was so high that it could not be attributed to dropping-out alone. Perhaps among the relatively few women who go to graduate school, there are a large proportion of poor marriage risks. Moreover, once such women get divorced, their chances of remarrying are markedly lower than similarly educated men who have gotten a divorce. Roughly four times as many graduate-educated divorcees were living alone in 1960 as of graduate-educated divorced men (most of the latter having already remarried by the time the census takers asked them their current marital status). This slowness in remarrying may reflect the fear of recently divorced men (who are the chief men available) that such highly educated women would be aggressive, domineering wives (similar to the women they just divorced). It may also reflect the ability of graduate women to support themselves while waiting for the "right" man to come along the second time.

So, for women, it appears that education generally contributes to marital success up through the four years of college, but that some uncertainty arises beyond that point.

CASTE STATUS

Strictly speaking, a caste system involves two or more classes of people whose social status is inherited from generation to generation, who are forbidden to intermarry, and who monopolize a customary way of life including distinctive occupations. The Indian caste system was the best known example, with its Brahmin caste at the top and untouchable caste at the bottom. The nearest American equivalent is the division between whites and blacks.

In the modern world, caste systems tend to disintegrate. The geographical social mobility made possible and required by industrial economies undermines the fastidious restrictions of caste. Stratification ceases being determined strictly by heredity and becomes subject to change by one's own efforts. Castes tend to be replaced by classes.

Nevertheless, insofar as the color of one's skin or another hereditary characteristic subjects a whole group to discriminatory treatment, caste-like elements remain. And because caste is so rigid, it introduces new elements into family relationships which were not there on the basis of class stratification alone.

The Negro–white situation in the United States is the chief case in point. Insofar as differences exist between black families and white families, they are primarily a consequence of the stratification factors we have already reviewed. Because the average black man has fewer economic resources, a lower-status occupation, and less education than the average white, his family suffers from all the usual handicaps faced by any family which finds itself at the bottom of the stratification system. But the fact of being poor blacks rather than poor whites makes a further difference. Wherever blacks are discriminated against because of color, integration into the larger society becomes difficult, the way upward is barred, and discouragement sets in. Racial discrimination means that poor blacks are even lower in the stratification system than poor whites, and more hopelessly trapped there. As a result, caste introduces further differences between blacks and whites in their family life.

Marginal Men

To be a black man in a white society is to be shut off from full participation in that society. De facto segregated schools give the average black child a substandard education which ill prepares him to play adult roles in an increasingly complicated society. Segregation in housing crowds families together in inadequate space and extorts a toll of inflated rents and monopoly retail prices from families unable to take advantage of consumers' supposed right to choose in a free market. The shoddy vocational training and meager experience of black workers prejudice employers against hiring them except under the duress of an acute labor shortage or governmental compulsion. The black worker has traditionally been "last hired and first fired," the dregs of the American labor market.

These facts of ghetto life sap the vitality of family life and especially undermine the role of the man. Since the husband is normally the chief representative of the family in the outside world, the prejudice and discrimination of that world fall particularly heavily on his shoulders. If the world does not give him an opportunity to hold a steady job at a decent wage, he cannot play the role of breadwinner adequately. This "inability of the Negro man to earn a living and support his family" Liebow (1967) found to be "the central fact of lower-class Negro life" (p. 224). The men he studied in Washington, D. C., wanted to support their families and tried to at the beginning of marriage. But after frustrating experience with inadequate wages and unstable jobs, most of his unskilled workers became discouraged and gave up trying.

For a man of any color to be unable to play the crucial role expected of him is to emasculate him psychologically. The black man is no exception. His economic inadequacy demoralizes him and makes him an undependable husband and an unpredictable father. He becomes a marginal man in his own family, sometimes there but frequently absent. And even when he is there, he frequently reacts to his emasculation with indifference, apathy, and noninvolvement.

One illustration of the black husband's marginality is Rainwater's (1965) finding that he less often shared with his wife in household activities than white husbands of the same class level. Insofar as he carried any responsibilities around the house at all, he and his wife were more apt to perform their chores separately on a segregated role basis.

Table 2-16 illustrates another aspect of the black husband's marginality: his marginal power position. When family decisions have to be made, black husbands play a relatively passive role and their wives a correspondingly active one. The result is that in Detroit, 44 percent of all black marriages were wife-dominated, but only 20 percent of white marriages were (Blood and Wolfe, 1960:35). Although some of these wives may have seized

TABLE 2-16   Husband's Power by Occupation and by Race

HUSBAND'S MEAN POWER BY OCCUPATION	RACE		White/Black Direction*
	Black	White	
Low blue-collar	4.31	5.07	+
High blue-collar	4.60	4.98	+
Low white-collar	—	5.34	
High white-collar	5.00	5.52	+

Adapted from Blood and Wolfe (1969):60. Source: Representative sample of unbroken marriages in the Detroit Metropolitan Area, 1955. The number of black cases was respectively 78, 20, 0, and 5; of white cases, 162, 162, 79, and 151.
*Power scores cannot be compared in the form of a ratio because they do not form an even series of numbers. However, the direction of the difference between groups is meaningful. In this table, a "+" means that a white power score is higher than the comparable black power score.

power over their husband's protests, usually this shift in the balance of power seems to have resulted from the husband's abdication. In white families, on the other hand, the chief pattern was not dominance by the husband but an equalitarian sharing of power with the wife. Thus the contrast between castes resulted from the black man's dropping out of the normal sharing of power.

If relinquishing power were as far as black marginality went, its consequences for family life would not be so disastrous. But a man who has withdrawn from decision-making and segregated his activities from those of his wife is apt to leave his family altogether. Whether searching for a new job or for a new love, a man who has reached a dead end occupationally and maritally often finds his only hope in the belief that life might be better somewhere else.

TABLE 2-17   Father Absence by Social Class and by Race

SOCIAL CLASS	RACE		High/Low Ratio
	Black	White	
Lowest	44%	15%	0.34X
Middle	28	10	0.36
Highest	14	0	infinity

From Deutsch and Brown (1964):28. Reciprocal percentages of fathers were living at home. Source: 543 urban public school children (first and fifth grade) studied by a research institute of New York Medical College.

Table 2-17 shows how much more often fathers of black children were missing from the home than fathers of white children of the same class level. If such large numbers of black children have no father in the home at any one time, we can easily imagine how many more children are liable to lose their father at some point before they grow up. Sociologist Eric Lincoln estimated to the author in 1965 that more than half of all black children in the United States had lost at least one parent before reaching maturity. In most cases, the father was the one who disappeared.

I use the word "disappeared" advisedly. Whereas most white marriages in the United States are legally dissolved by a divorce, black marriages are more apt to end by the husband simply walking out without saying goodby. The contrast can be seen most vividly in the current marital status of blacks and whites in the U. S. Census. Whereas the 1950 Census found almost twice as many whites divorced as separated, for blacks the relationship was reversed, with more than three times as many separated as divorced (Hillman, 1960). Since approximately the same proportions of blacks and whites were divorced, the combined result was that six times as many blacks as whites were informally but not legally separated from their spouses. Although generally speaking desertion is the poor man's divorce, it is especially the poor black man's divorce.

Figure 2-4 shows that for each of the income categories previously portrayed in Figure 2-1, the proportion of black men separated from their wives was several times as great as for whites with the same income. Since divorce rates for the two races were about the same by income, the combined result was that total failure rates for black marriages were much higher than for white marriages. This is understandable in view of the extra stresses to which black marriages were subjected. However, the main point is that when black marriages fail, the form of dissolution is apt to be informal rather than formal.

What difference does it make when men leave home without benefit of divorce? One result is that the wife and children are less apt to receive support than if there were a legal financial settlement (but since the husband was a poor supporter before he left, that is hardly a new problem). The main difference is that liaisons with new partners must necessarily be nonmarital in form since neither partner is legally eligible to remarry. Informal desertion therefore contributes to nonmarital intercourse and cohabitation. These in turn leave the next man in a woman's life even more marginal than her husband was. So male marginality tends to be repetitive throughout the lifetime of a given lower-class black family.

Overburdened Women

Women whose husbands are only partially integrated into the family or whose non-husbands are even less dependable necessarily carry a heavy burden of responsibility for family affairs.

Because of the unskilled man's inability to earn a steady income, wives are forced to go to work to supplement the husband's wages or to replace them altogether if he loses his job. And when the man himself leaves, the wife shoulders the entire burden of financial responsibility for herself and her children. The U. S. Census Bureau found that in 1958, 61 percent of nonwhite women aged 35–44 were employed compared to 41 percent of the white women. Although that study was not limited to married women, most women in that age bracket tend to be married and to have children living with them. So black women often carry the double burden of outside employment and domestic responsibility during the child-rearing years.

If the black woman is the sole wage-earner for her family, she is subjected to double discrimination as both a member of the bottom caste and of the inferior sex (see Table 2-18). Hence her work is likely to yield es-

FIGURE 2-4. **Separated Men, by Current Income and by Race**

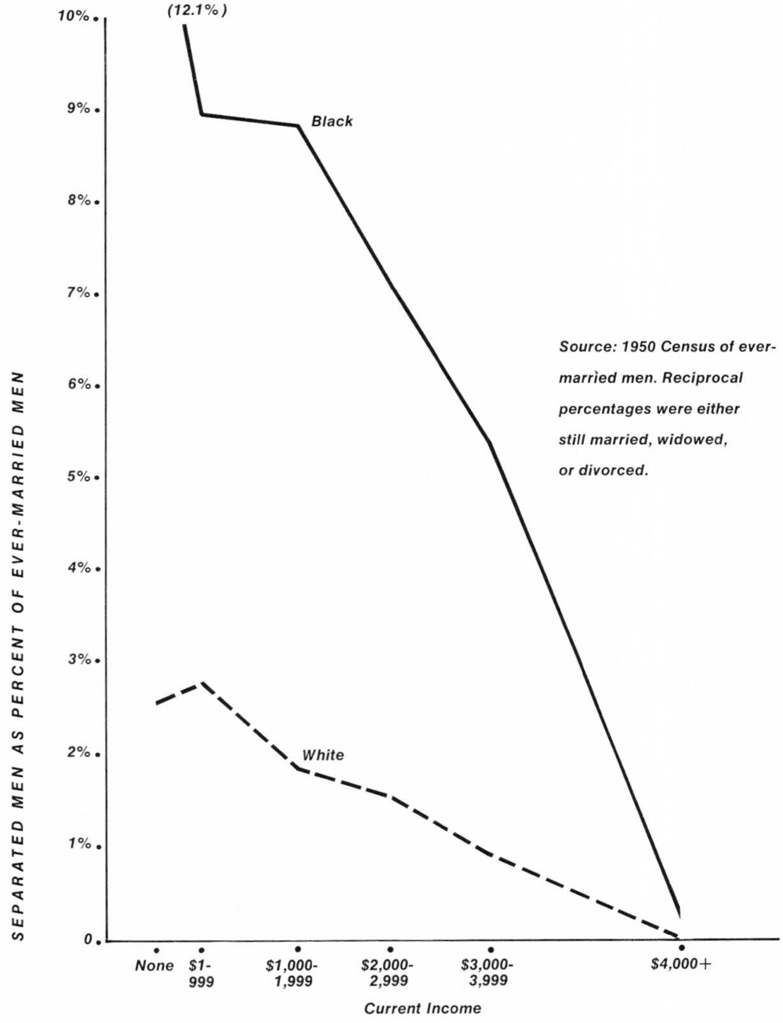

(12.1%)
10%
9%
8%
7%
6%
5%
4%
3%
2%
1%
0
SEPARATED MEN AS PERCENT OF EVER-MARRIED MEN
Black
White
Source: 1950 Census of ever-married men. Reciprocal percentages were either still married, widowed, or divorced.
None
$1-999
$1,000-1,999
$2,000-2,999
$3,000-3,999
$4,000+
Current Income

Adapted from Hillman (1960):41.

pecially meager returns. The only advantage she has over her husband is that her work is likely to be indoors and therefore steady, whereas his is apt to be outdoors and disrupted by rainy or winter weather. Financially it is to the Negro woman's advantage to work long hours to piece out her income, but she must be correspondingly absent from her family.

TABLE 2-18   Median Income Earned, by Sex and by Race

		RACE		White/Black Ratio
		White	Black	
SEX	Male	$5,137 ++ +–	$3,075	1.67X
	Female	$2,537 –+ ––	$1,276	1.98
Male/Female Ratio		2.02x	2.41x	4.02

Adapted from Peterson (1965):158. Source: U.S. Census, 1960. Median annual income for those with any wages or salaries during the year.

Supporting her family is difficult because the average black woman has more mouths to feed than her white counterpart. For instance, the 1960 U. S. Census discovered that nonwhite women who were married before the age of 22 to men who had not gone to high school and who were unskilled laborers had an average of 4.7 children, compared to only 3.8 for white women in the same circumstances (Moynihan, 1965:30). That extra child sharply reduces the per capita share of the already low income that the black worker brings home.

Finally, the cash a black man or woman earns will not buy as much in the ghetto as it would in the "outside" world. The fact that Negroes are trapped in the ghetto by housing barriers enables both landlords and shop-keepers to charge monopolistic prices. The poverty of their Negro customers gives those same businessmen extra risks in running their businesses. So businessmen and customers are trapped in a mutually exploitive relationship which could only be solved by breaking down the wall around the ghetto. In the meantime, the black parent faces the painful task of trying to spend his limited earnings in an unfavorable market to feed his extra mouths.

From what we already know of the consequences of poverty, we can appreciate that the impact of caste on family life is more than economic. Black families often have to live not only with extra children but with extra rats in an apartment necessarily small because of the high rental per square foot in the ghetto. Besides inflated prices, the landlord's monopolistic position enables him to get by without repairing or redecorating his properties so that the wear and tear created by overcrowding is not redeemed by repair and maintenance. The combined result is severe dilapidation of slum dwellings, leaving them unattractive shelters for family living and forcing family members to disperse out onto the streets for much of the day and night. For such reasons, even when parents are not away at work, family members see either relatively little of each other or (if they are home at the same time) too much of each other in their crowded quarters. They are seldom able to get along easily with each other.

In recent years, black slums have been the chief target of urban renewal. The physical appearance of American cities has been improved by demolishing obsolete buildings and replacing them with high-rise apartments. However, urban renewal has characteristically meant replacing apartments which black families can afford with new ones they cannot afford. Thus, urban renewal has spelled "black removal," forcing families to move again and again, adding a new dimension of uncertainty to their already precarious existence. Since urban renewal has rarely meant better housing for black families, it has simply added to the environmental insecurity of black children and to the burden of practical problems encountered by their parents.

Neglected Children

Black children cannot have marginal fathers and overburdened mothers without suffering the consequences in inadequate socialization. Moynihan (1965) summarized the evidence that children without fathers (1) had lower IQ's, (2) dropped out of school younger, (3) were more apt to become delinquent, both as first offenders and particularly as repeated offenders, and (4) sought immediate gratification of their desires. These findings are symptomatic of a general failure of many black homes to provide children with the intellectual stimulation, the moral training, and the supervision necessary for them to be fully socialized into American society. Parents who are second-class citizens can hardly serve as first-class models. The result is that children growing up in lower-class black homes grow into adults who will suffer the same handicaps as their own parents in a generation-after-generation cycle of personal and family disorganization.

Premarital Intimacy   One of the desires which black young people tend to gratify especially early is sexual desire. Although this illustrates the general problem of the inadequate socialization of black children, it is especially pertinent to our discussion of black family life because it affects both the marital and reproductive behavior of the young people involved.

TABLE 2-19 Premarital Sexual Permissiveness of Adult
Men and Women, by Social Class and by Race

PERCENTAGE HIGHLY PERMISSIVE BY SOCIAL CLASS	MEN		WOMEN	
	Black	*White*	*Black*	*White*
Lower class	70%	32%	33%	5%
Middle class	46	26	13	6

Adapted from Reiss (1967):50. Reciprocal percentages were not highly sexually permissive, *i.e.*, did not believe that premarital intercourse is acceptable under any circumstances. The measure of social class was Duncan's Socioeconomic Index which combines occupational prestige, education, and income. Source: National U. S. sample of adults over age 21 (80 percent were married; 20 percent, single). The numbers of cases in the lower class were 49, 202, 63 and 221, and in the middle class 11, 254, 15, and 271 respectively.

Table 2-19 shows how sharply American blacks and whites differed within the same social class in their attitude toward premarital intercourse. Roughly twice as many blacks as whites (and in the case of lower-class women more than six times as many) believed that premarital intercourse was permissible under some circumstances.

To believe that intercourse is permissible is not necessarily to act on that belief. Direct evidence on racial differences in premarital behavior is not available from the Kinsey reports. However, striking differences in illegitimate births for blacks and whites suggest that adolescent behavior generally coincides with the philosophical differences apparent in Table 2-19.

For instance, in 1963 almost one-fourth of black births in the United States were illegitimate compared to barely 3 percent of the white births (*Vital Statistics of the United States*). However, we cannot infer from this difference in illegitimate births that black girls had eight times as much premarital intercourse. Black young people may well be less apt to practice contraception effectively in premarital intercourse. And once a premarital conception is discovered, black girls are less apt to secure an abortion. (Among Kinsey's respondents, 79 percent of the white girls who became premaritally pregnant, but only 39 percent of the Negro girls, secured an illegal abortion as a way out of their dilemma—Gebhard, *et al.,* 1958:57;161). Much of the difference between black and white illegitimacy rates reflects greater tolerance of unmarried motherhood in the black community and less financial ability to resolve the problem by other means.

Nevertheless, the very acceptability of illegitimacy testifies to the pervasiveness of nonmarital sexual and reproductive behavior in the lower caste. In any case, the frequency of nonmarital sexuality and reproduction among lower-class Negroes means that intimate relationships tend to be relatively casually contracted, relatively informal, and easily severed. "Easy come, easy go." And the frequency of nonmarital reproduction means that a considerable proportion of the fatherless black families in the United States result not from the father's desertion but from his never having entered into a stable relationship in the first place.

Black women not only bear more children out of wedlock, but also are more apt to have conceived premaritally even when they do marry. For Americans married between 1955 and 1959, 41 percent of black brides compared with only 16 percent of white brides, bore their first child less than nine months later (Grabill and Parke, 1961:38–39). Even though these children escaped the stigma of illegitimacy, they came prematurely into homes ill-prepared to cope with them and (as we will see in a later chapter) more likely to crack up because of them.

So the inadequate socialization of black children leads them into sexual involvements in which the man is marginal and the woman is liable to bear the biological consequences alone, unable to give those children the care and attention they need if they were to be adequately socialized in turn. And so on, from generation to generation.

The casualness of involvement reflects the fact that lower-caste young people have nothing to lose because they are already at the bottom of the social scale. It contrasts with the supervision given young people in higher castes who have much to lose by involvement with the "wrong" person. In

India, the complexities of the caste system required that children be deprived of the opportunity to associate freely in their mixed communities, that they be chaperoned and sheltered through the vulnerable years of adolescence, and that they be safely married off by their parents as early as possible. Goode (1963) pointed out that "maintenance of caste was too important a matter to be left to the young," so the higher castes tabooed love-matches as subversive and insisted on parental control of mate selection (p. 208). Even though higher-caste parents emphasized the proper upbringing of their children, a mixed marriage would have been so disastrous to a high-caste family that it could not afford to trust even well-socialized children with so momentous a matter.

Once a marriage was contracted by a high-caste family on behalf of its children, that marriage tended to be stable because the whole kin network and beyond that the nonrelated members of the caste provided social support for conformity to the high code of the caste.

In essence, then, low-caste status gives young people freedom, but that freedom in turn leads into circumstances which are often precarious and seldom happy. High-caste status, conversely, is set about with many restrictions, but simultaneously is replete with economic and social resources which reward family members for their conformity to the caste code.

ROYAL LINEAGE

The extreme case of high-caste status is that of the nobility. Their special ancestry sets them apart from the ordinary people of their society. Because royal status is inherited, the family life of royalty becomes critically important. The royal family must perform two key functions in order to transmit the royal line from one generation to the next. First, it must preserve itself from contamination which would dilute the purity of the royal line. Secondly, it must bear fruit in potential heirs to receive the royal mantle.

Royal Purity

To safeguard the royal line, adolescents must be protected from involvement with the wrong people, *i.e.,* with commoners. Common people may associate with whomever they wish. But for royal offspring, such freedom would risk emotional or, worse yet, sexual involvement. Sexual involvement is particularly dangerous because it might introduce into the genetic stream inferior genes. That danger involves the royal females who are the potential bearers of the heirs to the kingdom. Hence it is the female rather than male adolescents whose chastity is closely guarded.

Even in Samoan villages with only loosely hereditary chieftainships, virginity was required of the girl designated by the chief to be the ceremonial hostess of the village (Mead, 1949). This emphasis contrasted with a general pattern of utter casualness in sexual relations for all other young people. The purpose of the sexual restrictions seems to have been to preserve not so much her biological purity as her social purity. By cutting her off from the sex play of ordinary boys and girls, the community set the hostess apart as a special person worthy of esteem. When she reached the age of marriage, her virginity guaranteed her willingness to be married off by the chief to the son of a chief in another village.

Royal Incest   Royal children are restricted not only in their premarital associates but even more in the persons they may marry. Since the spouse will be the progenitor of the next generation, that spouse must have proper social and biological credentials to maintain the royal line.

Generally speaking, royal endogamy is the rule, *i.e.,* mixed marriages with commoners are prohibited. Only members of the nobility of their own or another country are eligible for selection. And the royal elders have an extraordinarily large voice in determining which of the eligibles shall be chosen.

In the modern world, royalty form an international set and intermarriage across national boundary lines with distant cousins is the common European pattern. In the ancient world, travel was more difficult and royal families sometimes turned to members of their own households in preference to marrying commoners. One case was Hawaii, cut off by the Pacific Ocean from access to other nobility, whose kings frequently married their sisters. Another was ancient Egypt where one pharaoh married not only two of his sisters but at least two of his daughters (Middleton, 1962). And more than half of the Macedonian kings of Egypt (the Ptolemies) married either their half-sisters or their full-sisters. This was a new dynasty (founded by one of the generals of Alexander the Great) whose incest can perhaps be attributed to the small number of kin available to a new dynasty. Thus Ptolemy II (who married his sister) would otherwise have had to marry either into the deposed Egyptian royalty or to ally himself with foreign adversaries. He apparently felt safer in marrying someone who presented fewer political complications.

In the Egyptian case, incest was a stratified phenomenon, most common among the royal rulers, but also found to a lesser extent among the wealthiest families in Egyptian cities. In the latter case, Middleton attributed the motivation to the effects of the law requiring family property to be divided equally among all children of both sexes. Incestuous marriages preserved the family estate intact, as well as emulating the royal example.

In modern societies, by contrast, incestuous marriages and even incestuous sexual relations are prohibited. Rather than a royal or elite phenomenon, incestuous intercourse under such circumstances becomes the deviant behavior of only the lowest-status people.

Royal Continuity

Although elite families in feudal societies generally are eager to bear children who can carry on the family line and administer the family estate, this emphasis is especially strong in royal marriages. In modern times the Shah of Iran replaced a whole succession of barren wives until he found one capable of bearing him children. Moreover, in societies which do not recognize the right of women to inherit the throne, it may be necessary for the queen to bear not simply children, but specifically sons, if she is to fulfil her mission.

In polygynous societies, kings are spared the necessity of divorcing barren wives. They simply add their new wives to their household. Indeed such kings normally demonstrate their royal preeminence by acquiring more wives than anyone else in the kingdom. It would be inconsistent with political and social stratification for the head man to be outstripped by anyone else in so important a status symbol as the size of one's harem. So royal marriage and royal reproduction under such circumstances go far beyond the requirements of mere continuity. Only in monogamous societies is continuity something for kings to worry about.

chapter three
THE POLITICAL SYSTEM AND THE FAMILY

Sociologists have paid relatively little attention to the effects of the political system on the family. One reason, perhaps, is that the unit of analysis is larger. Since political systems are primarily national systems, an international comparison is necessary to assess cause-and-effect relationships. Few sociologists have the time and money to devote to multination studies, whereas almost every community offers opportunities to study the effect of stratification on family life.

To be sure, there are descriptive studies by legal experts who have written voluminous tomes on family law. But such volumes tell us more about what the government tries to do than about how family life is altered as a result. In other words, we could read at great length about the supposedly relevant aspects of our independent variable (the political system) but can find few systematic tests of the relationship to our dependent variable of family life.

Nevertheless, it is necessary to try to explore this relationship in however preliminary a fashion in the hope of gaining a tentative understanding of the impacts of government. First we will look at two unintentional impacts of government on family life via the model of the government itself and the repercussions of governmental policies focused on non-family objectives. Then I will devote the bulk of the chapter to a review of explicit governmental programs for the control and support of family life.

POLITICAL MODELS FOR FAMILY POWER STRUCTURE

Nations like to describe themselves as families, "brothers under the skin," nephews of the same "Uncle Sam," or children of the imperial father. To live in a society governed by a particular type of power structure and devoted to a particular philosophy about the exercise of power might affect the power structure of the family. A family, after all, is a social organization, too, and while its political apparatus is informal, it nevertheless must be governed. The example of the governmental structure and the concepts of the national political philosophy should have some influence on the way the average man rules his household. So we should find a correspondence between national power structure and family power structure.

Table 3-1 supports this hypothesis. Kingdoms in which the king ruled his people with a tight rein tended to have families ruled by the father and husband. Tribes, by contrast, had little governmental machinery. Chieftains were frequently chosen from among the tribe on the basis of their personal competence rather than on the basis of heredity. Chiefs have often been described as "first among equals." Modern democracies have a large governmental apparatus, but the rulers are subject to the consent of the governed. In both tribal and democratic societies, the head of the family typically had relatively limited power.

TABLE 3-1   Family Domination by the Husband/Father, by Political System

| | POLITICAL SYSTEM | | |
MEAN DOMINANCE	Tribe	Kingdom	Democracy
Father/son*	2.2	3.8	1.0
Husband/wife**	1.5	2.7	1.4
Number of societies	13	25	6

Adapted from Stephens (1963):332–333. Source: Interviews with expert informants (mostly anthropologists).
* Father/son dominance was rated according to the number of the following characteristics present: son may not address father by his first name; son rarely expresses verbal aggression toward his father; son rarely disputes with his father; son must speak softly to father; son either kneels or bows when greeting his father.
** Husband/wife dominance: wife kneels or bows to husband; wife rarely disputes with husband; husband dominates family decision-making; has seating priority (sits down first or sits in most honored place); wife is excluded from many social gatherings.

Table 3-1 shows that the political system is more closely related to the father–son relationship than to the husband–wife relationship. This suggests that a king or chief is perceived more as the father of his people than as the husband of his people.

The differences portrayed in Table 3-1 are not due to political influences alone. There is a close correspondence between the political system and the economic system. Tribes may gain their subsistence in a number of ways (including hunting and gathering), but almost all the kingdoms in Stephens' sample were agrarian and all the democracies were industrial. Some of the variation in family system was probably due to economic differences. But there is substantial consistency between the political system and the family system as far as their power structures are concerned.

Sometimes a government tries explicitly to align families with its own style of operating. During the era of the rise of European kings, royal legislation strengthened the control of the father over the marriages of his children (Aries, 1962). Encouraged by this royal sponsorship, the man's authority increased over both his wife and children. Indeed, the family was described as "the basis of the State, the foundation of the monarchy" (p. 356).

Conversely, the revolutionary era which marked the demise of kings, kaisers, and czars introduced democratic ideas and equalitarian legislation which emancipated women and children from the control of the family patriarch. We will examine the effect of Marxist revolutions when we come to the topic of social change. Here I will only mention that the nineteenth century Napoleonic Code legislated primogeniture out of existence as inconsistent with the French Revolution's ideas of justice and equality. Instead, the post-revolutionary family law insisted that all children must inherit equal shares of the family estate, applying the concept of equality to the group of siblings (Habakkuk, 1955).

In sum, then, authoritarian rulers tend to encourage male-dominated and elder-dominated families, whereas democratic governments tend to modernize the family system by abolishing the special prerogatives of the patriarch.

UNINTENDED CONSEQUENCES OF POLITICAL POLICIES

Some governmental actions which supposedly have no direct bearing on family life actually have marked repercussions. Government is such a powerful force that it can easily bring great pressure on family life without being aware of what it is doing.

Aries (1962) attributed the very creation of the concept of adolescence to the nineteenth- and twentieth-century invention of military conscription. Whereas in earlier centuries boys had moved directly from childhood into adulthood, universal military training for a term of several years interposed a new stage in life when the young man was no longer a child, but still unable to enter adult vocational and marital roles. This ambiguity of the adolescent —half man and half child—created social difficulties for the individual, the society, and particularly for the family. Parents who knew how to deal with children when they were young and dependent or to release them when they moved into adulthood hardly knew how to treat their adolescents when that borderline category was created by the state. Ever since, parents and adolescents have struggled to find appropriate definitions of their relationship.

In the chapter on social change we will explore the unintended consequences of the political system when governments go to war against each other. Then the disruptive effects of conscription on family life are multiplied.

Just as the military machinery of government intervenes in the relationship between parents and children, the legal machinery of government alters the relationship between husbands and wives. In the case of Polish immigrants to the United States, Thomas and Znaniecki (1958) were convinced that American legal processes had a disastrous effect on marital solidarity. Whereas in the old country, the kin group intervened by pressuring a couple to resolve their marital problems and preserve their solidarity, in the new country the courts operated to preserve the rights of the individual man or woman in a conflict of interests with the spouse. This new resource placed a powerful weapon in the hands of immigrant wives. Whereas previously they had had to conform to the patriarchal husband's wishes, now they could appeal to the police when they were dissatisfied with the husband's behavior. If the man was drunk or violent or neglected his family, the wife could take him to court and bring the coercive power of government to bear upon him to force him to "behave."

This legal procedure protected the rights of women in a situation where extended kin were no longer available to intervene informally on their behalf. Nevertheless, the unintended by-product of this legal protection of the individual was the destruction of the marriage bond. Immigrant men fiercely resented the intervention of the police, the probation officer, and the judge, especially since they usually were "foreigners" who had little understanding of Polish ways. Though the man might lose in court and be told to "cease and desist" his misbehavior, the wife's "victory" was likely to be hollow. Offended by his wife's impertinence in publicly humiliating him, the man frequently retaliated by deserting his family. This denouement was intended neither by the government in establishing its legal machinery nor by the wife in invoking it. Nevertheless, said Thomas and Znaniecki, "we have not found a single instance where official interference strengthened the conjugal bond" (p. 1747).

In both cases, then, a government with its eyes focused on other objectives (military strength in the one case and individual rights in the other) placed strains on the family system without realizing what it was doing.

The success of a national or imperial government in dealing with the outside world is another political force which unintentionally affects family life. In the heyday of the Roman empire, the ruling families of the imperial capital enjoyed luxurious living based on the financial tribute of the far-flung empire and the personal service of captured slaves. Their wealth and political security fostered a hedonistic philosophy of life which led them to search for diversion through sexual escapades in extramarital affairs. Eventually, the Empire fell in a collapse which was partly the result of the collapse of the Roman family system into decadence. Perhaps we can draw an analogy between what happens to families under conditions of political monopoly and what happens to economic enterprises when they have no competition: In both cases the entrenched group becomes flabby, decadent, and eventually tends to collapse. Conversely, a healthy competition between social groups tends to foster a responsible family life as a basis for social strength.

LEGAL CONTROL OF FAMILY LIFE

Governments sometimes try deliberately to shape family behavior in ways they believe to be in the best interests of both the families themselves and society as a whole. As social life becomes more complex and delicately balanced, the state becomes more concerned that families should supply it with recruits well qualified to fit into the delicate network of social roles which compose the society. Conversely, the costs of deviant behavior and of social incompetence rise exorbitantly, making the state increasingly anxious that families should build into their children's character restraints against antisocial behavior.

Modern societies also develop new technical and scientific knowledge which gives the state new standards of family welfare and new instruments for enforcing those standards. In an era of specialization, the jack-of-all-trades parent can no longer be trusted to function adequately without expert help. So the state enacts minimum standards of family welfare and employs practitioners to intervene in family life when those standards are not maintained. Thus the government becomes the agent of the society in promoting family welfare by legal fiat and social services.

Premarital Association

Some governments attempt to control the premarital association of boys and girls, especially by prohibiting premarital sexual intercourse. The attempt takes the form of passing laws but laws are not always enforced. Although policemen in some American communities patrol the lovers' lanes and order young people to "break it up," they rarely arrest anyone for this offense as long as the sexual experience is voluntary.

Rape is another matter. Most societies treat involuntary intercourse as a serious crime carrying severe penalties. Among 110 primitive societies less than half punished premarital intercourse as long as it was voluntary, and the typical punishment was a small fine. By contrast 95 percent punished the rape of an unmarried woman and the typical punishment involved knifing the offender (Brown, 1952). In modern societies, rape continues to be treated as a serious offense, especially when the victim is a high-status member of the community and the offender of lower status.

Between ordinary premarital intercourse and ordinary rape is "statutory rape," *i.e.,* intercourse between an adult man and a juvenile girl. This is seen as quasi-rape, involving the possibility of domination of the girl by the man and therefore deserving the special protection of the state. The greater the discrepancy in age and the younger the absolute age of the girl, the greater the danger and the more severe the penalty tends to be.

Although laws against premarital intercourse between consulting participants of the same age have little effect because they are seldom enforced, the laws governing statutory rape are more often enforced and therefore have more impact on actual behavior. Among Appalachian migrants in Chicago, Rosenberg and Bensman (1968) found that young men generally avoided underage girls in order to avoid charges of statutory rape. Such charges were especially likely to be preferred by the girl or her parents if she became pregnant. If the boy himself was underage he was legally immune from prosecution and so young boys excused their consistent failure to use contraceptives on the ground that no harm could come to them personally should their intercourse leave a girl pregnant. Such attitudes suggest that premarital behavior is indeed affected by legal controls, provided that those laws are enforced.

Family Formation

Although premarital intercourse (short of rape and perhaps of conception) is a matter of relative unconcern to modern states, marriage is another matter. The family, after all, is the basic unit of society and society is interested in controlling its formation. As long as extended families or kin groups exercise that control by arranging marriages for their young people, states can afford to delegate that responsibility. But once young people take marriage arrangements into their own hands, the state begins to be concerned. The higher the divorce rate rises, the more concerned the state becomes.

The first phase of governmental intervention in family formation is sometimes to try to bolster the power of elders over the marriages of their children. During the feudal era in Japan, arranged marriages were confined to the elite. But when the first modern government took control, it decided to encourage the lower reaches of the society to emulate their superiors by adopting their matchmaking system. By legislation giving power to the elders and especially to the man's family, by "moral education" in the new public schools which taught Confucian ethics, and by adult education through speeches and newspaper articles, the government tried to persuade the masses that their old freedom of mate-selection was uncouth. This made many of the old customs of the ordinary people "such as the relatively free relations between young men and women, seem crude and countrified" (Goode, 1963:327). Not only did attitudes change but family formation practices conformed to the new government-sponsored attitudes, so that in most of Japan save the most remote mountain and fishing villages self-selection almost disappeared by the early twentieth century and the only love-matched couples left in most communities were old people who married before the modern era.

Not only did the Japanese government discourage love-matches, it even prohibited marriages which would interfere with the feudal ideal of family continuity. Specifically, Goode discovered, the 1898 Family Code forbade marriage between a man and a woman who were both the last survivors in each family since marriage would mean that one family line would die out. Instead the law required sole heirs to bring new spouses into their households so that the family line could be continued (even if this meant that a man would have to adopt his wife's family name to continue her line unbroken).

In India, Goode noted that the government had a tougher time altering old customs of family formation. In a country so poor that it could not afford mass education, the government was deprived of a major instrument for reaching the masses of the next generation. Thus the legislature passed laws (for example, raising the minimum age at marriage) which were "consistently ahead of folk practice" although eventually they resulted in "considerable" change. The government was in an even more difficult position with respect to the taboos on intermarriage between castes. It could not force people to marry across caste lines but it could and did prohibit the punishment of those who chose to do so. The progressive members of the legislature thus made it easier for young people to violate the conservative attitudes of their elders and gradually freed mate-selection of some of the old restraints.

In the United States, the legislatures of the several states initially passed rather mild restraints on age at marriage. In Tennessee as recently as the 1940's the minimum age was only 12 for girls and 14 for boys (with consent of parents). Gradually, however, the minima have been raised as legislators have become aware of the extraordinary fragility of youthful marriages. Nevertheless, this law too is not self-enforcing. Unless government officials require such foolproof evidence as a birth certificate, underage young people who wish to marry are apt to falsify their ages. In Tippecanoe County, Indiana, Christensen, Andrews, and Freiser (1953) found that one sixth of those claiming to be old enough to marry without parental consent were under the minimum age (18 for girls, 21 for boys). And even among those too young to marry with parental consent, parents and children connived to cheat the law in an appreciable number of cases. One reason for cheating was a higher than usual number of forced marriages due to premarital pregnancy. Conversely, the state's concern to prevent marital failure by imposing age limits was shown to be justified by divorce rates more than double the normal level among couples who falsified their ages in order to get married.

Legislative attempts to prohibit youthful marriages thus may be evaded by lax bureaucratic enforcement. They also may be impaired by opportunities for migratory marriage. If couples too young to marry in one state may marry in an adjacent state with lower minima, a considerable proportion of eager young people will take advantage of that opportunity.

In Japan, the discrepancy between law and actuality is even greater with respect to the registration of marriages. The 1898 Civil Code required that marriages be registered with the local government in order to be legal. But as recently as the 1940's, only 1 percent of marriages in Japan were registered on or before the wedding day, and couples typically waited six months after the wedding before they actually registered (Fueto, 1956). There the customary belief in the desirability of completing a trial period to discover whether the new bride would fit into the husband's family and bear children was hardly affected by passing a law which carried no penalties for late registration. By contrast, the Turkish government, which had had similar difficulty persuading its citizens to register their marriages, suddenly achieved results when it decided not to pay dependency allotments to wives and children of soldiers engaged in the Korean War unless their marriages were registered.

One curious feature of both the Japanese and the Turkish cases is that many of the marriages which violated the registration law were contracted by religious ceremonies (Shinto or Islamic respectively). In the United States, a clergyman will not ordinarily conduct a wedding ceremony unless the couple produce a marriage license which guarantees that they have already begun the process of registration. The discrepancy between law and custom in the case of the U.S.A. comes in determining when a couple actually marry. As a result of long-term secular changes, increasing numbers of young couples have begun having intercourse, have become pregnant, and have even begun living together prior to the time when they ceremonialize their relationship. Given such informal ways of forming families, couples may by-pass governmental restrictions like those on age at marriage. Again the limits of governmental powers of enforcement are apparent.

In addition to attempting to delay family formation until a certain age, many governments attempt to prevent precipitous marriages by requiring waiting periods between the time a marriage license is applied for and the time the wedding may be enacted. Usually a matter of three to five days, these waiting periods allow recovery from the intoxication of alcoholic beverages or other momentary enthusiasms. How much they prevent "quickie" marriages has yet to be measured by before-and-after or comparative research.

Family Growth

Reproduction and child-rearing are more difficult for governments to control than marriage. Nevertheless governments are often vitally interested in both the growth of their population and the socialization of children, so they try to influence families as best they can.

A government may be interested in either expanding or limiting its population. To promote expansion and reduce the strain of children on family resources, more than sixty governments have instituted family allowances and other financial compensation. Stalin gave Russian mothers of ten or more children awards as "heroines" of the Soviet Union. And of course there is always propaganda. One cannot be sure how successful any of these methods is if other conditions are not right. If life is difficult, housing is short, and adults are more interested in raising their standard of living than in having large families, incentives are not likely to be very persuasive. In France, for example, family allowances have not been adequate to overcome a long-time sluggishness in population growth. An international study by Christopher Green for the Brookings Institution concluded that ". . . there is little or no statistical evidence that family allowances affect the birth rate. . . ." (Christenson, 1969). Perhaps only if governments raised their per-child payments substantially above current levels would any appreciable effect on birth rates become visible.

Governments seem to be somewhat more successful in contributing to population control, especially if families want to achieve that goal but need assistance. One variable over which governments have some control is the availability of abortion. If abortion is illegal, it may nevertheless be available to desperate patients on a fairly large scale. Among the American women studied by Kinsey, almost one fourth had had at least one induced abortion (usually illegal) although the proportion declined toward 10 percent after the Great Depression ended and children became less of a financial hardship (Gebhard, et al., 1958). To ban abortion does not make it disappear. Nevertheless, to define it as illegal tends to raise the price, to impose a social stigma, and to make it less available than would otherwise be the case.

If a government wishes to reduce the birth rate it may make abortion most readily available not only by legalizing it, but also by providing it as a public health service. Since the Japanese government adopted this policy in 1948, the number of abortions has equaled the number of live births, so that the birth rate has been approximately half what it otherwise would have been. The actual birth rate fell from 28 per thousand in 1950 to 18.5 in 1956 with abortions clearly the major factor in the rapid drop (Gebhard et al.). In Scandinavia, by contrast, the legalization of abortion was restricted with so many conditions and the practice of contraception was so effective (unlike in Japan), that only about 5 percent of all conceptions were legally aborted in the 1950s. Hence the effect of the legalization of abortion on child-bearing depends on how freely it is available and on how great the family demand for it is.

At the same time that Japan legalized abortions, it also attempted to promote contraception as a less drastic way of solving the population problem. Clinical and educational efforts gradually resulted in more widespread and more successful use of contraceptives. Other countries which did not legalize abortion have also sought to promote contraception. Such newer methods as intrauterine devices were adopted with considerable success in a number of countries, including Taiwan. In India, on the other hand, the limited health facilities and low educational level of the population made the voluntary sterilization of males whose families had achieved the maximum desired size particularly effective. In this case, however, it was necessary for the government not only to provide the sterilization without charge but to compensate the man for his lost day's wage in order to make it economically feasible for poor people.

So far, governments have intervened by offering voluntary aid. As the world's population grows more dense, it seems likely that the future will see increasingly powerful incentives designed to force families to limit their reproduction. Some scholars have already suggested that it may be necessary for families to secure a governmental license before they may have the two children which would maintain a stable population. When that time comes, legal control of reproduction will have become far more severe than it is now.

Family Dissolution

A government can hardly compel people to go on living together if conflict within a family becomes sufficiently severe. However, governments differ greatly in the extent to which they allow marriages to be legally terminated, and even more in the process they provide for that termination.

Italy, for example, until recently allowed no divorce. Marriages might be terminated only by annulment, *i.e.,* by a court determination that no "true" marriage ever existed in the first place. Such a determination was relatively easy in those rare cases where a marriage never was "consummated," *i.e.,* where the husband and wife never had sexual intercourse. But annulments could also be granted for marriages contracted on an invalid basis, *i.e.,* if it was discovered that one party was still married to someone else. Countries which do not allow divorce place a major impediment in the way of remarriage while the first spouse is still alive. In effect, they require their citizens to emigrate if they wish to enter such a remarriage.

Differences in the grounds on which divorces may be granted also affect the availability of divorce. Some governments allow divorce only on the basis of adultery. In New York State as long as divorce was limited to that single ground, couples who wished to end their marriage for other reasons were faced with difficult choices. They had either to (1) forego all chance of divorce (perhaps the least likely choice), (2) migrate to another state (such as Nevada) or country (such as Mexico) which would grant a divorce after a short period of residence, or (3) meet the provisions of the New York law. In some cases the law presumably encouraged couples to commit adultery in the form of premarital intercourse with their next prospective partner. However, a popular alternative was to pretend. Fake adulteries could be secured through the services of shady "businesses" which provided the necessary photographic and recorded "evidence" with which the divorce could be secured. Since the evidence was illegally concocted, the price was correspondingly inflated. Nevertheless for divorce-seeking couples unable to go elsewhere, an illegally simulated adultery often seemed preferable to committing the crime of real adultery. At least it shifted most of the criminal responsibility to the paid agents even though one partner (normally the man) had to "participate" to some extent in the crime.

In recent years the necessity for such fabrications has decreased. South Carolina, the last state to prohibit divorce altogether, now permits it. New York now allows divorce on grounds other than adultery.

Nevertheless, most states in the U.S.A. still require couples to cheat at another point—they must pretend not to be in collusion. Divorce laws are generally based on the premise that one party is guilty of the crime and the other innocent, that the innocent party has not condoned the crime by forgiving it either in words or through sexual intercourse, and that the two partners have not conspired together by agreeing on the desirability of getting a divorce. These ancient legal provisions require couples and their lawyers to hide from the judge the fact that both partners contributed to the breakdown of the marriage. They discourage couples from attempting a reconciliation (which would technically involve condoning the "crime") or force them to pretend that they didn't try to solve their problems. And they require the pretense that there has been no mutual agreement on the desirability of divorce as a way out of their marital impasse.

One consequence of the unilateral-crime philosophy is that couples must choose which partner is to blame. Due perhaps to the Western tradition of chivalry, most American couples decide that the husband is the villain whom the "innocent" wife will sue for divorce. Any evidence that both parties are guilty may prove to the outsider that a divorce is doubly needed but proves to the judge only that the case must be dismissed since there is no "innocent" party who deserves to be "awarded" a divorce.

The following news item was carried over UPI wire services in September 1965:

> DENVER (UPI)—Mrs. Barbara Prieto, 18, testified at her divorce trial that her husband, Anthony, had slapped her and threatened her life.
>
> As she stepped from the witness stand, Mrs. Prieto approached her husband, yelled "I hate you," and knocked him to the floor with both fists. The judge dismissed the case.

To say that Mrs. Prieto doesn't deserve a divorce because she hates her husband is absurd. Yet this is precisely the absurdity of most contemporary American divorce laws. So archaic are these laws that a 1965 joint conference of the American Association of Marriage Counselors with members of the Family Law Section of the American Bar Association agreed unanimously that current divorce procedures were "grossly unsatisfactory":

> Divorce law in theory and in practice are two completely different entities, and the whole divorce situation in the United States today involves a gross travesty of the best principles of law, of justice, and of humanity. . . . Marriage counselors cannot accept the view that in any average marriage failure it is possible to identify an innocent and a guilty partner. Lawyers admit that in practice nearly every divorce is either planned by mutual consent on the part of the couple or represents the capitulation of one

party to the persistent pressure of the other; and that then a matrimonial offense has to be "framed" to fit the law of the particular State. All were agreed that this is an unrealistic and in fact immoral situation.

Much of the marriage counselors' criticism of American divorce procedure centers around the "adversary" system. This means that in contested cases the husband and wife must battle each other to prove each one's innocence and the other's guilt. David Mace described the consequences of this legal process for the relationship between the two partners:

> The "adversary" concept of divorce inevitably tends, not toward easing the conflict between the spouses, but toward intensifying that conflict. Once involved in divorce proceedings, husband and wife find themselves in a climate which encourages them to fight each other for all that they can get. This is degrading, and may in fact destroy any last remaining chance of softening their hearts and bringing them together again. (1965:185–186)

Thus the provisions of the law interfere with the kind of approach to marital dissolution which would be appropriate in view of modern equalitarian philosophy and the equalitarian structure of contemporary marriages.

To replace the traditional concept of unilateral guilt and the associated legal myths, Mace recommended substituting the concept of "marriage breakdown" as a basis for divorce. This would require expert testimony based on clinical examination by a qualified marriage counselor "that the marriage relationship has degenerated to the point where it has become intolerable for one or for both, and it cannot be rehabilitated (p. 182)." This concept is the sole basis for divorce in the U.S.S.R. and in most other Communist countries. It is one basis among others in a number of other countries such as Switzerland, Yugoslavia, Greece, and Japan. This concept seems to be the most rational approach to marital dissolution and is likely to spread to other countries in the future.

Recently some American states have sought to modernize their divorce procedures. Some jurisdictions required marriage counseling either of all couples seeking divorce or of couples with children (based on the assumption that the latter have more of a vested interest in maintaining their marriage or that the state has an interest in protecting children from the collapse of their home). Despite the fact that such counseling comes very late in the process of marital dissolution, some reconciliations were effected. In a sense the counselors provided by courts of domestic relations are like the physicians provided in public health clinics: a public service to aid families in achieving their desired objectives.

Some states have experimented with compulsory waiting periods in the divorce process, either prior to trying the case or prior to the decree's taking effect. The former period is designed to allow an opportunity for reconciliation to occur spontaneously, which is not as far-fetched as it may seem since a sizeable minority of applications for divorce are withdrawn before the cases come to trial. The latter period is designed mostly to prevent hasty remarriages and is analogous in intent to the waiting period required after applying for a marriage license. Little is known about the actual effect of these legal provisions on the fate of marital dissolutions.

Generally speaking, insofar as stiffer divorce requirements (such as waiting periods and fines) function as barriers to marital dissolution, they may encourage couples to attempt reconciliation and enhance marital stability among those who succeed in solving their marriage problems. However, once a marriage has ended through desertion or permanent separation, easy divorce promotes marital stability by making remarriage possible. It is not in the public interest to have men and women floating around unattached and unable to remarry because they have been unable to free themselves legally from their former spouses. That simply promotes nonmarital involvements which are inherently unstable. It therefore seems useful to provide marriage counseling services and to encourage reconciliation where a clinical examination suggests that reconciliation may be possible. On the other hand, once it becomes apparent that there is no hope of reconstructing a particular marriage, prompt divorce and easy remarriage seem more conducive to family stability.

For couples with children most divorce decrees require support payments from the father until the children reach maturity or the mother remarries. Like many other provisions of the divorce law, this is widely violated. Many ex-husbands move out of the state to escape the jurisdiction of their home state's judicial system. Even for those who stay home, the enforcement procedures of most states are inadequate to compel compliance. When weak enforcement is combined with the poverty of many of these fathers, a large proportion of children fail to receive the support they might have expected.

In general, then, the divorce machinery of the U.S.A. might be described as archaic and inappropriate. Clients, lawyers, and judges have been forced to enter into a grand conspiracy to defraud the law in order to achieve the ends which they mutually agree are desirable: namely that couples should have an opportunity to end unworkable marriages and to contract new ones. The cumbersomeness of this circuitous approach impedes the cooperative approach between partners which might save some marriages and dissolve others less painfully. Hence American divorce laws may be described as a point of friction between the political system and the family system.

In this section on the legal control of family behavior, I have suggested that the state is often an inefficient instrument, especially when the wishes of the state run counter to the wishes of families. If the state tries to keep families from doing what they would like to do, the families usually can get around the law by devious, illegal means. If the state tries to force families to do something they don't want to do, stubborn resistance can often be successful. This does not mean that the political system has no influence on families. Even a widely violated law tends to be honored by some families. And even though the coercive power of the state is not automatically effective unless it is ruthlessly applied, the educative and service functions of the state are often persuasive or facilitative.

GOVERNMENTAL SUPPORT OF FAMILIES

With the evolution of the Welfare State, governments have shifted their emphasis away from merely controlling families to trying to serve them. Some of these services will be treated at the end of this book in the discussion of therapeutic intervention in family life and educational programs designed to equip people for family life. Here I will focus on economic and other tangible programs intended to provide resources for family living.

A large and growing number of countries support families directly by what are often called "family allowances." These are normally computed on the basis of the number of children in the family, sometimes increasing with the age of the child. They are usually paid to all families, regardless of need, though their chief purpose is to benefit families whose resources are inadequate. They have the greatest effect on poor families with the largest number of children, whereas for wealthier families the marginal increment in family income may make little difference in the family's standard of living.

Countries which do not subsidize families through cash payments may nevertheless affect families financially in other ways. For example, the U. S. federal income tax allows a deduction of $650 per dependent from taxable income. However, this deduction is worthless for families so poor that they owe no tax anyway and most valuable for families in the highest tax brackets. The net effect is to help those families most which need it least.

Governments which do not subsidize families must nevertheless find some way to aid families in desperate straits (unless nongovernmental agencies such as religious bodies and kin groups are strong enough to provide such support). Unfortunately, welfare policies supposedly designed to aid families may sometimes have destructive effects on family unity. The U.S. Aid to Dependent Children program in the 1950s required that there be no man in the home in order that a mother and her children might qualify for relief payments. As a result one Louisiana study found that in 39 percent of ADC families the husband/father had left home "for our benefit" (Schorr, 1960). If an unemployed man had left home to search for a new job, ADC regulations tended to prevent him from returning home empty-handed since his family's ADC payments would be cut off if he reappeared. Nor could he encourage his wife and children to join him in his new jobless location since families which moved across state lines lost their eligibility for relief programs dependent on having lived within a state long enough to be considered a citizen ("resident") of that state. Thus a whole series of welfare regulations had the effect of accentuating the tendency of poor families to be split by desertion of the husband. These side-effects of the ADC program (subsequently amended as the Aid to Dependent *Families* and Children program to try to resolve some of these problems) show that governmental efforts to aid families do not always achieve their intended results and like untested drugs sometimes have dangerous side-effects.

We saw in an earlier chapter that governmental pensions for the aged have a happier effect on family life by reducing conflict between the generations and enabling older couples to maintain their autonomy as a separate family unit instead of having to live with their married children.

Government housing policies have had ambiguous effects on family life. Where housing is short, public housing programs remove a major obstacle to the formation of new families. But if the allotment of housing is done on a purely individual basis (as is usually the case) an unintended consequence is to disperse units of the kinship network who would rather live in close proximity to one another. (Rosser and Harris, 1965). Also in the last chapter I noted that urban redevelopment has intensified the problems of black families in American ghettoes by disrupting their ties with their neighborhoods and forcing them to move at frequent intervals.

Thus, governmental programs designed to achieve certain values on behalf of some families may have negative repercussions on those families or on other families. Governmental support of families must be carefully planned and evaluated if it is to maximize the positive effects and minimize the unintended negative effects. Presumably as welfare states acquire more experience with their family programs, they will be able to strengthen the support which those programs provide.

chapter four
THE RELIGIOUS SYSTEM AND THE FAMILY

As with the political system, sociologists have paid little attention to the effect of religious systems on the family. Many sociologists have studied religious systems only as dependent variables responsive to other social forces. Others view religion as merely reinforcing the status quo rather than having independent influence in its own right which merits attention.

Nevertheless, societies with pluralistic religious establishments, such as the U. S. and Britain (where most of the world's sociologists are located), offer opportunities for making religious comparisons within national samples or even within local communities. Moreover the sharp difference between Catholicism and other faiths within these Western countries in its regulations concerning family life have attracted attention to specific features of family life such as contraceptive practice. The impact of religious institutions on certain aspects of family life is beginning to become apparent even though other aspects remain unresearched.

We will examine first the influence of religious values or ideology on family life and subsequently turn to the influence of religious institutions through their normative control systems and supporting services.

RELIGIOUS VALUES AND FAMILY LIFE

Perhaps the most important aspect of religious values is the ethical norms which determine the codes by which religious institutions seek to govern family life. However, religious concepts affect family life in other ways than just through the exercise of ecclesiastical control. Churches are socializing agents which seek to shape the character of children. When they succeed, they have a profound indirect effect on the behavior of those children throughout their lives. And even religious ideas which seem at first glance to have little to do with family life may have considerable impact insofar as they change the perceptions which family members have of one another and of their common family membership.

For instance, such a seemingly esoteric question as whether the individual has a soul may affect family relationships. If the individual is not perceived as having a transcendent soul, the family may control his body and mind more securely and do with it whatever it wills, less subject to ecclesiastical intervention. If he is seen to have a soul, the individual must be treated with more respect.

Aries (1962) believed that not until the seventeenth century A.D. did Christians apply the doctrine of the soul to children. The immaturity of children makes them especially vulnerable to family control and exploitation. Hence it was peculiarly important to the welfare of children when parents came to realize that they deserved to be treated with the respect due the possessors of immortal souls. From his study of history, Aries concluded that "there can be no doubt that the importance accorded to the child's personality was linked with the growing influence of Christianity on life and manners" (p. 43). In this way Christianity contributed to the emancipation of the individual child from his feudal bonds—one of the important features of the transition from the medieval to the modern family system.

By contrast, the Hindu concept of the soul is less individuated than the Christian concept and provides less basis for personal emancipation. Minturn and Hitchcock (1963) noted that the Rajputs of India did not believe that the human body housed a unique soul, but rather one that had been incarnated in other bodies previously and would be in other bodies in the future. Moreover, even that multiple-lived soul was not believed to have an independent existence, but rather was a mere "fragment of the universal world soul." This fitted the general view of the individual person as relatively unimportant in himself but primarily a member of a group, namely of his family: "Whereas a mother who conceives of her child as a unique individual emphasizes how he differs from other children, the Rajput mother, for whom all people are but transient elements in a permanent group structure, insists that 'all children are alike' " (p. 316). As a result, children tend to be treated alike, their distinctive needs ignored because their individuality is not recognized, much less encouraged.

The same emancipation from unlimited subjection which benefited children also benefited women. Feudal family systems perceive women as their husband's or his family's property in much the same way they do children. The fact that women are adults may give them greater opportunity to run away if their treatment becomes too severe, but if a society is sufficiently authoritarian, there may be no place to hide and the only escape may be suicide.

Christianity has often had a conservative influence on the position of women, but there have been several ways in which it spurred the emancipation of women. One was the same perception of women as individual human beings which benefited children. Today it seems difficult to perceive them in any other way, but from the standpoint of feudal societies it is not difficult. In addition to possessing souls, women have also benefited from the extraordinarily high status of the Virgin Mary in the Catholic pantheon. (In India, the female goddesses of Hinduism gave women—especially mothers—a higher symbolic status than did religions with only masculine deities.) To have a soul of one's own and to be of the same sex as a deity or the mother of a deity is to be doubly protected against the contempt which feudal men bestowed on women.

A third contribution of medieval Christianity was to provide a refuge for women fleeing their parents, their husbands, or prospective husbands. The Catholic Church's celibate orders for women provided an institutionalized alternative to permanent subjection to men in the family. The existence of such an alternative provided the individual with bargaining power. By threatening to leave the family, a woman might persuade her superiors to accede to her wishes (if they wanted her to stay). If she failed to persuade them, she could breach their authority by becoming a nun. This safety valve moderated the authority of the medieval man over his wife and daughters.

Although most religious institutions have been dominated by males and have therefore provided a conservative model for family life, some religious bodies have been exceptions. One was the Society of Friends (Quakers) who from their beginning in the seventeenth century granted women substantial equality with men in both worship and business meetings. Having experienced equality within their religious organization, Quaker women were dissatisfied with the restrictions to which they were subjected elsewhere in British and American society, and contributed a remarkably large share of the leadership to the Women's Suffrage movement in both countries (Flexner, 1959).

This is not to say that all religions or even that religion in general tends to emancipate either children or women. It is to suggest that certain religious ideas and program institutions may have a powerful influence in this direction.

THE SANCTIFICATION OF FAMILY LIFE

One contribution of some religions has been to sanctify the individual as an entity apart from his family or any other social institution. An analogous (and far more frequent) function of religion has been to sanctify the family itself.

This does not mean that religion has taken the familial status quo and made it sacrosanct. Rather it has taken the highest ideals of family life at the time the religion was founded and made them goals for all families. This means that initially religion had an ethicalizing effect on family life. However, it also means that after social conditions changed those religious ideals often became obsolete and exerted a conservative force resisting the development of new ideals appropriate to the new conditions. Since most of the world's great religions arose under premodern conditions, those ideals tend to be feudal ideals more appropriate to agrarian than to industrial societies. Nevertheless, they are ideals, and it is their idealistic character that we shall examine first.

The value of female deities for women has already been mentioned. There is a similar value for families in the concept of a "holy family." Campbell described how this served as a model for family life among Greek Orthodox shepherd families:

> In the popular mind [the family] is an earthly reflection of the Heavenly Family of God the Father, the Mother of God, and Christ. Relations between members of a family ought to be modeled on the attitudes which, it is imagined, inspire the relations of the Heavenly archetype Family and its members. A father ought to have wisdom and foresight, a mother compassion, a son courage and respect, a daughter virginity, and so on. Through grace, which descends in the sacrament of the Eucharist and through the icons, and in other ways, they are helped to achieve these modes of being.

> . . . Through reference to a divine model, a man or woman in family life participates in a reality that transcends individuality. . . . (1964:37)

Note that Campbell used the word "ought" throughout this statement. The families of man ought to be modeled after the family of God. How much they actually are cannot be definitively answered. But we can assume that a model bearing the prestige of divinity could not be preached for centuries without being practiced to some extent. Yet there is always a danger that divine models may be perceived as suitable only for divine beings, so for family life to be influenced most persuasively the family must be sanctified more directly.

Aries (1962) concluded that the Roman Catholic Church did not fully sanctify family life until the end of the sixteenth century. Before that, the church sanctified only what it labelled the "religious life," *i.e.,* the life of priests and monastics who escaped the corruptions of the world, and especially the corruptions of family life with its sexual involvements, to live a pure life of celibacy. Even that, as I have suggested with respect to the status of women, had an indirect effect on family life. The demonstration that it was possible for men to live a celibate life took some of the automatic compulsoriness out of the sexual aspect of marriage. If men were capable of refraining from sexual intercourse when they were not married, they were also capable of refraining from demanding it of their wives whenever they wished. Thus the sexual aspect of marriage, which had long been the point at which women were expected to be most obedient, became more optional and therefore a more considerate aspect of the relationship between husband and wife.

Nevertheless, the medieval Catholic emphasis on the superiority of "religious vocations" left family life as the apostle Paul had seen it centuries before, a mere concession to the weakness of the flesh. With the beginning of the modern era, Aries noted a major shift in church attitudes both within the Catholic Church and within the Protestantism which arose amid this new ferment of thought and bore its stamp. The marriage ceremony was brought inside the sanctuary from its former position "in front of the porch." This symbolized the new Catholic emphasis on marriage as a sacrament (a means by which God dispenses grace to the participants) and the Protestant emphasis on the legitimacy of all vocations under God, including the vocation of marriage.

With marriage as a sacrament came new emphases in the relationship. Marriage was idealized in itself, not just as part of a larger family life. The "marriage" of Christ and his church became the model for husband and wife. Emphasizing the husband–wife relationship undermined the vertical emphasis in feudal extended families and paved the way for shifting from arranged marriages to love matches. Sacramentalizing marriage distinguished it more sharply from other male–female relationships, undermining the feudal male prerogative of concubinage and developing a broader role relationship in marriage. Finally, sacramental marriage, because it was divinely ordained, undermined the patriarchal freedom to change wives at will. Henceforth a man must try to make his marriage work by exercising ethical responsibility in it. In such ways, the concept of the sacramental nature of marriage contributed to the qualitative improvement of husband–wife relationships.

Once family life became a vehicle for divine grace, religion was no longer restricted to special places and special officials but assumed importance within the home. Aries noted that Christmas became a family celebration instead of the communal celebration it had formerly been. And worship, too, began to be conducted within the home, especially in Protestant families. Indeed, when the revocation of the Edict of Nantes deprived French Protestants of the privilege of public worship, it forced Protestant families to worship at home. Such family worship and family Christmas celebrations contributed a ritual richness to family living which modern research suggests must be viewed as a significant contribution (Bossard and Boll, 1950).

The Conservation of Old Practices

In the preceding section I described ways in which religion enriches and changes family life. New religions particularly stimulate innovation, challenging families to raise their functioning to ideal levels. Such values as love and faithfulness, obedience and responsibility are incorporated into the religion as ethical commandments enjoined on devotees.

Once such ethical principles are enshrined in the faith, however, they resist subsequent change. Although they may have enriched family life originally, if conditions change sufficiently, they block the further evolution of family life. This problem is particularly severe insofar as family principles are recorded in written books (such as the Bible) which are considered divinely inspired and therefore not subject to change. By contrast, religions which rely on oral traditions are more flexible in adapting to changing circumstances.

An even more difficult problem is that religious teachings incorporate not only ideal principles but mere descriptions of family practices which happen to be current at the time. Certain aspects of family life are thus frozen into sacred writings, not because there is any particular concern to advocate them as ideals, but simply because they are taken for granted as current practices. Such "accidental" absolutizing of the status quo constitutes a particularly severe obstacle to progress and gives supernatural sanction to practices which otherwise might have more quickly been abandoned.

Examples of this combination of accidental and intentional conservatism can be found in any religion which has existed for very long. The ancient branches of Christendom are replete with illustrations. Islam provides another example of these processes.

Islam began in seventh century Arabia and reflected a combination of tribal and feudal conditions of the seminomadic pastoral Arabs of that day. These were incorporated into the Koran as a series of permissions and prohibitions which were appropriate to the seventh century but which have long since become outmoded. For example, Jeffery (1959) reported that the marriage bond had been held lightly by the pagan Arabs, as in many primitive societies. This de-emphasis on the marriage bond was incorporated into Islam in permitting polygyny (a maximum of four wives at once) and easy divorce. To a greater extent, however, Islam incorporated a feudal design for family life. The patriarchal authority of the husband–father was praised, along with a corresponding submissiveness for women and filial piety for children. Marriage was to be arranged between families of the bride and groom who were to sign a marriage contract that specified the terms of the economic transactions to be involved. Women were to be secluded from public view by cloistering in the harem and by veiling themselves outside the house. The rights of men to divorce their wives and to boss their wives and children were extended by asserting a patrilineal right to children in the event of divorce (the husband retained the children, the wife had to surrender them). Moreover, men not only had a tribal right to multiple wives but a feudal right to concubines and even to temporary marriages when they were away from home. Muslim men had the best of two cultural worlds.

Incorporating these tribal and feudal family customs into its teachings made family life in Islamic countries quite different from other countries. Polygyny has existed longer and divorce rates have been higher in such countries as Indonesia than would otherwise have been the case. Women and children, conversely, found Islamic teaching a major obstacle to their emancipation. This does not mean that the modernization of family life can be delayed indefinitely in Islamic countries, especially as they become modernized in other respects. But modernization is clearly retarded by the conservative influence of this ancient religion.

Do old religions ever change? In some case, old teachings are reinterpreted. In others, they are ignored. Eventually, industrialization, education and urbanization force old patterns to adapt to new conditions when the discrepancy becomes too great. If such adaptation is sufficiently thorough, a religion can even become a source of further innovation, at least temporarily. Perhaps we should conclude that any religion tends to be an innovative force early in its history and then tends to be a conservative force later, but that the relationship between religion and family life varies depending on the balance of reformist and conservative forces at any particular time.

Attitudes Toward Sex and Reproduction

Islam and Catholicism have been polar opposites in their attitudes toward sex and have caused corresponding differences in sexual behavior. Goode (1963) noted that "one of the moral lessons derived from Mohammed's comments or actions during his lifetime states that every time a man engages in sexual intercourse he carries out an act of charity" (p. 112). This positive interpretation contrasts with the negative attitude toward sex which Catholicism inherited from a dualistic philosophy which emphasized the distinction between body and mind (or soul).

One evidence of the impact of this difference in sexual philosophy is shown in Table 4-1. Although the differences between families in their monthly frequency of intercourse were not always large, the Islamic families consistently reported a higher frequency than Christian families of similar education and residence. Moreover, Goode saw in these data further evidence of the effect of Islam because even the Christians in Lebanon had intercourse more often than the Americans studied by Kinsey. In other words, Islam seems to have raised the frequency of intercourse for Lebanese generally, regardless of their current faith, through its pervasive influence on Arab culture. If we were to compare the frequency of intercourse in predominantly Christian America to that in Arabic Lebanon, the contrast would be even sharper.

TABLE 4-1   Frequency of Marital Intercourse in a Lebanese Village and City, by Education and by Religion

MEAN MONTHLY FREQUENCY OF MARITAL INTERCOURSE	RELIGION		
	Islam	Christianity	Islamic/ Christian Ratio
Village			
Uneducated	24.5	18.2	1.35X
City			
Uneducated	19.8	19.1	1.04
Educated	21.2	17.9	1.18

Adapted from Yaukey (1961):128.

Although the Catholic attitude toward sex is revealed partly in its tendency to idealize celibacy and to see marital sexuality as a lesser state of perfection, Catholicism frowns most sharply on nonmarital sexuality. Irish Catholicism is particularly emphatic at this point and has a corresponding effect on working-class recreation. Humphreys (1966) noted that in comparison to other European cities, Dublin men spent extraordinarily little time "fooling around" with other women. To their wives this did not mean that they were more virtuous, because there was what Humphreys' informant called "a great deal of drinking and a great waste of time and especially of money that could be used by the family" (p. 143). Nevertheless, sexual infidelity was extraordinarily rare in that Irish Catholic community.

Although Catholicism (and some other branches of Christianity) has a somewhat negative attitude toward sexual intercourse, its attitude toward reproduction is very positive. Indeed, most old religions arose under feudal conditions which gave them a typically feudal attitude toward large families. The Catholic Church often cites the Biblical admonition to "be fruitful and multiply" as a divine injunction, and faithful Catholics tend to prefer large numbers of children (see Table 4-2).

TABLE 4-2   Ideal and Expected Number of Children, by Religion

AVERAGE NUMBER OF CHILDREN	RELIGION		
	Catholic	Protestant	Jewish
Ideal for average American family	3.8	3.3	2.9
Wanted if life could be relived	4.4	3.4	3.1
Most likely expected	3.7	2.9	2.5
Number of wives	668	1,596	106

Adapted from Whelpton, Campbell, and Patterson (1966):90. Source: U. S. national sample of white wives, aged 18–39.

Table 4-2 shows that Catholic women consistently preferred the largest number of children both for themselves and for the "average American family" and that they expected to have the largest number. Differences in preferences are important because they show that differences in the actual size of Catholic and non-Catholic families are not due to differences in contraceptive practice alone, but to the value Catholics attach to large families. Indeed, Westoff, Potter, and Sagi (1963) found in a similar study that the larger number of children born in Catholic families was due *primarily* to the larger number desired and only secondarily to lesser effectiveness in family planning. The Jewish wives in Table 4-2 had the smallest preferences and expectations, although they differed from Protestant Christians less than the Protestants did from the Catholics. The biggest difference between the latter two groups was in the number preferred if their life could be lived over again, whereas when asked about the average family regardless of religion, Catholics moderated their statements in the direction of the average American norm.

The importance of religion in family growth can be seen in Westoff, Potter, and Sagi's finding that religious preference (Catholic, Protestant, or Jewish) was more influential than any other "major social characteristic" in determining the number of children born to white women in seven American metropolitan communities. Indeed they found not only a Catholic large-family norm, but also a Protestant small-family norm; *i.e.*, the more devout a Catholic family was, the larger its preferred and actual family size, whereas devout Protestant families had the smallest preferences and bore the fewest children. They attributed this to "the increasing dissemination of a moral theme of responsible parenthood" (p. 238). In any case, it is important to recognize that we cannot generalize that all religions value large families, but only that this is true of most old religions, whereas some newer ones advocate the opposite.

Another old religion which places a high value on children is Hinduism. Goode (1963) reported that Hinduism has traditionally required a man to have sons in order to gain entrance into heaven. This religious dogma gives a transcendental urgency to the impulse to bear children. And, noted Goode, since Hindus could not necessarily assume that their sons would survive to maturity in view of the high Indian infant mortality, the number of children necessary to guarantee the father's salvation was substantial.

Solidarity with Family and Kin

Although Jewish families in the United States prefer fewer children, this does not mean that they do not treasure the children they do have. Indeed the evidence suggests that Jewish couples get together with their primary kin (parents, siblings, and married children) more often than Catholics and far more often than Protestants. Family and kin solidarity is extraordinarily high among Jews and rather weak among Protestants.

The reason for this difference seems to be a difference in religious orientation. Judaism stresses the collective identity of the Jewish people. Jewishness is inherited from generation to generation through the family line. Catholicism recruits converts but stresses the collective solidarity of the parish and the duty of the family to raise their children to be Catholics. Moreover, salvation is not so much an individual affair, but is dispensed through the institution of the church. Protestantism on the other hand stresses the necessity for individual conversion even among the children of Protestant parents and stresses the direct relationship of the individual to God without institutional mediation. This gives an individualistic flavor to the Protestant personality and allows Protestants to choose between friends and relatives, often at the expense of the latter if they prefer the friends.

These differences in religious orientation are reflected in corresponding differences in family solidarity. Winch and Greer (1968) found that Jewish families had the most frequent contact with relatives, that Catholics were intermediate, and that Protestants had the least. Differences among these religious groups were greatest when two conditions occurred together: (1) maintaining contact with kin was difficult because both partners had migrated from the countryside to the city; but (2) their financial resources were great enough to permit contact across that geographical distance if their motivation was high enough. Under such circumstances, Jewish families suffered the least loss in contact, and Protestant family contacts declined the most, creating a major contrast between religious groups.

Similarly in Vicksburg, Mississippi, Brav (1940) found that Jewish men and women were more eager to see their siblings and their siblings' children than were non-Jewish adults. However, there was a sex difference in the desire to see their mothers: Jewish men were unusually eager to see their mothers, but Jewish women were not only less eager to see them than Gentile women were, but also less often kissed them or bragged about them to others. This suggests that Jewish households were dominated by the mother and that daughters rebelled against this domination. With the exception of this point of tension between mothers and daughters, however, kin solidarity among the Vicksburg Jewish families was remarkably strong, as symbolized in sending birthday messages and giving birthday and anniversary gifts to one another.

Thus in a variety of ways, the religious concepts of Judaism, Christianity, Hinduism, and Islam affect the patterns of family life of their devotees and, indirectly, of all who live under their influence.

ECCLESIASTICAL CONTROL OF FAMILY LIFE

So far we have examined the philosophical influence of religious systems on family life. But most religions are not content with such indirect influence. They take the family lives of their members too seriously for that. Authoritarian religions especially lay down rules and regulations either to control family life or at least to guide it. At the dynamic points of family formation, growth, and dissolution, religion tends to intervene in family life, characteristically to sanctify its formation, to encourage its growth, and to prevent its dissolution.

Rules to Sanctify Marriage

Most religions define the formation of a new family as a religious event which they clothe in ritual and ceremony. But their concern with family formation is more than merely ceremonial. They regulate eligibility for marriage and the possibilities of multiple marriage, and emphasize the distinctiveness of the married state.

Prohibition of Premarital Intercourse   One way of distinguishing marriage from non-marriage is to reserve just for marriage one of its most distinguishing characteristics: sexual intercourse. Many religions seek to enhance the significance of marriage by prohibiting unmarried persons from behaving sexually as if they were married. Although my description of the uneven effectiveness of governmental regulations on family life should not lead us to expect complete conformity with ecclesiastical legislation, religious affiliation is one of the best predictors of premarital sexual behavior.

TABLE 4-3 Premarital Intercourse of Men and Women Aged 16–20, by Religious Affiliation and Activity

| | RELIGIOUS AFFILIATION | | |
	Catholic	Protestant	Jewish
College-educated men			
Active	39%	27%	39%
Inactive	59	45	46
All women			
Devout	15	17	10
Moderate	32	21	11
Inactive	· 43	29	25

Adapted from Kinsey (1948):480 and (1953):343. Reciprocal percentages did not engage in premarital intercourse between age 16 and 20. Definitions of the degree of religious activity were not the same for the two sexes.

Table 4-3 shows that for three major religious groups in the United States, the more often young men and women attended church, the less apt they were to engage in premarital intercourse when they were in their late teens. Although the differences between religious groups were not consistent, the effect of religious activity was always conservative in each of the nine comparisons. The table suggests that the Catholic taboo may have been stronger than the other two. At least for both sexes the difference between active and inactive Catholics in the percentage engaging in premarital intercourse was greater than the difference in the other two religions. However, my main interest is not in the difference between religions but rather in the similarity: for all three religious groups, the greater the religious activity, the less the premarital sexual activity. Thus for all three groups, the distinction between the premarital and the marital state is greater for those most influenced by the church's teaching. Ehrmann (1959) found similarly that for both men and women students at the University of Florida, the greater the frequency of attending church, the smaller the proportion who had engaged in premarital intercourse, again suggesting the influence of religious teaching.

Among low-status groups, religious instruction may be less effective in preventing premarital intercourse, but church influence is revealed in the response of the individual to an accidental premarital pregnancy. Rosenberg and Bensman (1968) found that Catholic Puerto Rican boys in New York

City were no less promiscuous than Protestant Negro or Appalachian boys but that the influence of Catholicism became apparent when a girl became pregnant. Then a Puerto Rican boy was more willing "to accept the responsibility" for either marrying or at least helping the girl, whereas boys from the two Protestant subcultures were less apt to feel any responsibility.

Soon or late, then, many religions (and more especially Catholicism) stress the necessity for being married before engaging in complete sexual relations or at least for marrying to legitimate the biological consequences of those relations.

Standards for Mate Selection   Many religions limit the freedom of choice of the individual, defining some potential partners as unsuitable or prescribing others as obligatory. Catholicism, for example, defines a divorced person as ineligible for marriage as long as the former spouse is alive. Ancient Judaism prescribed the levirate (the obligation of a deceased man's brother to marry his widow). Most religions either prohibit or discourage marriage between one of their devotees and someone of a different faith.

Under some circumstances, however, religion increases the individual's freedom of mate selection. This was true where Christian missionaries encountered tribal restrictions in Africa. For instance, among the Ashanti, Fortes (1950) reported that missionaries undermined the customary prescription that a young man must marry his cross-cousin (his father's sister's daughter or mother's brother's daughter). And in Africa generally, Goode (1963) listed child betrothal, bride price, polygyny, and widow inheritance as tribal restrictions which missionaries attacked directly through their teaching and indirectly by pressing colonial administrators to pass and enforce laws against them. In abolishing the bride price young people were freed from a major economic obstacle to marriage and the role of elders in negotiating the economic exchange was reduced. Abolishing the inheritance of an elder brother's widow and the betrothal of children before they reached the age of discretion similarly freed individuals to make their own choices when they reached maturity. Only the attack on polygyny represented a restriction of freedom of mate-selection, but even here Christians emphasized the importance of the husband–wife tie against the familistic, economic, and prestige considerations which ordinarily motivated the acquisition of additional wives. (Although Islam permitted four wives, even that rule represented a limitation on the number of wives a man could acquire and thus was analogous to the Christian stress on having only one wife.) The changes which Christianity introduced into African mate selection were designed to enhance the solidarity of the husband–wife pair as against the power of elders and kin. These changes fit the widespread religious tendency to sanctify the institution of marriage.

The Ceremonialization of Marriage   Most religions develop rituals for the wedding ceremony which are designed to enhance the significance of the occasion and underline the significance of marriage. In general, the more elaborate the wedding ritual, the greater the distinction between the pre-married and the married state. The wedding ceremony is a kind of initiation ceremony, a rite of passage from one social status to another. The solemnity of the occasion impresses the couple with the seriousness of the responsibilities which they are undertaking to each other, to their future progeny, to their relatives and to society at large.

In most societies which offer a choice, secular ceremonies are less elaborate than church weddings. Landy (1959) noted that poor Puerto Ricans prefer a civil marriage as a way of avoiding the expenses of a church ceremony and the associated festivities which are expected to follow. But for those who can afford something more elaborate, the very cheapness and barrenness of a civil ceremony is precisely its disadvantage. In the Soviet Union the government was so disturbed by the tendency of young people to prefer church weddings that civil ceremonies were expanded to include many church-like features. Ornate wedding "palaces" were built by the government. The former procedure of mere registration was elaborated to include a short "sermon" by a representative citizen. The bride and groom wore special clothing and brought relatives and friends to the new weddings (Mace and Mace, 1963). Thus in an officially atheist country the influence of churches over the solemnization of marriage permeated even the civil ceremonies.

Rules To Encourage Growth

Religions which originated in feudal times usually share the feudal belief in the desirability of large families. They often prohibit contraception or other methods of family limitation.

The Catholic preference for larger numbers of children is limited to an official stand by the Catholic Church against the employ of any "artificial" methods of birth control. Within Protestantism, some fundamentalist sects also oppose birth control. Indeed Stycos and Back (1964) found that devout Jamaican converts to sectarian Protestantism were more hostile to birth control than Jamaican Catholics. The opposition of Catholic laymen to birth control is greatly weakened in Latin American countries where the masses are merely nominal Catholics. For example, in Puerto Rico, Hill, Stycos, and Back (1959) found that Catholicism had a "minimal" influence on contraceptive practice.

It cannot automatically be assumed that just because the Catholic Church prohibits contraception, that prohibition will be honored by Catholic families. What determines whether families will adhere to that ban? (1) The less population pressure there is on a family, the greater their willingness is to eschew contraception. Blake (1961) found that the men and women who gave the most religious objections to contraception had either completed their child-bearing, were no longer fertile, or had not yet borne their ideal number of children. Similarly in the U. S., many Catholic couples rely on the rhythm method as long as their families are small but shift to more effective methods as their families approach or pass their desired family size.

(2) The better they can afford children, the greater their willingness to rely on rhythm. For instance, Whelpton et al. (1966) found that most Protestant couples expected to use the pill regardless of income, but among Catholic couples, the percentage expecting to use this tabooed method declined from 34 percent of those with incomes under $3,000 to 15 percent of those with incomes over $10,000.

TABLE 4-4   Contraceptive Methods Used by Catholic Wives
by Frequency of Church Attendance

METHOD OF CONTRACEPTION	FREQUENCY OF CHURCH ATTENDANCE		
	Once a Month or Less	2–3 Times Per Month	Once a Week+
None	20%	35%	32%
Rhythm or abstinence only	7	15	37
Other methods	74	50	31
Total	101%	100%	100%
Number of wives	91	52	525

Adapted from Whelpton, Campbell, and Patterson (1966):285. Source: National U. S. sample of white wives aged 18–39 in 1960.

(3) The greater the exposure to Catholic teaching, the greater the conformity with it. Table 4-4 shows that Catholics who adhered to the church norm of attending Mass every week were most likely to practice the only method of family limitation sanctioned by the church (rhythm or more extensive abstinence). Conversely, a majority of those who went to Mass as little as once a month had used forbidden methods of contraception. Even these weak Catholics, however, showed the influence of Catholic teaching since they more often used the rhythm method or no method than the average non-Catholic.

I mentioned before that Irish Catholics have a particularly negative attitude toward sex. Humphreys (1966) found the average Irishman inclined "to a jaundiced view of sex and a generally ascetic outlook which places a high premium upon continence, penance and, in most spheres of life, on abstemiousness" (p. 26). One consequence is a strong emphasis in Catholic Ireland on the taboo on birth control, an attitude which survives for several generations after Irishmen are transplanted to the United States. A secondary consequence is that Irish citizens at home and Americans of Irish descent remain celibate longer (*i.e.,* marry later) than any other national group. Moreover, this effect of the birth control taboo on age of marriage applies generally to second-generation immigrants from Catholic countries in comparison to those from Protestant countries. Heer (1961) found that both men and women from seven Catholic countries were more apt never to have married by age 24 than their peers from five Protestant countries.

Closely related to the Catholic taboo on birth control is the taboo on abortion, but wherever that taboo is enacted into civil law, more than ecclesiastical control is involved.

In some religions the concern for growth extends not simply to the obligation to have children but to an obligation to marry off those children at an early age in order that growth may be sustained over succeeding generations. This concern for multi-stage growth was particularly strong in Hinduism. According to Goode (1963), one Hindu view was that if a girl was not successfully married off before she reached puberty, not only her parents but also her eldest brother would suffer divine wrath. Even the girl herself was forbidden to undergo ritual purifications and was considered no better than an outcaste as long as she remained unmarried. The chief consequence of this religious emphasis on early marriage was that it placed the girl's parents in a poor bargaining position and the groom's parents in a correspondingly strong position, increasing the size of the groom price the latter could expect to receive.

Rules To Prevent Dissolution

Most religions view marital dissolution askance—even if they do not prohibit it altogether (with the possible exception of Islam). Even Islam tries to prevent conflict from originating on the female side, even though it does little to impede masculine initiative.

Specifically, Goode (1963) noted that Islamic tradition called for removal of the female clitoris. This operation was intended to remove the temptation for women to engage in extramarital intercourse by reducing the physical pleasure experienced in sexual intercourse. Although from an equalitarian point of view, this seems like cruel discrimination against women, from the standpoint of a patriarchal religion concerned about safeguarding wives from marauding men, removal of the clitoris was an appropriate way to enhance the stability of the family.

Goode asserted that even the male prerogative of divorce was not as unqualified under Islam as is often supposed. Although the Koran allowed divorce, it did not praise it: "Of all that he has permitted, God detests nothing more than divorce." Moreover, the Islamic divorce ritual (saying "I divorce thee" thrice before witnesses) was not as abrupt as it sounds. Goode noted that "The ethical injunctions of the Koranic tradition assumed that a man would not express this formula three times at a single conflict, but might say, 'I divorce thee' and then retract that divorcement. That is, it was assumed that only after successive trials would a man finally and irrevocably divorce a woman" (p. 155). If the emphasis therefore is placed not on the simplicity of the verbal formula, but on the necessity of three stages before the dissolution is completed, even Islam seems to have viewed divorce critically. However, the extraordinarily high rate of divorce in Islamic countries suggests either that the discouragement of divorce is not enunciated clearly in the religious tradition or else that it is not taken seriously by the average Muslim.

In Catholicism, neither ambiguity exists. The ban on divorce is almost absolute (the only exception being the possibility of an annulment) and enforcement of the ban is so rigid that any Catholic who violates it by entering a second marriage contaminated by divorce on either side is excommunicated from the church. In other words, for all practical purposes, a Catholic cannot act as if he were divorced (by remarrying) and still remain a Catholic. Although some Catholics choose to leave the Church when faced with this dilemma, most conform to the norm.

One reason for this conformity is that most Catholic-dominated countries do not allow any of their citizens, Catholic or non-Catholic, to secure divorces. The religious system controls the political system, which thereby reinforces the control of the religious system over its adherents (and over others as well). The new Catholic state of Ireland incorporated into its 1937 Constitution a prohibition against all forms of divorce and annulment.

So extreme was this rule that it even prohibited Irish citizens from having their marriages nullified by the papal court in Rome! (Humphreys, 1966).

If divorce is unavailable to Catholics, what do men and women do when they can't get along with each other? One possibility is separation (which even Ireland legitimizes). Separated couples are still considered "married" in the eyes of the Church but are recognized as maintaining separate households.

Another possibility is that one or both partners may seek in extramarital relationships what they are unable to give each other. This seems to have been the pattern in a West Coast American city studied by Roebuck and Spray (1967). An expensive cocktail lounge in the finest hotel served as a rendezvous for middle-aged business and professional men, two thirds of whom were active Catholics (the remaining third were active Protestants). Almost all the Catholic men were married (whereas half the Protestants were divorced). Yet the Catholic men behaved as if they were divorced, joining the non-Catholics in regular sexual intercourse with the lower-status young women who frequented the lounge.

The men claimed to be "good husbands and fathers" who were loved by their families and loved them in return. They maintained this myth by allowing neither themselves nor their mistresses to get emotionally involved. Nevertheless several bits of evidence cast doubt on the meaningfulness of their marriages. The men visited the cocktail lounge an average of ten times a week, which means they must rarely have been at home. Their preferred forms of recreation (aside from sex) were not likely to involve their wives either: golf, hunting, and fishing. And most conclusively, they complained about their wives and families, suggesting that all was not well at home. Their wives were too "busy" to attend to their husbands' needs when the husbands *were* home. Apparently the chief business of the wives must have been with domestic responsibilities because the husbands complained about "family pressures," which probably came from the characteristically Catholic problem of excessive reproduction. Finally the husbands complained that their wives were "cold," which may have reflected the Catholic emphasis on virginity. (We can infer this from Kinsey's finding that active Catholic wives were considerably less responsive to orgasm than Protestant or inactive Catholic wives [1953:404].)

In general, Roebuck's Catholic men seem to have been thoroughly disengaged from their wives and families (despite their assertions to the contrary). They used their extramarital affairs as a substitute for the divorces which they might otherwise have obtained had their faith not forbidden it. This is one of the by-products of a rigid taboo on divorce: By making remarriage impossible, it makes extramarital behavior more likely. So while the Catholic ban on divorce effectively prevents divorce, it does not necessarily prevent marital instability and all-but-technical dissolution.

ECCLESIASTICAL SUPPORT FOR FAMILY LIFE

Religious organizations not only lay down laws for families but provide services designed to benefit family life. Such services could be described at great length. For example, Christian churches have provided charity for families in financial distress. Prior to the rise of the welfare state, churches were the main resource to which families could turn in time of trouble. Even where the state takes over the main burden of financial support, churches provide psychological support to families in trouble. Pastoral counseling has become a major activity of modern clergymen, and it is to clergymen that Americans studied by Gurin, Veroff, and Feld (1960) were more apt to turn than to any other professional person when they had marital problems.

We know little about the effect of ecclesiastical support on family life. However, Gurin and his associates found that people who had been to clergymen for help were enthusiastic about the amount of help that they were given. The help given by clergymen was especially often in the form of advice about what to do, or of supportive comfort which enhanced the couples' ability to endure their problems. Clergy were more apt than doctors or psychiatrists to help their clients break relationships in which they were involved, but we do not know whether these were premarital, marital, or extramarital relationships. On the other hand, clergymen were rather poor at "curing" problems either by changing the individual or by improving the relationship between him and his partner. So ecclesiastical support was considered helpful, but the nature of the help was primarily either to maintain the status quo or terminate it, rather than to improve its quality.

Although clergymen may have limitations in curing family problems, they are in a strong position to prevent problems. They are strategic premaritally because most couples who are to be married in a religious ceremony have an opportunity to confer with the clergyman in advance. This is the only institutionalized opportunity which exists in most modern societies for couples to be counseled in advance of marriage. A secondary consequence of this premarital contact is to make the clergyman an appropriate place to turn after marriage when further counsel is needed.

Religious institutions also provide education for marriage and family life. The courses in preparation for marriage which are now an established feature of American college curricula were originated extracurricularly by campus ministers. Many ministers continue to supplement academic courses with classes which emphasize their religious philosophy about marriage. Some councils of churches provide similar courses in metropolitan centers for young couples who have not had access to college courses.

Educational programs do not end with marriage. The Catholic Church sponsors "Cana Conferences" on marriage and family life in which married couples participate. And a new service of American churches has been family camps during summer vacations which offer a mixture of family-based recreation and family life education. Little is known about the effectiveness of these educational programs in preventing marital difficulties and improving the quality of family life. But the evidence is clear that religious institutions in many countries devote more energy than any other social institution to the support of family life.

THE EDUCATIONAL SYSTEM AND THE FAMILY

Education has many influences on family life. We have already seen in Chapter 2 some effects of varying amounts of education, and we referred in the last chapter to the efforts of religious institutions to provide specific education for family living. The purpose of this chapter is to focus on the consequences for family life of the participation of family members in educational institutions. Primarily this refers to the impact on family life of schools which take children away from home during the day and return them filled with information and attitudes which may not coincide with those of their parents.

Schools did not exist in primitive societies. There the responsibility for the education of children lay in the hands of their parents (with or without the cooperation of other parents). The same was largely true for agrarian societies. But with the rise of literacy among elite families in such societies came the need for specialized tutors and eventually for specialized schools. Finally in modern societies, mass schooling has deprived the family of many of its educational functions. The family now must coexist with educational institutions which assume primary responsibility for the technical education of children and compete with parents for children's basic socialization with respect to norms and values.

THE ORGANIZATION OF EDUCATION AND THE ORGANIZATION OF THE FAMILY

Schools came into existence in medieval Europe at a slow pace and in a series of stages (Aries, 1962). The first schools were not graded. All pupils of whatever age studied the same subject simultaneously. This reflected the tendency of parents to think of children as "little adults" without distinction as to age. Later as school curricula were arranged in sequences and school pupils were subdivided into classes, age-grading emerged. And when curricula ultimately were lengthened beyond the rudimentary instruction with which they began and were subdivided into elementary, secondary, and higher education, both pupils and parents began to think in terms of subdivisions of a child's life. Childhood proper was distinguished from adolescence, and the latter in turn, from young adulthood.

With the development of these distinctions, parents began to perceive changes in their children to which they had been oblivious before. Moreover changes were created which had not been there before. Aries noted that the middle class can still be distinguished from the working class throughout France by their differential relation to schools. In the middle class, adolescence is a period of secondary and higher education. But in the working class, the elementary school graduate goes directly to work and associates with men of all ages rather than belonging to a segregated age group.

Thus the schools produced a grouping among children by age which distinguished them from their older and younger siblings and which gave them an alternative basis of support outside the family. In the next chapter we will examine some of the consequences for family life of the creation of peer groups.

In addition to creating age grades, schools had profound effects on the child's physical relationship to his family. Prior to the rise of schools, the medieval European pattern involved the child's apprenticeship to a master who taught him a craft. This required the child to leave home at an early age to move in with his master's family as a quasi-adopted son. Henceforth he had little contact with his own family because he became the master's responsibility.

With the creation of schools, the separation of the child from his family was reduced. Even though the first schools were few and far between (which meant that most pupils had to leave home in order to attend them), parents maintained closer contact with their children than they had with apprentices. Aries found that children living in the vicinity of the early schools were brought food and money by their parents on market days. As schools became more firmly established, however, they began to provide dormitories so they came to function more extensively *in loco parentis*.

Only when schools became so widely established that they were available everywhere could the final rapprochement between the child and his family become possible. When private education gave way to public education and boarding schools to day schools to which pupils commuted from home, children were finally able to stay home and parents became once again the dominant moral authority in the lives of their children.

To put these changes in propositional form, the younger the age at which children leave home and the greater the responsibility assumed by an educational institution, the less influence the family has over its children. Conversely, the development of local high schools, junior colleges, and even municipal universities which allow young people to live at home in a financially dependent position until they are well into their twenties, prolongs the influence of parents over children.

Although mass education brought families back together and extended their years of intimate interaction, it must be acknowledged that there is still a sharp distinction between the modern family separated by the daily trek to school and the peasant family where children never leave the family plot. To be home at night is not the same as being home constantly. So even local education daily separates parents from their children and reduces parental control. Peasant children home all day long tend to be involved in chores under their parents' direction. Such children are in a very real sense employees of the family and subject to the discipline and authority exercised by employers everywhere. When children escape this discipline by their exodus to school, parental influence is inevitably reduced.

This exodus affects the family not simply because the children are absent but because they are involved in a competing social institution. That institution makes demands upon parents that the parents must honor. The children must be sent to school every day at a certain time and every year until they complete the prescribed curriculum. This limits parents' freedom to sleep late, to employ their children in crises, or to take their children off on whimsical holidays. The children must be properly clothed and shorn to fit the school's standards. The home must furnish the child with study facilities. In short, a whole series of intrusions on the autonomy of the family and infringements on its authority results from the child's involvement with an outside agency. Even though some parents win the contest of authority with the teacher for control of the child, the very fact that the teacher can challenge the parents is evidence enough of the loss of the old unquestioned authority of parents over the child which existed as long as the family was the only institution in which children were involved.

EDUCATION: THE GREAT EMANCIPATOR

One consequence of the school's intrusion into the family is a partial emancipation of children from parental auhtority. However, education has additional effects on family life besides supplying a competing authority. The task of education is to inculcate knowledge. Insofar as that knowledge involves new ideas, it tends to alter family relationships. This can be seen in the emancipation of children from their parents, of women from patriarchal subjection, and of nuclear families from entrapment in extended families.

The Emancipation of Children

We will see in a later chapter that whichever member of a family has more education than the others tends to have the most authority. Before the rise of schools, parents had the most knowledge because they had lived the longest. Even if parents taught children everything they knew, the children by definition could not learn more than the parents could teach. Thus children could never achieve an educational advantage.

With the invention of schools, however, this parental advantage was lost. When schools are first introduced or expanded to higher levels, children learn what their parents never had an opportunity to learn. And when an educational system becomes so highly developed that a "knowledge explosion" occurs (with new knowledge invented), even parents who have had as many years of education as their children are qualitatively disadvantaged. Parents who mastered conventional math a generation before cannot teach their children the "new math." With the expansion of knowledge, parents discover with mixed dismay and delight that their children are learning in grade school what the parents learned in high school, and in high school what the parents learned in college (leaving college free to teach things the parents never learned). Once an educational system reaches this advanced state, the rapid obsolescence of knowledge means that parents who completed their schooling some years before are correspondingly outdated in their knowledge.

This inversion of the normal parental advantage undermines parental authority. That authority can no longer be taken for granted "just because I say so." Parents are forced to replace their authoritarian stance with a democratic, bargaining stance. Children must be persuaded by marshalling evidence. And there is always a danger that the children will produce better arguments than the parents.

This does not mean that children are completely emancipated from parental influence. It does mean that the older they grow and the more education they acquire, the more their relationship with their parents tends to be transformed.

This decreased influence of parents applies more to technical fields than to moral influence. Hartshorne and May (1927) found that parents were more influential than teachers in determining children's values with respect to such moral matters as honesty and cheating. Parents have an advantage because they have first contact with the child: a monopoly of influence during the pre-school years before any teacher intrudes. Secondly, parents have continuous influence over many years whereas elementary teachers change every year and secondary teachers change with every class, diluting their influence. Thirdly, teacher influence is diluted by the size of classes. One teacher with 30 pupils has less contact per capita than two parents with three children. Moreover, family and school do not "play in the same league" but differ in their teaching emphases. Parents specialize in teaching human behavior, whereas teachers specialize in teaching algebra and biology, *i.e.*, the technical matters. Finally, the parent–child relationship is more emotional, more affectionate, and there-fore correspondingly more influential than the distant relationship of the teacher to his pupils. For such reasons, parents still maintain a powerful po-sition when it comes to socializing the child with the parents' values.

Modern parents may still have more influence than the teacher, but the fact that they must share that influence means that they have less control than if their children had not been influenced by the school system. One place where this decreased control shows is with respect to choice of marriage partner. It is easier for uneducated children to accept their parents' choice than for chil-dren who have been to school, especially if children have thereby acquired new standards. In Africa, Goode (1963) noted that educated young people asked for a voice in choosing their own marriage partner. Indeed among the Mende tribe of Sierra Leone, even the girls who had attended school were con-sulted by their parents as to their wishes in a husband. Boys, I assume, would have been consulted even earlier in history since they normally have a higher status in the family before receiving a boost from education. Presumably edu-cation also increases a child's freedom to choose his vocation and to make de-cisions generally.

The Emancipation of Women

Educated wives ordinarily marry men who received the same sort of education at the same time, so the balance between the two partners is not affected by differential obsolescence. Wives who receive no education, especially if their ignorance is compounded by segregation from even informal opportunities for learning, must depend on their husbands for practical knowledge and wisdom.

As women become educated, they acquire a base for critical thinking and independent judgment which leads them to challenge their husband's views when they disagree with him. Education develops the wife's independent in-terest in the world around her and her desire to continue to experience that world even after her schooldays are over and she is committed to keeping house and raising children. Educated women are less content to devote them-selves exclusively to domestic tasks and more interested in outside activities. Less submissive to the husband's will and more interested in the outside world, educated women have two bases for external activity. If the husband is willing to release her into the outside world, fine. If not, she will be less willing to stay home just because he tells her to. Nor does an educated husband who appreci-ates the value of external special interests and who has learned to understand human feelings seem as likely to insist that his wife stay home "doing nothing."

So an educated woman's excursions from home do not seem likely to meet with as much opposition if her husband has benefited from similar education.

TABLE 5-1 The Emancipating Effect of Education on Japanese Wives

	WIFE'S EDUCATION				
	HIGH SCHOOL		COLLEGE		HIGH/
	Non-		Non-		LOW
	Graduate	Graduate	Graduate	Graduate	RATIO
Husband and wife go out together for a good time (per year)	12.4	19.6	22.2	28.9	2.33X
Talks to husband's friends*	2.48	3.05	3.16	3.38	1.36X
Employed outside the home	33%	24%	43%	69%	2.09X
Number of wives	21	279	96	48	

Adapted from Blood (1967):149. Source: Young middle-class wives in Tokyo, 1959.
*Always = 4, usually = 3, half the time = 2, seldom = 1, never = 0.

The Japanese data in Table 5-1 support these hypotheses. Husbands of college graduates took their wives out on dates more than twice as often as husbands of high school drop-outs. Presumably at least part of the difference was due to greater eagerness of better-educated wives to "go places and do things," an eagerness to which the husbands responded.

Traditionally Japanese wives were not expected to join the conversation when the husband's friends came to visit. They were supposed to wait on the husband and guests, plying them with food and drink. The table shows that the Tokyo middle-class wives had departed substantially from that submissiveness, with even the least-educated wives joining the conversation more than half the time. Education directly affected the frequency of participation. The longer wives had stayed in school, the more interested they were in "men's" talk, the more able to keep up with it, and the less willing to play a merely passive role.

So far we have examined two settings within which educated wives are more active and equalitarian in the prescence of their husbands. The ultimate emancipation is doing things away from the husband. Table 5-1 shows that education emancipated Japanese wives in this way also. The number of college-educated wives employed outside the home (mostly fulltime) was roughly double the proportion of high-school-educated wives. This major external involvement reflects both the greater independence of educated wives and the salable skills they have acquired through their schooling. The percentages of college-educated wives who were employed was extraordinarily high by American standards, reflecting the fact that these couples had been married a relatively short time and were postponing child-bearing for a relatively long time until they could become well-established financially. Even so, the high-school-educated Japanese wives were equally young and childless, but their lack of education gave them less motivation and less ability to work outside the home.

Even though taking a job is a highly independent act, it usually takes the wife away from home during the same hours the husband is away. Hence the ultimate test of emancipation is whether the wife is able to leave home

TABLE 5-2   Wife's Evenings Away from Home, by Education

| | WIFE'S EDUCATION | |
EVENINGS AWAY FROM HOME	Under 12 years	12 years
At least weekly	28%	42%
1–3 times/month	13	29
Less often	22	16
Never	37	13
Total	100%	100%
Number of wives	32	24

Adapted from Komarovsky (1964):372. Source: Blue-collar wives under age 40 in an Eastern U. S. city.

when the husband is there. To do that is to desert him, depriving him of the companionship he ordinarily expects in his leisure. No data on this are available from my Tokyo study, but Komarovsky's study of blue-collar American marriages showed that wives who had graduated from high school were considerably more apt than drop-out wives to spend the evening away from home. Unfortunately this is not a full test of our argument because the husbands of women who finished high school may also have gone out more often. We cannot assume that they stayed home, fuming. But Komarovsky's data clearly show that these wives were spending leisure time away from their husbands that could otherwise have been spent with them. They thus demonstrate conclusively the emancipating effect of education on women.

At first glance it may seem paradoxical that educated wives in Table 5-1 spent more evenings out with their husbands, while educated wives in Table 5-2 spent more nights out without them. However, Komarovsky found that high-school-graduate wives had more dates with their husbands as well as more separate nights out than drop-out wives. The same may be true in Tokyo, although the taboo on separate evening activities for wives is stronger there.

Education promotes activity of many kinds, both joint and separate. Emancipation, then, should not be thought of primarily as emancipation from the husband but from the home and from subjection to the husband. Education frees the wife, but a free wife will choose to do things with her husband as well as apart from him. Without education, she is less able to do either.

Emancipation of Nuclear Families

Within extended family households, men are subordinated to the authority of their parents. This kind of family involves another kind of subjection which can be undermined by education. If education tends to emancipate children who are still young from their parents, how much more can we expect them to resist parental control when they become adults and marry and have children of their own. To be submissive to one's elders when one is already an adult and when one's education is more up-to-date than that of one's elders is particularly irritating. The fact that the elders in an extended family system in a developing country are likely to have less education than their adult children compounds the problem. Extended families exist primarily in agrarian societies and are therefore peculiarly subject to the upsetting influence of the educational revolution. Caught between the doubly conservative influence of parents who are at once elderly and uneducated and the emancipating force of education, sons are likely to be eager to establish homes of their own where they will no longer have to kowtow to anyone.

India is one place where education is destroying the extended family system. Gore (1961) found that only 20 percent of his main sample of Delhi area residents preferred nuclear families but 34 percent of his better-educated sample hoped to live apart from their elders. These were still minorities, but the emancipatory push of education was clear.

In general, then, education emancipates all the members of the family —men, women, and children—from control by their elders and by the dominant sex. When education is introduced into traditional societies, old family ways do not disappear overnight, but their eventual doom is sealed.

EDUCATIONAL INSTITUTIONS AS MEDIA OF CULTURAL DIFFUSION

School systems often are channels for diffusing new ideas about family life. Because teachers are well-educated, they quite unconsciously advocate those new family patterns with which they are most comfortable. When they write textbooks, they portray their own views of family life. When they teach classes, their attitudes influence the choice of subject matter, the choice of textbooks, and the way they treat their students. Both by describing more democratic human relationships and by practicing them in the classroom, teachers promote more democratic relationships in the home. But since teachers are not always democratic in either their philosophy or their methods, perhaps I should state the relationship propositionally: The more democratic a teacher's methods and materials, the more he will influence the family life of his students in a democratic direction.

In Africa, the fact that schools were established by European administrators (whether under the colonial government or a foreign missionary society) meant that the educational system was European in form. This meant that textbook portrayals of family life also were European in form, so the school became a propaganda agency on behalf of European styles of family living (Goode, 1963).

Even when schools do not teach new styles of family life explicitly, they indirectly accelerate cultural diffusion. Studies of the spread of small family ideals and of family planning methods show that they spread fastest among educated people. They are able to read printed materials, are more receptive to oral communication, and are more expressive in passing new information on to others.

Stycos and Back (1964) found that educated Jamaican women had more favorable attitudes to birth control. On Taiwan, Freedman (1963) found an even closer correlation between the wife's education and her likelihood of having actually practiced birth control (see Figure 5-1).

Freedman believed that literacy and education were more influential than either industrialization or urbanization in decreasing the birth rate in

FIGURE 5-1.   Use of Family Planning Methods, by Wife's Education

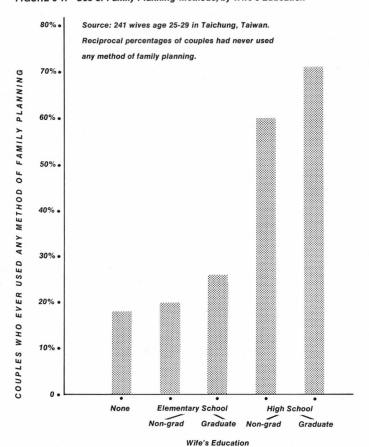

Source: 241 wives age 25-29 in Taichung, Taiwan.
Reciprocal percentages of couples had never used
any method of family planning.

Adapted from Freedman (1963):238.

Europe over the past century. He discovered several countries in which the birth rate fell even though the proportion of people engaged in agriculture remained constant; in every case the educational level of the country's population had risen.

Closely related to rising education is the development of mass media of communication and of communication networks such as postal systems and telephones. Freedman found that on Taiwan both the use of contraceptives and reductions in the number of births were closely related to exposure to these media of communication. For instance, contraceptive usage was directly related to the regularity with which wives read newspapers, and the number of births fell as the per capita number of long distance phone calls increased.

Presumably only a small proportion of the messages transmitted involved family planning as such. But, Freedman believed, families who became linked with the wider world through these communication networks developed new interests which transcended the limitations of the traditional preoccupation with bearing and raising children. In much the same way that education emancipates women from confinement to the home, education and communication networks emancipate whole families from satisfaction with traditional pursuits. As new interests develop, not only does knowledge of family planning increase, but also the desire to use it to keep from becoming too burdened with children increases. Thus education provides both motives and methods for modernizing family life.

EDUCATIONAL INSTITUTIONS AS GENERATORS OF INNOVATION

In the preceding section, schools served as a medium for transmitting the patterns of a foreign culture to another society. For most countries, this analysis is sufficient. But what about the pioneers? What role do educational institutions play in inventing new patterns in the most advanced countries? Are educational institutions not only transmitters but creators of culture?

Most are not. But at the apex of the educational system are universities which create new knowledge through research. Insofar as research is a function of educational institutions, they become a source of change in family patterns.

Many kinds of research affect family life. Innovations in housing, nutrition, medicine and other technical fields bear directly or indirectly on practical aspects of family living. However, since my focus is on the social aspects of family life, the social sciences are of greatest interest.

The fledgling science of family sociology has not had much of an impact on family life, but child psychology is another matter. Throughout the twentieth century, the researches and the opinions of child psychologists have influenced mothers in their child-rearing practices. Ideas have been consumed directly via books and magazine articles and indirectly via the pediatricians and other professional practitioners researchers have trained. As a result, many of the changes in child-rearing practices which have occurred in advanced societies and more especially in the United States can be traced to the innovative influence of scholars who have studied parent–child relationships.

It would be a mistake, however, to jump to the conclusion that changes in popular child-rearing practices represent a direct application of conclusive findings of scientific research. The most accessible mass media, such as women's magazines, rarely have articles written directly by scientists. Most are written by so-called science writers who are primarily writers and only secondarily trained in science (and not at all scientists in the creative sense of that term). Studies of the content of such mass media publications suggest that much of what purports to be scientific writing actually is a considerable distortion of scientific findings. This is apparent in the wide but nearly unanimous swings of opinion represented in such writing (see Table 5-3).

TABLE 5-3 Method of Scheduling Infants Recommended in Three Women's Magazines, 1890–1948

RECOMMENDED METHOD	YEAR						
	1890	1900	1910	1920	1930	1940	1948
Loose scheduling	100%	78%	23%	0%	0%	0%	0%
Tight scheduling	0	22	77	100	75	33	0
Self-regulation	0	0	0	0	25	67	100
Total articles	100%	100%	100%	100%	100%	100%	100%

Adapted from Stendler (1950):126. Source: Analysis of all articles dealing with infant scheduling during the year in question.

The table shows that every 30 years there was a complete revolution in the child-rearing method advocated by these magazines. Perhaps it is no accident that 30 years is almost exactly a generation. Apparently these science writers reacted against the preceding generation of parents and/or of science writers at least as much as they reported new scientific data. However, perhaps I should not criticize the writers too much, because even scientists who turned their attention to writing books applying their scientific findings to the tasks of raising children seem to have been plagued by faulty inferences. A notorious paragraph in the 1920s was written not by a journalist, but by a distinguished psychologist, John B. Watson:

> There is a sensible way of treating children. Treat them as though they were young adults. Dress them, bathe them with care and circumspection. Let your behavior always be objective and kindly firm. Never hug and kiss them, never let them sit in your lap. If you must, kiss them once on the forehead when they say goodnight. Shake hands with them in the morning. Give them a pat on the head if they have made an extraordinarily good job of a difficult task. Try it out. In a week's time, you will find how easy it is to be perfectly objective with your child and at the same time kindly. You will be ashamed of the mawkish, sentimental way you have been handling it. (1928:81–82).

Ludicrous as it seems, Professor Watson thought he was recommending exactly what his researches on behavioral conditioning had taught him. One consequence of the wisdom which the passage of time throws on such recommendations (and on the broader fluctuations in scientific fads) has been a growing cautiousness in scientific writing (see Table 5-4).

TABLE 5-4 Degree of Dogmatism of Articles on Breast Versus Bottle Feeding, 1920–1949

DEGREE OF DOGMATISM	YEARS					
	1920–1924	1925–1929	1930–1934	1935–1939	1940–1944	1945–1949
Absolute dogmatism	69%	81%	76%	53%	20%	19%
Positive but not absolute	20	10	9	28	36	27
Suggestive (alternatives recognized)	11	8	14	17	43	54
Total	100%	99%	99%	98%	99%	100%
Number of articles	49	49	42	39	52	48

Adapted from Vincent (1951):208. Source: Articles in *Reader's Guide to Periodical Literature* and *The Journal of the American Medical Association* and University of California library books published during the same years.

The table shows that Watson wrote at exactly the time when scientific dogmatism on at least one topic was at its height. Since that time writers on child care have become considerably chastened with the result that writing may be less dramatic in its impact on child care practices than in earlier years.

So far however I have only assumed that child-rearing practices change in response to changes in psychological advice. Is there any evidence that parents actually are influenced by changes in the literature? Table 5-5 shows that middle- and upper-lower-class families did change their child-rearing methods in the same direction as the baby manuals. Probably the middle-class families were primarily responsible for these fluctuations since they were the best educated and best-read families.

TABLE 5-5 Changes in Maternal Behavior, 1940–1960

MATERNAL BEHAVIOR	YEAR		
	1940	1950	1960
Babying the child	59.5	61.5	45.1
Protectiveness	57.5	64.5	50.0
Affectionateness	69.0	71.5	58.0
Giving approval	53.0	62.5	45.0
Number of mothers	40	32	35

Adapted from Waters and Crandall (1964):1031. Source: Yellow Springs mothers of 3-to-5-year-old children observed in the home. The numbers represent median ratings on a 90-point scale.

For each of the variables portrayed in Table 5-5, the peak period was 1950. In that year, mothers were the most nurturant and the most affectionate toward their children. In each case the 1960 behavior fell to an even lower level than it had been in 1940. According to the researchers, 1940 should be interpreted as a time when American child-rearing literature was already engaged in an upswing away from the "cool" period of the 1920s and 1930s. Unfortunately no data were available prior to 1940 to test this assumption. However, the content of the single best-selling baby manual of the era, Spock's *Baby and Child Care,* suggests that his advice changed earlier than mothers changed their behavior, so he must have been at least partially responsible for those changes. In the 1940s Spock was one of many advocates of warmth and permissiveness, whereas by 1957 he explicitly advocated a more moderate position which the 1960 mothers applied to their children. This link between the content of Spock's bestseller and the actual behavior of several dozen Ohio mothers suggests the influence of pediatrics and, more broadly, of child psychology generally on family life. A university researcher's work increasingly influences contemporary family life, it seems, once it is transmitted (in however distorted form) to an eager audience of conscientious parents.

As the world becomes better educated and research facilities more highly developed, I expect this educational influence to spread beyond the American middle class to embrace more of American society and more of the world's countries, despite the moderating effect of increased caution in scientific writing. The era of maximum educational influence on families is just dawning.

chapter six
THE COMMUNITY AND THE FAMILY

This chapter will assess the effect of the local community on the family. My primary concern will be with ordinary or "natural" communities, but I will also examine utopian communities.

An analysis of natural communities may be divided between the community as a whole and the specific neighborhood which surrounds the family. In both cases, the family is affected by the people and social institutions who happen to be in its environment. However, families exercise some discrimination in choosing which persons within that environment they will associate with most closely. So it seems appropriate to include friends as a selected aspect of the local community.

THE URBAN ENVIRONMENT

First I will consider the city as a whole and examine the impact on families of crowding in a densely populated space. What difference does it make when families live anonymously among a great mass of human beings instead of entrenched in a rural village where everyone knows everyone else? What difference does it make that housing costs rise as land utilization becomes more intensive? That families live far from the city center as the commuting area enlarges? That families face competing attractions in the bright lights of the city? These are some of the issues which arise when families live in cities instead of in the countryside.

The Housing Crisis

One consequence of the growth of cities is that land values rise. The larger the city, the greater the rise, and the closer one goes to the center of the city, the greater the rise.

This increased cost of land makes it less available for residential purposes. Family life cannot develop as freely as when land costs little or nothing. Even in a rural area, land gets expensive when population pressure becomes severe, so the same problems may arise in rural areas, though usually in less acute form. Rural land prices are primarily barriers to entering farming as a career, whereas urban prices may become so high that they prevent a family from acquiring a roof over its head.

Rising urban land prices eventually make family housing either too expensive or too small. Either way, the family's range of options about where to live and range of activities within the home are narrowed. Although the acuteness of a housing crisis varies with the particular family's financial resources, it does not seem exaggerated to say that urban families all over the world face a housing crisis. Or to put it less flamboyantly, housing everywhere limits the behavior of urban families in ways that lower-density rural families do not experience.

Barriers to Family Formation Just as farm boys in thickly settled Ireland could not marry until land became available through the retirement of their fathers, young men in the biggest city in the world could not marry until their late twenties because only then could they afford to rent an apartment. Whereas most American couples of similar age were already living in a home of their own, many Tokyo couples would never be able to buy a house or the land on which to build a house, since even a remote suburban plot would cost two or three times as much as the house which might be built on it. Correlatively, Tokyo families which eventually secured a home of their own could rarely afford one of more than minimal proportions since most of their capital had to be invested in the land under the house.

Barriers to Family Growth If families must live in small houses or tiny apartments because anything bigger would cost too much, there are limits to the number of people who can be added to the household. Neither children nor other dependents can be brought into such a home without infringing on the living space of those already there. We have already seen that within a given community, the smaller the housing unit the less the ability to accommodate relatives. Besides being one consequence of low status in a stratification system, the same phenomenon is a more general consequence of urbanization. The pressure of urban land values on housing size is another factor (in addition to the inability to employ child labor in non-farming occupations) which makes urban families smaller than rural families.

Slater and Woodside (1951) found that urban conditions discouraged British working-class families from having children in the housing-short years of the Depression and the Nazi blitz. Nor was this simply a question of sheer cubic footage inside the home. Housing was unsuitable for children forced to live in apartments rather than houses and in neighborhoods with no place for children to play without disturbing all-too-close neighbors.

Similarly, a family already crowded into a small space can hardly provide accommodation for an elderly parent. If housing is sufficiently tight, aged dependents will be forced to resort to institutional care, though in a rural community they might have lived with one of their married children.

In cultures where extended families are the norm, cities seldom offer enough housing to accommodate complex families. Goode (1963) noted that in African cities this prevented families from expanding into multiple-generation households like those which were common in the tribal reserves. Thus urban families were barred by the housing crisis from assuming the form they would have preferred.

Family expansion in Africa more often took the form of adding extra wives. But this horizontal expansion was also generally impossible in the cities. Government officials in charge of urban housing projects often made it a policy not to rent apartments to polygynists. Even apart from policy barriers, urban housing was seldom spacious enough to accommodate the complexities of polygynous living. Thus the urbanization of African tribesmen restricted families to nuclear households.

Barriers to Family Interaction   Just as grandparents for whom there is no room may have to be institutionalized, even children may have to be accommodated outside the family. When housing pressures become too severe, systems of adopting-out or "farming out" children tend to develop. In African cities, "surplus" children were sent to relatives living in less crowded quarters or better yet sent back to the rural "native reserve" where space was freely available (Goode, 1963). And even in Paris, Michel (1960) found that 40 percent of working-class families living in furnished hotels had sent away one or more of their children "because their living space [was] too small" (p. 288). Such forced expulsion of children from the family destroys all possibility of family interaction.

Even where families do not remove children entirely from their home, crowding may have a similar effect. Family members who somehow find space to sleep at home (even though they are crowded into the same room or even the same bed) are likely to avoid one another during their waking hours by escaping into the streets. In slum neighborhoods, children spend most of their time outside. Less apparent is the fact that husbands as well escape from the confusion of the family flat to the neighborhood tavern and that even wives flee when they can.

The more time the family members spend away from home, the less the opportunities for that interpersonal interaction on which family solidarity depends. The point is not that all urban families experience enforced dispersal, but that this is a characteristic consequence of the urban housing crisis.

Barriers to Family Autonomy   If one's home is too small for the whole family, individual members may be squeezed out and other relatives will be prevented from moving in. But if one's own home has extra space, however slight, and other housing is unavailable, invasion by hard-pressed outsiders is likely. This most often takes the subliminal form of failure of grown children to move out. I have already suggested that if housing is sufficiently scarce, it prevents new families from forming. But if there is room at home and none elsewhere, new families may form within the old home but be prevented from moving to an independent location. Not only is the new family unable to achieve autonomy, but the old family has its autonomy (or at least its privacy) infringed upon by the introduction of the new bride or groom into the household. In extended family systems, this is merely customary, but when a family system is supposedly neolocal, the strain on both generations is liable to be acute.

The intense housing problem in Javan towns studied by Geertz (1961) made them seem more traditional than rural villages in their household composition. Because of the urban housing shortage, families doubled up in the towns, whereas in the villages, nuclear families had more chance of acquiring a separate house. Therefore there were more compulsorily extended households in the towns than in the countryside.

If a shared house is big enough, partial autonomy may be achieved by maintaining separate households (in the sense that household economics and activities like cooking and eating are kept separate even though the families must use the same kitchen). Geertz found that even two sisters sharing the same building with their respective husbands and children might maintain functionally separate households in this way. Presumably where doubled-up families are not related to each other they are even more apt to try to keep their distance.

To keep out of each other's hair under crowded circumstances is extraordinarily difficult. Even to share the same apartment house is difficult if walls fail to prevent the transmission of sounds from one apartment to another. In an old American city, Komarovsky (1964) found a sharp difference between blue-collar families living in private houses and those in a low-rent tenement. Homeowners could be selective as to what they told their friends about what went on in their homes. Tenement dwellers, however, knew all about each other's affairs because crying children, drunken husbands, and marital disputes could be heard in the adjoining apartment. This lack of audio-privacy destroyed the individual family's sense that "Our home is our castle." Perhaps this situation was even worse than that of families sharing the same room because listeners on the other side of the wall could not always understand how the marital spat or disciplinary problem originated. Komarovsky's families lived in constant fear of "unfair gossip" which would give a distorted picture of events in their home and subject them to unjustified criticism.

To achieve complete autonomy, therefore, a family needs to have its own living quarters, and either these need to be completely detached from the quarters of other families or else the walls need to be impervious to sight and sound for the times when the family wishes to hide from public view.

Besides infringing on the nuclear family's autonomy, the urban housing crisis also makes the achievement of segregation within the family extremely difficult. Children can rarely have rooms of their own. Even married couples cannot count on the separate bedroom needed to enable their relationship to flourish. And in India, where upper-caste custom calls for separate living quarters for men and women, urban families find it difficult to conform to custom. Gore (1961) found that at least half of his rural families were able to provide separate quarters for the two sexes, but among his urban families only 20 percent of the joint families and 7 percent of the nuclear families were able to achieve internal segregation. Thus the housing crisis imposed compulsory modernization on Indian family patterns.

Barriers to Kinship Solidarity   In many societies, families who do not want to share the same house with relatives nevertheless want to live near them in order to be able to see them easily. Yet in cities where old housing is so tight that even the rented quarters are "inherited" from generation to generation, new housing is liable to be built only on the urban fringe, so far away that kin networks are dispersed and almost completely severed. I will examine the consequences of geographical mobility in greater detail in Chapter 9. The point here is that some of the mobility within a given city is forced on nuclear families against their will because the housing crisis offers so little choice. For example, in the Welsh city of Swansea, Rosser and Harris (1965) found that a severe housing shortage forced young couples to move to new housing projects on the opposite side of town from their parents. Only a fortunate few were able to find accommodations in the same neighborhood with their parents. The housing shortage thus enforced a dispersal of kin networks when nuclear units were able to find separate housing at all.

In a London suburb to which middle-class couples had moved it was not so much an absolute shortage of vacancies which prevented elderly parents from settling near their married children, but a shortage of the right kind of houses. Willmott and Young described the suburb as just as limited in its variety of housing as "the most hide-bound municipal estate" (1960:124). Because most of the suburban houses had three or four bedrooms, they were too big and expensive for an elderly couple seeking a one- or two-room apartment or a tiny one-bedroom house. Paradoxically, the London slum of Bethnal Green offered greater possibilities of kinship solidarity because it provided a mix of housing units of all shapes and sizes. The diversity of stages in the family life cycle represented in a network of kin requires a rich mixture of housing opportunities if every family is to be accommodated to maximum advantage within the preferred proximity.

To solve the urban housing crisis therefore requires not only building many more housing units, but also more diversified units within the same area. Unfortunately both the economies of mass production and the processes of housing segregation militate against diversification in new construction. And the more planned and large scale the construction, the more uniform the product tends to be. Thus the outlook for diversified housing opportunities in modern cities is rather bleak in most countries.

Rising land costs in urban areas make housing not only too expensive a commodity for the individual family to be able to purchase, but also in all save the most affluent countries too expensive for private enterprise to develop. Therefore urban housing tends increasingly to be a governmental responsibility which suffers from the narrowness of vision and monotony of form which bureaucratic planning so often entails. The same economic factors which force private housing into narrow straightjackets limit the freedom of governmental planning as well unless that government is extraordinarily wealthy. Finally a rapid flow of population from rural to urban areas and a rapid rate of natural increase of urban populations create such critical housing shortages that most governments are hard pressed to provide any housing at all, much less free to worry about such luxuries as varied housing to meet the needs of kin networks. Only if the population explosion were muffled and urban populations stabilized in an expanding economy could governments be expected to turn their attention to such sophisticated housing problems.

Anomie

Anomie is a French word for normlessness, a social condition in which traditional or conventional norms have weakened or disappeared leaving people in a social vacuum. Normlessness is never complete, but one characteristic of cities is that the individual person and the individual family are less tightly bound by social norms than in smaller communities. One reason is that the urban environment is relatively impersonal and anonymous. The individual may be known in his immediate neighborhood, but only a few celebrities will be recognized outside that neighborhood. The average city-dweller moves about most of his city alone, rarely encountering anyone he has ever seen before. Even if he recognizes the policeman on his beat or the clerk in the grocery store, his relationship is so narrowly limited to the latter's occupational specialty that neither party has any appreciable influence on the other as far as his family life (his "private" life) is concerned.

By contrast, one characteristic of a rural community is that everyone knows everyone else. So interested is everyone in each other's affairs that very little truly private life is available to anyone. A rural village is a kind of family in itself which controls the behavior of its members by informal processes of social control: the threat of gossip and the inevitable mutual chaperoning which occurs in a situation of mutual knowledge. This high level of social control means that the community provides strong support for adhering to mutually accepted norms.

In the city this informal social control over family life is weakened as soon as the individual escapes his neighborhood. Secondarily, the very inability of the city to enforce informal norms on its families means that norms tend to change. Those which depended on the ability of the community to command the loyalty and devotion of its citizens to rigorous requirements tend to weaken. Norms which may have been appropriate to a rural way of life adapt to the urban environment. In general these new norms give family members more freedom from subjection to one another. The individual is freed from his family and the nuclear family from its network of kin. The situation may not become entirely normless, but when the new norms' weakened content and weakened enforcement are compared with the tightness of the rural community, the label of anomie seems only a bit too strong.

Premarital Freedom   Freedom of dating, freedom of sexual involvement, and freedom of mate selection are characteristically urban.

In post-war Japan, the older generation viewed dating askance, but young people in cities circumvented that barrier by arranging to meet away from home in urban coffee shops where parents need never know of their trysts.

Stycos (1955) found that rural Puerto Ricans still stressed the necessity for girls to remain chaste until marriage, so most of their rural respondents believed that "all" the girls in their area adhered to the norm. By contrast half of his urban working-class respondents believed that either some or most of the girls they knew were no longer virgins at marriage. Similarly Reiss (1967) found that those adults in his national sample—and especially students from selected American colleges—had more permissive attitudes toward premarital intercourse if they came from large cities. Specifically 61 percent of students from cities of over 100,000 population believed that premarital intercourse was permissible under at least some circumstances, whereas only 39 percent of those from cities of less than 10,000 were so liberal. Reiss interpreted the effect of city size on premarital permissiveness as probably due to "its encouragement of courtship autonomy" (p. 74). Since urban young people viewed dating and courtship as their own affair and not their parents' business, they tended to be less bound by parental conservatism. (The gap between adult values and student values was substantially greater in big cities than in small towns.)

Even though a large city is generally a permissive environment, it is important to remember that vestiges of local social control still survive in some neighborhoods of even the largest cities. Whyte (1943) found this in an Italian slum in Boston. Local controls were still strong enough to prohibit premarital intercourse with Italian girls. But the lower-class code allowed (indeed encouraged) sexual involvement with non-Italian girls elsewhere in the city. The greatest premarital freedom is either in a city away from home or else in those parts of one's home city which are sufficiently remote from the home neighborhood to allow personal anonymity.

The same circumstances which allow "invisible" dating and sex relations also allow young people freedom of mate selection. In societies where parents ordinarily control mate selection by arranging marriages for their children and where they restrict their children's choices to highly eligible partners, urban young people have more freedom to make their own choices and to violate their elders' criteria of eligibility. Goode (1963) found that cross-tribal marriages were becoming more frequent in African cities as a result of both forms of freedom of mate selection. On the one hand, more urban youths were free to choose their own partners because their leisure could be spent beyond the watchful eye of their parents. At the same time, they were less bound by parental norms of tribal endogamy and more apt to choose their partners on the basis of such new criteria as membership in a common urban church or other urban institution.

Equalitarianism Equality between husbands and wives and (to a lesser extent) between parents and children is a characteristically urban norm which replaces the old rural emphasis on patriarchy and parental authority. We have already seen how authority is undermined in the city with respect to control of children's mate selection. Another way in which the community undermines the influence of parents is by offering more relaxed norms than some parents seek to instill in their children. Particularly if parents are divided in the values they seek to teach their children, the weight of the community is likely to give the more conventional parent the victory.

Putney and Middleton (1961) found that almost two thirds of those American college students whose parents disagreed about religion inclined to the views of the parent who held the modal American ideology ("modernist Christianity"). In this case, the external influence did not seem to be specifically urban in form, nor was the direction of influence necessarily toward freedom "from" religion. Rather, the community undermined whatever value position was more extreme. Neither conservative Christian parents nor skeptical parents were able to counteract the combined influence of a middle-of-the-road spouse and a middle-of-the-road society. The larger society gave children of mixed marriages freedom to choose a more moderate, less extreme position than the minority parent advocated. Only in a tightly knit conservative or radical community could children be expected to share their parents' extreme views.

The patriarchal domination of wives by husbands, which was the rule in feudal societies, tends to disappear with the growth of cities. In transitional societies, just emerging from their feudal pasts, equalitarianism appears first in the urban centers while patriarchal domination survives longest in remote rural areas.

In Puerto Rico, Hill, Stycos, and Back (1959) found that patriarchal domination was still strong in the mountains, was weakening in the plains, but was almost gone in the cities (save for face-saving lip-service). In Yugoslavia, Buric and Zecevic (1967) found that the longer men and women had lived in a city of 50,000, the lower the husband's power over family decisions fell and the higher the wife's rose (see Figure 6-1).

Why should the husband's power fall the longer he has lived in a city? One answer is the shift from farming as an occupation (with the husband the boss of the family enterprise). Another presumably is the urban opportunities for the wife to work and engage in social activities outside the home. But there can be little doubt that the urban environment offers equalitarianism as a new norm to replace the rural norm.

Freedom of Divorce   In countries which traditionally tabooed divorce (especially Western "Christian" countries), that taboo was heavily supported by rural social pressure. The rise of cities offered divorced people a place to escape from the critical eye of their neighbors. A later consequence was the gradual relaxation of social criticism of divorcees in the urban environment even when the individual's marital status was known. With the weakening of the ban on divorce, being known as a divorced person became socially tolerable and even socially acceptable.

One consequence of increased freedom of divorce with the steady urbanization of the United States has been a tendency of divorce rates to fluctuate more widely with changing economic conditions. Pinard (1966) attributed this fluctuation to the anonymity of the urban environment within which an increasing proportion of Americans live, leaving them free to get divorced when they are financially able to do so. More basic has been an absolute increase in the divorce rate itself. The long term trend in American divorce rates has been upward (once the complications introduced by wars

FIGURE 6-1.   Husband's Power, by Length of Urban Residence

Source: 117 auto workers' families from a factory of 10,000
workers in Kragujevac, Yugoslavia (a city of 50,000+).

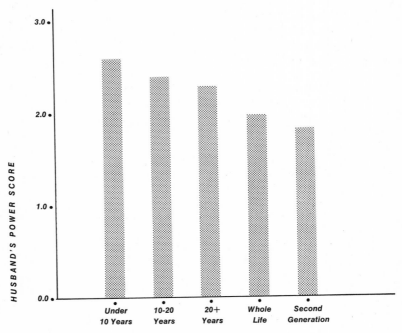

Adapted from Buric and Zecevic (1967):330.

and depressions are ignored), reflecting not so much a worsening of the state of marriage as a steady relaxing of the taboo on divorce for couples whose marriages are going badly. This relaxation is one of the major effects of the urbanization of American society on family behavior.

Urban Facilities

So far I have discussed a physical aspect of the urban environment (housing) and a cultural aspect (changing norms). Now the issue is the difference between city and countryside in the variety of social institutions available. In rural villages, families must depend on themselves for services which can be bought on the urban market. Whereas rural men, women, and children have no choice but to depend on their families, city people can choose between family services and commercial services. Hotels, apartments, and rooming houses offer alternative places to sleep, restaurants for eating, laundries and dry cleaners for clothing maintenance, commercialized recreation for leisure.

The effects on the family of these commercial services are diverse and complex. Family formation becomes less necessary since a bachelor or a single girl can survive more comfortably. Conversely, family dissolution is easier because a husband, wife, or child can survive more easily apart from his family.

Family members who are not interested in leaving permanently may nevertheless find in urban facilities opportunities to leave temporarily (if only for a few hours). The possibility of going to the movies or having dinner alone or with friends gives family members an independence which rural people do not have. Less dependent on one another and freer to leave when they wish to do so, urban family members develop a less cohesive style of family life, more fluid and open. Family members come and go in a less unified pattern, drawn out of the family by competing attractions in the community or driven from the family by internal conflicts into easily available places of refuge.

One consequence of these competing attractions is less preoccupation by urban women with such family functions as bearing childen. Slater and Woodside (1951) noted that urban distractions seemed a major cause of the lower birth-rate among urban working-class families in Britain. Living in the city supplied external interests and raised aspirations for the family's standard of living. Therefore families with modest incomes were forced to choose between having extra children and spending their time and money on other objects and activities.

Finally, whole families take advantage of certain commercial services in preference to doing their own work. Ogburn (1938) in a classic article noted the transfer of many functions away from the family to other social institutions. Foremost among these was the economic production which farm families perform but which most urban families (save those with family businesses) do not. Not only has the man's occupation been transferred to an alien employer; much of the women's home production has been abandoned in favor of commercial products.

Table 6-1 shows that even in a highly modern farming area immediately west of Detroit, Michigan, most wives produced most of their own food and clothes (grew their own vegetables, canned and froze fruits, vegetables, and sometimes meat, baked bread and pies, and made their own dresses). Conversely, barely one percent of the urban wives studied produced more than half of these goods. In the case of vegetables, urban land values prevented city families from growing their own if they had wanted to (depriving them of land suitable for gardening). For canning and freezing, the farm wives had an economic advantage insofar as they processed their own produce, rather than buying it at retail prices. For baking and dressmaking, however, the urban wives were not disadvantaged at all, yet even in these areas city wives relied heavily on commercial products.

TABLE 6-1 Home Production of Selected Food and Clothes by Rural and Urban Wives

Proportion of Selected Food and Clothes Produced at Home	Rural Wives	Urban Wives
All or nearly all	11%	*
Most	44	1%
About half	33	9
Less than half	11	77
None or almost none	1	11
Total	100%	98%
Number of wives	178	724

Adapted from Blood (1958):172. Included were baked goods, canned and frozen foods, fresh vegetables, and dresses produced at home. Source: Southeastern Michigan farm families and Detroit Metropolitan Area families, 1955.
*Less than one-half of one percent.

What is it about living in a city which makes wives surrender their productive functions? One factor is ease of access to retail stores, in contrast to the relative isolation of farm families. Another is the contrast between the cash economy of cities and the self-reliance of families living on the soil. The very physical layout of the city, with large numbers of families clustered together, makes it possible for commercial bakeries to mass produce goods as cheaply as the housewife could bake her small quantities at home (especially if she counted the value of her labor). While few city wives may think very much about what their time is worth in dollars and cents, they are quite apt to value their time in terms of alternative uses to which it could be put. Indeed the existence of the multiplicity of urban institutions of all kinds makes city wives turn to labor-saving institutions in order to free themselves to participate in leisure-oriented institutions.

The transfer of leisure activities from home to community was a second change noted by Ogburn. This change is not so much the substitution of commercial services involving the same activities, but rather the addition to life of new activities which families were incapable of providing alone. Dances, concerts, big league sports, or motion pictures require too much organization to be available within the home. Many of the city's most interesting attractions also require too much talent to be available to the average man. So the city serves as a focal point where large crowds can enjoy the talents of the outstanding few.

Paradoxically, further technological progress in the years since Ogburn wrote has returned some leisure functions to the home. Long-playing records, stereo sets, and FM radio have turned the home into a concert hall. Television has made it a movie theater and sports stadium. So affluent families in advanced societies can enjoy urban talent without leaving home. Nevertheless, for first-hand enjoyment of these talents and for access to those forms of urban activity which have not been packaged for home consumption, the city remains a place where recreation is more often engaged in away from home than in the countryside.

It is not necessary to analyze in detail the transfer of protective functions to the state, of educational functions to the school, of religious functions to the church, of medical functions to the hospital. The preceding chapters have given us an understanding of the impact of many of these characteristically urban institutions on the family. The general point is that the city provides a social base (with its large concentration of people) for the development of specialized institutions. In most cases the reason the family has surrendered these functions is that full-time specialists could do a better job than the jacks-of-all-trades whom we call "husbands" and "wives." Insofar as specialized institutions do a better job than families, the change is not simply a transfer of functions but a development of improved functioning. The result is an enrichment of the lives of city dwellers with higher levels of education, culture, etc. than could have been achieved if families tried to do everything themselves.

However beneficial these institutional contributions may be, the fact remains that families have been relieved of the necessity of performing many functions. What happens to family life as a result of this? It was suggested earlier that one consequence is a lessening of the mutual interdependence of family members as they rely more on outside services. But there is an important secondary consequence. Insofar as family members are emancipated from such prosaic burdens as chopping wood and baking bread, they have more leisure which can potentially be spent together. Free time has made it possible for urban families to develop their interpersonal relationships more extensively. The affectional relationship between husband and wife and the caretaking relationship between parents and children have flourished with these new resources of time. The result is that the urban family has become what Parsons and Bales (1955) noted is "a more specialized agency than before" (p. 9). In other words, the rise of specialized non-family institutions has made it possible for the family itself to become more specialized in those functions which it can perform better than any other social institution: raising children and providing emotional sustenance to family members through long-term primary relationships. This has made the family less independent of its social environment than the self-sufficient rural family but better able to perform its distinctive functions. Thus the urban family benefits not only from an enriched social environment, but also from a qualitatively enriched life of its own. The total product may be less stable than a rural family, but like a high-strung race horse, the urban family might be described as a thoroughbred capable of outdistancing its plodding rural cousins.

Urban Ecology

Ecology refers to the spatial pattern of the city. It is a complex network of streets, parks, banks, businesses, and police stations. Most of it affects family life only peripherally. But a few aspects are crucial: where the family lives, where the husband works, where the wife shops, and where the children go to school. These determine each family's daily pattern of dispersal and re-union. Social scientists have paid little attention to the impact of these patterns on family life, so we will be forced to speculate in the absence of data.

Commuting Time   With growth in size of cities came a corresponding extension of the time required for the average citizen to get to work. Within the urban community, however, there are enormous variations in commuting time. A privileged few work at home or within walking distance. Many an unlucky suburbanite must fight rush hour traffic in his car or with his body on crowded subways and trains. The farther away he lives, the earlier he must leave home in the morning, perhaps before his children are up, destroying breakfast as a potentially sociable family occasion (however rushed it may be at best). The same man faces the reciprocal necessity of arriving home equally late. Some families postpone dinner until 7:00 or later, but the younger children are, the less possible postponement is. Few long-range commuters get to eat any meals with their children except on weekends.

Wives must choose whether to eat with the children or the husband. The latter has the advantage of freeing them to assist small children with the complexities of eating. In any case, they must serve double-time with two rounds of cooking and two rounds of sitting at table. Both children and fathers suffer communication losses from their failure to eat together, leaving the wife the only link between estranged segments of the family. This places the wife in a strategic position which some writers have labelled "momism," noting that the exodus of men from the suburbs during the day leaves these areas populated almost exclusively by women and children.

Many years ago, Bossard (1943) argued that family meals were an occasion for socializing children into the family culture. The systematic absence of fathers from these occasions deprives children not only of half the normal teaching staff (altering the teacher–pupil ratio to their disadvantage) but of the opportunity to listen to, and observe, communication between their parents. Presumably such "one-parent" families have more child-centered and less adult-centered conversations since it takes two adults to talk about adult subjects.

Most conspicuously the children are deprived of "man talk" about events at the office and in the outside world. Insofar as the mother talks "adult talk" at all, it is likely to be drawn from the women's world of detergents, soap operas, and babies. The children who suffer most from this distortion are sons. (When fathers are absent for long periods of time sons acquire a relatively feminine or reactively hyper-masculine sex role identity [Tiller, 1957].) However, even daughters are deprived of opportunities to develop their feminine identity in interaction with a man. So the children of commuters are partially deprived not simply of a second adult, but of an adult of the opposite sex from the mother. To some extent at least this impoverishes the family as an incubator for personality development.

Suburban families feel that there are compensating advantages in the spaciousness and peacefulness of suburban living. But that is not the issue. The question simply is what happens to family life when extensive commuting forces the husband to "desert" his family five days a week.

For children the time required to get to school is normally minimal. Even here, however, urban ecology affects family life. Some school systems have abandoned the neighborhhood school concept in favor of busing children to remote schools or of requiring children to commute to centralized school campuses or "educational parks." Such developments may weaken the hold of the mother over her children, leaving her at home alone for more hours of the day.

Suburban Shopping   One counterforce to the centrifugal effect of urbanization on the family has been the construction of suburban shopping centers. Wives who earlier made major shopping expeditions downtown now find it possible to shop more conveniently at nearby shopping plazas. The means of transportation changes from the same commuting train used by the husband in going to work to the family automobile. Pratt (1960) found as one consequence that mothers more often took their children with them on shopping expeditions (since cars convey children more conveniently). The location of these shopping centers also made it possible to substitute more frequent brief expeditions for more ambitious major ones. A further consequence was that husbands, too, became more involved with the wife and children in shopping trips which could more easily be fitted into evenings and weekends. Thus the decentralization of shopping facilities made it possible for families to add shopping as another activity (like TV movies) which has returned to a family basis.

THE NEIGHBORHOOD

Husbands are away from home so much that where they live matters little save for the distance which must be spanned between home and work. Although wives often form mid-morning kaffee klatsches within the neighborhood, they may escape from an uncongenial neighborhood relatively easily. Children, however, invariably are stuck with neighborhood peers as compulsory associates. If they don't like them, they may retreat into solitude, but there is hardly any way of finding congenial alternatives. In early childhood, they are too immobile to contact remote friends. In later years, they may be trapped in neighborhood gangs whose "turf" boundary lines offer no freedom of choice. Everyone in this block belongs to the Rangers whether he wants to or not. To go outside the block would invite attack from both the rival group and one's own. In ghetto neighborhoods it is no more possible to escape the consequences of one's geographical location than for a citizen of one country to go over to the enemy in the midst of war. Indeed perpetual war is precisely the state of male adolescent society in many slum neighborhoods.

Cross Pressures

If for children the neighborhood provides a given set of associates, the only question is whether those associates will be friends or enemies. Ordinarily one can expect them to be playmates and gangmates. But under special circumstances children get caught between their families and their peers. What then?

One dilemma is when the child's religion clashes with his peers. Jewish children in a predominantly Gentile neighborhood or Catholic children in a predominantly Protestant neighborhood are liable to find that their ethnic–religious ties stand in the way of full acceptance. How disastrous this is depends on the severity of the ostracism. The smaller the number and proportion of fellow-believers in the neighborhood, the greater the isolation. The stronger the prejudice, the greater the persecution.

TABLE 6-2   Adolescent Psychosomatic Symptoms, by Religious
Affiliation of Child and of Neighborhood

| | *RELIGIOUS AFFILIATION OF NEIGHBORHOOD* | | *ALIEN/ SUPPORTIVE RATIO* |
PERCENTAGE WITH MANY SYMPTOMS BY ADOLESCENT'S RELIGION	*Supportive*	*Alien*	
Catholic	55%	65%	1.18X
Protestant	48	54	1.13
Jewish	51	55	1.08

Adapted from Rosenberg (1965):67. Source: Juniors and seniors in selected public high schools in New York State. Reciprocal percentages of students had relatively few psychosomatic symptoms such as headaches, dizziness and stomach upsets. Supportive neighborhoods contained at least 50 percent co-religionists. Alien neighborhoods contained at least 75 percent members of outgroups. Other mixtures have been omitted from the table. The numbers of Catholic adolescents were respectively 467 and 37; of Protestants 245 and 164; of Jews 77 and 42.

Table 6-2 shows that adolescents in a minority position in their neighborhood experienced more psychosomatic symptoms than those who lived in neighborhoods where at least half their peers were of the same faith. It is important to note that Rosenberg found no difference between completely homogeneous neighborhoods and those which were evenly divided. But he consistently found that adolescents suffered psychosomatic difficulties whenever less than half their neighbors were of the same faith. He also found that feelings of self-esteem were undermined under the same conditions. Both types of stress were particularly acute for those who actually experienced discrimination in childhood, such as being teased, called names, or excluded from activities because of their religion.

These data show what happens when children are caught in the middle right between parental influence and contrary neighborhood influences. The parents win the initial victory by giving the child his religious identity. Their influence is strong enough to enable the child to tolerate considerable diversity as long as the outgroup is in the minority. When a majority of peers share the individual's faith, peer group values and family values reinforce each other and there is no conflict. The individual's identity is supported by the neighborhood.

As soon, however, as the outgroup reaches majority proportions, peer group pressure conflicts significantly with family influence. Then the child feels cross-pressures. He wants to be loyal to both family and peers but he can't. Either he must side with his family and be ostracized by his peers or side with his friends and be criticized by his family. Rosenberg does not tell us which is worse, but either one seems likely to cause emotional stress and damage self-esteem. Nor does Rosenberg tell us what happens to the religious identity of children raised in nonsupportive neighborhoods. Presumably such children are more apt to marry out of the faith and to change (or lose) their own religious identity. In any case, the cross-pressures to which children are subjected by an alien environment tend to tear not only the children apart but (whenever the peer group wins) the family apart. Thus, directly or indirectly, the family's cohesiveness is threatened by an unsupportive neighborhood.

Gang Versus Spouse Cross pressures are most acute when neighborhood values clash with family values, but conflicting loyalties also arise when family and gang compete not for the individual's value system but simply for his time. The more totalitarian the claims of the gang, the more difficult it is to belong to a family at the same time.

During childhood this isn't much of a problem in lower-class families. Parents don't expect their children to stay home that much. The older the child becomes, the less claim the parents feel they have over him, so the gang commands his total allegiance.

Marriage, however, is another matter. In the United States even lower-class wives are sufficiently imbued with the romantic complex to expect a new husband to spend most of his leisure at home. Especially at the beginning of marriage, her demands are likely to be almost as total as the gang's. If wives were prepared to ease into marriage gradually, the collision would be less head-on. But marriage doesn't work that way. The desire for companionship is most acute when love is new. So just at the age when a young man has severed his ties with his childhood family, a love affair threatens his total allegiance to the boys on the corner.

This conflict of loyalties frequently produces paralysis. Since the gang already has him in its grip, the question is whether any girl can ever pry him loose. The girls are likely to be interested in marriage before he is, but the claims of the gang make him resist their overtures and resist any reciprocal feelings which may be stirring within him.

This does not mean that he has no contact with girls at this age. But that contact is likely to be gang contact. Rosenberg and Bensman (1968) found for example that Appalachian migrants to Chicago jointly exploited young girls who had run away from home or young wives already disillusioned with marriage. This sexual exploitation was "absolutely affectless," not only because ganging up on a girl is hardly a setting which encourages affection but because to allow oneself to become emotionally involved would threaten the very companions with whom one is engaged.

Constant involvement in the gang delays pairing off with girls. Rosenberg and Bensman found that boys who belonged to gangs married substantially later than individuals of the same ethnic background who had no gang ties to stand in the way.

How then do gang members ever manage to marry? Miller (1963) found one gang which had developed an ingenious solution to this problem.

Rather than openly betraying the gang, these boys "accidentally" impregnated their girl friends (by ceasing to use condoms in intercourse) when they were ready to get married. Then the girl, her family, his family, and their respective churches could be counted on to "force" them to get married. Miller felt that these marriages were not really forced because truly accidental pregnancies with undesirable partners did not result in marriage. Rather this strategy was tacitly recognized by the gang as a face-saving way of avoiding the charge of deserting the group.

To get married, however, does not solve the problem of conflicting loyalties. In some ways marriage intensifies it. Especially the first gang member to marry is caught between the continued vitality of the group (now composed of $N-1$ members) and the claims of his wife. Miller found that gang members used the myth of "the old lady won't let me" as an excuse for not participating in gang activities.

Just because a man is married does not guarantee that he will give priority to his wife. Komarovsky (1964) found that many blue-collar husbands participated in gang activities almost as much after marriage as before and their wives were acutely jealous of the gang's grip. One young man who married at 20 while his buddies were still single drank and gambled with them four or five nights a week just as though he were still single. Only after the others had married did his marriage have a chance to become firmly established. Another husband's conflict of loyalties was solved only by going on the night shift which gave him an excuse for dropping the gang even more persuasive than marriage, an excuse, incidentally, which was not accepted without challenge by gang members in Komarovsky's community. If a husband claimed domestic responsibilities, the gang would taunt him with being "hen-pecked," a charge guaranteed to prevent most working-class men from surrendering to their wives.

Bott (1957) found similarly that British men and women who belonged to tightly knit social networks where everyone knew everyone else (*i.e.,* to segregated male or female gangs) had segregated role relationships in marriage. They depended primarily on their pals for emotional support and had comparatively weak marital bonds. Conversely, couples whose social networks were loose-knit (whose friends did not know each other very well) depended on each other and did more things together both in and outside the home. For example, they shared more housekeeping tasks, finding companionship with one another despite their sex differences because they lacked close involvement with a group of their own sex.

In general, then, gang membership tends to delay family formation in the first place, to require circuitous maneuvers before family formation becomes possible, and to retard the consolidation of the marriage relationship even after the wedding has been performed and the couple are supposedly married.

The contradiction between the two relationships can be seen conversely in the tendency of gangs to dissolve once a majority of their members are married. This does not mean that ties of friendship with gang members are severed, but that the gang as a collective entity which spends most of its leisure time together cannot coexist with widespread external involvements of gang members through marriage. Sooner or later, one social relationship must lose out, and eventually it is the gang which tends to collapse.

Social Control

At the opposite extreme from urban anomie is the tightly knit social control which rural communities exert over their member families. Urban neighborhoods seldom provide much control over their resident families, but this varies from neighborhood to neighborhood. The more homogeneous the neighborhood in its commitment to common norms and values, and the more tightly knit its interaction patterns, the greater its ability to function like a rural enclave in the midst of a larger city.

One famous suburban "village" was Park Forest, Illinois, a new town of 30,000 people 30 miles south of Chicago (Whyte, 1957). Thirty thousand people are too many to form a single neighborhood, but within Park Forest neighborhoods sprang into existence almost instantly after sales and rentals began in 1948. One reason was its very newness. The early settlers faced common problems of unpaved streets and the organizational vacuum of a new community. Neighborhoods developed as neighbors joined together to solve their common problems. A second reason was homogeneity. Because the housing was comparatively uniform in size and cost, families at the same stage in life (young parents of young children) and with similar economic resources (junior executives and professionals) dominated the social mix. Problems of compatibility were few and friendships sprang up among families with similar education, occupations, etc.

The microecology of the housing units determined where neighborhood lines formed in this homogeneous mass of people, any of whom could potentially have befriended one another. The rental section of Park Forest consisted of rows of apartments centered about a common courtyard where cars were parked. Because fathers and mothers from adjacent apartments met frequently in this courtyard, it became the focal point for the formation of neighborhoods. The existence of these neighborhoods could be seen in the frequency with which leisure-time activities involved the same cluster of families. So tightly knit did these neighborhoods become that adults felt as much pressure to participate in neighborhood activities as juveniles in any ghetto gang.

Once Park Forest's neighborhoods acquired this high degree of informal social organization, they exercised a correspondingly high degree of social control over the behavior of their members. Families entering these neighborhoods felt the force of neighborhood norms and adopted them rapidly if they did not already hold them. For instance, Democrats converted to Republicanism, fundamentalists to liberal Protestantism, and members of other social classes to middle-classness. Keeping up (or down) with the Joneses was heavily enforced by a norm of "inconspicuous consumption."

Most important for our purposes was the enforcement of norms governing family behavior. Generally speaking these were not norms to which people had to be converted. Most middle-class families, after all, believe at least theoretically in marital fidelity and parental responsibility. But whereas urban anomie allows many a resident of an anonymous neighborhood to violate these norms, no such freedom existed in the tightly knit neighborhoods of Park Forest.

Whyte graphically described the court as "the greatest invention since the chastity belt." This protective function was performed by the network of neighbors who constantly observed the individual's activities as long as he was at home. Whyte saw the neighborhood not only as chaperone but as supplier of group affection. Insofar as the husband and wife were embedded in a secure group of sociable neighbors, there was less of the loneliness which might otherwise have motivated extramarital friendships. Since everyone was supplied with group friendship and group activities, there was less temptation for any of them to develop paired love affairs.

Parental responsibility also was supported by the neighborhood. With so many adults engaged in bearing and rearing children, deviant couples felt heavy pressure to acquire children too (by adoption if necessary) and to join the daily round of child-rearing. Moreover, the collective concern for the welfare of each other's children in the neighborhood encouraged couples to stick together when they might otherwise have broken up. Observed the minister of the United Protestant Church: "Few people . . . get divorces until they break with their groups. I think the fact that it is so hard to break with a group here has had a lot to do with keeping some marriages from going on the rocks" (p. 393).

In general, then, the more cohesive the neighborhood and the more familistic the values of that neighborhood, the more help a family receives in preserving its solidarity in accordance with those norms and values.

FRIENDS OF THE FAMILY

Neighbors are determined by sheer propinquity, whereas friends are chosen, either from among neighbors or from persons farther afield. This self-selected character of friends distinguishes them from the "given" character of neighbors.

One consequence of the distinction is that friends almost by definition tend to be more compatible than neighbors. What friend would behave like Rosenberg's neighborhood children: teasing, calling names, or excluding an individual? If an erstwhile friend begins to persecute someone that way, he ceases to be a friend. Nevertheless friends are not always homogeneous, so cross-pressures may arise with friends as with neighbors.

Unilateral Involvements

Cross-pressures are most acute when one family member is exposed to influences which other family members do not experience. This may happen whenever one family member participates in a unilateral social relationship which other family members do not share. The consequences of unilateral relationships are not inevitably divisive; that depends on whether the new relationship reinforces or challenges the family one. But insofar as a unilateral relationship introduces conflicting values into the family, it inevitably troubles the family. And even without conflicting values, the same problems of conflicting loyalties arise with unilateral friendships as with gang membership.

Children by virtue of the age gap have different friends from their parents. Husbands and wives, however, are the same age and potentially have the same friends. Their friends may be either shared or unshared in addition to being compatible or incompatible.

Children's Peers   Most children join peer groups which hold the same values as their parents. Peck and Havighurst (1960) found in one mid-Western American city that peer groups tended "to reproduce the moral atmosphere set up by the parents."

What happens in the exceptional cases? What if a teenager associates with peers from a different social background or with conflicting values? Then I assume he would experience the same psychological stresses as Rosenberg's minority children in alien neighborhoods. Perhaps he would have psychosomatic symptoms and low self-esteem. But the results for the child are not always negative.

TABLE 6-3   Vocational Ambitiousness, by Class Status of Father and of Three Best Friends

PERCENTAGE AMBITIOUS BY CLASS STATUS OF FATHER	STATUS OF BEST FRIENDS' FATHERS		
	Working-Class	*Mixed*	*Middle-Class*
Working-class	12%	32%	71%
Middle-class	18	57	72

Adapted from Simpson (1962):520. Source: High school boys in two Southern cities (whites only). Ambitiousness was defined as enrollment in a college preparatory curriculum plus expectation of entering a high-level professional or executive occupation. Reciprocal percentages were not ambitious by one or both of these criteria.

Table 6-3 suggests that occupational mobility is one possible benefit of cross-class peers for working-class children. We cannot attribute all the upward mobility to the influence of the friends themselves. Presumably much of the choice of middle-class friends was dictated by the mobility aspirations of the working-class boys. Nevertheless there can be little doubt that when such a boy associates exclusively with middle-class friends, they serve as socializing agents, teaching him how to become a middle-class person.

Of special interest in Table 6-3 is the strong influence of the peer group when all friends are members of the same class. If all are middle-class, the boy tends to be almost as ambitious as if he came from a working-class family. Conversely, if all are working-class, family background hardly saves a middle-class boy from being unambitious. However, if friends are mixed, the parents tip the balance. Thus 57 percent of middle-class boys with mixed friends are ambitious, and 68 percent of working-class boys with mixed friends are unambitious like their fathers. In other words, parents determine the child's vocational expectations either when the whole peer group has the same status as the parents or when at least some peers have that status. But if all three best friends belong to a different group, parents don't stand much of a chance. If a child is working-class, this cross-pressure produces upward mobility; if he is middle-class, it produces downward mobility. In either case, it moves the child away from his parents, pulling the family apart. Perhaps from the standpoint of the child and certainly from the standpoint of society, upward mobility is beneficial, but from the standpoint of the family, cross-pressures cause family stress.

Adult Confidants   Komarovsky (1964) defined a confidant as someone with whom a married individual shares such matters as "suspicion of his spouse's infidelity; his own unfaithfulness; pleasant or unpleasant facts about his sexual life; regrets about marriage; details of serious quarrels; some of his deeper disappointments in himself; disappointments about the spouse's ambition, intelligence or other traits; and confidences about the spouse's relationships with relatives and in-laws" (p. 207). Using this definition, Komarovsky found that most blue-collar wives had confidants but that most husbands did not (see Table 6-4).

TABLE 6-4   Confidants of Blue-Collar Husbands and Wives, by Education

| | HUSBANDS | | WIVES | |
	Under 12 Years	12 Years	Under 12 Years	12 Years
Isolates	15%	6%	6%	3%
Spouse only	65	61	26	26
Confidants	5	27	68	71
Tavern or clique	15	6	0	0
Total	100%	100%	100%	100%
Number of cases	40	18	31	23

Adapted from Komarovsky (1964):364. Isolates were those who communicated neither with the spouse nor with anyone else. Source: Young blue-collar white couples in an American city of 50,000.

Confidants were especially rare among men who dropped out of high school. They were more apt to confide in a clique, in tavern mates, or in no one at all than to share confidences with a special friend. Presumably finishing high school enabled both husbands and wives to express themselves more openly with friends as well as spouses.

Because confidential relationships are primarily woman-to-woman affairs, it will be appropriate to focus on the feminine case from now on. What difference does it make whether a wife has a confidante? The answer depends partly on whether she communicates with both her husband and her friend, or only with the friend. Since most of the messages involved represent complaints against the husband or secret information about her own betrayal of him, it is not surprising that more than a third of Komarovsky's wives talked about at least some segments of their lives more with their confidantes than with their husbands. Although some husbands professed not to care, many were jealous of the wife's greater intimacy with her confidante than she was willing to establish with him. Other husbands, especially those with the least education, did not especially want their wives to talk to them, but were equally touchy about the confidential relationship with an outsider. They simply wanted the wife not to talk to anyone. They were not so much jealous of the confidante as afraid she might gossip about his family affairs or attack him in league with his wife.

In general, then, unilateral communication with confidantes threatened marriages. The chief exception seemed to be marriages so thoroughly disunited already that the husband hardly cared what his wife did. Under such uncommunicative circumstances, some wives could tolerate their marital disappointment more easily because of the emotional support they received from the confidante. The external involvement enabled them to make the best of a bad situation. Nevertheless, unilateral confidential relationships seem generally to provoke more tension in marriage than they release.

Intimate Families

Not only friends of the child but friends of his parents may affect his behavior. Figure 6-2 shows that the more similar parental friends were to the parents themselves, the less likelihood that the child or any of his siblings had ever been arrested for juvenile delinquency. The table also shows that parents themselves were less likely to have divorced or deserted one another if their friends were similar to themselves.

Both relationships imply that homogeneous groups of friends reinforce a family value system and support conformity to conventional norms. By contrast, the more diversified the friends, the more they tend to pull the family apart, leaving the child and the parents freer to engage in deviant behavior.

Most of these close families were either relatives or neighbors, while "other friends" ran a poor third. In this sense friends were not wholly distinct from neighbors and relatives but reinforced the social control function of both those "given" groups.

Belonging to the same religious faith by definition involves similar values. Being in the same income bracket is an index of common status in the stratification system and therefore of common class values. Whether region of origin within the United States is also an index of common values is less evident, but insofar as there are regional subcultures, such as distinctive attitudes toward racial groups, this too is a source of value reinforcement.

Zimmerman and Cervantes' data suggest that insofar as a family surrounds itself with friends who share their values, the family will be strengthened and supported. Parents can socialize their children more effectively because their teaching is reinforced by both the friends and the friends' children who in turn are likely to become playmates of the child. Parents are likely to find their dyadic relationship buttressed by the sympathetic concern of their circle of friends. Conversely, when friends of the family hold different values, they undermine the socialization process by counteracting the parents' teaching, and even contribute to the dissolution of the marriage itself. Contrary friends may fail to provide support and may even offer foci of contention which line husband and wife up differently, for and against the controversial views of their friends.

Friends seldom functioned, according to Zimmerman and Cervantes, by forming a social group comparable to a gang or peer group. The five families which were a given family's closest friends were not necessarily

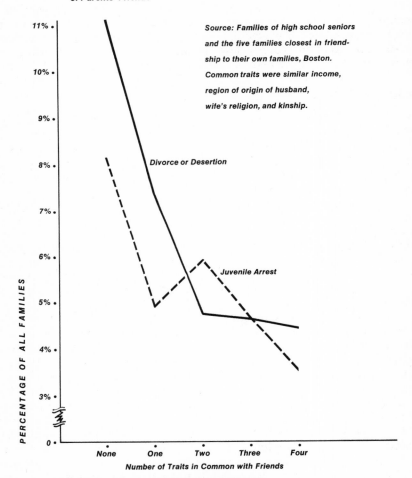

FIGURE 6-2.   Juvenile Arrests and Divorces or Desertions, by Similarity
              of Parents' Friends

Source: Families of high school seniors
and the five families closest in friendship to their own families, Boston.
Common traits were similar income,
region of origin of husband,
wife's religion, and kinship.

Divorce or Desertion

Juvenile Arrest

PERCENTAGE OF ALL FAMILIES

Number of Traits in Common with Friends

Adapted from Zimmerman and Cervantes (1960):76,95.

friends of one another. Indeed when the friends of the key family were asked what families were *their* best friends, they tended to name new families. So each family was surrounded by a spongy network of families, two (or more) layers deep. This suggests that most contact was on a family-to-family basis or that when more than two families gathered together, it was not always the same combination. It means that the social control function of family friends was not exercised by a corporate group. Presumably this means that social control was not as tight from this source as it was from the Park Forest neighborhood or from adolescent gangs. Nevertheless, both close friends and more remote friends (known through friendship with the closest friends) affected each family by the homogeneity or heterogeneity of their values. When homogeneity was high, families benefited from almost as much social control as if they had been embedded in a cohesive organization.

The Crowd

Although most families are surrounded by only a loose network of intimate families, some couples belong to closed groups of couples which are comparable to peer groups or gangs. Komarovsky (1964) found that one fifth of her blue-collar couples belonged to such a "crowd." Perhaps we can assume that this is a more common working-class than middle-class phenomenon since it may be an extension of the adolescent gang. Komarovsky's crowds typically consisted of three or four couples who spent most of their leisure together and whose couple-oriented recreational activities required both partners to be present if either was to be able to participate. This paired basis of membership in the crowd promoted marital solidarity by forcing the husband and wife to be together during much of their spare time and by correspondingly reducing opportunities for separate activities which might be divisive.

Komarovsky found that the crowd functioned as far more than just a place for leisure-time companionship. It became an informal therapy group, offering many of the same services to its members that couples in marital difficulties find in counseling with a group of married couples. (1) The crowd set norms for marital role performance, enabling couples to compare notes with each other about what each husband and wife expected of each other. (2) The crowd offered a setting for indirect marital communication. It allowed one partner to convey something to his spouse by telling his friend in her presence what he wanted her to hear. Or it served as a referee, enabling husband and wife to communicate directly with less fear that a quarrel might develop than if they were home alone and unchaperoned. Both functions Komarovsky subsumed under the heading of "the socializing role of the crowd." The crowd socialized new husbands and new wives into the roles of marriage and supported their solidarity.

UTOPIAN COMMUNITIES

Natural communities give family members a choice whether to depend on solidarity with their family or their friends. Utopian communities allow neither option. They eschew both familism and individualism in favor of communalism. Often explicitly rejecting the narrow limits of "tight little families," they attempt to establish a paradise on earth in which all will belong to "one big happy family." Sometimes families in the usual sense are completely abolished. In other cases, they are tolerated within severe limits. Either way, family life is deemphasized and priority given to the claims of the total community.

Communities Without Families

A book about families can hardly find communities without families of very much direct interest. Nevertheless, they may indirectly enlarge our understanding of family life insofar as quasi-family relationships (or eventually real family relationships) emerge within them. If attempts to institutionalize love in an entire community fail due to the reappearance of decentralized special relationships, something will have been learned about the limits of the human capacity to extend love relationships and the converse tendency of human relationships to coagulate into familistic clusters.

Non-reproductive Communities Monasteries, convents and other communities which extend themselves from generation to generation by "adoption" can more easily maintain their communal emphasis than those which reproduce themselves biologically. If it is necessary to gain "converts" to a utopian way of life, a community can be sure that its new recruits are dedicated to that way of life. But there is no guarantee that children born and raised in a utopian community will share the dedication of their parents.

Communities which do not depend on biological reproduction need not allow the sexual intercourse necessary to reproduction. Intercourse is such an intimate relationship that it tends to create feelings of attachment between couples who are thus involved and feelings of jealousy between those who are not privileged to share the relationship. In ordinary circumstances, these feelings are the foundation of the distinction between married pairs and outsiders. They tend to disrupt the undifferentiated love which utopian communities prefer. So vows of chastity and celibacy are conducive to maintaining an undifferentiated community.

The monastic vow of poverty also facilitates utopian communalism. Poverty does not usually mean a complete absence of food, clothing, and shelter, or even of such luxuries as books, T.V.'s and tennis rackets. Rather it means that property belongs to the community, not to the individual. This rule resembles the vow of chastity in removing a basis for interpersonal jealousy and for invidious distinctions within the community.

The final monastic vow—obedience—may also contribute to the familistic quality of a community, although the connections are less clear. If all members of a community must accept whatever assignments are handed out and cannot vie with each other for preferred assignments, another potential basis for jealousy, rivalry, and divisiveness is removed. In any case, a large proportion of utopian communities have come into existence around a charismatic father figure and have operated on an authoritarian basis. Most utopias have been patriarchal families.

To summarize: Such rules as chastity, poverty, and obedience force the members of a community to maintain an undifferentiated equality among rank-and-file members (with the exception of the patriarch). And the non-reproductive character of the community enables it to avoid the danger of dilution which comes with inherited membership in favor of the purity of communal dedication which can be assured by admitting only true believers.

Communal Reproduction   A few rare communities have devised ways of reproducing biologically without allowing families to form around the repro-ductive function. One notable case was the Oneida Community in the Mohawk Valley of central New York from 1848 to 1879 (see Kephart, 1963 and 1966). Oneida was a Protestant community whose charismatic founder was John Humphrey Noyes (and which lost its utopian non-family character within a few months of his departure from the community in 1879). Like Catholic monasteries, the community abolished private property and economic distinctions. All members wore the same clothes and lived in the same house, each in his own cubicle. To minimize functional distinctions, work assign-ments were rotated. Unlike monasteries, however, Oneida was coeducational. And unlike the Shakers (another nineteenth-century American coeducational religious community) Oneida allowed both sexual intercourse and reproduc-tion.

How then did Oneida prevent the emergence of families? The answer lay in a series of institutional controls designed to prevent the rise of familism and to insure the continuing priority of the community. So elaborate were these regulations that Noyes' term of "free love" hardly fits save in the nega-tive sense that this was sex without marriage. Noyes preferred the term "com-plex marriage" with its connotations of group marriage to the more anarchic conception of free love.

(1) Sex distinctions were minimized. As in the early days of Israeli kibbutzim and of Soviet and Chinese Communism, femininity was tabooed and women were largely transformed into men. Oneida required its women to bob their hair, replace their skirts with pantaloons, and wear no jewelry.

(2) Suggestive behavior was forbidden. The very fact that everyone was potentially free to have intercourse with everyone else made sex a touchy subject to be carefully avoided in public. Kephart reported that "inappropriate behavior, suggestive language, overt displays of sexuality" were strictly taboo (1966:174). Speculation about who might be having intercourse with whom was considered so offensive that one inquisitive man became the only mem-ber ever expelled in the colony's history.

(3) The community restricted sexual partnerships, especially the sex-ual initiation of new members. Young men were initiated by old women and young women by old men. One reason was to lessen the danger of accidental pregnancies (with women who were post-menopausal or men who had learned how to avoid ejaculating). Another reason was philosophical. As the 1875 Oneida *Handbook* put it:

It is well understood by physiologists that it is undesirable for persons of similar characters and temperaments to mate together. Communists have discovered that it is undesirable for two inexperienced and unspiritual per-sons to rush into fellowship with each other; that it is far better for both to associate with persons of mature character and sound sense. (Kephart, 1963:270)

(4) The community supplied a go-between in every pairing for inter-course. Especially the first time a man wished to have intercourse with a woman, he applied to a Central Committee which sent one of its older woman members to inquire of the intended partner as to her willingness to receive the man. This bureaucratic procedure was supposed to make it easier for the woman to decline without straining good relationships in the community. An un-intended side-effect, however, was to make the community's presence felt in what otherwise might have been a private affair. Privacy was just what the community must avoid if monogamy was not to creep in.

(5) The community severely limited the sexual and affectional in-volvement of its members. Intercourse was restricted to a one- or two-hour visit to the woman's room after which the man was required to return to his own room. Affectional involvement was not supposed to develop alongside the sexual relationship. All members of the community were supposed to love each other equally, and no special love was allowed, no matter whether particular couples were physically intimate or not. Sexual relations (as the *Handbook* suggested) were supposed to be sensible, not passionate.

(6) Despite these regulations, special love occasionally erupted in the community. When this happened, the ultimate sanction was banishment of one partner from the community. Conveniently there was a branch colony in Connecticut to which offenders could be sent. Had that option not been available, it seems likely that total expulsion from the movement would have been necessary—so sinful was the offense.

Similar mechanisms controlled reproduction in the community, except that this was even more restricted. (Intercourse was separated from reproduc-tion by requiring men to stop short of ejaculation in intercourse with any woman still young enough to conceive. Only with post-menopausal women were men ordinarily allowed to reach a sexual climax.)

(1) Reproduction was forbidden altogether for the first 20 years of the community's existence in order to enable both sexes to concentrate on economic production until the community was well established.

(2) Community permission was necessary before any man or woman could engage in reproduction. Reproduction was restricted to those mem-bers deemed by two community eugenics committees to be suitable as po-tential parents. Each of the women chosen bore an average of only 1.1 chil-dren apiece during the entire decade when the eugenics program was in operation (Kephart 1963:267). Thus the community restricted not only the personnel eligible for reproduction, but also the number of children each could have. So stringent was the entire program of reproduction that the community would have been able to reproduce itself only partially, had it survived its founder's departure. While there is nothing intrinsically neces-sary about this heavy restriction on reproduction, many utopian communities find themselves so fully engaged with more immediate problems that repro-duction tends to be deemphasized.

Finally, the children born of these carefully supervised unions were not allowed to become the nucleus of special families:

(1) After 15 months, the child was taken from the mother and raised in a communal nursery. This severed the special relationship of mother and child.

(2) Demonstrations of special affection between mother and child beyond that point were as thoroughly forbidden as special affection between a man and a woman. Just as all men and women were supposed to love one another equally, all children were supposed to be loved equally. For the biological mother to single out her own child for special attention would have been to discriminate against the other children of the community.

By communalizing sex, reproduction, and child-rearing, the Oneida Community was able to preserve its communal character for three decades. However, the very complexity and rigidity of the rules surrounding these familistic functions suggest how dangerous they seemed to members of this community. They threatened to destroy the equality of all men, all women, and all children as members of one "family."

The seriousness of that danger can be seen in the reasons why the community finally broke up. The younger generation revolted against the restrictions which had enabled the community to reproduce without marriage. Young men protested against being restricted to old women as sex partners, and young women objected to having their children taken from them. The unwillingness of the younger generation to accept restrictions imposed thirty years earlier by their elders suggests the tendency of sexual and reproductive behavior to reinvoke family life within a community once the early fervor and original leadership of that community have disappeared. Perhaps for a generation communal reproduction can avoid the decentralizing tendencies of special love. It seems unlikely that such a combination of communalism and dyadic biological relationships can coexist much longer than a generation. And once the coexistence ends, almost always the communalism goes and the privatism takes over.

Communities with Limited Families

Communities with limited families may be just as antifamilistic in ideology as those which ban families completely, but they choose a different way of resolving the conflict between communalism and privatism. The best-known contemporary example is the Israeli kibbutzim. These vary in size from less than 100 to more than 1,000 members. Some were founded as long ago as the early twentieth century, providing an opportunity to observe their evolution from initial collective enthusiasm to later compromises with privatism.

Many kibbutzim were inspired by a secular Marxist philosophy but some were religiously motivated. Spiro (1956) noted that kibbutzim without a transcendent value system succumbed to familism fastest, whereas those based on faith in Jewish or Marxist absolutes retained their dedication to communalism longer. Nevertheless, even the most radically Marxist kibbutzim (such as the one which Spiro studied) have weakened their collective emphasis over time.

Limited Sex Differentiation   The early kibbutzim deemphasized distinctions between the sexes in appearance and function.

Their original ideal was that men and women would have equal opportunities to receive any assignment in the communal division of labor, and that job assignments would be rotated to bar the development of social differences within the community based on differences in occupation. This ideal broke down because some tasks were too strenuous for women to perform (especially for pregnant women) and because nursing women could not be given assignments very far from their infants. The removal of women from the more technical jobs for the duration of their maternity leaves meant their replacement by men who could be counted on to stay more permanently so that their expertise would not be lost. As the kibbutzim prospered and mechanized their agricultural production, women who had performed unskilled farm work reasonably well were replaced by men capable of operating complex machinery. The combined effect of these forces was that women were assigned less frequently to farm work and more often to domestic communal enterprises: cooking, laundry, and raising children (Talmon, 1965b).

During the early years, women were forbidden to emphasize their femininity. Make-up was strictly taboo and women preferred wearing slacks or shorts which symbolized their ability to work as hard as the next man. However, Spiro discovered that the onset of middle age made women dissatisfied with their fading natural charms and led them to resort to hair dyeing, wearing dresses, and using make-up to prolong the appearance of youth. Talmon (1965b) similarly found that concern over their appearance led women to avoid outdoor work for fear their complexion would be roughened by the sun and their figure bent by hard labor. Spiro believed that the weak institutional support for the marriage bond in the kibbutz made wives unusually insecure and anxious about their looks. Since family life was functionally weak, wives were afraid their husbands might abandon them in favor of younger, more attractive partners.

Sex differences were also ignored in room assignments and shower facilities. However, neither experiment lasted very long. Of particular interest is the fact that segregated showers were instituted in Spiro's kibbutz at the initiative of teenagers whose changing bodies made them too self-conscious to share a communal shower.

Thus communities which began with the principle that men and women are simply human beings with interchangeable functions found that differentiation and segregation of the sexes gradually emerged. These trends contributed to a reemergence of family life itself.

Limited Family Formation   The early kibbutzim were founded by young single immigrants, often still in their teens. Living conditions in frontier deserts or swamps were arduous. The only shelters were tents. Faced with hostile elements and surrounded by hostile Arabs, the kibbutzniks were too busy trying to survive to have time for the niceties of life. Besides, they didn't believe in niceties anyway.

For both practical and ideological reasons, family formation was postponed. It is not clear from Spiro and Talmon whether this allowed a pattern of free love. Apparently the more radical kibbutzim frowned on premarital intercourse as a private indulgence and encouraged all the members of the community to spend their leisure together dancing the hora and singing pioneer songs.

It is clear, however, that once a couple became serious about each other, they were expected not to get married, but simply to start living together in the same room. Even this was not always easy since the communal housing shortage sometimes necessitated a considerable wait before a room became available. That housing shortage was partly ideologically motivated because the scarce resources of the community went first to expand communal facilities, especially productive facilities, and only after that to expand the housing available to individuals or couples.

When a couple applied to the community for a common room, that deed signified publicly their seriousness of intent. The absence of any ritual meant that couples merely drifted into a sort-of marriage with little emphasis on the significance of the transition. Not until a child was born was the relationship legalized, and even then only to conform to the legitimacy laws and not for the sake of cementing the marriage bond.

In later years, marriage came to be emphasized more: "Normally, marriage now precedes the beginning of life together in a family apartment. Quite a number of couples postpone regular sexual relations until they marry. Most couples attach considerable importance to their marriage and want it to be a meaningful and memorable event" (Talmon, 1965a:274). In Spiro's Marxist kibbutz, one couple even held a religious celebration of their marriage. And the old minimizing of the significance of marriage symbolized in the failure of the wife to abandon her maiden name later gave way to adopting the husband's name.

The pattern of drifting into marriage was associated with easy divorce. Divorces were frequent in the early years, supported partly by an ideology of marital freedom and partly by the postponement of child-bearing which minimized the complexities of changing partners. As child-bearing became a normal part of marriage, attitudes toward divorce shifted. Talmon (1965a: 274) reported that "divorce of couples who already have children is severely censured and condemned by public opinion." So strong did social pressure become that divorce rates fell almost to zero even in kibbutzim which earlier had had relatively many divorces.

Even worse than divorce was an extramarital affair within the kibbutz. Like Park Forest's courtyards, kibbutzim were so small that extramarital liaisons could not be kept secret. Even though the original antibourgeois philosophy of the kibbutzim advocated marital freedom, the practical consequences of extramarital entanglements were too severe and painful to be tolerated. Just as the children raised collectively in a kibbutz marry outsiders because it would be too "incestuous" to marry one's "roommate," extramarital affairs placed too much strain on the tightly knit social relations of the community: "Since life in the kibbutz entails close cooperation and frequent contacts between all members, the neglected spouse is exposed to recurrent encounters with the rival. Bitter jealousies which tear members apart and breed long-drawn enmities have a corrosive effect on interpersonal relations and impair the functioning of the system as a whole" (Talmon, 1965a:274). The defensive response of the community to this internal threat effectively prevented most extramarital affairs from taking place in the first place and forced the expulsion from the community of at least one member of the triangle in cases where adulterous affairs or divorces and remarriages did occur.

In sum, the general trend in the kibbutzim was to repeal the initial restrictions on family formation and to emphasize the importance of both getting married and staying married.

Limited Reproduction   If the early days were so difficult that couples could hardly afford to get married, they could even less afford to have children. The labor of every man and woman was needed to make the new settlements viable. Women could not be spared either to bear children or to raise them. At first, then, the kibbutzim functioned largely as nonreproductive communities dependent on new recruits from the outside world to replenish their numbers.

Only when the original work camps housed in tents were replaced with permanent settlements did having children seem feasible. Even then, reproduction remained for many years below the replacement level. Only with affluence did having children in any considerable number become economically appropriate. At the same time the drying up of European sources of recruits made childbearing more important to the survival of the kibbutzim. In any case, the history of these communities involved a gradual increase in the birth rate.

The consequences of a rising birth-rate for the importance of family life were profound. The involvement of a growing proportion of adult women in bearing and nursing children accelerated their withdrawal from an undifferentiated sharing in the division of labor, leaving them physically "closer to home" throughout the day. Secondly, we have already seen that communal taboos on divorce were particularly strong for couples with children. Talmon (1962) asserted that children were "the main focus of segregated family life in the Kibbutzim." Husbands and wives who otherwise would have been held together only by the more ephemeral ties of love acquired in children more enduring responsibilities. And as children became the hope of the continuity of the community, the families which produced those children came to be seen as no longer ideologically alien but fundamentally important.

Limited Child-Rearing   Kibbutzim have always maintained a pattern of collective child-rearing. Typically the individual mother retained custody of her child for only 15 months. After that, she was expected to return to full-time employment and leave her child in the communal nursery. The child henceforth saw his parents only a few hours a day in the late afternoon or evening. Even meals were eaten separately with peers rather than with parents.

Even though this basic pattern has endured, mothers have increasingly complained about their sense of bereavement when giving up their child at the tender age of 15 months after having had his entire companionship up to that time. Spiro reported that mothers found it particularly difficult to leave their children in the children's house at night and to be unable to see them in the morning. In other words the trauma of separation and the impossibility of early reunion were difficult to bear emotionally.

Mothers felt jealous of a child's custodian. Knowing that another woman was with her child made a mother anxious lest the child become more attached to the teacher than to her. But mothers had several built-in advantages in competing with the teacher. The mother had the exclusive custody of the child during those 15 months to build on. She had tenure in office, whereas teachers changed frequently. She had only one or two children to cultivate, whereas the teacher might be responsible for a dozen or more. Finally, the teacher had educational responsibilities which required her to put pressure on the children, whereas the mother could play a purely affectionate role in the time she spent with her children. That mothers could doubt their children's love despite all these competitive advantages indicates the strength of their separation anxiety.

While no kibbutzim abolished their collective nurseries in response to this maternal unhappiness, many allowed marginal increases in the mother's freedom to be with her children. Parents have intervened more in the life of the school, taking turns staying with the children at night, caring for them when they were ill, and helping prepare special festivals for the children. Afternoon tea and the evening meal were originally communal functions but came to be served by parents in the home at least on special occasions. Some kibbutzim even made the radical concession of allowing children to sleep at home, so they were at school only during the parents' working hours. Once reform had gone that far, the balance between family and community had shifted almost all the way from utopianism to naturalism.

Limited Housekeeping   Partly because of poverty but also in line with the collectivistic ideology, the original family "apartment" was simply a single room furnished with hardly more than a bed and a chair (Spiro). There were no private cooking facilities, not even a teapot. All food was prepared in the communal kitchen and consumed in the dining hall. Clothes were owned by the community and cleaned in the laundry.

The concept of collective clothing was the first to prove unworkable. Since human beings are not all the same size, they need clothing which varies correspondingly in size. The original policy failed to take sizes into account. The next step was to label and sort clothing by sizes so that individuals could receive back from the laundry the same size clothes. Even this turned out to have disadvantages, however, and was eventually replaced with privately owned clothing. Spiro's kibbutz made this policy change in order to encourage people to take better care of their clothing. Although theoretically clothes still "belong" to the community, their permanent consignment to a particular person creates an attachment which benefits the clothes (and indirectly the community).

The decentralization of food consumption seems not to have been motivated by economic considerations but by desires for family unity as opposed to collective unity. Gradually kibbutzim relaxed their insistence on communal eating and allowed families to prepare their afternoon tea, supplying them with both equipment and ingredients. Similarly, many kibbutzim allowed families to take prepared food from the communal kitchen to eat in the privacy of their apartment.

The apartment has expanded from the original barren room to a multiple-room suite equipped with private sanitary facilities and a kitchenette. This increased size and complexity has increased the time which family members must devote to their housework. It has also increased the attractiveness and range of family activities to which the apartment is conducive, accelerating the withdrawal of the family from communal facilities to the privacy of its own home. Not only were new apartments regularly equipped with teapots, but they were also given radios. Cooling fans for summer heat and heating stoves for winter cold were increasingly installed in the private apartments (Spiro).

With increased attractiveness in the family's living quarters, the tendency of the community to break apart into family units accelerated. Talmon (1965a) reported that some kibbutzim fought back by improving the dining hall. It seems unlikely however that any communal facility, no matter how attractive, can compete effectively with family facilities once the latter reach a minimal threshold of convenience. In most kibbutzim that threshold has long since been crossed.

Dispersion of Family Members   The final limitation which the early kibbutzim placed on families was to separate family members from each other. Partly this limitation was intended to prevent any family ties from disrupting the larger community. The remainder simply resulted from neglecting to coordinate the work schedules of family members. The community treated husbands and wives as unrelated persons, with the result that they often got conflicting schedules which prevented them from sharing a common leisure.

Talmon (1962) reported that uncoordinated work schedules put husbands and wives to work on different shifts so they were not free at the same time during the day. Similarly the single holiday per week might differ for the two partners and even their annual vacation leaves might not coincide. Couples were so dissatisfied with this failure to take their needs into consideration that they forced the kibbutzim to coordinate their assignments. As a result of this pressure, the communities now recognize the right of married couples to spend their leisure together.

So strong was the intial taboo on marital segregation within the community that couples went out of their way to avoid being seen together in public. Spiro reported that husbands and wives were "ashamed" to be seen entering the dining hall together, so they avoided this embarrassment by entering through different doors and eating at separate tables. Similarly, when an individual returned from a trip outside the kibbutz, he would "greet everyone in the kibbutz except his mate." This reflects the fact that the strongest taboo was on public expression of affection between husbands and wives. This was not because the kibbutzim had an explicit ethic of collective love like Oneida, but simply an unconscious reaction to the pressure for collective unity which characterized the kibbutzim when they were new.

Rather than being free to associate with one another as a couple, husbands and wives were expected to spend their entire leisure with the collectivity. Members spent their evenings in the dining hall, in the library or on the central lawn. They engaged in common activities: business meetings, political discussion, folk singing and folk dancing. The religious rituals of Judaism which had been centered in the family were transferred to the community and celebrated collectively if they were celebrated at all.

Spiro believed that the collapse of collective leisure was due primarily to the transformation of the community's leaders from youth to middle age. The early emphasis on collective activity was congenial with the needs and abilities of young adults emerging from adolescence. But by the time those same people reached middle age, their interests shifted to "children, friends, and personal concerns," all decentralized interests.

Presumably a variety of casual forces were at work: biological aging and declining ideological fervor were certainly among them. However, the most significant conclusion to be derived from the experience of the kibbutzim seems to be a natural tendency of family life to emerge within a larger community. The limited capacity of human beings to embrace a large number of people with equal affection promotes the gradual differentiation of more intensive from less intensive relationships. The family represents the most intensive of these differentiated relationships, surrounded by concentric circles of kin and friends within the larger community. The larger the community becomes and the longer it exists, the more sharply this internal differentiation tends to emerge. It can be resisted only by intense ideological dedication to collective values and by rigid regulation of collective involvement. In the case of most kibbutzim (like most utopian communities), neither the collective commitment nor the social control mechanisms remained intact for very long. As a result, family life which had been severely repressed gradually emerged into the open and began to flourish at the expense of collective involvement. Whether this transition is good or bad depends on one's value system. The point for our purposes is the inherent incompatibility between strong families and utopian communities. The latter need not abolish families altogether, but the greater the priority they give to the community, the less room there is for family life (and vice versa).

FAMILY–COMMUNITY BALANCE

It is apparent from the last section that the strength of family and community tends to vary inversely. It is also clear that the weight given to the family or the community varies enormously from one situation to another and from time to time. Hence family and community are not necessarily evenly balanced, but may strike quite different balances.

The Emergence of the Family

In utopian communities, the balance is far to the left. Communal values require either the abolition of the family or at least its confinement within a straight-jacket. But such artificial communities are not the only circumstance within which families have a hard time existing. Even natural communities are sometimes constituted in such a way that the family hardly exists as a social unit (though it still may be the unit of reproduction).

Aries (1962) claimed that the concept of family was not invented until the seventeenth century. Before that, people spent so much time in public that they had very little time for their families. If their house was big enough, it served as a place of business and sociability. Clients and friends felt free to call at any hour of day or night, indeed to drop in unannounced. So constant was the flow of outsiders into the home that family meals (that central family gathering-time) were often impossible. And if the house was not big enough to serve as a "public house," most members of the family spent their time in the street like members of a street-corner gang.

Aries discovered that the concept of the family came into clear focus only as other specialized institutions relieved the family home of the necessity of serving such a confused melange of functions. The growth of the tavern, the club, and the cafe provided alternative gathering places for sociability. The establishment of separate business and professional offices relieved the home of the flood of clients.

The strengthening of the family was to be seen both in increased privacy for family life and in increased internal intimacy within the shelter of that privacy. Whereas previously wedding guests invaded the bedroom when the newlyweds were already in bed and retired only to adjacent rooms to make intentionally disturbing noises throughout the wedding night, aristocratic manners frowned on this behavior as coarse and indecent. Similarly, the home ceased to be invaded without warning as families of good breeding sent their calling cards in advance of their visits.

Thanks to this gradual separation of family life from outside life came a growing awareness that members of the family were especially intimate friends who deserved to be addressed in a distinctively intimate fashion. Whereas literate men and women had previously addressed one another in their letters as "Sir" and "Madame," the same way they addressed everyone else, with the rise of family-consciousness, formal terms gave way to terms of endearment such as "my dear love," "my dear child," and "my dear little one" in one man's letters to his wife. Children, similarly, were given nicknames and pet names. "This increasingly widespread use of nicknames corresponded to a greater familiarity and also to a desire to address one another differently from strangers, and thus to emphasize by a sort of hermetic language the solidarity of parents and children and the distance separating them from other people" (Aries, p. 400). These distinctive terms of address used within the family circle symbolized that the family had at last achieved a secure niche in the community.

A Tyranny of Families

At the opposite extreme from a utopian community emphasizing communal solidarity at the expense of the family would be a natural community where family priority was so strong that interfamily solidarity could not exist. This would be a community in name only, in actuality only an aggregate of isolated families (however close they might live to one another physically). Like Hobbes' uncivilized man, every family's hand would be raised against every other family. The family would rule supreme over its homestead, but that rule would be tyrannical, a fascist dictatorship, the right-wing triumph of family over community.

Banfield (1958) found such a situation in a community called Montegrano in southern Italy and labelled it "amoral familism." Not that there was no morality at all. Individual family members exhibited great loyalty to one another. Parents were extraordinarily benevolent to their children and made all sorts of sacrifices for their children's welfare. The very strength of the family's internal relationships meant a greater willingness of parents to help their children than would be found elsewhere because (1) parents had no conflicting interests outside the family, and (2) they knew that if they didn't help their children, no one else would.

The converse of this benevolent concern of family members for one another was a corresponding urgency for family members to come to each other's rescue, especially in emergencies. Children were expected to sacrifice their individual welfare for the sake of their siblings in time of need. Children were expected to be obedient to their parents and were the only security the family possessed in a hostile environment of "enemy" families.

The greatest tragedy in such a society was to lose a parent. In most societies, this crisis is cushioned by turning to relatives, friends, or social agencies for help. But in Montegrano, social institutions scarcely existed because to organize to aid the poor would be to betray one's own family by aiding the "enemy." So-called "friends" were not to be trusted and especially not to be aided financially when one's own family's financial resources were meager. The belief in familism did not extend even to relatives. The most graphic evidence of this was the failure of Montegrano emigrants to the United States to share their affluence with relatives back home. Thus the loss of a family head was likely to be an unmitigated disaster.

The isolation of the Montegrano nuclear family created a pervasive anxiety about premature death. Banfield found that most local residents told stories about the unexpected death of a parent in response to Thematic Apperception Test pictures. By contrast few North Italians told such stories, perhaps because most of them lived in stem families with built-in parent-substitutes and because the North Italian ethos was less hostile to interfamily cooperation. Banfield found individuals raised in stem families not only less anxious about losing a parent, but also more sociable toward outsiders and more socially responsible in their attitude toward community problems (perhaps as a result of being raised in a larger extended family unit).

In any case, the "amorality" of the Montegranisi characterized their attitude toward everything outside their tight little family units. Every family was a law unto itself. Even government officials used their office to aggrandize their own families at community expense—and were routinely voted out of office at the next election. The result of this lack of social concern was a potential "war of all against all" which was restrained only by the existence of Montegrano within the larger framework of the Italian nation. But for the modicum of law and order imposed on the community by the central government, Banfield believed the local community would fall apart, burying the individual families under its collective debris.

Even though outside political and police control maintained a modicum of "peace," it was a stagnant peace. Lacking any basis for cooperation, the community could do nothing for its mutual betterment. Hence the title of Banfield's book: ". . . A Backward Society." In this sense, Banfield believed that Montegrano was just as "unnatural" a society as a utopian community. Just as utopia represents a temporarily extreme emphasis on collective interests, so Montegrano represented a temporary overemphasis on family interests. But it was not a viable balance. Only the intervention of the larger society enabled it to survive.

A Shifting Balance

Somewhere beween the anarchy of Montegrano and the totalitarianism of Oneida lies the normal range of community influence over families. Within that range we have already discovered some factors which determine the particular balance to be struck. Ordinarily the smaller the community, the stronger the informal influence of its members on one another. Indeed, Gerrit Kooy has coined the relationship as "open families in closed communities," by which he meant that families located in tight little communities tend to have no secrets but to be open to external intervention and control by the community. Conversely, in open communities characterized by large-scale mobility, families tend to close their doors in the face of the flood of strangers and to retreat into autonomy.

Another relationship seems contradictory to the previous one. The more heavily populated a society, the stronger its formal regulations over all sorts of social units (including families) tend to become. As societies become more densely settled, people begin to infringe on each other's lives more often, and the individual family must be protected from that infringement by the formal intervention of the community. A man's home may once have been his castle, to do with as he saw fit, but the latter-day laws of urban sprawl say he cannot build out to his lot line, cannot cut sunlight off from his neighbor, cannot hold noisy parties which disturb his neighbor, cannot conduct a business on his premises, cannot even sell it to whomever he pleases. The longer the population explosion continues and the more delicately interdependent the social fabric becomes, the greater the limits imposed by the community will become.

Paradoxically, these increasing restraints have come precisely in those urban centers which I earlier characterized as releasing families into the freedom of normlessness. This contradiction can be resolved by distinguishing between the informal freedom conferred by a state of anomie and the formal restraint imposed by urban government. Nevertheless, even legal restraints on families have gradually eased with respect to the private behavior of adult men and women. The law considers it less and less its business whether men and women divorce and remarry (whatever their reasons) or choose to have an abortion rather than bear an unwanted child, and in the future seems likely to take the same attitude with respect to whether they have sexual relations with members of their own sex.

The crucial distinction is between what people do as consenting adults and what they do which infringes on the welfare of others. The balance between family and community is gradually shifting toward increased freedom to do what family members have consensually determined they wish to do, but toward increased community concern that the exercise of freedom by one person should not infringe upon the welfare of another.

This suggests then that the balance cannot be described as shifting universally in the direction of increased community influence. Rather the community is strengthening its formal controls to compensate for its loss of informal control and at the same time discriminating more sophisticatedly between the legitimate concerns of the community and those which are merely private affairs.

chapter seven

THE KINSHIP SYSTEM AND THE FAMILY

In the history of mankind, kinship was the first social system with the possible exception of the community (or group of families) to develop outside the family. Because kinship is an extension of the family system, the two are almost inseparable from one another. Once a given family has been in existence for more than one generation, it acquires relatives by blood and marriage. Regardless of whether relatedness ties are constructed into formal organizations, they are likely to be defined by the family members and by the wider society as the basis at least of informal patterns of interaction.

Kinship systems are not only the oldest of extrafamilial influences. In many primitive societies they are either the only external system or at least the strongest one. In hunting and gathering societies, the division of labor tends to be by sex. Another way of saying this is that there are no other specialized social institutions: no economic, political, religious, or educational institutions. Since families are composed of both men and women and since kinship systems are built from family units, those systems are the only type of larger social organization (save such territorial aggregates as villages or tribes) consistent with such a limited degree of role specialization.

Primitive societies are usually small and their local communities smaller still. This means that the members of such societies tend to know one another as individuals, including knowing about family relations and interfamily relations. This knowledge makes it possible to act on that basis, *i.e.,* to differentiate in personal encounters between persons on the basis of kinship ties and to discriminate between kin and non-kin. Not only are kin ties well known in small communities, but the very smallness of the community throws the same groups of kin and non-kin into repeated contact, making possible the development of elaborate behavior patterns based on who people are.

Who people are means their place in the network of kin. Behavior in such societies is ascribed on the basis of ancestry. Since no alternative forms of social organization exist to compete with kin relations, they have an extraordinarily powerful influence.

These circumstances combine to make kinship in primitive societies not just a matter of interpersonal relations but of group relations. Where the same kin are thrown together repeatedly and the boundaries between kin and non-kin are well known, kin tend to become crystallized into a formal group. Since life in primitive societies is unusually hazardous, since few families can be depended upon to meet all the exigencies of life, and since no alternative institutions are available for emergency relief, families come to depend on their relatives for a broad range of services. And with dependence always comes a surrender of power to that which is depended upon. Thus for a variety of reasons, the kin group in primitive societies achieves an importance which it is difficult for modern men to imagine unless they have steeped themselves in anthropology.

The impersonality and mobility of modern cities destroys kinship as an effective basis for formal social relations. The rise of specialized institutions weakens the exclusive grip of kin over families. As a result, voluntary kin relations replace compulsory membership in formal kin groups.

This means that modern man can pick and choose which relatives he will associate with and which he will shun or ignore. The more remote the relationship, the greater this option becomes. The more the individual has the power to choose, the less powerful kin influence becomes, since attempted influence can be spurned. He may not only choose which relatives to interact with but even choose not to associate with any of them. Friends may replace relatives for personal companionship, and institutional support may replace kinship support. Social security systems, company retirement programs, hospitals for the sick, and homes for the aged have reduced the necessity for children to care for their aged parents.

Nevertheless, even in modern societies, kinship remains one basis for personal and family interaction with outsiders. Generally speaking, relatives are preferred over nonrelatives for leisure-time interaction and for mutual help. The more important the occasion, the larger the role relatives are likely to play. Especially on familistic occasions associated with family formation (weddings and anniversaries), family growth (birthdays and christenings), and family dismemberment (illness and funerals), priority goes to kin ties. The more critical the help that is needed (the larger the loan, the more intimate the nursing care, the more extensive the invasion of family autonomy by adding an outsider to the household), the higher the priority of kin ties over "mere" friendship.

One reason for the continuing importance of kinship in modern societies is the priority of those ties in the life of the individual. The parents and siblings who were members of one's family in his childhood become his relatives in adulthood. Those with whom one lived so intimately for the first few decades of life are designated one's "primary" relatives in contrast to all others who are secondary kin. The very strength of family ties explains the continuing strength of ties with primary kin.

Studies of contemporary societies show that ties with secondary kin are the main ones weakened by modernization. This does not mean that primary kin have the same function today as before. The same transformations which have affected parent–child relations in childhood necessarily affect those relations after the child has been launched into independence. Shifts from authoritarianism to equality between the generations affect kinship as well as they affect family. But despite these structural changes, primary kin remain important to most people in even the most modern societies.

KINSHIP AND RESIDENCE

At the beginning of marriage, kinship may determine where couples are allowed to live.

Rules of Residence in Primitive Societies

In primitive societies where kinship is extraordinarily important, it is rare for a couple to be allowed to live anywhere they choose. Almost always, the kinship system determines where the new family should be located. And that location is almost always within the immediate vicinity of either the man's family or the woman's.

TABLE 7-1 Rules of Residence in Primitive Societies

Rule of Residence	Percentage of Societies
Patrilocal (husband's family)	58%
Matrilocal (wife's family)	15
Matri–patrilocal (wife's at first, then husband's)	9
Ambilocal (husband's or wife's)	8
Neolocal (independent location)	7
Avunculocal (husband's maternal uncle's home)	3
Total	100%
Number of societies	250

Adapted from Murdock (1949):17. Source: World-wide sample of primitive societies (70 North American tribes, 65 from Africa, 60 from Oceania, 34 from Europe and Asia, and 21 from South America).

Table 7-1 shows the frequency of different rules of residence in a world-wide sample of primitive societies. Clearly one rule was overwhelmingly common: the newlyweds in most societies were expected to live with the husband's family. This did not necessarily mean that they lived in the same household in an extended (three-generation) family. They were, however, supposed to live at least in the vicinity of the husband's family, even if they were allowed a separate house. This meant that the wife made the major move at marriage whereas the husband either stayed where he was or moved next door. The differential impact of marriage on the two sexes is analogous to the tendency of wives in most societies to adopt their husband's family name at marriage (whereas men seldom change their names). Both patrilocality and patronymy illustrate the general tendency of males to dominate females in family and kinship systems.

A poor second after patrilocal residence is the opposite extreme—matrilocality. Probably one reason for the preeminence of these two systems is that if one is going to require couples to live with relatives at all, the simplest arrangement is to require them to live with one childhood family or the other. To require the couple to live with the wife's family is just as simple and straightforward as to require them to live with the husband's. Both systems have the virtue of maintaining residential continuity through a single sex— from father to son to grandson, or from mother to daughter to granddaughter. To be sure, at the same time that a man stays with his father, he also stays with his mother, but the unbroken continuity in residential location is through the male line (or in the matrilocal case through the female line).

I assume, in general, that any kin group prefers to retain its own children and grandchildren, rather than to lose them at marriage; however, the incest taboo forbidding intermarriage within a single family means that every marriage system requires children to marry across family lines. And systems of residence do not mean that one family gets to keep all its children, and others lose all of theirs; they determine rather which children (whether sons or daughters) will stay. The choice is whether a family gets to keep its sons or to keep its daughters. Patrilocal families keep their sons, and matrilocal systems keep their daughters.

Some primitive societies developed more complex systems which took into consideration the competing interests of both sets of families. Matri–patrilocal systems are an interesting compromise. They require the couple to live temporarily at the wife's home, either for a specified period of time such as a year or until the birth of the first child. Then the couple, having discharged their obligation to the wife's family, move in with the husband's family and settle down.

Ambilocality and neolocality are the only systems which allow any choice. Ambilocal systems specify that the couple must live with either the husband's family or the wife's but allow circumstances to dictate which family will win. The choice is not necessarily left to the couple. Some ambilocal societies award the couple to whichever family has more wealth or higher status, regardless of personal preferences. From the standpoint of the families, it makes sense to place the couple in whatever family can best support them, especially when we remember that survival cannot be taken for granted in many primitive societies. Ambilocality at most restricts the couple's choice to two alternatives and sometimes gives the power of even that decision to the two groups of kin.

Only neolocal systems universally give the couple a free hand in determining where they will live. Their choice need not necessarily be a new location, away from both families, but it may be. Neolocal systems allow the couple to choose one of the two options open in ambilocal societies or a completely new location away from either family. This freedom is universal in modern societies but rare in either primitive or feudal societies since kin groups in these societies are rarely prepared to surrender that much power to their children or to face the possibility of losing the services of both their sons and their sons-in-law. In both primitive and feudal societies, wealth is too dependent on the cooperative efforts of the family group in hunting together or farming together to allow children the luxury of spurning their elders. As parents age, they are likely to become more dependent on their children for their own survival. Keeping married children within the family was a form of life insurance in the days before the rise of insurance companies and government pensions. Thus neolocal systems of residence were quite rare under premodern conditions.

Finally, Table 7-1 shows that the most complex system of all, avunculocal or "uncle" residence, is the least common (only 8 tribes out of the 250). Both sons and daughters in these cases must leave home but parents can look forward to receiving in return the husband's sister's sons and their wives.

Since sons wind up in the mother's kin group, avunculocality contrasts sharply with the continuity through a single sex in the most popular systems. The double complexity of taking both sexes away from their immediate families and assigning sons to the custody of the maternal kin group while daughters go with their husbands suggests some of the psychological and socio-structural reasons why avunculocality is so rare a solution to the problem of residence.

With sons assigned to the mother's kin group, the avunculocal system is related to the matrilocal pattern. Both result in creating communities composed predominantly of matrilineal kin. Conversely, both patrilocal and matri–patrilocal systems produce patrilineal communities. Out of these matrilineal or patrilineal communities tend to grow larger kin groups, either in the form of extended families living together or in the form of clans. Neolocal systems, by contrast, allow no basis for the growth of larger kinship organizations and leave the nuclear family of husband, wife, and children independent of formal kin control though not necessarily cut off from informal influence.

For the sake of simplicity I have concentrated on general systems of residence, but exceptions to the rules may be allowable under particular circumstances. For example, Romney and Romney (1963) found that the Mexican Indian ideal of patrilocality gave way to matrilocal residence if the wife's family had more economic resources and more space to accommodate the new couple than the husband's family. Such matrilocal residence quite regularly occurred in mixed marriages between a low-status-man and a high-status woman.

In a Filipino village, Nydegger and Nydegger (1963) found the same tendency to live with the wife's family in order to take advantage of greater resources. They also noted that matrilocality solved the continuity problem of families with sons but no daughters. In this patrilocal community, exceptions were far more apt to be matrilocal than neolocal in form. If a family had a remote tract of land which needed to be occupied, newlyweds might settle there, but this hardly seems neolocal since whichever family owned the land controlled the child's residence. The only truly neolocal cases resulted from kin group quarrels, *i.e.,* from the breakdown of the normally harmonious relations with kin. Even then, however, such independent families usually became the focal point of new patrilocal households once their sons grew up and married. The matrilocal exceptions, similarly, remained matrilocal for only a single generation, resuming patrilocality in succeeding generations. Thus the Filipino norm of patrilocality held firm, the exceptions to it being only temporary and with good reason.

Community Residence and Family Residence   So far I have suggested only that most kin groups prefer to keep their sons at home and that the male group usually wins in competition with the female group. The emphasis on retaining sons suggests another principle which contributes to the popularity of patrilocality. I have already referred to the cooperation of males in wresting a livelihood from the land. Similar cooperation is required in defending that land against marauding enemies. Teamwork is facilitated when boys who have grown up in the same household can work and fight together as adults. In matrilocal systems strange men are imported as husbands so their cooperation with one another and with their father-in-law is more problematic than the cooperation of brothers with one another and with their own father.

One way of minimizing this strangeness is to insure that brothers-in-law have at least grown up in the same community. If matrilocal families are required to recruit their men locally, husbands will have known each other even if they didn't grow up in the same home. The limited size of most primitive communities assures that fellow-villagers are well acquainted.

TABLE 7-2   Community Residence, by Family Residence

COMMUNITY	FAMILY RESIDENCE		
RESIDENCE	Patrilocal	Neolocal	Matrilocal
Exogamy (marry out)	53%	0%	21%
No rule	40	69	8
Endogamy (marry in)	7	31	71
Total	100%	100%	100%
Number of societies	101	13	24

Adapted from Murdock (1949):19. Exogamous societies either require or at least tend to marry outside the community, and endogamous communities marry inside. Other systems of family residence have been omitted for the sake of simplicity.

For the sake of simplicity I have shown in Table 7-2 only the simplest rules of residence where either the woman or the man must move to the other's home or both may leave. In the matrilocal cases, where the man must move, the table shows that he rarely moves out of his own community. He is almost always protected against leaving the village by a rule or at least by a general tendency to community endogamy. While he changes families, he is usually safeguarded against having to change communities.

Presumably endogamy minimizes the economic strain which might otherwise occur and at the same time minimizes the losses which the "superior" sex would incur in becoming a low-status novitiate not only in the wife's family, but also in a strange community. Perhaps even more importantly village endogamy protects men who join their wives' families from having to fight against their own brothers when war breaks out. Their brothers will still be fellow-villagers even though they belong to other matrilocal households. Finally, endogamy enables men to discharge the avuncular responsibilities which men in matrilocal societies normally carry for their sisters' children, especially for their sisters' sons. If they had had to leave their own village at marriage, they would no longer be close enough to their sisters' domiciles to be "good" maternal uncles responsible for overseeing and training their nephews. Men who must leave their families have a combination of economic, military, and kinship responsibilities which prevent them from going beyond their village boundaries when they marry into matrilocal households.

Conversely, in patrilocal cases, such protection is rarely given the bride. Her major responsibilities are in the home—the inside of one home is much like the inside of another. Another way of putting this is that if either sex is expected to change communities, it is almost always the woman, not the man.

In neolocal systems, couples are free to choose their residence without restriction. It should not surprise us to discover that unregimented choice applies to the community from which the partners are drawn as well as to the particular location where they will settle.

Compensation for Unilateral Loss　　Patrilocal systems frequently impose a double hardship on the bride. Not only must she leave home to join her husband's family, but she frequently must leave her village as well. While the hardship is most severe on the bride herself, this double removal is also mourned by the family she leaves behind. Kinship systems have often sought compensation for this surrender. If the daughter must be given up and the family must do without her presence and services, kin groups have devised compensatory devices for alleviating the pain.

TABLE 7-3　　Compensation for Bride by Rule of Residence

| | RULE OF RESIDENCE | | | |
| | | Matri– | | |
COMPENSATION	Patrilocal	Patrilocal	Matrilocal	Neolocal
Exchange of women	7%	0%	0%	0%
Bride price	74	29	11	0
Bride service	1	62	22	12
None	18	10	67	88
Total	100%	101%	100%	100%
Number of societies	140	21	36	17

Adapted from Murdock (1949):20. Selected rules of residence in 250 primitive societies.

Table 7-3 shows that patrilocal systems usually required compensation, whereas matrilocal systems seldom did and neolocal systems almost never did. An exchange of women occurred only in strictly patrilocal systems: You give me your daughter and I will send one of mine in return. Such a system of reciprocal exchange is remarkably fair but difficult to institutionalize because of the lack of an equal number of sons and daughters. The easiest compensation to arrange is monetary or material. Hence if compensation is to be made at all, it is most apt to be in this easily procurable and transferable form. The bride price is normally given from the man's family to the bride's family, though in unusual circumstances, the man himself may earn the funds.

Matri–patrilocality is almost by definition a system of bride service, since the main purpose of living temporarily with the bride's family seems to be so the groom can perform useful services for them.

In matrilocal societies, the surprising feature is not that so many dispense with compensation altogether, but that some require the groom's family to surrender their son and to send material wealth as well. Bride service in matrilocal marriages should be particularly easy since the husband is living near the bride's family anyway. Presumably, bride service would not be necessary if the couple were actually inducted into the bride's family household, but only needs to be prescribed when a separate household is established nearby.

Neolocality involves interfamily transactions so seldom because it is more an individual affair than a family one and because both families "lose" their children equally, leaving neither side deserving of compensatory reimbursement from the other.

In general, then, transfers of goods and services between families at marriage tend to be adjustive mechanisms which correct imbalances between the two groups of kin.

Residence and Inheritance   In most primitive societies not only are there rules concerning which family a couple must live with, but also rules governing the inheritance of family property. Under primitive economic conditions, the amount of property is not likely to be very great, but the worse the poverty, the more valuable the inheritance. Just as societies choose the simplest mechanisms for assigning residence, so they prefer the simplest mechanism of confining inheritance to one family line. And just as the man's family most often is preferred residentially, so the male line normally gets the inheritance, too.

I have already suggested that the man's role in economic subsistence is a major reason for giving his family preference in residence. If the man is primarily responsible for producing the wealth to be transmitted at his death, it is not surprising that wealth is handed on from father to son rather than from mother to daughter. An American Indian's horses, a South Sea islander's ceremonial flutes, the carefully guarded equipment for magic and warfare— these are treasures which could only be used by another man and which a man would rather bequeath to his son than to his son-in-law (as in matrilineal inheritance). In Murdock's sample, three-fourths of all tribes prescribed patrilineal inheritance, leaving only 17 percent matrilineal and 8 percent with a more complex system of mixed inheritance to both sons and daughters.

One might expect inheritance to be closely connected with residence. A son who lives with or near his father and works with him day in and day out is in a strategic position to take custody of his father's wealth at his death. Similarly a woman who lives with her father is likely to be his favorite heir, even though it may be her husband who actually manages inherited matrilineal wealth.

TABLE 7-4   Inheritance Pattern, by Rule of Residence

RULE OF INHERITANCE	RULE OF RESIDENCE		
	Patrilocal	*Bilocal*	*Matrilocal*
Patrilineal	89%	73%	25%
Mixed	5	27	10
Matrilineal	6	0	65
Total	100%	100%	100%
Number of societies	98	11	20

Adapted from Murdock (1949):38. Other rules of residence have been omitted for the sake of simplicity.

This expected relationship is confirmed in Table 7-4. Almost all the patrilocal societies confined inheritance to the male line. Among matrilocal families the grip of residence on inheritance patterns was not quite so strong, but still a solid majority of these societies restricted inheritance to matrilineal kin. The masculine bias in primitive societies is apparent in the deviant quarter of matrilocal societies which bequeathed property to their absent sons rather than to the sons-in-law who were living with the family. Mixed inheritance, though never the dominant pattern in any residential system, was most common in ambilocalism, a system which potentially kept both married sons and married daughters within the family.

In general, then, living with or near parents lays the ground work for inheriting their property, with the important qualification that the general patrilineal preference for inheritance of masculine-oriented property sometimes outweighs the influence of residential proximity.

Residence and Descent   If tangible property is usually handed down within the residential locality, one would expect descent also to be traced through the people who live most closely together. Modern men and women generally think of themselves as descended equally from both sides of the family. But this is rarely the case in primitive societies. To trace descent equally on both sides in a primitive tribe would soon make everyone related to everyone else and then kinship could no longer serve as a principle of social organization. If tribes are to be divided into separate clans, some method of selection must be found which will allow an individual to emphasize his descent from certain ancestors and to ignore his descent from others. The easiest way to do this is to trace descent either through the male line or the female line.

There is an analogy between the inheritance of property and the inheritance of genes. Hence I expect to find similar patterns with descent to those I have already shown with inheritance: (1) The male line should be emphasized more than the female one; (2) simpler systems should be found more often than complicated ones; and (3) the choice of line should be affected by the residential pattern.

TABLE 7-5   Descent, by Rule of Residence

DESCENT SYSTEM	RULE OF RESIDENCE		
	Patrilocal or Matri–patrilocal	*Ambilocal or Neolocal*	*Matrilocal or Avunculocal*
Patrilineal descent	58%	22%	0%
Double descent	10	3	0
Bilateral descent	23	64	28
Matrilineal descent	9	11	72
Total	100%	100%	100%
Number of societies	168	36	46

Adapted from Murdock (1949):59.

Table 7-5 confirms all these hypotheses. The most complicated system is the rarest. Double descent means that the individual traces his ancestry both through his father's male line and his mother's female line (but not through his other two grandparents).

Bilateral descent is less complex in the sense that all ancestors are equally important, but in primitive societies it is confined primarily to the rarest residential systems where new couples live either equally far from both families or have an opportunity to live with either one.

The most common systems are the unilateral systems, and generally speaking descent is reckoned through the line with which the couple lives. The exceptions are unimportant in the case of matrilocal and avunculocal systems since they retain the matrilineal descent but add the husband's line as well. Only in patrilocal and matri–patrilocal systems do we encounter extraordinary cases of neglecting the family entirely with which the couple lives and choosing the alternate family line. Those exceptions are comparatively rare and do not mask the general tendency for residence to influence descent.

How one reckons descent may not seem very important to modern people, for in modern societies ancestry is simply a matter of idle curiosity. In most primitive societies, on the other hand, descent is a powerful organizational force since people with common ancestry tend to form lineages which engage in common ritual, economic, and political functions. The rules of descent determine which kin primitive men will collaborate with and which equally close biological kin they will ignore, avoid, or even oppose.

Although the correlations are not perfect, residential patterns in primitive societies are powerful determinants of many other aspects of family life: who will marry whom, who will inherit from whom, which relatives will be treated as members of the same lineage, and which relatives (if any) will be compensated at marriage for losing a child.

Residential Patterns in Modern Societies

There is no such thing as a set of rules of residence in modern societies because the family's grip loosens too much under the impact of mobility and equalitarianism. Theoretically, modern societies allow freedom of choice of residence and therefore the basic pattern is neolocal. Nevertheless, the question remains whether contemporary couples choose to live near or far from relatives and, if near, which set of kin is chosen. If, even in the absence of rules, couples tend to live near their primary kin and choose the kin of one spouse more often than the other, the implications for the structure and vitality of kinship in modern societies should be impressive.

In the absence of explicit norms regulating residential behavior, such patterns would imply that residence is determined by the wishes and desires of married couples to live near enough to certain relatives to be able to interact with them with minimal difficulty. Presumably this would reflect the strength of parent–child ties before marriage, but perhaps also the anticipation of creating a certain style of interaction with primary kin after marriage. Whether consciously intended or not, such residential tendencies would be symptomatic of past, present, and future kinship interaction patterns.

Propinquity to Kin   The answer to the first question is easy: Even in modern societies, couples generally live close to their relatives. How close depends on the availability of suitable housing. In communities where housing is short, newly-married couples may have no choice but to settle in new apartment houses on the urban fringe. Other things being equal, they would have preferred to live closer to their parents, but other things are seldom equal, especially in housing.

How close they live also depends on the availability of jobs. If jobs are scarce locally and plentiful elsewhere, couples may experience economic pressures to leave that are as great as housing imbalances which create physical pressures to move. Societies vary also in the amount of occupational mobility they allow. In Japan, the ordinary employee remains with his initial employer until he "retires" at 55. But in countries where people can change jobs freely and where the route to better pay is often a zigzag from one employer to another, economic incentives to move will conflict with kin ties.

Despite the physical and economic pressures to leave, the average modern man does not move very far from his closest relatives. And if non-family factors were removed, it seems clear that most modern men and women would settle down within easy access to their kin. This does not mean that they want to live in the same household with either set of parents. The neolocal norm in modern societies forbids that except in hardship cases. But the "new" household of a newly-married couple does not have to be remote from both sets of parents. The ideal from the standpoint of kin ties alone is to live close enough to primary kin so that contact can be easily maintained.

TABLE 7-6   Propinquity of Husbands and Wives to Closest Kin

LOCATION	Parents	KIN Age-Near Sibling	Best-Known Cousin
Same city	35%	29%	20%
Within 100 miles	25	23	28
Within adjacent states	21	20	23
Elsewhere	19	28	29
Total	100%	100%	100%
Number of respondents	444	697	682

Adapted from Adams (1968):38, 100, 143. Source: White men and women married 20 years or less, Greensboro, North Carolina. Adjacent states included North and South Carolina and Virginia.

Table 7-6 shows the geographical distribution of the close kin of a mixed group of married men and women in a southern U. S. city. Although only one third lived in the same city with their parents, a majority lived within 100 miles (or two or three hours' drive). The table also shows that more remote kin lived somewhat farther away. Yet perhaps the surprising feature of the table is not the decrease in propinquity with decreased kinship, but rather the fact that even as remote a relationship as the best-known cousin was found within a 100-mile radius almost as frequently as the age-nearest sibling. Thus not only primary kin (parents and siblings), but even secondary kin were fairly accessible.

Studies in other cities and countries show essentially the same picture. Generally speaking, married couples prefer to establish their independent homes within either daily or weekend driving distance of their closest kin.

The Matrilocal Tendency   The second question is not so easily answered. If we examine which relatives are closest—whether the husband's or wife's—the answer is not always the same. In some studies, a patrilocal tendency appears, but it is rarely strong. More often, a matrilocal preference emerges and the magnitude of that preference (while never overwhelming) is somewhat larger.

TABLE 7-7   Matrilocality and Patrilocality of Newly-Married Couples Living With or Near One Set of Parents

	PROXIMITY	
	Same Household	Same Neighborhood
Patrilocal (husband's family)	35%	39%
Matrilocal (wife's family)	65	61
Total	100%	100%
Number of couples	383	111

Adapted from Rosser and Harris (1965):250, 253. Source: Newly-married couples in Swansea, Wales, who were living with parents or near only one set of parents. Those living in the neighborhood of both parents or outside the neighborhood of either set of parents have been eliminated. Due to a housing shortage, a majority of couples lived in the same house with relatives.

Table 7-7 portrays a Welsh community with a marked matrilocal preference. The table is limited to couples who lived with or near one set of parents, but not near both. As evidence of their general proximity to relatives, it should be noted that as many couples lived in the same neighborhood with both sets of parents as in the husband's family's neighborhood. My purpose now is to examine which set of parents is chosen in circumstances when both sets cannot be equally close. Under those circumstances, these Welsh newly-married couples more often chose to live in the neighborhood of the wife's family— or even in the same house with them. While the difference was not great, the matrilocal preference was especially strong when couples lived in the same house.

In primitive and feudal societies, the greatest point of strain in patrilocal extended families is the conflict between mother-in-law and daughter-in-law who must share the same housekeeping role. However, the system requires those two women to make the best out of the situation because there are urgent reasons why father and son need to live together. With industrialization, those masculine priorities fall away. Father and son work for separate companies and are away from home all day. The only adults who are thrown together in a composite household are the two women. So it is that the intrinsic strain between mother-in-law and daughter-in-law acts as a barrier to the formation of patrilocal households except where no alternative is available. Other things equal, contemporary couples almost always choose to live with the wife's parents. After all, mother and daughter have shared the same house, the same menus, and the same housekeeping operations ever since the daughter was a little girl. To bring the groom into this already-established household introduces no new personnel into the intergenerational housekeeping team. The work load increases, to be sure, but mother and daughter can be expected to team up effectively in meeting it. But when a new bride moves in with her mother-in-law, the clash of domestic methods can be expected to provoke chronic tension. Hence it seems that the patrilocal exceptions in Table 7-7 were occasioned more by differential space and economic resources than by preference for that arrangement.

Although Table 7-7 is limited to newly-married couples, the same matrilocal tendency appears throughout the family life cycle. In Chapter 9 we will see that even couples who move away from home tend to pull their parents after them when the latter reach retirement, widowhood, and senility. At that time, a new reason arises for moving in with a married daughter rather than a son. The daughter's affectional ties will make it easier to provide the intimate nursing care which is liable to be needed by old people in their declining years. For a daughter-in-law to have to empty bed pans would be more embarrassing to both generations. Both would sense the strain of what might literally be called "un-familiarity" (*i.e.,* not members of the same family). Such strain spoils the atmosphere of love and emotional security which is treasured by those whose grip on life is slipping. There is a tragedy for both generations in a patrilocal termination of life, but for an old man or woman to be cared for by one's own daughter on one's deathbed is at least the nicest way to go.

The preceding discussion has assumed that families can choose between sons and daughters or between the husband's parents and the wife's parents whenever doubling up is necessary. In exceptional cases where no alternative is available, patrilocality may be accepted more positively. For example, Townsend (1957) found that women who had lost their own mothers often were glad to move in with or to live near their husbands' mothers because they could be mother-substitutes. For these women, a mother-in-law was preferable to no mother at all. Similarly, if an elderly couple had sons but no daughters, Townsend found that at least one of those sons normally remained at home or nearby in order that he and his wife could provide the parents with the desired care and companionship. The more urgent the need, the greater the willingness of married sons to respond. Townsend found that this exceptional patrilocalism was most common when the husband's mother had lost her husband and was all alone save for the companionship which a son and his wife could supply.

Although some sociologists would recommend matrilocality for contemporary societies whenever neolocal existence is impossible, this norm is not explicitly recognized by contemporary societies. Therefore it seems preferable to call it a tendency rather than a rule. Families stumble into this arrangement partly out of unconscious anticipation of potential trouble with patrilocal arrangements, but mostly as a result of stronger matrilineal ties, the same ties which determine a matrilineal bias in kinship interaction after marriage.

When family lineages are traced for three generations in modern societies, it is found that family members rarely remain in the same community. But in those cases where three-generational lineages can be found within the same community, the matrilineal tendency is accentuated by the dual links between generations. For example, in Minneapolis and St. Paul, Aldous and Hill (1965) found more than twice as many pure matrilineages (grandmother–mother–daughter) as patrilineages. Cross-sex lineages, as might be expected, were intermediate between those extremes in frequency. The larger the number of generations through which residence is traced, the more the matrilineal tendency is likely to be accentuated.

KINSHIP LATERALITY

Many of the factors which determine the residential location of family units with or near one set of relatives influence kinship interaction patterns across greater distances. To live together is to interact most frequently. To live nearby is to make frequent interaction possible but not inevitable. To live outside the neighborhood is to free interaction from the constraints imposed by propinquity.

In this section we will be concerned primarily with interaction under freedom of choice. However, in premodern societies, the concept of interaction includes a wide range of patterns, some of them obligatory. Such questions as who may or must marry whom are often determined by kinship ties in such societies. Hence, this section will be concerned with ways in which kinship determines both involuntary and voluntary interaction, with the exception of where people live.

Our focus will be on the comparative influence of the husband's and wife's kin. The question is *which* partner's kin are the focus of interaction? "Which side are you on, brother?" is the meaning of the concept of kinship laterality. Nor is this just a question of quantitative distinctions. If the nature or quality of interaction with one set of kin differs from that with the other side, that too is relevant. So the basic question may be formulated: How does interaction with different sets of kin vary, and more particularly how does interaction with the husband's kin differ from that with the wife's relatives?

Differential Interaction in Premodern Societies

Just as premodern societies often assign residence to one set of relatives, they also utilize kinship as a basis for prescribing other forms of interaction. The prescriptions may be either positive or negative. With some relatives, interaction is compulsory; with others, taboo, though such societies are seldom indifferent to the fact of kinship. Only with nonrelated persons are such societies sufficiently unconcerned to allow unrestricted choice.

Marriage Taboos   At the beginning of the family cycle, kinship universally determines who may not marry whom. In every known society some kind of kinship taboo specifies who is too closely related to be eligible for marriage. The common element in incest taboos is that whoever is considered most closely related is *ipso facto* defined as ineligible.

The precise content of the taboo varies from society to society. Primary kin in the sense of one's parents, siblings, and children, are always taboo in general (though occasional societies have allowed a limited number of exceptions without abandoning the rule). The variability comes beyond the nuclear family. Generally speaking, those who share a common household are ineligible. Cousins in an extended family are normally prohibited from marrying. (Although not formulated into a rule, it is interesting to note that boys and girls raised in the same utopian community seldom marry one another, preferring partners from other communities, *e.g.,* from other Israeli kibbutzim or from other Hutterite colonies in North America.)

Beyond the immediate household, incest taboos gradually disappear as the kin ties become more remote. For example, first cousins are taboo more often than second cousins. But sheer biological proximity of kinship is less important than functional proximity. Kin who belong to the same kinship organization are likely to be forbidden to intermarry, whereas equally close kin who belong to the unimportant side of the family may be allowed to marry.

The function of the incest taboo seems to be chiefly to preserve harmony among kin who must either live together or at least cooperate closely. Competition within the group for sexual favors and affectional preeminence would create dangerous tensions. Any group which depends for survival and prosperity on the undifferentiated loyalty of its members can hardly afford to allow the favoritism which would be involved if two members of the group paired off in the intimacy of sex and marriage.

To be sure, the husband and wife who are the center of the nuclear family have such a special relationship but that relationship did not represent a withdrawal from the family but the recruitment of an outsider as an addition to the family. Because the incoming spouse is an outsider, marriage does not alter the existing set of relationships within the family.

Incestuous marriage, by contrast, not only creates potential jealousy among the remaining members of the family but introduces conflicting relationships into the family. To the child of an incestuous father–daughter marriage, the father would be at once father and grandfather. Among the African Nuer, Evans-Pritchard (1951) reported that marriage prohibitions were seen as useful because "They prevent confusion between one relationship and another and the contradictions such confusion would cause between the patterns of behavior in which the relationships are expressed. . . . Were marriage with the wife's sister permitted, to the child of it the mother's sister would also be the father's wife" (p. 46). To us, such confusion might not seem disastrous, but to an African tribe which prescribes very different behavior in dealing with one's mother and one's aunt, the confusion could be serious indeed.

Marriage Prescriptions At first glance it seems strange that kinship should ever prescribe in favor of marrying relatives in view of what has just been said about the confusion such marriages cause. Nevertheless, some premodern societies have such prescriptions. They are seldom as rigidly enforced as incest taboos. More often they are merely preferences. Nevertheless, the apparent violation of my interpretation of incest taboos needs to be reckoned with.

Easiest to understand are prescriptions favoring the marriage of close in-laws when entering second marriages either after losing the first spouse or in addition to the first. In patrilocal, patrilineal systems, the levirate (marriage of a man's widow to his younger brother) is a logical solution to a difficult problem. Goode (1963) pointed out that in Arabic Islam, a widow could not be left unmarried because she needed a man to protect her and take responsibility for her. She could return to her own family, but in that event she would have to leave her children behind (since they belonged to the male lineage). The only alternative was for her to marry someone to take her husband's place. If that could be someone from the husband's family (who could therefore keep mother and children together), the younger brother would be the logical candidate. Moreover, widow and brother-in-law would already be well known to each other, so adjustment problems for the new marriage would be minimized.

The value of this mechanism for family stability is suggested by Ackerman's study of a sample of societies from the Human Relations Area Files. Every one of nine societies practicing the levirate had a low divorce rate, in contrast to only 27 percent of 22 societies without it (1963). He believed the levirate contributed to marital solidarity by guaranteeing the woman a permanent place in her husband's lineage, severing radically her ties to her own lineage. By contrast, a woman whose ties with her own kin remained strong was more apt to be torn between conflicting loyalties to her husband and her family of childhood.

Many of the reasons for the levirate and for the matrilocal bias in contemporary residence patterns are similar to the reasons for sororal polygyny. If a man is to add a second wife, many societies encourage him to marry the younger sister of his first wife. This simplifies negotiations between families—no new in-law ties have to be formed. It simplifies relationships between the two wives because they have already worked out an older sister–younger sister relationship in childhood. And the already established kin ties between the man and his sister-in-law and between his children and their aunt simplify the new wife's entrance into the household.

More difficult to explain is the preference in some societies for marriage with a relative not by marriage but by blood. The most commonly preferred spouse is one's cross cousin: either one's father's sister's child or one's mother's brother's child. One key to cross-cousin marriages is that they require marriage outside the lineage. Such societies would forbid a man to marry his patrilineal parallel cousin (his father's brother's daughter) for that would be too incestuous, bringing people together from within the same lineage. But in a patrilineal society, matrilineal kin are sufficiently distant functionally to raise fewer incestuous feelings. Moreover, matrilineal kin in a patrilineal society are particularly "nice." Unlike members of one's own lineage toward whom one must show respect because those are powerful individuals, matrilineal kin are like modern grandparents: permissive and doting. Whereas patrilineal kin are too powerful to be loved, matrilineal kin are particularly lovable.

Although cousin marriages encroach on the incest taboo, they have the advantage in familistic societies of presenting the marriage arrangers with known quantities in family background and with equal status since members of the same kin network are likely to be similarly placed in the social structure. Anthropologist Robert J. Smith commented in a personal communication that cousin-marriage in Japan was "one device by which both families to the match could begin negotiations with some feeling of security about background and prospects for future interrelations." And Beardsley, Hall and Ward cited a Japanese expression that cousin-marriage is the "safest way to make sure the marriage is even." They found that more than 10 percent of the marriages in one Japanese village involved cousins and stressed the adjustment advantages of couples who were sure to be from similar backgrounds: "Cousins usually have less adjustment to make in a new household; so people still marry cousins if they think their own house is especially troublesome to adjust to" (1959: 323).

That this preference for cousins produces greater marital solidarity is suggested in Ackerman's (1963) study of 62 primitive societies. Societies which permitted marriage with first or second cousins had lower divorce rates than societies which forbade marriage with cousins. Ackerman interpreted this as a reflection not simply of greater compatibility between partners from similar backgrounds, but of the supportive influence of common kin (whereas couples with separate kin groups may be pulled apart by their "disjunctive affiliations").

The influence of kinship on future marriages is foreshadowed in pre-marital relationships. If a society has already prescribed whom one's next marriage partner is likely to be, this encourages a quasi-marital relationship with that person. In India, Goode (1963) reported that in areas where the levirate was customary, the relationship between a woman and her husband's younger brother was particularly close. Toward her husband, the patriarchal norm required her to show too much respect to feel very intimate. But the younger brother's closeness in age and nonauthoritative position combined with his propinquity within the household made him a source of solace and tender feeling. So close did this relationship become that Goode found it a frequent focus of extramarital (or should we say premarital?) sexual relations.

Congenial Relatives   In skewed kinship systems which emphasize patrilineal kin more than they do the matrilineage (or vice versa), whichever set of kin dominates tends to be treated with greater deference and less affection than the other. The same factors which make a man prefer his matrilineal relatives as a source of eligible marriage partners also make them preferable for in-formal companionship. Three different patrilineal societies in as many regions of the world may be cited to illustrate this principle.

On the South Seas island of Tikopia, little children run to their maternal relatives as an indulgent refuge to escape punishment at home (Homans, 1950). Similarly when the mother's nurturant behavior toward her son must be ended at puberty because of sex taboos against contact between women and their adolescent sons, the mother's brother takes over her "maternal" role while the father intensifies his disciplinary role.

Among the Rajputs of India, Minturn and Hitchcock (1963) found that running to maternal relatives was not confined to children: "When a Rajput is in such serious trouble that he wishes to leave his family and village, he is very apt to go to his mother's brother" (p. 239). Moreover, friendly relation-ships with maternal kin extended even to sons-in-law. Rajput wives had periodic opportunities to return home to live with their families. Since custom required wives to be chaperoned on such expeditions, the husband normally accompanied her both going and returning. He frequently spent a day or so at her home, visiting with her father and brothers. The comradely, unstrained character of these visits contrasted with the restraint and deference which would have been required had he been at the home of his patrilineal kin.

Among Greek shepherd families, wives similarly visited back home once or twice a year for a number of years after marriage. Campbell (1964) noted that these visits enabled children to establish close friendships with their matri-lineal cousins. When these children grew to maturity, their cousins remained their favorite confidants outside the immediate family. Seventy percent of Campbell's shepherds named a matrilineal cousin as the most intimate and trusted friend. Moreover, these cousins were not only a source of friendship and advice but an important source of financial aid in crises.

The converse of this preference for matrilineal kin is that feared and hated relatives tend to be found on the patrilineal side of patrilineal systems. For instance, Campbell found that "the wicked uncle" was almost always a paternal uncle with whom the father had quarreled and who vented his hostility not only on his brother, but also on his nephews.

Thus we may conclude that members of powerful lineages tend to have "authority-tinged" relationships with each another. Conversely, that side of the kinship system with whom one is merely related, but to whom one is not subordinated, is the side on which ties of affection are uncontaminated by problems of power. In general, then, the differential role of kin in unilateral kinship systems introduces qualitative differences into the types of interaction and the types of affect felt toward the two sides.

We should be careful, however, not to infer from this differential congeniality that pre-modern men spent most of their time with their congenial relatives and avoided their respected ones. Quite the opposite was the case. In a patriarchal society, a man and his wife spent most of their time with his family in the tasks of everyday life. Even when the man traveled afar, if his trip was on business, he would depend primarily on patrilateral kin for assistance.

For example, Campbell found that kin supplied the shepherds of the Greek mountains with hospitality unavailable in a region without hostelries. They also supplied inside information in a competitive economic and political system:

> . . . the price that he should ask for his milk, his wool, and animals for slaughter, the intrigues of others with merchants and officials which often vitally affect his own affairs, the ever-pressing problem of where winter pasture is to be found, this is the kind of information a man exchanges with his kinsman or, more rarely, with a close and trusted affine. (1964:38)

A matrilateral kinsman was more to be trusted than an unrelated person, but the natural place to turn on business matters in a patrilateral system was to the men with whom one was most closely involved. Nor was this mutual assistance limited to commercial transactions. Marriage negotiations, too, relied heavily on kinsmen living in the prospective partner's village. Here again, the most valuable assistance was reliable "intelligence" about the girl's chastity, physical vigor, industriousness, and temperament. Not only could kinsmen be trusted to provide more reliable information, but they could also be trusted not to allow others to learn prematurely of the prospective match.

Kinsmen then are extraordinarily useful but "useless" in-laws may be more enjoyable for that very reason.

Differential Interaction in Modern Societies

In many contemporary societies, kin interaction is almost as skewed as in primitive societies, but the reasons are different. Modern societies have no formal kin groups to bias interaction one way or the other. So new reasons must be sought to explain the failure of kinship interaction to be evenly balanced in supposedly bilateral societies.

The Matrilateral Bias   Just as we saw that couples forced to choose between living with the husband's and the wife's parents tend to choose the latter, and as we have seen a preference among families for living closer to the wife's parents than to the husband's, interaction should be expected to focus on those same parents. This is partly a consequence of the matrilocal residential tendency. But data from several studies suggest that even when differential proximity is controlled, the wife's relatives tend to be preferred.

For instance, three times as many of Komarovsky's blue-collar couples celebrated such special occasions as Christmas, Thanksgiving, birthdays, anniversaries and joint vacations with the wife's parents as with the husband's (1964). In East London, Townsend (1957) found that the wife's parents had "first claim" on married couples at such festival times and also for grandchildren visiting. Apparently the husband's parents could not expect to see their son and his family either until after the matrilateral kin had exercised their claims or when the latter were unavailable.

So strong was this norm in the British case that it avoided conflicts to which bilateral systems are potentially exposed. Both husband and wife and the two sets of parents simply took it for granted that the matrilateral kin had priority. In the American case lip-service was paid to an ideal of bilateral equality. When asked, couples almost always said that both sides of the family should be treated equally. Because it violates the ideal norms of modern society, the matrilateral bias in interaction patterns is especially significant, suggesting that powerful social forces intervene between the mental ideal and actual behavior.

One reason for this matrilateral bias is that girls are more dependent than boys on their parents. They spend more time at home, consult their parents more, and are given more attention by their parents. As a result, girls and their parents feel closer to each other than do the girls' brothers and the same parents. The matrilateral emphasis in interaction after marriage is simply an extension of more intensive interaction between the girl and her parents before marriage. No new factor needs to be introduced to explain what is simply a continuation of prior activity.

Contemporary societies vary in the extent to which this matrilateral interaction involves only the female partners (wife and mother) or the male spouses as well. In some cases, the wife does most of the visiting and her contacts with her father seem largely incidental to seeing her mother. Hence, closely related to the matrilateral bias is the specifically feminine bias in modern kinship interaction.

The Feminine Bias   The focal point of contemporary kinship interaction is contact between mother and daughter. These two generally see each other more than any other two relatives. Insofar as other family members are involved in kin interaction, they frequently are responding to initiative exercised by these two women.

This, too, is an extension of an earlier relationship. Just as girls are closer than boys to their parents, they are closer to their mothers than to their fathers. This was expressed by Komarovsky's married women when 62 percent said they felt "close" or "very close" to their mothers but only 34 percent felt that close to their fathers. This special closeness to the mother reflects her central role in raising children and also indicates the special kinship felt by persons who occupy the same role in life.

To play the same role is to have more than a psychological affinity, however. In very tangible ways, mothers and their married daughters assist one another with their housekeeping and child-rearing tasks. In a later section we will see that most of the help modern kin provide is feminine help: baby-sitting, nursing care, help with housework. Even the more psychological help tends to be feminine: exchanging Christmas gifts, writing letters, talking on the telephone, even visiting itself. The latter receives a special assist insofar as women are ladies of leisure and can visit their mothers during the day while their husbands are at work.

Conversely, the removal of the man's work from his home has eliminated most of the basis for masculine help. Whereas a farmer still sees his male kinfolk when they team up for harvesting and barn-raising, urban man has few chores to perform at home and even fewer which require more assistance than his wife could provide. To be sure, some forms of kin assistance involve masculine services, principally the loan or gift of money in financial emergencies. But important as such assistance may be, masculine projects occur infrequently in comparison to feminine activities. In a sense removing the man's occupation from the home has left family life centered around the woman's housekeeping and child-rearing.

Another way in which the mother–daughter relationship is central to contemporary kinship interaction is the way women initiate even the interaction of their husbands or children. Preschool children have no choice but to accompany their mother on visits to her mother. But husbands could refuse to go along if they wanted to. Yet the evidence from American data is clear that most visiting between families is on a family-to-family basis with the husband included. For example, my Detroit study in 1955 found that more than 90 percent of family visits included the husband. The mother–daughter link not only is strong, but also is the foundation on which ties between other family members are established.

Kin ties are most appreciated in crises, and so crisis brings out the greater strength of the feminine ties. For example, when couples are divorced, the wife is apt to return home to live with the parents with whom she has maintained close ties all along. The husband, however, is less likely to move in with his parents since his relationship with them has often atrophied. For example, Geertz found that married sons in Java "tend to drift away emotionally and rarely return home as adults," even after divorce (1961:45).

Finally in old age, human biology introduces another feminine bias into kinship patterns. The fact that women outlive men and that this differential is widened by the tendency of men to marry younger wives leaves old women with a monopoly under precisely those circumstances when kinship interaction is intensified. Many studies show that after the death of the spouse, old people tend to move in with their children or at least to see more of them than they had when the spouse provided companionship. The coupling of this factor with female longevity means that at the very end of the family life cycle, the concluding phase of kinship interaction is heavily feminine in focus.

The Parental Focus To suggest that the central kinship link is between mother and daughter leaves open the question of whether this relationship, too, is asymmetrical. The answer is clearly affirmative. The grand focus of the contemporary kinship system is the maternal grandmother.

This, too, is a continuation of the antecedent pattern of childhood. To visit the mother is to *go home* with the pleasant connotations of returning to the womb. If there are two or more children, the old home is the natural place for reunions with siblings as well as parents. Thus the childhood family tends to be reconstituted on special occasions in the old home place. The maternal grandmother thus supplies the focal point not only for relationships with each child individually, but for all the children (especially the female children) and their children collectively. The whole structure of sibling ties and cousin ties clusters around the grandmother.

In Greensboro, North Carolina, Adams (1968) found a direct relationship between the number of parents who were alive and the proportion of young adults who said that kin generally were "very important" to them. For married women, the proportion rose steadily from 42 percent (those with neither parent alive) to 51 percent (those with a single parent) to 62 percent (those with both parents alive). Men conversely were more apt to say relatives were "unimportant" if they had no parents alive than if they had at least one alive (26 percent versus 14 percent). These differences reflect the importance of parents in the kinship system. They also show, in the data for women, that the mother is not the only parent who matters. To be able to visit with both parents is even more preferred than to visit only the mother. Nevertheless, if one were to have to choose which parent was the center of attention, the answer would unquestionably be the mother.

Insofar as the interaction pattern is an extension of childhood patterns of sharing the same home, that pattern tends to be limited to adjacent generations and their dependent children. Once the grandchildren grow up and have spouses and children of their own, the kinship network begins to reorganize around the new set of grandmothers in the second generation. If grandparents lived forever, it is doubtful that the kin network would be able to ramify indefinitely. Rather it tends to focus at any one time on the range from dependent children up to their grandparents and rarely extends meaningfully all the way to great-grandparents.

The centrality of the parent–child bond becomes most apparent when parents die. Adams found, for example, that the total number of kin known by his young adult respondents shrank from a median of 31 (those with two living parents) to 23 (those who had lost one parent) and to 20 (those who had lost both). The reason why the death of a parent diminishes the number of known kin beyond the loss of the immediate person is that that parent often served as an intermediary link to other relatives. With the death of a parent, ties with that side of the family (the matrilineal or patrilineal kin) tend to weaken. At a later stage in life, Townsend (1957) found that the death of a spouse tended to sever ties with siblings-in-law, especially with those of the opposite sex.

The consequences of the death of parents are especially severe for ties between siblings insofar as they were based on common interaction with the parents. If children have children of their own, the death of parents is the signal for the decentralization of the kin network. The children become new focal points themselves. With their attention focused on their own children and grandchildren, these new heirs to the family presidency can no longer spare the time to get together with siblings who have their own responsibilities to children and grandchildren. Thus sibling ties tend to weaken.

The only exception is for siblings who have no children, especially those who never married. For them the death of the last surviving parent precipitates an intensified dependence on their siblings as the only surviving primary kin. Indeed, if two siblings remain unmarried at that point in life, they turn particularly strongly to each other after the parents' death (Townsend, 1957).

Townsend found that one other aspect of the death of parents sometimes weakened the tie between siblings. If siblings quarreled over who was to inherit the family home or other possessions, this drove the siblings apart. Even if the parents did not own their home, in working-class East London there was often rivalry over who would inherit the right to rent the parents' flat. When housing is scarce, such rights of succession to tenancy can be as serious a source of conflict as inheritance of money or tangible property.

Conversely while parents are still alive, they often serve as mediators in disputes among siblings, healing breaches which otherwise might have fragmented the sibling group. Campbell (1964) found that even if brothers had publicly insulted one another (the most unforgivable offense among Greek shepherds), parents might be able to bring the warring brothers back together.

The converse of the special importance of the mother–daughter tie is that the husband tends to be involved primarily in his wife's network and to become estranged from his own relatives. Townsend (1957) found that the man's ties to his own siblings were particularly vulnerable after the death of his parents. If both partners had surviving siblings, the wife's preference for her own siblings led her to express hostility to the husband's siblings. Most of Townsend's working-class British husbands surrendered to their wives' preferences and antipathies by dropping their own siblings in favor of the wives'. Only when the wife had no accessible siblings did she take a more positive attitude toward the husband's siblings. Especially if he had sisters and she didn't (and doubly so if those sisters were widowed), the wife might come to see more of his sisters than the husband did himself.

Normally, then, parents remain, until they die, the focus of the kin network for their children and for their unmarried grandchildren. However, whenever members of this network fail to become parents themselves, they are forced to turn to the next closest alternatives—their siblings—as the central features of their kin network.

Kin Selection   A term like "forced" must be used carefully in referring to modern kinship interaction. When no relative of a particular type is available, individuals are forced to turn elsewhere. But whereas the absence of a relative necessarily prevents interaction, the presence of a relative does not compel interaction, although it may predispose people to take advantage of the opportunity. Generally speaking, modern man prefers to associates with relatives rather than friends, especially on the most important and most familistic occasions. But *which* relatives he associates with depends only partly on biological and geographical propinquity. In effect, the network of kin provides a "field of eligibles" from among whom a man can select those he will interact with in a fashion analogous to mate-selection (Blood, 1970). And just as marriage partners are chosen on the basis of personal affection and compatibility, so kin "partners" are chosen on the same bases.

TABLE 7-8 Frequency of Interaction with Parents Living Outside the Community, by Affectional Closeness and Value Consensus

FREQUENCY OF INTERACTION	*FEELS CLOSE TO PARENTS*		
	To Both	*To One*	*To Neither Parent*
At least once a week	26%	19%	7%
2–3 times per month	54	45	26
Once a month	17	29	39
2–11 times per year	2	7	16
Less often	0	0	13
Total	99%	100%	101%
	VALUE CONSENSUS WITH PARENTS		
	With Both	*With One*	*With Neither Parent*
At least once a week	30%	14%	7%
2–3 times per month	54	49	19
Once a month	14	32	41
2–11 times per year	2	5	19
Less Often	0	0	15
Total	100%	100%	101%
Number of men	44	37	27

Adapted from Adams (1968):75. Source: Young married men whose parents lived outside Greensboro, North Carolina. Interaction might be face-to-face, by telephone or by letter. Value consensus represented agreement on ideas and opinions about things considered "really important in life."

Table 7-8 shows a close relationship between affection for parents and interaction with them. The more a man liked his parents, the more he made an effort to see them even though they lived outside the community. (If they lived in the same city, almost everyone saw his parents frequently, no matter how cold he felt toward them.) If they lived too far away (more than 250 miles), it became difficult to see them no matter how much he might wish to. Geographical location was a constraining force either when proximity was so great that contact was unavoidable or so remote that it was almost impossible. In the intervening range, freedom of choice was available and the man's subjective feelings governed his behavior.

The bottom half of Table 7-8 shows that consensus on values was even more closely related to frequency of contact than feelings of affection. Men who agreed with both parents on substantially all the things they considered really important were especially apt to contact them at least once a week whereas those who shared no values with either parent were apt to contact them only once a year or less.

Presumably value consensus is an important form of compatibility between people and determines how close they feel and how much they want to associate with each other. If consensus is lacking, not only is a potential basis of solidarity missing, but divergent values will be a potential source of conflict. The easiest way to avoid conflict is to avoid contact.

Table 7-8 suggests, then, that Greensboro married men chose how often to contact their parents on the basis of personal liking and mutual compatibility, especially under circumstances where moderate but surpassable barriers intervened. Presumably such factors would have even more sharply affected contact with remote kin. Indeed Adams found that married men and women were more selective with their nearest-aged sibling and closest cousin than with parents. Moreover, his female respondents felt so great an obligation to keep in touch with parents that they continued to do so regardless of their emotional feelings or value discrepancies. Only with kin other than parents did those women show the same selectivity which men showed even toward parents.

This gradient of obligation also expressed itself in relation to geographical propinquity. The high level of obligatory contact which Greensboro men maintained with parents living in the same city did not extend to siblings. Both men and women who were affectionally alienated from their siblings discriminated against them in deciding how to spend their leisure time despite the fact that they lived within the narrow confines of a relatively small city.

In general, then, contemporary men and women exercise freedom of choice in deciding which kin to interact with and how often. Selectivity is greatest with remote kin, with men rather than women, and over intermediate distances which offer appreciable but not insuperable barriers. Conversely, contemporary kinship interaction most nearly resembles the obligatoriness of pre-modern societies when kin live so close together that interaction is practically unavoidable or when kin have established such close dependency relations (as in the case of women and their parents) that interaction has become habitual. This combination of male choosiness and female involvement with relatives contributes to the matrilateral bias in contemporary kinship patterns.

KIN AS SUPPLIERS OF RESOURCES

Although kin interaction in modern societies is based mostly on free choice, that doesn't mean it consists only of pure sociability. To belong to a kin network is to exchange many resources besides love and companionship. Even those could be called forms of help, especially in the case of widows, for example. But kin supply far more tangible forms of help according to the old familial formula: from each according to his ability, to each according to his need.

Practical Help

In primitive and feudal societies, kin depend heavily on one another for assistance in staying alive and making economic progress. In modern societies, most families depend on an unrelated employer for subsistence and even in emergencies have alternative institutional resources like banks and welfare agencies to which they can turn. Nevertheless, even when formal institutions are theoretically available, kin often come to the rescue first, and for many of the more intimate services required by families, formal agencies may not be available or may charge high fees. For such reasons, families often turn first to relatives when their resources for coping with life are exhausted, and even in less critical circumstances, kin often volunteer their services.

TABLE 7-9   Help Exchanged with Parents

| | DIRECTION OF HELP | |
TYPE OF HELP	From Parents	To Parents
Help during illness	46%	47%
Financial aid	47	15
Child care	21	4
Valuable gifts	18	3

Adapted from Sussman (1959):336. Source: 53 middle-class and 27 working-class families in two areas of Cleveland, Ohio. Reciprocal percentages had not received or given the specified form of help.

Table 7-9 shows that almost half the families studied in Cleveland had received financial aid and help from their parents during illness. Conversely, an equal proportion of parents had been aided by their children when ill, though far fewer had received any other forms of aid. This difference between illness-help and other types reflects the fact that illness strikes all families, old or young, whereas most other needs are concentrated in the younger generation. Few parents have children young enough for their married children to help with, but grandparents relieved of their own children are correspondingly available to baby-sit with their grandchildren. Financial aid and valuable gifts tend to flow from the older generation to the younger partly for the same reason. Parents whose children have left home have a smaller dependency burden than married children whose family size is at its peak. At the same time, an older man's income is normally higher than a young man's, and the former's inventory of equipment for family living (house, car and appliances) is complete. The older generation is abundantly supplied with money just when the younger generation is most pinched—and money flows downward accordingly.

To some extent, illness is unpredictable. But the loss of the wife's resources to the family during the time when she bears a child is a predictable hazard. And since few husbands have either the skill or the time to manage the home alone (especially if there are other small children), kin are regularly called upon to resolve this problem. Siddiqui (1962) found that most Detroit wives received such assistance from their own mothers and/or from their mothers-in-law (especially if their own mother was not available).

Although all forms of help in Sussman's sample were received most from parents, siblings were a secondary resource of considerable importance. In this case, however, the flow of resources tended to be more symmetrical since siblings faced the same problems at about the same time. However, the very fact of simultaneous need limits siblings' ability to respond to one another.

At the end of the life cycle, the flow of help tends to be reversed. In old age, illness strikes more often than earlier in life and nursing care is more urgently needed. For couples without adequate resources, retirement may create financial dependency. According to the principle of need, help then flows "uphill," reversing the life-long pattern which began with the initiation of the parent–child relationship many years before.

Although help normally flows downward from generation to generation, the reason behind this unidirectional flow is that parents normally have more resources than children. The basic principle is that resources flow from kin who are most amply endowed to kin who have the greatest need. One basis for estimating the resource-status of the generations is to look at their comparative social status.

TABLE 7-10   Tangible Gifts Given Each Other by Young Married Men and Their Parents, by Comparative Social Status

| Tangible gifts | COMPARATIVE SOCIAL STATUS | | |
Given 3+/year	Parents Higher	Equal	Sons Higher
By parents	40%	28%	29%
By sons	20	14	33
Net difference	+20%	+14%	− 4%
Number of cases	10	119	52

Adapted from Adams (1968):57. Source: Young married white men in Greensboro, North Carolina. Reciprocal percentages of sons and their parents had given less than three tangible gifts per year to each other. Social status was classified by occupations into blue collar and white collar categories.

Table 7-10 shows that when parents and their adult children had the same social status, help flowed in the normal way from parents to children. For children with lower status than their parents the parental resource advantage was accentuated and the downward flow increased to mitigate the children's distress. Conversely, when the children's social status was higher than the parents', the children's giving rose so markedly that parents received more than they gave.

In households where the husband works and the wife does not, men are the chief suppliers of money and women of time and energy in kinship exchanges. Rosser and Harris found that where services rather than goods were the currency exchanged, "in nine cases out of ten the tasks concerned are performed by women—and this of course is not surprising since we are dealing with such things as domestic nursing, child-rearing, house-cleaning, washing, shopping, and the whole gamut of household affairs and skills. It is the world of the mothers' union" (1965:230). Another way of saying the same thing is that most of the tasks normally done around the house are done by the wife. So if an outside helper is needed, it is natural to import another expert of the same sex.

The tighter the supply of money, however, the less possible it is for families to purchase services on the market. Therefore poor families even in the richest country in the world still supplement the normally feminine exchange of services with masculine services. For example, Komarovsky's blue-collar husbands "frequently" exchanged such services as "house painting, carpentry, repair, laying linoleum, building partitions, and help in moving." All these except the last are fairly technical in nature so the help provided by relatives is probably shoddier than professional experts would supply. Nevertheless, when a family is sufficiently poor, the help of a jack-of-all-trades is better than no help at all, so kin exchange is appreciated. Even so, it is important to recognize that for most families repairs, improvements, or moves are only an occasional crisis, whereas the services women provide are more nearly everyday affairs. Therefore even in the poorest families, the balance of help is still heavily feminine.

Reciprocation Systems of exchange by definition require some sort of reciprocation. Assistance to kin is no exception. We have already seen that assistance among siblings tends to be bilateral and that the same holds true for intergenerational help during illness.

Townsend (1957) found that even old people who he assumed would only receive help actually gave many forms of help in return. Although aging women had to surrender their shopping first and then the heavy cleaning and washing, they clung to their cooking longest. This meant that they could prepare meals and baby-sit for their daughters while the latter went shopping for them. Such services could be given most easily when elderly women lived with relatives, but they were also performed by mothers who lived nearby.

We have also seen, however, that most forms of help during most of the life cycle flow unidirectionally from parents to children. How, then, can children reciprocate? The two main answers are that reciprocation need not be in kind and that it need not be to the same person.

The very fact that resources flow down the family tree means that the same couple who receive help from their parents while the couple are young must expect in turn to aid their own children after the latter marry. Aid in this sense is like a family estate handed down from generation to generation. The heirs are not expected to repay their ancestors directly, but they have an obligation to their benefactors to preserve the inheritance intact for succeeding generations. Parents who aid their children with substantial wedding presents and subsequent assistance are happy in the thought that the children in turn will do the same for *their* children a generation later.

Unlike bank loans which must be repaid in cash, kin help can be repaid in other forms. We have seen that grandmothers baby-sit in return for getting their shopping done. But repayment need not be so tangible. Sussman (1953a) found that middle-class parents in New Haven expected affection from their children in return for helping them tangibly. Not that they were trying to bribe their children to get affection, but that they were satisfied to receive affection as their only return.

The transaction was not a simple exchange of affection for tangible help. The parents, after all, bestowed affection as well as summer cottages on their children. But they would have been hurt to be spurned by their children after their double generosity. Normally children could be expected to be spontaneously affectionate under these circumstances. But if they were tempted not to be, the parents hoped their help would overcome that temptation and guarantee their affection. Rarely was that a conscious thought. The parents helped their children because they loved them, and assumed that the children would love them in return.

Affection, then, is a latent rather than an intended consequence of parental help. And parents who receive that affection need no other compensation.

Marital Benefits   The previous discussion suggests that those who help their relatives (especially parents who help their children) normally enjoy both the satisfaction of being helpful and of being loved. What about the children? Do they resent being kept in a dependent position? Do they wish their parents would let them grow up and "stand on their own two feet"? Do they quarrel over in-law meddling in their marriage? Although individual cases of such negative reactions can be found, Figure 7-1 suggests that the impact of kin helpfulness on marital solidarity is more apt to be positive than negative.

Figure 7-1 doesn't give the last word on the subject since it gives no direct evidence of the husband's satisfaction and deals only with the number of types of help ever received, not with the frequency of help. Moreover, it does not specify which relatives gave that help. Perhaps there are hidden sources of stress in such unreported directions, though that seems doubtful.

For one thing, most of the things that relatives supply are needed. So without that help, the marriage would be strained anyway. Insofar as help is a response to need, it apparently reduces strain on the marriage more than it creates it.

For another, help comes mostly from relatives of the person helped: patrilateral help to the husband, matrilateral help to the wife. Hence even if in-law help were resented, it seldom represents the dominant pattern.

Thirdly, the paper on which Figure 7-1 is based gives other data which imply that husbands as well as wives respond positively to help from kin: (1) The larger the number of types of help received, the less segregated the role structure of the marriage. This means that husbands with helpful kin and in-laws are more helpful to their wives around the house. (2) The more help received, the more often the husband tells his wife about things that went on during the day. This means that helpful kin are associated with communicative husbands. (3) The more helpful the kin, the more often the wife tells her troubles to her husband. This suggests that wives not only receive more help from their kin, but more psychological help from their husbands in a pervasive pattern of responsiveness to need. No wonder, then, such wives are generally the most satisfied. With this multiple evidence it seems possible to generalize that marital solidarity is strongest where kin networks provide the widest variety of types of help.

Family Security   If husbands and wives feel closer when they are surrounded by helpful relatives, it seems likely that their sense of solidarity extends to the whole nuclear family. Cushioned against unexpected emergencies by the readiness of their relatives to come to their rescue, couples are blessed with a free insurance policy.

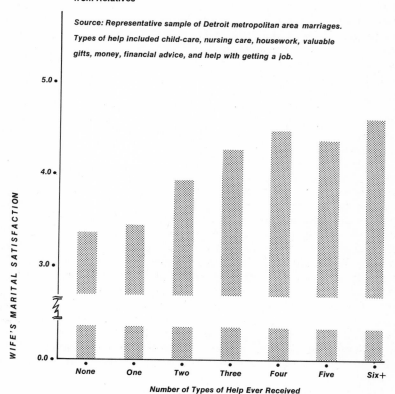

FIGURE 7-1.   Marital Satisfaction by Number of Types of Help Ever Received
from Relatives

Source: Representative sample of Detroit metropolitan area marriages.
Types of help included child-care, nursing care, housework, valuable
gifts, money, financial advice, and help with getting a job.

Adapted from Blood (1969a):182.

When couples bring children into such an environment, they can trust that no matter what disasters occur, the children will be well cared for. As in extended families with built-in parent-substitutes available in case of the premature death of one or both parents, kin networks offer both concerned personnel and practical resources to couples who encounter difficulties in rearing children.

Given this security, couples can afford to extend themselves further in deciding how many children they can afford to have. They need not set aside so much money for formal life insurance or to tide themselves over temporary financial reverses. Other things being equal, couples with the most helpful kin can be expected to bear the most children.

Figure 7-2 gives one test of this hypothesis. It deals with the availability of mothers under very limited circumstances, namely their willingness to help when a child is born. Having a mother or two come to replace the incapacitated one not only helps immediately, but presumably sets a precedent for continuing help. If we had a full picture of not just mothers but all relatives and all types of help, we would discover an even greater impact of kin resources on willingness to risk having children.

Shelter for Old Age   We have seen that newly-married couples without alternative housing are apt to settle down with their parents. Although most couples see this as a temporary arrangement and move into their own quarters as soon as possible, if housing is sufficiently short or the family's financial resources limited, the joint arrangement may be maintained indefinitely. When Rosser and Harris (1965) examined the living arrangements of old people in Swansea, Wales, they found that half the old people who lived with relatives were simply continuing an arrangement which began when the junior couple moved in at marriage. Even when the joint arrangement did not begin until the parents reached old age, there were just as many cases in which children had moved back into the parental home as in the opposite direction. This heavy emphasis on doubling up in the parental home shows that parents were often assisting their children or that the relationship was mutually beneficial. In only one third of these cases was joint living solely for the benefit of the aged family members.

The main turning point in the direction of movement and in the emphasis on the beneficiary party is the death of a parent. As long as both parents survive, they tend to maintain their old home intact and use it not only for permanent shelter to needy children, but for temporary accommodations on briefer visits and for family festivals such as Christmas. Shanas and her associates (1968) found that in Britain, Denmark, and the U.S.A., widowed (and divorced) parents tended to move in with their children. Moreover, single old people almost as often moved in with a sibling.

To provide a refuge for an elderly parent or sibling who might otherwise have to live alone is a very practical way of helping. It may also be at least as valuable a psychological benefit. In any case, we shall see shortly that patterns of residential assistance in old age exactly parallel the patterns of nonresidential companionship, suggesting that there is a close parallel between these two kinds of resources supplied to older relatives.

FIGURE 7-2.   Expected Number of Children, by Number of Mothers and Mothers-in-Law
Who Help after Childbirth

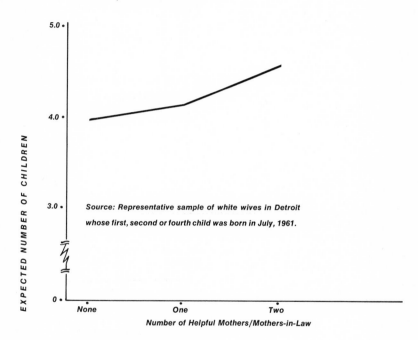

Source: Representative sample of white wives in Detroit
whose first, second or fourth child was born in July, 1961.

Adapted from Siddiqui (1962):26.

Protection Against Institutionalization Regardless of whether families open their homes to relatives or simply help them in their own homes, the kinship network is a bulwark against either extramural or intramural institutional care. Studies of institutional treatment suggest that it rarely compares favorably with home care and frequently is depressingly inadequate. In the great majority of cases old people seem to prefer to avoid institutional treatment or to postpone it as long as possible. Yet in the aged persons' declining years, it becomes steadily less possible to function without outside help.

A choice eventually must be made whether to turn to institutional care or to call for help from relatives. The choice is seldom difficult for the old people. Almost always known kin are preferred to unknown professionals. But kin are not always available, and in the event that they are not, institutionalization is forced on the isolated minority.

TABLE 7-11 Parental Status of Old Persons With and Without Institutional Care

MARITAL/PARENTAL STATUS	None	INSTITUTIONAL CARE		
		Visiting Homemaker	*Geriatric Hospital*	*Municipal Homes for the Aged*
Married or widowed				
With daughter	71%	54%	39%	29%
With sons only	11	16	19	18
Without surviving children	9	18	21	27
Unmarried	9	11	22	27
Total	100%	100%	100%	100%
Number of Old People	203	464	280	188

Adapted from Townsend (1957):192. Source: Selected categories of old people (men 65+ and women 60+) in a working-class East London neighborhood. Those with no institutional care were either living independently or living with kin. Surviving children were not necessarily geographically near.

Table 7-11 deals only with surviving children, disregarding other relatives who may come to the rescue when children are not available. A complete census of the community would have been more useful in showing the consequences of the presence or absence of children for elderly parents. However, the marked differences in the composition of groups receiving different kinds of institutional care suggest how crucially children affect their parents' ability to survive without outside help.

The table suggests the overwhelming value of daughters in giving parents whatever help they need without turning to the social services or to social institutions. To be useful, however, daughters must live with or near their parents. Townsend reported that a substantial proportion of those in the geriatric hospital and in homes for the aged whose daughters were still alive were unable to benefit from them because they lived too far away. Surviving sons, by contrast, are less useful because they are less able or willing to perform the housekeeping and nursing tasks their parents may need. Even when sons are married, their wives are apt to have responsibilities to their own mothers, and the family is apt to live in the wife's home neighborhood rather than the husband's.

Worse than having only sons, however, is to have no surviving children at all. Indeed married or widowed old people without surviving children suffer a fate strikingly similar to that of old men and women who never married. Both types of "childless" individuals make up a sizeable proportion of the institutionalized population, several times as large as would be expected from their proportion in the general elderly population.

The visiting homemaker service deserves special comment. This is a community service which sends a woman into the home to perform house-keeping functions which the inhabitants are unable to perform. In a sense, the visitor might be called a "daughter-substitute" or a supplementary "daughter." She performs services similar to those which daughters and daughters-in-law ordinarily perform. In Townsend's research, she often saved old people with-out surviving daughters from institutionalization. As a socially supplied quasi-relative, the visiting homemaker represented a nice compromise between the preferred care of one's own daughter and the dreaded alternative of institution-alization.

In general then relatives, and more especially daughters, offer their aging parents refuge either by caring for them in the same household or by supple-menting their skills sufficiently to enable them to maintain their own home without outside unrelated "interference."

Psychological Help

When practical help is reciprocated with affection and attention, kin supply psychological and social resources to one another. But these "soft currencies" are not merely an alternative way of "repaying" practical assistance. They are the main element in contemporary kin transactions.

We discussed in a preceding section the emphasis on voluntary choice in contemporary kin interaction. Under certain conditions that voluntary inter-action becomes so valuable to the participants that it is properly labelled a resource in its own right.

Confidantes Most women (and some men) want a confidante outside of marriage with whom they can discuss their marriage problems in particular and deeply meaningful experiences in general. The lower the social status of the family, the less the wife can afford a professional consultant and the less apt she is to have friends with whom she feels sufficiently close. The less such alternatives are available, the more heavily kin are relied upon to supply this need. And the more heavily a particular confidante is relied upon, the more apt that person is to be a relative rather than just a friend (see Chapter 2).

"Friends" In most contemporary societies, the nuclear family is not a self-sufficient social universe. Members of the family have some kind of contact with others in their leisure time. For low-status people, however, we have already noted that friendship is not easily achieved with strangers. Neither the lonely seekers nor the potential friends warm easily to new relationships. Under such circumstances, relatives play a crucial role because they become the chief "friends" outside the immediate family.

One third of Komarovsky's blue-collar couples belonged to no organizations and spent no leisure with nonrelatives save on the rarest occasions. Even for those with some unrelated friends, relatives were the chief source of sociability. The larger the circle of relatives, the richer that sociability became until any need for friends was quite preempted:

> One man who has five siblings is married to a woman who is one of seven children, and the two families happen to be congenial—they enjoy picnicking together; "Sometimes we'll have thirty or forty people out there, all coming from the same families, all whooping it up and having a wonderful time." (1964:238)

With that many relatives, who needs friends?

Solace in Old Age   When young parents and children are living happily together, neither extra help nor extra companionship seems needed. Life might be further enriched by associating with kin, but it may seem rich enough as parents enjoy the preadolescent years when children are still content to go places and do things as a family.

Once children reach adolescence, however, the home fast empties. By the time they have gone off to college or the army or have gotten married, it is characteristically labeled an "empty nest." Bereft of children, the parents need substitute companions. This new urgency intensifies the appreciation of kin. The children themselves (now reclassified as primary kin) will hopefully return to visit, and other relatives who have been neglected gain in value.

The "empty nest" stage is only the beginning of this growing appreciation of kin. For most couples, children are launched while the parents are still vigorous. The father is still employed, perhaps with more responsibilities than ever. The mother may resume employment if she has not already done so. So leisure time may not yet be abundant, and financial resources may be abundant.

When the couple passes out of middle age into old age, the need for relatives becomes most urgent. With the retirement of both partners from active work, leisure may become unwontedly abundant. With declining vigor, more and more help will be needed. And with the death of one marriage partner, the survivor's need for substitute companionship becomes acute.

Relatives are a more dependable source of companionship in old age than either neighbors or other friends. Rosenmayr and Kockeis summarized their review of the literature thus: "All studies have revealed that old people's most frequent visitors are members of their family" (1963:414). They also noted that most old people preferred primary kin rather than comparative strangers when they needed such intimately personal services as advice or bodily care. Relatives, thus, are the biggest source of companionship and service by choice, not by necessity.

When old people lose their marriage partner, they need a replacement, and tend to recruit a relative to play a quasi-marital role. Townsend found that widows or widowers with several close relatives singled out one in particular for personal services (especially those of a more intimate character). He felt this concentration on a particular individual created a more intimate tie, helping to fill the gap left by the death of the partner.

Townsend reported a case showing how ritualized interaction became with a complex network of kin:

> Mrs. Mayhew was a widow of 70 living alone. That morning her daughter-in-law had visited her. This happened six days of the week. Just before I left, her daughter arrived (a regular call after she finished a part-time job). Mrs. Mayhew saw these two every day, and the son, who had a market stall, nearly every day. In addition to these visits there were the following rituals: Monday afternoon, old people's club; Tuesday afternoon, tea with her son, his wife and children; Wednesday, visit to cinema with sister; Friday, old people's club; Saturday, tea with daughter; Sunday, day with daughter. (1957:39)

Mrs. Mayhew thus had at least one living sibling, but gave most of her time to her children. Both represent primary kin, the one in the family of childhood, the other in the family of marriage. This is one case where priority in time does not produce stronger relationships but rather opportunity for old relationships to fade. During the child-rearing years, parents (especially mothers) are far more intimately involved with their children than with their siblings. Indeed, the parent–child relationship characteristically assumes a depth of dependency and an intimacy of involvement greater than the sibling tie ever assumed. Hence old people who have both children and siblings to choose from tend to interact more with their children than with their brothers and sisters.

TABLE 7-12 Percentage of Brothers and Sisters Seen Daily by Old People With and Without Children

SIBLING *SEEN DAILY*	*MARRIED OR WIDOWED*		*SINGLE*
	With Children	*Without Children*	
Brothers	2%	13%	10%
Sisters	4	33	28

Adapted from Townsend (1957):104. Source: Working-class men age 65 or more and women age 60 or more, East London. Reciprocal percentages did not see the specified sibling every day.

Table 7-12 shows the usual feminine bias in kin contacts. But for both sexes, sibling contacts are many times as common for old people without surviving children as for those who have children to fill their days. I conclude that vertical contacts are the normal ones, whereas horizontal contacts are chiefly a substitute when vertical ones are unavailable.

So close is the relationship between unmarried siblings in some cases that Willmott and Young (1960) labelled their relationship the equivalent of a "family of marriage." Regardless of whether they were single or married, those who had a close relationship with siblings thereby acquired a link with any children or grandchildren the siblings had. In this indirect manner, child-less old people acquire (if they can) nieces and nephews whom they treat as if they were their own children, and grandnieces and grandnephews whom they treat like grandchildren.

Despite this tendency of old people to convert their nearest kin into substitutes for missing spouses, children, and grandchildren, this does not mean that substitute-relationships function as effectively as the real thing. Whereas 73 percent of an American sample of old people said they were "very close" to their children, only 48 percent of those without children felt that close to their siblings (Streib and Thompson, 1960). Perhaps distant kin resist being converted into intimate kin and perhaps even for those who try to do the converting, the transformation never seems entirely genuine. However, the very fact that replacement occurs testifies to the importance which old people attach to kin.

KIN AS AGENTS OF SOCIAL CONTROL OVER FAMILIES

Corporations, governments, churches, schools, and neighborhoods all attempt to control their captive families. Sometimes these controls are intended to benefit the family, sometimes to protect the nonfamilial institution from disruption by hostile family activity, sometimes to coopt the family into serving the ends of the agency. These efforts are not entirely successful. Families have a stubborn way of resisting the efforts of outside agencies to control them. They also resist control by relatives. However, relatives are so much closer emotionally and so much more often present inside the family's "castle" that kin control tends to be more powerful than control by more remote agencies.

The most powerful control comes when kin live within the same household, especially when it is a parent's home within which the family members reside as dependents. That situation I will examine in a later chapter exploring the effect of complex families on the nuclear families of which they are composed. Here I will focus on control exerted from outside the home by kin who may live nearby but do not form a joint household.

The amount of control by "outside" kin depends on how formally they are organized. When they are organized into unilineal kin groups which have exclusive responsibility for their patrilineal (or matrilineal) membership, control is tightest. The kin group may hold regular meetings for the purpose of making decisions about the welfare of their members or may delegate to a smaller group of officers the responsibility for policing the activities of members and meting out punishment to offenders. The group code may be concerned with many matters, but one of its central elements is apt to be rules about such aspects of family life as mate selection, husband–wife relationships, child-rearing responsibilities, and inheritance. In general, those rules are likely to be conservative, enforcing conformity and responsible behavior upon members who might otherwise be tempted to put their individual welfare ahead of the welfare of their family and kin.

Without formal kin groups, the power of kin is much reduced. When kin control depends on intervention by individual families or even by individual relatives rather than collective intervention by the whole network, it can be more easily ignored. Nevertheless, even in modern societies if the behavior of the offender is sufficiently flagrant, relatives may mount collective pressure on him. And even if pressure is not organized, the responses of successive individual kin to deviant behavior are likely to be so nearly uniform that they reinforce each other.

The sanctions available to contemporary kin are relatively mild in comparison to the death penalty, banishment, and other punishments invoked by organized kin groups. Nevertheless to an individual who feels affectionate toward his relatives and who sees them regularly, the possibility of being shunned, criticized to his face, or talked about behind his back may exert a very real influence over his behavior. Nor are the sanctions in either primitive or modern societies all negative. To win the praise and esteem of one's most intimate circle of associates (namely, primary kin) is intensely rewarding. So the norms of family behavior exemplified in the lives of related families and reinforced by the positive and negative sanctions of close kin powerfully influence the behavior of most nuclear families. Or, to put it propositionally, the closer a family is to relatives, the more that family tends to be subject to the relatives' control.

Control over Mate Selection

The selection of a marriage partner vitally concerns relatives because it involves recruiting into the kin network a new in-law and a co-progenitor of future descendants. In small communities, such as Polish villages, it also means establishing an official link between two kin networks (Thomas and Znaniecki, 1958). Primary kin are especially interested in the new person with whom they will frequently associate and who will vitally affect the life of their child or sibling. But even secondary kin have an interest in the new recruit, as attested by the frequency with which they are involved in wedding procedures. Hence we should expect to find few societies in which young people are given a completely free hand in choosing a partner.

TABLE 7-13 Parental Control of Mate Selection, by Presence of Unilineal Kin Groups

| | UNILINEAL KIN GROUPS | |
FORM OF MATE SELECTION	Present	Absent
Arranged marriage only	48%	27%
Both arranged marriage and self-selection	44	7
Self-selection, but parental approval required	8	27
Self-selection, parental approval not required	0	40
Total	100%	100%
Number of societies	25	15

Computed from Stephens (1963):199. Source: Primitive, feudal, and modern societies in various parts of the world.

Table 7-13 shows the effect of formal kin groups on the control system for mate selection. Where unilinear kin groups were present, not a single society allowed individuals to choose their marriage partner without at least giving parents the right to veto that choice. On the contrary, the most common system was to allow only arranged marriages, which meant that parents were actively involved in the very process of selecting the partner. Indeed in some societies *only* the parents were involved, the prospective couple knowing nothing of who was in store for them until arrangements had been completed. A few cultures did not even allow the groom to discover the identity of his bride until her veil was lifted during the wedding ceremony.

In general, then, societies with powerful kinship organizations tend to give the power of mate selection to parents and not to entrust young people themselves with much of a voice. This does not mean that even the parents are necessarily given full authority in such an important matter. Formal kin groups frequently require the parents to secure their approval before they proceed with the marriage negotiations. In some cases the whole process from beginning to end is essentially a kin-group activity rather than a family activity. The kin collectively discuss whom their young man should marry and then ask a trusted kin member other than the parents to negotiate with the family of the prospective bride.

Table 7-13 also shows that societies without unilineal kin groups are less apt to require kin control of the mate-selection process. This does not necessarily mean that relatives are unimportant in determining who marries whom. Even in societies where parental approval is not formally required, most parents keep in touch with their children's progress toward marital commitment. They usually meet the prospective partner before the relationship is formalized in an engagement. And although they may not be explicitly asked for their approval, their views are frequently sought and frequently listened to. Even if such views are not expressed in words, the positive or negative reaction of the parents is sure to be evident in the corresponding warmth or coolness of their reception of the visitor.

In the United States where mate-selection is supposed to be notably free, Bates (1942) found that most men and women reported that their parents (especially mothers where daughters were concerned) had been actively involved in the process of choosing their marriage partner. Even though parental discouragement is presumably most influential prior to engagement, Burgess and Wallin (1953) found that broken engagements were more than twice as common when both parents disapproved of a girl's fiance as when both approved. Some of this difference may be a reflection of the girl's own discovery of the problems to which the parents objected, but that objection itself presumably helped sever the relationship.

Hence, even in societies which supposedly allow free choice, close kin are apt to play influential roles in the selection of marriage partners.

Effects of the failure of kin to perform this social control function can be seen in African cities where young people left their native reserve to seek employment in the cities. Goode (1963) noted that immigrant young people living away from their elders tended to enter into consensual unions (*i.e.,* to begin living together without marriage). Moreover, even after the girl became pregnant, the man would not necessarily marry her as he would have been forced to do by the kin network had he been subject to normal control. A large number of illegitimate births resulted from the inability of absent relatives to exert their normal control over the family formation process of young people.

Control of Marital Behavior

Although the recruitment of a new kinsman is a time of special interest to the existing set of kin, the social control function does not end with the wedding ceremony.

Broadly speaking, relatives are concerned with the whole range of behavior of any of their adult kinsmen insofar as that behavior may bring either esteem or disrepute upon them. Although kin sometimes unite to sponsor achievements in a young protege (as by pooling their funds to send him to professional school or to launch him in business), kin ties seem more often activated defensively when someone threatens to violate the norms not only of the kin network but of the whole community and thereby to bring shame upon his relatives.

Campbell (1964) noted that among groups of Greek shepherds, kin were the most powerful agent in enforcing community norms of behavior. When a man violated a major value, kin generally sided with the community in ostracizing him both because they shared the community's value system and because only thus could they hope to minimize public disapproval of themselves. The threat of losing both the moral support and the practical cooperation of kinsmen was a powerful deterrent to deviant behavior.

One way of preventing this disaster from happening was for an individual shepherd to consult his kinsmen in advance before making a major move. Similarly whenever a man found himself in difficulty, his first thought was to seek the advice of his kinsmen about how to extricate himself. This continuous process of consultation with kin before taking action and of criticism by kin whenever any individual's behavior seemed questionable involved each man in such a tight system of social control that few individuals deviated sufficiently to merit disinheritance or social ostracism.

Although kin groups are concerned about all sorts of behavior (especially in small communities where knowledge about deviant behavior spreads like wildfire), *family* behavior is especially important because families are the basic units of the kinship system. Among the Polish peasantry, Thomas and Znaniecki (1958) found great concern that husbands and wives should treat each other respectfully because that respect reflected on the social status of the kin group. To disobey one's husband or mistreat one's wife would betray a lack of respect not only for that individual as a person, but for the whole kin group to which he belonged. Hence relatives demanded that proper respect be shown for them through respect for their representative in the marriage.

The larger the role of kin in arranging a marriage in the first place, the greater their involvement in the success of the marriage. Kin control over mate selection tends to promote control over the marriage. Thomas and Znaniecki noted that each kin group exercised control over both partners: Not only was the "outsider" chastised when he failed to show due respect for the kin group's representative, but the latter was subject to constant scrutiny by his own group to be sure that he gave no grounds for criticism from the other group.

In most societies, the greatest disrespect that a man or woman can show is to commit adultery. Many feudal societies which practice rigid segregation of the sexes and which prize both premarital chastity and marital fidelity, expect the kin group to defend itself against this ultimate dishonor by punishing both offenders. Among Campbell's Greek shepherds "a father (or brother) must first destroy his daughter (or sister) and only afterwards turn his attention to the lover. Similarly, a husband ought first to kill a wife taken in adultery and then the paramour" (1964:199). This retaliation was considered necessary to restore the honor of the whole kin network. Needless to say, the socially enforced automatic nature of this capital punishment served as a powerful deterrent to this form of deviant behavior.

In modern urban societies, the social control functions of kin are less effective in preventing deviant behavior, just as kin have lost much of their influence over mate selection. The emancipation of women from cloistering in the home and their increasing integration into the occupational system have made it more difficult for relatives to control their movements. The general anonymity of the urban environment robs relatives of the opportunity to supervise the behavior of one another. Urbanization has shifted the administration of capital punishment from kin to governmental agencies and has loosened the kinship bonds which made adultery seem so heinous an offense. The kin network has lost much of its ability to punish its members and much of its desire to do so.

This does not mean that the social control function disappears entirely under modern conditions (except where mobile kin lose contact with one another). It does mean that both the absolute importance of kin and their relative importance in comparison with other institutions tend to decrease. And as these control functions weaken, the nuclear family and the individual members of that family acquire correspondingly greater freedom—including freedom to violate their marriage vows when they so desire.

Control over Parent–Child Relationships

Insofar as kin are concerned with the fate of an ongoing lineage, they may have even more interest in parent–child relations than in husband–wife relations. Although most men and women (especially those who married with the approval of the kin group) can be counted on to be successfully socialized into acceptable patterns of behavior, the same cannot be said for children. Children come into the world unsocialized and must be carefully nurtured if they are to bring credit to the kindred and are to be able in turn to assume responsibility for raising their successors.

Thomas and Znaniecki noted that among Polish peasants the whole kin group supported parents when they were challenged by a child:

> . . . a rebellious child finds nowhere any help, not even in the younger generation, for every member of the family will side with the child's parents if he considers them right, and everyone will feel the familial will behind him and will play the part of a representative of the group. (1958:91)

This did not mean that parents could do anything they wanted to with the child. If they were too severe or too lenient, parents could expect kin to intervene on behalf of that happy medium which was expected to result in the most successful socialization. Kin thus controlled both the older generation's tutelage of the young and the latter's acceptance of that tutelage.

Sometimes control is exercised not simply by living kin but even by departed ancestors (though living kin act as the ancestors' agents). Plath in a 1964 article on "The Role of the Dead in Japanese Households" cited a paragraph from a 1962 Japanese sociology book: ". . . we often are dragged by dad or mom to the front of the household (ancestral) shelf and asked, 'Do you think you can give any excuse to the ancestors for doing that?' " (p. 42).

By contrast, urbanization and modernization undermine parents' and more remote relatives' control over children. In Dublin, Ireland, Humphreys (1966) found that urban families were less authoritarian than rural families in handling their children. City parents lacked support from a circle of kin who could back them up as fully as Polish kin had and as rural kin did for farm families in Ireland. Thus urban kin tend to lose touch with each other's child-rearing problems and parents must shift from relying on strict controls to more democratic methods.

In general, tightly knit kinship systems exercise strong control over many aspects of their members' behavior, but the looser the kinship system becomes, the weaker that control becomes.

KINSHIP VERSUS MARRIAGE: CONFLICTING LOYALTIES

Marriage involves one of the greatest discontinuities in the history of any family. If residence is neolocal, both partners leave home. If the couple take up residence with one partner's parents, the other partner leaves home. Even for the child who stays at home, marriage establishes a tie with an incoming stranger, a tie which conflicts with his tie to his parents. The parent–child tie may predominate as long as the parents survive, leaving the new relationship in an all-around precarious state. If the family system subordinates the new tie sufficiently, the established family may hardly feel threatened by the newcomer. Nevertheless, systematic ways have been invented of controlling the newcomer, implying the potentiality of a threat to established bonds. Where systematic ways of controlling the threat do not exist, the conflict between ties to parents and to spouse often becomes more than potential.

Barrier to Family Formation

If parents and children are sufficiently close, they may satisfy so many of each other's needs that the child feels little need to get married and the parent little willingness to let him. Excessively close relationships between parents and children thus function as a barrier to the formation of a new family.

In arranged marriage systems, overinvolved parents simply procrastinate in taking the initiative to negotiate a match for the beloved child. In Jamaica, Blake found that poor parents depended on their children for economic and practical aid. The old saw about parents not losing a daughter but gaining a son depends on the expected closeness of a son-in-law. Most Jamaicans expected him to be less dependable than the child who would be "lost" through marriage. As a result, parents were tempted "to procrastinate in their efforts at matchmaking" (1961:137).

The emotional dependence of parent on child is intensified when the parent's marriage is shattered. A parent who loses his partner through death, desertion, or divorce coopts a child into becoming a substitute partner who will provide the companionship and affection which had previously been supplied by the spouse. Because fragmented families more often consist of mothers-and-children than of fathers-and-children, and because women generally become more emotionally involved in their children than men do, the problem is particularly acute following the loss of a husband. Although mother–daughter ties are normally close, the loss of a male marriage partner increases the importance of a male child to replace both the practical and the affectional services of the father. So the last remaining son of a widow is a typical candidate for bachelorhood (or perhaps we should say for lifelong "quasi-marriage" to his mother).

Humphreys noted that many Irish countrymen postponed marriage until after the death of their widowed mother, by which time they were sometimes too old to be any longer interested. They postponed marriage so long not simply because the mother opposed it, but because they were personally concerned about the mother's welfare. They did not wish "to bring another woman in on my mother" (1966:21). This reflects a patrilocal family system where a wife would have to share the farmhouse with her mother-in-law and where conflict between the two women could be almost as intense as if the man were a bigamist. The fear of such potential conflict led both mother and son to see forming a new family as a threat to the solidarity of the old family, and therefore best postponed.

Barrier to Marital Solidarity

Although in extreme cases, ties to parents prevent family formation altogether and in intermediate cases delay marriage, the most common consequence is to bar the way to complete marriage. Technically a man and a woman may be married, but if either of them is still tied to the mother's apron strings, they will be only half-married. Caught between ties to the mother and ties to the spouse, the latter tie can only half develop with the result that the marriage is weak and jealousy produces conflict between the competing parties.

Marital Weakness   Within certain limits, ties with kin and with spouse are mutually compatible. However, beyond those limits they interfere with each other. If ties with kin are sufficiently strong, they prevent the development of strong ties with the spouse.

The crucial ties, in this respect, are those with parents. When one partner continues to live either near his parents or in the same home with them, his old dependence on them tends to persist unattenuated, preventing the development of a new dependence on the spouse.

I found (1969a) that the marital satisfaction of Detroit wives declined when as many as half their relatives lived in the same neighborhood (implying that either they or their husbands had not left their home neighborhood). Similarly, regardless of residential propinquity, marital satisfaction declined for couples who saw their relatives excessively often (more than once a week). One clue to the cause of this declining satisfaction was a corresponding decline in the frequency with which wives told their troubles to their husbands after a bad day. Presumably the more deeply involved these people were with their relatives, the more apt they were to rely on their relatives instead of on their spouses. If kin dependencies were sufficiently strong, there was very little chance for marital dependencies to grow.

In view of the matrilateral bias of modern kinship, I assume that the wife's ties with her mother are especially often the barrier to marital development. In societies with extended family systems, the nature of the barrier depended on whose family was lived with.

Patrilocal systems required the wife to leave her mother and frequently enforced this departure with extremely rigid rules. If the wife's tie to her mother was completely severed, interference from that quarter was minimized. However, the tie between the husband and his mother was apt to be strong and (as we will see in Chapter 18) the rules of the extended household suppressed overt displays of affection between the young bride and groom. Emphasizing the importance of filial obedience of the son to his parents correspondingly deemphasized the marital bond. And if parents were displeased with their new daughter-in-law, many cultures gave them the option of sending her home. Thus patrilocal marriage inhibited the development of the marital bond and created ways of disrupting it.

In matrilocal systems, the problem was even more acute. A man imported into his wife's home could be integrated less easily than when the sexes were reversed. Moreover in matrilineal systems, the man ordinarily had continuing responsibilities to his own lineage which meant that his sisters' children were his chief responsibility rather than his own children. Such arrangements were severe barriers to the husband–wife relationship.

Among the matrilineal Ashanti tribe in Africa, Fortes (1950) pointed out that "it is to his sister that a man entrusts weighty matters, never to his wife. . . . Women, again, agree that in a crisis they will side with their brothers against their husbands." Similarly among the Ismailis of Tanzania, Nizarali (1968) reported that husband–wife ties were so weakened by the wife's involvement in her kin group that wives seldom addressed their husbands as "my husband," preferring instead to refer to him as the father of a favorite son, *e.g.*, "Aziz's father."

Matri–patrilocal systems presented an even more acute problem in this regard. The longer the couple lived with the wife's parents, the stronger the mother–daughter tie became. Richards (1950) discovered that among the African Bemba, some wives became so entrenched in their family of childhood that when the time came for the couple to move to the husband's home, they refused to leave, preferring to divorce their husbands instead. (Similarly Goode has noted that child betrothal in India speeded the induction of the girl into her husband's family, whereas the rising age of marriage in recent years strengthened her ties with her own family.)

This marital weakness and instability of couples heavily involved with their kin may be contrasted with the strength and stability of marriages without strong external involvements. For example, Colson (1958) found that the Rhodesian Tonga were neolocal, emphasizing their independence by settling apart from their families. This forced the husband and wife to depend on each other for cooperation in managing the household, making the husband–wife tie central. Goode (1963) saw a general trend throughout Africa toward stronger husband–wife relationships. As mate selection shifted from parents to the young people themselves, there was a corresponding weakening of the tie to parents after marriage and strengthening of the tie to the self-chosen partner. And in some localities, Goode observed that households were so isolated not only from kin, but from any other families, that a man could not even find another male for companionship and was forced to turn to his wife as the only available adult. In such ways, the isolation of the nuclear family from kin and other social contacts forces the husband and wife to develop their relationship with each other.

Although parents particularly stand in the way of marital development, other close relatives may do so, too. The closest relatives other than parents are siblings. The tie to siblings is rarely strong enough to prevent family formation, but for wives who have sisters available for comfort and companionship, that relationship may be more vital than the tie to the husband. Especially in later life when marital ties tend to weaken, the wife may find more in common with a same-sex sibling than with an opposite-sex spouse.

In a study of older Kansas City residents, Cumming and Schneider (1961) found that the marriage bond was remarkably weak and that the bond between sisters was often stronger. So weak had the marriage bond become for these women in general that it was more a nuisance than a help. Thus, morale was higher for widows than for those with husbands still alive. Widows were free to go places and do things with their sisters, sisters-in-law, or other friends with whom they had developed a quasi-sisterly relationship. Wives, on the other hand, found that marriage got in the way of such sociability because husbands had to be cooked for three times a day and complained if their wives were out too much between meals. Presumably if the marriage bond had remained more meaningful, it could have had a more positive connotation in old age. But under the actual circumstances of these American marriages, the vitality of the sibling tie further weakened the spousal tie.

Competitive Conflict How does a man feel when his wife becomes more involved with her sister than with him? The answer is quite simple: he feels jealous. Nor is the problem simply male possessiveness. When scarce resources are involved (for example, when there is only a limited amount of wealth to be shared), members of the nuclear family may be engaged in a zero-sum game with members of the kin network: The more I get, the less you get— and vice versa. In an intrinsically competitive situation, the involvement of the spouse with his kin threatens the individual's interests, breeding defensive counter-measures and precipitating open conflict between the two sides.

For instance, among the matrilineal Ashanti of Africa, Fortes (1950) found that the typical husband was caught in the middle between the demands of his wife and the demands of his sister, each of whom wanted him to provide well for her children. This crossfire often resulted in divorce when wives resented the loyalty a husband gave his sister and the sister's children.

A matrilineal system is peculiarly apt to create conflict between the husband and wife, but it is not unique in this respect. In patrilineal Greece, Campbell (1964) found a similar conflict between the sibling relationship and the marriage relationship. In this case, the key tie was not between brother and sister but between brother and brother. Before marriage, the group of brothers acted together like an urban gang, defending each other's honor and making whatever personal sacrifices were necessary for each other's welfare. After marriage, each man's loyalty was expected to be transferred to his own children, which meant he could no longer give his undivided loyalty to his brothers. Indeed, while he was not expected to abandon his brothers altogether, they were expected to lose out in case of direct conflict between their interests and those of the children. We can easily imagine that such a drastic shift did not always occur easily and that if a man failed to make the shift to his wife's satisfaction, she and all her family would respond bitterly to his betrayal.

In the nominally bilineal U.S.A., any tendency to favor one set of kin over the other is correspondingly resented by the neglected kin and by their representative in the nuclear household. Komarovsky (1964) found in-law conflict twice as common among households with close wife–mother ties as where the wife was normally independent. Dependence of the wife on her mother was especially common among wives who had dropped out of high school. These dependent wives confided their marriage troubles to their mothers, supplying them with ammunition to use against their sons-in-law. Husband–wife conflicts under these circumstances tended to balloon into in-law conflicts which exacerbated the tension between the partners.

So far we have portrayed only one set of in-laws involved in marital conflict (namely the set to which one partner is especially attached). However, the problem may be compounded by compensatory involvement of the neglected set of kin. Rogers and Leichter (1964) detected retaliation among Jewish families in New York City. Most couples had the usual matrilineal bias in their kinship patterns, but mother–son ties were sufficiently strong to leave patrilineal kin resentful. Moreover, wives not only saw more of their own kin but complained if their husbands even visited their parents by themselves. For wives, the ideal marriage allowed them to visit their mothers in the daytime and to have their husbands' undivided attention at night (leaving the husbands and their families furious).

The failure of the husband and his relatives to accept this one-sided bargain produced intense conflict between the partners, echoed by their respective kinfolk. The husband's mother resented the wife's intervention in the mother–son relationship (and the wife reciprocated with correspondingly bitter feelings toward her mother-in-law). Rather than attacking the wife openly, however, the husband's family characteristically criticized her role performance, calling her a bad housekeeper and a poor mother. So hostile did they become to the wife that even when opportunities arose to include the young couple in kin activities, the kin group pointedly excluded them in a vicious cycle of growing mutual alienation. What matters to us, however, is not the growing estrangement between the nuclear family and kin (indeed such kin might better be placed at a distance), but the fact that such alienation was emotionally intolerable to all parties concerned. So the conflict with in-laws strained the relationship between the husband and wife.

Threat to Family Peace

Given the danger that kinship ties on one or both sides of the marriage may become a source of conflict, many family systems devise precautionary measures to prevent the outbreak of war. In primitive societies these often took the form of rules of avoidance, *i.e.,* taboos either on having any contact at all with in-laws or on coming close enough (*i.e.,* interacting informally enough) to be dangerous. In other words, if in-laws could be kept sufficiently remote either literally or by confining interaction to rigidly straight-jacketed formality, the danger of violence breaking out would be minimized.

Anthropological literature is replete with descriptions of avoidance rules which frequently focus on the husband and his mother-in-law. In some societies, a man is not even supposed to look upon his mother-in-law; one party must avert his/her eyes or even hide in the bushes when the other approaches. Stephens (1963) noted that such taboos were especially common in societies with unilineal kin groups which made strong claims upon one partner and which therefore were liable to threaten the husband–wife relationship. They were also common in societies with a long postpartum sex taboo forbidding the couple to have intercourse for months or years after the birth of a child.

The latter taboo creates problems of unsatisfied sexual needs and suggests that one aspect of mother-in-law taboos is the potential jealousy which would arise between mother and daughter if the man were to be sexually attracted to his mother-in-law. Another index of the sexual aspect of this kinship threat is the fact that societies which do not prescribe avoidance of the mother-in-law frequently require a joking relationship which is explicitly sexual in nature. By requiring the man to tease and pretend to seduce his mother-in-law in public, such societies create an effective barrier against either party taking the seduction seriously.

Avoidance and joking are not simply alternative solutions to the same problem but frequently exist side by side in the same society as behavior prescribed for alternative kin. Radcliffe-Brown (1950) noted that avoidance was often prescribed toward members of older generations, whereas joking more often applied to members of the same generation. One's mother-in-law (and perhaps the father-in-law, too) were to be treated respectfully and kept literally at a distance. Sisters and brothers-in-law, however, were supposed to be treated disrespectfully and so consistently insulted that no one could ever take offense at what was obviously "just a game."

Conflict between ties to the marriage partner and to kin is normally most acute at the beginning of marriage when the new ties are just being formed. Hence it is understandable that in some societies, avoidance rules are especially stringent at that time. For example, among the Nuer, Evans-Pritchard (1951) found that men could not appear openly in their in-laws' homes until after the birth of their first child. Not until several children had been born could they eat with their in-laws. By then, the children had so cemented the marriage relationship that in-law ties were no longer so threatening. Even so, highly formal respectful language was still enjoined upon both sides at all times.

Societies which require neither avoidance nor joking nevertheless may require respect. The Javanese language (Geertz, 1961) had a whole vocabulary of respect which was used with one's superiors generally but which was also supposed to be used with one's in-laws. The importance of respect toward in-laws was dramatized in the use of this special language even toward one's inferiors (i.e., toward a son-in-law or daughter-in-law) even though they were technically "children" and therefore not ordinarily entitled to respectful treatment from their elders. Nor was respect restricted to language alone. Geertz found that wives were expected to send "a fairly steady stream of little gifts" to the mother-in-law as a way of showing their respect and desire to please.

Among the patrilineal Greek shepherds, Campbell (1964) found that the men carried the burden of cultivating good relationships with in-laws. For example, when the new bridegroom came to visit his wife's family, his father-in-law would honor him by killing a prize lamb so that they might feast together in better-than-usual style. Own kinsmen, Campbell reported, could not be sure of such extraordinary hospitality as this stranger whose favor needed to be courted so he would be kind to the daughter he had been given in marriage. In addition to this "courtship" between father-in-law and son-in-law, brothers-in-law tried hard to please one another in order to promote the welfare of the new marriage. When the whole network of kin on both sides established good relationships with each other, the peace of the married couple was safeguarded against conflict over in-laws.

In supposedly bilineal systems, I have suggested before that any lateral skew is a potential source of trouble. But what if everyone concerned accepts matrilineality as a "natural" (even if not an ideal) state of affairs? The replacement of an impossible ideal by a norm which coincides with reality should reduce resentment by the neglected kin. Townsend's report (1957) from the London slums suggested that this adaptation to reality was made successfully there: ". . . conflict with in-laws is reduced or avoided . . . by acknowledging the primacy of the wife's mother's claims." If, whenever a choice must be made between kin, the wife's mother automatically gets priority, such choices are removed from the sphere of potential conflict between husband and wife.

Finally, a variety of distancing mechanisms may be utilized to keep in-laws at a "safe" distance. In neolocal societies, establishing a separate residence prevents the conflicts which arise when different nuclear families live under the same roof. When doubling up with in-laws is necessary, distancing requires greater-than-usual segregation of activities within the home. For example, Geertz (1961) found that Javanese families behaved quite differently when a divorced woman and her children doubled up with her parents than when she doubled up with her sister and brother-in-law. With parents there were no barriers to resuming an economically dependent relationship. Even if she was earning money, she would turn it over to her parents to administer as a single household economy. However, a brother-in-law could not be expected to be so hospitable, and so such households tended to be decentralized, with the original nuclear family and the returning broken fragment keeping their finances separate even though they might share the same roof for the rest of their lives. Such decentralization minimized feelings of exploitation on the part of either family.

Such patterns of respect, ritualized disrespect, avoidance or extraordinary kindness protect the new tie between husband and wife against disruption from tension between families related only by marriage.

Threat to Family Autonomy

In the preceding sections, the major threat to marital solidarity has been the one-sided involvement of one partner with his own kin at the expense of the other partner and his relatives. But one-sidedness is not the only problem families face in relation to kin. If kin generally invade the privacy of the nuclear family or swallow it up in mass activities, the integrity of the nuclear unit suffers.

One way relatives may violate the integrity of the family is by invading the home unannounced. I found in Detroit (1969a) that the larger the proportion of visits from relatives which were unplanned, the lower the solidarity of the married couple. When relatives "dropped in" without warning, they might disrupt activities which the couple had planned for themselves. Their failure to ask permission represented a lack of respect for the autonomy of the couple. One might say the relatives failed to acknowledge the couple's right to say no to proposed visits, and to respect their home as the "castle" encasing their family life.

How much unplanned visits will infringe upon the autonomy of a family depends on how often they occur. Taking all kinds of visits together (planned and unplanned) I found that marital solidarity declined for couples who saw their relatives more than once a week.

Another variable which threatens the integrity of the family unit is the number of relatives with whom they are involved at any one time. The larger the swarm of relatives, the greater the danger that the nuclear unit will be overwhelmed and lose its separate identity. Thus I found that "large family gatherings" were more "dangerous" than simple family-to-family visiting. (Marital solidarity declined for couples who saw whole masses of kin more than once a month.) Presumably in large family gatherings, husband and wife are more apt to become separated from one another, the husband joining the men and the wife the women in sex-segregated activities. The larger the gathering, the more difficult it must be for a family member to resist advice from kin which may be antithetical to the interests of the spouse. In any case, the evidence seems clear that sociability with kin can become so intense that it gets in the way of marital solidarity.

Thus, not only is it essential for families to maintain a certain distance from in-laws to avoid divisive conflict, but it is necessary to maintain enough independence of kin generally to be able to achieve and maintain a sense of their identity as a family. Just as the identity crisis for a teen-ager involves learning to see himself as an autonomous individual apart from his parents and peer group, so a nuclear family (especially a fledgling marital dyad) must achieve a sufficiently autonomous existence to be able to become internally strong and cohesive. The boundary lines between the family and all others (even the closest kin) must be sufficiently clear-cut so that all parties know to whom the family members "belong." These boundaries are symbolized by a separate home whose privacy is respected by potential visitors when they ask in advance for permission to come.

KINSHIP VERSUS FRIENDSHIP

In the modern world, there is a rough equivalence between kin and unrelated friends. Yet the two are not identical. The purpose of this section is to compare the ways families relate to these two sets of associates and to note the conversion of friends into quasi-kin when true kin are not available. The latter transformation is the most effective testimonial to the continuing significance of kin ties in the modern world.

Differences Between Kin and Friends

Differentiation between kin and non-kin varies with the importance of kin relations in a society. The more diverse the social relations in a society, the more the distinction between kin and non-kin tends to become blurred. But if kinship is the only or almost the only organizing principle in a society, the distinction between kin and non-kin is correspondngly sharp.

Intimacy   In kin-based societies, kin are those with whom one may be intimate because they can be trusted, whereas non-kin must be held at a distance just as in-laws must be treated with care.

The sexual connotations of the word "intimacy" are relevant. For example, among Muslim Arabs who ordinarily stress the segregation of the sexes, Goode (1963) noted that girls were permitted to remove their veils in the presence of their brothers or of any relative whom they were forbidden to marry. Similarly young Ashanti tribesmen were reported by Fortes (1950) to feel that their cross-cousins (their mother's brother's daughter) were too closely related to them to be sexually attractive because they were almost like a sister. An unrelated girl would have more sex appeal than such a familiar relative.

Paradoxically, then, close kin (especially those subject to the incest taboo) are too close to marry, too well known to be sexually attractive, and so can be treated informally and affectionately short of overt sexual involvement.

Among Greek shepherds studied, similar intimacy was possible among kin. For example, Campbell noted how a younger brother might lean his head against the shoulder of his older brother's wife, an unforgivable insult were the brothers not bound so closely by their ties of kinship. For unmarried shepherds, even to talk to a girl was forbidden outside of the family and kin. By contrast, with a girl cousin not only might he talk but he might even have physical contact: "Particularly among first cousins of opposite sex between the ages of thirteen and sixteen familiarity is expressed in playful wrestling, bottom smacking, and cheek pinching" (1964:101). Significantly, the more remote the kinship, the less free this sexual play might become since the relationship was less protected by incest taboos and more liable to conversion into sexual involvement.

However, intimacy among kin is more than just heterosexual intimacy. Among members of the same sex there is also a special closeness and informality. Campbell's Greek shepherds did not think true friendship was ever possible with an unrelated person because he could not be trusted. But a man's best friends were normally chosen among his cousins, especially those with whom he did not have direct business dealings and could therefore maintain a pure friendship uncontaminated by economic responsibilities. With these cousins, men enjoyed the only pure sociability outside the immediate family which they ever experienced.

Partiality   One consequence of special intimacy with relatives is that they tend to be sympathetic listeners. Sympathy is supportive and appreciated when that is what the individual wants. But if he wants objective advice, kin may be too partial to supply it.

Komarovsky (1964) found that some blue-collar wives preferred unrelated confidantes because their mothers automatically sided with them in every dispute. Particularly when a woman had a problem with her in-laws, it was difficult for her mother to be objective. Another similar situation in which the mother was often disqualified to serve as a confidante was when the wife's problem concerned her parents-in-law's son, *i.e.,* her own husband. Here again the normally competitive feelings between in-laws left the mother liable not only to sympathize with her own daughter but to become enraged at her son-in-law. Thus to confide in one's mother about one's marriage problems was liable to make the problems worse. Of course, friends too may be partisan, but they are less automatically predisposed to one side than are relatives who "belong" on that side.

Priority   In certain societies for certain purposes, friends and relatives are interchangeable. But for many purposes, families turn first to kin and then to friends only in the absence of effective kin. Feelings of mutual obligation among kin give them a legitimacy which mere friends may lack as a source of assistance and advice. The more urgent the claims, the greater the reluctance to go to friends and the higher the priority of relatives. For example, when children are orphaned and need a permanent home, relatives are frequently the exclusive resource. For major loans of money, the same reluctance to approach a friend may appear. Friendship, after all, may be "spoiled" by commercial transactions. No one thinks that kinship may be spoiled because that is the responsibility of kin.

TABLE 7-14   Relationships of Married Adults with Their Parents and Their Best Friends

Relationship	Parents	Best Friends	Parent/Friend Ratio
Interact on special occasions (birthdays, Christmas, holidays, vacations)	88%	20%	4.40X
Feeling of obligation to keep in touch is an important reason for doing so	73	28	2.61
Provide tangible mutual aid	88	43	2.05
High value consensus ("agree on things I consider really important in life")	65	75	0.87
Engage in social activities together outside the home	43	74	0.58
Number of men and women	724	737	

Adapted from Adams (1967a):72–73. Source: White married men and women married 20 years or less, Greensboro, North Carolina. Reciprocal percentages did not have the specified relationship with the parent or best friend.

Table 7-14 shows that a feeling of obligation was important in keeping in touch with parents but relatively unimportant in the case of friends. One consequence of this difference is that relationships with close kin are kept alive regardless of such hindrances as geographical mobility, but friendships tend to come and go as people move.

Indicative of the priority attached to kin is the tendency in Table 7-14 for parents to be the focus of attention on important occasions. Friends may be seen on ordinary occasions, but the more important the festival, the greater the chance that it will be spent with close kin to the exclusion of friends.

Tangible mutual aid is an example of the kind of practical help which one hesitates less to ask of kin than of non-kin who are mere friends.

On the other hand, the table shows that certain relationships were closer with friends than with relatives. The high value consensus among friends reflects the fact that friends are chosen on that basis. (If my friend and I don't have much in common, why be friends?) Relatives, on the other hand, one has to keep in touch with regardless of how much one's values may change. Again this suggests the greater stability of kin ties in comparison to friendship.

The social activities outside the home which loomed so importantly in the activities of friends included such things as going to movies or going shopping together. These might be thought of as the "ordinary" activities in which friends engage in contrast to the special occasions for relatives. On the other hand, it may also be that these friendships depended somewhat more on the assistance of commercial recreational facilities for their very existence, whereas relatives were more content simply to visit in each other's homes. In that sense, kinship may be a more domesticated relationship whereas friendship is more akin to a special interest such as develops among those who share a hobby or club. Kinship in this sense is relatively diffuse whereas friendship is a more specific relationship centered around a narrower range of activities.

In the light of Table 7-14, we cannot say that kin have priority for all types of activities but that the more urgent the need, the greater the tendency to turn to kin.

THE CONVERSION OF FRIENDS INTO QUASI-KIN

Nuclear families which have no kin tend to substitute friends instead. In so doing, they alter the quality of the relationship with those friends, making it into a kind of kinship which can be labelled "quasi-kinship." The more urgent the family's need for outside resources, the greater the tendency to convert friends into kin.

Two family situations involve particular need: those at the end of the family life cycle (aged couples and widows), and those at the bottom of the stratification system (poor families generally and black families in particular).

Townsend (1957) found that old people without relatives turned to non-kin for both companionship and the help which relatives normally supply. This tendency to substitute non-kin for missing family members was conspicuous in the case of widows and widowers who needed companions and help-meets to take the place of their missing spouses. Short of actually remarrying, the bereaved persons sometimes established quasi-marital relationships with similarly situated persons of the opposite sex who lived in the same block. For those whose spouses were still alive but who had no children with whom to interact and on whom to depend in old age, younger friends sometimes became substitute children (especially young women who took the place of daughters).

Table 7-15 shows the alteration in the quality of old people's ties with their friends when they lose touch with their brothers and sisters. Those without siblings were far more apt to describe their friends in the comprehensive terms which normally characterize ties with siblings: "She's my old friend and would do anything for me," or "He is a nice, likeable man." By contrast, those who maintained diffuse ties with their siblings were more apt to describe their friends in specific terms such as "We play bridge together," or "We go fishing together." This shows that families normally maintain a comprehensive relationship with kin and a specialized relationship with friends, but when kin disappear, ties with friends become correspondingly diffuse.

TABLE 7-15   Diffuseness of Relationship with Friends
by Presence or Absence of Siblings

DIFFUSENESS OF RELATIONSHIP WITH FRIENDS	*SIBLINGS*	
	Present	*Absent*
Diffuse relationship	53%	78%
Specific relationship	47	22
Total	100%	100%
Number of old people	186	34

Adapted from Cumming and Schneider (1961):504. Source: Random sample of Kansas City residents over age 50.

Liebow (1967) found that conversion of peers into quasi-siblings occurred among impoverished black men and women in Washington, D. C., throughout their adult lives and not simply in old age. The most common sibling tie was established between persons of the same sex. For example, two men would announce to the world that they were "going for brothers" which meant that they were especially close friends, better than ordinary "best friends," committed to the reciprocal obligations that normally apply only to kin. For men short of money and of dependable friendships in an unstable community, to acquire a brother in this way was to gain a resource of greatest value.

Less common but even more interesting was the establishment of quasi-kin ties between men and women. Sometimes this was labelled a brother–sister relationship, sometimes "going for cousins." In either case, it enabled the man and the woman to establish an extraordinarily close relationship without arousing the jealousy of any marriage partners who might be involved. For example, a married man and his divorced unrelated "cousin" borrowed money from each other and visited back and forth so frequently that the divorcee's son thereby acquired a benevolent "uncle." Another man, himself divorced, was able to place his motherless daughter in the home of a married woman whom he called his "sister." In both cases, the kinship label enabled a man and woman to establish a close affectional and practical relationship with each other and yet protected the couple from becoming sexually or romantically involved. Thus all the benefits of kinship—both intimacy and the incest taboo

—could be imported into a heterosexual friendship which otherwise would have threatened the marriages involved. It is perhaps significant that in each of these cases, one partner was not living with a spouse and had a child to care for, so to some extent these "conversions" resembled those for old people who have lost a spouse. The unique feature of Liebow's cases, however, is that the "bereaved" parents looking for spouse substitutes were not limited to unmarried persons but could link up with married persons as well in this fictional kinship. The acute needs of an impoverished black community produced an accepted way of enlarging the benefits which kinship normally satisfies in more stable societies.

CHANGING RELATIONSHIPS BETWEEN
SOCIETY AND THE FAMILY

The preceding chapters have shown how family life varies in different segments of the social structure and under different social conditions. These have been static comparisons—how the middle-class family compares with the working-class family, how the family in primitive societies compares with the family in modern societies, or how farm families compare with city families.

The purpose of this section is to trace the impact of change on family life. How do changing social conditions affect families who undergo them (Chapter 8)? And how does movement by a given family from one location to another in geographical space (Chapter 9) or social space (Chapter 10) affect the family's internal and external relationships?

In each chapter, our main interest will be in transitional phenomena. We already know the before-and-after conditions of a working-class family which becomes middle-class through upward mobility. What we do not yet know is what happens to the family during the process of transition, while it is moving, still half-way between its original pattern and its destined pattern. What are the strains and structural alterations which families experience when either they or their environment change so fast that the old secure relationship between the family and its environment no longer exists? These are presumably temporary phenomena which usually alter family life only for a generation or two, after which life goes back to normal (though perhaps on a new basis). But even though eras of rapid social change or drastic family movement may be brief epiphenomena against the whole sweep of human history or family history, they are particularly valuable for purposes of scientific understanding because they constitute the nearest thing to an experiment on the relationship between the family and its environment. Whereas the preceding chapters could be little more than classification schemes like the botanist's genus and species, changing social relationships are our best source of experimental evidence about the effect of social relations on family life.

chapter eight
SOCIAL CHANGE AND THE FAMILY

Most families throughout history have lived under reasonably stable social conditions. They may not have had the same amount to eat every day or every year. But their circumstances fluctuated about a fairly steady norm. Or if the norm shifted, the change was so gradual as to be imperceptible save to the historian looking back from the perspective of future generations.

As long as the relationship between families and their environment remains stable, the patterns of family life can continue to function in their traditional ways. Parents bear children and raise them in the accustomed ways. Children accept their parents' tutelage and model their lives after their parents. Older people have high status because they know best the traditions of the society. Adolescent rebelliousness is rare.

But when a society changes rapidly, the normal relationship between the generations is destroyed. Parents who grew up in "the old days" become old-fashioned, whereas children growing up under new circumstances acquire new ideas. The society tends to become stratified into an older generation clinging to the past and a younger generation grasping the future. The younger generation looks on its elders as obsolete and a hindrance to social progress. The elders' teaching no longer seems relevant. Indeed, the younger generation feels that it should become the teacher of its parents. Yet this attempt to reverse the normal age-grading of the family is seldom received gracefully. So conflict ensues or else the generations are so alienated from each other that they cease to have significant contact.

This internal polarization of the family into contending generations means the loss of control over youth by their elders. When the socialization function of the family is weakened, and the social control of children by their elders is weakened or destroyed, symptoms of social disorganization appear.

The normal processes of family formation may break down. Young people relieved of parental controls may drift into premarital sexual involvements (with such secondary consequences as venereal disease, premarital conceptions, abortions, illegitimate births, and forced marriages). These may be either casual affairs or quasi-marriages devoid of the security and stability promoted by ritualized, legalized marriages. When families are formed, they may be less stable than usual because of a larger proportion of mixed marriages between persons of different class, racial, or religious backgrounds. And if weddings are held at all, they may be relatively informal elopements shorn of the usual participation of family, kinfolk, and friends.

Once formed, family units may be discouraged, by uncertain social conditions and inadequate socialization into family ways, from the performance of normal family functions. Voluntary childlessness is apt to increase and children's socialization to be neglected so that juvenile delinquency and other evidences of unsuccessful socialization increase.

Marriages contracted under unfavorable circumstances and faced with an unstable social environment tend to fall apart. Most forms of family disorganization tend to increase: divorce, desertion (whether permanent desertion or that temporary desertion known as an extramarital affair), marital conflict, and unhappiness. Partly these result from impaired functioning in the mate-selection system, partly from the differential impact of the changing environment on the marriage partners. Just because husband and wife are members of the same generation does not guarantee that they will be affected equally by new social conditions. The wife, for example, may be less exposed to new ideas if she stays home while the husband goes to work. Thus tension may arise between husband and wife analogous to the split between parents and children.

The faster the society changes, the more severely the family tends to be disorganized. This broad generalization will henceforth be examined in terms of specific forms of social change (modernization, revolution, war, etc.), and documented in terms of the evidence for the specific effects that these changes have on various aspects of family life.

MODERNIZATION

Under ordinary circumstances, the pace of social change is too slow to cause the types of disorganization listed here. This is not to say that family life is not affected by changes in the wider society. The preceding chapters implied vast changes in family patterns resulting from industrialization, urbanization, and other pervasive forces in the modern world. The emancipation of women and children, reduction in the birth rate, and other profound changes in family life have resulted from those sweeping social changes.

But if the pace of change is slow enough, the family system adapts itself to new circumstances with extraordinary ease. In 1958 I went to Japan hoping to study role conflict between husbands and wives growing out of the profound changes in post-war Japan but had to abandon the project because there was little evidence of overt conflict despite the drastic experiences that nation had so recently been through.

One circumstance under which families fail to keep pace with change is when the family system is trapped in the rigidity of feudal attitudes which prevent the older generation from adapting to change. Unwilling to listen to the new voices of their children, the elders resist change and risk the danger of forcing their family into revolution.

The most dramatic instances of modernization-induced conflict were reported by Thomas and Znaniecki (1958) from their study of Polish peasant families prior to World War I. There the individualistic tendencies fostered by modernization encountered such stubborn resistance that young men sometimes resorted to murdering their fathers or other obstructive family members in a desperate attempt to break through the barriers they encountered. This was not a widespread "solution." Far more young men simply left the scene by emigration or by isolating themselves from contact with their elders. Even those solutions were further evidence of the limited adaptability of the Polish peasant family to change at the critical juncture between feudal and modern times.

In the contemporary world, Africa is probably the continent with the most disorganized families. Goode (1963) concluded his review of African family life by pointing out that "much of the African industrialized and urbanized population is living in a state of social disorganization." The reason for that disorganization seems to be that families were uprooted from rural subsistence cultures and plunged abruptly into urban industrial communities. They were caught between tribal values such as polygamy and urban values such as monogamy without fully subscribing to either. They were also caught between contradictory forms of social organization—still being members of tribes but also company employees and urban citizens at the same time. The process of modernization gave them little opportunity to achieve a satisfactory new way of life because they had neither employment security, adequate housing, nor any other prerequisite for successful family life in an urban environment.

A second disorganizing feature of the African scene in the process of modernization was the migration of large numbers of men (either married or unmarried) from rural villages to urban locations for employment in mines and industries. Since few jobs for women were available in these locations, and since housing for families was not provided, normal family life was impossible. In the face of this abnormal situation, Colson found in Zambia (1958) that prostitution sprang into existence. The demand came from unaccompanied males whose industrial wages enabled them to purchase sex. The supply came from divorced and widowed women who were similarly unattached and needed money. Not only did the modernization of Africa undermine old family patterns, but it also created a family vacuum which was filled by promiscuous and commercialized (and therefore unfamilistic) sexual relationships.

REVOLUTION

Although the pace of modernization is only occasionally rapid enough to disorganize family life, any bona fide revolution can be guaranteed to turn the family upside down. Revolutions turn the whole society upside down, replacing the ruling class with a previously subordinate class. The new government adopts policies of planned change which accelerate many of the old spontaneous changes. In general, revolutions involve the most rapid, deliberate change in social structure. They grow out of the failure of feudal aristocracies to allow change to come with due speed. After sufficient strains build up in the old system, the revolution explodes, destroying that system in a sudden burst of collective effort.

Although revolutions profoundly affect family life, they are primarily politico-economic events. Government changes the most, families the least Since families are the smallest, most decentralized social institution, they are least subject to manipulation from the revolutionary headquarters. But the very fact that the family lags behind in a time of revolutionary change is one source of strain in family life. Limited though its ability to control the family may be, the revolutionary movement sees the family as a recalcitrant obstacle to its success and mounts a vast effort to destroy it. Even though in the long run family systems may not be greatly changed by a national revolution, there may be much hostility and hardship to endure in the thick of the struggle between family and state.

The Acceleration of Modernization

Marxist revolutions like the Russian and Chinese revolutions occur in crumbling feudal societies. Even though the cause of revolutionary violence is frequently the stubborn resistance of the feudal aristocracy to change, this does not mean that forces for change were not at work in such societies. Indeed the very fact that they can be labelled "crumbling" suggests that changes were at work under the surface even though the old regime may have tried to "keep the lid on."

The most powerful ingredients in modernization—industrialization, urbanization, and education—are all active in pre-revolutionary societies, building dissatisfaction with obsolete patterns and transforming them into newer ways. The very decentralized nature of family life which makes it difficult for revolutionary movements to control also makes it difficult for reactionary regimes to control. Pioneering families experiment with modern patterns of family living long before the revolution takes place. The function of the revolution is not so much to originate new family patterns as to accelerate their diffusion from the pioneering minority to the entire nation.

In pre-Communist China, Lang (1946) saw the traditional patriarchal family disintegrating as early as the 1920s under the influence of urbanization, industrialization, and Western ideas. Although wealthy rural landlords continued to maintain extended, three-generation households, and most rural peasant families continued to rule their nuclear families in a patriarchal manner, urban families were extensively modernized before the revolution. The emancipation of women was well under way in the cities and arranged marriages had widely been replaced by love matches. Indeed, the prerevolutionary Kuomintang government (which considered itself reformist) passed legislation in the 1930s embodying many of the same reforms as the Communist marriage law of 1950. Perhaps the difference between the prerevolutionary government and the postrevolutionary government was not in their legislation but in the vigor of executing those reforms at the grass roots level via propaganda and mass education, plus the unintended consequences of other governmental policies.

Specific elements of this accelerated modernization included prohibiting concubinage, arranged marriage, and bride purchase, plus guaranteeing freedom for widows to remarry and for wives to sue for divorce. None of these was a uniquely revolutionary innovation, even though the coming of the revolution speeded their implementation.

Another way of assessing the impact of the revolution on the Chinese family is to compare developments in China with those in Japan, a country similarly affected by modernization but untouched by revolution. At least three of the "changing patterns in the Communist Chinese family" described by Huang (1961) are paralleled in Japan. (1) In both countries, freedom of mate selection was underway in the 1950s but had been only partially accomplished. Matchmakers, introducers of potential partners, and advice-giving parents were still widely relied upon in both countries by those who failed to find their own partners. (2) In both countries, dating was relatively rare apart from courtship and courtship itself was short. Especially couples given the blessing of their elders through a sponsored introduction moved quickly into marriage. Huang cited individual cases of marriage within 10 or 15 days, and I found among Tokyo arranged marriages an average of less than 10 dates between a formal introduction and the decision to get married (Blood, 1967). Related to this truncated courtship were warnings from elders in both societies against the dangers of romantic love. (3) Both countries experienced what Huang called "exploitation" by females or what might better be labeled "bargaining" during mate-selection. In China this included requests for guarantees of their own economic welfare after marriage and in both countries reluctance by rural girls to become farm wives forced to work in the fields or to live with their mothers-in-law.

These three elements represent transitional phenomena in societies experiencing the modernization of feudal systems, in the Japanese case under the impact of rapid industrialization, in the Chinese case the same industrialization compounded by a revolutionary social movement dedicated to the twin goals of economic development and social reconstruction.

The Emphasis on Revolutionary Goals

The primary interest of a revolution is not in family life but in economic development and an equalitarian society. The most tangible of these goals is the economic one. To achieve a great leap forward in industrialization and economic growth requires effort and sacrifice. Revolutionary governments generally sacrifice family values to economic values in their effort to achieve economic success. In so doing they often resemble utopian communities in the priority they give to communal welfare at the expense of family welfare.

Half a dozen features of the Communist Chinese family reported by Huang are by-products of the emphasis placed by the regime on economic production. (1) Wedding ceremonies were simplified in order to conserve scarce resources which might better be devoted to industrial development. (2) Workers were encouraged to postpone dating or even marriage in order to concentrate on industrial production. In the case of female workers, the postponement of marriage had the further consequence in a society unused to contraception of postponing pregnancy and childbirth. (3) Young people were encouraged to choose their marriage partners for their social value (war heroes, production heroes, and political stalwarts) rather than for their personal attractiveness. (4) Maternal health was sacrificed to the needs of production, curtailing maternity leaves for women who were pregnant or who had had a miscarriage so production would not have to be curtailed. (5) The health and welfare of children were sacrificed to the desire to keep mothers engaged in full-time employment. The regime gave low priority to nursery facilities and to time off from work for breast-feeding. (6) The husband–wife relationship was ignored when work assignments were made. Husbands and wives might be assigned to work in widely separate locations, not intentionally but just because marriage was not worth considering in comparison to the overwhelming importance of the economic effort.

Chen (1953) similarly noted the Chinese Communist effort to deemphasize sex (in this case, a reversal of the tendency under pre-Communist modernization). By abolishing cosmetics, replacing "feminine" dress by overalls, and attacking romance as a selfish preoccupation with subjective feelings, the regime hoped to shift attention away from small-scale interpersonal relationships toward devotion to the needs of the economic system.

In the early decades of the Soviet Union, there was a major effort to emancipate women from child-rearing responsibilities in order that they might join the industrial and agricultural labor force. Since institutional child-care facilities were no more available in impoverished Russia than in impoverished China, the easiest way to emancipate women was to lower the birthrate. By legalizing abortion and promoting contraception, the government sharply reduced the Soviet birthrate, enabling women to concentrate on economic production and reducing the number of dependent mouths to be fed so that profits could be plowed back into the expansion of productive facilities. How extensively the legalization of abortion curbed reproduction is suggested by a League of Nations report cited by Mace and Mace (1963) that in 1934 there were 371 abortions for every 100 live births in the Soviet Union. Although the method of curtailing reproduction differed, the basic objective of freeing adults for the building of a new society was similar to the postponement of reproduction in the early years of the Oneida colony and Israeli kibbutzim.

In general, then, many of the policies of revolutionary governments which seem to represent attacks on family solidarity and family functioning are motivated not so much by hostility to the family as by the priority attached to achieving the revolutionary goals of a better economic and political life for the whole society.

The Attack on the Prerevolutionary Family

The fact that revolutionary family policy mostly accentuates previous trends or simply ignores the family does not mean that the family is viewed with affection. Most revolutions involve the overthrow of elder statesmen by young rebels. This easily turns into an intergenerational conflict. Regardless of the age of the establishment and its challengers, the very fact of revolution tends to split the generations apart because of the inevitable contrast between the prerevolutionary and the postrevolutionary generation.

The prerevolutionary generation (those who grew up prior to the revolution) are conservative because they were socialized in the norms of the old society and because they held positions of power in the society or at least in the family. As a result, they provide few recruits for the revolutionary movement and are the chief bulwark of the status quo and the chief threat of counterrevolution to restore the status quo ante.

Conversely, children of the prerevolutionary generation tend to flock to the revolutionary standard in an idealistic revolt against the corruption of the powers-that-be. Depending on their age at the time of the revolution, they are either resocialized in the revolutionary movement or receive their initial political socialization in the school system and youth movement established by the revolutionary regime. Being younger makes them more malleable so that insofar as the new regime tries to resocialize the whole society, the younger generation learns the new values the fastest.

Anti-Parents   To win the revolution and consolidate it against its enemies, revolutionary movements everywhere have tried to capture the loyalty of the young and to use it against their elders. To do this, it is necessary to remove the young from the influence of their elders, *i.e.,* to destroy the social control and socialization functions of parents over their children.

This was accomplished in the Soviet Union by establishing the Komsomol pioneer youth corps, a kind of Communist boy scouts movement which indoctrinated the young in their spare time. Secondly, the public schools were utilized for political indoctrination as well. Although schools continued to teach the usual subject matter, the illustrations in math problems and the stories in literature classes were selected for their political value. And besides there was explicit political teaching in the classroom as schoolteachers counteracted the reactionary influence of parents. Finally, the mass media were monopolized by the revolutionary regime and utilized for propaganda purposes.

The effectiveness of this multiple-pronged attempt of the Communist movement to capture the minds of children can be seen in Geiger's 1956 study of Russian refugees. Only 40 percent of these anti-Communist parents succeeded in persuading their children to adopt their anti-Soviet point of view. For the remaining 60 percent, the state won. In half of these cases, parents had tried explicitly to teach their children to be anti-Communist but failed to counteract the teaching of the state. In the other half, parents didn't even try to teach their children (for fear the children might deliberately or accidentally betray them to the authorities). In the absence of any parental teaching, the revolutionary influence naturally succeeded. In some of these cases, parents even paid lip-service to Communism, so fearful were they of betrayal. If anti-Communist parents failed that often to socialize their children, we can easily imagine how much less the apathetic masses of parents could hold the loyalty of their children in competition with the new regime.

The betrayal which refugee parents feared is a real threat in a revolutionary society. In addition to capturing the loyalties of the younger generation, new regimes fearful for their survival against the threat of counterrevolution frequently exhort young people to place their allegiance to the revolution ahead of their filial loyalty and report suspicious activities of their parents to the secret police:

> In celebration of the International Children's Day in Nanking on June 1, 1951, a number of model children were selected to symbolize the new ideals of youth in "the age of Mao Tse-tung." One of the models was a twelve-year-old boy who exposed his father as a counter-revolutionary and "demanded his execution." To his brother who tried to protect the father he explained, "He is our class enemy, not our father." When he heard that his father had been shot, he exclaimed, "It serves him right!" When his mother asked him to take off the red scarf he was wearing and to wear mourning for his father, he replied, "The red scarf is the glorious symbol of the Pioneer Corps, and I absolutely refuse to take it off. Besides, what is there to mourn in the death of a counter-revolutionary?" (Chen, 1953:344)

This was an extreme case, but it is significant because the revolutionary regime used it to demonstrate the loyalty which it felt young people should give the state at the expense of their parents.

In summary, then, revolutionary movements tend to undermine the authority of parents over children (especially their teaching authority) and even to reverse that authority insofar as children become more revolutionary than their parents.

Anti-Marriage   The same subversion of family ties occurs with respect to marriage bonds insofar as marriage partners are unequally devoted to the cause. Contradictory reactions to a fanatical movement inevitably strain the relationship between partners, but that strain is frequently encouraged by the movement itself. In China women joined the Communist movement as a means of emancipation from patriarchal husbands and a patriarchal society. In Islamic Algeria, similarly, Goode (1963) found that some women were more ardent revolutionaries than their husbands. But in the Soviet Union, Geiger (1965) noted that most women remained old-fashioned because of their isolation from political developments, whereas their husbands became more rapidly socialized into the new outlook.

Perhaps the Russian experience is more normal, but the lower the prerevolutionary status of women, the more they are likely to respond to the revolutionary movement as a means of expressing a feminist protest against the status quo. Regardless, however, of whether the woman or the man is more devoted to the new cause, rapid changes in political conditions strain the marriage bond, causing marital conflict and destroying what otherwise might have been stable relationships.

In the Soviet case, the regime freed marriage by making divorce freely available. All that was necessary to secure one's emancipation from an antirevolutionary (or any other) marriage partner was to send a postcard to the government, certifying that husband and wife no longer intended to live together (Hindus, 1949).

Given this hostility to prerevolutionary families, it was a small step for the Soviet government to minimize the importance of new marriages as well. Wedding ceremonies were not forbidden but deceremonialized and stripped of their bourgeois luxuriousness. Not only were weddings made optional, but even the registration of marriages with the government was temporarily discontinued. In effect, the government institutionalized a policy of free love which (according to Hindus) many urban young couples took advantage of to engage in successive informal relationships.

Limits to Change   Even when the anti-family campaign was at its height, however, most families in Russia and China remained remarkably stable, especially in rural areas.

Goode has suggested that no matter how hostile a revolutionary government may be to the family, it can hardly afford to destroy that institution altogether because it serves too many social functions. In the Chinese case, he noted that the government carefully refrained from taking over responsibility from families for the care of aged dependents because governmental resources were not adequate for such a heavy burden. Thus while the revolutionary regime no longer encouraged children to be subservient to their elders, it still asked them to provide retirement security for them. Similarly, Geiger (1968b) observed that the Soviet Union belatedly found it necessary to reemphasize family responsibility for children and male responsibility for wives because government facilities were inadequate to care for homeless children or for divorced mothers with dependent children. Because the state was unable to provide enough asylums, it proved necessary to encourage the adoption of orphaned children. Because the state was unable to provide financial assistance to divorced mothers, it was necessary to abandon the policy of unrestricted divorce.

Insofar as revolutionists triumph in underdeveloped countries and come to power amid the shattered ruins of the old society, they can ill afford to replace those functions which families can perform more cheaply. The preoccupation of revolutionary regimes with industrialization requires that provision of welfare services to the aged, to women, or to children be long postponed.

Revolutionary governments, then, tend not only to discount the importance of family values but to explicitly attack those values, though only within limits. Much as revolutionaries might like to do away with organized family life, once they achieve power they are forced to compromise with reality and accept the fact that a new society must develop some form of "peaceful coexistence" between the family and the state or else the state will collapse from attempting to do too much.

The Restoration of Family Authority

Whereas the political exigencies of a revolution require the emancipation of revolutionary youth and revolutionary spouses from the shackles of their families, a generation later the situation looks very different. By that time, the revolution has long since been won and the danger of counterrevolution from the prerevolutionary elite has disappeared. The stalwarts of the revolutionary movement have become middle-aged and are raising children of their own. Do they want their children to have the same freedom to rebel which they had when they were revolutionary youths challenging reactionary parents? Of course not. No longer is there any need for children to rebel against their parents. Quite the contrary. Now rebellion is counterrevolutionary. Now the danger to the revolution is that it will fail to be maintained by the oncoming generation in the pure form it achieved in its early days.

As a result of this new situation, the revolutionary movement rediscovers the old family virtues. In the Soviet Union most of the anti-family legislation of the new era was repealed two decades after the revolution. Spurred partly by the rise of Hitler but reinforced by the conservatism of aging men and an aging revolution, the Soviet Union reversed its attitude toward the family. One 1939 Communist publication even claimed that "so-called free love is a bourgeois invention and has nothing in common with the principles of conduct of a Soviet citizen" (Timasheff, 1946:198). To implement this new philosophy, the Soviet government abolished free divorce and reinstituted divorce courts capable of denying requests for divorce and levying financial penalties against those granted divorces. Free love was replaced by compulsory marriage registration and by abolition of the recognition granted to unceremonialized common-law marriages. Wedding rings, marriage licenses and other symbols of marriage were reinstituted. Family stability became the foundation of the stability of the postrevolutionary society.

At the same time, family growth was encouraged by changes in policy and propaganda. Abortions were made illegal except for therapeutic reasons. Even contraception (while still legal) was officially frowned upon with the result that birth control literature vanished from the newsstands and government doctors systematically discouraged their patients from practicing contraception. Conversely, the mass media extolled large families, and the state ceremoniously awarded medals to "Mother Heroines" who had borne ten or more children. Although one purpose of this remarkable shift in attitude toward reproduction may have been to provide cannon-fodder for future wars, it also became necessary for a society which had concentrated briefly on the immediate problems of economic and political change to turn its attention to the problem of providing a continuing labor supply and replenishing the political leadership of the country.

If children are to become useful workers and dependable citizens, it is necessary not only to produce them but to socialize them into the ways of the new society. We have already seen that revolutionary societies can mobilize sufficient resources to socialize their young people quite apart from assistance by the family and can even, in many cases, overcome opposition from the family. Nevertheless, by the time the revolutionary generation become parents, they can be utilized as dependable assistants in the socialization process. No longer are the interests of family and state potentially contradictory. Hence the state changes its attitudes toward parental authority and encourages its restoration. Beginning in 1935 Soviet propaganda began to include such statements as "Young people should respect their elders, especially their parents" (Timasheff, 1946:202). Shades of Confucius!

This second phase of revolutionary movements tends to go to the opposite extreme from the first. Partly to counter the effect of the preceding policies and partly to strengthen the concern of the revolutionary parents about the complacency of their offspring, the emphasis on family stability and family authority tends to become quite reactionary: authoritarian, puritanical, and Victorian.

The Relaxation of Family Authority

It seems unlikely that any revolutionary movement can successfully restore an authoritarian family system for very long when it is based only on ideological grounds. Parents, to be sure, can be counted upon to retain their revolutionary fervor for the rest of their lives. But children cannot be expected to share their parents' enthusiasm for the revolution. Those who have grown up taking the revolution for granted and who have no memory for the injustices of the prerevolutionary era cannot be expected to share their parents' enthusiasm for the collective cause. Just as in utopian communities time undermines dedication to collectivism, so in postrevolutionary societies, the concerns of individual families within the society and of individual persons within the family gradually reassert themselves. Indeed the very success of the revolution in modernizing the country eventually dooms the struggle of revolutionary elders to maintain the dedication of their youth.

Eventually, every successful revolution breeds its own undoing. Eventually, every Stalinistic era is followed by de-Stalinization. Eventually the families of the new elite begin putting the welfare of their own children ahead of the welfare of the society at large. Eventually, the children of the new society develop hedonistic recreational interests to their elders' dismay. Both tendencies represent betrayals of the revolution but not in an explicitly counterrevolutionary sense. Rather they result from forgetting the revolution as families reassert their normal concern with their own welfare and as educated, prosperous young people engage in their usual enjoyment of the distinctive culture of youth.

This does not mean that the postrevolutionary situation is identical with the prerevolutionary one. It does mean, however, that the eventual form of the family is not likely to differ greatly in a society which passed through the fire of revolution than in a society which modernized by more peaceful means. But in the midst of that fire, a generation or two of families have experienced such wrenching social changes that their collective life was temporarily subjected to severe stress.

Pseudo-Revolutions   Parenthetically it should be noted that not every Communist takeover is preceded by a genuine revolution. In Eastern Europe at the end of World War II, the conversion of national governments to Communist states was more a foreign conquest by the Soviet armies than a grass roots revolution. Under such circumstances, the progression from anti-family Communist policy to the restoration of normalcy occurs spontaneously as soon as a "thaw" allows the reassertion of free expression.

In Poland, Kloskowska (1958) reported that family themes in the popular magazines changed sharply in the brief interval between 1951 and 1957. In 1951, a Polish government still subject to heavy Soviet dictation was using the mass media to emphasize the employment of women, the subordination of the older generation to the younger, and the subordination of the family to political, economic, and social issues. Forbidden topics included romance, emotional feelings, sex appeal, and other individualistic and subjective personal phenomena.

Six years later, Kloskowska found that the very same magazines were no longer publishing revolutionary literature. They reasserted marriage and family life as the highest values. Love, affection, and subjective feelings were again of interest. In many ways, the magazines seemed to have resumed publication where they had left off when the war broke out in 1939, the only major change being that the old Catholic taboo on divorce had been broken.

What had happened in the meantime to bring about in half a dozen years a change which in the Soviet Union required three generations? The answer is that in 1955, Gomulka succeeded in achieving sufficient independence from Soviet rule to be able to allow popular magazines to publish whatever family themes they wished instead of being forced to publish Communist anti-family propaganda. The very fact that family values so rapidly reasserted themselves proves how superficial the Polish revolution had been, enabling the Russian three-generation cycle of revolutionary change to be short-circuited as soon as freedom of the press was restored.

WAR

The violent phase of a revolution sometimes lasts only a few weeks or months but the rigors of the postrevolutionary regime last for decades. With major wars, this relationship tends to be reversed. The war itself may last for years but most postwar governments emphasize returning to prewar normalcy as fast as possible. Whereas the emphasis in the previous section was on the impact of the postrevolutionary regime on family life, the impact of war must be assessed primarily in terms of the wartime period itself.

There is one major exception to this generalization. Insofar as war kills off a whole generation of men, it leaves their potential wives stranded. The drastic alteration of the sex ratio in Germany after World War II led to serious advocacy of polygyny as a humanitarian solution. Since this solution was not formally adopted, women unable to marry could only enter into informal liaisons when they sought affection and sexual satisfaction.

This instability injected into the system of monogamous marriage as a result of the war-induced alteration of the sex-ratio parallels the temporary alteration which results from the mass removal of young men to the battlefront. This exodus speeds up family formation, separates husbands from wives and drives a wedge between the older and younger generations. Some of the subtler consequences of this separation for marital and parental relationships I will reserve for Chapter 22. Here, however, I will discuss the more grossly disorganizing effects of war on family life.

Distorted Family Formation

When war disrupts the life of young people, it threatens to deprive them of the chance for family living. Afraid they may not live long enough to experience life in due time, young men anticipating conscription into active military service feel impelled to rush into sexual involvement, marriage, and parenthood "before it's too late." The girls of their generation, equally aware that their young men will soon leave, perhaps never to return, are almost as driven to taste these experiences before life passes them by. Consequently, the outbreak of a major war stimulates premarital sexual involvements, hasty marriages, and precipitate child-bearing.

In studying fluctuations in the marriage rate in the United States, Pinard (1966) noted that World Wars I and II were responsible for extraordinary peaks in the number of young people marrying at any one time. In each case, however, there were two peaks for each war, one at the beginning of the war in a rush to marry before induction, the other at the end when demobilized men who had not succeeded in marrying in advance made up for lost time. At either point, the pressure of time does not allow judicious mate-selection or thorough courtship.

Even in the midst of war, marriages are contracted, sometimes under the worst possible circumstances. Slater and Woodside found that British soldiers who married during World War II were married only in a technical sense. Separated from their wives from the very beginning, they had only 10- to 14-day reunions which were "more like honeymoons than normal married life." Their wives continued to live with their parents and to work as they had before marriage, their living habits hardly changed by the wedding ceremony. The only major change was that they were no longer eligible to date and were forced into a loneliness worse than before. Indicative of their sense that they were only half-married were such comments as "it's a funny position, to be married and yet not married" and "war wives are like a single girl" (1951:215).

In short, couples married during wartime are only half-married at best. The process of family formation begins with a wedding and honeymoon, but is disrupted right there before there is any chance to consolidate the new relationship. No wonder such marriages tend to be unstable.

Disrupted Marriages

Wartime marriages have unusually fragile beginnings but war threatens pre-war marriages as well. For millions of couples, war removes the husband from home for years on end. Such physical destruction of the relationship, however temporary it may ultimately prove to be, cannot help but weaken the relationship between the partners, at least for the time being.

Deprived of any opportunity to depend on each other for emotional and sexual satisfaction, both partners are liable to become involved in extra-marital relationships of an ephemeral or more lasting nature. Given the divergent experiences to which they are subjected, husband and wife are liable to find their attitudes and values changed in different directions.

As a result of such factors, the reestablishment of the marriage relationship on the husband's return cannot be simply taken for granted. At the end of both world wars, American divorce rates reached new peaks which were only partly an accumulation of deferred divorces. The eruption of divorces at the end of World War II was too great to be accountable only as an accumulated backlog of court actions. Rather the twin handicaps of inadequate family formation and wartime separation took their toll of marriages which might have survived under more stable conditions.

Alienated Generations

Wars are fought by young men in response to political problems created by the old men who are heads of state. The contrast between the hardships endured by the young and the comparative safety of the old, together with the sheer physical separation of the generations due to the mobilization of the young, gives the young a self-consciousness which thrives on their sense of being exploited by the old. Aries (1962) noted that in World War I, hostility between the troops at the front and the older generation at the rear caused French society to become aware of youth as a distinctive group worthy of anxiety.

More recently the controversial nature of the Vietnam War widened the gap between generations in the United States. Young people who believed that American intervention in Vietnam was unwise or, worse yet, unjust protested against a war which their parents supported or at least accepted. The characteristic split between the conservatism of middle age and radicalism of youth was accentuated by the prolonged impasse of the longest war in American history, the heaviest bombing, the undeclared nature of the war, and other bitterly controversial features. Among the results was the exodus from home and family of thousands of young men to Canada, symbolizing the rejection by hundreds of thousands of others of the policies and values which their parents advocated.

The extent to which war alienates the generations depends on the popularity of that war. Presumably in an Arab–Israeli conflict, war might unify the generations. But whenever war affects the generations differentially, burdening one generation while the other is safe and even profits from a boom economy, such differentials can be expected to widen the gap.

SOCIAL COLLAPSE

Some wars end, for one side at least, in collapse of the whole social structure. Especially countries defeated in a major war may find not only their physical facilities but their morale so shattered that the country comes apart at the seams. This may also be the fate of a country torn by prolonged civil war or wracked by economic collapse in a great depression or a run-away inflation. In any case, if the complex machinery of civilization comes tumbling down, individuals and families are forced to shift for themselves in a social vacuum.

In the Middle Ages, the dissolution of the State resulted in renewed reliance on kin (Aries, 1962). Stripped of the protection of formal government, men resorted to the time-honored refuge of primitive man in the lineage. Knights who otherwise would have given their allegiance to larger political entities fell back on the ties of blood which survive every social crisis. With the collapse of large-scale social institutions, the family and its network of kin became the basic units out of which the social order was painfully reconstructed.

In modern times, the economic paralysis of the Great Depression of the 1930s and the destruction wreaked upon both Germany and Japan in World War II forced family members to rely on whatever resources were available within the kin network. Families liable to be bombed or already short of food evacuated their children to the security of rural relatives. Families fortunate enough to have financial resources shared them with relatives who did not.

Although kin networks were widely utilized under these difficult circumstances, nuclear family functioning was severely handicapped. Family formation was so widely postponed due to lack of housing and other facilities that the marriage rate fell sharply. Couples already married postponed having children so long in the case of the American Depression that their completed family size was lower than either pre-Depression or post-Depression families. Even divorce rates fell throughout the world because families could afford neither to pay the necessary legal fees nor to establish separate households.

Social collapse, then, is one of the few forms of social change which has a conservative effect on family life. Rather than the disorganization which results from other forms of change, social collapse forces family members to cling to one another for sheer survival. This does not mean, however, that family members are necessarily happy about their enforced mutual dependence.

Much of the classic literature on intergenerational conflict written by American sociologists was based on their observations of parent–adolescent relations in the United States during the Depression era. For instance, Davis (1940) and Parsons (1942) saw conflict as the essential feature of the relationship between parents and their adolescent children. Although some conflict is an inevitable concomitant of the constantly changing character of any technological civilization, the extent of conflict varies with the rate of change and the character of change. The peculiar character of the Depression was that economic change particularly frustrated young people. Employers preferred experienced men for the few jobs that were available, so unemployment rates among young men who had never held a job were many times higher than among their elders. Even young people still in school knew that they could look forward to a bleak prospect of postponed and shattered hopes. Under the circumstances, young people naturally begrudged the older generation for its failure to provide them with opportunities. They may not have been able to leave home because they couldn't afford to live independently, but their attitude toward their parents was hardly one of appreciation.

Social collapse then often forces family members to depend upon one another but that does not mean that family life flourishes under these painful circumstances. Rather the ideal setting for family life is social stability which allows families to pursue their goals leisurely and voluntarily.

FOREIGN CONQUEST

When war ends in the conquest of one country by another, the conqueror's views about family life are imposed on the defeated power. Another consequence is that family life is demoralized by the frustrations of domination by a foreign power, no matter how well intentioned that power may be.

After World War II, Japan was occupied by the American army and ruled by an Occupation government. One purpose of the Occupation was to democratize the Japanese people by reforming the family system. All efforts of the mass media, schools, and other agencies were bent toward this end in a fashion reminiscent of a revolutionary regime. At the same time, thousands of American men and their families settled in Japan to administer the Occupation. Through their treatment of Japanese women and the example of their own family life, these foreigners provided other lessons in the Western style of family life.

The combined effect of these teachings by precept and example was to accelerate the modernization of the Japanese family system. Although members of the same generation changed similarly enough to minimize marital disorganization, the damage to intergenerational relationships was severe. During the 1950s I noticed that Japanese young people characteristically referred to their parents as "feudal," while the parents recoiled at the brash behavior of their children. So wide was the gap between the prewar and postwar generations that intergenerational communication in many families broke down completely. Having experienced too many difficulties trying to understand each other, both generations ceased trying. Although the younger generation might still depend on their parents for food, clothing, and shelter, socially and psychologically the family had been split asunder.

A few years later, however, the Occupation came to an end, the postwar generation had children of their own whom they could understand more easily, and family life returned to normal (even though that normalcy was not the same as the prewar, pre-Americanized pattern).

Colonization

What happens if the occupying power doesn't leave? In the colonial era, dozens of poor countries were appropriated as colonies by the industrialized countries of Europe and the United States. What happens to family life when an occupying power rules generation after generation? What family patterns do the colonial administrators attempt to change—and how successful are they? What are the consequences, for family life, of living in a country ruled indefinitely by a foreign power interested in exploiting the colony's natural resources for the benefit of homeland industries?

Under the heading, "Factors of Social Change in Africa," Goode noted that no matter how much European administrators might try to accept the family customs of native peoples, they could not tolerate practices which they felt were "repugnant to common decency" (1963:172). Among the censured practices were inheritance of widows by younger brothers, betrothal of infants, payment of bride prices, and sometimes polygyny. Although administrators in some colonies did not attempt to wipe out all these practices immediately and in other cases did not succeed even where they tried, the administration of tribal territory by foreigners unsympathetic to basic elements of native family systems had an unsettling effect. Through school systems with European curricula and court systems presided over by foreign judges or by foreign-trained native judges responsible for interpreting laws modelled after European codes, the colonial administrators hoped to overturn un-European family practices.

I have already referred to African cities where Goode found extensive disorganization of families caught between native and European patterns. Another place where imperial conquest and rule destroyed family patterns was the Caribbean area and, to a lesser extent, the mainland countries of South America. In another article, Goode (1961) pointed to extraordinarily high rates of illegitimacy and of common-law or "consensual" unions of cohabiting unmarried couples as evidence of severe disorganization. He cited Jamaica, for example, where 72 percent of all children born in 1954 were born outside of wedlock (compared to less than five percent in the U.S.A. according to a 1960 report of the U. S. Bureau of Vital Statistics).

Goode ascribed this fragmentation of Caribbean family life to "cultural penetration," *i.e.,* the destruction of native cultures by the British, Spanish, and French conquerors. Both the normative structure (the culture) and the social structure crumbled under the impact of foreign conquest. Both socialization and social control mechanisms broke down, plunging society back into a relatively uncivilized state of irresponsible promiscuity.

This destruction of the native culture was sometimes a deliberate policy designed to keep the natives or imported slaves down by obliterating the traditions about which their resistance might have been mobilized. Sometimes it was simply a byproduct of imperial economic measures which ignored indigenous family units in determining breeding programs designed to produce more slaves or in the separate sale of husbands and wives to different masters. The normally disruptive effects of foreign conquest were compounded in these cases by the appropriation of individual people into slavery as well as of the whole society into colonialism.

The surprising feature of the Caribbean is not that family life fell apart at the time of colonial conquest but that several centuries later it was still so disorganized. To be sure, illegitimacy rates have begun to fall in most Caribbean countries, suggesting that those societies are beginning to recover from the worst of their colonial disorganization. But why didn't they adapt sooner to the colonial era? What kept them disorganized for hundreds of years even when no longer confronted with sudden invasion from abroad but simply with the persistence of foreign rule? Normally, family life finds a new equilibrium in a generation or two after disruption. In the next chapter we will see that families which migrate to a foreign country are usually disorganized for two generations but then adapt to their host country with relative ease. Why then when the pattern was reversed—when the rulers came from abroad—did the native families of the Caribbean remain disorganized almost indefinitely?

Goode suggested three major causes for the frozen disorder of the Caribbean. (1) The native peoples were allowed neither upward mobility into the dominant ruling group nor acculturation into their normative structure. Colonial rule, slavery, and caste (racial) barriers kept people subjugated and apart. (2) When immigrants settle in a foreign land, they usually form a small minority which is absorbed into the dominant culture of the overwhelming majority of the society. But the ratio between imperial rulers and native peoples is less favorable. Especially in rural areas, there are few opportunities for natives to observe and therefore to learn the ways of the dominant group. With their native culture destroyed, there is little opportunity to acquire a replacement culture from abroad. (3) Because the Caribbean Islands were not economically developed but simply exploited for their agricultural resources, the administrators provided little incentive for learning more stable family patterns. In an impoverished society, stable family life is difficult if not almost impossible. Only with the growth of industrialization in such a setting would there be sufficient resources to underwrite a stable family life and sufficient reward for those who adopted the European way of life. In the meantime, the ordinary people of those islands continued to live in a state of cultural anomie and social disorganization.

The situation in the Caribbean may be contrasted with that in Wales (which Welsh nationalists consider a colony of England). In the coastal city Swansea, so many families had already learned to speak English that Rosser and Harris (1965) found the number fluently speaking Welsh declining precipitously from 31 percent in the older generation to 16 percent among their children. Similarly, the high-status Anglican Church already embraced a majority of the population with the result that a rapid exodus of the younger generation was underway away from the Welsh chapels. This intergenerational linguistic and religious mobility could not help but leave the older generation feeling deserted. Yet in this case the process of adaptation to the impartial culture had proceeded so far that the reconsolidation of "Welsh" families around a common English culture could safely be predicted for the near future.

In almost every respect, the Welsh situation differed from the Caribbean one: (1) No barriers of caste or slavery prevented intermarriage, intimate social contact, or mobility into the English community. (2) English migration to nearby Wales was considerably greater than to the remote Caribbean, giving a population ratio more favorable to Anglicization. (3) The industrialization of Wales gave opportunities for participation in the British economy as well as a firmer basis for a stable family life. Thus foreign rule does not inevitably trap a society in a state of indefinite disorganization provided the native populace is given free access to assimilation into the dominant culture.

Decolonization

If colonial rule has been sufficiently long to destroy an old culture, the liberation of a country from foreign rule may be just as disorganizing initially as the original invasion was. If a newly independent nation decides to revive a culture which almost everyone has forgotten the culture shock may be almost as great as when an alien culture is imposed from abroad.

In the Republic of Ireland, Humphreys (1966) found that the government's decision to reintroduce Gaelic into the public schools brought the same kind of linguistic split between the generations which normally happens in immigrant families. When schoolwork must be done in a "foreign" language, parents cannot even understand what their children are studying, much less assist them with their homework. However, this "chasm" between the generations (as Humphreys called it) will disappear as soon as today's children become parents themselves and can share the new–old Gaelic culture.

Another consequence of decolonization resembles the effects of revolutionary movements. Insofar as women join in the resistance against imperial rule, their status in the society tends to rise. In India, where women previously had been cloistered and forbidden to take part in political activity, the anticolonial movement was an exception. So great was the hostility of Indian men to British rule that they even allowed their women to join the independence movement. But women cannot participate in a movement for freedom from foreign rule without being infected with a desire for freedom from domestic masculine rule:

> The political movement launched by Mahatma Gandhi brought women from their hearths to face lathis and bullets, and gave them not only a consciousness of their own strength, but a new vision of their true place in society. . . . Gaining a new confidence in their own capacities and abilities, they now became conscious of the fact that they had to fight for their proper place in home and society. (Kapadia, 1958:254)

To fight for their proper place in home and society is to fight against husbands and fathers—in other words, to disturb the family. Yet, as in the Irish case, the disorganization of decolonialization is likely to be far less prolonged than in the colonization case because a viable new pattern of family life can be established. The departure of a foreign conqueror, especially if he resists leaving, is therefore another drastic change to which family life must adapt. But the prospects for a satisfactory adaptation are far more hopeful after he departs than they were after he arrived.

CULTURAL DIFFUSION

It is sometimes difficult to separate the diffusion of Western cultural patterns into non-Western countries from the effects of foreign conquest, especially when the diffusion takes place under colonial rule. I shall attempt to distinguish, however, between the impact of imperial administrative policies and of missionaries, educators, and other foreigners who rely on persuasion and example rather than compulsion.

Cultural diffusion is not limited to the colonial context but may occur quite independently. The channels of diffusion may be books and movies originally intended for Western consumption and the agents of diffusion may be natives traveling to Western countries rather than vice versa. In any case, the question is whether the clash of cultures is sufficiently critical not only to change family patterns but to disorganize them. Or is cultural diffusion so gentle that families can adopt new ideas gradually without being disorganized in the process?

Comparable research in the United States, France, Greece, and Yugoslavia (summarized by Buric and Zecevic, 1967) showed the effect of the diffusion of modern family patterns into quasi-feudal countries of Southeastern Europe. Whereas in the U. S. and France, high-status husbands wielded more authority in the home than low-status husbands, the reverse was true in Greece and Yugoslavia. The reason apparently was that the latter countries were still feudalistically patriarchal and only high-status men (better-educated, white-collar, and higher-salaried) were sufficiently exposed to cosmopolitan ideas to grant their wives a voice in decision-making.

One way of ascertaining whether this diffusion had occurred without disorganization is to examine the subjective feelings of husbands and wives about their marriages. In Greece, the wives of college-educated husbands were highly satisfied with their marriages, suggesting that the transition to new patterns of marriage in response to cultural diffusion had been successfully made. However, in Yugoslavia, marital satisfaction fell for wives of better-educated men. Even though educated Yugoslavian husbands were partially responsive to new concepts of marriage, they had not adapted sufficiently to please their wives who also were infected by the new ideas.

Buric and Zecevic noted that strains in Yugoslavian marriages were most severe where the greatest change had occurred, *i.e.,* where wives were employed outside the home. This suggests that where family patterns change very rapidly under the impact of cultural diffusion, it is difficult for the husband and wife to adjust to the pace of change. Yugoslavia was a particularly backward country undergoing a crash program of modernization under the leadership of a quasi-revolutionary Communist government. Thus the dissatisfaction of emancipated Yugoslav wives with their marriages may have been due to several other factors in addition to sheer cultural diffusion.

In some countries, religious institutions have been a major support for the status quo in family life. For instance, Islam and Catholicism have tended to uphold the patriarchal rights of men and enforce the subjugation of women. However, in other settings, the intrusion of foreign missionaries brought the emancipation of women and children from the subordination to which they were subjected under feudal conditions. For instance, in countries which offered higher education only to men, foreign missionaries have established institutions for women which educated them for emancipation and coeducational schools which fostered equality and communication between the sexes.

Missions have had more success in freeing subordinate groups than in imposing restrictions on native peoples. For example, in Northern Rhodesia, Colson (1958) found that missionaries successfully advocated freedom of mate-selection for young people, but failed in their efforts to curb premarital sexual freedom. Even girls who had attended mission boarding-schools for years and who had been exposed to the full impact of mission teaching had as many illegitimate children as girls unexposed to mission influence.

Cultural diffusion, then, is uneven at best. Because of the differential receptivity of the receiving culture, foreign patterns are taken over piecemeal. Even though the whole world seems to be adopting a Western style of family life under the influence of modernization and cultural diffusion, exposure to these influences sometimes changes certain facets of family life while leaving no observable change in other facets.

One consequence of this erratic pattern of change is that different aspects of family life may become poorly articulated with one another, which strains family life in addition to the very fact of change itself. If change were more evenly balanced, it might be less disorganizing. But in a world whose transportation and communication networks are accelerating cultural diffusion from modernized countries to the rest of the world, the processes of change can hardly be coordinated, much less prevented. Until the world becomes culturally homogenized, cultural diffusion across cultural boundaries will continue to have an unsettling effect on older patterns of family living.

chapter nine

MIGRATION AND THE FAMILY

Most families never move. Once the family is formed, it lives in the same house throughout its life cycle. If people move at all, they change houses in response to housing pressures and opportunities, but the new house is usually close enough to the old one to involve no significant change in ties with kin or friends. For those few families who leave kin and friends behind, the move is apt to be to a similar environment so that while the people may change, the culture does not.

Only a minority of persons ever move from a rural to an urban environment within their own country or migrate from one country to another. Yet from the standpoint of this chapter, these very cases are the most interesting. The farther the move and the greater the change of cultural environment, the greater the strain on the family. So we will focus primarily on those exceptional moves which wrench the family from its environment.

FAMILY STABILITY

Other things equal, most families don't like to move. Those who do move, do so reluctantly, hoping that the pain of moving will be outweighed by economic or other gains. If the husband is the chief determiner of the family's economic welfare, he is apt to advocate the change, whereas the rest of the family may prefer to stay put.

In most feudal societies, families remain fixed in one location for many generations. Younger sons may leave to seek their fortune elsewhere, but the ancestral home remains in the stem family indefinitely.

In feudal Poland, according to Thomas and Znaniecki, one consequence of geographical stability was social stability:

> When a family has lived from time immemorial in the same locality, when all its members for three or four generations are known or remembered, every individual is classified first of all as belonging to the family, and appreciated according to the appreciation which the family enjoys, while on the other hand the social standing of the family is influenced by the social standing of its members, and no individual can rise or fall without drawing to some extent the group with him. And at the same time no individual can so rise or fall as to remove himself from the familial background upon which social opinion always puts him. (1958:96)

When the individual is closely bound up with his larger family, his ability either to climb the social scale or to fall is hampered. Because he is not judged as an isolated individual, he cannot achieve upward social mobility without pulling his whole network of kin up with him—an extraordinarily difficult feat. Such an interdependent setting is a safeguard against downward mobility but a deterrent to upward mobility. As a result, the social standing of an individual when he dies is very likely to be little removed from that at his birth. Indeed, in a geographically stable community, social status is far more ascribed at birth than achieved by one's own efforts.

Geographical mobility does not make social mobility inevitable, but makes it far more possible. The smaller the community and the better known the individual's family, the more he must leave the community to free himself to achieve his own destiny. This is not just a question of the individual versus the family. (An upwardly mobile man normally carries his wife and children with him.) The crucial effect of geographical stability is to freeze the nuclear family, whereas geographical mobility makes it possible for that whole unit to move independently of its kin network.

Home Is a House   A society does not have to be agricultural to breed attachment to the family homestead. Wherever families have homes of their own, the house shelters so many family experiences that family memories are bound up with the building. The longer a family lives in a particular house (especially during the child-rearing years), the more it comes to symbolize the family's identity. In old age, when the store of family memories is full and parents live more in the past than the present, the tie to the old house becomes strongest. *Viz.,* this report on East London working-class couples' reluctance to move in with their children:

> Old people's wish to live independently was reinforced by a deep attachment to their homes. It was rare for widows or widowers in the district to join a married son or daughter. Only three, all widows, had done this, and

even these three had been reluctant. Others said they were invited but had refused to go. Home was the old armchair by the hearth, the creaky bedstead, the polished lino with its faded pattern, the sideboard with its picture gallery and the lavatory with its broken latch beyond the rain. It embodied a thousand memories and held promise of a thousand contentments. It was an extension of personality. To the married children it was also the reminder of their history and achievements—this the paper where you looked for animal shapes, that the doormat which had to be lifted at the corner if the door was to be shut. "We always go over *home* to see Mum on Sundays," said a married daughter. Part of what the children felt for their parents was what they felt for the parental home. It was not only the place where associations with the past and long usage provided comfort and security in old age. It was a symbol of family unity and tradition. (Townsend, 1957:27)

INTERNAL MIGRATION

Against this background of normal stability, we turn to the exceptional families who move. There are two major types of migration, those confined within the boundaries of the society and those which cross those boundaries. Internal migration may involve no change in the cultural environment—the new locale may be almost identical with the old. Only the people are different. They may be the same kind of people as before—with the same way of life—but they are strangers initially, whereas old neighbors were friends and relatives. Thus even a move to a culturally and socially identical community severs social ties.

Movement within a given society is not always so painless. Regional differences in culture and rural–urban differences may free the family to be resocialized into a new way of life. For hillbilly families in Chicago the culture shock may be almost as profound as for European peasant immigrants half a century ago. The strain of geographical mobility therefore depends on such factors as the frequency of moving, the geographical distance moved, and more especially the cultural distance moved.

Nomads: Migration as a Way of Life

Under some environmental conditions, a settled way of life is impossible. If the subsistence afforded by a given locality is too meager to feed a family for very long, survival may require adopting a migratory way of life, moving from pasture to pasture or hunting ground to hunting ground as natural resources are exhausted.

Within settled societies, some occupations require seasonal or perennial migration. Migrant laborers in American agriculture follow the crops from South to North with the changing seasons. For them, migration becomes an almost chronic state to which the family must adjust.

The larger and more complex the household, the harder it is to pull up stakes and migrate together. At the same time, the very scarcity of resources which makes migration necessary in the first place prevents the development of large masses of people (as in extended households). For such reasons, the more migratory the subsistence pattern, the less likely the society is to have extended families as its normal household arrangement. Conversely, a sedentary way of life does not make extended families necessary, but it facilitates their development.

If the family is accustomed to moving, it is psychologically easier for a new unit to split off and establish an independent household. On the other hand, if the family never strays from home, it is easier for a marrying child to bring his bride into the home base than for both partners to launch out into a new domicile. Thus the close correlation between migratory households and nuclear households in Table 9-1 can be interpreted as a correlation between two forms of migration: of elders to new locations and of newly-married couples to independent locations.

TABLE 9-1   Household Composition by Migratory Pattern

| | MIGRATORY PATTERN | | |
HOUSEHOLD COMPOSITION	Sedentary	Seasonally Nomadic	Nomadic/Migratory
Extended	60%	51%	28%
Nuclear only	40	49	72
Total	100%	100%	100%
Number of societies	410	78	61

Adapted from Nimkoff and Middleton (1960):219.

Nomadic tribes carry their rudimentary social institutions with them. However, a nomadic way of life prevents the development of very specialized institutions, leaving the family, the kin group, and the village as the chief forms of social organization.

For modern migrants, the necessity of moving from farm to farm every few weeks rips the family loose from other social institutions. Children may be enrolled in a whole series of schools during the migratory seasons but stay at any one hardly long enough to get much benefit. If all schools studied the same books at the same time, migration from school to school would be less disruptive. But in a decentralized school system, successive schools may be studying such different topics that the child is only bewildered, not educated. Similarly, migrant families have few opportunities to establish meaningful ties with churches, labor unions, or other organizations. If they are fortunate, they may be able to migrate en masse with friends and relatives in a caravan of cars. But even this "village" is likely to be less stable than among the Saharan Bedouin.

This isolation of migrant families from social facilities further impoverishes an already deprived group of adults and children. Only if there is a base camp in the South where they settle down for the winter is there much opportunity for such families to benefit from the educational facilities of an advanced society, and then unemployment may pose economic barriers to utilization of temporarily accessible facilities.

Migrant parents have little hope to offer their children. This undermines the parents' influence. On the other hand, families cut off by their perennial wandering from meaningful contact with outside groups are especially dependent on internal cooperation. Children work in the fields with their parents from an early age, especially during the summer "vacation" from school. Families travel together in the narrow confines of the family car and frequently sleep together in the single rooms of tar-paper shacks. Given their poverty of inter-action with outsiders and their intensity of interaction with each other, family ties may be strong even though often strained by conflict.

Migration of Individuals

When unmarried individuals leave their families to seek their fortunes else-where, they free themselves from family controls and win a chance to make their way as individuals. The fortune they seek may be wealth, social status, a marriage partner, a sexual partner, or simply freedom from parental control. In any case, attenuation of that control comes automatically with departure from home, regardless of whether that departure is permanent or temporary. As long as the child is away and the farther away he is, the greater his freedom from parental supervision, admonition, and control.

If a migrating individual is already involved in a quasi-marital relation-ship, his departure similarly frees him from control by the person or persons with whom he has been involved. In this case, migration is often criticized as an escape from responsibility, rather than as freedom from control. But the basic process is the same. Leaving home gives the individual a chance to assert his individual wishes against the claims of others with whom he has been involved in a family or quasi-family. The full-fledged desertion of a bona fide marriage partner I will postpone for the chapter on "Leadership Impair-ment," but it has many elements in common with other cases of migration by individuals.

Premarital Migration   Single adults leave home more for economic motives than for any other. We have already seen Thomas and Znaniecki's description of the freedom which this gave Polish peasants to become socially mobile, without the necessity of raising the status of their entire network of local kin-folk.

Sometimes, the motive for leaving is sexual. For example, an elopement involves running away from home to get married. Its motivation is usually parental opposition to a proposed marriage—either because the child is too young to marry anyone or because the proposed partner is unsuitable. In either case, the child asserts his freedom and independence by travelling to a distant community or another state.

Parallel to elopement is the temporary migration of young men from their home town or neighborhood to another community in search of sexual partners. In this case, not only the parents' but the neighbors' supervision is evaded. Insofar as the home community exerts social control, as in a rural village, migration may be necessary to achieve the freedom of action which is available locally only in urbanized anomic areas. So if one wishes to engage in behavior which is forbidden at home, a "foreign" locale permits deviant behavior with greater impunity.

In a Polish–American farming community of 3,000 in the Connecticut River Valley of Massachusetts, Green (1941:345) found that "the local boys usually drive to the surrounding towns and villages for their pick-ups, so that the village's Main Street is the hunting ground for out-village boys." Mobility between villages depended on the ownership of a few cars among the single young men. A car was shared by two or three boys who used it to pick up a corresponding number of girls from the adjacent community. The first group date normally consisted of necking in a secluded place. Subsequent individual dates progressed rapidly to sexual intercourse. According to Green, these out-of-the-village relationships were completely loveless and not uncommonly bordered on rape. "This is the social jungle . . . a situation approximating open warfare" between the sexes (p. 345).

Although Green did not emphasize the effect of migration, he implied that it contributed to the anomic character of the sexual behavior. He noted that serious courtship (the type which eventuated in marriage) was usually between partners who lived in the same village. These steadier relationships within the home community involved more conservative, socially accepted patterns of behavior: "Usually, the girl who goes steadily with a boy is more reserved, less promiscuous and foolhardy than those who date indiscriminately" (p. 345). In general, I conclude that the closer to home dating is, the more subject to family norms it is, whereas dating in remote places is free to be more anomic.

When young Africans leave their villages to seek employment in the city, the resulting estrangement from their parents results from more than simply geographical separation. Goode (1963) noted that in the city, migrants became exposed to "European" ways of life unfamiliar to their parents so that they became culturally estranged in much the same way as the children of migrants to a foreign country. The greater the cultural difference between the target community and the home base, the greater the value dissonance injected into the parent–child relationship.

LeVine and LeVine noted the breakdown of parental control over the premarital behavior of young Kenyans who migrated from their rural villages to urban areas: "While traditional means of controlling sexual behavior remain effective at the local level where kinship sanctions are operative, increased contact between persons of different localities has resulted in a rise of premarital sexual activity, including rape" (1963:104). In this case both partners were removed from the influence of parents and kin. Note the researchers' emphasis on the freedom of behavior of persons from different home communities. If both partners had migrated from the same community, they would still be somewhat restrained by their common origin. On the other hand, couples who have no common ties are least restrained by family teachings.

In many African cities, only the fortunate few are able to marry, because labor migration has imbalanced the sexes. In Salisbury, Rhodesia, Goode (1963) reported that there were seven black men for every woman. Most men could not hope to marry as long as they were in the city. Even the few women available for marriage there might find it less attractive financially than the income provided by prostitution to this overwhelming number of unattached males. The result was an almost complete breakdown of stable family patterns and the substitution of prostitution, temporary liaisons, and concubinage for marriage, and of illegitimate child-bearing for legal reproduction.

E. Franklin Frazier, writing an early article about the impact of urban civilization upon black family life, stressed the consequences of recurrent migration for unattached men and women who wandered from the rural South to an urban ghetto and then from city to city in search of the employment which was so elusive for black men and women during the Depression. Some of them had been married back home. Some entered into temporary liaisons in the city. But the frequency of moving on discouraged the development of even tentative commitments in common-law relationships. Frazier (1937:312) felt the blues expressed the "disappointments and disillusionment in the city" of these "homeless, wandering, intermittent black workers." Although occasional couples "mated" in the sense of settling down to live together briefly, neither partner knew when the other would leave to continue his/her wanderings. The uncertainty of the situation contributed to the fighting and quarreling which Frazier found characteristic of these brittle impulsive unions. So chronic was the tendency to migrate that norms of stable relationships could hardly emerge.

Migration does not inevitably prevent single men and women from establishing stable relationships—but it tends to have that effect. It would be possible to cite young people who have gone away to school or work and moved smoothly into stable marriages. The point is that insofar as migration makes a difference, it tends to reduce the stability of relationships.

In rural Poland at the turn of the century, unmarried girls attempted to use their seasonal labor migration into Germany to land a man whom they hoped would become a faithful husband. An article in the *Gazeta Swiateczna* for 1907 described the frequent betrayal of these hopes:

> In parishes near the Prussian frontier it often happens that girls, and even widows, who went to Germany to work, bring thence their companions of work, compatriots, boys or widowers, in order to tie up in matrimonial bonds with them. More than one girl actually bought wedding-clothes for such a boy or widower brought from Prussia and coming from a different part of the country; she bears all the cost of the wedding and festival herself only in order that he should marry her. But it does not always end in marriage. For among such candidates to matrimony there happen to be worthless fellows and sometimes even rogues, married men pretending to be bachelors or widowers. Such a rogue, having wheedled his betrothed out of as much money as he can, disappears before the banns or during the time of the banns, and does not return any more. (Thomas and Znaniecki:1159–1160)

Seasonal migration brought these women into contact with supposedly unattached men whom they otherwise would have had no opportunity to meet. Their aggressive attempts to snare the men was not a product of their own migratory behavior alone but of the fact that their chances for marriage had been sharply reduced by the emigration of young men to the United States.

On the other hand, Thomas and Znaniecki felt that a girl's temporary emigration to Germany not only brought her into contact with new men, but also emancipated her from family control enough to have the courage to pursue the men forthrightly. The fact that she returned home at the end of the harvest brought her again within the scope of a family system which placed a heavy premium on the regularization of relationships through marriage. Perhaps the discovery of these strong family ties was enough to scare many men away as soon as they encountered them! The men had been emancipated from conservative patterns by their own seasonal migration to Germany and were hardly prepared to stomach a return to the tight controls of married life in an old peasant village.

Migration, then, threw men and women from different communities together in a strange place where women were able to exercise extraordinary initiative toward contracting what they hoped would be the stable relationships demanded by their home communities. But contact with the wedding process frightened the men out of the marriages that Thomas and Znaniecki believed they had usually intended. Thus seasonal migration failed to offer a basis for contracting substitute relationships for the marriages prevented by the emigration of local young men. Even when migration seems to offer new opportunities for marriage, it may bring concealed dangers.

Desertion of Quasi-Families Wandering individuals sometimes form quasi-families and then abandon them as they go on their way. The ability to migrate repeatedly is prized by such individuals as a means of escaping familistic responsibilities when they become burdensome.

Probably the most common burden to be fled is an unwanted pregnancy. For a man living temporarily with a girl for the sake of her sexual and domestic services, but with no intention of founding a dynasty, her missed menstrual period is a warning that it is time to move on. Rosenberg and Bensman found that Appalachian boys in Chicago were extraordinarily mobile because most of them owned cars: "In a crisis, occasioned, say, by the impregnation of a girl friend (scarcely a rare occurrence), they can always take to the road, ranging widely over Illinois and adjacent states" (1968:65). In other words, they could disappear from public view until the crisis was resolved by an abortion or at least until the girl gave up hope that the father would assume responsibility for the child.

Although relatively few Chicago couples were actually living together when such migration-inducing pregnancy occurred, informal living arrangements were common in Blake's study of Jamaica. However, a common domicile hardly deterred the man from abandoning his woman when she became pregnant (unless he felt ready to begin raising children): "The instability of employment on the island and the resulting itineracy frees many men from local controls. . . . The itinerant male can therefore avoid both family and community sanctions" (1961:92).

Blake reports that Jamaican men "often" departed hastily when they discovered an unintended pregnancy. Since these cohabiting couples engaged in sexual intercourse without benefit of contraceptives, the pregnancy-and-abandonment sequence was a standard feature of premarital liaisons.

Migration was not only a means of terminating relationships but sometimes a cause for desertion. In a vicious circle, the geographical mobility of young islanders resulting from employment instability provided an inauspicious setting for the development of stable family or quasi-family patterns. Accustomed to moving on in search of employment, young men easily acquired the habit of moving on in search of unencumbered sexual partners. The encumbrance of pregnancy was partly financial (frightening men incapable of supporting an extra mouth), partly social (frightening men unready to assume the role of husband, much less of father), partly sexual (since the growing fetus eventually interfered with the woman's ability to have intercourse). Migration therefore fed upon itself, preventing the establishment of secure relationships in the first place and precipitating the abandonment of insecure relationships as soon as they threatened to levy claims upon the man.

In some family systems, young men are not the only ones who find migration a convenient escape from family pressures. In some African tribes, Goode (1963) found that old women who had lost their husbands fled from home to escape pressure from the husband's family. If tribal custom called for widow inheritance (requiring marriage to the deceased husband's younger brother) and the widow did not wish to marry him, the opportunity to run away and support herself elsewhere became a means of escape. Goode noted that in recent years, travel had become not only easier but safer (though he did not specify whether the hazards had been animal or human). In any case, improved travel provided alternatives to the customary acceptance of kin-determined remarriages.

For both never-married and formerly-married individuals, therefore, migration offers an escape from being trapped in unwanted marriages. Freedom of movement prevents individuals from being forced into forming unwanted family ties. Family formation thus becomes more purely voluntary than it would otherwise be. Although in extreme cases, migration offers opportunities for lifelong bachelorhood, studies in most of these communities show that the average man or woman eventually settles down to marriage. Migration is not so much a means of avoiding marriage ultimately as a means of escaping marriage before the individual feels ready for it.

To put it another way, the availability of desertion enables men to experiment with quasi-family relationships when they are too young or too poor for full-blown family ties. Presumably if their financial resources were greater, such young men would find migration less necessary either for occupational or for familistic reasons. Under the circumstances, recurrent migration is an adaptive solution to the frustrations of being caught between desire for sexual intimacy and ability to accept the consequences of that intimacy.

More broadly, the migration of individuals allows them to escape either imposition of unwanted family ties (as in the case of the African widows), escalation of the degree of commitment involved in quasi-family relationships, or the frustration inherent in family disapproval of deviant behavior in which the individual wishes to engage. In every case, migration frees the individual from family influence.

Dispersion of Kin

There is a close analogy between the effect of migration on an individual's relationship to his family and on a nuclear family's relationship to the circle of kin. When the migrating unit is not a solitary individual but a whole family, the effect is the same—freedom from control by the larger unit. The motives are less often to escape from kin or to engage in what relatives might call deviant behavior. Nevertheless, the very fact that kin perform a social control function (Chapter 7) suggests that families might have much the same freedom-seeking motives as young men or widows.

Adams (1968) found a difference between middle-class and lower-class Americans in the extent to which moving was motivated by a desire to escape from kin. For blue-collar white males during a time of relative prosperity, it was rarely necessary to change communities to find satisfactory unskilled or semi-skilled employment. So if a blue-collar family moved at all, it was almost always for the sake of escaping from unsatisfactory kin relationships. On the other hand, middle-class men often found it necessary to change communities in order to advance their more specialized careers. For them negative relationships with kin less often were the main reason for moving, and positive ties less often prevented them from moving. For blue-collar men, by contrast, kin ties normally took precedence over vocational concerns as their motive for either staying or leaving.

Regardless of motives, however, the effect of migration away from relatives is much the same. Freedom from control and reduction of contact are produced by geographical mobility.

Attenuation of Kin Ties By definition, the movement of a nuclear family away from home means establishing a neolocal residence and abrogating the possibility of being part of an already established extended family. In American history, the existence of an open frontier until 1890 made it possible to avoid developing an extended family system despite the fact that most of the men were farmers. Generation after generation, sons moved West to establish their own independent families. Even those who stayed behind could resist the attempts of their fathers to dominate them by threatening to go West. American families remained remarkably equalitarian under economic conditions which in settled countries produced domination by elder kin. Just as the frontier closed, industrialization and urbanization swept over the American scene to prevent any freezing of kinship ties. Thus, the perennial possibility of internal agricultural or urban migration loosened kin ties enough to affect the whole character of the American family system.

In neolocal family systems, migration does not change the already decentralized character of the family–kinship system, but simply attenuates the amount of contact with kin. Other things being equal, the greater the distance moved, the less the contact with kin.

TABLE 9-2 Presence of Kin in the Local Community by Migration Status of Husband and Wife

KIN HOUSEHOLDS IN THE LOCAL COMMUNITY	NUMBER OF MIGRANT PARTNERS		
	None	*One*	*Both*
Both primary and secondary kin of both partners	47%	23%	10%
Some kin households	52	76	60
None	2	1	29
Total	101%	100%	99%
Number of cases	124	150	230

Adapted from Winch and Greer (1968):42. Source: Representative sample of Wisconsin households. A husband or wife was classified as migratory if he/she had arrived in the community after the age of 18.

Table 9-2 illustrates the impact of migration prior to marriage on the presence of primary or secondary kin in the local community. When both partners still lived in the same community they were born or grew up in, almost half the couples were surrounded by not only primary but also secondary kin on both sides of the family. This full set of local kin was usually left behind when families migrated. Only half as many families had bilateral kin when one partner had migrated and removed himself from his central cluster of kin. And when both partners had migrated, the proportion with bilateral primary and secondary kin dwindled almost to nothing. Conversely, the latter were almost the only couples who lived apart from all relatives. Migration, then, profoundly affects the presence or absence of kin in the local community.

TABLE 9-3   Frequency of Interaction with Parents, by Geographical Distance

FREQUENCY OF INTERACTION	GEOGRAPHICAL DISTANCE			
	Same Community	100 Miles	Adjacent States	Elsewhere
At least once a week	84%	17%	0%	0%
At least once a month	16	61	35	10
At least twice a year	0	20	57	46
Once a year or less	0	2	8	44
Total	100%	100%	100%	100%
Number of young adults	155	113	93	83

Adapted from Adams (1968):38. Source: Young married white men and women in Greensboro, North Carolina.

Table 9-3 shows how sharply contact with the most intimate primary kin is reduced by the barrier of geographical distance. For those whose parents lived in the same community 48 percent of the men and 72 percent of the women saw their parents at least *twice* a week. At the opposite extreme, parents living outside the adjacent states of Virginia and South Carolina were seldom seen more than a few times a year.

The same disruption of contact by mobility appears in numerous studies of kinship. For example, Townsend found that East London old people were sharply affected by the location of their children:

> If the children lived in the same district, the old person often spent one or two days of each week, particularly Sundays, with them, quite apart from any visits the children made on other days. If the children lived several miles away in London suburbs or housing estates he or she often spent a weekend with them. And if they lived far outside London he or she often spent a week or more with them once or twice a year. (1957:37)

The reduction of visiting by geographical separation correspondingly affected the kinds of services which aging parents could receive from or give to their children. Parents and children who lived nearby "exchanged all kinds of services and helped one another in the daily problems of life" (p. 38), whereas children living furthest away provided nothing more than hospitality for holiday travellers and attended only the most urgent gatherings of the clan (weddings, funerals, and golden weddings).

The fact that distance reduces the ability to assist aging parents produces what Litwak (1960a) labelled "push and pull" migration. Parents who earlier in life may have sponsored the child's departure for greener pastures are later drawn to the child's new community in order to receive the intimate care they need in old age. Willmott and Young noted that for former East Londoners who moved to the suburbs this often meant that parents moved into the child's home itself:

> . . . the reason why so many old people live with children in [the suburbs] is, paradoxically, because they used to live so far away. The old people of Bethnal Green were down the street; their children had only to walk over the road to look after them or keep them company. But [suburban] children lived so far off that even with cars they could not keep an eye on parents all the time, nor give them that assurance which old people need, of someone close by to call on in an emergency. (1960:43)

Somehow distance had to be dissolved either by the younger family returning home or by parents moving to the suburbs. Since suburban families owned their own homes, they were too firmly rooted to leave. Most urban families were tenants so it was physically easier for them to move. Psychologically, however, moving was hard on old people since it stripped them of their old friends and thrust them into a new community where everyone save their child was a stranger. To have to move into the same house with a son- or daughter-in-law was not easy, but the suburban community offered no apartments or houses small enough to meet the needs of an elderly couple. So if elders followed their children to the suburbs, they had to follow them right into the house.

Although at the end of life migration may reunite once-separated kin, in the meantime separation presents a barrier to interaction. At first, separated relatives make a valiant effort to maintain the contact they are used to. At great cost to themselves in time and money, they travel long distances to see each other. But after a while, the cost begins to weary the traveller. For practical reasons, he finds it impossible to maintain the pace which was natural when he lived in the same neighborhood. As his visits fall off, he begins to feel less close to his relatives.

Before the move, frequent interaction and intense affection sustain one another. After the move, the intensity of affection brakes the expected decline in interaction for a time, so that interaction declines gradually rather than abruptly. But decreased interaction tends to undermine the intensity of affect so that motivation to visit declines, making a further decline in visiting psychologically possible. Eventually a new equilibrium is established on a lower level of affect and interaction appropriate to the time/cost facts of life at the new distance.

One example of gradual reduction of contact comes from India, where Goode reported that after nuclear families had moved to the city, "frequency of contacts with kin grow progressively less with longer periods of residence in the city" (1963:244). In other words, the longer the interval following migration, the greater the decline in frequency of interaction. However, this statement needs to be qualified by the premise that eventually a plateau would be reached from which there would be no further decline.

Figure 9-1 shows how kin contact declined over a two-year interval some years after couples moved from a London slum to a new housing project in the suburbs. Presumably by the time of the study the level of kinship interaction had not yet reached its new equilibrium. However, the curves are drawn beyond the terminal date for the statistics to suggest how that new plateau might appear in subsequent years.

A new feature of Figure 9-1 is the differential impact of migration on the kinship contact of men and women. Back in the slums, kin contact was skewed in a feminine direction. But after migration to the suburbs, men had more contact than their wives. Migration reduced the ability of women to maintain face-to-face contact with relatives more than it interfered with men's contact. The reason is the occupational roles of the two sexes. Most wives did not work, which meant that as long as they lived nearby they could visit their relatives several times a day. After moving, they could not afford the expensive trip all the way into London more than once or twice a week. Many of their husbands on the other hand still worked in London and could sometimes visit relatives after work. This produced an unusual patrilateral bias in the post-migration interaction pattern. It should not be assumed, however, that migration has universally patrilateral effects. In Swansea, Wales, both husbands and wives originally lived close to their kin in the same neighborhood. The opening of housing projects on the fringes of the city proved more attractive to sons than to daughters, because sons felt less tied to their parents than did their sisters. The result was a selective migration of sons out of the neighborhood, leaving behind a matrilateral cluster of kin (Rosser and Harris, 1965).

Another way in which mobility produced matrilaterality in Swansea was by bringing unmarried middle-class men to the community for employment. Whereas most working-class men found jobs within the community, making bilateral kin available locally, middle-class men travelled farther in search of specialized employment. They married local girls and settled down in Swansea, close to the wife's kin but far away from their own.

Only when an already-formed nuclear family migrates away from both sets of kin does their pattern of contact sometimes shift in a patrilateral direction. Even that, however, may be restricted largely to poor families where the wife cannot afford to travel and to a transitional period when the husband continues to work at his old job. Eventually we might expect the husband's employment to shift toward the suburbs if suitable jobs are available there, for the very same reasons why kin contact is curbed by mobility. If it costs too much time and money to visit relatives in the old location, it is too expensive to commute to work, too. When a shift in employment occurs, we might expect the husband's kin contact to fall off sharply and an overall pattern of matrilaterality to reemerge.

Continued postmigration contact with kin due to sentimental ties will depend on the strength of those ties. Presumably contacts with secondary kin

FIGURE 9-1. Frequency of Kin Contact Before and After Migration

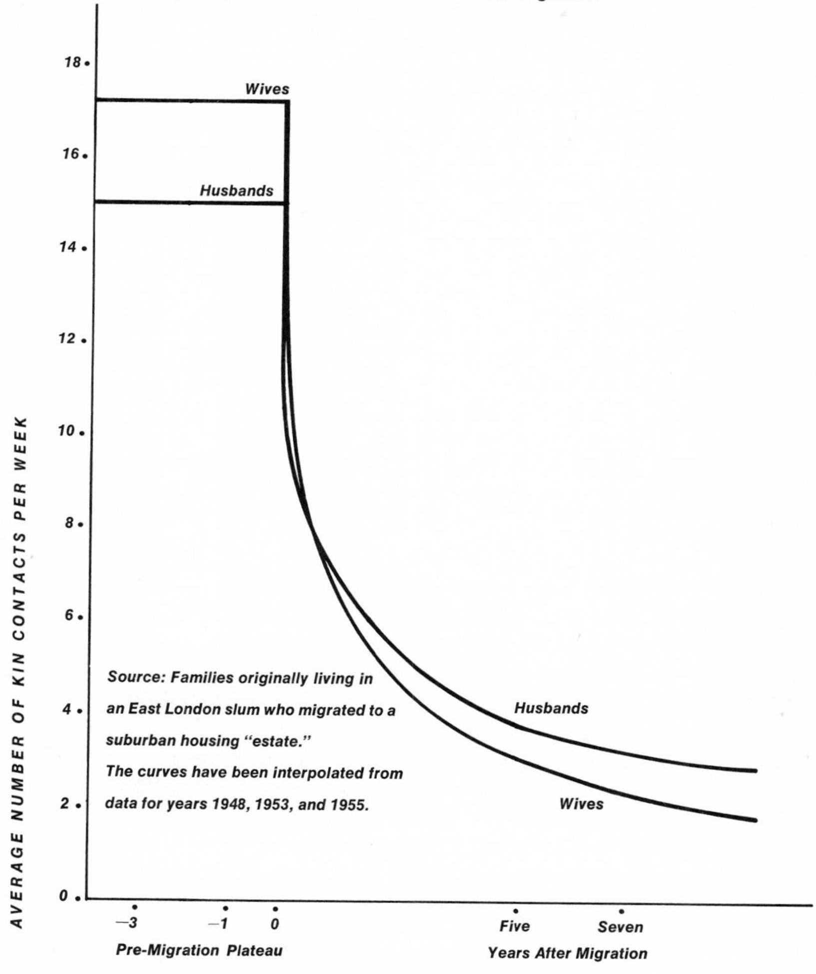

Adapted from Young and Willmott (1957):106.

will suffer a sharper reduction than those with primary kin; and within the latter group, interaction with siblings should decline more rapidly than with parents.

TABLE 9-4 Percentage of Young Adults Who Interact at Least Monthly with Kin and Percentage Reduction of Interaction, by Closeness of Kin and by Geographical Distance

PERCENTAGE INTERACTING AT LEAST ONCE A MONTH	*None**	*GEOGRAPHICAL DISTANCE*		*Elsewhere*
		100 Miles	*Adjacent States*	
With parents	100%	78%	35%	10%
With age-near sibling	89	53	20	2
With best-known cousin	41	23	4	2
Percentage Reduction from Local Level of Interaction				
With parents		−22%	−65%	−90%
With age-near sibling		−40	−78	−98
With best-known cousin		−44	−90	−95

Adapted from Adams (1968):38,110,143. Source: 799 young married white men and women in Greensboro, North Carolina. The percentage interacting monthly in the local community was treated as the base (100%) and the percentage loss at a given distance computed.
* Kin living in the same community.

Table 9-4 shows that the more remote kin are socially and geographically, the lower the frequency of interaction. The only exception is that monthly interaction with the closest sibling is just as rare as with the closest cousin. The test of the hypothesis is presented in the lower part of the table which shows that a given distance affects remote relationships more severely than close relationships. Ties with parents survive the impact of mobility more than ties with siblings, and those in turn more than with cousins. Again, the only exception results from the survival of monthly interaction with a very small number of cousins living "elsewhere." Presumably, the effect of mobility on unrelated friends would be even more disastrous.

Ability to maintain contact with kin across distances depends on the resources available for bridging that distance. These resources include time, money, and technological facilities for transportation and communication.

The more leisure time available, the more often families will be able to undertake lengthy weekend or holiday trips to visit their relatives.

The more money they have, the more they will be able to spend on transporting themselves or on other forms of communication. Lack of financial resources perhaps explains why Litwak's working-class families (1960b) who had recently moved to new houses in Buffalo, New York, had less contact with the kin they left elsewhere in the city than middle-class families who had also recently moved. In Dublin, Ireland, Humphreys (1966) similarly noted a sharp decline in kin contact when working-class families who could not afford automobiles moved from country to city.

Technological progress has increasingly made it easier for families with time and money to bridge what previously would have been unbridgeable distances. Rosser and Harris (1965) found that improved Swansea bus services and roads had made suburban relatives more accessible to central-city kin than in earlier eras. Faster trains and airplanes link kin in widely separated regions or even in different countries. Improved telephone communications have already brought kin ear-to-ear and may soon bring them face-to-face on video screens.

Thus, technological and economic development have softened the extent to which mobility reduces kin interaction. However, we should beware of assuming that such changes will ever wipe out the effect of distance completely. Distant kin may become more accessible than they used to be, but propinquitous kin will always be the most accessible of all.

Substitution of Pseudo-Kin   We already know from Chapter 7 that families without kin tend to convert unrelated friends into pseudo-kin. Perhaps the most common cause of loss of kin (except by death in old age) is migration. Thus families who have migrated are particularly apt to substitute non-kin for absent kin.

Although kin ties are maintained as much as possible, the greater the distance moved, the greater the attenuation of contact. Therefore, the greater the dispersion of kin, the more we can expect the substitution of non-kin.

Figure 9-2 illustrates the substitution of non-kin for kin as a source of help in old age. The more remote the daughter (normally the chief source of such services), the greater the tendency to turn to non-kin.

Ease of substituting non-kin depends on their accessibility. In Michel's study (1960) of rural migrants living in Parisian furnished hotels, not only were kin inaccessibly remote but non-kin were extraordinarily propinquitous. Sharing the same building meant meeting one another in the halls, at common faucets, and in the courtyard where children played. The inadequacy of their cramped living quarters forced these migrants into greater association with one another than would have been the case with larger apartments. This high intensity of contact with non-kin sped their conversion into pseudo-kin.

Presumably substitution occurs less rapidly when non-kin live in more dispersed dwellings such as row houses (like Park Forest), detached dwellings surrounded by lawns, houses surrounded by hedges or by garden walls, or on widely separated farms or estates. This isolation of neighbors from one another retards the development of substitute pseudo-kin ties and favors the predominance of kin ties which have always characterized aristocratic estate dwellers and ordinary farm families.

The balance between kin and non-kin is not simply a matter of geographical distance. Kin ties normally have priority, other things (like distance) being equal. But the farther kin are removed by migration, the more their social priority is offset by the propinquity of non-kin until eventually a point of equilibrium is reached after which substitution of non-kin begins to predominate.

Strengthening of Internal Ties   In addition to depending on outsiders when kin are unavailable, husbands and wives and parents and children also depend on each other more. In Chapter 7 we saw that nuclear families who are relatively distant from kin have stronger internal bonds than those where in-

FIGURE 9-2.   *Help Received from Nonrelatives by Old People, by Availability*
of Daughters

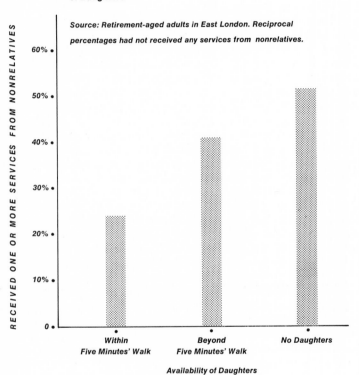

Adapted from Townsend (1957):131.

dividual family members have intense relationships to their external kin. In order for nuclear families to achieve this independence, it is necessary for them to migrate away from their childhood homes sometime before or after marriage. The migration need not be very far—it may be only to the next village or the next neighborhood. But some movement is necessary if the autonomy necessary to internal cohesiveness is to be achieved.

There is no need to repeat my earlier statements about neolocal residence patterns. My interest now is in the effect of post-marital migration on internal cohesion. Insofar as migration attenuates kin ties, it *ipso facto* strengthens ties within the nuclear family. If external relationships previously interfered with the development of internal relationships, severing the former allows the "substitution" of the latter. If intrusive relatives preempted the attention of husband and/or wife, moving away gives the partners a chance to devote that attention to each other. Ditto for parents and children.

In Bott's classic study of *Family and Social Network*, the larger the number of places the husband and wife had lived, the looser their social networks and, in turn, the more cohesive the marital bond:

> . . . if a family with a close-knit network move out of their old area to a new housing estate, their network will rapidly become less connected and for a time at least husband and wife will develop a more joint relationship with each other. (1957:109)

The fact that increased interdependence may not last reflects the establishment of external ties in the new community. Increased cohesion is likely to be most pronounced precisely when the family is in transit from one location to another. This transitional character of internal cohesion fits our broader concept of the temporary character of many consequences of changes in the relationship between the family and its environment. After a period of internal preoccupation, the family returns to a normal balance between internal and external dependencies. But since the new locale is not likely to contain relatives for a long time to come and since friends are normally less intrusive than relatives, the new equilibrium may involve more internal cohesion than existed before the move.

Willmott and Young similarly found that families which moved from the slums to the suburbs became more cohesive as a result. They found a new "partnership" between husband and wife because the wife's mother no longer preempted her time and attention. This partnership was further strengthened when not only the grandmother but also the couple's own children were not around to distract them. When a married couple have left their parents behind and their own children have left *them* behind, they achieve the maximum isolation and the maximum interdependence. Willmott and Young wrote: "Middle-aged mothers and fathers, with their children off the scene, are much more likely than in (the slum) to lead shared lives, to develop common interests, to deepen their attachment to each other" (1960:65).

Another example is reported by Goode (1963) from India. In the traditional Indian household, the married man was so close to his brothers that he neglected his wife. However, couples who migrated away from their extended family to establish nuclear households so the husband could work for the Seta-Raam steel mill experienced a sharp alteration in his behavior. No longer able to depend on his brothers for emotional gratification, he was forced to turn to his wife and children as substitutes. The previous censorship by his parents of any expression of affection toward his wife was now lifted. Thus he was both free to love his wife and children and impelled to do so by the loss of his previous affectional ties.

This is not to say that the more times a couple move, the stronger their marriage necessarily becomes. My study of "Kinship Interaction and Marital Solidarity" (Blood, 1969a) implies that the relationship is curvilinear. (Mobility probably increases internal cohesion only up to a point, beyond which additional mobility may become too much of a strain.) However, my primary purpose here is to contrast families which are completely stable with those who engage in *some* geographical movement. Under these circumstances, the evidence seems clear that the effect of migration on marriage is generally positive.

Migration of Families

In the preceding section my concern was with the effect of migration on weakening kin ties and on the strengthening of ties with non-kin and within the family. However, these are not the only effects of internal migration. If the new environment is hostile or costly of family resources, it may impose such heavy burdens that the integrity of the family is destroyed unless kin or kin-substitutes come to the rescue.

The Costs of Urban Renewal   Slum clearance is theoretically designed to benefit the families which are removed from overcrowded dilapidated housing and relocated in bigger new homes somewhere else. But if the new location is too far away from the old, and if the new housing is more expensive than the old, the new arrangement may be physically comfortable but functionally disastrous.

One such disaster occurred in Lagos, Nigeria (Marris, 1960). Forced removal from a downtown slum to a new housing project five miles away destroyed many families and damaged most of the rest. Not only was the cost of living higher in the suburbs, but also wives were cut off from the income they had earned as traders in the downtown markets. In response to financial crisis caused by this forced migration, some wives deserted their husbands and others were sent by their husbands back to their parents. Some children similarly were dispersed among relatives willing and able to take them in. The poorer the family, the greater the likelihood that the costs of urban removal would plunge them over the brink into disorganization.

For black families moving from the rural South to northern cities in the United States, migration was often equally costly (Frazier, 1937). Although migration in this case was voluntary and motivated by a hope that it would bring new resources to the family, that hope was often unfulfilled. The urban labor market offered few opportunities for unskilled employment, and urban living conditions were more congested than farm cabins no matter how ramshackle. For the poorest and least educated families, migration to the city often destroyed their cohesiveness. In America, it was more often the husband than the wife who deserted. Just as in Lagos, the children were sometimes scattered. More often the children remained physically in the home but were lost to parental control, resorting to delinquent behavior—organized crime for the boys, sexual delinquency and unmarried motherhood for the girls. Such families could have preserved their integrity had they never moved but remained on the farm where they could eke out an existence from the land.

Strengthening Ties with Available Kin   In view of the crises to which impoverished families are subjected when they migrate from one home to another, we should expect families to turn desperately for help from any kin who may live at their destination. We have already seen this reliance on kin in Lagos when families sent their wives and children to live with kin elsewhere in the city. But if kin were available in the immediate vicinity of the new home, it might be possible for the family to survive the trauma of moving without falling to pieces.

One way kin become available in the target community is by push–pull migration. Save for the first member of the kin network to migrate, subsequent migrants to the same community are assured that they will not be alone but can depend on the hospitality, guidance, and other assistance of their predecessors. For migrants from the hills of Kentucky to southern Ohio, Seggar and Schwarzweller (1964) found that the receiving kin group cushioned the stress on subsequent migrants. For migrants faced with worries, anxieties and despair generated by a strange environment, to turn to kin for emotional support was a great relief.

Thus, if kin are available in the new location, migrant families are eager to turn to them to reduce the strains caused by migration. If a network of kin is available there, the kin will protect the nuclear family from the shock of too sudden an immersion in the new urban culture in much the same fashion that ethnic enclaves (like "Little Italy") in American cities cushioned the shock for immigrants from abroad.

Although the removal of one nuclear family attenuates kin ties, the serial or multiple migration of kin to the same target area may intensify dependence on kin so that the migrant cluster develops even closer ties than they had prior to migration. The effect of migration therefore varies from one extreme to another, depending on whether migration removes the nuclear family from kin left behind or brings it into intensified dependence on co-migrating kin.

Perhaps the most graphic evidence of comigration was reported by Talmon (1962) among North African Jewish immigrants to Israel. Initially Israeli officials deliberately dispersed kin throughout the country, but so great was the need to rely on kin that families persuaded their relatives to move to common settlement areas. The final result of this consolidation of kin in the new homeland was a far tighter kin grouping than existed prior to migration.

In Israel, the migration was not internal to one country but international, yet the same processes are at work whenever migration places sufficient strain on the nuclear family and when kin are a potential relief for that strain.

INTERNATIONAL MIGRATION

If migration within a culture strains the nuclear family and more markedly affects the kin network, international migration can be expected to have even sharper effects. The fears and anxieties of Kentucky mountain families who moved to Ohio cities were mild in comparison to the bewilderment of families who move to an entirely different culture. Especially if the new country speaks a different language and if family members do not know that language, adaptation to the new environment is extraordinarily difficult. For purposes of this analysis, I will focus on migration across language barriers.

Severed External Ties

Because international migration generally involves longer distances than domestic migration, ties with kin left behind are weakened correspondingly more. Visits home may not be possible at all or may be postponed until retirement. Contact may be reduced to correspondence, to money remitted home, and to occasional presents. Only with improved transportation and sufficient economic resources do kin ties stand much chance of surviving the separation trauma of international migration.

The one exception I have already mentioned. If kin migrate together to the same country, their interdependence may be strengthened rather than lessened. Similarly, interdependence within the nuclear family may be intensified by moving to a foreign location. The more hostile the new environment, the more the members of the family will be forced to depend on one another. They may be the only persons who speak the same language and understand one another. The loss of external ties makes the members of the family depend on whatever ties remain—whether within the family or with kin fellow-travellers.

If kin are not available in the new land, the substitution of non-kin may be less easy than with internal migration. Talmon (1962) reported no quasi-kin ties among families who migrated from Europe to Israeli cities comparable to the substitution which Michel (1960) found among French peasant families migrating to Paris. One reason for the failure of these Israeli immigrants to find kin-substitutes may have been the "deep yearning for privacy" which developed during their enforced collectivism in German concentration camps. Another may have been the polyglot character of Israeli cities where immigrants from many national backgrounds spoke different tongues. Only with the mastery of Hebrew could a linguistic basis for developing quasi-kin relations be laid. In any case, Talmon found that these urban immigrants from the concentration camps depended exclusively on intensified family relationships during their earliest years in the new land. Only after some years had passed did ties begin to develop with neighbors and work colleagues.

For high-status Cuban refugees to the United States, Lahey (1967) reported the loss of a special kind of quasi-kin who existed in the old country before the revolution, namely mistresses. After migrating to the U.S.A., the problem was not the unavailability of fellow nationals who might be recruited as "second wives" but the loss of income occasioned by starting a new life in a foreign land. A professional man who had been able to maintain a separate apartment for his mistress before the revolution could no longer support such a "quasi-spouse" after being reduced to driving a taxi or waiting on tables in Florida. In this case, lack of economic resources prevented the development of outside ties and enforced dependence on the nuclear family, much to the latter's pleasure.

When a migrating family settles down in an ethnic enclave, fellow nationals are available for conversion into quasi-kin. Among Italian immigrants to American cities, MacDonald noted that *padroni* (bosses) often served as godfathers to immigrants whom they assisted with housing and employment. In serving as "banker, landlord, foreman, scribe, interpreter, legal adviser, or ward boss" for his men, a *padrone* performed many of the functions which kin would have served had they been available (1964:86).

In general, the ability of immigrants to create kin-substitutes in a foreign land depends on the availability of fellow-migrants from the same country. If compatriots are not available, no one else outside the family can serve that purpose effectively.

Altered Family Roles

Not only does migration alter the family's relationships to outsiders, it frequently alters the internal role system. This has already been implied in the statement that migration intensifies mutual interdependence. But family relations may change not simply in degree, but also in kind.

Differential Migration   Many European migrants to America initially could not afford to bring their wives and children with them. For impoverished peasant families, it was difficult enough to find the money to pay the passage of the husband/father. Many immigrants were able to travel only through loans advanced through prospective employers and other agents.

The inability of the family to travel together meant long periods of separation. Presumably this emancipated the women and children left behind and must have made them resist submission to their former patriarch when they finally arrived in the new country. I also assume that the wife and children became strongly dependent on one another and on their homeland kin, whereas the husband became equally involved with kin and kin-substitutes in the new country. These differential external involvements compounded the strain on the relationship between the man and his absent family.

In the new country, there were few unattached girls of peasant origin. For Italians, MacDonald noted that "an unmarried female travelling alone was inconceivable in a culture which took extremely restrictive precautions to safeguard family honor" (1964:89). If the migration of unattached females was impossible, the only females in the new land were wives of men who had migrated earlier. Both Italian and Polish immigrant males preferred to board with compatriot families in order to enjoy some of the comforts of home, including feminine companionship.

Thomas and Znaniecki found many cases in which this living arrangement among Polish immigrants to the United States resulted in sexual relations between the boarder and his landlord's wife. In some cases, the role of boarder in the home became quasi-institutionalized in an informally polyandrous relationship with both men contributing to the financial support of the household:

> The husband [in one case] after some revolt accepts the situation of the boarder but makes the latter share all his conjugal responsibilities, familial and economic, by alternating with him in living with the woman and supporting her and the children. It is a regular polyandric arrangement, which shows both the close connection that still subsists between sexual life and other marriage interests in the immigrant's consciousness and the decay of the institutional significance of marriage. As a solution of the given subjective situation it seems to work satisfactorily for all the persons concerned, since no higher ideals of love are active. (1958:1742)

Such complete sharing of one woman by two men was far from universal among Polish immigrants, but it illustrates the strains placed upon the institution of monogamy when a large number of males must compete for a small number of already-married women.

As they became integrated into the American economy, married immigrants were able to send home for their wives. For migrant bachelors, the shortage of unmarried compatriot girls meant that they had to return home to search for brides or send home for "proxy wives" (MacDonald, 1964). Thus the barriers to normal family formation and family living caused by international migration were eventually removed.

However, the long time required to resolve this problem completely is symbolized in the fact that even second-generation Americans (the children of the immigrants I have been discussing) are less apt to be married than "old Americans" of the same age and sex (Heer, 1961). Although no longer a product of differential sex ratios, their lower marriage rate reflects the incomplete assimilation of children of immigrants into the mainstream of American life.

Altered Economic Roles   For immigrants from peasant economies, the original pattern had been joint work by both partners in the fields. A Polish peasant wife's chores included caring for cows, pigs, poultry, and a vegetable garden—all of which enabled her to contribute to her family's prosperity.

In the new country, economic opportunities for wives were removed from the home if families settled in cities. For families moving from rural Europe to urban America, this was a double adjustment. Some wives found employment outside the home, but those who did not were often demoralized by the loss of their role in the family economy. This demoralization so embittered Polish immigrant wives toward housework that they neglected their residual tasks around the house.

Thomas and Znaniecki found that wives' unwillingness to do housework was so widespread that Polish men generally considered them "lazy." Returning home from a hard day's unskilled work to find their homes messy and their hard-earned cash spent by their slovenly, careless wives, the men were infuriated. They retaliated by spending their earnings on themselves instead of bringing them home and by attacks on the wives which sometimes destroyed the marriages altogether.

Another reason wives were demoralized was that they didn't know how to make housekeeping a creative task. Knowing little about cooking save boiling potatoes and cabbage, and nothing about interior decoration, these illiterate women were reduced to a mere holding operation, trying to keep the family from being ground down into poverty in the face of bewilderingly capricious circumstances.

Their sense of uselessness was compounded by exposure to the higher standards of living of the dominant American community. This raised their aspirations and exaggerated the frustration of their circumstances. Presumably wives who found outside employment under these difficult economic conditions felt more useful, even though this too would have created strains by altering the husband–wife relationship in an equalitarian direction.

Differential Socialization

When a family migrates to a foreign country, it must learn to function effectively in a new social environment. The biggest task is to learn a new language in order to be able to communicate with the new society, but there are other lessons to be learned: new money, new foods, new customs. Theoretically all family members might learn these lessons equally fast and equally well. But the diversified ages and sexes of family members make this unlikely. Differential socialization among family members must be expected, creating conflict within the family from the clash of internalized cultures. Sometimes this clash occurs between husband and wife. And almost universally it divides parents from children.

Husbands and Wives We have already seen one basis for differential socialization of men and women in the differential migration schedule of the sexes. Whenever men migrated first and women followed later, the men had a head start exposure to the new culture.

Even if husband and wife migrated together to the new land, differences in family roles gave the husband more learning opportunities than the wife. If the man was involved in the occupational system while the wife was confined to the home, he had an institutionalized external involvement which she lacked. The man's functions as representative of the family in the outside world and negotiator with government officials and other outsiders on behalf of the family gave him additional contacts.

The fact that most immigrant families came from patriarchal cultures accentuated this split between the private sphere of the wife and the public sphere of the husband. If the woman had outside involvements at all, they were apt to be limited to her fellow immigrants. Neighborhood grocery stores and neighborhood churches were more apt to be immigrant institutions than the political and economic organizations in which the man was involved. Hence the man was likely to learn both the new language and the new culture faster than his wife.

If the husband's attitudes were transformed while his wife's remained the same, the couple by definition grew apart. Insofar as they subscribed to progressively alienated sets of values, they found it increasingly difficult to achieve consensus in family decision-making. Yet paradoxically such consensus between the partners was needed in the American environment as never before in the old country. Back home, family life was ruled by customary patterns enforced by the kin network. In America, the family was torn loose from kin and thrust into a strange environment where old norms were no longer appropriate.

Because of the individualizing effect of the differential socialization of the partners and because of the disorganizing impact of the rapid resocialization of the man, Thomas and Znaniecki (1958) pointed out that the old basis of family living was shattered and a new basis appropriate to the new environment was difficult to find. American norms of love between the partners were too foreign and too subtle to be grasped by ex-peasants. No new ideals emerged to replace the old sense of familistic duty. The new individualism simply released both partners from obedience to old norms, freeing them to retreat into the hedonistic self-indulgence of working-class vices for the man and apathetic irresponsibility for the woman. The result was a vicious cycle of mutual recrimination which frequently ended in the disintegration of the family.

These disorganizing effects of migration on Polish peasant families in American cities in the early twentieth century should not be taken as universal consequences of emigration. The extent of family disorganization depends on the extent of the contrast between the two cultures and on the success of the immigrant in the new society.

For Polish immigrants, life was difficult on both counts. As illiterate peasants moving to urban slums in a foreign land, they were subjected to a wrenching cultural shock and had only meager access to the reward system of the new society. By contrast, immigrants who already speak English, who have skills needed in the American economy and who come from urban origins can fit into the new society more smoothly. Even so, migration at best changes the family's environment enough to raise at least the possibility of differential socialization of the marriage partners.

Parents and Children   There may be room for doubt about the universality of differential socialization of married couples through international migration. There can be no doubt, however, about universal differences between parents and children. The extent of the difference depends on the age of the child at migration: the younger he is, the greater his advantage over his parents because of (1) his greater speed of learning new ways and (2) his lesser stock of old-country habits that have to be unlearned. The classic case is the child born in the new country to parents who grew up in the old.

Although I have just emphasized the speedier transformation of the husband than of the wife, children often feel that neither parent has changed at all. For example, Polish parents continued to demand that their children turn over their earnings even though American culture taught the children to view those earnings as their own. Such conflict frequently resulted in "a complete and painful antagonism" between parents and children, according to Thomas and Znaniecki (1958:104). Unable to resolve their conflict, the children eventually resorted to "as complete an avoidance as possible" of their parents. The parents, in turn, tried desperately but unsuccessfully to retain control of their children, resorting to methods which expressed their exasperation but only widened the chasm:

> The mutual hate, the hardness, unreasonableness, and brutality of the parents, the contempt and ridicule of the child—ridicule of the speech and old-country habits and views of the parents—become almost incredible. The parents, for example, resort to the juvenile court, not as a means of reform, but as an instrument of vengeance; they will swear away the character of their girl, call her a "whore" and a "thief," when there is not the slightest ground for it. (1958:104)

Parents repelled the child in two ways. First, they imposed demands which were customary in Poland but unacceptable in America. Secondly, they made those demands in the traditional authoritarian manner which was as offensive as the substance of the demands. Instead of making their requests tactfully or explaining them rationally, parents imposed them flatly, expecting unquestioning obedience. This "tyrannical" approach goaded the child into open defiance and antisocial behavior.

With immigrant children (as with lower-class rebels, generally) this defiance usually took the form of thievery for boys and of sexual delinquency for girls. Since girls cannot be sex delinquents without the cooperation of boys, the latter were also involved in premarital promiscuity (though parents seldom worried as much about their sons as about their pregnancy-prone daughters). Parents in the old country safeguarded their daughters against hazards to their virginity. In the new country, parents lost their ability to protect their daughters because of the anonymity of the urban environment and the rebelliousness of the girls.

Green (1941) found that Polish–American boys not only took full advantage of this situation, but also conducted what he called "open warfare" against the opposite sex. He felt that these sons of Polish immigrants aggressively exploited girls not just because they enjoyed sexual intercourse but as an expression of economic frustration in a community whose only factory had been closed during the Depression, five years before. Under hopeless economic conditions, young men not only had their parents' authoritarian irrelevance to rebel against, but the whole economy of their supposed "land of promise." For children who had prided themselves on adopting new-country ways to find that the country gave them no rewards for what they had learned was bitterly disappointing.

Campisi found that conflict between Italian parents and their American children was most severe during the second decade after arriving in the United States:

> This is the period of great frustration and of misunderstanding between parents and children. In this undeclared state of war between two ways of life it is the parents who have the most to lose, for their complete acceptance of the American way of living means the destruction of the Old World ideal. (1948:448)

Although parents mostly clung to their old ways and tried to impose them on their children, sometimes roles were reversed. Children tried to teach parents the proper English and the right way to dress. Parents were forced to turn to their children for help in fathoming the unfamiliar ways of the new environment. When children become the teachers of their parents, not only is the authority of parents as representatives of the outside society surrendered, but the authority of the children is recognized, however temporarily. This turns the whole generational structure of the family upside down. Unless parents can accept this revolution gracefully, it only adds to the confusion within the family.

The position of oldest child in an immigrant family is similar to that of oldest child in an oversize family (as we will see in Chapter 14). From the standpoint of the younger children, their big brother or big sister is a better teacher of the new culture than their incompetent parents. Because the oldest child has learned the new ways faster than his parents, he tends to replace them as chief advisor, mentor, and role model for his siblings. This strengthens his position in the family but brings him into sharper conflict with his parents. From their point of view he is undermining all the old-country values they are trying to teach. Only where the parents themselves reject old-country values and prefer the new (however imperfectly they may understand them) can this preeminence of the eldest child be welcomed rather than resisted. Willingness to delegate authority to a child is rare among adults socialized in a traditional agrarian culture which prized obedience to parental authority.

In general then even parents who expect to remain in the new country for the rest of their lives tend to be more oriented toward the culture they left behind than to that of their newly adopted home. For families which emigrate only temporarily a backward orientation is more understandable. The fact that a family plans to return home after a few years does not prevent children from being deeply affected by the new environment. For one of the author's students, a Japanese girl who lived in the U. S. during her grade school years, differential socialization brought conflict with her parents:

> Although my parents provided me with all of my desired material benefits, within reason, they should have given me more support, understanding, sympathy, and confidence in the problems I encountered. Much of their inadequacy as parents was due to the fact that not only are we two different generations apart, but we are also almost two different cultures apart. Although they are definitely not typically Japanese in ideals but in fact are quite liberal and Westernized, there still exists a great gap in our values.
>
> In my childhood, I was always slightly repressed from enjoying normal childhood pleasures by constant reminders to not "play outside always" and be more lady-like, to practice the hated piano while everyone else was playing, etc. My not quite perfect English, my race, my lack of religion and my "queerness" (children regarded my quietness, which was actually a fear that my English would not come out correctly and my staying home always, which was just the fact that I wasn't allowed to "run about" and my "great love for the piano," which I never really loved but was forced to accept, as "queerness") all contributed to my alienation from the other children. I staunchly believe that if I hadn't left the States two years ago, I would still be wallowing in a twilight of lack of identity, self-esteem, and confidence for a happy future.

Buffered Migration

The effect of emigration is cushioned insofar as the new community contains supportive elements of the old. We have already seen such cushioning provided by comigrating or push–pull migrating kin of migrants from the Kentucky mountains to Ohio. Similar kin-cushioning occurs in international migration (as with Talmon's Jewish migrants from North Africa to Israel).

Kin are not the only potential cushion. To stand between a migrating family and the full force of an alien culture, all that is needed is a compatriot, not a kinsman. To accomplish this, migrants from the same country must settle close to one another. Drawn not only by a desire for help after arriving in the new country but by help with the travel itself, migrants have usually settled in clusters, whether on contiguous farms in rural areas or in ethnic neighborhoods of urban centers.

MacDonald (1964) found that the "Little Italies" of American cities were populated not only almost purely by Italians, but by families from the same town. Where the pattern of settlement did not bring blood relatives together in the new world, it at least tended to reassemble old neighbors. For the latest arrivals, such erstwhile neighbors were readily available for the creation of quasi-kin in the absence of true kin. Both kin and quasi-kin can be expected to be extraordinarily helpful to new arrivals in providing temporary shelter and assistance in getting established in the new environment.

Ethnic enclaves offer a transitional culture less shocking than a completely foreign environment. By offering informal sociability and formal institutions conducted in the native tongue, the new neighborhood removes the language barrier which thwarts understanding elsewhere. By duplicating native institutions, ethnic organizations require no learning of new social forms. The parish church, the ethnic sports club, the grocery store stocked with native foods provide the immigrant family with a reassuring sense of being "at home" in the midst of an alien city. The man may have to venture into a strange world to work, but at night he can go home not only to his old wife, but also to a near replica of his old home town.

One institution which Thomas and Znaniecki (1958) found particularly useful in Polish neighborhoods was the parochial school established by the Catholic Church. Children who attended public schools were estranged from their parents by rapid socialization into American culture. Children in parish schools, however, were taught their parents' language, religion, and national history, reinforcing the parents' informal attempts to pass on their ancestral customs. By teaching children the elements of Polish identity, the parochial school retarded their Americanization enough to enable parents and children to keep in reasonable touch with each other during the course of their mutual adaptation to the new society.

In general, the more effectively ethnic institutions isolate the nuclear family from contact with the new culture, the less the strain on family ties. In extreme cases, migrant groups set up self-sufficient communities like those of the Pennsylvania "Dutch" which ape old-world patterns so much that international migration becomes as harmless as if they had moved to another region of the fatherland.

In the long run, most immigrant families move out of the ghetto into the wider community. The crucial question is not whether families ever become assimilated, but when. If the "long run" is long enough, husbands and wives and children may move together with relative ease. But if exposure to the new culture is unbuffered—and especially if some family members are handicapped in learning the new culture because they do not know how to read and write— the family is apt to be plunged into a severe crisis and torn apart.

chapter ten

SOCIAL MOBILITY AND THE FAMILY

Social mobility refers to the vertical movement of the family through social space (in contrast to the horizontal movement of the family through physical space in geographical mobility). Vertical movement may be either up or down. In many societies, more families move up than down because lower fertility in the higher strata creates room at the top. Moreover, if the occupational system is improving, there may be long-term increases in the proportion of white-collar jobs at the expense of blue-collar jobs. This means that even if all social classes had the same birth rate, many families would need to move up the scale in order to respond to the skilled-job opportunities which the system is creating.

Upward mobility is not only achieved by more families, but it is aspired to by many more. Descending the social scale is rarely intentional. Most families which lose status do so because of crises such as the death, desertion, or crippling of the breadwinner. These traumatic causes of downward social mobility will be discussed later in this book in connection with family crises. Because downward mobility seldom occurs under normal circumstances, I will have less to say about its effect on families than about upward mobility. For most of the chapter, social mobility will be practically synonymous with upward mobility.

In general, movement through social space seems to have similar effects on the family as movement through physical space. In both cases, the family cuts its ties with its original environment and moves to a new environment. Both movements weaken ties with the old setting and risk differential socialization to the new.

Some of the same strains on the nuclear family and on kin relations during and after vertical mobility occur that we have already seen with horizontal mobility. However, one element is new. Whereas movement through physical space often causes the family to withdraw within itself in response to a hostile new environment, upward social mobility demands participation in the external system. Without a heavy emphasis on ascending the ladders of the stratification system (achieving an education, getting a better job, earning more money, etc.), the family cannot move. Therefore, social mobility requires the family to turn its attention away from family matters and concentrate on achieving outward success.

EMPHASIS ON THE EXTERNAL SYSTEM

In utopian communities, we saw that the community urges the family to sacrifice its own individual welfare to group goals. To be socially mobile, a family must give priority to non-family matters. The only difference is that in the one case, all families within the community simultaneously turn their attention to the needs of the external system, whereas upward social mobility ordinarily involves the movement of a single family while its neighbors and relatives stay behind. In both cases, the question is the relative priority of family versus non-family activities. In both, non-family activities are given top priority.

Giving priority to non-family matters delays or curbs such family activities as getting married and having children.

Delayed Family Formation

Generally speaking, social mobility is a masculine task. Since the family's place in the social structure usually depends on the husband's job position, we can largely ignore the question of female efforts to climb the social ladder (except through marriage) and concentrate on male aspirations.

If a man is to climb from the lower class into the middle class, he will have to begin very young to study hard, work hard, and learn the speech and manners of his target class. So busy will he be with these tasks that he will have little time to worry about getting married and little energy to devote to those heterosexual preliminaries which pave the way to marriage. His premarital behavior is apt to be restrained and his marrying delayed.

Premarital Restraint We have already seen in Chapter 2 that higher social classes are more sexually restrained before marriage than lower classes. Kinsey (1948) found that these differences were especially marked among boys in their early teens. Low-status boys begin having sexual intercourse at younger ages than their high-status peers. This class difference suggests that boys who subsequently move into higher social classes are more restrained than their class equals in conformity to the norms of their target class. Kinsey's data shows that the higher a boy's ultimate social status, the more restrained he was prior to age 16 (see Figure 10-1).

In Figure 10-1 not only were the boys more restrained the more mobile they eventually became, but boys who eventually climbed into the high-white-collar and professional classes were even more restrained than boys born in those classes. For example, of the boys who climbed all the way from the skilled-worker class to the high-white-collar class only half as many had had intercourse by age 16 as boys who were born into the latter class and who could reasonably expect to stay there. Such "excessive" restraint was not manifested by all the upwardly mobile groups in Kinsey's study, but it was particularly common among those whose upward mobility was most extreme. The more herculean the efforts required to achieve upward mobility, the greater the likelihood that the individual's sexual behavior will be even more restrained than that of peers who merely inherit their high status.

FIGURE 10-1.   *Premarital Sexual Experience of Young Teenage Sons*
of Skilled Workers, by Eventual Mobility Status

Source: Adult males born to skilled manual workers, recalling their
experience in premarital intercourse prior to age 16, classified
by their occupational level at time of interview. Reciprocal
percentages had not had premarital intercourse by age 16.

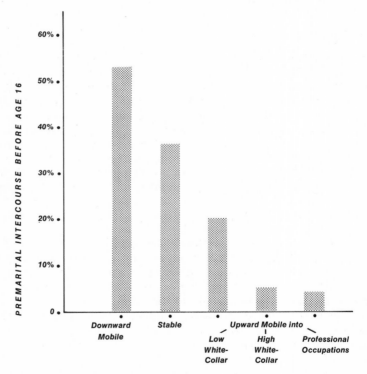

Adapted from Kinsey (1948):430.

It should be emphasized that sexual restraint in this context does not mean refraining from all forms of sexual behavior, but rather from sexual intercourse. Other data in Kinsey's study suggest that upwardly mobile boys are unusually apt to release their sexual tensions by masturbation, again even more than their target-level peers. Thus upward mobility does not reduce the frequency of sexual activity so much as it shifts attention from sociable to solitary forms of sexual behavior. Mobile boys may be too preoccupied with their studies and other vocationally oriented activities to have time to become sexually involved with girls.

Delayed Marriage If upwardly mobile boys are too busy to have intercourse in their early teens, it is not surprising if they are too busy to marry in their later teens. They may be expected to marry later than stable or downwardly mobile boys and in a larger fraction of cases never to marry at all. If they remain sufficiently involved in the world of business, dating and marriage may always seem too frivolous to be indulged in.

One study which supports this line of reasoning is Heer's (1961) study of the marital status of children of people who had migrated to the United States. Holding migration status constant (*i.e.*, all of their parents were foreign-born), the higher the occupational status of sons, the greater the chances they were not yet married by age 24. This implies that such sons were so busy making their way in the American occupational system that they had put off the prospect of marriage.

One reason for delaying marriage is presumably lack of involvement with potential partners. Another, however, may be the fear that marriage might involve incurring financial obligations which would prevent the individual from investing the resources he needed for his education and his occupational future.

Delaying marriage is also a way of postponing child-bearing for occupationally mobile young men unable to rely on contraception because of religious scruples. Heer (1961) found that second-generation Americans from predominantly Catholic countries were less apt to marry by age 24 than those from non-Catholic countries at the same level of occupational achievement. To be upwardly mobile doubly requires delaying marriage if marriage can be expected to be followed almost immediately by child-bearing. Conversely, if marriage and child-bearing can be separated, marriage will not need to be delayed so long.

Limited Family Growth

We have already seen that ambitious children of immigrants to the U. S. delayed their marriages in order to prevent having children before they were financially ready. Similar motives should lead already-married upwardly mobile men to postpone child-bearing and limit it to modest proportions so they may conserve their resources of money and time for occupational advancement.

One study of Australian professors (Tien, 1961) found that upwardly mobile men who did not marry until after age 24 postponed the birth of their first child almost 50 percent longer than occupationally stable men who married at the same age.

Delayed child-bearing among upwardly mobile men is also suggested in Table 10-1. At every occupational level, the proportion of couples usually or always using contraceptives was greater for upwardly mobile men than for occupationally stable men. Since the data were restricted to contraceptive practice at the time of conception, this means that if an upwardly mobile couple conceived during the Depression years of the 1930s, it was far more apt to be an "accidental" pregnancy than for an occupationally stable couple.

TABLE 10-1   Use of Contraception, by Occupation and Mobility Status

PERCENT "USUALLY" OR "ALWAYS" PRACTICING CONTRACEPTION BY OCCUPATION	MOBILITY STATUS		MOBILE / STABLE RATIO
	Stable	Upwardly Mobile	
Professional	0%	35%	infinity
Managerial	20	43	2.15X
Clerical	19	31	1.63
Skilled	27	37	1.37

Adapted from Kantner and Kiser (1954):1000. Source: Indianapolis couples married 1927–1929, interviewed in 1941. Reciprocal percentages only "sometimes" or never practiced contraception at the time of conception.

Postponement of child-bearing usually results in smaller completed family size. Table 10-2 shows that upwardly mobile couples had fewer children than occupationally stable couples. This difference held both for couples who were successful in planning the number and spacing of their children and for those who did not plan their last child but who nevertheless did not consider it unwanted.

TABLE 10-2   Average Number of Children Born, by Family Planning Status and Mobility Status

AVERAGE NUMBER OF CHILDREN BORN BY FAMILY PLANNING STATUS	MOBILITY STATUS		MOBILE/STABLE RATIO
	Stable	Upwardly Mobile	
Number and spacing planned	2.22	2.08	0.94X
Quasi-planned*	3.15	2.83	0.90

Adapted from Kantner and Kiser (1954): 982. Source: Indianapolis couples married 1927–1929, interviewed in 1941.
* Last child was not deliberately planned but was "wanted."

Similarly, Baltzell (1953) found that upwardly mobile Philadelphians listed in *Who's Who in America* had fewer children than colleagues whose parents had been socially prominent. Those whose ancestors had been in the Philadelphia Social Register for 40 years or more had an average of 3.1 children, whereas those whose parents were not in the Social Register had only 2.6 children. Presumably mobility interfered with fertility in this case because of the extraordinary efforts necessary to break into the pages of *Who's Who*. Perhaps we can hypothesize that the more strenuous the man's involvement in the occupational world, the more he tends to neglect his family roles, including child-bearing.

In a sense, the same Philadephia data show the delayed positive effect of successful mobility on family size. The social mobility of their ancestors enabled some men to combine occupational achievement with having large numbers of children. In societies with extended family systems, upward mobility similarly makes it possible for subsequent generations to be retained in the household who otherwise would have had to live independently because of inadequate financial resources. Thus Freedman (1961–62) noted that upward mobility in feudal China was followed by increased family complexity. Conversely, downward mobility caused extended families to fall apart as they lost their wealth.

In general, then, postponing and limiting family growth may be necessary in order to make upward mobility possible, but once mobility has been achieved, the family subsequently is able not only to remove these limits, but may even grow more than would have been possible had the mobility not taken place. Conversely, downward mobility may be caused initially by premature or excessive child-bearing, but subsequently it may curtail family growth insofar as families are able to respond adaptively to straitened economic circumstances. The latter response is enforced on extended families which cannot afford to live together once their source of subsistence is curtailed. However, unplanned child-bearing sometimes results in extensive family size even when economic conditions are no longer satisfactory. Thus the impact of downward mobility on child-bearing can be seen only when contraception is successfully practiced.

DIFFERENTIAL MOBILITY

Whenever a family moves to a new position in the stratification system, new behaviors must be learned for getting along in their new location. Just as with international migration, the members of the family may learn the new ways at different speeds. But whereas with immigration, family members will usually move together physically and differ only in the pace of learning the new culture, in the case of social mobility, the very process of resocialization determines whether the members of the family are mobile. If they learn at different speeds, they will move at different speeds. And if they occupy different positions in social space, they will lack that communality of location which we normally assume for families.

Social mobility, then, involves a risk that members of the nuclear family will become alienated from one another by differential rates of mobility. And since it would be unusual for the members of a whole kin network to move up together, the social mobility of a nuclear unit almost inevitably puts social distance between them and the kin they leave behind.

Strains on Family Cohesiveness

Normally, the members of a single family unit move up the social scale together. At least that is the ideal to which families aspire. In a few cases, however, the partner may lag behind an ambitious man or woman, and in a larger number, the children may forge ahead of their parents. Either way, the differential mobility of family members may be expected to reduce the cohesiveness of the family unit.

Husband–Wife Strains   In Chapter 11 we will examine the consequences of mixed marriages between partners of different social backgrounds. In this section, the question is what happens to a couple who were initially homogamous when one partner is socially mobile and the other fails to move or lags behind. In such cases, a marriage which was initially homogamous in its social characteristics (though perhaps not in psychological attitudes) becomes heterogamous as a result of unilateral change.

McGuire found that differential mobility in the working class usually took the form of ambitious wives married to lethargic men, whereas in the middle class, it involved ambitious men married to lagging wives. In both classes, differential mobility produced what he called "divergent families," characterized by disagreement between the husband and the wife "in certain essential aspects of their frames of reference." He noted that ". . . one parent is motivated by role expectations characteristic of one life style, while the second parent is attached to the role images of another" (1952:110). Under such circumstances the normal congruency between role expectations of the marital pair gave way to contradictory expectations.

Little evidence is available about the consequences of such divergence for the husband–wife relationship. In scattered cases, the husband may be socialized by his colleagues into a higher occupational position while his stay-at-home wife clings to old friends and an old way of life. In extreme cases, the husband may divorce his wife as a handicap to his continued mobility and marry a new wife more suitable to his destination.

Even more rare are cases where the wife is so spectacularly successful that the husband is overshadowed by her fame. This reverses the usual case in which the family's position in the community depends on the husband's success. Because this situation breaks the usual rules, most men dislike their dependent position. Therefore differential mobility in which the wife forges ahead of the husband seems especially disastrous for marital satisfaction.

It should be apparent by now that upward mobility after marriage does not necessarily separate the husband and wife. In some cases, the partners are equally motivated toward mobility and move forward smoothly together. In others, the aggressive partner involves his spouse in external learning situations (taking her to parties, conventions, and other locations where she can meet his new friends) and coaches her privately in the new ways he has learned elsewhere. Only in exceptional circumstances does one partner lag behind. But in those cases, differential mobility will strain the marriage.

Parent–Child Strains   Just as with international migration, the more rapid socialization of children than of parents to the new social position can be taken for granted. The evidence is substantial that parents who initiate social mobility are likely to see their children eclipse their own mobility. Hard as they may try, parents are never likely to find the new ways as natural as do their children. And having learned those new ways later in life, they are seldom likely to have learned them so well. As a result, occasional lapses in moments of thoughtlessness can be expected from parents which would be impossible for children who have always lived in the new environment.

If children are to learn things their parents do not know, they cannot rely on their parents as teachers or as examples. They must turn to teachers supplied by the school system and the community. For working-class children, the most accessible teachers are the middle-class professional personnel of the public schools. For the children of the *nouveaux riches,* they are the teachers—and more especially the pupils—of private schools. In either case, parental authority is undermined by the parents' inability to be their children's chief socializing agents—and even more by the reversals of role to which successful children subject their parents. Even for parents who have sponsored the mobility of their children, it is not easy to experience the impatience and superciliousness of "young upstarts" who know better than their parents.

In rural Greece, educational progress enabled a whole generation of shepherds to eclipse their parents' educational achievement. Whereas the older generation were completely illiterate, the younger generation could read government regulations and fill in government forms:

> It is easy to understand that if the head of the family must be constantly asking his young son to read, explain, and advise on all written documents, he finds it difficult to maintain his authority until his son has reached the customary age of marriage. (Campbell, 1964:163)

Among families of students at the University of Wisconsin, LeMasters found that even where the family supposedly moved up the social scale together, "there was some evidence that children acculturate more completely to the new class patterns than do the parents." When this occurred, he observed that "a type of social distance is created which seems to hinder effective inter-generation communication and control" (1954:229).

In upward mobility, then, children tend to outstrip their parents and this reduces understanding between the generations and undermines the authority of the parents. An even more severe form of family disorganization was discovered by Myers and Roberts (1959) when they studied mental patients at New Haven hospitals and clinics. A very large proportion of their lower-middle-class neurotic patients were emotional casualties of unsuccessful or only partially successful mobility. Their parents had encouraged them to be upwardly mobile, but when the patients outstripped their parents' social position, they felt estranged from their parents and robbed of the emotional security which their nonmobile siblings had found at home. If later for one reason or another they found further advancement blocked, they turned against their parents for launching them on an impossible journey.

The patients resented their parents' low social status (including their ethnic background in the case of recent immigrants, and their religion in the case of Catholics and Jews) which handicapped their upward mobility. They also resented their parents' lack of appreciation of the importance of higher education and their inability to finance the liberal arts education the children so much desired. The parents, conversely, felt rejected by their child and unappreciated for the financial sacrifices they had made on his behalf.

In general, then, patients and parents were estranged and embittered toward each other even though the parents had deliberately launched these children on their upward-bound career. The contradiction between parental sponsorship and parental thwarting of mobility placed the patients in an emotional bind which expressed itself in neurosis whenever the desired mobility failed to be achieved.

Such psychological casualties are avoided when families move up the scale together or when a child's unilateral mobility is so successful that emotional rewards from the external system compensate for the loss of home ties. But regardless of whether a mobile individual becomes neurotic, if he outstrips his parents' social position, he is liable to find it difficult to remain close to them psychologically.

Despite the inevitable strain introduced into the parent–child relationship by divergence of social position, the more the left-behind generation prizes the achievements of the mobile individual, the less the strain. Parents take pride in their children's successes even when they carry the children away from home.

Where mobility is downward rather than upward, family ties are particularly jolted. In these cases not only has the child moved away from home socially but he has rejected the parents' efforts to teach him to be respectable. His new way of life constitutes a visible violation of the parents' standards, painful for them to witness. Hence parent–child relations suffer more from downward than from upward mobility.

Strains on Kin Ties

When mobile children grow up and leave home, family ties are transformed into kin ties. Much of what we have already described as strains in parent–child relations is exacerbated after the child leaves home and has the opportunity of reinforcing his feeling of social distance with geographical distance. A similar tendency may be expected where differential mobility involves one child changing social strata while his siblings stay behind. In both cases, the looser character of kin relations in modern societies allows the consequences of social mobility to be revealed more clearly than relations within the nuclear family.

Parent–Child Strains   The relationship of married children with their parents suffers from differential mobility. One illustration is the reduced proportion of children named after kin by upwardly mobile couples. Rossi (1965) found that whereas almost all children (94 percent) were named for kin in stable American middle-class families, significantly fewer (79 percent) were kin-named in mobile families. She felt this reflected strained feelings within the kin network (whereas geographical mobility had no such effect on kin-naming). This suggests that upwardly mobile young couples feel somewhat alienated from the families in which they grew up.

Table 10-3 shows that strains do not affect all relationships equally. In

TABLE 10-3 Contact of Married Men and Women with
Their Fathers and Mothers, by Mobility Status

| | MOBILITY STATUS | | MOBILE/STABLE |
WEEKLY CONTACT	Stable	Mobile	RATIO
By Men			
With father	66%	43%	0.65X
With mother	66	56	0.85
By Women			
With father	75	65	0.87
With mother	69	66	0.95

Adapted from Willmott and Young (1960):166,167. Source: Married adults living in a
middle-class London suburb; data restricted to those with the specified parent still living.
Reciprocal percentages had not seen the parent during the previous week. The number of
stable cases was respectively 49, 73, 28, and 48; of mobile cases, 76, 98, 78, and 123. Mobility
was defined as movement either up or down a sixfold classification scheme.

this British study, mother–daughter contact was hardly reduced at all by
social mobility, whereas contact between fathers and sons was reduced the
most. This indicates that social mobility interferes with relations between
male kin more than between female kin. Willmott and Young commented
that "men naturally judge each other according to the jobs they hold, and
they are liable to feel uneasy with any close relative who has in the worldly
sense succeeded more than they have themselves" (1960:84).

Most of the women in this study did not participate directly in the
stratification system. Their social position was determined largely by their
husbands. Even daughters who had achieved more education than their mothers were not by and large utilizing that education to enter a different social
position. Mothers and daughters shared the same roles in life: Both generations were wives, mothers, and housekeepers and shared many of the same
jobs and problems, no matter what their social standing.

We cannot assume that mothers and daughters will never be affected by
differential mobility. Young and Willmott found relatively little effect in a
middle-class suburb. But Townsend found that working-class families in a
London slum felt less happy about daughters who had "gone up in the world,"
leaving their old Mum behind. "The daughter often had a different view
about house- and mother-craft, she had strange friends, and she usually lived
in a completely different environment" (1957:93). These differences made
mothers feel uneasy when their daughters came to visit. Moreover, working-
class mothers could not take pride in a son-in-law's accomplishment the way
they could in a son's. Moreover, contact between upwardly mobile sons and
their working-class mothers was often reestablished after the fathers' deaths
removed the basis for invidious comparisons between fathers and sons.

Although these British studies differed over whether the son or the
daughter was more alienated by social mobility, they agreed that ties with
the father were affected more than with the mother. Men whose accomplish-
ments are outstripped by their sons do not take easily to their eclipse.

Does this mean, then, that men whose sons fall below them take secret
delight in their superior position? Perhaps. But positive feelings (if they exist
at all) are likely to be more than offset by both the parents' and the child's

sense of failure. The parents failed to bring the child up properly, and the child has disappointed his parents' expectations. Data from Willmott and Young show that contact with the father was depressed more by downward mobility than by upward mobility. (Only 41 percent of downwardly mobile men and women had seen the father in the previous week, compared to 60 percent of upwardly mobile and 70 percent of nonmobile adults.)

In general, then, social mobility places strains on contact and subjective feelings between adults and their parents. The strain ordinarily focuses more on members of the kinship system who participate most directly in the stratification system (*i.e.*, males) and is greatest when the direction of movement runs contrary to the values of the kin group (*i.e.*, in downward mobility).

Strains Between Siblings   Although parents take justifiable pride in the upward mobility of their children, siblings seldom sponsor each other's successes. Indeed, the rivalry of siblings within the nuclear family must be intensified when parents express pride in the superior achievements of a brother or sister. As members of the same generation, siblings indirectly compete with one another in school and the occupational system. They seem more likely than parents, therefore, to react negatively to losing out in that competition.

TABLE 10-4   Contacts of Married Men with Nearest-Aged
Brother, by Mobility Status

	MOBILITY STATUS		
CONTACTS (3+/YEAR)	Stable	Unilaterally Mobile	MOBILE/STABLE RATIO
Joint social activities outside the home	31%	18%	0.58X
Communication by mail or telephone	70	55	0.79
Home visits	65	59	0.89
Number of cases	113	44	

Adapted from Adams (1968):107. Source: Married men in Greensboro, North Carolina. Reciprocal percentages of men had less than three contacts per year of the specified kind.

Table 10-4 shows how differential mobility between brothers reduced contact between them in one American community. It may be no accident that the kind of contact which was most markedly reduced was social activity outside the home. Since differential mobility involves moving into contrasting positions in the larger social structure (in these cases one brother was a member of the middle class and one belonged to the working class), public activity might be expected to strain relations the most. Conversely, visits within the privacy of the home must be less humiliating for the lower-status brother and less embarrassing for the high-status brother.

Among Dublin Irishmen, Humphreys reported feelings of strain between siblings who were differentially mobile: "Toward siblings who are in the class above them they report feelings of jealousy and a margin of restraint, although sibling relations usually still remain close" (1966:199). Regardless of whether overt contact remains unimpaired, the existence of subjective barriers indicates the strain which mobility places on sibling ties.

In East London, similarly, Townsend found that class differences caused some siblings to avoid each other. Slum dwellers, left behind by successful siblings, "were self-conscious about their homes and, though their attitude to their siblings was sometimes tinged with envy and bitterness, their main concern appeared to be fear of being treated as inferiors" (1957:101). These working-class people felt that their middle-class siblings had somehow been "disloyal" to their background. They often ridiculed their mobile siblings for their "superior" ways. Such attitudes do not seem likely to make a successful sibling feel very welcome when he comes back "home" to visit.

TABLE 10-5 Changes in Closeness after Marriage for Differentially Mobile Nearest-Aged Siblings by Sex

| | SEX OF SIBLINGS | | |
CHANGE IN CLOSENESS	Brothers	Brother/Sister	Sisters
Closer since marriage	18%	31%	61%
About the same	23	33	16
Less close	59	36	23
Total	100%	100%	100%
Number of pairs	44	91	56

Adapted from Adams (1968):120. Source: Cross-stratum pairs (one white-collar, the other blue-collar) of married white adults in Greensboro, North Carolina.

In the preceding section we saw that mobility impaired kin ties between males but had less effect on female kin. Table 10-5 shows a similar difference in the effect of mobility on siblings. Assessing how they felt toward a differentially mobile sibling after marriage as compared to before marriage, girls reported that earlier feelings of strain had largely disappeared now that they were engaged in the common roles of wife and mother. While they were adolescents, their nascent differential mobility presumably caused tension in school and during dating. Marriage removed these women from competition in the stratification system and enabled them to find common ground in their domestic activities.

For brothers, by contrast, Table 10-5 shows that the passage of time only made matters worse. Their competition may have been bad enough in adolescence, but after entering the occupational system the contrast between the success of one and the failure of the other only sharpened.

Differential mobility, then, seems almost always to strain relationships between siblings. Even the seeming exception of sisters portrayed in Table 10-5 resulted from repairing an earlier gap between them. Nevertheless, the strain is greatest for those who compete most directly in the occupational system and whose chief source of self-esteem depends on their success or failure in that system. To a man concerned with how he has done in the outside world, a more successful brother is too vivid a reminder of what he might have achieved himself if he had only tried harder (or been endowed with better brains). That parenthetical disqualifier is less easy to assert between brothers born and nurtured in the same family than between strangers who can more easily assume that the other person "had all the breaks."

Shifts Between Secondary Kin   For an individual who was the first of his kin network to become upwardly mobile, a sense of alienation from his relatives might be expected. However, two factors reduce the strain: (1) Men usually feel less competitive toward cousins than toward brothers, so they make fewer invidious comparisons and feel less resentful of status differences; and (2) mobility is seldom limited to a single member of the network. Most American networks offer a choice of persons at various status levels. A mobile individual is therefore able to associate with relatives who share his new occupational level. Mobility reduces contact with the kin who are left behind but alternative kin at his new status level enable him to maintain a high level of interaction with *some* secondary kin. Adams (1968) found that interaction with secondary kin was highly segregated along class lines, but was not appreciably reduced for mobile individuals. Mobility within mixed-level networks shifts the kin chosen for contact more than it reduces the amount.

part two

THE FAMILY AS A
SOCIAL ORGANIZATION

In the first half of this book our focus was on the impact of outside forces upon the family and on changing relationships between the family and the external world. From this point on, the focus will be on what happens within the family. Outside forces can rarely be ignored, but instead of focusing on them as causal factors, they will be treated as control factors. The search for cause and effect relations will shift to the consequences of intrinsic features of the family itself: for example, family size, household complexity, or marital conflict. Though family size differs between agrarian and industrial societies, the new question will be: Within a given type of society, what are the consequences of variations in family size? The focus thus turns from the macroscopic cross-cultural and cross-institutional questions with which we dealt in Part I, to a microscopic, cross-family analysis. How do structural features of family life affect what goes on in those families? And how do families accomplish those tasks which are necessary to the survival of any organization: organizational formation and growth, internal social control, the resolution of organizational crises, and the utilization of expert consultants?

ORGANIZATIONAL FORMATION

From the standpoint of biological descent, every family can trace its existence to the beginning of time. Even if descent is treated as a social phenomenon (as in the lineage), it is difficult to say when the family tree first sprouted, save perhaps in the first known ancestor to bear the family name.

However, in a much more limited sense, families are formed anew in every generation. If marriage partners were not recruited from outside the family, inducted into the family, and socialized into the family's ways, the family would suddenly end. Only with the successful solution of this organizational problem can the family go on existing from generation to generation. Hence, mate selection provides a convenient starting point for analyzing family formation in any particular generation.

chapter eleven
MATE SELECTION: PERSONNEL RECRUITMENT

The incest taboo prevents recruitment of marriage partners from within the family. Consequently, partners must be found elsewhere. But not just anywhere. The choice is never purely random. The task of this chapter is to examine the patterned nature of mate selection: Who marries whom, and who does the recruiting? I will concentrate on social factors in mate-selection (those interested in psychological factors may see that section in my 1969 book, *Marriage*).The crucial question will be: "What are the consequences of different patterns of choice and of different agents of mate-selection?

THE AGENTS OF MATE SELECTION

The main agents of mate selection are either the bride and groom or their family and kin. A third alternative—an institutionalized or informal matchmaker—is normally used by one of those main agents, and rarely takes the initiative in promoting marriage himself. Thus for the sake of simplicity it is possible to focus on the differences between self-selection and kin-selection (with the understanding that the chief kin involved are usually parents).

Determinants of the Selection System

Before examining how these agents operate, we need to understand what features of family systems determine the system of mate selection. Self-selection is the simpler system and therefore needs less explanation. Why do some family systems prefer the more complicated procedure of kin-selection?

Parental Authority Family systems vary in the authority parents exercise over their growing and grown children. The greater the authority of parents in other matters, the greater their voice is likely to be in mate selection. Family systems which make a virtue of parental responsibility and children's obedience are likely to see personnel recruitment as another opportunity for parents to exercise their responsibility and a parallel opportunity for children to demonstrate their allegiance by accepting without question the parents' choice.

In such societies, the parents' sense of responsibility is sometimes a heavy burden. Aging parents whose children are still not married struggle valiantly against illness and old age, feeling they cannot afford to die until they have discharged their obligation to their children and their ancestors by successfully completing the marriage arrangements.

Children in such societies normally welcome their parents' concern. But occasional rebels worry their parents by not accepting their assistance. Geertz described one such case from the island of Java:

> . . . Juminah . . . had menstruated only once before she was married. No one asked her whether she wanted to marry or not, or told her the plans; and until three days before the wedding she was still attending school in the third grade. The parents of the groom, a young apprentice carpenter, sent her three sets of clothes, and her mother gave them to her to wear without telling her their significance. When she found out, she refused to wear them. There was a big wedding with a six-piece orchestra, but from the beginning she refused to serve food to her husband, to stay in the same room with him, or to sleep with him. Her father scolded her, and even hit her. She had been going to school every day on her bicycle, and the day after the wedding she started to go again. Her father did not like this and secretly damaged the bicycle so that she could not ride it. She missed one day of school, but the next day, determined to keep going, she walked the whole three miles to town. But her father meanwhile had been to see the teacher, and the teacher would not let her re-enter school. She was still unreconciled to the marriage, and every day her father scolded her. Her mother would have intervened on her behalf but was afraid of the father. Finally, without Juminah's knowing, her mother went to a magical curer and he gave her a charm which she gave to Juminah in a glass of iced drink. After that, although Juminah did not know about the magic charm till a year later, she became more reconciled, and by two months after the wedding her rebellion was all over and she moved to the house her husband had ready for her. Twelve months after the wedding she gave birth to her first child. She remarked that if it had not been for her parents and the magic charm she would have divorced her husband that first month. (1961: 74)

It is symbolic of Javan attitudes that Juminah was considered mentally ill. Any normal girl would not have given her parents and their hand-picked groom a hard time but would have meekly accepted what was done for her and would have done what was expected of her.

Goode noted that self-selection on the basis of love is "nearly always associated with a strong development of an adolescent peer group system" (1959:45). Perhaps one reason is that peer groups tend to undermine parental authority. If Juminah had been able to appeal to her peers against her parents, the parents might have treated her less severely. But, unsupported by anyone else, she had to be extraordinarily courageous to resist the combined efforts of father, mother, husband, teacher, and magician.

We have already seen in Chapter 6 that parents and peers tend to be pitted against each other in value conflicts. More important than any specific conflict of issues is the alteration in the power structure of family life when the child has an alternative social group. If he is home all the time, he can be controlled by his parents. But if he participates in an external group (no matter how informal), the support of the group nullifies the parent's influence and helps to emancipate him from their control. This social and psychological emancipation provides the child with the autonomy necessary to be able to exercise his own initiative and judgement in mate selection. By providing the child with a source of external participation, the peer group raises his status within the family, making him less subservient and able to function more independently.

Peer groups are ideally suited to perform this emancipation function since they are primary groups offering a powerful emotional alternative to family ties and an alternative membership group to which the individual may give his allegiance.

Peer groups are not the only possible basis for emancipation. Attending school, military service, independent employment, and living away from home are other external experiences which wean the child from depending on his parents. Regardless of the cause, the stronger the child's position *vis-à-vis* his parents, the greater his ability to choose his own partner. Conversely, the stronger the parents' general control over the child, the more likely they are to control his mate selection.

Family Residence   Although powerful parents are naturally interested in their child's mate selection, they are more personally involved if the mate is to move into their own household. Then it is not just the spouse who will have to live with the newcomer, but the whole family. Indeed, in a sex-segregated patrilocal household the man's mother more than the man himself may have to live with the bride. Counted simply in terms of the number of hours of interaction, wife and mother-in-law may be together far more than wife and husband. Nor is this simply a matter of rubbing elbows. The wife is likely to be a full-time servant to her mother-in-law. If she is a hard worker, she will ease her new mother's burdens, but if she is careless, incompetent or lazy, she will only cause trouble. Under these circumstances it is understandable that the mother should be vitally interested in the qualifications of her new "employee."

Even though the father is the head of a patriarchal household, he may play a relatively inactive role in the choice of his son's bride since she has little direct functional importance to him. On the other hand, he may be indirectly interested insofar as she represents a family with whom he wishes to establish a political alliance or economic partnership. For different reasons, the father and mother may both consider the selection of a spouse crucial to their own interests. However, the father's interest is not related to the patrilocal residence, whereas the mother's stake is intimately related to that pattern.

Matrilocal residence reverses the importance of mate selection to the two parents. If the groom is to join his wife's household, his qualification for work and his personal compatibility are of greater interest to the father than the mother. So fathers should be more involved in mate selection in matrilocal systems and mothers more involved in patrilocal systems, reflecting the sex of the mobile partner.

TABLE 11-1 Mate-Selection System in Societies with Extended and Nuclear Family Households

	IDEAL HOUSEHOLD	
MATE-SELECTION SYSTEM	Extended	Nuclear
Kin selection only	55%	30%
Both kin selection and self selection	18	39
Self selection but parental approval required	27	9
Self selection, parental approval not required	0	22
Total	100%	100%
Number of societies	11	23

Adapted from Stephens (1963):199. Source: Interviews with ethnographers familiar with a particular village or other subcommunity in a variety of primitive, feudal, and modern societies.

Table 11-1 compares societies with and without extended families. Those with extended families tend to give the heads of those families the whole responsibility for recruiting partners for their children. At the opposite extreme, none of these eleven extended-family societies allowed young people to choose for themselves without reserving the right to veto that choice.

In some family systems it is not the parents but antecedent wives who have to live with a new wife. In a polygynous household, the first wife is apt to be given a voice in the selection of subsequent wives. Even if she does not have to sleep in the same dwelling with a second wife (where wives each have their own hut), she is likely to be involved with the second wife in cooperative economic activities or to use her as a servant almost as much as the mother-in-law of a patrilocal bride.

Quite apart from questions of practical work, however, the first wife's jealousy is minimized if she can veto any extra wife whom she does not like. Again the division of labor may be such that women of the same generation in polygynous families spend most of their time together (like women of adjacent generations in extended families), so compatibility among women is of crucial importance.

Although they do not constitute a separate family system, children in one-parent households are similarly interested in choosing their new step-parent. Thus we can generalize that whenever persons other than the marrying individual will live with the spouse, they want to participate in selecting that person. Regardless of whether the spouse will be a son- or daughter-in-law, a co-wife, or a step-parent, these other persons have a stake in the selection of the new member of their family.

In neolocal systems, the problem is simplified. Only one person will have to live with the new recruit, so his interests are paramount. To be sure, parents will be interested because they are still acquiring a new son- or daughter-in-law. But if their interaction is to be confined to kin ties rather than to household ties, their stake is far less than that of the marrying child.

Even in the neolocal case, the basic principle is the same: The dominant members of the receiving household tend to become agents of mate selection. In the neolocal case, the receiving household is established as a result of the marriage itself. Both in these simple households and in complex ones, selection vitally concerns those whose welfare depends on finding a person competent to fill the role he/she is about to assume.

For an already-established household, adding a stranger threatens to disrupt already established routines and the existing family solidarity. For a new household to be established, mate selection will determine whether there will be any family solidarity at all or whether the new family will fall apart because of the inability of the spouses to establish a successful partnership. In both old and new households, the successful recruitment of a new family member can be a blessing to all concerned, but introducing a "bad apple" into the household can spoil the whole barrel.

Family Inheritance   A family with extensive property inherited from earlier generations or painfully acquired in the present will be correspondingly interested in the choice of the son/daughter-in-law who will share control of that property after the death of the parents and who will bear the children to receive the family estate after their own death. Some types of property interest parents more than others. Fixed, immovable property, especially land, invites parental involvement since land is a visible, tangible asset in whose management all members of the family participate. Conversely, intangible assets such as stocks and bonds are less likely to be transmitted intact from generation to generation and therefore less fatefully determined by the marriages of succeeding generations. Disregarding this distinction between types of property, we may generalize that the larger the amount of property held by the family, the greater the involvement of the elders in mate selection is likely to be.

Perhaps we can also assume that the longer the property has been in the family line, the more elders are likely to be concerned also. Old wealth creates a vertical time orientation toward the past and the future. Families able to recall generation after generation of prosperous ancestors can easily imagine the continuation of their wealth into the future through prudent marriages. Conversely, one of the hazards to new wealth is the danger that the children of a self-made man will waste his substance in a Doris Duke- or Tommy Manville-type series of misalliances with gold-digging gigolos or chorus girls. Even old wealth is not immune to such dangers, but old families are more likely to have developed ways of controlling the marriages of their younger members.

Family Status Closely associated with transmissible wealth is inheritable status. Faamilies with high prestige, with high caste status, or with royal blood take precautions about the marriages of their children since a bad marriage might destroy the special position which they received from their ancestors. In rigidly stratified societies, a nobleman who marries a commoner loses his eligibility to royal office, and a high caste person who marries beneath himself is reclassified at the lower partner's level. Even if the high caste partner does not lose status, his children are likely to bear the stigma of the lower parent's status (as contemporary American children of interracial marriages are considered "Negro" if either parent is black).

From the standpoint of high-status parents, the sacrifice of hard-won or long-cherished family status through such a mismatch is not only a personal loss to the child and the grandchildren but a loss to the family. The worst fate of all would be extinction of the family line should a sole surviving child choose to "throw away his birthright" in such a marriage. Therefore, the higher the family's status, the greater the supervision the family is likely to exercise. The greater the threatened loss through marriage to an extraordinarily low-status partner, the stronger the family opposition is likely to be. And the smaller the number of children on whom the transmission of the family name depends, the greater the family's interest in the marriages of those crucial few.

Conversely, in societies which are relatively equalitarian (with minimal distinctions between social strata), parents can afford to let their children do their own choosing because no one has much to lose (since no status is very high) and no one is much of a threat (since no status is very low). Similarly, if inherited status counts very little and personal achievement counts very much, marrying and bearing children has less relevance to placement in the stratification system. Even individuals who are somewhat penalized by the low status of a spouse or parent may be able to overcome that handicap by vigorous effort in the occupational system. In any case, the family line will not be doomed to permanently low status but can hope to recoup its social standing by upward mobility. Thus the less stratified and the more mobile the society, the less concerned the family is likely to be with mate selection.

Kin Selection of Marriage Partners

Having examined the general principles which determine the agents of mate selection, we turn now to a detailed examination of the way those various agents operate. If kin are to assert and maintain control over the human tendency of young men and young women to fall in love with each other, safeguards must be erected. Mechanisms have been devised by various societies which either singly or in combination guarantee that kin control will not be subverted.

Early Marriage If kin marry their children off young enough, they are less liable to face the dilemma of what to do about self-initiated love affairs.

Goode asserted that early marriage is "perhaps the most widely used structural pattern" for guaranteeing kin control (1959:43).

In Java, Geertz noted that parents accelerated their attempts to marry off their daughter soon after her first menstruation "especially if she begins to show a marked interest in men" (1961:56). In earlier generations, parents did not wait even that long but married off their daughters prior to puberty, fearing that interest in the opposite sex might then appear. Prepubertal marriage meant that a little girl was sent to live in her husband's household, to be brought up by him and his family until she was old enough to be initiated into full-fledged marital and sexual roles after puberty.

In societies where puberty is considered a prerequisite to intercourse, prepubertal marriage insures that parents neither have to marry the girl to a man who has seduced her nor be handicapped by any reputation for promiscuity which she might gain. The younger the daughter at marriage, moreover, the weaker her power position and therefore the less resistance she can put up to her parents' arrangements.

Because most societies have a double standard of sexual morality, early marriage is desirable for girls but less necessary for boys. If, as in Java, marriage is inappropriate for boys until they are financially self-supporting, that ability gives the boy a greater voice in his own decision than extra years alone would warrant. Under such circumstances, early marriage may involve a mixture of complete kin-initiative in the case of the girl plus limited self-initiative in the case of the boy. Geertz reported that Javanese boys could nominate candidates to their parents or veto nominations made by the parents. Nevertheless, the parents carried on the negotiations with the family of the girl finally chosen, and the boy's voice in the selection was discreetly screened from public view.

One consequence of emphasizing early marriage is to make it difficult for widows and widowers to remarry. If a widowed person must move into a new household after marriage, he or she is not likely to be easily adaptable after having lived so long in a different household. In rural Poland, this meant that families in the market for a spouse felt that "a widow or a widower is an undesirable partner, because more difficult to assimilate than a young girl or boy" (Thomas and Znaniecki, 1958:109). In patrilocal extended families, this principle created no particular difficulty in recruiting a new bride for a widower but left a young widow in a difficult position. We have already seen that many societies solved this problem by marrying the widow to a younger man from the same household so that she would not have to change families so late in life. Since such extended families generally consider the widow a member of their family, they wouldn't want her to leave even if she could. The levirate nicely solves the problem created by the death of the husband.

Segregation of the Sexes   If marriage has not been arranged by the time of adolescence, the problem of keeping young people from falling in love becomes more urgent. At this age, children who may have reasonably safely played together from infancy must be separated to prevent them from becoming emotionally and sexually involved.

To accomplish this segregation, coeducational primary schools are succeeded by segregated secondary schools and colleges. In cloistered societies, girls join their mothers in seclusion within the home. If they must leave the home, they may be shrouded from masculine view by veils which expose only their eyes, leaving them as anonymous as masked bandits.

Segregation may last throughout the engagement period so that bride and groom see each other for the first time when the bride's veil is lifted at the climax of the wedding ceremony. To continue segregation that long is intended less to prevent the betrothed couple from becoming positively involved than to prevent them from putting up resistance should they not like what they saw. The less the boy and girl know about the prospective partner, the stronger the parents' hands in the negotiations. Without knowledge, one can only trust or hope for the best.

Supervision of the Sexes   If a society does not separate the sexes, it may nevertheless guarantee the girl's chastity by chaperoning her at all times. If she is allowed to associate only with boys whom the parents would be willing to have her marry, love is confined to appropriate relationships. After parents have decided which person would be a suitable partner, they can afford to risk or perhaps even to encourage the development of affection, provided that the risk of premature sexual involvement is neutralized by the ever-present chaperone.

A supervisory system permits a far narrower range of contacts between the sexes than does a free system of self-selection. Such dating as occurs under supervision does not begin until both partners are old enough to marry. Whenever affectional attraction begins, the chaperone duly reports this to the parents (if she is not a parent herself) and they encourage the couple to move quickly into marriage. Dating unrelated to marriage is discouraged. Instead all dating tends to be a kind of courtship. The parents lurk in the background, kept abreast of developments by that member of the kin group who serves as chaperone, and thereby are able to keep the limited contact under strict kin control.

Prescribed Kin Choices   The three previous methods imply that parents take precautions to prevent their children from exercising choice but say nothing about restrictions on the choices. Kinship systems with highly developed lineages or other kin groupings often prescribe whom the marriage partner must be. In some societies, the preferred or even the compulsory partner must occupy a particular position in the kinship system. A popular position is the cross-cousin (such as the mother's brother's daughter or the father's sister's daughter). In kinship systems based on unilateral rather than bilateral descent, a cross-cousin does not belong to the same lineage and is therefore sufficiently remote to avoid an incestuous relationship, yet close enough to avoid marriage to an unknown, unrelated family.

Regardless of whether choice is confined to cross-cousins or some other particular persons, if the kinship system designates whom the individual must marry, it takes the choice of mate out of the hands of both the young people and their parents and places it in the hands of the system. To do so is to ban all love affairs outside the specified few eligible partners. Sometimes the system specifies only one potential partner, and one who is known from birth. Even if the mother's brother has two daughters, the system may require the older daughter to marry before the younger. If only one love is permitted, the danger of love with the wrong person is remarkably reduced, especially in societies small enough so that young people are rarely out of sight of kin. The only decision left to elders in these circumstances is when the predestined marriage shall take place.

The four systems of guaranteeing kin control of mate selection are each so powerful that it is seldom necessary for more than one or two of them to be used in a given society. Rather they are alternative ways of insuring that young people will be effectively prevented from exercising their own free choice.

Self-Selection of Marriage Partners

Self-selection sounds as though it is carried out independently of kin. In practice, however, close kin tend to play subordinate but significant roles. The difference lies not in their complete exclusion, but in their being relegated to subsidiary instead of primary roles. Whereas in purely arranged marriages, parents do the entire selecting behind the child's back, in self-selection the child does the selecting while the parent encourages or discourages particular relationships. This secondary role is analogous to the child's ability to veto parental nominations in contemporary Japan's modified system of kin arrangement (Blood, 1967).

In the United States, Bates (1942) found that the role of parents in their children's mate selection was normally positive and democratic. They assisted and encouraged the development of relationships of which they approved, and advised rather than dictated the child's choice. In exceptional cases where parents behaved in an authoritarian manner, attempting to forbid marriages of which they disapproved, children resorted to devious methods of by-passing their parents' blockade. They often eloped to marry outside the home community and sometimes kept the marriage secret from their parents even after the wedding. Authoritarian opposition from parents sometimes results in breaking a proposed relationship, but young people in modern countries are more apt to be persuaded by less arbitrarily expressed opposition than by unreasoned intransigence; as one once related to the author:

> Once I was unofficially engaged to a fellow of whom my parents did not approve. Rather than actively trying to force me to break off with him they used a thousand and one subtle hints about the mistake it would be to marry him. No attempt was made to stop us from dating, but it was not enjoyable without their approval. There were off-hand references to other people I had dated in the past, leaving an unspoken negative comparison. By consistently showing me that they were interested in my welfare and trusted my judgement "not to make such a mistake," they bound me tighter to them. This way I could not actually side with the fellow against my nonunderstanding parents, nor could I be angry with them. This "soft" approach, along with the logic of their arguments caused me to break off the relationship. A cousin in much the same circumstances, faced strong parental coercion, and eloped as she told me she thought her husband was the "only one on my side."

Sussman (1953b) found that parents more often discouraged than prohibited marriages of which they did not approve. They actively discouraged partners whom they feared would prove incompatible and marriages which they deemed premature in terms of the child's age.

Thus if parents intervene at all in systems of self-selection, their intervention is likely to attempt to encourage or persuade the child rather than to dictate his choice. In deviant cases where parents try to prohibit a marriage, their arbitrariness often backfires in rebellious circumvention of the prohibition.

Professional Selection: Matchmakers

Relatives searching for an eligible partner often turn to third parties to assist them in finding a good prospect. Even in self-selecting societies individuals may find formal agencies useful in providing contacts which might lead to marriage. By professional matchmakers I mean any persons—whether paid or unpaid—who specialize in locating potential prospects for persons other than their relatives.

Where mate selection is the responsibility of the whole family, matchmakers function as go-betweens, negotiating the delicate relationships between families and saving face in case the negotiations go wrong. Because each family tries to make the best possible match for its own child, negotiations resemble business deals or political treaties in which each side tries to exploit the other side's weaknesses and hide its own in order to strike the best possible bargain. Subtle matters of family prestige are at stake, influencing the conduct of the negotiations. In a tightly knit rural community, this can lead not only to failure in matchmaking but to feuds between families if anything goes wrong. In such a context, the go-between must be a skilled mediator. In rural Poland:

> Every family naturally tries to make the best possible alliance; at the same time it tries not to lower its own dignity by risking a refusal or by accepting at once even the best match, for the range of possibilities open to an individual is a proof of the high standing of the family. Thence also such institutions as that of the matchmaker, whose task is to shorten the ceremonial of choosing without apparently lowering the dignity of the families involved. (Thomas and Znaniecki, 1958:110)

In Japanese cities, Vogel (1961b) found that matchmakers were sociable women with a large range of contacts whom they utilized to find eligible young persons. My Tokyo research (Blood, 1967) indicated that the main function of introductions was to give couples a chance to size each other up rather than to actually "arrange" a match until the couple decided that they were interested. That Japanese young people widely exercised their veto rights was demonstrated by the fact that hardly more than 10 percent of the formal introductions experienced by my sample of married couples had led to marriage. And even though formally introduced couples were under considerable pressure to make up their minds as soon as possible, the average couple who married after a formal introduction required ten dates spread over five months before getting engaged. This was far short of the 41 dates over 19 months which the average self-selected couple experienced, but it indicated nevertheless how far the modern system of kin-sponsored professional selection had strayed from the original authoritarian form.

Urbanization and mobility make it harder for young people and their families to find potential partners. This has produced a gradual shift away from personal, unorganized matchmakers toward formal matchmaking agencies. In Japan, the municipal governments of the larger cities established "Marriage Consultation Centers" which offered an inexpensive public service to individuals wishing to find a marriage partner. The Tokyo Center in the early 1960s facilitated a thousand marriages a year via its contacts. Approximately one fifth of those registered at the bureau succeeded in marrying each year, the remainder being carried forward to the next year. Most applicants were office workers. A bare majority of the men were college-educated. One problem facing the bureau was that twice as many women as men registered, so the chances of finding partners were less for women than for men.

In addition to municipal governments, some segregated women's colleges in Japan established marriage bureaus for their alumnae. Since alumnae of such colleges had the reputation of becoming unusually "mild" (*i.e.*, submissive) wives, these bureaus attracted large numbers of men from the largely segregated prestige universities.

In the United States, technological sophistication made possible the development of computer matchmaking centers which functioned somewhat similarly to the Japanese agencies. However, the American approach emphasized the subjective, personal criteria more appropriate to a self-selection system instead of the objective family background criteria prized in a society accustomed to kin-selection. Moreover, American agencies gave their clients a free hand in arranging their own dates by phone or by mail, whereas the Japanese agencies sponsored formal introductory meetings at the agency headquarters presided over by a staff counselor. Thus professional selection adapts itself to the environment within which it operates.

Because American women are almost as handicapped as Japanese women in taking the initiative toward dating new partners, computer agencies also were flooded with female applicants and short of male applicants. For young women such agencies offered a satisfactory way of making new contacts, but for older women faced with the shorter life-span of males, the chances of marrying could hardly become bright by this or any other means.

Other institutions in American cities which functioned to promote introductions were recreational in nature. Date bars, summer resorts, and holiday cruises restricted to unmarried adults usually relied on the initiative of those in attendance to introduce themselves to each other but sometimes utilized "mixers" and computers to assist in the introduction process. How many marriages emerged from these facilities is not known, but in relatively anonymous urban environments like New York City they were a mecca for new migrants from the hinterland and for less sociable individuals whose own resources had not led them into marriage as fast as they wished.

In Japan, most young people preferred self-selection but found it comforting to be able to fall back on matchmaking women and matchmaking bureaus if their own efforts failed (Baber, 1958). In the U. S., similarly, the development of institutional facilities for professional selection of potential spouses supplemented self-selection in cases of special need. In the future, such supplementary facilities can be expected to become increasingly important in an increasingly impersonal world.

Consequences of Mate-Selection Systems

In the polar types of mate selection by kin or by oneself, there are characteristic differences in the criteria emphasized for a "good" partner, the role stressed after marriage, and the type of relationship developed between the husband and wife.

Criteria for Selection Young people choose their own partners on a quite different basis from that of kin or marriage bureaus in a kin-oriented society like Japan. Kin emphasize family background (*i.e.,* the characteristics of the *other* set of kin) and status in the stratification system. Self-selectors emphasize personal qualities of a comparatively idiosyncratic nature.

For example, women applying to the Tokyo Marriage Bureau wanted husbands with good incomes, with reliable occupations ("conscientious white collar" workers), who did not intend to live patrilocally with their parents after marriage. Male applicants preferred partners who were physically healthy (and likely to produce strong children to carry on the family line), cheerful and obedient to the husband's orders, and willing to work if necessary to supplement the husband's income. The stress on income by both men and women reflected the difficulties of achieving a high standard of living in a country with a relatively low salary level and galloping inflation.

In transitional mate-selection systems where young people have only the briefest opportunity to see one another, the criteria for selection must be correspondingly superficial. A young Javanese man traditionally paid a formal visit with his father to the home of the girl who had been selected as his potential bride:

> This visit is called "to look at," its purpose being to give the man and girl a chance to see each other and, perhaps more important, to give the parents of both an opportunity to size each other up. Traditionally, and frequently even today, neither of the two young people knows the other, and this is their only chance to make an appraisal.
>
> The role of the girl . . . is confined to silent serving of tea or coffee and snacks, and she usually is intensely embarrassed at the presence of her possible husband. The girl is supposed to walk with eyes shyly downcast. A man looking over a girl is said to pay special attention to her eyes and to the way she walks. If she looks around too much, if she does not walk demurely, these are signs that she will be disobedient and willful, and he may decide against her. . . . One government official . . . rejected a girl because her feet were too big. (Geertz, 1961:62–63)

Self selection stresses subjective feelings between the partners and reciprocally shared characteristics conducive to an equalitarian relationship. Burgess and Wallin's middle-class Americans had gotten engaged because they felt love and affection for each other, were personally compatible, and had many interests in common (1953). Kin-oriented criteria stress different traits for men and for women, traits reflecting the traditional preoccupation of the man with his occupational role and of the woman with her child-bearing and housekeeping functions. This tends to produce a male-dominated, patriarchal type of marriage.

In Japan, the criteria and systems are in transition from the traditional emphasis on the wife's ability to fit into the husband's family. Indeed, contemporary Japanese women are in widespread revolt against that old requirement, now that they no longer inevitably must accept that fate.

When kin select a daughter-in-law to live with them, one of the main criteria is her ability to fit into the family. In rural Poland, Thomas and Znaniecki reported that families were interested in finding not only someone of good character "but a set of habits similar to those prevailing in the family to be entered" (1958:109). In other words compatibility between the values and habits of the two families was necessary to insure a good fit for the "immigrant" spouse into her new home.

In addition to compatibility of character, the new spouse must be able to fulfill her family roles. This requirement is not unique to kin-selection systems but is masked in self-selection systems by more subtle concern with feelings and attractions rather than the practical concerns which kin emphasize. Kin stress the importance of the bride's health as an index of presumed child-bearing capacity and ability to work hard within the home. Kin also double the importance of obedience since the bride will have two generations of masters and not just one.

Even if kin wanted to emphasize the values which self-selectors stress, they would find it difficult or impossible to do so. Common interests they might be able to judge (though not so well as the couple themselves). Personal compatibility would be harder for outsiders to judge. Love and affection could hardly be predicted even by the couple themselves prior to its actual development during courtship. Kin, then, not only have different vested interests which affect their priorities, but they also have a different vantage point for gathering information which limits the kinds of data they could secure. Thus the system of mate selection inevitably affects the criteria to be emphasized.

This difference in emphasis can be seen even within a given society (which has the advantage of holding constant economic conditions and other societal differences). I found (Blood, 1967) that, within my Tokyo sample, those who were formally introduced stressed the husband's income and the wife's health and housekeeping ability, whereas couples who met on their own emphasized the importance of love between the partners.

In the United States, where matches are essentially self-selected, parents and children nevertheless differ in the criteria they emphasize. When coeds at Temple University (Philadelphia) were asked the most important trait to look for in a husband, 68 percent specified personality or physical attractiveness. Only 42 percent of their mothers, by contrast, chose these individual characteristics, whereas the majority thought the man's job or family background was more important (Bell and Buerkle, 1962).

Role Emphasis Closely related to the differences in criteria utilized in choosing the new recruit are differences in emphasis on the husband–wife or the parent–child relationship after marriage. Self selection builds a bond between the partners which becomes the key element in family life. Kin selection, conversely, deemphasizes the husband–wife relationship and stresses the couple's responsibilities to their antecedent kin and their descendant children. In other words, the horizontal emphasis involved in the process of self selection tends to continue after marriage, whereas the vertical emphasis in kin selection is similarly perpetuated.

Self-selection builds a relationship between partners by dyadic interaction during unchaperoned dates. The love which is an index of the couple's suitability for marriage also attests the strength of their relationship. When kin-selection systems ban dating, they make the establishment of any relationship between the partners impossible before marriage. Theoretically, love might develop after a kin-initiated marriage, but continuing involvement with kin prolongs the resident child's emotional attachment to his parents and discourages the development of a competing tie with his partner.

In my Tokyo research, formally introduced married couples failed to develop as much love for each other as couples whose whole relationship was self-sponsored, despite the fact that none were living with relatives and had no direct interference from relatives.

The title of Sussman's article (1953b) on "Parental Participation in Mate Selection and Its Effect upon Family Continuity" implies a greater emphasis on vertical relations in American marriages where parents play an active (even though subsidiary) role. Sussman found that couples who married despite the opposition of one or both sets of parents had more conflict and less interaction with them after marriage. To put it another way, parental approval provides a basis for predicting positive relationships with parents after marriage. To put the matter most simply, the vertical or horizontal emphasis which begins with the initial participation or nonparticipation of parents in mate selection tends to continue after marriage as long as the parents live. Even after they die, the vertical orientation persists as wives who have been weakly linked to the marriage partner turn their attention downward to their children and grandchildren.

Marital Satisfaction We have already seen that the participation of parents in mate selection tends to guarantee good relationships between kin and the married couple. The effect of parents on relations between the partners is less clear. We have seen that parental participation in mate selection foreshadows a continuing deemphasis on the marital relationship. However, parents may provide valuable assistance to their children in the mate-selection process. Young people, after all, easily can make unwise choices. Perhaps their parents can draw on the wisdom of their years of experience with life in general and marriage in particular. Certainly the parents offer the relative detachment of being less involved in the selection (at least in self-selecting systems), and therefore contribute a measure of objectivity which the couple may lack. In any case, couples who might have blindly contracted unpromising marriages may be aided by the supplementary judgements of both sets of parents. In this sense, six heads are better than two.

If self selection benefits from the supplementary participation of parents, can we also assume that kin selection benefits from the supplementary participation of children? If kin emphasize certain relevant criteria to the neglect of others, perhaps involving children will introduce the neglected criteria. Then, with both generations participating, the prospective match must pass the test of both kin-relevant and personally relevant criteria.

Evidence is not available to prove the superiority of the participation of both selves and kin over the involvement of only one set of agents. But this idea can be tested indirectly by examining the success of marriages in which both generations concur with the decision to marry with those in which one generation doubted the wisdom of the forthcoming marriage.

In my Tokyo research (1967), the happiest arranged marriages involved couples who did not rush into engagement after being formally introduced but dated at least ten times and were most intensely in love by the time they got engaged. These marriages combined parental sponsorship with personal validation of their compatibility. They could hardly fail to be extraordinarily successful.

The happiest love matches were not those which exemplified the romantic concept of marrying in the face of parental opposition, but those where parents were most enthusiastic about the pending match. Perhaps the nearest approximation to noninvolved parents were those "indifferent" to the proposed match. Those marriages turned out to be worst of all, even worse than those where parents responded negatively. Perhaps then the active involvement of parents in love-matches is generally auspicious. In any case, when a self-initiated match receives the unreserved blessing of parents, extraordinary success can be predicted.

In general, then, the most successful marriages involve neither kin alone nor children alone, but the cooperative activity of both generations, regardless of which generation initiated the relationship or is the prime agent in mate selection. At best, parents and children are not antagonists in the mate-selection process but collaborators whose combined efforts offer a more secure basis for marriage than either generation could achieve single-handedly.

I assume that marriages which are prevented by the successful exercise of their veto rights by either generation would have been even worse than marriages which are consummated despite the negative reaction of subsidiary agents. We have already noted that in Japan the great majority of the partners nominated by parents through a formal introduction are vetoed by the children after the introduction. In the United States, Burgess and Wallin found that almost a third of engagements disapproved by both parents of the girl were broken. In a decision as fateful as mate selection, perhaps the greater danger is that of entering a bad marriage rather than missing a good prospect. In any case, the evidence of heightened success in doubly endorsed marriages is unmistakable. This suggests that who the agents of mate selection are matters less in the long run than whether both generations participate in the decision-making, regardless of where the original idea came from.

THE CRITERIA OF MATE SELECTION

We have already seen that different criteria are employed by the two generations. Henceforth, one can largely disregard the question of who uses which
criteria and concentrate rather on the nature of the criteria and the effects on
marriage of adhering to or violating those qualifications.

Regardless of whether criteria are employed consciously or unconsciously, the actual patterns of mate selection in various societies answer our
central questions: Who marries whom? and what are the consequences?

The broadest possible answer is that like marries like, and that such
homogamous marriages are generally more successful than heterogamous
(mixed) marriages.

Horizontal Homogamy: Geographical Eligibility

Although like generally marries like, the most extreme case constitutes an
exception. Those who are most alike are members of the same family (as
computers recognize when they pair brothers and sisters on the basis of their
remarkably similar family background!). Yet the incest taboo is as nearly
universal a rule as one can find anywhere. Even though marriage between
siblings would be unusually cohesive, the effect of such dyadic withdrawal
on the parental family would be too destructive. The losses to the old family
outweigh the advantages to the new.

On a larger scale of social organization, cohesive communities also tend
to observe an "incest taboo." We saw in an earlier chapter how the Oneida
community placed elaborate restrictions on sexual intercourse in order to
prevent the development of dyadic ties within the larger "family". Of even
greater interest were the Israeli kibbutzim where young people who had
grown up together in the same kibbutz seldom married within their peer
group even though there was no rule forbidding such marriages. They usually
married someone from a different kibbutz. Apparently young people who
had grown up together in a "children's house" formed too cohesive a group
to allow pairing off to seem anything less than betrayal.

Talmon (1964) suggested that excessive familiarity in the kibbutz prevented couples from falling in love. In those rare cases where couples from
the same age group married, they had almost always been separated for several years by military service or some other absence, with the result that they
had a chance to rediscover each other. Fromm (1956) similarly suggested
that one of the motivating forces for marriage is the discovery of compatibility between two people and the excitement of "the collapsing of the walls"
between them. For never-separated kibbutzniks, there had never been any
walls to collapse so the excitement of new love was impossible.

Kibbutzniks faced with an informal ban on marriage within the group
were able to look for partners within other kibbutzim. In the United States
and Canada, marriage partners for members of Hutterite colonies have normally been recruited from other colonies. But what happens if a utopian
community has no parallel elsewhere? One community in Canada (the Breth-
ren of Early Christianity) felt so strongly that their children should not be

"yoked unequally with unbelievers" that they preferred marriage within the community to marriage with strangers. However, those marriages were conspicuously unromantic and focused on the necessity of reproduction to preserve the community. If the community had solved its problem of continuity by making new converts from the larger society, it seems likely that the new recruits would have been more popular and romantic marriage partners than the old community-mates.

The experience of nuclear families and utopian communities suggests that if propinquity is excessively close, marriage is less likely, rather than more likely, to occur. This conclusion should be qualified, however, by noting that if people are old enough to marry when they begin living in close proximity (and especially if they do not belong to a larger group to which they owe a conflicting loyalty), close proximity may be a positive factor in mate selection. In my Tokyo research I encountered several cases where girls had fallen in love with men who had come to board in their homes. For these girls no antecedent social group prevented propinquity from producing new ties. Conversely, once a family or a familistic group comes into existence, it resists threats to its unity from couples seceding from the group.

Adoption presents special problems since it recruits outside personnel who may become either a child subject to the incest taboo or an eligible spouse, depending on the age of adoption. Among the African Nuer, Evans-Pritchard (1951) found that captured children of an inferior tribe were ordinarily brought up within the household as legally adopted children in the case of boys or as informal members of the household in the case of girls. In either case, they were subject to the incest taboo in relation to their step-siblings and indeed to the whole lineage which they had joined. If a captured girl was desired as a spouse instead of as a daughter, she had to be handed over to another man to bring up outside the village because, as the Nuer expressed it, "if she were to remain in his homestead she would become his daughter" (1951:32).

By contrast, when an adult Japanese man was adopted into a family as an adult, he became both the husband of the daughter and the "son" of the family at the same time. He carried on the bride's family name and became the father of her children. This suggests that the problem with adoption is not one of "excessive propinquity," but one of timing. If the newcomer joins the family prior to marriage, he cannot subsequently marry within that family. If he is recruited as a marriage partner rather than as a spouse, he is not necessarily prevented from simultaneously becoming a child of the family he has just joined indirectly by marriage.

Village Endogamy   Only when we turn from families or familistic communities to larger social units does territorial homogamy begin to be permitted. Even here, however, there are exceptions. Many primitive societies require that mates be recruited from outside the village. This rule stems from conditions resembling those for families when villages are small and consist primarily of blood relatives. Conversely, the larger the village becomes, the greater the tolerance for endogamy.

Many primitive tribes find external as well as internal advantages in village exogamy. Establishing ties with another village offers security against armed conflict between villages. The new recruit becomes a hostage within the village, reducing chances of attack from without.

Perhaps for such reasons, Murdock (1949) found community exogamy in more than twice as many societies as required endogamy. Almost as many other societies had no rule either way, suggesting the ambiguousness of social forces at this level.

In societies subdivided into regions, endogamous preference arises insofar as those regions represent differentiated subcultures. In traditional Poland, for example, families hoped to recruit marriage partners "in the same district, since customs and habits differ from locality to locality" (Thomas and Znaniecki, 1958:109). In the United States, northern and southern cultures differ sufficiently to introduce culture conflict into marriages between typical representatives of those regional cultures. In such circumstances, endogamy brings together partners who are likely to have fewer conflicts with each other and with their in-laws.

National Endogamy In contrast to the indeterminacy of mate-selection preferences inside or outside the village is the widespread preference for marriage within the larger society.

For a migrating partner, an international marriage imposes many of the same learning assignments as for the migrant couples described in Chapter 9. But whereas migrating couples find solidarity in undergoing the hardships of emigration together, an international marriage imposes differential strains on the two partners. The foreigner alone must learn the new culture while the native becomes the chief cultural tutor. This alters the structure of marriage in favor of domination by the native partner (other things being equal).

The importation of a foreign spouse is frequently resisted by members of the domestic kin group and even more by the foreign kin who will lose contact with their emigrating offspring. Once the marriage takes place, however, the receiving group may tend to shift their focus from resistance (now that it is too late) to assistance in resocializing the stranger. Strauss found that American soldiers' parents "played an important part in the acculturation of the [Japanese war] bride, teaching her about shopping, about kitchen equipment and the like" (1954:105). The fact that these Japanese brides severed their ties with their own families removed one potential source of marital conflict which ordinary marriages face, namely conflict over which partner's kin to visit on special occasions.

However, the fact that conflicts over allocating time to in-laws are reduced does not mean that international marriages have fewer marital conflicts in general. Depending on the particular combination of cultures involved, clashes of customs are an inevitable concomitant of socialization in different societies. American soldiers living with their Filipino wives near an American base in the Philippines, experienced sharp conflict over child-care practices, housekeeping practices, and sexual attitudes and practices (Hunt and Coller, 1957). For example, wives refused to undress in front of their husbands, refused to engage in sexual foreplay, and did not expect sex to be pleasurable. These typically Philippine attitudes of modesty clashed with the sexual hedonism the husbands had learned from American culture.

Any attempt to resolve conflicts deeply rooted in childhood socialization is handicapped by the communication difficulties of partners with different native languages. Although one partner may learn the foreign language sufficiently to manage ordinary conversations, sexual attitudes are not likely to be effectively communicated in an unfamiliar tongue.

In addition to conflict over child care, housekeeping, and sex, Hunt and Coller found that husbands and wives agreed to differ in two areas of life— each eating his native foods and engaging in his native forms of recreation. Such internal divisions deprive marriage of what otherwise might have been joint activities. The remainder of marriage consisted of a peculiar combination of American and Filipino cultural traits, such as American-style education for the children and Filipino-style religious practices.

This fragile synthesis of American and Filipino elements made these families at home in neither American nor Filipino society. Like immigrants in a foreign land, their hybrid culture was buffered by associating with other mixed couples. Similarly Strauss found that American–Japanese couples in Chicago confined their social life almost exclusively to other mixed couples, and the same leisure-time segregation occurs among Eurasian marriages in Asia. Presumably the support of other couples faced with the same problems helps offset the internal strains faced by husbands and wives who must cope with cultural differences and language barriers.

Unfortunately, statistical evidence on the success of international marriages is not available. It seems reasonable to hypothesize that such marriages suffer from the strains to which they are subjected, but knowledge about the extent of this deterioration awaits future measurement.

One index of strain in international marriages is fewer children. Table 11-2 presents the results of a carefully controlled analysis of reproductive

TABLE 11-2   Average Fertility of Americans Married to American or Foreign Partners, by Religion

AVERAGE NUMBER OF CHILDREN BORN, BY RELIGION	NATIONALITY OF PARTNER		Exogamous/ Endogamous Ratio
	American	Foreign	
Protestant	2.48	2.26	0.91X
Catholic	2.76	2.42	0.88

Adapted from Bresler (1961):19. Source: Parents of alumni of Brown University and Pembroke College. The numbers of cases on which the means were computed were 281 and 34 for Protestant families and 67 and 19 for Catholic families, respectively.

differences between international marriages and endogamous marriages. The lower number of children born to international couples presumably reflects the greater difficulties which such marriages encounter.

It is for such reasons that, other things being equal, geographical eligibility for marriage is ordinarily limited to the boundaries of the cultural entity which we call a society or nation.

Vertical Homogamy: Social Eligibility

Although geographical eligibility is a variable phenomenon, changing from small-scale exogamy to larger-scale endogamy, eligibility within stratification systems is restricted to the same stratum, with the rarest exceptions. Vertical homogamy is therefore a more consistent principle than horizontal homogamy.

For the sake of simplicity, vertical strata will be treated under two classifications: inherited caste positions, and achieved or class positions.

Caste Endogamy   A caste system is composed of groups of people whose membership is defined by birth and who are ineligible to intermarry. The taboo on intermarriage between castes may not be quite so strong as the incest taboo on marriage within the family, but the parallel is close. In the latter case, the taboo bans endogamy between persons considered too close to marry. In the caste case, the taboo bans exogamy between persons too distant to marry. The classic case is the Hindu caste system of India. Weaker but relevant cases are the taboos on intermarriage between blacks and whites in the United States and, weaker yet, on intermarriage between Jews and Gentiles.

The Indian caste system was extraordinarily complex. Mate selection was restricted not only to one's own caste, but even to one's subdivision within the caste (Goode, 1963). The only leniency was that a girl could marry into a higher sub-caste (but not a higher caste) provided her family paid a larger dowry to compensate for her inferior status. To this modest extent, the caste system was flexible enough to assimilate a lower-status bride into a groom's subcaste, thereby permitting women a limited amount of upward mobility by marriage.

Caste endogamy protected not only the purity of the blood line but the solidarity of the patrilocal extended family. According to Gore:

> Marriage within the caste-group ensures that the bride's cultural background is similar to that of the husband's family. Castes lay down a relatively unvaried and unambiguous code of conduct for their members. Marriage within the caste therefore provides the necessary homogeneity which makes adjustment easy. The young bride who belongs to the same caste is less likely to shock her in-laws by inadvertent actions. (1965:219)

Insofar as each caste had a unique subculture, endogamy prevented cultural diversity within the family.

Among black Americans, the equivalent of Hindu subcastes involve differences in shade of skin. Light-skinned blacks form an elite group to which the dark-skinned blacks have long felt inferior. Liebow (1967) found that dark-skinned lower-class men were afraid that light-skinned wives would turn on them with devastating racial slurs in an argument. So sensitive were they that they felt uncomfortable with light-skinned women even as casual sex partners.

Against this background of fear of light-skinned women, it is surprising how often black men marry white women. Unlike India, where high-caste men might marry slightly lower-caste women, American patterns of inter-caste marriage tend to involve lower-caste men marrying higher-caste women. For example, in four states in the early 1960s, black men married white women several times as often as white men married black women (Heer, 1966). Similarly, in Washington, D. C. and in Iowa, Jewish men married Gentile women more than twice as often as the reverse (Rosenthal, 1963).

This reversal of the Hindu pattern is unexpected because high-caste American women who marry low-caste men tend to lose caste thereby. Their children are classified in the husband's caste and even the women themselves may be reclassified. Pavela (1964) found that the children of black–white marriages were considered colored and that a majority of white wives became "black" socially—living in black neighborhoods and associating only with black friends.

In Jewish mixed marriages, wives and children are less often stigmatized as Jews. Indeed one Washington study showed that a majority of children were considered non-Jewish by their parents. This begs the question of how they were viewed by outsiders who seem more likely to attribute Jewish ethnicity to children bearing an identifiably Jewish name conferred by the father. Whereas the children of black–white marriages were treated as black regardless of whether the father or the mother was black, children of Jewish–Gentile marriages were twice as apt to be considered Jewish by their parents if the father rather than the mother was Jewish (Rosenthal, 1963).

From the standpoint of the wife, then, such marriages seem to be "bad" marriages. Why then do they occur so often? That the answer is somehow connected with prejudice and discrimination is suggested by the fact that interracial marriages in Hawaii are less skewed in the black male/white female direction than on the U. S. mainland, where they are much less common and less socially accepted (Heer, 1966). Similarly, Mayer (1961) found that as anti-semitism grew in Germany from 1876 to 1933, the proportion of Jewish–Gentile marriages in which the husband was Jewish steadily increased.

The hurdles to marrying "down" are implied in Pavela's finding that whites marrying blacks (regardless of sexes) were almost two years older than those marrying within their own caste. Similarly, Jewish–Gentile marriages a generation ago, when anti-semitism was stronger, occurred later than usual, whereas more recently this delay has disappeared as intermarriages have become more common.

Does the fact that high-caste women are older when they marry out of their caste mean that they are falling back on second choices after caste endogamy has passed them by? Perhaps, in some cases. Merton (1941) hypothesized that high-status men had sexual relations with low-status women but didn't marry them as often because they didn't have to, but this argument about white male exploitation of black women hardly applies to Gentile men and Jewish women.

Perhaps the older age of out-marrying women is necessary to enable them to be emancipated enough from normal social controls to be able to break the caste taboo. Intermarriages between blacks and whites frequently involved civil ceremonies which by-passed the normal family involvement in religious ceremonies (Pavela, 1964).

Perhaps low-caste persons of both sexes prefer to marry up but low-caste males are freer to exercise the sex-linked privilege of initiating such "good" marriages. By contrast, as caste barriers disappear, intermarriage becomes less sought for its own sake and therefore less dominated by low-status males.

Table 11-3 shows that inter-caste marriages in the United States failed more often than caste-endogamous marriages. In these five cities, Jewish men married to Gentile wives were five times as apt to desert or divorce their wives as men who married within their own group.

TABLE 11-3 Desertions and Divorces of Jewish Men, by Caste Status of Wife

| CITY | *Percentage of Marriages Ending in Separation or Divorce by Caste Status of Marriage* | | *EXOGAMOUS/ ENDOGAMOUS RATIO* |
| | CASTE STATUS OF MARRIAGE | | |
	Endogamous	*Exogamous*	
New Orleans	33%	57%	1.73X
Omaha	13	62	4.78
St. Louis	9	44	4.90
Boston	5	25	5.00
Denver	8	48	6.00

Adapted from Zimmerman and Cervantes, 1960:153–154. Source: Families of high school seniors and of friends of their families. In the five cities combined the total number of cases studied included about 1,420 endogamous marriages of Jewish men with Jewish wives and 450 exogamous marriages of Jewish men with Gentile wives. Reciprocal percentages of marriages did not end in desertion or divorce.

Presumably the hazards of black–white marriages are even greater than for Jewish–Gentile marriages in view of the greater American prejudice against blacks. While comparable statistics are not available, Smith (1966) found that black partners tended to be touchy about seeming racial slurs and to insist on the white partner's need to learn to "understand" blacks. This suggests inferiority feelings similar to those which plagued Liebow's dark-skinned men when they interacted with light-skinned women.

Smith also noted heavy external stresses experienced by black–white couples in New York City. The white partner tended to be ostracized by his relatives and both partners experienced hostile or curious stares from strangers wherever they went. Sometimes they were searched by policemen who suspected that they were engaged in illicit activities such as prostitution (interracial marriage is so rare that couples are seldom suspected of being married). In extreme cases, one or both partners were attacked and beaten in the streets by strangers infuriated by their violation of caste taboos. Such external strains presumably undermine the morale of most couples who experience them, magnifying whatever misunderstandings arise between them.

A second symptom of stress is limitation of family growth. Inter-caste marriages in the United States tend to have fewer children than endogamous marriages. Forty-three percent of Golden's (1954) black–white couples in Philadelphia were childless. Substantially more of Goldstein and Gold-scheider's (1966) Jewish–Gentile couples in Providence were childless than their endogamously Jewish couples. However, the increasing assimilation of Jews into American society diminished the impact of intermarriage on the birth rates of Jewish–Gentile marriages. Among women 45 years of age and older, there were 2.7 times as many cases of childlessness in the exogamous marriages, but among those under 45, there were only 1.8 times as many. Thus as caste lines soften, the negative consequences of intercaste marriages gradually disappear.

Class Endogamy   Social class is a more complex and subtle phenomenon than caste. As a result it is sometimes difficult to determine the difference between endogamous and exogamous marriages except in extreme cases. Moreover, the concept of a class system allows individuals to change positions. A man or woman can move to a higher class by greater achievement. The relatively fluid nature of class systems and the lesser emphasis on inherited position than in caste systems lowers the ban on exogamous marriages but does not remove it.

A sophisticated analysis of a U. S. national sample by Blau and Duncan (1967) demonstrated a high level of class endogamy, using the partners' own educational achievement as the measure of class status. A correlation of .6 between the education of the two partners means that 36 percent of the variance in the wife's education could be predicted from the husband's (or vice versa). Such a high correlation between partners suggests that there is a norm of class endogamy, even though it is impossible to differentiate the effects of organizational propinquity when partners meet at school from voluntary selection of endogamous partners from a mixed group of eligibles. In any case, like marries like as far as education is concerned.

Two studies by Hollingshead showed similar tendencies toward class endogamy when other measures of class status were used. In Elmtown (a small mid-Western community), Hollingshead found that most high school dates were between students whose fathers belonged to the same social class (1949). Since high school dating foreshadows eventual mate selection, this implies that marriages were similarly concentrated within endogamous class backgrounds. However, Blau and Duncan found that the extent of homogamy by family background was weaker than homogamy by education because father's occupation may not measure the achieved status of the child by the time he marries. Thus family background may govern dating in high school but an individual who goes to college may escape the limits of his background and find a partner who matches his own achievements.

In New Haven, Hollingshead (1950) used the prestige of the partner's residential area as a basis of classification and found that most couples came from areas with the same classification. Contributing to this class endogamy is residential propinquity (the fact that partners tend to come from the same area, not just from the same type of area). For whatever reasons, New Haven young people rarely married someone from "across the tracks."

To summarize these findings with respect to social class, there is a marked tendency for husbands and wives to marry within the same class as measured by their personal achievements, and a weaker tendency for them to come from the same class as far as childhood origins are concerned. The more mobile the community, the less relevant family background becomes, but this does not nullify class restrictions on the *personal* qualifications of the partner. Middle-class people, regardless of family background, tend to marry middle-class people.

In exceptional cases where people marry across class lines, the deviations are as heavily sex-linked as with inter-caste marriages—but in the opposite direction. Whereas inter-caste marriages in the United States primarily involve low-caste men marrying high-caste women, inter-class marriages occur more often between high-class men and lower-class women. For instance, 23 percent more New Haven men came from a better residential area and 18 percent more men had superior educations compared to the number of mixed marriages in which the wife was superior. These differences are modest in comparison to the doubly or triply male-biased inter-caste marriages—yet they are consistent enough to deserve a separate analysis. It will not be enough simply to compare endogamous and exogamous marriages, but the latter will need to be subdivided between husband-high and wife-high marriages as far as possible.

I have already said that one reason for the occurrence of husband-high marriages is that they do not threaten the husband's position. However, this is a negative reason which does not explain the positive attraction of low-status women. In eighteenth century France, impoverished aristocratic men married wealthy bourgeois women because the latter offered handsome dowries to compensate for their inferior status (Barber, 1955). However, when American middle-class men marry down, their wives are relatively poor so such mixed marriages occur in spite of financial deprivations rather than because of financial compensations.

Presumably, the compensating advantages of lower-status women are of a more personal nature: beauty, sex appeal, and vivaciousness. Such characteristics are not class-linked. They can be found at any social level. And since the stratification system allows men to marry down without damage to their social position, men attracted to beautiful women who happen to be socially inferior may marry them in spite of the class difference. The possibility of marrying down enlarges the pool of eligible females among whom men may choose their partners. In this sense, the down-marriages of high-class men are not motivated by the vertical difference in the same way that the up-marriages of low-caste men are. Rather the class system is permissive toward out-marriages based on non-class factors.

For men who marry up, class factors may be a motivating force. However, in this case, the marriage potentially threatens the self-esteem of the man (men are touchy about such things because they are constantly involved in the competitive status-assessment process of the stratification system). Moreover, wife-high marriages threaten to be wife-dominated, a state which few men or women desire to see actualized. Greek movies, for example, frequently have shown relations between poor men and rich girls ending in disaster: the woman consistently rebellious, domineering, promiscuous, and unfaithful (Safilios-Rothschild, 1968). Although such fears are greater in quasi-feudal societies which idealize submissive women, even equalitarian societies rarely consider the superior wife attractive to either sex. So psychological factors discourage the contracting of wife-high marriages. Hence the lesser frequency of this form of exogamous marriage.

How do inter-class marriages work out in actual practice? Barber

(1955) found that marriages between bourgeois wives and aristocratic French husbands "were often not successful". They suffered from a lack of intimacy between partners due to their lack of social equality. Husbands frequently escaped from the strains of the marriage into extramarital adventures while wives mourned their fate in their chateaux.

In modern America, studies by both Roth and Peck (1951) and Blood and Wolfe (1960) showed that husband-high marriages were less successful than endogamous marriages and that wife-high marriages were worst of all. Table 11-4 uses the most sensitive criterion, the partners' education, and shows that from the wife's point of view, the best marriages in both the U.S. and Japan were endogamous, and the worst were those in which the husband had an inferior education.

TABLE 11-4 Marital Satisfaction by Comparative Education of Husband and Wife

MARITAL SATISFACTION BY SEX AND SOCIETY	COMPARATIVE EDUCATION			
	HUSBAND MORE			
	4+ years	*1–3 years*	*EQUAL*	*WIFE MORE*
Detroit wives	4.89	5.01	5.09	4.58
Tokyo wives	5.20	5.26	5.50	4.92
Tokyo husbands	5.61	5.88	5.55	5.03

Adapted from Blood (1967):154. Source: Detroit couples with children below age 13; middle-class Tokyo couples under age 40. The scales for marital satisfaction in the two cities were not identical. Numbers of couples were 41, 96, 126, and 140 respectively in Detroit and 172, 145, 99, and 28 in Tokyo.

Japanese husbands agreed with their wives in finding wife-high marriages the worst of all. However, they differed from wives in both countries in preferring to be slightly superior. Presumably this was a quasi-feudal attitude which may give way to greater appreciation of equality in subsequent generations. In any case, we can confidently assess the unsatisfactoriness of wife-high marriages in two different countries and for both sexes even though we can be sure of the superlative satisfaction of educational endogamy only for wives.

Organizational Homogamy

Some organizations encourage their members to marry within the membership. Notable among these are religious organizations which are actively involved in organizational formation for new families through their ritualization of the wedding. The degree of endogamy varies with the organization's commitment to a distinctive value system and with its exclusion of non-members from access to its sanctuaries and sacred rites. Nevertheless, all religious organizations are committed in some degree to a norm of organizational endogamy.

The ability of a religious organization to enforce such a norm depends upon its ability to provide eligible members of the opposite sex as potential recruits. In Japan, endogamy among Christians was limited by a shortage of males for Christian girls to marry. In the next chapter we will see that the smaller the religious group (and therefore the smaller the number of eligibles to choose from), the less endogamy. Nevertheless, even in difficult circumstances, organizations ordinarily encourage endogamy whenever possible, other things being equal.

Although most religious organizations welcome the conversion of exogamous partners to the faith, nonconverted partners create problems for both the organization and the marriage. Divergent organizational membership means that husband and wife must either attend separate church services or that one must inhibit his own attendance at the church of his choice. In either case, the family lacks that unity of organizational participation and loyalty which endogamy fosters. Some inter-organizational marriages create value conflicts about marriage. Conspicuous among these are the Catholic–Protestant controversy over "artificial" methods of birth control. Thirdly, every inter-organizational marriage which produces children faces the question of which parent's organization the children will join. Whereas children in endogamous marriages bring their parents into greater joint organizational participation, in exogamous marriages they intensify the alienation of the partners. For such reasons, exogamous marriages seem likely to fail more than endogamous ones.

TABLE 11-5 Divorces of Catholic and Protestant Women
in Endogamous and Exogamous Marriages

| | PERCENTAGE DIVORCED BY RELIGIOUS HOMOGAMY | | *Exogamous/* |
| | *Endogamous* | *Exogamous* | *Endogamous* |
MEMBERSHIP OF WIFE	*Marriages*	*Marriages*	*Ratio*
Catholic	3.8%	20.2%	5.31X
Protestant	13.8	25.2	1.83

Adapted from Burchinal and Chancellor (1963):357. Source: All Iowa marriages between 1953 and 1959 which had ended in in-state divorce by 1959. Reciprocal percentages were presumably still married. The numbers of marriages on which each percentage was based were 14,193 and 2,957 Catholic wives and 52,720 and 2,615 Protestant wives respectively.

Table 11-5 shows that exogamous Iowa marriages cracked up several times as often as endogamous ones. The sharp difference between Catholic–Catholic marriages and Catholic–Protestant marriages is partly due to the lesser taboo on divorces among Protestants than among Catholics. This differential taboo makes the increased divorce rate of Protestant women married to Catholic men especially interesting. One might expect the husband's attitude to reduce the divorce rate below the normal Protestant level, but the conflict created by the organizational divergence more than offset the presumed reluctance to resort to divorce as a way out. The same study, incidentally, found that high-status (professional and managerial) marriages were more severely affected by the organizational split than low-status marriages. This may be related to the fact that the authors in another analysis of the same data (1962) found that high-status couples less often entered exogamous marriages in the first place, suggesting that the norm of religious endogamy is especially strong at high-status levels. Presumably high-status people are more organizationally committed and have higher expectations of marital solidarity so they react more strongly to organizational diversities than lower-status people.

Contributing to these higher divorce rates in Catholic–Protestant marriages are conflicts over birth control and over the children's religious affiliation. The Catholic church attempts to prevent conflict in mixed marriages by insisting on the Catholic ban on artificial methods of birth control and on Catholic affiliation for the children. However, many mixed couples violate these rules, suggesting that even more must have argued over whether to abide by them or not. Freedman (1959) found that 70 percent of Catholic men and 46 percent of Catholic women in exogamous marriages had used forbidden methods of contraception, compared to 35 percent of endogamous Catholic couples. Similarly, Landis (1949) found that more than 70 percent of Catholic men and roughly one third of Catholic women in exogamous marriages failed to transmit their Catholic faith to their children.

One method of resolving such conflicts is conversion of one partner to the faith of the other. Even this, however, does not entirely resolve the problems created by exogamy since it intensifies conflicts between the convert and the "bereaved" set of kin. In Landis' sample, marriages between converts to Catholicism and ordinary Catholics ended in divorce 2.4 times as often as endogamous Catholic marriages, and marriages resulting in conversion to Protestantism produced divorces 1.8 times as high as usual. Both these rates were lower than if conversion had not taken place, but true endogamy requires that both partners belong to the same church independently rather than joining under marital pressure.

Longitudinal Homogamy: Biological Eligibility

The weakest endogamous norms apply to biological characteristics. With respect to such characteristics as height, weight, age, etc., there is some tendency for like to marry like, but the norm primarily discourages extremes and more especially wife-dominated extremes (*e.g.*, wife older or wife taller). With respect to height, the average man is taller and heavier than the average woman and therefore male superiority characterizes the average marriage. With respect to age, the average man tends to die younger than the average woman, so one might expect men to "marry up," but patriarchal tendencies encourage "marrying down," instead. The rule with respect to age is not equality, but husband-dominance within relatively narrow limits. The concept of homogamy is therefore applicable only in the loosest sense to biological factors.

Age Homogamy By longitudinal homogamy is meant similarity in the husband's and wife's stage in life. Are they members of the same generation, endowed with similar resources of youth or faced with similar problems of aging? Or are there discrepancies in their physical capacities?

In order to avoid such discrepancies, it is necessary to limit the range of persons from whom marriage partners are chosen. Table 11–6 shows that in my Detroit and Tokyo samples, only one tenth of married couples were exactly the same age, but almost half the husbands were not more than three years older. For the husband to be more than three years older was more common than for the wife to be at all older. Even so, relatively few husbands were as much as a decade older which may be taken as the outside limit of age homogamy in these two societies.

TABLE 11-6   Marital Satisfaction by Comparative Age of Husband and Wife

MARITAL SATISFACTION BY SEX AND SOCIETY	Comparative Age						
	HUSBAND OLDER					WIFE OLDER	
	11+	7–10	4–6	1–3	EQUAL	1–3	4+
Detroit wives	4.26	4.67	5.10	4.89	5.00	4.89	4.38
Tokyo wives	5.48		5.42	5.16	5.26	4.44	
Tokyo husbands	5.41		5.98	5.38	5.81	6.00	
Number of couples							
Detroit	23	42	85	147	36	37	11
Tokyo	4	48	125	158	47	22	2

Adapted from Blood (1967):144. Source: Detroit couples with children below age 13; middle-class Tokyo couples under age 40. The scales for marital satisfaction in the two cities were not identical. Because of the small number of cases of extreme age discrepancy in Tokyo, they were combined with the adjacent category to form "husband 7+" and "wife older" categories respectively.

The structural consequences of age discrepancies are fairly clear, as will be seen in Chapter 19. However, the impact of age discrepancies on marital success is less clear. In equalitarian societies, age homogamy seems to contribute to marital success. At least in my Detroit sample, marriages where the wife was markedly older (more than three years) or the husband markedly older (more than ten years) were conspicuously unsatisfactory for wives. In Tokyo, however, women married to husbands more than three years older were more satisfied than those married to men of about the same age, and husbands married to older women were also surprisingly satisfied (even though men married to women four to six years younger were also highly satisfied). This suggests that in some post-feudal societies, age-homogamous marriages may be less appreciated than discrepant marriages, particularly from the standpoint of a younger person able to establish a dependent relationship on an older partner. More importantly, however, these contradictory findings between American and Japanese samples suggest the weakness of age homogamy as a general principle and the extent to which it seems to be a culture-bound concept.

Astrological Compatibility   In some feudal societies, the date of birth of the man and woman establishes other limits within which marriage is either possible or taboo, preferred or discouraged. This may be a question of the sign of the zodiac under which the child is born or of the year in which he is born. In Java, for instance:

An important magical restriction on choice of mate . . . has to do with the dates of birth of the couple. As soon as serious marriage negotiations are under way, both families confer with a man who knows about such things to see if the birth dates of the couple are in harmony, for it is believed that compatibility between their birth dates, as indications of their characters, is essential to compatibility in their marriage. (Geertz, 1961:60)

In Japan, similarly, the 1968 birth rate was markedly below normal because that was an inauspicious year for a girl to be born in. Parents who wanted to insure the best possible marriage chances for their children therefore deferred their child-bearing until the more auspicious following year.

In both countries, however, matchmakers did not always take astrological compatibility seriously. Sometimes the astrological incompatibility of prospective mates was used as a convenient excuse for turning down matches which really were being rejected on other grounds.

Homogamous Mate Selection

We have seen that mate selection tends to be restricted to persons with similar characteristics and that, in general, the more homogamous the marriage, the more successful it is. The basic task of mate selection is to find a partner who will fit into the kin-group, mesh with the husband, and join with him in socializing children with a minimum of conflict. All three objectives are best realized when the two partners are homogamous.

The reasons for the widespread occurrence of homogamy include the realization of the agents of mate selection that these objectives will be best achieved thereby. Another factor is ethnocentrism (the preference for persons who share one's own way of life). This is a universal human characteristic save for alienated rebels who reject their family's values in favor of those of outgroups or children of mixed marriages whose identities may be so ambiguous that they drift into mixed marriages themselves. For example, the child of a Protestant–Catholic may be nominally Catholic yet marry a Protestant because his Catholicism is weakened by his parents' dual allegiance.

Just as individual attitudes normally promote endogamy, so do group pressures. Most groups prefer that their members marry within the group. The strength of their norm of endogamy varies somewhat from group to group:

1 In general, the smaller the group, the more its existence is threatened by outmarriage (this appears to contribute to the strong endogamous norm among Jews).
2 The more the group depends on biological reproduction rather than on conversion for recruiting new members, the stronger the pressure for endogamy to safeguard the identification of the children (this also applies to Jews).
3 The more distinctive the culture of the group, the greater the desire to safeguard its purity by endogamy. (We may contrast the weak endogamy feelings of third generation ethnic groups in the United States whose national cultures are disappearing in the American melting pot with the stronger feelings of American religious groups noted by Kennedy, 1952).
4 Finally, the lower the social status of the group, the weaker the norm

of endogamy tends to become because of the social advantages of marrying out.

These norms are learned by group members and therefore are partly self-enforcing. They are also enforced by kin, especially when the kin are the agents of mate selection. Friends and strangers supply social pressure when heterogamy is visible (as in interracial marriages) or otherwise publicly known. Perhaps the most vigorous enforcers of homogamy are the official leaders of endogamous organizations. Religious leaders in particular dissuade their parishioners from marrying out. Among Polish peasants, Thomas and Znaniecki noted the heavy social pressures exerted against intermarriage:

> . . . for a territorial, professional, national, or religious group, such an individual is lost, and, since no group likes to lose its members, every kind of exogamy which involves a passage into another group incurs a social condemnation. This condemnation is particularly strong if the individual, by passing into another group, renounces the essential values of his first group—customs, traditions, ideals. . . . the family is influenced by the larger social group to which it belongs; the national and religious groups usually require that the family shall disown a renegade member, and the family in general complies with this demand and rejects such an individual, even if he wishes to keep the familial solidarity. (1958:115)

Marital Strain Endogamy provides a common membership in an external group which supports and buttresses the solidarity of the marital pair. Conversely, exogamous marriages not only lack such external support but are subject to cross-pressures because of the partners' conflicting affiliations. Exogamy is not just a question of belonging to different organizations (*e.g.*, the wife to a garden club, the husband to a professional organization) but of belonging to rival categories of the same external system. An individual can be a citizen of only one nation, a member of only one race, committed to only one faith, or assigned to only one class position at a time. To marry someone who belongs to a different group is to cross a boundary which normally unites a family but which in this case divides it. Such strains are most acute in the case of religious affiliation insofar as membership is voluntary and subject to competitive pressure from the partner for conversion and insofar as religious activity is institutionalized in organizations which place conflicting claims upon the husband and wife for scarce resources like time (for church attendance), money, and loyalty to conflicting behavioral norms (such as contraception).

The points of strain in family life are three-fold:

(1) Ties are strained between the kin group and the "foreign" in-law. This conflict frequently is intensified by the birth of children whose affiliation becomes a source of dispute between grandparents and their children.

(2) Husband–wife relationships are strained in competing for scarce resources to be allocated between their respective organizations. Because of their differential external affiliations, there is either pressure for conversion or at least for the disaffiliation of one partner to resolve the tension in their relationships. Continuing dual affiliation strains the marriage so that increased

energy must be devoted to maintaining it or the relationship itself will suffer. We have seen in numerous tables that, on the average, marital dissatisfaction and in a larger number of cases, marital failure tend to result.

(3) The third point of strain is in parent–child relationships. In many types of mixed marriages, the children's social identity is in doubt. If they have a choice between identifying with the mother or with the father, the general tendency is for the majority to identify with the mother (in view of her greater role in child-rearing), especially in the case of girls for whom the mother is the psychological identificand. However, the fact that a substantial minority identify with the father shows that mother-identification is not automatic, but problematic. Under such circumstances each parent has some influence over the child, so his identification with either parent is weakened by his cross-identification with the other. The conflicting influence of the two parents therefore complicates the socialization process at least as far as the child's group identification is concerned and perhaps in other senses as well. Such socialization problems may lie behind Zimmerman's and Cervantes' discovery (1960) that juvenile delinquency is greater among children of interfaith marriages than in endogamous families.

INITIAL SELECTION/RESELECTION

The previous section assumed that a single person's first mate was being selected. But a substantial minority of adults marry more than once. Either they lose their original partner through death or divorce, or they add extra partners to their existing household through polygamy. How do second choices compare with the first?

The Agents of Reselection

Since reselection occurs later than original selection, it undermines one of the conditions for kin-selection, namely early marriage. Individuals who may have been subject to kin control in their first marriage are freer to choose their own partner the next time. If they still live with their parents, they are in a more powerful position within the family insofar as they have grown from childhood into adulthood. If they live apart from their parents they have become more aware of their own preferences and less willing to depend on their parents' advice. In Arab countries where women normally have little influence, Goode (1963) found that widows and divorcees had some voice in remarriage. Similarly, Geertz found that Javanese girls who had already been married once were freer to move about in public and could take more initiative in promoting their subsequent marriages than in the sheltered circumstances prior to their first marriage.

We cannot generalize however that reselection is always free of kin control. Some kinship systems prescribe second partners even more definitely than the first. A common form of polygyny is sororal polygyny, which means that if a man acquires a second wife, it must be the next younger sister of his first wife. Similarly, the levirate and sororate respectively prescribe that after the death of the spouse, a widow must marry her husband's younger brother or a widower his wife's younger sister.

Prescriptions for remarriage within the same family save both kin groups the necessity of starting all over again in negotiations with a brand new family. Indeed, one characteristic of remarriages in Java even with new families was that negotiations were less formal than for first marriages (Geertz, 1961). Thus even where kin are the agents of reselection, they tend to simplify their activity once they have gone to all the trouble of marrying off their protege the first time.

For a man interested in acquiring an additional wife, another possible agent is his first wife. In a polygynous household, the first wife occupies a position similar to the husband's mother in a patrilocal extended family, *i.e.*, she employs the housekeeping services of subsequent wives. And insofar as (like a resident mother-in-law) she must associate closely with this new wife, she owns a vested interest in choosing the new bride which rivals her husband's interest. For such reasons, a wise husband seeks his first wife's approval of subsequent choices (just as a dutiful son secures his parents' approval in extended family systems).

Perhaps the only generalization which can be made about agents of reselection is that they tend to differ from those involved in first marriages insofar as the family structure has changed in the interval.

The Characteristics of Second Partners

One consequence of the lesser role of kin in reselection is that second partners are less endogamous than first ones. Variance is particularly marked with respect to age. When a man remarries, he tends to choose a relatively young girl of the more-or-less normally eligible age. Since the man is past the normal age for marriage, the gap between their ages is correspondingly wider. Among the African Yako, Forde found that whereas "young men usually marry girls of their own age in the first instance, on the other hand, in later marriages men often take women who differ widely from them in age, and the general tendency is to marry younger women" (1950:290).

In adding extra wives, the superior position of the first wife is safeguarded by choosing subsequent wives who are younger or of lower social status than she. In India, Goode (1963) noted that extra wives were usually from a lower caste than the first wife. Among the African Tonga, Colson (1958) found that second wives had often had their reputations damaged by the desertion of lovers who had fathered a "bush-child" outside of marriage.

In many societies, dependent children from a previous relationship are a major obstacle to remarriage. In Jamaica, the larger the number of children, the greater the difficulty a woman had in marrying (Blake, 1961). Jamaican men fathered many children outside of marriage but rarely wished to assume legal responsibility for any children other than their own.

For the woman, on the other hand, children create heavy economic pressure to marry/remarry. Goode (1956) found that divorced mothers in the U.S.A. were so eager to remarry that they did so just as often as childless divorcees. I assume, however, that the childless women were in a stronger bargaining position than the child-burdened women.

Single people are less apt to marry than previously married people of the same age. In the U.S.A., Landis (1950) found that divorced women

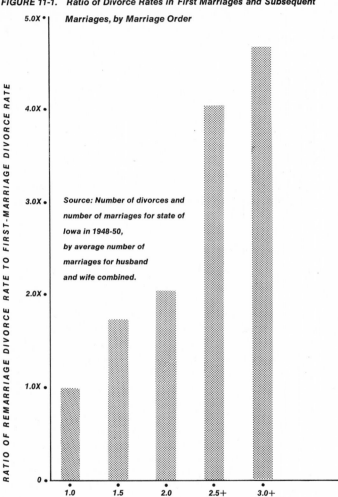

FIGURE 11-1. Ratio of Divorce Rates in First Marriages and Subsequent Marriages, by Marriage Order

Source: Number of divorces and number of marriages for state of Iowa in 1948-50, by average number of marriages for husband and wife combined.

Average Number of Marriages per Couple

Adapted from Monahan (1952):287.

were far more likely to remarry than single women of the same age. "For example, at age 40, the divorced woman has 65 chances in 100 of remarriage; the widowed woman, only 29 chances in 100 of remarriage; and the single woman, only 16 chances in 100 of remarriage." One reason for the extraordinarily high marriage rate of divorced people is that their interest in marrying an extramarital partner sometimes caused the divorce in the first place. A second reason is that previously married persons are less apt to prefer being single. Most "confirmed" bachelors and spinsters didn't wish to in the first place. A third factor is the desire of divorced persons to overcome their sense of failure by trying again. Such factors predispose divorced persons to jump even at exogamous opportunities for remarriage.

The Success of Reselection

Given the exogamous tendencies of second marriages, one might expect reselection to produce less successful marriages than first marriages. From the standpoint of the participants, to be sure, the fact that most second marriages succeed whereas all of their first ones by definition failed represents progress. But from the standpoint of the comparative effectiveness of systems of mate selection, the total process of original selection is more effective than the mate selecting of those who try a second time after failing once.

Figure 11-1 shows that divorce rates approximately doubled in Iowa when second marriages were compared with first marriages, and doubled again in third and subsequent marriages. How much of this is due to increasingly exogamous selections and how much to the fact that only the poorest marriage "risks" get divorced is impossible to assess. Certainly these are increasingly divorce-prone groups of people. Nevertheless, I hypothesize that at least part of the difference between the low divorce rate in first marriages and the higher rates for subsequent marriages reflects the known exogamous tendencies and the lesser participation of kin in the reselection process.

chapter twelve
COURTSHIP AND MARRIAGE: ORGANIZATIONAL ENACTMENT

In the preceding chapter we have seen who marries whom: what kinds of mates are selected, by whom, and with what consequences. But we have hardly touched upon the process by which marriages are contracted. In this chapter, we will examine the processes by which people meet and become involved progressively more deeply until their relationship is cemented in marriage.

In some societies, this process begins with dating which may not be marriage-oriented. In most societies there is a period of courtship, either between the partners themselves or between their representatives, during which efforts are made to contract a successful relationship. If courtship takes place between the partners, it lays the foundations for an interpersonal relationship which will be elaborated in marriage. If the focus is on negotiations between kin, the emphasis is more likely to be on tangible transactions such as the exchange of money and goods. In either case, a successful courtship is signalized by a more or less formal betrothal or engagement to marry. Finally, in almost every society, the new family is officially formed with a wedding ceremony.

In contrast to this normal sequence of events are two cases in which the process is short-circuited and individuals engage in marriage-like behavior prior to marriage. Premarital sexual intercourse and premarital housekeeping blur the normal distinctions between non-marriage and marriage and therefore may be called quasi-marital states.

CONTACT: OPPORTUNITY FOR INVOLVEMENT

Under systems of self-selection, people who never meet cannot marry. Conversely, the more often people meet (with certain exceptions noted in the previous chapter), the greater the opportunities for getting acquainted, becoming friends, and getting married.

Frequency of contact depends on propinquity. Those members of a society who live nearest to one another, work for the same company, attend the same school, or belong to the same organization will be thrown together most often. These examples of propinquity can be boiled down into two key types: residential propinquity and organizational propinquity.

Residential Propinquity

The influence of geographical proximity on mate selection has been observed in numerous studies (see Katz and Hill, 1958). Typically, American couples lived within 20 blocks of one another when they first met, with the largest fractions located at the shortest distances. In other words, the shorter the distance between two people, the higher the probability that they will marry. This is due partly to a greater chance of meeting in the first place and partly to the lower cost in time and money required to associate with each other throughout the dating and courtship period.

However, residential propinquity involves more than sheer geography. The segregated residential patterns of most cities mean that persons who live close to one another are also more apt to be socially homogamous. Insofar as persons of the same race, religion, or social status live in the same neighborhood, propinquitous contacts will be more socially compatible than contacts at greater distances. Thus social homogeneity reinforces the time–cost economy of interacting and marrying nearby partners. One illustration of this correlation between homogamy and propinquity is Kennedy's finding (1943) that homogamous marriages between members of the same ethnic group in New Haven (*e.g.,* Italian–Americans or Polish–Americans) were consummated at shorter distances than inter-ethnic marriages between persons of different nationality backgrounds.

But what if one's neighbors are not homogamous? Then the larger the proportion of the community who are outsiders, the greater the difficulty of marrying within the group and the greater the chances of out-marriage. We saw in the preceding chapter that people tend to marry within their own religious group. But if there are few co-religionists in the vicinity, it may be impossible to find a partner of the right age, sex, social status, etc. The larger the number of adherents of other religions nearby, the greater the chances of getting involved with and marrying one of them, despite the religious difference.

Figure 12-1 shows that most Canadian Catholics married other Catholics when there were plenty to choose from in their province. But in provinces where non-Catholics were in the majority, the shortage of co-religionists meant that a large proportion of social contacts were with non-Catholics, and a correspondingly large proportion of marriages were with those same non-Catholics. These violations of the religious endogamy norm testified to the importance of propinquity in marital choice.

Organizational Propinquity

Many features of homogamous marriages involve selecting fellow members of the same organizations. This may be accomplished by asking persons met under other circumstances what organizations they belong to. But organizations promote marriages directly by providing contact-points for their members. To attend the same school, go to the same church, work in the same office, or belong to the same hiking club means that persons are thrown into regular contact with each other. Within such organizational settings, friendships tend to grow which may eventuate in marriage. Insofar as organizational memberships involve shared values and shared interests, they are even more likely to promote marriage than sheer residence in the same community.

One illustration of the effect of organizational propinquity on contact is the role of coeducational colleges in mate selection. Many Americans marry persons whom they met in college. Such marriages tend to be homogamous in education and social class in contrast to the greater mixture of dating patterns in high schools (Alan Kerckhoff, 1964).

Although universities are relatively homogeneous compared with high schools, they tend to be subdivided internally into different organizational worlds. One subdivision is between the "Greek" world of fraternities and sororities, and the alternate world of "independent" students. Scott (1965) suggested that fraternities and sororities played a relatively active role in mate selection, in contrast to most other college organizations where mate selection was a by-product of membership rather than a conscious goal. Sororities restricted the contacts of their members by keeping them involved with organizational activities and by confining vulnerable novitiates to the sorority house on weekday evenings. Those restrictions reduced the hazard of contracting exogamous affiliations on campus. More positively, sororities sponsored parties and exchange dinners with closely matched fraternities (with corresponding ethnic affiliations—Jewish/Gentile, black/white, and of similar social status). These organizational activities provided repeated opportunities for association which tended to blossom into intensive dating activities.

Although sororities often planned their activities for the specific purpose of providing auspicious heterosexual contacts, sexually integrated (coeducational) organizations provide such contacts automatically without any special effort. Joint play rehearsals, lab assignments, or newspaper writing serve the

FIGURE 12-1. Exogamous Marriages by Proportion of Outsiders in the Population

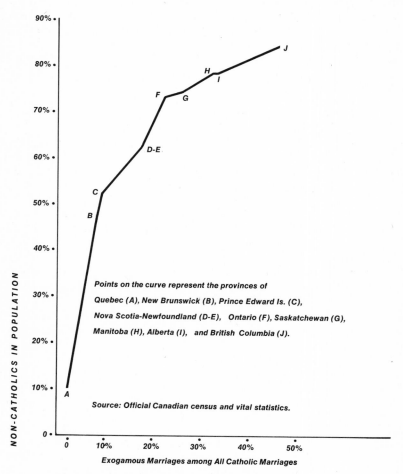

Points on the curve represent the provinces of
Quebec (A), New Brunswick (B), Prince Edward Is. (C),
Nova Scotia-Newfoundland (D-E), Ontario (F), Saskatchewan (G),
Manitoba (H), Alberta (I), and British Columbia (J).

Source: Official Canadian census and vital statistics.

Exogamous Marriages among All Catholic Marriages

Adapted from Locke, Sabagh and Thomes (1957):331.

same purpose without the necessity of any deliberate matchmaking intent. To belong to a heterosexual organization is to be guaranteed the kind of contact which is liable to lead to forming a new family.

DATING: PRELIMINARY INVOLVEMENTS

Dating patterns vary enormously from one society to another. In some primitive societies, the chief recreational activity after dark is sexual intercourse. In post-feudal Puerto Rico, Hill (1955) reported that adolescent girls walked around the town square every evening while the boys watched them go by. The only interaction consisted of smiles or flattering comments which the girls pretended to ignore.

In the former case, involvement is so easy and so physical that little social or emotional attachment is generated (Blood, 1952). In the latter, contact is so superficial that involvement hardly begins. Indeed one characteristic of feudal and post-feudal societies is that they allow little opportunity for preliminary involvements. Instead, once involvement begins, it tends to be heavily marriage-oriented both for the participants and for their relatives, who push the relationship toward total commitment in marriage.

If dating is defined as paired association between persons of the opposite sex for the purpose of companionship with no necessary intention of marrying, it is a uniquely modern phenomenon. In Japan, dating was just beginning to be distinguished from courtship in the 1950s and not until the 1960s was it unambivalently accepted as a legitimate activity (Blood, 1967). In the United States, dating has long been socially accepted, but increasing affluence has resulted in earlier and earlier dating so that it now may begin even before adolescence. Broderick and Fowler (1961) found that children in a precocious southern U. S. town began dating in the sixth or seventh grade. For the U. S. as a whole, the typical beginning was slightly later (Douvan and Adelson, 1966), but nevertheless substantially earlier than had been the case prior to World War II.

Another change in American dating has been a shift from pre-war patterns of dalliance (holding the partner figuratively at arm's length) and of "playing the field" to avoid being trapped in a relationship (Waller, 1937). After the war, American young people generally lost their fear of being trapped and began "going steady" with a succession of exclusive partners in a pattern which had previously been restricted to couples seriously considering marriage (Herman, 1955). Although the majority of steady relationships terminated short of marriage, this new pattern encouraged deeper emotional and sexual involvements than the previous casual pattern. It provided a more relevant background out of which serious courtship and marriage might eventually emerge as the terminal steady relationship developed into courtship and marriage.

In contributing to family formation, dating is not simply the place where mate-selection begins but a facility for socializing young men and women in patterns of heterosexual association. Douvan and Adelson found that dating spurred the growth of girls "in both sensitivity and good sense as regards . . . relations with boys" (1966:206). Insofar as the dating system is divorced from the marriage system, the norms into which it socializes young people may not be entirely relevant to marriage. But generally speaking the post-war changes in the nature of the dating system narrowed the previous gap between systems and made dating more relevant.

Douvan and Adelson found that only 4 percent of girls under age 15 were going steady. That deviant minority was usually insecure and dependent (which may explain why they were going steady at such an early age).

TABLE 12-1   Attitude Toward Boys by Dating Experience

	DATING EXPERIENCE		
ATTITUDE	*Do Not Date*	*Date*	*Go Steady*
Source of popularity with boys			
Appearance	45%	39%	34%
Sensitivity, understanding	30	39	48
Response to boyfriend's criticism			
Broken relationship	26%	7%	2%
Unconditional surrender	16	11	8
Compromise	7	15	26
Number of girls	76	344	139

Adapted from Douvan and Adelson (1966):408–415. Source: National sample of high school girls age 16 or older, U.S.A. Reciprocal percentages of girls did not give the specified response to open-ended questions.

Table 12-1 shows that steady daters among older adolescents had achieved a more mature relationship. They placed the least emphasis on appearance and the most on sensitivity as a basis for popularity with boys, presumably because they had developed an understanding relationship with their steady partner. Similarly, they were less inclined to go to either extreme of breaking the relationship entirely or surrendering completely when confronted with criticism from the boy friend. Instead they were more willing to compromise on a give-and-take basis.

Douvan and Adelson's research suggests that casual dating may be an appropriate learning experience during the early teens and that steady dating promotes more mature heterosexual relationships during the later teens. Perhaps another way of saying the same thing is that by the time older girls go steady, they are so deeply involved that an understanding and mutually giving relationship becomes possible. It must be noted, however, that dating at this point shades over into courtship since 39 percent of Douvan and Adelson's older steady-dating girls daydreamed about marriage, home, and family.

Table 12-1 also demonstrates that girls who were not yet dating by the time they reached age 16 were almost as deviant a group as those who began steady dating prematurely. Their extraordinary willingness to break relationships in the face of criticism suggests a corresponding unwillingness to get involved with boys, which may help to explain why they were not dating. Other data show that they also were notably hostile toward girls who were "too boy crazy" or who had a "bad reputation." How much of this was a rationalization of their lack of dating experience and how much a defense against sexual fears is impossible to disentangle. But the positive experience of the girls who dated and especially of those who were going steady suggests the contribution of dating to understanding the opposite sex.

COURTSHIP: DEVELOPING A MARRIAGE-ORIENTED RELATIONSHIP

To court means to seek the favor of a woman. In earlier days, the man's task was to persuade the woman to marry him. In modern societies, the equality of the sexes reduces this persuasive element and makes it a reciprocal responsibility. Within an equalitarian relationship, courtship is less a task of persuasion than a process of developing that relationship.

Truncated Courtships

In many post-feudal societies, the courtship process is severely circumscribed. Social pressures force the couple toward quick decisions once they begin relating to each other. For example, in rural Puerto Rico, Landy (1959) found that once a boy became seriously interested in a girl and visited her home "a few times," the whole community expected them to marry and condemned them if they did not. This did not mean that courtship was necessarily brief (averaging almost a year and a half), but rather that the compatibility testing function of courtship was short-circuited by the difficulty of terminating the relationship once it began. In a sense, the rural community trapped couples in a relationship which might or might not prove compatible as they grew to know each other better. Such freezing of relationships destroys one of the potential functions of courtship—to provide an opportunity for evaluating the marriage potential via intimate interaction within a steady relationship. Only when an individual chooses among several steady relationships can husband–wife relationships rest on a firm foundation. Without a period of tentative exploration, courtship allows the development of a relationship, but not the sorting out of promising relationships from unpromising ones.

Although we might expect external pressure for commitment to be particularly powerful within a small community, Hill (1955) found that even among university students in Puerto Rico, almost half moved directly into "going steady" without any previous uncommitted dating and decided to marry after only five dates.

Such abbreviated courtships allowed little time for mutual exploration and had the additional disadvantage of being so thoroughly chaperoned that few kinds of interaction could occur. Hill noted, for example, that chaperoned dates were not likely to allow the free expression of opinion which might test the couple's problem-solving ability. Thus, rigidly confined by time limits and watchful third parties, even the relationship-building function of courtship was hampered.

To avoid falling into such courtship traps, young men and women must be careful not to allow courtship to begin until they are financially and otherwise ready to marry. Humphreys noted in Dublin that Irish boys in their late twenties and early thirties who did not feel ready to marry avoided girls for fear of becoming trapped. According to one young man:

> Around here if a boy were to take a girl out once a week for a month or six weeks, well the girl and the parents and even the boy's friends would think they were thinking of marriage. . . . If you take a girl out five or six times, you are considered as doing a line and some night soon the parents will invite you in for tea, and believe me, once you have gone in for tea, you have had it. They'll want to know what your intentions are. . . . Most of the boys are quite honourable. They do not want to do a line until they are in a position to support a girl because they honestly feel that they might be hurting a girl's chances. They feel that if they are going around with a girl she will pass up other fellows whom she could marry, and unless they feel sure that they can eventually marry her they will stay away from her entirely. (1966:174)

Marital Consequences   Courtship is the foundation of marriage. If courtship is abbreviated, the marriage is likely to suffer accordingly.

At their worst, inadequate courtships lead to broken marriages. Geertz suggested that the extreme brevity of Javanese courtships was "one of the most important structural reasons" for the phenomenally high divorce rate:

> . . . with the arrangement of the marriage by the parents, the young couple has little chance to know one another before the wedding, and . . . even after the first marriage, when the individual is more free to choose his own spouse, the choice is rarely given very serious thought. It would appear that, more often than not, a Javanese couple have the wedding first and then, in the months following, find out whether or not they will get along together. (1961:139)

Regardless of whether truncated courtships lead to the complete breakdown of marriage, they tend to produce weak husband–wife relationships. The weaker the boy–girl relationship during courtship, the weaker the relationship between the partners is likely to be in the years after marriage. Relationships during courtship set patterns which persist into the future.

TABLE 12-2   Marital Informative Companionship by Premarital Informative Companionship

ANNUAL FREQUENCY OF TELLING PERSONAL EVENTS AFTER MARRIAGE, BY SEX	FREQUENCY OF TELLING PERSONAL EVENTS BEFORE MARRIAGE				Often/ Never Ratio
	Never	Seldom	Sometimes	Often	
Husbands	135	140	165	208	1.54X
Wives	213	171	229	253	1.19
Number of cases					
Husbands	45	71	97	148	
Wives	39	42	106	172	

Adapted from Blood (1967):107. Source: Tokyo middle-class husbands and wives under age 40, married relatively few years.

Table 12-2 shows that Tokyo men and women who most often told each other what had happened to them since their last date told each other the same sorts of news most often after marriage as well. The one exception was girls too shy to talk before marriage but who blossomed out after marriage somewhat more than the "seldom-tellers."

Similar continuity between premarital and marital patterns appeared with respect to frequency of telling one another their troubles after a bad day, frequency of contact with relatives, and frequency of contact with friends. In general the intensity and style of relationship established during courtship sets the pace for marriage. If the courting relationship is deep and close, the marriage will tend to be also. But in truncated courtships, the relationship tends to be shallow and distant, leading to a correspondingly superficial relationship in marriage.

Premature Marriages

If marriage follows an abbreviated courtship, it is premature in terms of the development of the relationship. If it follows an abbreviated life-span, it is premature in a far more serious sense. At the youngest ages, people do not have the maturity necessary for marital success. Rushing into relationships for which they are not prepared, they are like early adolescent girls who rush into steady dating too soon. In both cases, the motivation for premature involvement is likely to be personal insecurity or other personal and situational inadequacies. Such factors make early involvement understandable, but they doom it to almost inevitable trouble.

Causes of Early Marriage   In earlier chapters I pointed out that broad social forces like affluence and wars lower the average age of marriage. Here my concern is not with general trends but with individuals who marry younger than usual.

Many of those who marry early have low educational and occupational aspirations so they have no incentive to defer marriage to complete their education. This removes one of the barriers to early marriage, but it does not explain why such people choose to marry early.

Burchinal (1960) found that a majority of Iowa high school students who married in 1958 were involved in a premarital pregnancy: 57 percent of the girls and 87 percent of the boys who married while still in school. This suggests that a large proportion of premature marriages occur earlier than they otherwise would have if pregnancy had not intervened. Nor can we assume that these couples would necessarily have married eventually. Pregnancies short-circuit the courtship process in much the same way as external pressures in post-feudal societies. Indeed, it is often the parents of pregnant youngsters who pressure them into marriage. Had the pregnancy and the early marriage not occurred, the most fragile of these relationships would have terminated prior to marriage. But when poor relationships are catapulted into premature marriages saddled with the extra burden of premature pregnancies, the outcome is bound to be unhappy.

A second pressure forcing young people into early marriage is unhappy home life. Young people marry in hopes of escaping from parental restrictions into a happier existence in a home of their own. Martinson (1955) found that females who married soonest after high school graduation had had significantly poorer family relations than those who married later.

If those who marry early have poor relationships with their families, it should not surprise us to discover that they are poorly adjusted emotionally. Just as girls who began going steady before age 16 tended to be emotionally insecure, so those who married before age 19 were found by Moss and Gingles (1959) to be less emotionally stable than those who married later. Martinson, similarly, found that early marrying girls had poorer social and emotional adjustment, were less self-reliant, felt less personal freedom, and more often tended to withdraw from social contact or to commit anti-social acts. Such findings suggest a general tendency to emotional and social maladjustment which leads young people to flee prematurely from the uncertainties of life into the hoped-for blessings of marriage.

Problems of Early Marriage Those blessings seldom materialize for couples married under such inauspicious circumstances. For most, premature marriage means the proverbial jump "from the frying pan into the fire." At worst, poverty-stricken couples can't even leave home but must live doubled-up with the boy's or the girl's parents because they can't afford a home of their own. In a study of high school marriages in Columbus, Ohio, Inselberg (1962) found that 59 percent lived with parents from the beginning of marriage and an additional 17 percent moved in with parents within the first few years of marriage. Thus 76 percent of the premature marriages failed to achieve consistently neolocal marriages contrasted with only 28 percent of an equally low-status working-class "control group" who married later (in their early twenties).

To live with parents produces conflict between the generations. Three times as many premature marriages as normal marriages in the Columbus study experienced interference from their parents-in-law or felt rejected by them. Three times as many felt either hostile or ambivalent toward their parents-in-law. Such feelings are symptomatic of difficulties for both generations in freeing the child from dependence on his parents and transferring his loyalty to the marriage partner. When young people marry prematurely, neither they nor their parents are ready for this transfer of loyalties. And if they live with one set of parents, the conflict of loyalties for the partner caught in the middle between his parents and his partner is especially difficult. Columbus wives who had married prematurely felt that their in-laws more often "won" whereas the partner usually "won" in the post-high school marriages. Among wives reporting in-law conflict, 70 percent of the younger wives felt that their husbands sided with their parents rather than with them and reported that their husbands became hurt or angry when the wives criticized their in-laws. By contrast, only 17 percent of the older wives were dissatisfied with their husbands' reactions to in-law conflict or felt any emotional disloyalty from him.

Early-marrying wives also thought their husbands were disloyal in other ways. Three times as many complained that their husbands had not settled down and were running around too much. Presumably some of this running around was with men, but some of it was with other women. This was suggested by the fact that 10 percent of the younger husbands (but none of the older ones) said their wives were "unduly jealous." To marry prematurely is liable to mean getting trapped into marriage before one is ready to settle down.

We have seen a number of signs that premature marriages are entered into under pressure of external circumstances before young people are ready either personally, or mutually, to take on the responsibilities of a new relationship and to leave behind old ties to families and friends. Under such inauspicious circumstances, we should not expect such marriages to be very strong. Figure 12-2 shows how extraordinarily often marriages of young men and young women ended in divorce. The younger the age at marriage, the likelier the failure of the relationship.

Normal Courtship

In industrial societies, the division of labor has become so complex that individual personalities are widely differentiated. No longer, as in primitive societies, is any marriage partner as good as any other. No longer, as in feudal societies, is marriage to anyone within the right stratum a safe bet. Rather the concept of the "one and only" emerges to symbolize the emphasis on individuality in the choice of partner. One need not believe that slogan literally to recognize that its emphasis on the uniqueness of the individual is distinctively modern.

Compatibility Testing Diversities of temperament, values, life styles, and interests offer a bewildering array of possibilities to the individual "shopping" for a marriage partner. Although he may be assisted by relatives and friends or by a computer, ultimately the individual must choose for himself. But choice cannot be made at a glance. Even instances of "love at first sight" must be tested to see if they will last. In the absence of such spontaneous convictions, certainty about the decision to marry emerges only gradually through a long process of getting acquainted and discovering what kind of relationship can be built. The decision whether to marry is not so much an intellectual one based on knowledge of the partner's characteristics as a reflection of the growth of a rudimentary marital relationship between the partners. By interacting in a variety of ways, the couple allow themselves an opportunity to develop a multifaceted relationship which can be further extended after marriage.

In the early stages of courtship, the types of interaction are barely distinguishable from ordinary dating activities. Indeed, it is often difficult to say where dating leaves off and courtship begins. Later, courting couples become less concerned with immediate enjoyment and more oriented toward long-range possibilities. They converse about educational and vocational plans. As they dream about the possibility of getting married, marriage-oriented topics emerge—weddings, honeymoons, family-planning, and child-rearing. Such exploratory conversations help the partners imagine what life together might be like.

But mutual daydreaming is not the essence of courtship. Rather it requires a widened scope of joint activities. The more serious the courtship, the

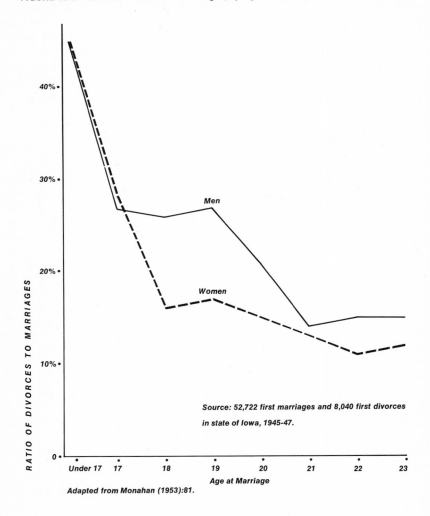

FIGURE 12-2.   Ratio of Divorces to Marriages, by Age at Marriage of Men and Women

Source: 52,722 first marriages and 8,040 first divorces in state of Iowa, 1945-47.

Adapted from Monahan (1953):81.

greater the likelihood that the couple will visit in each other's homes, laying the basis for in-law relationships. Eating out is likely to be supplemented by meals cooked by the girl in her apartment or even by the boy in his. Spectacular entertainment gives way to opportunities to be alone, to talk and make love. Gradually the couple focus more intensively on one another, withdrawing from wider social involvement as they develop their dyadic relationship. Such increasing concentration provides an opportunity to develop the bond which becomes the key relationship of the nuclear family: the husband–wife relationship.

The concept of testing for compatibility implies that some courtships will end in failure. The deeper the relationship between any two people goes, the greater the possibility that new features of the relationship will alter the situation. Either those features will strengthen the attraction between the partners or they will cool it. Modern courtship at its best allows couples to terminate relationships which turn cold.

Farber (1964) has suggested that a distinctive feature of modern societies is that more and more people consider themselves "permanently" available for courtship, regardless of whether they are already married or not. In this sense, compatibility testing is a permanent process. When the results are favorable, they lead to intensified relationships. When they are unfavorable, they lead to broken engagements and broken marriages. In either case, trying out new experiences is a major characteristic of the courtship process.

Falling in Love Although an expert can point to objective features of a relationship such as homogamy and say that they offer a basis for predicting a successful marriage, the ultimate basis for the decision to marry is subjective —do I or don't I love her/him enough to marry her/him? I have elsewhere (1969) defined love as "an intense emotional attachment." Courtship provides an opportunity for the growth of this feeling between the partners. The more fully the relationship between the partners develops, the greater the opportunity for the sentiment of love to grow.

There is no standard degree of intensity which can be accepted as prerequisite to marriage. Among Burgess and Wallin's engaged couples (1953), 24 percent described themselves as "head over heels" in love, but the great majority (70 percent) felt that was too strong a term and that "very much" in love more appropriately described their feelings. At the other extreme, 7 percent were only "somewhat" or "mildly" in love, despite the fact that they were engaged. Probably these individuals contributed disproportionately to the one third of all couples whose engagements were later broken. In general, subjective feelings of attraction to the partner and enthusiasm for the prospect of marrying him are the crucial evidence which most contemporary individuals seek in courtship.

Intense attraction is rarely instantaneous. More than half of Burgess and Wallin's couples were not sufficiently impressed by one another when they first met to be even "interested" in each other, much less emotionally involved at first sight. The median experience was to become acquainted first and then interested, but a significant minority did not become romantically interested until after a platonic friendship had developed (see Table 12-3). Obviously, there is no uniformity about the development of affection in heterosexual relationships, but these data suggest that more often than not, the relationship is established first and only subsequently does affection confirm the positive qualities discovered in the relationship.

TABLE 12-3 Degree of Acquaintance at First Becoming Interested in the Fiance, by Sex

Degree of Acquaintance	Male	Female
On first meeting	46%	34%
After becoming acquainted	34	37
After becoming friends	20	29
Total	100%	100%
Number of cases	226	226

Adapted from Burgess and Wallin (1953):160. Source: College-educated engaged couples in Chicago, 1937–39.

Differences in the speed and intensity of falling in love depend upon the temperamental volatility of the partners, and the romanticism of the circumstances of meeting. Another factor is the individual's freedom to fall in love, depending on his lack of involvement with other love objects such as parents or dating partners. Most liable to enter dramatic emotional involvements are those recently bereaved of parents or fiances and who are therefore vulnerable to "rebound" love affairs. Similarly the more negative relationships are with parents or the more an individual's self-esteem has been shattered in a previous love crisis, the more attractive a new love becomes.

Such extraneous factors mean that feelings cannot always be taken as proof of the compatibility of a relationship. In this sense, feelings of love are sometimes "false positive evidence." On the other hand, the absence of feelings of love usually indicates that something is missing in a relationship. In this sense, love is a necessary but not a sufficient condition for an auspicious marriage. This is perhaps what people mean when they say that "true love" is a sufficient basis for marriage, as distinguished from infatuations based on superficial characteristics.

In a classic passage, the anthropologist Ralph Linton many years ago likened love to epileptic fits:

All societies recognize that there are occasional violent emotional attachments between persons of opposite sex, but our present American culture is practically the only one which has attempted to capitalize these and make them the basis of marriage. Most groups regard them as unfortunate and point out the victims of such attachments as horrible examples. Their rarity in most societies suggests that they are psychological abnormalities to which our own culture has attached an extraordinary value just as other cultures have attached extreme values to other abnormalities. The hero of the modern American movie is always a lover just as the hero of the old Arab epic is always an epileptic. A cynic might suspect that in any ordinary population the percentage of individuals with a capacity for romantic love of the Hollywood type was about as large as that of persons able to throw genuine epileptic fits. However, given a little social encouragement, either one can be adequately imitated without the performer admitting even to himself that the performance is not genuine. (1936:174)

This cynical statement fails to recognize that love is more appropriate to the new conditions created by modernization than to the primitive and feudal societies which are the special interest of most anthropologists. Secondly, Linton failed to recognize that the socialization processes of modern societies create in young people an ability to love as an expected form of behavior which is real and not just simulated. To be sure, love for the average modern person may be less ecstatic than the romantic extreme which Linton had in mind. But we should beware of jumping to the conclusion that just because love is not always spectacular enough to be portrayed in a Hollywood movie, it is not a significant element in modern courtship.

TABLE 12-4   Marital Satisfaction of Husbands and Wives
by Betrothal Love and Mate-Selection System

| MATE-SELECTION SYSTEM | LOVE AT BETROTHAL | | | |
	Little	Considerable	Strong	Intense
Self-introduction				
Husband's marital satisfaction	3.38	4.64	5.30	6.46
Wife's marital satisfaction	3.25	4.13	5.54	6.64
Formal introduction				
Husband's marital satisfaction	4.73	5.08	5.77	7.83
Wife's marital satisfaction	4.28	5.18	6.03	8.00

Adapted from Blood (1967):88. Source: Young middle-class Tokyo married couples. The total number of self-introduced couples was 212 and of formally introduced couples, 127.

Vivid testimony to the value of love as a criterion for courtship success can be seen in Table 12-4. Among my Tokyo married couples, there was a high correlation between their remembered feeling of love at the time they got engaged and their present feelings of satisfaction with their marriage. This was true not only for self-introduced love-matches but for couples whose marriages had been initiated by formal matchmaking introductions. This suggests that even in Japan where the mate-selection system had not yet been fully modernized, love had become an index of successful courtship.

BETROTHAL: NEGOTIATING THE MATCH

Although the transition from dating to courtship may be imperceptible, organizational enactment eventually requires more solid commitments. The first public commitment is the betrothal or engagement to be married. In most societies this is the crucial decision. Once a couple have decided to marry (or their relatives have decided to marry them), the wedding follows almost automatically. Since the betrothal is the turning point in the relationship, it is often highly formalized to safeguard the interests of all concerned against misunderstanding and betrayal.

In self-selection systems, the betrothal follows such a long period of interaction that it mostly formalizes an already-existing commitment. For a couple already deeply in love, to get engaged seems almost superfluous save as public notice of their decision to make their relationship permanent.

The weaker the relationship between the partners, the greater the significance of the betrothal itself. Among lower-class black men in Washington, D. C., Liebow found that marriages universally failed to provide the security and mutual satisfaction which American culture advocates. Knowing that their chances of failure were overwhelmingly great, these men moved with the greatest reluctance into marriage despite their sense that marriage was a "big thing," a way of attaining manhood. Caught in this ambivalence, they decided to marry reluctantly, with a feeling of uncertainty and anxiety. As a defense against the tension generated in undertaking a journey filled with so many hopes and so many pitfalls, they hid their feelings from public view:

> Men . . . hedge against probable failure by camouflaging their private readiness to marry with the public fiction of coercion. Hedging takes the edge off failure. The hedge asserts that the man does not enter fully and freely into the marriage contract; that he was forced into it, went into it reluctantly, or was merely "going along with the program." Thus, marriage becomes, in part, a hold that is not a hold. The hedge permits a more passive participation than the obligation that total public commitment carries with it. It gives the man a partial defense against those who would hold him strictly to the terms of the contract; and it somewhat lightens the onus attached to breaking up the marriage by permitting him to say, in effect, "I didn't really want to get married in the first place." (1967:115–116)

This may not seem like a statement of the importance of the betrothal, and certainly there is no reference to any ceremonialization of the step. Nevertheless, the decision to marry under those ambivalent circumstances was psychologically more important than under normal circumstances. Perhaps one could even say that buttressing the decision with appeals to the necessity of marrying because of premarital pregnancies or illegitimate children is a kind of ritualization which provides the betrothal with firmer support.

In kin-selection systems, a pre-betrothal relationship between the partners does not exist. Excluding the young people from the mate-selection process places the burden of negotiating the betrothal on their parents. But in feudal societies, such negotiations may be too delicate even for parents to perform directly. To seem to be interested in another family's daughter and then to change one's mind is too much of an insult to be tolerated in a society whose highest value is family honor. To avoid such embarrassments, societies rely upon third parties to act as "go-betweens" until the contract has been sealed in the betrothal. In Java, for example, "preliminary negotiations are made by a friend or relative of the young man in order to avoid the embarrassment of being refused" (Geertz, 1961:62).

Mistrust between families is endemic in feudal societies where kin boundaries represent the limits of ethical behavior. Among Greek shepherds, Campbell described the marriage contract as "in the nature of a peace treaty between two previously opposed social groups" (1964:124). To negotiate a treaty in the face of inter-family rivalry and hostility was a delicate matter, fraught with suspicion and mistrust up to the very last minute. Contemporary custom called for the betrothal to be celebrated by feasting attended by both families in the village of the girl. But feasting did not insure that hostilities would not break out between the proposed affines:

> In the modern betrothal feast, the future bride appears only about an hour before the groom's party are due to depart, that is between four and five o'clock in the morning. By this time the rings have been exchanged [between the two heads of family] and there is no way of retreat left open to the bridegroom. . . . The groom's kinsmen invariably demand that the girl should appear much earlier in the proceedings before the rings have been exchanged. . . . Invariably, the girl's father and brothers refuse the request, and it is often this refusal which is the beginning of the brawling and quarrelling between the two groups. (Campbell, 1964:126–27)

Thus, betrothal ceremonies were no guarantee of good relations between the parties. Nevertheless, the very existence of a high level of hostility between the families made such ceremonies as an exchange of rings and the holding of feasts attended by so many relatives appropriate means of strengthening the fragile new bond between the families. Indeed, if the question of when the girl should appear had been more thoroughly ritualized, that particular basis for quarreling would have been removed.

Financial Transactions

One way of bolstering relations between families is to exchange not simply rings but larger objects or sums of money. I hypothesize that the more valuable the property exchanged, the more secure the relationship becomes.

In unilinear kinship systems, marriage takes one partner from his kin and adds him to the partner's kin. One way of compensating for the lost member is to transfer wealth to that kin network. In patrilocal systems, this often takes the form of a bride price paid to the bride's kin to compensate for her loss.

This is not exclusively a compensatory device. Sometimes it is a means of endowing the young couple with wealth so they can start their marriage more affluently. For example, the dowry represented wealth conveyed by the bride's family to the daughter which she took with her into marriage as a capital fund. Sometimes, it took the form of a trousseau, linens, cooking equipment and other utensils needed for keeping house, guaranteeing that no household would lack this equipment.

It presumably does not matter whether the primary purpose of the financial transaction is to compensate kin or to endow the next household as far as cementing the betrothal goes. In either case, the larger the amount of wealth invested by one or both kin networks, the greater the incentive to continue the new relationship. It would be awkward both for the couple and for the kinfolk if the property had to be returned. Indeed, where bridewealth takes the form of cattle, tracing the increase of that wealth may be difficult.

In Nuer society, Evans-Pritchard (1951) found that the betrothal period lasted until the first child was born. Only then was the couple considered truly married. It was precisely during this long betrothal period that the largest number of broken relationships occurred and that the maximum repayment of bridewealth was necessary. The larger the number of children, the less the repayment. The fact that most "divorces" occurred during the betrothal interval shows that bridewealth did not guarantee stability. On the other hand, the concentration of financial penalties on the interval when couples had the fewest children suggests the role of the financial element in tiding a new couple over until their relationship could become firmly established.

In a comparative study of two African tribes, one with a high divorce rate and one with a low rate, Gluckman (1950) found that marriage payments were correspondingly low and high, respectively. In his opinion, "the amount of goods transferred and the divorce rate tend to be directly associated" (1950:192). He was not sure which came first, historically. Once a high rate came into existence it would be impossible for kin to invest much wealth in fragile marriages. I would assert, however, that—other things being equal—the larger the investment, the more stable the match.

In the case of Gluckman's stably married tribe (the South African Zulu), so powerful was the effect of the marriage payment that it outlasted the life of the donor. The bride-payment gave the man's group legal rights to all the bride's children, not "so long as we both shall live" but as long as the bride lived. Even if the wife deserted her husband and bore children by another man; even if he died and she bore children after his death; even if he was impotent and she bore children sired by another man; all those children were claimed by the kin group which had given cattle at the betrothal. Indeed so powerful was the impact of the bride-payment that it tended to carry over even beyond the death of the wife into sororal replacement of her reproductive services. In other words, the transaction linked two families in such a way that the husband's family acquired reproductive rights which extended as long as eligible spouses in the same generation were available on either side. This transcended an emphasis on the stability of the betrothed dyad to emphasize the stability of the relationship between whole kin groups:

> Marriage endures beyond the death of the husband and father, for he is still married to his widow now living either in leviratic marriage with a kinsman of his, or in widow concubinage, and he is still father of her future children. . . . The death of the wife may break the marriage, but, though it is not compulsory, it is considered proper, if the husband has been a good spouse and son-in-law, that she should be replaced by a younger sister who steps into her place under the sororate. This sister is now the dead woman and the family is reconstituted. (Gluckman, 1950: 184)

Gluckman summed up the effect of the Zulu financial transaction by saying that "The marriage payment transfers the woman's procreative power absolutely to her husband's agnatic lineage for her life, *and therefore divorce is rare*" (1950:192). I have italicized his conclusion because it epitomizes my conclusion.

Alternatives for Impecunious Families High financial requirements for betrothal are all very well for those who can afford to pay them, but they create problems for those who cannot.

For families with equal numbers of sons and daughters, one solution is to use the wealth received by marrying off a daughter to pay for a bride for a son. Even simpler where two families have one daughter and one son each, is a direct exchange of daughters which enables the families to consider themselves even without having to make any payments at all. Goode (1963) discovered that in Arabic Islam, marriage by exchanging sisters was a rather common solution to the problem of poverty in the lower classes.

If the rules of incest permit marriage within the same lineage, betrothal payments may also be by-passed since there is no point in transferring wealth within the lineage. Goode found that this too was sanctioned in Arab culture:

> A further structural element in the Arab kinship system was . . . the preference for marrying father's brother's daughter . . . since in such a marriage brother would be giving money to brother, the bride-price was much lower. Since both sides were interested in maintaining the honor of the same lineage, the husband could be sure that her chastity would be guarded adequately after the marriage. Land and any other property would remain in the same agnatic lineage. (1963:93)

Unfortunately, poor young men and women do not always find the right combinations of eligible siblings or cousins. LeVine and LeVine (1963) found that bride prices among the Kenyan Gusii were the equivalent of several years' wages for poor plantation workers. This tempted fathers to marry their daughters off to rich old men as secondary wives in polygynous households. To escape that fate, girls eloped as concubines with young men who could not afford to pay the bride price. Such informal liaisons might eventually be legitimated if the husband managed to pay off the bride price in installments. Meanwhile the choice between polygyny and concubinage offered an unattractive pair of alternatives for low-status girls.

Financial requirements for betrothal, then, seem to have a stabilizing influence on fragile relationships, provided those requirements can be met. For those unable to meet them, the system has dysfunctional consequences which may produce marriages less stable than they otherwise would have been.

In modern societies, financial transactions disappear as dyadic relationships become stronger. Nevertheless the engagement ring remains a symbolic equivalent of the bride price and a reminder that even in African tribes, the chief value of an exchange of cattle was symbolic and ceremonial rather than materialistic.

Broken Engagements

In some societies, broken engagements are unthinkable because they would offend the families concerned. Campbell's Greek shepherds assumed that a submissive girl would never have the nerve to break an engagement but that a callous man might. So punitive procedures had been devised for rectifying such an act:

> . . . to break an engagement is a violent affront to the honour of all the members of the bride's family, and as such it carries the ultimate sanction

of vengeance killing, which the girl's brothers, if they are men of honour, ought to carry through against the person of the bridegroom. (1964:128)

Even to refuse a betrothal in this honour-conscious context was considered an insult. This was an act which a girl's kin might commit against a man's family seeking to negotiate a match. If the man felt he had been sufficiently insulted by this refusal, the culture provided a customary way of wiping out the insult (though not without risk to everyone involved)—namely to abduct the girl:

> The captured girl is taken without delay to a prepared hideout in a cave or forest clearing. Here she is held by the bridegroom for three days and three nights. On the fourth day, the man takes the girl to the nearest police post and gives himself up, explaining that he took the girl from her home because he wished to marry her. The police at once send for the father or brother of the girl, and in his presence the police officer asks her if she wishes to marry her abductor or return to her home. She is asked this question three times and gives her answer three times. If she says that she is willing to marry the man they are taken immediately to the church and the service is celebrated. If she elects to return home, she is handed over to her kinsmen while the man is held to await trial on a serious charge which may send him to prison for a number of years. [In five cases of abduction] there is only one instance of the girl choosing to return to her own people. During the days and nights when she is detained by her abductor, the situation is carefully explained to her. If she refuses to marry the man, nobody will believe that after three nights in the wilderness with an ardent lover she is any longer a virgin. In any case, she cannot expect to be sought in marriage except by a man of low prestige or a widower. Secondly, if she goes back to her family, it inevitably obliges one of her brothers to seek vengeance on the abductor when he emerges from prison. And, in this case, the brother in turn may lose his life in counter vengeance or, at least, be forced into voluntary exile. Thirdly, she is asked if it is not pleasant, despite the sudden shocks, to be married to a man who is willing to risk his life to take her as his wife. For these reasons, and especially for the first of them, the girl is more likely to say "Yes" than "No." (Campbell, 1964:130)

In modern societies, broken engagements are an expected part of the system. Although theoretically the major compatibility testing takes place prior to engagement, there are always exceptional cases where testing was inadequate and cases where new incompatibilities emerge with the changes which betrothal brings.

The general assumption in modern societies is that a broken engagement prevents what otherwise would have been a broken marriage. In this sense, broken engagements are viewed as the lesser of two evils.

Between societies, however, there tends to be a positive correlation between the frequency of broken engagements and the frequency of broken marriages. In post-feudal societies, both rates tend to be low, whereas in highly developed societies, both tend to be high. Cultures which expect a great deal of the man–woman relationship create critical attitudes which lead to terminated relationships whenever in the process of organizational enactment those expectations are disappointed. The same attitudes which lead some people to break their engagement lead others to break their marriage. Both breaks result from the perfectionism and idealism with which modern people approach marriage. Broken engagements therefore are an intrinsic and necessary characteristic of the modern system of mate selection.

WEDDING: LEGITIMATING THE RELATIONSHIP

If there is any one point at which the new family organization is definitively formed, it is the wedding. The total process may involve a whole series of ceremonies, beginning with a betrothal ritual and culminating in a consummation ritual or in the birth of the first child. But in the wedding, the new marriage is officially authorized and given the stamp of legitimacy by the society.

Normal Weddings

Two main features are involved in weddings. As rites of passage marking the transition between different statuses in life, weddings are ritualized. At the same time, if weddings are to legitimize an otherwise private relationship, the public must participate in the ceremony. In general, I assume that the more ritualized and public the ceremony, the greater its impact on the participants.

Ritualization Weddings are characteristically the most elaborate ceremonies in which families are ever involved. Other family ceremonies such as those marking the birth of a child or the death of an elder are seldom as elaborate.

Marriage rituals vary from culture to culture. A frequent element is the sacred character of the ritual. Weddings are often held in religious buildings, and conducted by religious functionaries who recite sacred rites. Age-old formulas invoke traditional sentiments about the meaningfulness of marriage and add solemnity and dignity to the occasion.

Presumably the more elaborate the ritual, the greater the awareness in both the couple and their relatives and friends that the wedding signifies a major change in relationships. One characteristic of cohesive social organizations is clear-cut boundary lines. One way of sharpening the boundary between not being married and being married is to elaborate the ceremonies which mark the time of crossing the line.

Participation of the Public A second way of dramatizing the occasion is to involve a large number of people. In primitive tribes where most events are family events, weddings assume great significance. Among the Nuer, weddings were "important public events":

> Preparations for them are made days, even weeks, ahead, and they are talked about, especially by the young people, long before they take place.
> . . . A whole district attends them, the mere coming together of so many people making marriage a memorable event. Neighbours thus bear witness to the creation of the new social ties and by their presence sanction them. (Evans-Pritchard, 1951:59)

Nor are the only Nuer participants those who are still alive. Even the ghosts of ancestors are invited to attend:

> Before the wedding dance begins, or as soon as it has begun, the kin on either side signify their approval of the marriage by calling out the spear-names of the clans or . . . lineages of the bride and bridegroom and invoking the ghosts of their ancestors to look upon the cattle of the bride-wealth—a rite which makes the ghosts partners to the union and witnesses of it. (1951:65)

Although participation by large numbers of people and ghosts adds to the significance of the wedding, the crucial public participant may be a single official representative of the larger society. A clergyman or governmental official symbolizes the larger public's interest in the newly formed marriage. By his attendance and central role in the proceedings, he symbolizes the importance which society attaches to the married state and the distinction society draws between being single and being married. Presumably the participation of representatives of the larger society adds further significance to the wedding.

Mini-Weddings

Not all weddings fulfill the conditions which characterize organizational enactment at its most formal and public best. Couples who are not prepared for so much formality may elope as a way of by-passing the normal ceremonies. Secondly, individuals marrying for the second time usually invest less in their second wedding than they did in the first.

Elopements   To elope means to by-pass the normal wedding procedure and marry less formally than usual. For young people whose marriage is opposed by one or both families, this eliminates kin from participation. For couples too poor to afford a big wedding, marrying away from friends as well as relatives may be a way of saving money. In societies offering both religious and civil ceremonies, the latter may be a cheap substitute for the former. For example, the Nydeggers (1963) found that Filipinos turned to civil marriages as an inexpensive alternative when the normal big church weddings did not seem appropriate.

Although class differences and parental disapproval contribute to the instability of marriages contracted by elopement and by civil rather than religious ceremonies, it seems likely that diminished wedding ceremonies provide a weaker beginning point for marriage even when other factors are held constant. Locke (1951) found that compared to his happily married couples more than twice as many of his divorced respondents had been married by justices-of-the-peace. Similarly, Burgess and Cottrell (1939) found that more than twice as many couples married by a clergyman were well-adjusted after marriage compared to those married by a civil official.

Remarriages   When people get married for the first time, they tend to make a big thing of it. The second time around, they tend to make a little thing of it. Regardless of whether the second marriage involves a polygamist adding a second wife or a monogamist replacing a partner lost by death or divorce, it seldom equals the first in elaborateness.

After describing the elaborate rituals of first marriages among the Tonga, Colson pointed out the omissions which characterized second marriages:

> If the bride has been married before, she will still be taken to her husband by his messengers, but she is not expected to protest nor will she be dragged from the house of her guardian and enticed along the route with small presents. Theoretically no offering should be made at the door when she goes, for she has already been detached from her father's household at the time of her first marriage and divorce does not reestablish her membership in it. When she is taken to her husband, her face will not be covered nor will she make her formal visits home. Already she has been weaned from her relatives. (1958:340)

Though the reasons differ, much the same diminution of wedding ceremonies occurs in the United States.

TABLE 12-5 Ritualization of Organizational Enactment
in First Marriages and Remarriages

| | MARRIAGE ORDER | | | |
| | | | REMARRIAGE | |
	FIRST MARRIAGE FOR BOTH	Man's	Woman's	Both Partners
Courtship				
Months of pre-engagement dating	18	17	13	12
Betrothal				
Months engaged	10	9	7	5
Formally engaged	89%	74%	69%	54%
Engagement ring	84%	64%	60%	43%
Wedding				
Church wedding	81%	45%	23%	25%
Reception	88%	79%	52%	45%
Guests at wedding/reception	169	80	38	26
Honeymoon				
Honeymoon trip	95%	79%	76%	62%
Days on trip	9	9	6	6
Number of couples	715	58	62	65

Adapted from Hollingshead (1952):310–311. Source: Random sample of New Haven residents married in 1949 and 1950. The two middle columns involve mixed marriages between a previously married partner and a never-married partner. Numbers other than percentages represent averages (means).

Table 12-5 shows how extensively wedding behavior was curtailed by Americans entering remarriages. This curtailment was not limited to the wedding alone but extended to every phase of the enactment process from pre-engagement courtship to the honeymoon. In mixed cases where only one partner had been married before, the woman's previous experience was more depressing than the man's, perhaps because getting married is a woman-centered experience in the United States.

The diminished ritualization of remarriages presumably provides a weaker foundation and a diminished significance in the eyes of the participants and the surrounding society. To put it another way, most people (especially girls) look forward to the excitement of getting married. Among Liebow's Negro men, for example, marriage was ". . . a rite through which one passes into man's estate. For the young, never-married male, to get married is to become a man" (1967:114). But one does not become a man twice in one lifetime, nor is a second marriage as exciting as the first. So it is understandable that remarriages should be faint echoes of their predecessors.

HONEYMOON: CELEBRATING THE ENACTMENT

The celebration of the wedding begins with a public event—the reception or wedding feast. In some cultures this is a gala affair with music and dancing, eating and drinking which may last for days. The newlyweds in many societies take part in the reception as guests of honor. On the other hand, in kin-based societies, the emphasis is on celebrating the alliance between families, in comparison to which the couple's relationship is relatively unimportant.

The honeymoon involves the withdrawal of the couple from public view for a period of undisturbed intimacy. Its privacy contrasts with the public character of the betrothal and the wedding. Slater has suggested that popular customs which interfere with the couple's withdrawal reflect society's ambivalence about tolerating such privacy:

> A great deal of hostility is expressed directly toward the departing couple in the form of diffuse anal-expulsive gestures such as throwing rice and confetti. Some of the customary jokes unveil the basis of this hostility, in that they have the covert purpose of hindering the couple's departure. These include tampering with the couple's automobile, hiding their luggage, etc. Furthermore, a number of devices, such as signs, streamers, or tin cans fastened to the automobile, stones placed in the hub caps, and, again, the confetti, serve to make the couple conspicuous, and thus have the effect of minimizing or negating the sense of privacy which has been granted to them. . . . Finally, attempts are often made to invade the privacy of the couple directly, and to forestall, by symbolic means the breaking of peer group bonds. Thus objects may be placed in the couple's suitcases, or the couple's clothes may be tied in knots—a rather pathetic blending of hostile and wistful sentiments. In the more extreme case every effort is made to find out the couple's destination, and to communicate with them in some way. (1963:356)

Hostile though society may be to the couple's escape into privacy, the fact that the couple must surmount such ritualized barriers intensifies the excitement and therefore the psychological significance of their withdrawal.

Honeymoons are not a universal custom. They tend to be incorporated in the organizational enactment process by societies which put the biggest emphasis on the change of status at marriage. Societies in which wedding ceremonies are most elaborate tend to add the honeymoon as another boundary-marking episode (Rapoport and Rapoport, 1964).

American weddings may be finished in as little as ten minutes and receptions seldom last more than half a day, but a week-long honeymoon adds a major time interval to the transition. In another book (Blood, 1969:198) I quoted a student's comment about the psychological value of taking a honeymoon:

> There is a very dismal aura to the thought of getting married on Wednesday and going to work on Thursday. It is almost as if someone could ask you, "What did you do yesterday?" and you could answer, "Oh, nothing much. I just got married!"

To be able to take a holiday from ordinary responsibilities requires a certain degree of economic affluence. The development of honeymoons is one element in the heightened significance attached to marriage in post-primitive societies. It both symbolizes that significance and contributes to it by accentuating the discontinuity between the premarital and the married state.

In order to emphasize this discontinuity, the honeymoon must differ from the sheer beginning of marriage. Some American couples hide away in their new apartment during a so-called honeymoon, but this waters down the distinction between the honeymoon and the rest of marriage. In this sense, a honeymoon ideally involves a wedding "trip," not that the couple must go far away but rather that if they choose a distinctive location (away from their parents and from their own new home), their role transition is accentuated.

This is not to say that marriage does not begin during the honeymoon. It provides the traditional setting for initiating the sexual aspect of marriage. In societies which demand that the bride be a virgin, the sexual initiation may require public proof in order to insure the honor of all parties concerned:

> . . . in Morocco, a woman used to be stationed in front of the wedding chamber, and as soon as the bridegroom had deflowered his bride he handed to her the bloodstained napkin, which she thereupon showed to all the assembled guests, proclaiming in a loud voice that the bride was found to have been a virgin. (Patai, 1959:67)

Even where the sexual initiation of marriage has no public significance, the honeymoon is considered important to the initiation or the development of the sexual relationship between partners who have not previously lived together. Even couples who have already engaged in occasional episodes of sexual intercourse have rarely had the opportunity for leisurely, undisturbed intercourse which the honeymoon offers.

In other ways, little and big, the marriage also begins during the honeymoon: patterns of dressing and undressing, sharing bathroom facilities, and sharing responsibility for money begin to be worked out. Nevertheless, the major function of the honeymoon is to celebrate the fact that the couple are finally married.

QUASI-MARRIAGE I: PREMARITAL INTERCOURSE

Throughout this chapter, I have emphasized the discontinuity between single life and marriage. To "enact" an organization means that beforehand it did not exist. Nevertheless, no organization ever springs instantaneously into being, and family formation is clearly a multistage process.

Insofar as marriage is an extension of courtship, the question arises, "What is the difference between being married and not being married?" Other than that the couple have formalized their relationship through a wedding, it is difficult to give an absolute answer since premarital and marital customs differ widely around the world.

Two possible differences are that unmarried couples may refrain from sexual intercourse and from living together, whereas after the wedding intercourse is the expected "consummation" of marriage and establishing a common household (with or without relatives) is also expected. If couples engage in sexual intercourse or begin living together before the wedding, they will be half-married already. For them, the boundary line between not being married and being married will be blurred.

In many cultures, premarital intercourse has been socially permitted or even socially encouraged. Seventy percent of Murdock's world-wide sample of societies permitted premarital intercourse for both sexes. Most of the remaining 30 percent were permissive for men even though they prohibited it for women. Indeed, Murdock concluded that "There is . . . nothing in man's social experience to indicate that the ideal of premarital chastity has any scientific value" (Murdock, Woodward, and Bolman; 1950).

In evaluating this statement, it is important to remember that most of Murdock's societies were small, primitive tribes. In Chapter 1 we saw that premarital intercourse is especially common in such simple societies. By contrast, most of the world's population lives in feudal and modern societies which are less permissive. Feudal societies have characteristically placed an extraordinarily high value on premarital chastity. Hence if we look at the question in terms of the total history of mankind, we cannot so easily dismiss chastity as irrelevant. Indeed, the frequency or infrequency of any particular custom contributes relatively little to our understanding of the consequences of a behavior pattern, no matter how rare it may be.

Double standards of sexual morality reflect the fact that the sex drive is stronger in males than females, especially during adolescence (Shuttleworth, 1959). Boys are more biologically driven to sexual expression than girls the same age, and inhibiting their drive is a more difficult cultural achievement. Cultures have adapted themselves to a biological fact in allowing boys greater freedom.

But there is another biological fact which is more responsible for placing restrictions on girls, namely the fact that they may become pregnant. In Chapter 14 some of the consequences of illegitimate births will be dealt with. Earlier in this chapter the negative consequences of premarital conceptions for forced marriages were mentioned. Neither placing a child for adoption, nor getting rid of it through abortion, is viewed with equanimity by very many societies. For such reasons, many societies have tabooed premarital intercourse for girls.

Many of the premodern societies which permitted premarital intercourse experienced relatively few conceptions because the average girl married before she became fertile. Due to dietary deficiencies, girls in primitive societies mature late. Even after menstruation begins, relatively few ova are capable of fertilization at first. Thus, if the average girl in such a society marries in her mid-teens, the chances of conception are relatively slight no matter how often she has premarital intercourse (Ford and Beach, 1951:172).

The delayed age of marriage and accelerated rate of physical development in modern societies increase the risk of pregnancy. Technological improvements in methods of contraception and abortion have reduced this risk although they have by no means eliminated it entirely. In many modern societies, premarital conceptions have risen due to increased premarital intercourse, despite the invention of improved methods of contraception. Even for married couples, contraception is not yet generally fool-proof. For young unmarried persons, it is less widely and less consistently used.

Like contraceptive usage in marriage, taking precautions before marriage may be expected to be a stratified phenomenon, most widespread among high-status people. Nevertheless, 22 percent of the sexual liaisons of Kirkendall's Oregon State University men students had involved no contraceptive precautions (1961). Among Kinsey's single women (most of them college-educated) who ever had had intercourse, almost 18 percent became pregnant. Nor did one pregnancy guarantee effective contraceptive precautions under the conditions then existing (prior to 1950), since 15 percent of those who became pregnant once did so again prior to marriage.

The proportion of those having intercourse who become pregnant may have fallen with improved contraceptive effectiveness. However, as recently as the late 1950s, the U. S. Census Bureau reported that the proportion of all brides whose first babies were born less than nine months after the wedding had risen to the highest point in American history and did not yet show any signs of abating.

In order for social attitudes toward premarital intercourse to change, it is not necessary for premarital conceptions actually to disappear, but only for people to think they have. The invention of improved contraceptives has already spurred a more tolerant attitude toward premarital freedom for women. This is reinforced by the modern tendency to feel that a double standard is unjust. With the emancipation of women from traditional restraints and the growing equalitarianism in man–woman relations resulting from the education and employment of women, the double standard increasingly seems discriminatory. Although it might theoretically be replaced by a conservative single standard, the very changes in social relations which have made the double standard seem obsolete all point toward increased sexual freedom for women rather than increased restraint for men. Such reasoning led Reiss (1960) to forecast increasing sexual permissiveness for American society. Nor is this a uniquely American trend. It seems likely that the modernization of post-feudal societies and the growing affluence of industrialized societies will liberalize sexual attitudes in many parts of the world.

The question in the most advanced societies is not whether sexual standards are softening, but rather how far and how fast that liberalization will go. Reiss (1967) found that change tends to be progressive. Those who abandon a philosophy of abstinence rarely jump to complete permissiveness. Rather, people (and presumably societies) tend to accept first of all intercourse within engagement or with strong affection. (In Scandinavia, for example, Christensen [1966] observed that permission for premarital intercourse had traditionally been restricted to engaged couples and was only recently extended to couples who were "going steady.") Later they may come to tolerate intercourse between casual acquaintances. I predict that social attitudes will change slowly but steadily in this direction during the coming generations.

My concern here, however, is not with the extent of premarital intercourse or with the conditions under which it occurs, but rather with its effects on the process of family formation.

Blocked Enactment

Under certain conditions, premarital intercourse barricades or at least obstructs the path to normal family formation.

In societies where quasi-marital relationships are freely available, the motivation for men to marry is correspondingly reduced. For Jamaican men, quasi-marriage offered many of the privileges of marriage with few of the responsibilities. It was an alluring by-pass on the road to marriage:

> Comparatively speaking, Jamaican males undergo relatively less deprivation by not marrying than is true for bachelors in more adequately functioning social structures. In most societies, life outside of marriage is made relatively undesirable, infelicitous, and lonely. If nothing else, people tend to get repelled into wedlock. In Jamaica, however, a man is deprived of neither regular sexual association nor feminine companionship by remaining single. Young girls can . . . be seduced with relative ease and their seduction may even be facilitated if the man is considerably older and of high socio-economic status. Once these girls are burdened by illegitimate children, their services—sexual and household—do not have a very high price. There is thus available to men a free-floating supply of women who are tired, hungry, and eager for help. Hence, although marriage may be a man's long-term goal, life outside of wedlock is not so boring or lonely or statistically deviant for him that he is typically motivated at an early age to . . . get married. . . . (Blake, 1961:142)

Whenever quasi-marriage is substituted for marriage, certain consequences tend to follow. First of all, the sexual relationship may become fixated on a level lacking the positive ingredients of marriage. Secondly, individuals known to have engaged in premarital intercourse may lose some or all of their eligibility for marriage.

Stunted Relationships   In some social circles, premarital sexual relationships are extraordinarily exploitative and irresponsible. Among working-class people on the island of Jamaica, Stycos and Back found that "visiting relationships involve rather erratic patterns of sexual union, with frequent periods of separation on the part of the partners. This seems attributable not only to the difficulties inherent in the relationship, but also to its tenuous nature, involving little responsibility on the part of one partner to the other" (1964:171). Rosenberg and Bensman found that unmarried male Puerto Ricans in New York City, Appalachians in Chicago, and Negroes in Washington had impoverished sexual relationships:

Neither emotional and material responsibilities, nor their opposite, pure joy in unrestrained sexuality, is much in evidence. Sexual fulfillment is experienced merely as a physical release . . . in which the female is the necessary but unequal partner. Otherwise, sexual conquest provides a trophy calculated to enhance one's prestige in peer-group competition. Masculinity is affirmed as part of a game whose competitors must incessantly prove themselves before an audience of others engaged in the same pastime. Since it is a competitive game, the boy who plays cannot expect to earn points for scoring over an easy mark, a "pig." Victory consists in overcoming the largest possible number of inaccessible girls. The conversion of females into trophies reduces them to nonpersons. Their personal, sexual, or simply human, needs do not matter. They exist to be tricked, deceived, manipulated—and abandoned. Skill in all these techniques is a sign of stylistic virtuosity. For a boy to abuse his sexual partner in many ingenious ways makes him a big winner. (1968:75)

These are extreme cases of sex without love. They are presented not as evidence of inevitable consequences of premarital intercourse but rather to illustrate the depths to which premarital relationships may sink when unbuttressed by broader commitments. Although marriage does not guarantee either responsibility or love, it provides a structural framework within which exploitation is less likely to occur. To engage in sexual intercourse outside engagement or marriage is to place the weight of responsibility for humanizing the relationship on the effectiveness of the socialization of the individual personalities involved. If that socialization has been weak, the sexual relationship is liable to fall short of the reciprocity expected of marriage.

Impaired Eligibility for Marriage If social norms specify that one or both sexes should refrain from sexual relations before marriage, violation of those norms will impair the individual's eligibility for marriage. In some cases, the disqualification is complete, so that the violator is permanently restricted to nonmarital relationships. In some, the individual becomes ineligible for a first-class marriage, but he may still be able to enter a second-rate marriage. In still others, an ordinary marriage may still be possible, but it may be more difficult to find a partner willing to overlook the sexual defect. Conversely, even if premarital freedom is generally accepted, the exceptional person who remains chaste may thereby acquire greater attractiveness as a potential marriage partner (just as Rosenberg and Bensman's boys gained prestige if they seduced a virgin).

Rosenberg and Bensman's Appalachian boys held a double standard, differentiating between "good girls" whom they dated and married and "bad girls" who were mere sex objects. To those who take the double standard literally, a girl must never engage in premarital intercourse if she wishes to be eligible for marriage. In the Appalachian case, however, the distinction lay in the degree of resistance which the girl put up:

Asked whether he still considers girls decent if they go to bed with him, a Chicago boy answers, "It's a matter of how hard I have to work. If I have to work real hard, I think a lot of them. If they give it to me right off, I think they're pigs." (1968:66)

Substandard marriages may result either from becoming trapped with an inferior partner or from reduction of eligibility with subsequent partners. These consequences are particularly likely when intercourse results in pregnancy. Among the Zambian Tonga, for example:

> Some Plateau parents . . . look upon the premarital affairs of their daughters with a somewhat jaundiced eye. . . . They see in such affairs . . . a possible lessening of the girl's chance to make an advantageous marriage should she conceive by her lover, who may be either less well endowed with wealthy relatives or with formal education than she is. Or, if he refuses responsibility for her and her child, she may find it difficult to marry a young man of equal status, for such a man may be reluctant to take her, at least as a first wife. (Colson, 1958:292)

The last phrase suggests than an unwed mother who lost her chance for becoming a head wife might be reduced to becoming a secondary wife in a polygynous household.

Tongan society generally allowed bachelors the freedom to have sexual relations with several girls at once, whereas girls were supposed to restrict themselves to a single lover in order to be able to name the father if and when they became pregnant. Even for young men, however, there was some danger that excessive promiscuity might impair their eligibility for marriage:

> Young men who are known to be completely promiscuous, especially if they have frequented the women of the railway as well as the village girls, may have their characters scrutinized when they make proposals of marriage to the guardians of the girl of their choice. Her elders may need to be reassured about some sort of reform, and the man's own relatives may be reluctant to undertake marriage negotiations in his behalf if they think his subsequent behaviour is apt to endanger the success of his marriage. (Colson, 1958:293)

Here it was not the difference between chastity and unchastity, but the degree of promiscuity which affected the man's chances for marriage. Since Tongan society generally tolerated premarital freedom, only unusually avid exploitation of that freedom was deviant by their cultural standards.

Even in such permissive societies, the most desirable wife may be one who has managed to keep her "virtue" intact by refraining from intercourse completely. In Jamaica, Blake noted that "Although men do not seem to respect virginity in the sense of refraining from casual intercourse with virgins if this is possible, they nonetheless seem to prefer virginity when looking for a wife" (1961:101). And in Samoa where sex play was the chief form of adolescent recreation, Margaret Mead (1949) likewise found that virginity was a source of prestige whenever it occurred (which was not very often) and was prescribed for the village princess who served as the ceremonial hostess of the village. The Samoan case is especially interesting since the preference for virginity did not result from any belief in a double standard but existed in the midst of a generally permissive attitude toward premarital experience for both sexes. To put the matter crassly, there seems to be a widespread tendency for "unused merchandise" to command a higher price in the mate-selection market.

Blurred Enactment

Couples who have had intercourse with each other already feel partly married. So they tend to feel that their enactment rituals are less important subjectively and to make them less elaborate objectively than couples whose marriages initiate their sexual relationship.

Among the Zambian Tonga, this principle is illustrated by the diminished wedding rituals of women whose sexual involvement had produced an illegitimate child. Colson (1958) found that whereas a woman normally was expected to protest when she was taken to her husband for the wedding ceremony, one who had already borne a child was not supposed to protest, presumably because the visible evidence of her motherhood attested that she had already psychologically left home.

Even without the complication of premarital pregnancy, Rapoport and Rapoport noted that societies which allowed premarital sexual involvement generally deemphasized marriage rituals and also had less clearly demarcated honeymoons:

> This seemed to relate to the degree of discontinuity the individuals experienced in leaving their unmarried roles and entering their married roles. In groups where considerable premarital sexual experimentation was allowed and the couple were publicly known to be intimately involved with one another, the actual marriage tended to be marked with little fanfare and little need for removal of the couple from their usual round of activities. (1964:35)

At an Indiana university, Kanin and Howard (1958) found that premarital intercourse reduced the proportion of students who took a honeymoon trip from 87 percent to only 47 percent. Apparently a majority of the couples who had already had intercourse with each other felt that the wedding was something of an anti-climax, hardly worth celebrating with a honeymoon trip. This suggests that to initiate sexual relationships prior to marriage is to engage in a quasi-wedding stripped of the usual public and ritualized features. Under the circumstances, much of the significance of the wedding and honeymoon seems to have been lost.

In general, the more intimate the couple prior to marriage, the less significant the formal marriage.

Repetitive Enactment

Breaking the chastity barrier is relatively difficult. But once an individual has had intercourse with a first partner, it becomes psychologically easier to do so again. The result is that the speed of moving into intercourse with successive partners tends to increase. In Jamaica, for example, the median length of courtship prior to first intercourse declined steadily in successive relationships:

from 4.2 months of acquaintance prior to intercourse with a woman's first partner, to 2.9 months with her second partner, 2.4 months with the third, and 2.1 with the fourth (Blake, 1961:165). This suggests a gradual cheapening of the relationship for these women, reflecting their deteriorating bargaining position in the courtship market. Thus, one consequence of premarital intercourse is a tendency for repetitive enactment with other premarital partners.

The same tendency toward repetitiveness applies in lesser degree to extramarital intercourse and to marriage itself. Insofar as premarital intercourse muddies the process of organizational enactment, it weakens the boundary lines between marriage and non-marriage. This applies especially to the sexual boundaries of marriage. Individuals who have not deemed it necessary to be married in order to have sexual relations before marriage are less apt to deem it necessary in order to have sexual relations outside of marriage. I therefore expect premarital intercourse will be followed by extramarital intercourse and, secondarily, by divorce. In those two senses, premarital intercourse tends to produce repetitive sexual involvement with new partners and repetitive marriage.

Extramarital Intercourse   The most direct evidence of the relationship between premarital and extramarital intercourse comes from Kinsey's study of married women (1953). Twenty-nine percent of his premaritally experienced women compared to only 13 percent of the premaritally chaste women had engaged in extramarital intercourse up to the time they were interviewed.

Anthropologists from various cultures have reported widely held beliefs that virgin brides make safer wives. Oscar Lewis (1962) reported that Mexican peasants preferred to marry women who were disinterested in sex because they were believed less likely to become sexually involved with other men in the village while the husbands were away working in the fields. Similarly, a typical Jamaican male attitude was to mistrust women who are "easy marks":

> Some people are a decent type and if you want to approach a decent type of person that way you should have to wait. In the country you see a decent woman's daughter and you want to approach her you would have to wait even six months.

And, said another Jamaican man:

> It ought to be a good while before sexual relations because too much hastiness not good, for if you is looking a good wife he should wait. Like me, if I wasn't married and talking to a girl and put questions to her and she consent too early, I would say she not good. I would feel that she would consent easily to any man and she wouldn't make a good wife. (Blake, 1961:164–165)

Divorce   Extramarital intercourse is a more direct threat to marital solidarity than intercourse which occurred previous to the marital union in question. If the latter is restricted to the eventual marriage partner, no third parties are involved. Extramarital intercourse, by contrast, involves at least one third party by definition. If the innocent partner knows about it, it tends to create feelings of jealousy toward the outsider and of resentment toward the mate. The ultimate result need not necessarily be the destruction of the marriage, but in American society at least, that is a frequent outcome.

I am not concerned here with the direct consequences of extramarital intercourse but rather with the repercussions of premarital intercourse (which may be mediated indirectly through extramarital intercourse as well as in other ways).

Focusing on intercourse with the future spouse only, the study by Burgess and Wallin (1953) indicated that the more frequently couples had intercourse with each other before marriage, the less they loved each other after marriage, the less happy and satisfied they were in their marriages, and the less confident they were that their marriage would last. Marriages were most successful by these criteria for those with no premarital experience, progressively less for those with increasing amounts of experience between the partners, and least for those who had relations with other partners besides the future spouse. These findings suggest that the more promiscuous the premarital history in terms either of frequency of intercourse or more especially of number of partners, the less successful the marriage is likely to be.

In a comparison of happily married and divorced men, Locke (1951) found that three times as many of the happily married men had had no premarital intercourse (37 percent versus 12 percent). The divorced men were much more apt to have had intercourse with "many" women whereas most of the happily married men who had had premarital relations at all had had only a few partners.

Since most Americans whose marriages fail subsequently remarry, some of the extramarital intercourse to which I have referred might better be described as pre-remarital intercourse. From the standpoint of the concept of "reenactment," this is just the point: Premarital intercourse leads indirectly to involvements with other partners outside of marriage which in turn result in the dissolution of the first marriage and its replacement by a new marriage. Regardless, however, of whether the first marriage is legally terminated, extramarital intercourse becomes easier when premarital intercourse has weakened the boundaries around marriage. The more frequent the intercourse and the larger the number of partners, the weaker those boundaries become.

Given these threats to marriage, some of the societies which supposedly allow premarital freedom actually circumscribe that freedom by limiting it to certain times and certain persons. If sexual access is restricted to persons who are already engaged or who are at least socially eligible to marry one another, the threat to marriage is more effectively controlled (short of complete chastity).

QUASI-MARRIAGE II: PREMARITAL HOUSEKEEPING

Closer to marriage than isolated episodes of intercourse is setting up housekeeping "without benefit of clergy." This regularizes the sexual relationship and resembles marriage in so many ways that a stranger could hardly tell the difference from a genuine marriage. The only universal difference is legal (and in some societies, even this disappears after couples have lived together long enough—in English common law, seven years). Secondly there is a psychological difference if the couple have not committed themselves to a permanent relationship. This is not necessarily distinctive, since some housekeeping couples hope to marry eventually and some married couples do not expect to stay married indefinitely (though few start out on such a temporary basis). These however are exceptional cases, so in general joint housekeeping is a tentative experiment whereas marriage is a permanent commitment.

Experimental apartment living is a growing practice among American college students freed from dormitory requirements. No studies are yet available of the results of these experiments. However, concubinage, "consensual unions," "domiciliary unions," and common law unions are interchangeable terms for patterns which can be found in many premodern societies and in the disorganized sectors of modern societies. In the black ghettoes of American cities and among the lower-class peoples of most Caribbean islands, a large minority or even a majority of the adult population lives in nonlegalized relationships at any one time, even though most of them will enter a legal marriage at some point in their lives. In order to assess the consequences of premarital housekeeping, it is necessary to turn to such cultures and subcultures, comparing these quasi-marriages with true marriages within the same societies.

One element in premarital housekeeping is the sexual relationship, so living together may be presumed to produce the same effects as premarital intercourse under other circumstances—namely blocked, blurred and repetitive enactment of marriage. We can assume, however, that sexual activity is usually intensified for couples who are living together in comparison with those who have only a dating relationship. For example, in Jamaica Stycos and Back (1964) compared couples who had originally had only a "visiting" premarital relationship but then began living together. Ninety percent of the couples increased their frequency of intercourse and 70 percent increased the regularity of intercourse under the more convenient circumstances. Living together made intercourse not only more convenient but more difficult to avoid since the woman could not send the man home if she was not interested on any particular occasion.

Although increased sexual access may have been a prominent motive for the man to move in with the woman, her motivation was likely to be quite different. Blake (1961) found that most initial Jamaican housekeeping ventures resulted from pregnancy (just as premature marriages in the United States were usually caused by pregnancy). Since premature quasi-marriages increased the frequency of intercourse, pregnancy was a frequent outcome of living together. The larger the number of children, the more desperate the unmarried mother's economic plight became and the more eager she was to acquire a quasi-husband who would assist her financially if she could not persuade him to become a full-fledged husband. (Stycos and Back [1964] found a direct relationship between the number of children born to the first sexual union and a woman's likelihood of entering a housekeeping relationship with her next partner. Whereas only 28 percent of the childless women set up unlegalized housekeeping with their second man, 34 percent of those with one child and 44 percent of those with more than one child "settled for" such an arrangement.) For the man, then, living together was a convenience; for the woman it was a desperate necessity.

Such desperation drove more than twice as many of Blake's women with children as of those without (39 percent versus 15 percent) to succumb to intercourse in less than one month after meeting their second man. In order to rid themselves of this handicap to marriage, some women placed their children out for informal adoption by someone else. A few other women had children who died. For the remainder, increasing numbers of children progressively eliminated the preferred alternatives of remaining single or getting married and forced them to settle for the disliked alternative of entering a quasi-marriage.

An Unrespectable Status

Quasi-marriages differ from complete marriages in two respects: They are not socially respectable and they are not secure.

Blake (1961) asked her working-class Jamaicans whether they preferred informal or formal marriage. Ninety-seven percent preferred to be legally married for the reasons shown in Table 12-6.

TABLE 12-6 Reasons for Preferring Legal Marriage Instead of Unmarried Housekeeping, for Men and Women

Reason for Preferring Marriage	*Men*	*Women*
Respectability		
Marriage is more respectable; people have more respect, treat you better	45%	57%
Religion advocates marriage	20	14
Legitimate children have more opportunities, a better chance in life	22	5
Marriage sets a good example to children	4	11
Security		
Woman has financial claim on man; security, protection; he cannot leave her without support	—	78%
Man can expect woman to take better care of him, house, and children; can trust her more	54%	—
Inheritance assured for wife and children	16	22
Can expect fidelity from mate	22	9
Children better cared for, trained	*	12
Number of cases	51	95

Adapted from Blake (1961):121. Source: Lower-class Jamaicans.
* For men, this item is included in the 54 percent who expect the woman to take better care of the children in marriage.
Totals add to more than 100 percent because respondents could give more than one reason.

For men, the reasons for preferring marriage were evenly divided between respectability and security. Women were equally concerned with respectability but appreciably more concerned with security than the men.

To say that nonlegal cohabiting is unrespectable is circuitous. To legalize a relationship is to place the official stamp of approval on it. To live together without the normal sanction of society is to invoke social disapproval even in places like Jamaica or Liebow's black ghetto, where consensual unions are widespread. To live together is even more unrespectable than to engage in premarital intercourse because living together cannot be concealed.

Indirectly testifying to the sensitivity of Jamaican women about the low prestige of consensual unions is the resentment Blake reported they felt toward their quasi-husbands. Women were resentful "because the man did not ask her to marry him . . . instead of 'testing her out first.' " Indeed, marriages preceded by informal cohabitation with the same partner often were ruined by the "deep injuries to pride and self-respect" inflicted on the woman by the early relationship (1961:146).

Although living together was considered deviant enough when a couple had no children, it worsened with the arrival of children who (like the "marriage" itself) were illegitimate. For the parents, the larger the number of children born out of wedlock (even if their relationship was reasonably stable), the greater their loss of social respect, reported Stycos and Back (1964). For the children themselves, the half-married state of their parents was also a source of embarrassment. The older the children got, the more urgently the parents felt a need to legalize their relationship to remove the stigma from their children. This benefited not only the children (by relieving them from embarrassment and from discrimination by employers and other outsiders), but it also improved the parent–child relationship:

> We would go on living together if we were not having children. But no matter how poor you are, while you are married you can chastise your children . . . because they can't throw back bad life at you when you speak to them. It don't look well for the children to grow up and see us living a bad life. They will not respect us, and we parents cannot talk to them when they do anything wrong as our way of living is no example to them. (Stycos and Back, 1964:98)

In other words, quasi-marriage is unrespectable not only in the eyes of outsiders but of insiders, both parents and children. All these problems are resolved by a wedding ceremony.

Insecurity

Less obvious than the unrespectable character of quasi-marriages is their insecurity. Theoretically, a man and woman might devote themselves as wholeheartedly to each other without marriage as with it, yet the data from the Caribbean suggest that in general relationships tend to be strengthened when they are legalized. Unlegalized relationships are weaker both between the man and woman and between parents and children.

Weak Parent–Child Relationships   Not mentioned directly in Table 12-6 as a reason for marrying but clearly stated in the quotations from Stycos and Back is a weakness in parental authority over children when parents do not have a legally authorized relationship.

What undermines the parent–child relationship the most is not the low moral status of the parents but the instability of their relationship. Blake found that common-law marriages typically broke up in less than four years, far less than the time required to raise children to maturity. As a result, children born into quasi-marriages usually experienced a whole succession of "fathers" whose relationship to them was made even more difficult by the fact that they were only stepfathers. Actually, men often tried to avoid assuming responsibility for children they had not sired because the problems involved were so difficult:

> Children knowing that he is not father may not be respectful, may be impertinent. The children will never accept him as the father and he may not be able to subject them or get them to obey his orders. (Blake, 1961: 103–104)

Jamaicans have such checkered sexual histories that step-parent relationships pervade the entire working-class, affecting not only individuals currently involved in quasi-marital relationships, but also those who marry after earlier premarital sexual episodes. Figure 12-3 shows that the only Jamaican males whose entire child-bearing was confined to marriage were those who married youngest and were still married to the same partner when they were interviewed. On the other hand, married men past age 40 had sired children by other women almost as often as quasi-married men, so apt were they to have had multiple partners prior to marriage. Nevertheless, Figure 12-3 shows that the more solid the man–woman relationship, the less likely the man was to have sired outside children requiring his financial support.

In general, then, parent–child relationships are weakened within quasi-marriages by the low prestige of the parents' marital status and are weakened even more between fathers and children when men abandon their quasi-families.

Weak Husband–Wife Relationships　Table 12-6 showed that the chief insecurities in quasi-marriages (from the standpoint of the adult participants at least) were not those affecting the children but those for the adults themselves and more especially those affecting women. One source of anxiety stems directly from the complexities of parent–child relationships in societies where quasi-marital relationships are widespread, namely the possibility that ties with children by former relationships may promote sporadic reinvolvement with the former sex partners. This was described colorfully by one of Blake's male respondents in expressing his dislike for having children supported by another man within his own home:

> When [the other] man supports them, [the mother] have to run after him fe get the money. People believe she da play with him still. I don't like it. (1961:104)

Quasi-marriages provide less insurance against extramarital involvement, quite apart from contacts "outside" children may stimulate with former partners. Liebow noted that there was no consensus in his Washington ghetto about whether couples living together were supposed to confine their sexual relationships to one another whereas the rights and duties of married couples were clear-cut:

FIGURE 12-3. Men Supporting Children Outside the Current Relationship,
by Age and Marital Status

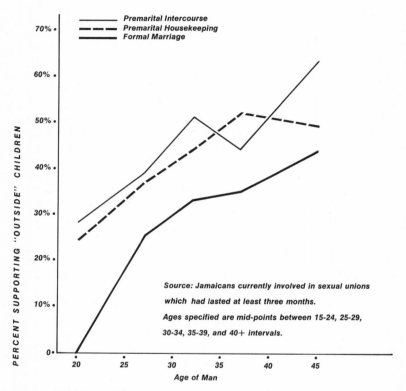

Adapted from Stycos and Back (1964):336.

The right to exclusive sexual access to one's spouse . . . is freely acknowledged to be a right which attaches to marriage. But there is no consensus
on sex rights in consensual unions. Some streetcorner men feel that a partner in a consensual union has a right to demand exclusive sexual access;
others deny this. Perhaps the majority feel that one has a right to expect
sexual exclusiveness but not to demand it. (1967:104)

The ambiguity in quasi-marriages with respect to sexual fidelity is merely
one facet of a larger picture of uncertainty in this half-married, half-not-
married state. Sometimes this uncertainty has advantages. Among the Nuer,
Evans-Pritchard (1951) found that concubines were sometimes treated more
considerately than wives. With no legal hold over his concubine, the man must
continue to court her or he might lose her to another man. On the other hand,
this same uncertainty led some Jamaican quasi-wives to exploit their men
financially since they could not depend on their support indefinitely. Women
tried to "drain the man financially, or to steal from him outright, in order to
secure a private cache for the inevitable 'rainy day' " (Blake, 1961:123).

Quite apart from such extraordinary features of quasi-marriages, they
suffered some of the same disillusionment and disenchantment that affect
ordinary marriages as time goes by, yet they were more vulnerable because
of their lack of institutional support. In Blake's words, premarital housekeeping "offers as full an opportunity for antipathy and ennui to develop as marriage itself offers, and yet it provides none of the institutional protection
against environmental interference (for example, "the other woman") that
marriage affords" (1951:145).

This lack of institutional support would weaken the stability of quasi-
marital relationships even if other things were equal. However, there is plenty
of evidence to suggest that ties between partners in quasi-marriages are seldom
as close as in real marriages.

TABLE 12-7   Cohesiveness of Quasi-Marital and Marital Relationships

| | MARITAL STATUS | | |
COHESIVENESS	*Premarital Intercourse*	*Premarital Housekeeping*	*Legal Marriage*
Woman feels closer to her man than to anyone else	20%	25%	43%
Mean communication score	4.4	5.8	6.3
Highly satisfied with partner's affection, understanding	46%	50%	64%

Adapted from Blake (1961):154 (the first item) and Stycos and Back (1964):341. Both studies
dealt with Jamaican respondents.

Table 12-7 shows that Jamaicans felt closer to the sexual partner the
more formalized their relationship was. Most women who were not legally
married felt closer to their mothers than to their partner. Such factors as less
communication with the man, less expression of affection, and a less understanding relationship contributed to the weakness of the man–woman relationship when couples were only keeping house temporarily or had only a sporadi-

cally visiting relationship. The effect of marriage on communication was especially interesting because married couples communicated frequently regardless of how satisfied they were with their relationship. In both kinds of quasi-marital relationships, however, couples communicated only if their relationship was relatively successful. In other words, the relationship tended to stand or fall on subjective feelings if couples were not married, whereas the more secure relationship of marriage sustained communication regardless of the feelings of the partners. This attests to the greater ability of marriage to survive the vagaries of subjective feelings.

Thus marriage is not only a stronger relationship from the standpoint of external approval but from the standpoint of the durability of the interpersonal relationship between the partners. Only legalization of the relationship firmly establishes a new family tie.

chapter thirteen
SOCIALIZATION OF THE MARRIAGE PARTNERS: ROLE INTEGRATION

Individuals who have survived the selection process and been formally inducted into their marital status then face the crucial test whether they will be able to function effectively in their new role. No matter how compatible the two partners are, there is always an adjustment to be worked out between the new recruit and the rest of the family (whether that remainder consists of only one spouse, an extended family, or a polygynous household). In order to work out a mutually satisfactory integration of family roles, one or more members of the family will have to alter his behavior. This alteration may be encouraged by explicit coaching or worked out by trial and error. If the new family consists of only two members, the accommodations are more likely to be mutual (but not, even then, if the culture requires one sex to submit to the other). If the new recruit joins a preexisting household, the newcomer will have to do most of the adjusting since she is a minority of one in a long-established social group. The more one-sided the adjustment process, the more explicitly the dominant side may be expected to teach the raw recruit what is expected of her.

In societies where marriage is preceded by a period of courtship, the process of working out an accommodation has already begun. The dating couple have gradually worked out patterns of decision-making, communication, lovemaking, and etiquette which carry over into marriage. Since courtship is when the foundations of marriage are laid, it is then that the partners' socialization begins. But since the formal enactment of the marriage markedly intensifies the relationship, much of the socialization process can only begin after that boundary line is crossed. Establishing a division of labor in the home, extending decision-making patterns to a wider range of issues, extending lovemaking to more intimate depths or at least to a new setting—such new tasks require the couple to work out new accommodations in the early years of marriage.

NEWLY-WEDDED: A CRITICAL PHASE

In most societies, newly-married couples are recognized as different from those who have been married longer. In some, they are even set apart in a separate category and given special privileges. To grant newlyweds special status is to recognize that they face special problems in making the transition from one status to another. So difficult are those problems that to be newly married can appropriately be called a critical phrase, even if in particular cases the crisis happens to be weathered smoothly.

The fatefulness of this phase can be seen in the frequency with which marriages fail at this juncture. In Java, for example, almost half (41.5 percent) of all divorces which ever occurred fell within the first year of marriage—and the most critical month was the very first, when 6 percent of all divorces were contracted (Geertz, 1961:73). In the United States, the concentration of marriage failures during the newlywed period is not quite so heavy. Nevertheless, Figure 13-1 shows that in the States also, separations leading to divorce form a J-curve with its peak in the first year.

For at least one partner if not both, marriage involves a transition from one family to another. To complete this transition successfully requires two processes. The individual must (1) leave his childhood family behind and (2) enter his new family. Each of these steps constitutes a potential crisis.

Crisis of Departure

For a young person who has lived all his life in one home and whose very life depended initially on his parents, dependency ties may be very strong. In most societies they are stronger for girls since girls are more apt to have been kept close to home to help with household chores and for protection against alien involvements. In any society, the earlier the marriage, the stronger the dependency feelings. For dependent young people as well as for parents, the departure of a child from the home may be almost as traumatic as bereavement.

One sign of difficulty in letting go is the frequency with which newly-married women visit their mothers. In Komarovsky's blue-collar American marriages, 92 percent of wives married less than seven years saw their mothers either every day or at least several times a week. For women married longer than that, the proportion seeing their mothers so intensively declined to 59 percent. For their less dependent husbands, the corresponding figures were 60 and 48 percent (1964:27).

This decline in intensive contact parallels the declining divorce rate portrayed in Figure 13-1, in part because excessive ties to parents sometimes prevent marriages from becoming successfully established in the first place. When one partner is overdependent, the other partner tends to be jealous and to develop hostility toward the in-laws.

Blood and Wolfe (1960) found that in-law conflicts were a major source of difficulty for newly married couples but declined rapidly in importance in later years. Specifically, they were 15 percent of the disagreements between newly-married couples but only 8 percent for couples with preschool chil-

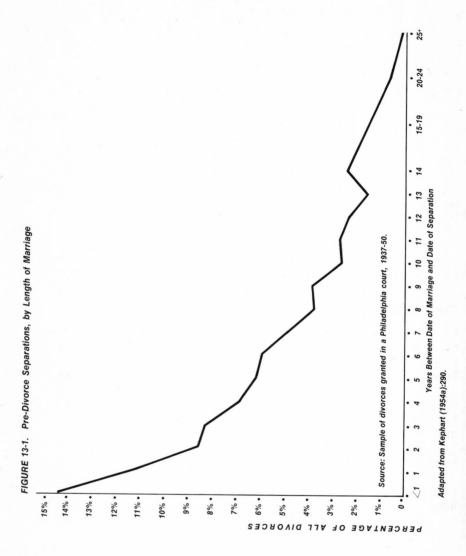

FIGURE 13-1.   Pre-Divorce Separations, by Length of Marriage

Source: Sample of divorces granted in a Philadelphia court, 1937-50.

Adapted from Kephart (1954a):290.

dren, 5 percent for couples with grade-school aged children, and a residual 2 percent for couples married longer than that.

As a cause of dissolution of Catholic marriages, Thomas (1956) found that in-law problems were especially prominent in marriages which broke up in their first year, declining in importance for marriages which dissolved later. Such findings do not mean that family-leaving problems are the most important single cause of difficulty in new marriages but that this problem tends to be concentrated in that transitional phase of marriage.

Some societies cushion these transitional problems by allowing new wives an interval of continued contact with their families. Characteristically this period ends with the birth of the first child, perhaps because a new mother must give so much attention to her child.

Among the Nuer, Evans-Pritchard found that both bride and groom remained with their own families until the birth of the first child. The only change for the bride during this interval was that she was given a hut of her own:

> When her husband comes to visit her in her father's homestead he sleeps with her in this hut. She continues in all other respects to lead the life she led before marriage, and after her husband's visits she hangs up the . . . domestic utensils and sleeps with her unmarried sisters. On these visits her husband stays at a neighbouring homestead as he cannot eat in the home of his parents-in-law and ought not to be seen there at all. When someone tells the wife that her husband has come, so that she may prepare for him, she feigns annoyance or lack of interest, pretending that she is still unmarried, a shyness she keeps up with third persons, though she is at ease when alone with her husband. When everyone is asleep he visits her and spends the night with her, leaving before any of the bride's people are about. Her parents are supposed to know nothing of his visits. . . . (1951:72)

Such surreptitious visiting is an extreme arrangement but one which buffers the departure crisis for both bride and groom.

Crisis of Accession

To marry is not always to precipitate a crisis of departure because some people leave home prior to marriage. However, marriage always creates a problem of accession because sooner or later the husband and wife must begin living together. Then all the problems involved in working out a smoothly functioning relationship inevitably are confronted. If a couple have had a long and thorough courtship, they may be well prepared to face those problems. If their courtship has been brief or nonexistent, the crisis may be severe. In Java, Geertz believed that it was a major source of the brittleness of new marriages:

> The young couple, often unacquainted before marriage, inexperienced in sex, and forced to make a rapid transition to adult life, experience considerable emotional strain. . . . The difficulty of emotional adjustment, especially for a very young girl married to a strange man, is recognized in

the folk belief that during the first thirty-five days the couple are suscep-
tible to attacks by evil spirits and for this reason should remain secluded
in the house of the girl's mother. (1961:73)

The less the couple know each other before marriage, the more difficult a
sudden plunge into complete marital intimacy must necessarily be.

For wives joining a compound family the Filipino Ilocos cushioned the
shock by allowing considerable autonomy during the newlywed period:

> The emotional transition at marriage is eased by the autonomy of the
> new household. No in-law would presume to take over the management of
> the new bride's house unless specifically requested during illness or child-
> birth. This is particularly true of the kitchen, which is a woman's private
> domain. Advice is constantly given, but there is no authority to lend it
> weight unless the husband chooses to argue in favor of his family's attitude.
> In general, however, a husband should and does stay aloof from such
> "women's" disagreements, and they rarely reach a serious state. After her
> first child is born the new wife relies with greater frequency on the advice,
> help and friendship of her husband's relatives, and soon she is a part of
> this intimate group—"we who share the same yard" replace those com-
> panions to whom she said goodbye on her wedding day. (Nydegger and
> Nydegger, 1963:745)

In this decentralized compound where only the yard is shared and not
the whole household economy, a multistage transition to family living was
possible. The newly-married period was devoted to working out relations
with the husband. Only subsequently were intimate relations established with
his surrounding relatives. Such gradual integration is not possible if the whole
family lives as a single unit. Then the newcomer is exposed all at once to
an established family structure which she enters as an outsider.

Although in nuclear families the main crisis involves establishing a
working relationship between the husband and wife, a subsidiary task is
to learn to get along with in-laws even when they do not live in the same
house. Insofar as modern societies have a matrilateral bias, this may require the new husband to do most of the adjusting. He is the stranger in a
family whose center is the maternal grandmother. In any case, whichever
partner has the most frequent contact with his in-laws will face the greater
test of his ability to adapt to new relatives.

SOCIALIZATION BY THE SPOUSE

Once a marriage begins, the most appropriate teacher for most aspects of
marriage is the partner (though we will see that for certain purposes, teachers
of the same sex may be more useful than of the opposite sex).

Sexual Relations

The most intimate aspect of marriage is an area where the partners can be
helped least by outsiders because of the private nature of sexuality, and
helped most by each other. It may be no accident that sexual and affectional

needs head the list of trouble spots in the relatively new student marriages portrayed in Table 13-1.

TABLE 13-1 Complaints of Role Expectation Violations, by Newly-Married Husbands and Wives

| | PARTNER COMPLAINING OF ROLE EXPECTATION VIOLATION BY SPOUSE | |
BEHAVIOR	Husband	Wife
Frequency of sexual intercourse	23%	15%
Verbal expression of affection	20	19
Care of the home	17	19
Sharing of ideas	16	14
Spending family income	12	11
Personal neatness and appearance	9	8
Spending time at home	3	14
Total complaints	100%	100%
Number of complaints	94	134
Number of respondents	60	60

Adapted from Cutler and Dyer (1965):198. Source: Campus marriages at Brigham Young University (Utah) in which the husband was less than 23 years old.

Each complaint in the table represents an area in which one partner's expectation for marriage was disappointed by the other. All represented discrepancies which either had to be resolved or would be a continuing source of difficulty.

The table shows that husbands were more apt than wives to complain that their expectations about the frequency of intercourse were violated by the spouse. Presumably in most cases the wife was not willing to have intercourse as often as the husband expected. Indeed, for most of the items listed in the table, it seems likely that the chief difficulty was failure of the partner to perform an expected act (except in the financial area where the problem may have been spending too much money).

To reach an accommodation about when to have intercourse is the most obvious of the sexual tasks of newly-married couples. More fundamentally, inexperienced women must learn how to respond to sexual stimulation. In contrast to men whose sexual climaxes normally begin in infancy and occur frequently throughout adolescence in "wet dreams," masturbation, heterosexual petting and/or intercourse, most American girls come to marriage with relatively little experience in orgasm. (Kinsey [1953] found that the typical single girl had not had her first orgasm until she was 20 years old.)

Figure 13-2 shows that only half of Kinsey's women experienced orgasm during the first month of marriage despite the intensive sexual activity of the honeymoon. By the end of the first year, the typical wife was still having an orgasm less than two-thirds of the time, but in each succeeding five-year period this physiological response became more regular.

While much of the wife's response depends on having had intercourse sufficiently often, I assume that the husband's cooperation is also helpful. For both partners, techniques of foreplay can only partially be learned from

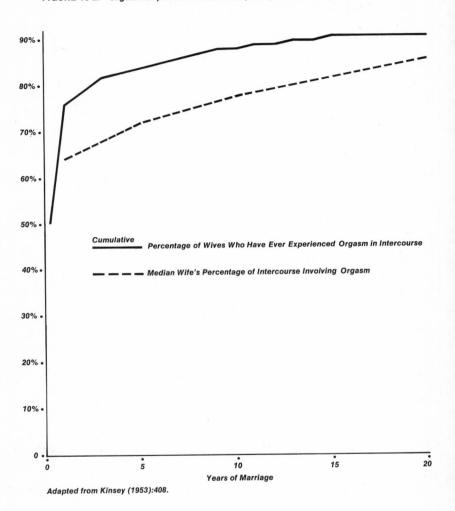

FIGURE 13-2.   Orgasm Experience of Wives, by Length of Marriage

Cumulative _____ Percentage of Wives Who Have Ever Experienced Orgasm in Intercourse

— — — — Median Wife's Percentage of Intercourse Involving Orgasm

Years of Marriage

Adapted from Kinsey (1953):408.

marriage manuals. Success in arousing the partner depends on responding to his/her idiosyncratic preferences. This can be discovered only by communication and feedback between partners. This involves learning both what the partner likes and what he dislikes. The dangers of not learning the latter lesson can be seen in Kephart's (1954b) finding that a large proportion of Philadelphia wives who initiated divorce suits between 1937 and 1950 blamed their husbands for demanding oral-genital contact.

Whereas the main problem for wives is to learn to respond sexually, the problem for husbands is precisely the opposite—to learn to control their response in order to coordinate their sexual experience with the wife's. The problem of "slow" wives and "fast" husbands is most acute in the early years of marriage. Age slows down the male response so that eventually the problem of coordination becomes less difficult. Nevertheless in the critical early years of marriage, men may have to teach their wives how not to overstimulate them at the same time the wives are teaching their husbands how to stimulate them most successfully.

Practical Matters

It would be possible to discuss at length the complexities of socializing the partner into the individual's wishes for affection, companionship, and emotional therapy, but perhaps the previous discussion of sexual socialization will suffice to illustrate the lessons to be learned in such interpersonal areas.

Three of the seven topics complained about by Cutler and Dyer's married students were very practical matters: care of the home, spending money, and personal appearance. Although courtship offers opportunities for learning one another's social and psychological expectations, most practical matters cannot be worked on until joint housekeeping actually begins. Even personal appearance acquires new dimensions for couples no longer restricted to carefully prepared dates but who face each other across the proverbial breakfast table on "the morning after."

Keeping house with no mother around to help out means that any task the wife doesn't wish to do, the husband must (and vice versa). In traditional societies, there may be no dispute about who does what if jobs are assigned uniquely to one sex or the other. In modern societies, however, such a sex-linked division of labor tends to break down as different families work out different patterns. One consequence is that each partner may come to marriage expecting the other to carry out the rubbish because the man's mother did it and the wife's father did it. Marriage means discovering which tasks are left undone because neither partner wants to do them. Such gaps must be plugged quickly if the household operation is not to break down.

Wolfe and I (1960) found that newly-married Detroit couples shared a relatively large number of tasks at the beginning of marriage but the longer they were married, the fewer they shared. Presumably couples initially work together partly because they enjoy each other's company. Partly, however, the beginning of marriage is a trial-and-error period of discovering which partner can do things best. Gradually each partner ceases to be a jack-of-all-trades and masters the ones he can do best. In the process, an increasingly rigid division of labor emerges between the partners.

Learning to live within one's income is difficult enough for a single person but more complicated when two people are spending for their separate and joint needs. Keeping accounts and budgeting are new tasks for most couples. Filling out income tax forms becomes more complicated after couples buy their first house. Managing a joint checking account is a delicate feat in interpersonal coordination.

There is little point in listing all the lessons which newlyweds must learn. I hope by now it is apparent that husband and wife have much to teach each other and much to learn from experimenting with alternative solutions to their new problems.

SOCIALIZATION BY THE HOUSEHOLD ELDERS

In a neolocal home where husband and wife live alone together, no one else is available to give instruction in marriage roles and no one else need be considered in dividing up responsibilities. In the complicated situation presented by extended and polygynous households, other tutors are not only available but they tend to assume the main responsibility for role induction. Typically the partner moving into such a household is the wife and the person who becomes her coach is the top woman in the household. In extended families, the head woman is the family matriarch (the wife's mother-in-law); in polygynous families it is the Number One Wife.

The Mother-in-Law

In extended families, the emotional aspects of the husband–wife relationship are suppressed by the presence of many chaperones. The division of labor follows rigid sex lines so there are no ambiguities to be worked out between the partners. But the new recruit alters the division of labor among the women of the household. If she is the first bride to be added in the junior generation, she becomes her mother-in-law's only servant. If there are other women already in the family, she becomes the servant of all. In either case, her mother-in-law is the mistress of the house and must train the new servant to become a useful member of the household.

The responsibility of the matriarch for socializing her daughter-in-law has been a standard feature of extended family systems. Among Greek shepherds, a new bride had many tasks to perform:

> . . . the new bride is subordinate to all other adults in the extended family. Even the five-year-olds try with varying success to boss the new "bride." As a worker her services belong to the whole group. She is, as they often say, "our bride." Not only does she care for the comfort of her own husband but she is responsible for washing, mending, and darning the clothes of all his unmarried brothers. In general, it can be said that any hard or unpleasant work will be delegated to her. A mule to be rounded up, water to be carried —the new bride is certain to be sent. "She must learn our ways," the other women explain, "and she must take root in her new family. Besides, she has no children to care for." The bride takes most of her orders from her

mother-in-law under whose critical and watchful direction she works. But she must be prepared to carry out requests from any brother, sister, or other more senior bride of the extended family. (Campbell, 1964:64)

Extended families are hierarchical social structures which new recruits enter at the bottom and gradually climb to the top. One reason why new brides are given undesirable tasks is simply that no one else wants to do them and the novice is the most defenseless member of the family. Like new soldiers assigned to K.P. duty or the boss' son starting out as office boy, such assignments are also supposed to be good for the novitiate's character.

Another reason why new recruits are given the dirty work is a displaced retaliation against the mother-in-law's own harsh induction a generation earlier. Like fraternity members determined that new pledges not escape the hazing they experienced at the hands of their elder "brothers," mothers-in-law seize the opportunity to wreak revenge on the helpless newcomer.

The bride is helpless because neither her relatives nor her husband dares challenge her mother-in-law's tutelage. In China, for example:

> The young bride [had] the duty of adjusting to her in-laws, especially to her mother-in-law, and her husband was not supposed to interfere, or even to establish a close emotional tie with his wife. Since she came from another geographical area, and was not surrounded by her own kin, she had no external kin support (except under extreme conditions). . . . A middle-class bride might be forced to make shoes for her husband's family as a symbol of her subservience, and she was supposed to rise before anyone else and bring tea to her mother-in-law. (Goode, 1963:309)

Another motive for exploiting the daughter-in-law is simply jealousy. In extended families, mother–son ties are very strong. The young bride is a threat to this intimacy. Levy (1949) noted that the feudal Chinese mother-in-law's treatment of her daughter-in-law was "quite frequently harsh, vindictive, and unjust." Matriarchs took advantage of their position not simply to teach their daughters-in-law the necessary skills but to remove the scars left by their own traumatic experiences a generation earlier.

In China the penalties on a young bride for failing to learn her lessons properly were severe. Whereas in neolocal families, divorce results from failure of the couple to work out a mutual accommodation, in extended Chinese families, the chief cause of divorce was the inability of the mother-in-law and daughter-in-law to achieve a satisfactory relationship. Even though the matriarch normally played an active role in selecting the new bride, this did not guarantee that the newcomer would swallow the bitter medicine she was liable to be administered under the guise of teaching her what she needed to know. Levy reported that "there were many cases of a daughter-in-law forced out of the family because she had incurred the disapproval of her mother-in-law" (1949:110). The mother-in-law was both the main educator of the bride and the main judge of whether she passed the test.

In extended families, thus, the process of socialization was initially severe and the consequences of failure particularly harsh. But what if the new

bride performed her functions well? What if she bore a son to carry on the
family line and thereby made the whole family indebted to her? Then she
would be graduated from the role of novitiate into an accepted member of
the family and her treatment would correspondingly improve. Once she became a mother, her socialization for all practical purposes was finished.

Campbell described this ultimate role transition for Greek shepherd
families:

> After one or two years most brides have become mothers. This . . .
> brings about a great change in the bride's position in the extended family.
> Previously . . . she remained a stranger even in the eyes of her own
> husband. After the birth of her first child it is said that the new bride "takes
> root in the new family". . . . The arrival of the child is received with joy
> by the whole extended family whose attitude towards the bride shifts from
> tolerance to acceptance and affection for her as the mother of their tiny
> kinsman. . . .
> At this time the husband's behaviour towards his wife undergoes fun-
> damental changes. He now begins to talk with her more freely before other
> members of the family. She is not any longer merely the conjugal partner
> with whom he has sexual relations, which even in marriage possess a sus-
> pect if not exactly shameful quality. She is now the mother of his child;
> and in this role, especially if her infant is a son, the husband openly rec-
> ognizes his wife without the ambivalence which previously attached to their
> relationship. . . . After the birth of the first child the bride does not
> usually continue to address her husband's brothers and sisters as . . .
> "master" and "mistress"; instead she uses their Christian names. And if,
> by this time, a younger brother of her husband has been married, the family
> no longer address her as "bride" but use the name of her husband with
> the suffix "-ina" added. . . . These changes . . . reflect . . . the growing
> equality in the relationships of the wife with the members of her husband's
> family of origin who are of her own generation. It is also significant that
> no member of the extended family, except the parents-in-law, any longer
> orders her about in peremptory fashion in the presence of her husband,
> let alone attempts to scold or discipline her. (1964:69)

The extended family's abandonment of scolding and disciplining certifies to
the wife's graduation from domestic socialization into full-fledged membership
in the group.

The Number One Wife

Polygynous households face some of the same problems in adding a new wife,
but they are more severe. If the mother in an extended family feels jealous
when her son marries, that jealousy is minimized by the knowledge that she
has a whole generation's precedence over the wife. Moreover wives and mothers do not compete directly for the husband's affection. Theoretically a man
may love these two women complementarily. But when a man takes on two
wives, they "compete in the same league." Problems of jealousy are so endemic in polygynous households that most polygynous societies have devised
institutionalized ways of minimizing the disruptive threat of this jealousy.

A common solution to the first wife's resentment is to give her some of the same privileges exercised by the matriarch in an extended family. By being given authority over subsequent wives, the first wife's psychological loss in having to share her husband's affection is offset by acquiring a maid-servant.

But whereas extended family systems universally assign socialization responsibility to the matriarch, polygynous societies differ in the extent to which they give authority to the first wife. Sometimes each wife is established in a separate hut, raising her own food and doing her own cooking. Under such decentralization, each hut becomes a neolocal household sharing half a husband. This gives the husband more responsibility for socializing the new wife since his contact with her may be greater than the first wife's.

Nevertheless, if the new bride is to fit into the complicated family she has entered, she will need to accept the tutelage of all the members of that family and more especially that of her senior wife. In systems of sororal polygyny where the husband is expected to marry sisters in order of birth, the authority of the elder sister is likely to have been accepted by the younger long before either of them ever thought of marriage. Where the new bride comes in as a comparative stranger to the first wife, integration is more difficult, but a tactful bride will learn how to get along with her co-wife (or co-wives) in order to minimize friction.

If wives were not born in the same family, they may differ in age enough to make it easier for the new bride to accept the authority of a first wife who is markedly older. In one Kenyan community, LeVine and LeVine found that three polygynous households were exceptions to the general rule of friction between wives. In all three, the first wives were much older than the newcomer, sometimes old enough to be like a mother:

> In these cases the younger wife has accepted domination by the older, working with her in the fields, asking her advice and help in child care, gossiping casually with her in the afternoon, and so on. Where co-wives are closer in age, they may be superficially polite and cooperative but harbor grudges which result in their not talking for months at a time. (1963:43)

The larger the age gap, the easier it is for the first wife to be accepted as the legitimate socializing agent of the junior wives. In any case, the more the first wife is able to play that role (for whatever reason), the more effectively the newcomer will be integrated into the family.

SOCIALIZATION BY EXTERNAL ROLE INCUMBENTS

The primary task of socializing new recruits belongs to members of the household, but outsiders sometimes assist in the process. Outside help is hardly needed in complex families already staffed with potential teachers, but in nuclear families a same-sex coach is sometimes needed. This must necessarily be someone from outside the marriage, and the natural place to turn is to others who play a similar role. Women turn to other wives and men to other husbands for advice and counsel. The chief difference between insiders and outsiders is that the former have a legitimate right to teach the newcomer how to fit into the family, whereas the latter are merely optional resources to be consulted at the novice's discretion.

Relatives

Even for those who do not live in extended-family households, relatives are a natural place to turn. Earlier chapters revealed how often women turn to their mothers and married sisters with their marital problems. They also turn to their mothers-in-law as experts on the care and feeding of the man who was once a son and has now become a husband.

Friends

If relatives are not available due to geographical barriers or for other reasons, friends are an alternative source of information about other people's marriages. In a study of the extent to which New Yorkers knew about other people's marital problems, Mayer (1966b) found that middle-class wives were especially familiar with the problems of friends rather than relatives. They had gained their information primarily from the friends directly (and only secondarily by "putting two and two together" or being informed by third parties). Direct communication presumably provides the best basis for socialization into both the problems and solutions which close friends have encountered. Learning that others have similar problems reduces the burden on couples who take their problems too seriously. Learning what solutions others have devised increases the repertoire of role behavior which the couple may apply in their own marriage. Where learning from relatives and friends is inadequate, group therapy with married couples may serve a similar socialization function (as we will see in Chapter 24).

RESOCIALIZATION TO CHANGING ROLES

It would be wrong to assume that one learns all there is to know about being a husband or wife in the first years of marriage. Even though the early years are crucial for discovering a *modus vivendi,* life is not static and role changes must be made throughout the entire span of marriage.

A Changing Partner

One reason the wife must change is that her husband changes (and vice versa). In a 20-year follow-up study of couples whose average age initially was 25, Kelly (1955) found that both sexes changed more than they remained the same. Specifically they changed 52 percent of their values, 55 percent of their vocational interests, 69 percent of their self-rated personality characteristics, and 92 percent of their attitudes. Although these changes had been gradual, an enormous amount of cumulative adjusting must have been required of their spouses. In some areas, couples grew more alike (chiefly in more positive attitudes toward marriage and the church as social institutions). But on the whole, changes were random, leaving the couples slightly less alike than they had been in the beginning. Obviously these couples had not succeeded in teaching one another to become more alike. Hence resocialization partly means learning to get along with differences, including new and unexpected differences which could not have been foreseen when the couple got engaged.

Nelson Foote (1956) pointed out that most friendships do not last a lifetime, so the problem of modern marriage is to find ways in which it can become an exception to the general rule. When interests change, friends grow apart. If married couples are not to do the same, they cannot rest content with having found a good partner, but must engage in a continuous process of matching their phases of development. Matching can occur only if couples communicate their emerging interests. Indeed, Foote suggested, married individuals can not only adapt to spontaneous changes in their partners but can become agents in each other's growth and development. By serving as sympathetic critics of each other's "performances," the couple can provide each other with invaluable feedback which could be obtained nowhere else save in a sensitivity training group. Thus marriage at its best becomes a life-long training center for the development of mutual sensitivity.

A Changing Relationship

Regardless of the random changes which occur in the partners as individuals, marriages undergo progressive changes by virtue of the passage of time. (The consequences of introducing children into the family will be reserved for the next chapter.) An old-established relationship tends to be different from a new relationship. Therefore part of the resocialization process after marriage involves adapting to the effects of time on the relationship.

Increasing Segregation   We have already referred to the fact that housework becomes more specialized in the United States the longer couples have been married. Table 13-2 shows that this applies even more strikingly to Tokyo than to Detroit, and to decision-making as well as to keeping house.

TABLE 13-2   Role Segregation, by Length of Marriage

ROLE	LENGTH OF MARRIAGE		DIRECTION OF CHANGE
	Newly-Married	*Older-Married*	
Unilateral decisions			
Tokyo	1.66	1.96	+
Detroit	3.70	3.76	+
Unilateral household tasks			
Tokyo	3.23	3.74	+
Detroit	4.92	4.96	+
Number of couples			
Tokyo	167	27	
Detroit	30	56	

Adapted from Blood (1967):225. Source: Middle-class Tokyo couples under age 40 and cross-section Detroit couples married not more than 15 years. Newly-married couples in Tokyo were defined as married less than five years, in Detroit less than four years. All data restricted to childless couples. Note that decision and task items were not identical for the two cities.

In general, then, couples begin their married life with a relatively high degree of sharing of family responsibilities, but as time goes on tend to specialize more and more in areas of their own interest and competence. The result may be increased efficiency of role performance but also less togetherness in the marriage.

Decreasing Interaction   In one sense, increased segregation and decreased interaction mean the same thing. However, in the former case I referred to specialization of objective task performance, whereas I now am interested in the purely sociable aspects of marriage. Presumably it does not destroy the marriage if chores are done or decisions made more unilaterally in the later years of marriage. But if the husband and wife have less of any kind of interaction, time clearly has corroded their marriage. Numerous studies demonstrate that decreasing interaction indeed generally occurs.

One cause of decreased interaction is old age. The older people get, the less energy they have for any kind of activity. The effect of aging is especially apparent in activities with a major biological component such as playing football or having sexual intercourse. For women, the capacity to have intercourse is hardly affected by age; indeed, we have already seen that orgasm capacity tends to improve with experience. For men, however, the contrary is true.

The capacity to achieve an erection and to ejaculate declined rapidly after age 55 for Kinsey's sample of American males. Moreover, the impulse to intercourse begins to wane far earlier in life. (Total sexual "outlet" of Kinsey's males declined steadily from a high point in the late teens.) The profound impact of the man's aging on the sexual life of married couples is visible in Figure 13-3.

Figure 13-3 shows that frequency of marital intercourse steadily declined as the husband grew older. However, it also shows that his total sexual experience declined even more sharply as nocturnal emissions and masturbation gradually disappeared from his repertoire and extramarital intercourse became less frequent. This suggests that the man's declining sexual capacity is a major factor in the decreasing frequency of marital intercourse, whereas boredom and other nonbiological consequences of length of marriage may be only secondarily involved.

Aging is a less meaningful explanation, however, for decreases in such simple activities as expressing affection and communicating information between the partners. Yet Table 13-3 shows that interspousal communication decreased in two different countries when older-married couples were compared with newly-married couples. These data are especially interesting because they are based on childless couples who differed only in the number of years they had been married.

The expression of affection, informative companionship, and therapeutic utilization of the partner portrayed in the table are not the only forms of interspousal communication which wane with time. In the same study, I found that Tokyo couples also discussed the news less often after the first few years of marriage. They also spent less time together on "dates," going out as a couple just to have a good time. Indeed, it may be significant that in Tokyo the decline in going out as a couple was partially offset by an increase in double-dating, *i.e.*, in getting together with other married couples. This shift

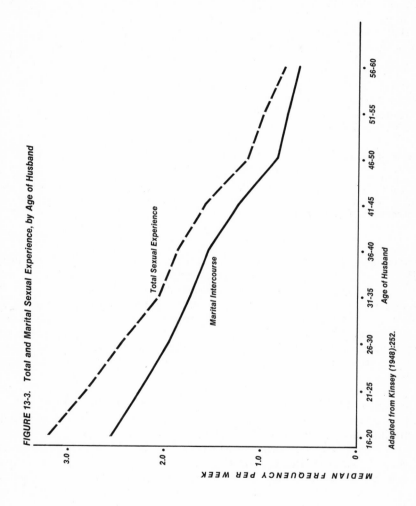

FIGURE 13-3. Total and Marital Sexual Experience, by Age of Husband

Total Sexual Experience

Marital Intercourse

MEDIAN FREQUENCY PER WEEK

3.0

2.0

1.0

0

16-20 21-25 26-30 31-35 36-40 41-45 46-50 51-55 56-60

Age of Husband

Adapted from Kinsey (1948):252.

TABLE 13-3 Interspousal Communication, by Length of Marriage

| | | LENGTH OF MARRIAGE | | DIRECTION OF CHANGE |
TYPE OF COMMUNICATION	CITY	Newly-Married	Older-Married	
Affection				
Husband expresses affection	Tokyo	178	133	—
Personal Events				
Husband tells events	Tokyo	194	164	—
	Detroit	220	184	—
Wife tells events	Tokyo	240	222	—
Personal Troubles				
Husband tells troubles	Tokyo	2.45	2.22	—
Wife tells troubles	Tokyo	3.18	2.96	—
	Detroit	2.63	2.34	—
Number of couples	Tokyo	167	27	
	Detroit	30	56	

Adapted from Blood (1967):226–227. Source: See Table 13-2. Frequencies of telling events which happened during the day and of expressing affection are estimated annual frequencies. Frequencies of telling troubles after a bad day are weighted on a scale from "always" = 4 to "never" = 0.

demonstrates that the problem is not entirely a lack of energy, but partly a shift in the focus of attention from the partner to a broader group.

Why, then, do married couples do less and less together, the longer they are married? One hypothesis might be that the more they have done together before, the less necessary it becomes to repeat those activities. For example, if a man has told his wife he loves her a thousand times, she should know it henceforth without needing to be told. When two people have discussed the day's events every day for years, "So, what's new?" may get a less enthusiastic answer.

Granted that couples may tire of saying the same things and doing the same things, the question is whether memories of past interaction suffice to replace present interaction. That they do not is suggested by sharp declines in marital satisfaction I found for both Tokyo husbands and wives and for Detroit wives. This decreased satisfaction affected almost all the interactive aspects of marriage. Indeed, the only areas where satisfaction generally improved had to do not with interpersonal relationship between the partners but rather with their ability to perform their separate roles: the husband's ability to support the family financially, and the wife's to spend his money wisely and manage the household successfully. In these practical areas where the partners do their own work separately, practice made perfect. By contrast, both husbands' and wives' satisfaction with each other's love, sex, companionship, and courtesy declined almost without exception.

Decreasing interaction, then, cannot be explained away on the grounds that it is not needed. Rather, each partner gives less and less to the other in spite (or perhaps because?) of his own growing dissatisfaction. Older couples make less effort to make their marriages work, even though the amount of effort which might be required to make the marriage grow might not be staggering. Sustained interaction in marriage is possible but exceptional. Most couples allow their marriages to "go to seed," once the novelty wears off and they begin taking each other for granted. This is an all too human reaction to the difference between fresh and accustomed relationships. In any case, decreasing interaction can be expected in the average marriage and makes some kind of resocialization necessary—either by learning to accept the growing estrangement or (for the vigorous minority) learning to respond to the threat of disengagement by new programs of marital revitalization.

The most comforting aspect of the passage of time is that disagreements between husbands and wives become less frequent. Wolfe and I (1960) found that whereas only 15 percent of newly-married couples had no major disagreements (and even fewer parents could report that they were trouble-free), 26 percent of older couples whose children had left home and 31 percent of those who never had children could report the same. Perhaps the later years of marriage are a bit sad, but at least they are more peaceful. Carried too far, however, the disengagement of older couples may doom the marriage even though nobody realizes what has happened. To have no disagreements may mean that conflicts have been resolved—or it may mean that couples no longer take the trouble to confront each other.

By recruiting a mate, a marriage can be established, but it takes children to make a family. The world around, children come in widely varying numbers and on equally diversified schedules. The consequences for family life vary accordingly. But children do not stay forever except in extended families, which those of either one or the other sex never leave. In nuclear family systems, children of both sexes leave, returning the organization to its original dyad.

Fundamentally, these processes of expansion and contraction are biological. But the family is a social organization, so children (like marriage partners) must be socialized into the organizational norms.

These twin processes of reproduction and socialization make possible the growth of families.

chapter fourteen
ACQUISITION OF CHILDREN: ORGANIZATIONAL EXPANSION AND CONTRACTION

In some families, the arrival of children is planned in advance and controlled in execution. But in most of the world's families, children come by chance. Even if they are planned for, they profoundly alter family life. The larger the number of children, the closer they are bunched together; and the more abnormal they are, the greater the alteration. The task of this chapter is to assess the consequences of acquiring varying numbers and types of children at varying points in the life of the family.

SOURCES OF CHILDREN

All children are born to someone, but not all children are raised by their biological parents. From the standpoint of family life, what matters is not the biological reproduction but the social induction of children into the families to which they will belong. Bearing one's own children and adoption are alternative ways of recruiting children into the family.

Reproduction

To produce one's own children has both advantages and disadvantages. The chief advantage is that the parents confer their own genes on the child, making him a biological member of the family. This means that his physical appearance is likely to resemble at least one of his parents and some of his siblings, making it easier for him to be identified as a member of his family. Secondly, the fact that he is a biological member of that family gives both him and his parents a feeling that he belongs there. This feeling is intensified for the mother by having grown him in her womb for nine months, given birth to him, and suckled him. These biological sources of membership in the family aid both generations in surviving later stresses in interpersonal relations.

The chief disadvantage of producing one's own children is that it is difficult to control. Despite improvements in the technical efficiency of contraceptives, Table 2-11 showed that as recently as 1960 hardly more than half of the college-educated wives in the United States succeeded in avoiding unwanted pregnancies (Whelpton *et al.* 1966). A large proportion of women of all educational levels had at least one "accidental" pregnancy while they were supposedly practicing contraception. Freedman *et al.* (1959) found that most failures resulted from temporarily discontinuing the method, rather than from failures of the method itself, with the chief exception being the relatively unreliable rhythm method. Nevertheless, such "human failures" must be accepted as part of the human condition.

The difficulty of coping with an unplanned first child is suggested by Dyer's finding (1963) that only 26 percent of middle-class couples who planned the birth of their first child experienced an extensive or severe crisis, compared to 92 percent of those whose plans failed or who had no plan.

Relatively few American mothers reported to Whelpton and his associates that they had had more children than they wanted, but that is a slippery figure because some women adapt their preferences to actualities once they are confronted with an unintended extra pregnancy.

The fact that an unwanted child is conceived does not necessarily mean that an unwanted child will be added to the family. Table 14-1 shows that

TABLE 14-1   Outcome of Pregnancy by Marital Status

| | MARITAL STATUS OF WOMAN AT CONCEPTION | | |
OUTCOME OF PREGNANCY	Premarital	Extramarital	Marital
Live birth			
Legitimate	15%	16%	66%
Illegitimate	5	—	—
Abortion			
Spontaneous	4	16	17
Induced	76	69	17
Total	100%	101%	100%
Number of conceptions	417	32	3,645

Adapted from Gebhard, Pomeroy, Martin, and Christenson (1958):77, 99, 137. Source: Nonrandom sample of white women interviewed between 1938 and 1955, U.S.A.

the great majority of children conceived out of wedlock by white American women were destroyed by induced abortion (usually under illegal auspices). Even for married women, contraceptive failure was often compensated for by abortion.

In some foreign countries, contraceptive practice is less effective than in the United States, and abortion is more extensively utilized to protect the family against unwanted children. In Japan, legalized abortions were estimated to be the fate of more than half of all *marital* conceptions in the 1960s. In most advanced countries, therefore, contraception and abortion (whether legal or illegal) provide defense in depth against unwanted family expansion. Only in underdeveloped countries is unlimited reproduction any longer a general hazard for families.

It is not enough, however, for contraceptives to be invented or even for them to be made freely available in public health clinics. To be effective, they must be understood and used. In many transitional societies, neither knowledge nor use is widespread.

In Jamaica, Blake (1961) found that most lower-class women knew little or nothing about sexual relations or pregnancy before experiencing them. The women were especially ignorant about the causal relationship between intercourse and conception—a fatal flaw if conception is to be prevented. Even in the United States, Vincent (1961) found that unwed mothers were unusually ignorant about sex.

In Puerto Rico, Hill, Stycos, and Back found that married couples frequently delayed using contraceptives until after they already had more children than they wanted. Even sterilization of one parent (the only fool-proof method of preventing births), was "typically performed after so many births that it does little to affect family size" (1959:248). For most of the world's families, then, protective measures against overreproduction are too little and too late.

A smaller number of families cannot rely on biological reproduction because of infertility. With advances in medical science, this problem is being reduced for those who are geographically and financially within reach of such services. Nevertheless, even in the United States, fertility impairments were still a hazard in the 1950s, increasing with the age of the wife (see Table 14-2).

Couples must have tried to conceive for a considerable time before their ability to conceive can be adequately tested. Table 14-2 therefore conservatively estimates the number of women who have difficulty in having children of their own. On the other hand, roughly half of the definitely sterile women were this way because they wanted to be: *i.e.,* they had been sterilized for contraceptive purposes. In any case, the ability to bear children cannot be taken for granted even in young marriages.

Adoption

For couples unable to have children of their own or who wish children of a particular sex or with certain qualities their own children lack, adoption is the alternative. On the other hand, adoption is sometimes motivated by the need

TABLE 14-2 Reproductive Capacity, by Age of Wife

REPRODUCTIVE CAPACITY	AGE OF WIFE			
	20–24	25–29	30–34	35–39
Definitely fecund	86%	79%	64%	53%
Possibly fecund	5	8	11	8
Possibly sterile	5	5	9	13
Probably sterile	1	2	3	7
Definitely sterile	3	6	13	19
Total	100%	100%	100%	100%
Number of women	440	600	624	677

Adapted from Whelpton, Campbell, and Patterson (1966):161. Source: U. S. national sample of white wives. The classifications are based partly on doctor's opinions and partly on the number of years the wife had failed to conceive in the absence of using any method of contraception (more than 10 years for the probably sterile, 3–9 years for the possibly sterile, up to three years for the possibly fecund).

of the child, rather than of his new parents. In that case, it may create as many problems for the parents as an unwanted child of their own.

Childless Couples   Couples unable to bear children must acquire them elsewhere. The most readily available resource is the unwanted children of others, especially those born to unmarried mothers. Secondary sources are the surplus children of large familes and those whose parents have died or become incapacitated. If such children are not available, the kinship system may require larger family units to share even wanted children with their childless relatives. Sometimes this obligation benefits even spinsters. One of my Japanese friends, an unmarried college professor, was given a niece to raise as a daughter in order that she would have someone to care for her in her old age.

In the Philippines, the Nydeggers found that even grandparents whose own children had already left home adopted grandchildren to fill the vacuum. In this case, adoption occurred when the child was old enough to make up his own mind whether he wished to stay with his parents or move to his grandparents. This required the latter to "court" the child in order to win his favor in a fashion analogous to recruiting a marriage partner.

> Parents will not allow adoption of their first-born, but the second child, especially if the second is of the same sex, is a favorite for this purpose. The process is gradual. The grandparents coax the child to eat with them more often, fuss over him a great deal more than his busy parents can, buy him expensive tidbits, nice clothes, encourage him to sleep at their house. After a period of six months to a year, during which time the child resides in both households, he either takes up permanent residence in the newer household or, if unwilling, is passed over in favor of the next child. (1963:853)

How do parent–child relationships after adoption compare with those resulting from natural reproduction? That there may be a difference is suggested by the Japanese use of the term "pseudo-family relations" for adoption.

A study of 100 adoptive children in the United States compared with a matched group of bio-children showed that more of the former were referred for psychiatric treatment because of uncontrollable behavior in school (Work, 1968). Examination of their family background showed that adoptive parents overprotected their children in much the same way that Levy (1966) found for parents whose bio-children had been conceived with difficulty, had been carried to full term with difficulty, or had narrowly escaped death through illness. Whenever children are hard won (as by waiting patiently to adopt) or nearly lost, those children tend to be viewed as extra special and given extra attention.

A second characteristic of adoptive parents is that they put heavy pressure on the child to conform to the family. This seemed to result from viewing the child as something of an outsider:

> The demands the adoptive parents make on the child for conformity, for being like the family, tend to be high. They stress family values and discipline and discourage independence. The parents seem to say, "Be like us. You're part of our family now." (Work, 1968)

Presumably with "normal" children, belonging to the family is taken for granted so children are allowed to speak their own minds and have the normal freedom of behavior. The point is not that normal children are undisciplined but that adopted children are over-disciplined.

Thirdly, Work found that adoptive parents were less apt than normal parents to turn to the usual sources of advice on children's problems—relatives and friends. Instead they more often turned to professionals. Presumably this stemmed from the involvement of professional agencies in the placement of the children for adoption. But it seems consistent with the overconcern and special anxiety which parents gave their adopted children.

Such findings suggest that family relationships are indeed affected by the process by which children are added to the family. Apparently, adoption tends to create special concern on the part of both parents and children.

Boyless Couples In patrilineal societies it is not enough to have children. It is necessary to have a boy to carry on the family line. For couples whose reproductive efforts have resulted only in girls, it may be necessary to adopt a boy in order to fulfill their duty to the family line.

Boys may be adopted in the normal fashion and raised as part of the family, groomed to take over the family estate after a suitable marriage partner has been recruited from outside. Or, in Japan at least, one daughter may be retained at home and her husband adopted into the family, assuming her family name and surrendering his "maiden" name. To lose one's name and leave one's family in a patrilineal society is an enormous sacrifice. To come as a stranger into one's wife's household is to risk being placed in a weak position in an otherwise patriarchal society. No young man would stoop to such an ignominious adoption were not the rewards sufficient to compensate him. In Japan, only a lower-status man could ordinarily be expected to accept such adoption, since for him the higher status and greater wealth of the wife's family would compensate for his psychological sacrifices. For the wife's family, however, this custom had the value of bringing only one stranger into the family instead of two. Thus the cultural continuity of the family could more easily be assured than if both an adopted son and his bride were brought into the family.

Surplus Children　If adopted children present problems of integration into the family even when they have been recruited to solve the parents' problems, how much more difficult adoption must be when the problem is the children's! When children arrive because they have lost their parents or because their parents cannot care for them, they are liable to be resented in much the same fashion as children born of accidental pregnancies. And since they are liable to have been already partly socialized in another family, they are less easily integrated into the family than children who enter at birth. In general, I assume that the older the child is when he changes families, the greater difficulty there is in resocializing him to fit his new home.

Surplus children are often taken on as extras by relatives who already have children of their own. In Tokyo, Vogel (1963) noted that adopted children were sometimes neglected and discriminated against by such relatives. He believed they would have been better accepted in the homes of childless nonrelatives where they would not have had to compete with biological offspring.

The disruptive effect of quasi-adoption on adolescent girls is evident in the fact that 15 percent of Blake's Jamaican respondents had been sent away from home to live with relatives or friends just prior to their first sexual liaison. A combination of resentment over having been expelled from home as unwanted surplus children and of unwillingness to accept the authority of the pseudo-parent made them vulnerable to seduction despite the "considerable effort" of the latter to control them and keep them away from men (1961: 85). Establishing new parent–child relationships was especially difficult under these circumstances because of the girl's feeling of having been rejected by her biological parents and her relatively advanced age at changing families.

To a lesser degree, similar problems may result whenever a parent–child relationship is disrupted and an attempt is made to substitute a new one. Adoption, then, seems to pose more difficult problems of family integration than biological reproduction. Nevertheless, all children present socialization problems to some degree, regardless of where they originate.

FAMILY EXPANSION

Adding children profoundly alters the way of life of all the family members. How much life is altered depends, however, on how many children are added, as well as how quickly and how definitely. The crucial increment, however, is the first child.

Advent of the First Child: Crisis of Accession

Prior to the first child's arrival, the family consists of two persons able to give their entire attention to each other. After he arrives, the comfortable reciprocity of the dyad is destroyed. Henceforth, each adult must compete with the child for the attention of the spouse.

The winner is likely to be the child. The younger he is, the greater his dependence on his parents. While he is an infant, his needs for food and clothing are at a maximum. Without attention, he would literally die. The spouse, however, can care for himself and therefore must be content with left-over time and energy after the baby's needs are met. Mature adults expect nothing else, but parents young enough or neurotic enough to have strong dependency needs may find the sense that "three's a crowd" disconcerting.

Since mothers concentrate on responding to the needs of infants, fathers are more apt to feel neglected. Dyer (1963) found that 62 percent of new fathers but only 12 percent of new mothers felt neglected "at least sometimes" as a result of the spouse's preoccupation with the child.

Both parents are confronted with strikingly new tasks. The new member of the family is not just quantitatively an addition but qualitatively different. Before, the family consisted entirely of adults. Now suddenly the least adult of all human beings has been added. Infants create entirely new problems with which the parents must learn to cope. Especially troublesome are the diagnostic problems: What is he crying about? What does he need (if anything)? Should we call the doctor? The infant's inability to communicate verbally with his parents presents them with ambiguous messages which are difficult to decode. The ability to interpret those messages may be a matter of life or death, so the parents' anxiety may be acute. Even if sheer survival of the child is not in question, the parents must figure out how to appease his demands if they are to have any life of their own. Even sleep is impossible when a child is wailing about an unknown problem.

Suddenly, then, new parents are confronted with a profound structural alteration of their family (from dyad to triad) and with complex new tasks to be performed. Faced with these striking changes, 83 percent of the middle-class American couples interviewed by LeMasters (1957) felt that parenthood had been either an "extensive" or a "severe" crisis of accession.

The critical nature of the transition may be symbolized in the abrupt doubling of housework for couples who acquire a child under age two (see Figure 14-1). With more detailed information for the first few weeks of his life, the jump would presumably have been even greater. In any case, housekeeping suddenly erupts from a low plateau to its highest peak, from which it declines only gradually as children grow up and leave home.

To have time for this extra housework, American wives typically quit working outside the home. This alters the power structure of marriage as they come to depend both financially and psychologically on their husbands. It also alters the division of labor as they contribute a far larger share to the total amount of housework done (Blood and Wolfe, 1960).

Despite the extra hours released from outside employment, most of the middle-class wives studied by Dyer (1963) found their sleep so disrupted by the baby's feeding demands that they were chronically tired and exhausted, especially during the first six to eight weeks of the baby's life. They also worried about neglecting their husbands and about their adequacy as mothers. Husbands found it difficult to adjust to their new responsibilities and to new family routines. Most couples also had trouble coping with loss of the wife's income at the same time that the child brought added expenses. Such stresses

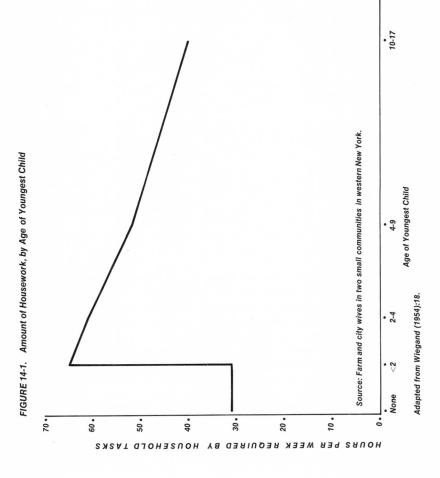

FIGURE 14-1. Amount of Housework, by Age of Youngest Child

Source: Farm and city wives in two small communities in western New York.

Adapted from Wiegand (1954):18.

suggest concretely what couples mean when they say that having their first child precipitated a crisis.

Resources for Coping with Children   The intensity of the crisis depends on the family's resources. Dyer found, for example, that college-educated couples were less apt than high-school-educated ones to be thrown for a loss by their new experience. Presumably, education enables people to reason their way through new problems.

Within American society, lower-class black couples are particularly ill-equipped to deal with the problems presented by adding children to their relationship. The weaker their relationship, the greater the hazard posed by children. And when the relationship is illicit, the problem becomes increasingly difficult as children get older:

> Children—one's own as well as someone else's—are . . . liabilities in the all-important world of man–woman relationships. Where eating, sleeping, child-rearing and lovemaking are frequently confined to a single room, children render privacy a scarce commodity. . . . Children threaten not only exposure of illicit relations but also active interference. Indeed, when Tonk and Earlene were kissing in the car, his daughter kept trying to pull them apart, screaming at Earlene "You're not my mother! You're not my mother!" Older children, in this respect, are bigger nuisances. . . . Once when Nancy and Clarence were fighting, Nancy's twelve-year-old son hit Clarence with a baseball bat. (Liebow, 1967:92–94)

The more crowded the space, the more the addition of a child interferes with the man–woman relationship, whether illicit or licit.

The slimmer the parents' resources, the more the addition of any child (and not just the first) constitutes a crisis. Morris studied the family backgrounds of British men imprisoned for minor crimes and was impressed by "the number of husbands who go into prison as their wives approach the end of a pregnancy. It seems as though they are unable to tolerate the additional responsibility that the birth may bring with it" (1965:112). For a man short of money and emotionally unstable, living in an already overcrowded house and married to a wife already complaining about the burden of the existing children, the need to seek refuge in prison from the strain of another baby is understandable.

In extended families, the advent of a first child makes hardly more of a dent than the arrival of the last child in a large family. An extended family is already large before the first child is born. The young husband and wife already lack privacy for mutual devotion. So the birth of their first child brings relatively little change to their already inhibited relationship.

The extended family's resources for coping with children are more ample. Their financial base is broader so that even if childbirth forces the wife to retire from productive work, the percentage loss is less severe. Their housekeeping base is equally broad, so the new mother can concentrate on her child-rearing tasks while the mother-in-law and other women of the household carry on with housekeeping routines.

The women of the household are also available to care for the child and give advice when needed. A woman raised in an extended family is less apt to need advice, however, since she has observed and even participated in child-rearing from early childhood.

In India, Minturn and Hitchcock were struck by the expertise of new mothers in extended families:

> . . . the village mother has had far more experience with children than a mother raised in an isolated nuclear family. She has grown up in a household where the advent of a new baby was a fairly common occurrence. She has seen babies born, seen them nurse, seen them live and grow up, and seen them die. She has probably cared for a younger sibling or cousin herself. Furthermore, she has her own children in the company of older women to whom childbirth is a familiar experience. Therefore babies are neither the objects of interest nor the objects of anxiety that they are in [the United States].
>
> A mother does not fear that her child is sick every time it cries; she knows better. But, by the same token, she is not delighted with its smile because she also knows that all babies smile. She therefore continues with her usual routine, attends to her infant's needs but does not hover over it or "drop everything" to rush to its side. If there is not sufficient help, she may resort to opium to quiet the child while she gets her work done or she may use some other device to amuse the child. (1963:317)

Whether the child is better or worse off under these unruffled circumstances is another question. But from the standpoint of the extended family, it is unlikely that the birth of a child would be as critical an event as in a nuclear family.

Child Timing: Phased Expansion

Since few families acquire their children all at once, expansion tends to be a multiphased process. Even in those exceptional cases where expansion occurs all at once, its relation to the initial enactment of the family is an important question of phase coordination. In general, I assume that the earlier children are acquired and the more swiftly they arrive, the greater the crisis they create for parents.

Premarital Births   We saw in Chapter 12 that housekeeping couples on Caribbean islands often bore children out of wedlock. Though such children were often unwanted, we cannot assume that that is always the case in disorganized societies. Liebow found that unattached black men in Washington customarily expected to establish quasi-marital relationships with women whose children they fathered. If they didn't mind the possibility of being linked indefinitely with their current partner, they stopped using condoms. Their chief motive may have been a desire to enjoy sex to the fullest rather than a positive desire to have children. But at least children were not sufficiently unwanted to motivate them to take steps to prevent them:

> I asked Sea Cat if he always used [prophylactics]. He said no, sometimes he does, sometimes he doesn't. "It depends on the girl. If she's nice, friendly

and all that, the kind I wouldn't mind helping out, then I don't use them. But if she's not nice, I don't take any chances." Acknowledging his responsibility to "help out" any woman whom he gets pregnant, he forestalls having to enter into an ongoing, helping relationship with the "not nice" girl by using contraceptives. There is no such pressing need to use contraceptives with the "nice" girl since he has no strong aversion to the continuing relationship with her that conception would entail. (1967:152–153)

Children born under quasi-marital circumstances (where the father is willing to enter into some sort of continuing relationship with the mother and children) are not so impoverished as children of what might be called "unwanted mothers." When women enter into such fleeting relationships that they do not know who is responsible for their pregnancies, or in relationships when the father is known but disdains to accept his responsibility, both mother and child are severely handicapped.

To avoid that fate, an unmarried mother may make desperate efforts to enter into at least a quasi-marital relationship either with the known father or with anyone else who will come to her aid. In a society which stigmatizes unmarried motherhood, a man is not only a source of financial support but a way of avoiding the shame of having mothered a bastard. In Kenya, for example:

> Illegitimacy, that is, the birth of a child to an unmarried girl, is regarded as an extremely disgraceful situation. The girl who discovers that she is pregnant may frantically plead with her lover to marry her or even come to live in his house without being invited. Sometimes this results in marriage or concubinage, but more frequently young men, cherishing an ideal of marriage to a girl with whom they have not had sexual relations, run away to plantations or the city to avoid such involvement.
>
> Most frequently the unmarried mother is simply taken as a secondary wife by an elderly man wealthy enough to pay a high bride-wealth rate for proven fecundity but too old to be able to demand a girl of high moral virtue. The child becomes a legal part of the family of his mother's husband, but he has a lower status in the eyes of many in that family. (LeVine and LeVine, 1963:132–133)

Women able to establish a relationship with any man are fortunate compared to those who must raise a child alone. For the latter, a quasi-family has been established, consisting of mother and child (or children). The difficulties of managing a quasi-family successfully are evidenced by the reliance of such family fragments on the woman's relatives (especially on her mother) or on social welfare schemes like Aid to Dependent Children.

To be able to support children financially and care for them personally ordinarily takes the combined efforts of a father and mother. When the father is missing, it is difficult for an unmarried mother to be able to manage unassisted. Given her remarkably meager resources, an unmarried mother has by definition been caught in a crisis, and one which will hardly disappear within a few months (as did the crisis for most of Dyer's married couples).

Premarital Conceptions   We have already seen that relatively few unmarried American couples who become pregnant get married to solve their problem.

Nevertheless, some do. As with premarital births, these are normally unwanted pregnancies and sometimes unwanted marriages. Insofar as pregnancy forces couples to marry who otherwise would never have married, it links poorly matched persons.

One way of distinguishing between the effect of the pregnancy itself and of the forced character of marriage is to compare couples who marry soon after their pregnancy is discovered with those who marry only late in the pregnancy. The latter presumably delay their marriage because of their incompatibility, succumbing reluctantly to social pressures and a hopeless sense that there is no other way out of their dilemma once the time for abortion has passed.

TABLE 14-3   Divorce Rate, by Timing of First Birth in Relation to Marriage

		TIMING OF MARRIAGE AND FIRST BIRTH		
		PREMARITAL CONCEPTION		
SAMPLE	*PREMARITAL BIRTH*	*Delayed Marriage*	*Undelayed Marriage*	*POSTMARITAL CONCEPTION*
Copenhagen	46%	34%	24%	19%
Indiana County	—	20	14	7

Adapted from Christensen (1960):37. Sources: Copenhagen couples married in 1938 and Tippecanoe County (Indiana) couples married in 1919–21, 1929–31, and 1939–41 followed for five years to determine date of birth of first child and rate of divorce. Reciprocal percentages of couples had not been divorced within the first five years of marriage. Copenhagen couples with premarital births had married after the wife had born a child out of wedlock, not necessarily by the same partner. "Delayed marriages" were where the child was born less than 140 days after marriage. In "undelayed marriages" the child was born 140–265 days after marriage (assumed to be premarital conceptions).

Table 14-3 shows that the earlier the pregnancy occurred in two different countries, the higher the divorce rate.

I have suggested that one reason for the higher divorce rate in premature pregnancies is that many of the marriages and childbirths are unwanted. A second factor is presumably the weaker state of the marriage when the child arrives. In postmarital pregnancies, couples have at least nine months to work out their marital relationships before readjusting to the little intruder. We will see shortly that if the first birth occurs even later than nine months, the couple need not cope with the problems of pregnancy during their "honeymoon" period. Conversely, the more pregnancy and child-rearing intrude upon the first months of marriage, the harder it is for couples to work out a satisfactory husband–wife relationship. No wonder, then, that marriages in both Denmark and the U.S.A. are remarkably brittle when there is no opportunity to build a solid marital relationship before family expansion begins. Some of these marriages would have collapsed anyway, even without the added burden of the child. But when family expansion occurs prematurely, the likelihood increases of overburdening the couple's resources until their relationship snaps.

Postmarital Conceptions   The effect of early conception on marriage does not cease even when couples are already married. The longer conception is postponed after marriage, the stronger the marriage has an opportunity to become. Christensen and Meissner (1953) found in an Indiana sample that divorce rates decreased steadily the longer the interval was between marriage and the birth of the first postmaritally conceived baby (from 9.1 percent in marriages invaded 266–391 days after the wedding, to 7.1 percent after 392–531 days of grace, to 5.8 percent after more than 531 days).

Dyer (1963) similarly found that all his couples whose first child came less than three years after marriage described parenthood as a crisis whereas only 32 percent of those married at least three years felt that way. Testing the influence of marital solidarity more directly, only 20 percent of those who considered their marital adjustment excellent experienced a crisis, compared to 82 percent of those who were less well adjusted. In general, then, the longer couples are married before they have their first child, the stronger their marriage has an opportunity to become. And the stronger the marriage, the less critical the effect of parenthood.

Delaying parenthood affects not only the husband–wife relationship but the parent–child relationship. The better parents can cope with their first child, the more the child benefits from their increased resourcefulness. Morgan and his associates (1962) found, for example, that the earlier parents had children, the less education those children completed (even when parents were carefully matched on education, income, and other background factors). Educational deprivation was particularly severe for children born to fathers who were not yet adults themselves (*i.e.,* who had not yet reached age 21). When children come too soon after marriage, everyone suffers, parents and children alike.

Spacing Between Children All the arguments for wide intervals between marriage and the first birth apply in similar fashion to intervals between children. If children born too soon tend to overburden both the husband–wife and the parent–child relationship, children born too close together have the same effects.

TABLE 14-4 Mother's Attitude Toward Pregnancy, by Birth Interval Between Children

MOTHER'S ATTITUDE TOWARD PREGNANCY	BIRTH INTERVAL BETWEEN CHILDREN			
	<22	*22–31*	*32–54*	*55+ Months*
Delighted	9%	28%	42%	52%
Generally pleased	23	40	35	16
Mixed or negative feelings	68	32	23	32
Total	100%	100%	100%	100%
Number of mothers	34	54	92	31

Adapted from Sears, Maccoby, and Levin (1957):40. Source: Mothers of public-school kindergarten children in two Boston suburbs.

Table 14-4 shows that the wider the interval between children, the more delighted the mother. (The only irregularity in the table is an increased number of mixed or negative reactions in long-postponed children which partially offsets the increased number of delighted mothers.) The attitude of the mother toward her child affects the way she treats the child. The same study found that the wider the interval between children, the more warmly the mother treated the child. Indeed this warmth was manifested not only toward infants but toward the same children five years later.

At a much later stage in the family life cycle, Townsend (1957) noted that families who spaced their children so widely that the last child was born late in life experienced the smallest discontinuity between the child-rearing phase and the parent-caring phase. When children married close to the age when their parents retired, there was less of a gap between the dependence of children on parents and the dependence of parents on children. Closing the gap may not be an unmixed blessing from the standpoint of the child's marriage (since the marriage is liable to be saddled prematurely with aged dependents). From the standpoint of the parents, however, wide spacing offers the maximum security since they can maintain contact with their last child without interruption.

Infant Mortality: Uncertain Expansion

So far I have assumed that children become more or less permanent members of the family, at least until they grow up. This depends on modern conditions of medicine and food, however. Under primitive conditions, infant mortality was so high that no assumption could be made about the survival of any particular child. Parents could only hope that *some* children would survive from the total brood.

Hedging Against Mortality   If enough children were to survive, more than enough had to be produced in the first place. In the absence of contraception, "overproduction" was normally easy. But once people become accustomed to the necessity of bearing large numbers of children in order to insure the survival of a few, the adoption of contraception is likely to be delayed for some years after the death rate begins to fall. Only after a society has experienced the survival of extra children for a whole generation is it likely to realize that the gap between the number of children born and the number reared has disappeared.

Such transitional ambiguity appeared in the Jamaican women interviewed by Stycos and Back:

> Since the average Jamaican woman thinks of about three children as ideal, we might expect that she would think of a family as "large" if it exceeded this number by two or three children. But when asked what they meant by a "big family," over a quarter of the women in the sample said twelve or more children, and the median was 8.9. (1964:30)

Perhaps such women thought of three as their ideal number of surviving children but were not prepared to feel sure that they had guaranteed the survival of three until they had borne six extra children. In any case, the memory of infant mortality in an underdeveloped country creates widespread uncertainty about the proper number of children to bear.

Non-Attachment   If parents bear extra children on the assumption that a considerable but unknown number are likely to die, it is not wise to become too deeply attached to any particular child during the hazardous youthful years. The larger the number of children, the more diffuse the parent's attachment is likely to be to any particular child anyway. But the uncertain destiny of each individual child imposes an extra barrier to the development of strong ties. In medieval Europe:

> No one thought of keeping a picture of a child if that child . . . had died in infancy. . . . it was thought that the little thing which had disappeared so soon in life was not worthy of remembrance: there were far too many children whose survival was problematical. The general feeling was . . . that one had several children in order to keep just a few. As late as the seventeenth century . . . we have a neighbor, standing at the bedside of a woman who has just given birth, the mother of five "little brats," and calming her fears with these words: "Before they are old enough to bother you, you will have lost half of them, or perhaps all of them." A strange consolation! People could not allow themselves to become too attached to something that was regarded as a probable loss. . . . This indifference was a direct and inevitable consequence of the demography of the period. (Aries, 1962:38–39)

And in Modern India, Minturn and Hitchcock found that Rajput parents felt ambivalent about becoming attached to particular children:

> The high rate of disease affects the attitudes of parents toward children. Almost every baby wears a necklace containing charms to ward off illness. Delicate children are objects of concern, and adults sometimes openly express their doubts for their survival. When discussing the future life of a child, a mother would sometimes add ". . . if he lives." One mother who had lost two daughters reported that she was reluctant to become too fond of her 8-year-old daughter or to buy good clothes for her for fear that this child also would be taken from her. (1963:285)

In other words, the higher the rate of infant mortality in the society at large, the less attached parents will be to their individual children.

However, non-attachment is replaced by overprotection under certain other conditions of mortality.

1   For women who experience difficulty in conceiving or in carrying their pregnancies to full term, such conditions heighten attachment to any child who happens to survive these hazards. If the chances of having enough children are slight, the survival of any one child becomes extra important. Levy (1966) found that 65 percent of his overprotective mothers had had some sort of difficulty in bearing children.

2   A similar effect can be derived from the threatened loss of a child once he is born. This applies to parents who have borne only the number of children they desire because they had assumed every child would survive. If this assumption is threatened by near-fatal injuries or illnesses, the mother's anxiety about the child's survival leads her to overprotect the

child in order to shelter him from further danger. (Levy's overprotected children had had twice as many illnesses and three times as many operations as a control group of normally treated children.)

Only when the survival of all children can be pretty well counted on do parent–child relationships have an opportunity to develop a happy medium between non-attachment and over-attachment. Then the size of the family is no longer uncertain but dependable and family relationships can develop accordingly.

Family Size: The Limits of Expansion

Eventually families reach their maximum size. For some, the number of children acquired is zero, for others a dozen or more. A basic sociological principle is that the size of an organization affects its structure and behavior. From the numerous studies which have been made of groups of varying size and families of varying size, we should be able to understand the effects of family expansion on the family.

Decentralization   The larger the family, the more it tends to subdivide into smaller subgroups. These subgroups may or may not be permanent or sharply segregated from one another. Nevertheless, the larger the family, the more difficult it is for them either to feel or function as a single undifferentiated group.

TABLE 14-5 Frequency Distribution of Informal and Work Groups by Group Size

| | NATURE OF GROUP | |
GROUP SIZE	Informal Groups	Work Groups
2	71%	71%
3	20	23
4	6	5
5	2	1
6+	1	*
Total	100%	100%
Number of groups	7,405	1,548

Adapted from James (1951):476. Source: Informal and work groups in public situations in Eugene and Portland, Oregon, *e.g.*, children on school playgrounds, workmen on a building construction project.
* Less than one-half of one percent.

The data presented in Table 14-5 were not derived from families but from spontaneously formed groups of people uncomplicated by differences of age or sex. They suggest nevertheless the tendency of people to form extremely small groups. The economy of human relations makes dyads less strenuous and more rewarding than larger groups. These same benefits make husband–wife dyads resist the intrusion of the first child. In social situations where there is a larger total group (as at a party), it tends to fall apart into smaller conversational sub-units unless vigorous leadership is exerted to hold it together.

In families, the same forces tend to divide large families into smaller subgroups. The pairing of husband and wife may persist to some extent. But parent–child dyads and sibling dyads and triads appear as more members are added to the family.

The fact that children are not born simultaneously and come in two sexes makes differentiation into sub-units even more likely than in homogeneous groups. Bossard and Boll (1956), in a study of families with five or more children, found that siblings tended to split into same-sex and near-age subgroups. Although they failed to report the distribution of these subgroups by size, the fact that the median family had three subgroups suggests that most of the subgroups were small.

TABLE 14-6 Number of Sibling Subgroups in Large Families

Number of Subgroups	Percentage
No clearly defined subgroups	20%
One cohesive subgroup	11
Two subgroups	19
Three	32
Four	11
Five	4
Six	4
Total	101%
Number of families	75

Adapted from Bossard and Boll (1956):189. Source: Families of University of Pennsylvania students with four or more surviving siblings (median, seven).

Bossard's families ranged in size from several with five surviving children to one with 16. Presumably, the larger the number of children, the greater the number of subgroups. Unfortunately, he failed to correlate family size with number of subgroups so I cannot demonstrate the relationship between size of family and tendency to decentralization. All we can be sure is that stable subgroups rarely failed to appear in families with five or more children (indeed the authors were skeptical of the accuracy of students who reported no subgroups).

One of the most dramatic evidences of the difficulty of holding large families together is their tendency to farm out older children when their financial resources are inadequate. Blake (1961) found that more than half the Jamaican children loaned to relatives and friends were spun off in later childhood or adolescence at an age when they consumed more food and required more expensive clothing. I also assume that by that age, their parents had acquired so many younger children that housing and financial pressures had intensified. Child dispersal presumably not only occurs in the largest families but occurs at that point in a family's life cycle when it has reached its maximum size.

Figure 14-2 shows that for poor families, the larger the number of children, the less they were able to retain all their children at home. The more insecure the parental relationship, the more these effects of family size were magnified. The ability of a family to cope with large numbers of children thus depends on the twin factors of marital solidarity and financial support. For lower-class common-law relationships, both factors are missing and the possibility of retaining children in the family is correspondingly undermined.

Even parents who keep all their children are less able to interact with each child as their family increases in size. In general the larger the number of children, the more attenuated the relationship between the parents and any particular child becomes. The mother may have just as much love to give, but she must divide that love into smaller pieces as the number of recipients increases. Actually, the larger the number of children, the greater the likelihood that the mother will inhibit her affection for any children, perhaps because there are so many children that she can't feel close to any of them. In any case, I will shortly show (in Table 14-10) that mothers with large numbers of children exhibit less warmth than those with fewer children. This does not mean that such mothers do not engage in an enormous amount of total interaction with all their children put together but rather that their relationship with any one child is inevitably diluted when there are so many children to share their attention.

Table 14-7 shows that diffused relationships with individual children persist throughout life in large families. Parents with larger numbers of children had almost four times the aggregate amount of interaction with their grown children. Nevertheless, they interacted less with each child than did parents with fewer children. The difference is between intensive relationships in small families and extensive relationships in large families.

Townsend found that the closer tie between only children and their parents produced both more frequent visiting when they lived apart and more frequent doubling up with elderly parents "not so much because they delayed marriage as because they continued to live with their parents" after they married (1957:28). Only children sometimes had so close a relationship with their parents that they established an extended family pattern in the midst of a neolocal society.

In less industrialized societies this tendency is even more pronounced. Rosenberg (1958) found that in an Arab village in Palestine, not a single only son left his father to live elsewhere. Conversely 82 percent of all sons who lived with their fathers after marriage were only sons. This suggests that in a society where one half to two thirds of all sons established neolocal households, it was almost exclusively sons from extraordinarily small families whose ties were close enough to their parents to keep them at home after marriage.

By weakening the parent–child relationship, increased numbers of children reduce the parents' ability to socialize them. Douvan and Adelson (1966) found that adolescents from small families felt closer to their parents and identified more with them. They spent more of their leisure time with

**FIGURE 14-2.   Child Dispersal, by Number of Children and Formalization
of Marriage**

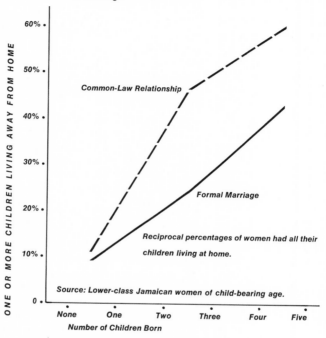

Adapted from Stycos and Back (1964):338.

TABLE 14-7 Contact of Old People with Their Surviving Children, by Number of Children

| | NUMBER OF CHILDREN | | | | LARGE/SMALL |
	One	Two	Three/Four	Five+	RATIO
Total contacts/week	5.2	8.5	11.7	19.1	3.67X
Average contacts per child	5.2	4.2	3.4	3.1	0.60
Number of old people	26	29	45	57	

Adapted from Townsend (1957):87. Source: Working-class London men aged 65+ and women aged 60+.

their parents, turned to them more for advice, and used them more as confidantes. For children from larger families (in this case with three or more children), all these signs of close parent–child relations were diminished or missing. Instead of relying on their parents, teenagers from larger families relied on their peers. Toward their parents, their attitudes were an ambivalent mixture of dependency and resentment.

The results of weakened parent–child relationships can be seen in the lower aspirations and poorer attainments of children from large families. The reason for lesser aspirations presumably is the lesser per capita mental stimulation by the parents. The parents' lesser ability to develop achievement motivation in their children can be seen in Table 14-8.

TABLE 14-8 Achievement Motivation, by Number of Children and Social Class

| | NUMBER OF CHILDREN | | | LARGE/SMALL |
SOCIAL CLASS	1–2	3–4	5+	DIRECTION
Upper, upper-middle	5.20	6.41	2.33	—
Lower-middle	6.49	6.14	5.83	—
Upper-lower	5.06	3.40	2.82	—
Lower-lower	4.57	3.67	1.48	—
Number of boys	178	193	54	

Adapted from Rosen (1961):578. Source: 8- to 14-year-old boys in the Northeastern U.S.A., including French–Canadian, Greek, Italian, Jewish, black, and white Protestant Americans. Higher numbers mean stronger achievement motivation.

Table 14-8 shows that achievement motivation was generally stronger in the higher social classes. However, within each class (with only one reversal), the larger the number of children, the weaker that motivation became. This suggests how the attenuation of parent–child relationships in large families deprives the child of the intensive attention which children receive when parents are able to concentrate on a small number of children.

Children handicapped by large numbers of siblings not only aspire less, but achieve less, too. For instance, their mental development is impaired as measured by intelligence tests. Lipset and Bendix (1962) reported that studies in many nations demonstrated that the larger the number of children per family, the lower their I.Q.

With lower aspirations and underdeveloped mental capacities, it is to be expected that children from large families would drop out of school sooner, even if we discount the possibility of their being drafted into occupational service on behalf of their family's financial needs. In a large national survey, Morgan *et al.* (1962) found that children from larger families dropped out of school earlier even when differences in parents' education, income, and other social characteristics were controlled.

TABLE 14-9   Educational and Occupation Achievement, by Number of Children

| ACHIEVEMENT | NUMBER OF CHILDREN | | | LARGE/SMALL DIRECTION |
	One	*Two to Four*	*Five or more*	
Education	5.0	4.7	4.1	—
First job	29.8	27.0	23.8	—
Current job	40.4	38.7	33.9	—

Adapted from Blau and Duncan (1967):299, 303. Source: Representative sample of U. S. men age 20–64. The total number of men was 20,700. The means shown for families of more than one combine the means published for different sibling positions (eldest, middle, and youngest). All means were controlled on father's occupation, and the first job was also controlled on father's education to rule out the effect of these stratification variables. Relevant codes were as follows:
Education: 4.0 = high school drop-out; 5.0 = high school graduate.
Occupation: 20–24 = shipping and receiving clerks; bus drivers, etc.
            25–29 = brickmasons; mechanics and repairmen; plasterers, etc.
            30–34 = gas station proprietors; plumbers; sheriffs, etc.
            35–39 = retail salesmen; TV repairmen; firemen, etc.
            40–44 = cashiers; clerical workers; electricians; policemen, etc.

Table 14-9 from a separate American study shows the same reduction in educational achievement and parallel reductions in occupational achievement with increased family size. Blau and Duncan commented thus:

> The greater the number of children in a family, the greater the strain on its financial resources, and the less the resources available for each, within a given range of family income. In an age in which the inheritance of a business, a farm, or a professional practice has become increasingly rare, a major channel through which affluent parents can transmit their superior status to their sons is by providing them with an advanced education. But many children restrict a family's ability to do so, just as they limit the property each child can inherit. (1967:302)

Blau and Duncan found that family expansion especially depressed the child's educational achievement and that in turn determined his ability to succeed or fail in his occupation.

In general, then, the farther a family expands, the harder it is to hold it together. At worst, some children may have to be farmed out to relatives or friends. Even for those who stay behind, the family tends to split apart into separate subgroups of children and into parents unable to maintain close touch. The concept of "one big happy family" seems to be a myth which masks internal structural decentralization.

Differentiation   So far I have simply made this point: that large families tend to subdivide into separate parts. Are those parts "separate but equal"? Or does the expansion of families create inequalities among the parts? As the family gets bigger, does it become more difficult to treat the children alike?

If families expanded instantaneously, there might be some chance of equality. The fact that children are added piece-meal means that family size varies over time. The first-born child and the last-launched child live temporarily in one-child households. Middle children live more of their lives in large families. Moreover, as we will discuss in more detail in Chapter 17, siblings in a given family differ in age, so they differ in the stresses or benefits incurred with increasing family size. It seems reasonable, therefore, to expect that the larger the family becomes, the greater the differentiation which may be expected among its sub-units.

Differentiation between first-born and last-born children increases proportionally with the number of intervening children. Cobb and French (1966) found that last-born children were underrepresented among medical students at the University of Michigan, but that the handicap of being a last-born child increased the larger the number of children was. Specifically, last-born children from two-child families were only 33 percent underrepresented, whereas those from three-child families were 68 percent underrepresented, and those from families with four or more children 95 percent underrepresented in comparison to first-born children.

Cobb and French dealt with a relatively narrow range of variation among families—few of them had more than four children. As families expand beyond that point, even first-born children begin to suffer. Humphreys (1966) found in Ireland and Bossard and Boll (1956) in the United States that eldest children in large families were pressed into assistant-parent roles. For boys, this meant that they must curtail their education and go to work to help support the family. For girls this meant becoming an assistant mother and helping with the housekeeping and child-rearing. In Wales, for example, Rosser and Harris noted that "the existence of large numbers of young children needing care combined with frequent pregnancies on the part of the mother creates a situation of recurrent domestic crisis. It is inevitable that in a large family . . . older siblings (especially daughters) will have to assume in times of crisis some of the parents' responsibility for younger children" (1965:175).

In six different societies, Minturn and Lambert found that the larger the number of younger siblings, the more an older child was expected to do chores around the house. In families where the number of younger siblings was below the societal average, only 37 percent had to do chores, but in larger families, 65 percent had to help out (1964:269).

In some societies girls too may be sent out to work if money is more urgently needed than their unpaid labor at home. Lambiri (1965) found that a large proportion of girls employed in a Greek textile mill came from large families with more mouths to feed or with a large number of girls needing dowries to be able to marry. In either case, the family's financial strain forced girls to work in socially degrading jobs.

Blau and Duncan (1967) found that oldest children from families with five or more children had less education and poorer jobs than their youngest siblings. Their study was consistent with the medical-school finding that achievement differentials in large families were greater than in small families.

The larger the family, the greater the differentiation between the husband's and wife's roles in marriage. When there are only a few children, husband and wife may be able to share responsibility for them. As size increases, however, the partners tend to divide responsibility for different children, the mother caring for the newest baby and the father for older children. On the other hand, increased financial pressure from extra children will take the husband away from home more if he takes on extra jobs or works overtime to earn crucial extra money. For example, Mott found that among blue-collar workers, "as the number of children increases, the probability of getting a second job also increases" (1965:300). This saddles the wife with an increasing share of the housework and forces the partners to specialize in separate tasks as they try to get the housework done.

TABLE 14-10   Division of Labor in the Home, by Number of Children

DIVISION OF LABOR	Zero	One	Two	Three*	Four+
		NUMBER OF CHILDREN			
Wife's task performance					
Detroit	4.74	5.26	5.35	5.84	5.19
Tokyo	4.23	4.55	4.67	6.05	—
Task specialization					
Detroit	3.70	3.44	3.93	4.48	4.15
Tokyo	3.30	3.60	3.74	3.84	—
Number of families					
Detroit	74	93	112	64	37
Tokyo	153	131	78	19	—

Adapted from Blood (1967):229. Source: Young married couples. Task performance refers to the proportion of household tasks performed by the wife rather than by the husband. Task specialization refers to the number of tasks performed unilaterally (rather than jointly) by either the husband or wife.
* For Tokyo families this means three-or-more children.

Table 14-10 presents a consistent picture of increased role differentiation in Tokyo. On the other hand, there was some tendency for the largest families in Detroit to reverse this trend once the size of the families got beyond three children. This suggests that in these largest families, the wife's capacity to complete the housework becomes overtaxed. Role specialization breaks down as the husband is forced to come to her assistance. The normal increase in specialization due to additional children is counteracted beyond that emergency point by the stresses of excessive size.

Strain   The "one big happy family" suffers not only from decentralization and differentiation of its unity but from strains on its happiness. We saw by implication in Table 14-10 that stresses became severe when four or more children were added to American households. From the standpoint of the satisfaction of the marriage partners, happiness may be impaired even sooner, but the degree of impairment and the point at which it sets in depend on the family's financial and other resources for coping with children. The scarcer those resources, the sooner the point of diminishing returns is reached.

TABLE 14-11   Wife's Marital Satisfaction, by Number of Children and Family Income

WIFE'S MARITAL SATISFACTION BY FAMILY INCOME	NUMBER OF CHILDREN				
	Zero	One	Two	Three*	Four+
Very low income (Tokyo)	5.90	4.76	4.52	**	—
Low income (Tokyo)	5.74	5.00	5.03	3.93	—
Moderate income (Detroit)	4.31	4.96	5.09	4.61	4.28
High income (Detroit)	4.71	5.10	5.00	5.43	5.00
Number of families					
Tokyo	153	131	78	19	—
Detroit	74	93	112	64	37

Adapted from Blood (1967):229. Marital satisfaction in Tokyo was based on ten facets of marriage and in Detroit on five facets, of which satisfaction with the number of children in each case was one element. Scores are not comparable between cities. Tokyo families were split at $1,000 per year (1958 income); Detroit families at $5,000 (1954 income).
* For Tokyo families, this means 3+ children.
** Less than 10 cases, so a reliable mean could not be computed.

Table 14-11 shows that marital satisfaction was greatest for childless wives in Tokyo. It fell more precipitately with increased numbers of children in families with the fewest financial resources. For families in affluent America, the relationship between marital satisfaction and number of children was curvilinear (partly because the American measure weighted children more heavily, and partly because American women valued childbearing more than Japanese women in a pinched economy). For families with relatively low incomes by American standards, the point of diminishing returns was two children whereas for those with higher incomes, satisfaction crested at three children.

Why should the effect of children on marital satisfaction depend on the family's income? Presumably because more money enables wives to cope with children more easily. With extra money, the family can employ more help with the housework, retain baby-sitters to enable the parents to have respites from their children, take the whole family on vacation trips, etc. Without money, the wife is tied down by the house and children.

In Japan, children impaired marital satisfaction more severely because baby-sitters were rarely available and were socially tabooed. Japanese wives were "good" mothers in the sense of taking their responsibilities seriously, but this meant sacrificing the husband–wife relationship as soon as a single child arrived.

Only in an affluent society, then, are children compatible with marital satisfaction. But even there, most family's resources are not unlimited, so children can be absorbed only within modest limits. Beyond these points of diminishing returns, children become so much the focus of concern that the husband–wife relationship tends to atrophy.

The marriage bond is not the only casualty of large numbers of children. Wives tend to become physical casualties of bearing and rearing too many children. The larger the number of conceptions, especially in primitive societies, the greater the likelihood of dying in childbirth. Even for those who survive, large numbers of children bring premature aging, so that mothers of large broods resemble the grandmothers of small families.

The physical strain on mothers of large families is paralleled by emotional strain. These twin stresses impair the ability of mothers to give their children the warmth, consistency, and freedom which they otherwise could.

TABLE 14-12   Maternal Child-Rearing Practices, by Number of Children

MATERNAL CHILD-REARING PRACTICE	NUMBER OF CHILDREN		LARGE/SMALL RATIO
	Small	Large	
Cold to child, seldom praises him	48%	61%	1.27X
Fluctuates in coldness, hostility	37	58	1.57
Punishes aggression against peers	41	68	1.66
Minimum number of families	67	57	

Adapted from Minturn and Lambert (1964):259, 263, 277. Source: Families in six cultures. Large families consisted of two or more children in the U. S. and the Philippines, three or more in India, four or more in Mexico and Okinawa, and five or more in Kenya. For the six cultures combined, the average number of children in the "small" families was 1.8, in the "large" families 4.3 (computed from detailed data kindly supplied by co-author William W. Lambert). Reciprocal percentages did not exhibit the specified practice.

Table 14-12 shows that children in large families suffered from strained maternal resources in six widely different cultures. Maternal coldness reflects the decentralization of parent–child relationships in large families. Fluctuations in maternal feelings reflect the exhaustion of the mother's emotional resources. Punitiveness for aggression against peers reflects the difficulty of keeping large numbers of children under control. Also mothers crack down more because of overcrowded housing and the noise of squabbling children.

Large families overtax personal resources in the same way they overtax the financial resources of parents. Indeed, the notorious difficulties of "solo parents" in coping with any children are matched by the difficulties of dual parents in coping with large numbers of children. After all, it is the ratio of parents to children that counts as far as care-taking is concerned. From this standpoint, two parents with four children may be worse off than a solo parent with only one.

Although the burden of large numbers of children falls heavily on mothers, fathers are not exempt from feeling the strain. In Tokyo, husbands' marital satisfaction fell almost as sharply as wives' with increased numbers of children. And in Puerto Rico, Landy found that most poverty-stricken husbands reacted negatively to the prospect of additional mouths to feed:

Only two fathers seemed genuinely happy, both of them [with] small families. Fathers of small families in general fear the birth least, or, put another way, families, when small at the incipiency of the family cycle, fear having children less than large families, which have already experienced the material and psychological costs of several children. Five husbands seemed more concerned with their wives' health than with the unborn child.

Some husbands, with their greater freedom and irresponsibility, will desert mates and children. When they remain with their families, some abandon the husband–father roles, ignore the needs of wife and children, and assume the role of a privileged guest whose slightest whim and need must be complied with. Anselmo . . . paid not the slightest attention to his wife when she returned from the hospital, weak and ill, with their tenth child. (Two had died of malnutrition and neglect. . . .) Anselmo is a stranger in his own home. His aged mother takes care of his children with his wife. . . . Anselmo spends a large part of what money he seasonally earns on rum. (1959:84)

In this case, excessive reproduction in a culture of poverty destroyed the morale of the father with the result that he retreated into an irresponsible abandonment of his family roles.

Finally, strain affects the children, themselves. We have already seen that older children tend to be pressed into wage-earning and child-caring roles which make them grow old before their time. For oldest daughters, Bossard and Boll found that this sometimes robbed them of the chance to marry:

The social activities of girls in large families . . . were interfered with and limited by the family chores imposed upon them. During the "courtship years," when other girls are out socializing with boys, large family girls are at home doing housework, taking care of the younger children, and in various ways sharing the responsibilities of a large household. . . . Of particular significance in this connection is the practice, seemingly followed in many large families, of "sacrificing" one of the girls to the care of the family. This is the dutiful daughter, the good girl, who stays at home with mother, who looks after father, who works to send a brother through college, and in various other ways devotes herself to her family to the exclusion of her own marriage and family development. (1956:263–264)

So, in general, the larger the number of children, the greater the strain on the capacities and resources of all the members of the family.

Coordination   The larger the family, the more difficult the task of coordinating the activities of the different members to insure that the mountain of housework gets done and to minimize conflict. In all sorts of groups, conflicts arise when members compete for scarce resources. Just as large families have fewer parents per capita, they also have fewer bathrooms, automobiles, TV sets, and other goods or facilities. Despite these increased possibilities of conflict, the number of parents available for dealing with them is reduced by the father's extra work load and the mother's extra housework load. Consequently, coordination in large families tends to break down.

The point is not that small families have no problems, but that conflicts arise more often in large families and that these have smaller reserves of time and energy for dealing with problems. In small families parents can afford to listen patiently to stories of how a particular conflict arose. They can reason with the warring parties hoping to teach them lessons in human relations, to socialize them into values of generosity and mutual consideration which may enable them to avoid conflict or resolve it themselves in the future. Moreover, small families can respond differentially to the individual needs of children of varying ages and temperaments.

The larger the family becomes, the less possible it is for parents to indulge in the luxury of such time-consuming approaches. To save time, parents in large families must forego the luxury of individualized attention. Decision-making must become authoritarian, arbitrary, and parent-dominated simply by virtue of the lack of time and energy to do anything more democratic.

TABLE 14-13   Paternal and Maternal Authoritarianism by
Number of Children and Social Class

| | NUMBER OF CHILDREN | | LARGE/SMALL RATIO |
	1 or 2	3 or more	
Father is authoritarian or autocratic			
Middle class	28%	39%	1.39X
Lower class	37	43	1.16
Mother is authoritarian or autocratic			
Middle class	22%	30%	1.36X
Lower class	27	35	1.30

Adapted from Elder (1962):253. Source: Seventh- to ninth-grade boys in Ohio and North Carolina schools. Reciprocal percentages of parents were democratic, equalitarian, or permissive with their sons.

Table 14-13 shows that even when the line between small and large families is drawn between two children and three or more children, parents in the latter category are consistently more authoritarian. The same differences held for senior high school boys as well and for girls as well as boys in both age groups. With the exception of the fact that mothers of older boys did not differ at all by size of family, 15 out of 16 comparison groups (including the four shown in this table) consistently showed more authoritarianism in larger families.

The value of this centralization of authority is suggested by Bales, Hare, and Borgatta's review of studies of the effects of group size on decision-making in non-family groups: "as size increases there is a tendency toward a more mechanical method of introducing information . . . , a less sensitive exploration of the point of view of the other, and a more direct attempt to control others and reach solution whether or not all group members indicate agreement" (1957:399). Since families are decision-making groups, the same tendencies toward authoritarianism necessarily arise there as well, even when very small families are compared with only slightly larger ones.

Another short-cut used by parents in larger families is punishment rather than reasoning. Douvan and Adelson found that teenagers from large families saw their parents as generally more punitive than adolescents with fewer siblings:

The parents of large families . . . are more traditional, strict, and punitive in their exercise of authority. Their youngsters are less likely to have a say in setting the rule at home; they expect obedience and respect for authority more frequently; their children . . . more often portray parents as strict, and . . . are more likely to characterize their parents' rules as hard. Finally the parents punish their children physically more often than do the parents with fewer children. (1966:275)

Paradoxically, teenagers are just at an age where punitive methods are most apt to provoke rebellion rather than conformity. Elder and Bowerman (1963) found that large families failed to adapt their disciplinary methods to the needs of the individual child. As the oldest child moved into adolescence, they hesitated to give him greater freedom because of the large number of younger siblings who still needed to be controlled. Thus, the larger the family, the less it adapts itself to the needs of the individual, and the more the needs of the group take precedence. It seems likely therefore that large families will suffer increasing breakdowns of their coordinative efforts as their older children approach maturity.

Closely related to this emphasis on punishment is a stress on formal rules. The larger the family, the less possible it is to rely on *ad hoc* decisions because they take too much time. Informal understandings are less likely to be understood by all members of the family because communication is more difficult. To insure clarity of understanding and to minimize the need for further discussion, decisions tend to be utilized as precedents and formalized into rules. The larger the family, the greater the likelihood that these rules will be written down in schedules for using scarce facilities, schedules of work assignments, codes of conduct and penalties for infractions. In short, the larger the family, the more it must operate like a business and like a government, rather than like an informal primary group. It must be bureaucratized to cope with the multiple demands originating in its many members. Otherwise, chaos is liable to ensue.

To direct this bureaucracy, a family needs an efficient administrator. Bossard and Boll (1956) noted that successful large families were headed by women of administrative and managerial ability. Best known of these women was Lillian Gilbreth, mother of the famous *Cheaper by the Dozen* (1949), who was an industrial engineer specializing in scientific management.

Given such effective coordination, the conflicts which threaten large families may be minimized and the strain of living reduced. But the emphasis on standardized rules, strict authority, physical punishment, and conformity means that parent–child relationships are less democratic than they tend to be in a small family. In effect, the larger the number of children added to a nuclear family, the more it comes to resemble a classical extended family which emphasizes respect for elders who exercise authoritarian control. In both cases, the size of the group is a contributing factor to the emphasis on hierarchical coordination.

Internal Preoccupation   The larger the family becomes, the more it tends to be preoccupied with its own internal problems at the expense of being able to meet the needs of outsiders. This can be seen in the decreased ability of a large family to respond to the needs of others in its kinship network. Parents who are barely able to meet the needs of their own children can ill afford to respond to anyone else.

Figure 14-3 can be looked at from two perspectives. In part, it reflects the desire of parents with no children or few children to adopt children of their own. But, from another point of view, it shows that the larger the family, the less it is able to assist surplus children by providing them with a

FIGURE 14-3.   Acquisition of Adopted Children, by Number of Children and
                      Formalization of Marriage

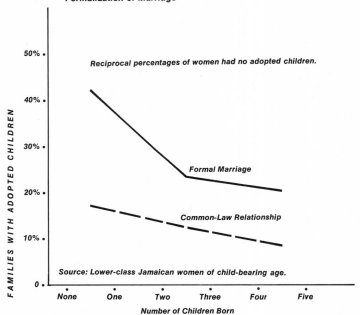

Adapted from Stycos and Back (1964):337.

new home. This figure is the converse of Figure 14-2 and shows that poor families unable to maintain their children will find it difficult to place them with kin who are already preoccupied with children of their own. It will be even more difficult, of course, to place them with families whose own future is doubtful because the man has never married and is liable to leave at any time. Nevertheless, Figure 14-3 shows that even among common-law marriages, the larger the family, the fewer the extra children given even temporary shelter. Conversely I assume that relatively wealthy families can afford the cost of absorbing extra children. But even for them it seems likely that the larger the number of children born, the more reluctant they will be to complicate their life by taking in outside children.

Earlier in this chapter, we saw that old people with many children had more visits from all their children put together than those with few children (even though the latter maintained a more intensive relationship). The converse of this large number of visits from grown children is that such parents are less free to interact with kin outside the nuclear family.

When children are young, Humphreys (1966) found that large Irish families had less interaction with relatives. Presumably after the children leave home, parents are so preoccupied with visits to and from their children and grandchildren that they have less contact with their own siblings and secondary kin. Having founded a major dynasty themselves, their attention is focused downward rather than laterally.

Presumably, internal preoccupation reduces the ability of parents of large families to give money to charity (they already are operating a child-feeding mission of their own), to participate in politics, or otherwise contribute to the life of the larger society. The chief exception may be child-oriented agencies such as the PTA or scouts, where such parents may feel extra involved because so many of their children benefit from these institutions. With that exception, in general the larger the family, the more its energies are absorbed internally and the fewer resources are left over for the larger society.

Deviant Children: Expanded Responsibility

Each normal child added to a family imposes an additional burden on parents and older siblings. If a new acquisition is abnormal, the extra strain may be the equivalent of a whole flock of children. And if the abnormality is incurable the dependency burden may last as long as the parents live, unlike the strain of normal children which eases as they grow up.

External Resources   Many of the effects of having a large number of normal children seem to be duplicated when one child is crippled or retarded. For example, strain, coordinative efforts, and internal preoccupation are likely effects of a deviant child. To give only one example, Farber (1960) found that adding a retarded child to a family with limited resources tended to reduce the parents' marital integration.

A unique feature of deviant children (unlike "surplus" normal children), is that welfare states provide institutional resources to assist over-burdened families. The value of this resource is seen in Farber's finding that families with equally limited resources which succeeded in placing their retarded child in an institution thereby managed to salvage the marital relationship.

From the standpoint of the deviant child, however, institutionalization spells his exclusion from the family. For retarded children, this exclusion may be permanent. In the case of children crippled with polio, during the period that children were hospitalized, they tended to be alienated from the family and integrated into the hospital organization. Doctors and other hospital personnel viewed parents as a threat to the institution's ability to manage the child—a real threat because parents violated dietary regulations to bring the child candy and other sweets. To protect themselves against parental interference, hospital officials tried to freeze parents out and cut them off from information about the child's condition and future prospects. This cast the parents and the institution in a battle for control of the child which the hospital usually won because they had him in their power 24 hours a day whereas the parents could visit only periodically. The end result of hospitalization was to create problems of reintegration into the family when the child was finally allowed to return home. This is not meant to imply that the family could possibly have coped with the child's medical crisis unaided, but that the assistance provided by the hospital relieved the burden of the child's illness only to create reintegration problems when it released him.

Other external resources which Farber found enabled mothers to survive the strain of living with a retarded child included hiring a full-time maid, calling upon the maternal grandmother for assistance, and taking a part-time job. The latter may have provided extra money for the extraordinary expenses of raising a deviant child. More importantly, perhaps, it gave the mother a legitimate excuse to escape from home and have time away from the constant anxiety of caring for an irresponsible child.

Discriminatory Treatment   A second difference between having a large family and having a deviant child is that the latter necessarily requires differential treatment from his normal siblings. The deviant child may need stricter handling. For example, a retarded child needs constant supervision to keep him from getting into trouble and strict, consistent rules because of his limited ability to make decisions. But to compensate for his handicaps, a handicapped child may seem to deserve extra kindness. Davis found that polio children were often overindulged to the point where they were spoiled and their siblings resented the favoritism they received. (However, the larger the number of normal siblings, the less parents were able to get away with discriminatory treatment; conversely "solo" children were the most overindulged.)

Just as we have seen earlier that older siblings in large families are pressed into caretaking roles, so normal siblings (whether older or younger) are expected to care for their deviant siblings. The greater the responsibility, the more the life of the caretaker is affected. Farber (1963) found that children who played with or cared for a retarded child every day developed different life goals than those who carried less responsibility. Both boys and girls with caretaking experience placed less value on having friends, getting married, or becoming a community leader. Instead, they valued devotion to worthwhile causes, making a contribution to mankind, and in the case of girls entering one of the helping professions such as nursing or special education. The unusual roles assumed in the family became a pattern which they would follow throughout their lives.

In general, then, deviant children affect families much like multiple normal children. However, if the deviancy is sufficiently severe, the welfare state may come to the rescue by removing the child from the home. Where children remain in the home, the special treatment they require is likely to alter the life of all the members of the family, but especially of those who carry major caretaking responsibility.

FAMILY CONTRACTION

For all nuclear families save those with a child so deviant that he will always be dependent, there comes a time when children are no longer children, but adults, and when they establish their own nuclear families. Even for families saddled with permanent dependents, the parents eventually die and the family contracts. In any case, families which begin with two members and expand to maximum size, eventually contract to the original two and beyond that to the last survivor.

The Departure of Children

Whereas the first child rather generally causes a crisis because he profoundly alters the lives of the parents, the departure of children is less difficult. It is questionable whether one should label the exodus of either the first or the last child a "crisis" for parents generally.

One reason why launching children into the outside world is less critical is that the strains and losses occasioned by the accession of children are removed by their departure. For some couples, the departure of the last child seems worthy of celebrating with a second honeymoon. Deutscher found that rather than becoaning their "empty nest," middle-class postparental couples welcomed their liberation from the responsibilities of child-rearing. Indeed more couples saw postparenthood as better than the preceding stages of family life than rated it just as good. Even fewer rated it worse than previous stages.

> . . . for some people, postparental life, far from being a time of crisis, is the "good" time—or at least it is better than the periods immediately preceding it. Primarily, to these couples, it is a time of freedom—freedom from financial responsibilities, freedom to be mobile (geographically), freedom to be one's self for the first time since the children came along; no longer do the parents need to lead the self-consciously restricted existence of models for their children. They can let their hair down: "We just take life easy now that the children are grown. We even serve dinner right from the stove when we're alone. It's hotter that way, but you just couldn't let down like that when your children were still at home." (1959:41)

Perhaps because the burden of child-rearing falls more heavily on mothers than on fathers, women in Deutscher's study were especially apt to see life without children as an improvement.

A second reason why launching is seldom a crisis is because it is a gradual process. In contrast to the abruptness of childbirth which suddenly imposes on a couple the most helpless of infants, children begin leaving home almost from birth. Nursery school and kindergarten, playgroups and cliques, evening dates and the college years all involve increasing absences from home and gradual loosening of family ties. By the time the age of marriage is reached, the change in parent–child relationships occasioned by the wedding may be hardly noticeable for a child who is already self-supporting and living away from home. Indeed, for such a child it is difficult to say just when launching does occur, since it is so multiphased. Moreover, the fact that children normally leave home one at a time also prepares the parents for the departure of the last one.

Thirdly, launching does not require the husband and wife to master new skills the way parenthood did. All they have to do is resume the *status quo ante* children—the life they knew at the beginning of marriage.

Lastly, the gradualness of launching seldom totally severs relationships. Generally the departure of children is cushioned by the visiting, phone calls, letters, and gifts which flow back and forth as long as the parents survive.

Contraction Difficulties   Only in exceptional cases is contraction as difficult as expansion. I will examine some of these at greater length in later chapters dealing with family crises. In general the weaker the parents' marriage, the greater the likelihood that parent–child ties will be so strong as to hinder launching. Especially mothers who have invested much of their lives in their children may resist their departure if the chances of resuming a meaningful relationship with the husband are meager.

The Death of the Spouse

Bereavement will be treated fully in the next to the last chapter of the book, again under the heading of family crises. Although for most old people, the loss of the spouse is an unmitigated tragedy, even here there are exceptions. If the husband–wife relationship has been bad enough, loss of the spouse means ending conflict and strain. From the standpoint of wives who must keep house for their husband, his death brings a freedom from responsibility similar to that obtained by launching children. Cumming and Henry (1961) found that the older women get, the larger the proportion is of their friends who enjoy a vigorous peer group of widows. Not until the death of their own spouse are such women free to switch from the shrinking circle of elderly couples to the group of widows. Especially for wives whose husbands have retired and are home all the time, the barrier to enjoying the company of widows is ever present.

On the other hand, if the wife dies first, contraction down to solitude is almost universally tragic. Few men know how to keep house for themselves and there is rarely a circle of widowers they can join (so rarely do men outlive women). Only a man who is willing to join a coed group dominated by women can solve his social problem. His housekeeping problem can hardly be solved short of remarriage. Fortunately there are plenty of eligible women to choose from. Otherwise, a married daughter may rescue her father by inviting him into her home or by visiting him frequently if he lives nearby. For widowers without such resources, the loss of the spouse is felt most acutely.

chapter fifteen

SOCIALIZATION OF CHILDREN: INTEGRATION OF NOVITIATES

The integration of children into the family is in some respects easier, but in others harder, than integrating a marriage partner. For children born into the family or acquired by adoption soon after birth, the advantage is that they come fresh to the family, uninfluenced by outsiders. Unlike marriage partners who (save in the case of child brides) have been socialized in a different family with a partly alien culture, new-born children are the proverbial "clean slates" with no habits to be unlearned, no conflicting values to be changed. Thus the task of the family is exclusively one of socialization with none of the complications of resocialization.

Linked with the lack of prior socialization is a lack of external ties. Whereas young adults face the problem of leaving their parents when they marry, infants have no competing ties to anyone. Their home is their horizon —for the time being, at least—and so the family can monopolize their social relationships.

While these characteristics place the family in a powerful position, there are also some disadvantages. The very fact that the infant is a "clean slate" means that he is completely unsocialized. Not only does he have no bad habits, but he has no good ones either. He comes into the family completely ignorant. He must be taught everything. He is worse than an unhousebroken puppy since animals have a wider range of instinctive behaviors. Nevertheless, in most respects, he comes to the family as a little animal who must be humanized and civilized if they are to be able to accommodate him. By comparison, the task of integrating an already civilized marriage partner into a new family is simple.

NURTURANCE

Relatively little can be done to socialize a baby during his first few weeks, yet from the very beginning the foundations of the socialization process are being laid. At first the baby must simply be accepted into the family as a helpless newcomer who is unable to govern his own behavior. The unconditional character of this acceptance is one of the unique features of the original situation of the child in the family. Most other social organizations have admission requirements which must be passed to gain entrance and behavioral norms which must be observed to remain a member. But to be accepted into a family, a baby must meet no conditions. He simply belongs.

The survival of the child requires that the family meet his physical needs. Food, clothing, and shelter must be supplied or he will soon die. He depends completely on his family for many months for sheer survival.

In depending on his parents, the child acquires a dependency relationship to them. Unconsciously, without realizing it, they come to mean the world to him and therefore acquire greater influence when they are finally ready to begin socializing him.

The creation of a firm tie with the parents depends on more than simply physical nurturance, however. The older the child becomes, the more sensitive he becomes to psychological forces in his environment. And while most parents supply their children's physical needs rather uniformly, parents vary greatly in the quantity and quality of their affection.

In the last chapter, I referred to wanted and unwanted children, to deficiencies and surpluses of children. I also described how high rates of infant mortality and the threatened loss of particular children affected their status in the family. For such reasons and many others, parents differ in their feelings toward their children, and the children's feelings toward their parents are affected accordingly. Some children have a marginal position in the family; they are likely candidates for doling out to interested kin, if that is customary, or for emotional rejection, if it is not. Other children are central to the mother's life, especially if her tie to her husband is weak. In this sense, the integration of the child into the family can be measured simply in terms of the emotional attraction or repulsion which his parents exert directly on him.

The older the child grows, the less unconditional his membership in the family remains. The more he is considered old enough to know better, the more offensive unsocialized behavior becomes. The emphasis gradually shifts from simple acceptance/rejection based on such extraneous factors as the size of the family and the extent of the family resources to an integration dependent on the child's own behavior. This means that molding his behavior becomes increasingly important, so the child's willingness to be socialized becomes more important.

With respect to socialization, the parents' emotional nurturance acquires a second facet. Numerous studies of child-rearing suggest that the child's ability to be socialized is profoundly affected by the parents' affectional relationship to him. If they have loved him abundantly, he will love them in return and respond positively to their child-training efforts. But if they have disliked him, he is liable to resist their efforts to socialize him.

Effects of Nurturance

One of the crucial aims of socialization is to instill a workable conscience in the child. Peck and Havighurst (1960) ranked adolescents on a continuum from those with underdeveloped consciences whom they labelled "amoral" to those with overdeveloped consciences, the "irrational conscientious." Amorality was caused by parental rejection. Irrational conscientiousness was caused by possessive, smothering love which trapped the child in a conscience so rigid as to paralyze him. In the middle with extensive but not excessive warmth were those whom they labelled "rational altruistic" personalities, well-socialized but able to adapt to changing circumstances. In general, then, the warmer the parents, the stronger the conscience.

In a study of nine- to eleven-year-old boys, Rosen and d'Andrade (1959) found that the biggest difference between high-achievement-motivated and low-motivated boys was in the warmth of the mothers of the highly motivated boys. Their fathers were also warmer, but the difference was not as great. Curiously, however, the mothers of the highly motivated boys were also somewhat more rejecting, though their rejection was small in comparison with their warmth and acceptance. Perhaps they manifested just enough rejection to prevent their warmth from being too sugary. After all, if one is completely accepted, why try to achieve anything more? Perhaps, as in the case of conscience, achievement motivation bears a curvilinear relationship to warmth. A good dose of warmth is needed but it is possible to have an overdose.

At the opposite extreme from warmth is hostility. Children whose parents are not warm but cold, rejecting, and hostile tend to become hostile toward others in turn. In part, this may be an imitation of the parents' example (which I will discuss shortly). But it also reflects the weakness of socialization in a cold emotional climate.

Bandura and Walters (1959) found that the warmer the parent (in this case especially the same-sex parent), the less aggressive teenage boys were toward peers, teachers, etc. Warm fathers spent more time doing things with their sons and were more emotionally expressive. Parental warmth enabled the son to establish positive human relations with the key figures in his environment—the father himself, teachers, and peers. Given these positive relationships, the boy was able to engage in mutual give and take without feeling threatened. I also assume that these boys had more effective inner controls against aggressive behavior as a result of their warm interdependent relationships with others.

In addition to overt aggression, hostility expresses itself in prejudice. To consider oneself categorically superior to blacks, Jews, women or other "lesser breeds" is to manifest a contempt often based on inner insecurity. Myers and Roberts (1959) found that lower-middle-class neurotics who felt rejected by their families in childhood were acutely status-conscious, emphasizing social conformity and respectability. One of their greatest fears was that blacks would invade their neighborhoods, lowering their prestige. Having failed to be accepted by their families of origin, they were eager to be accepted by the outside world and depended for that acceptance on super-conformity to middle-class norms and prejudices.

The obverse of hostility toward inferiors is gullibility toward superiors. Blake (1961) found that working-class Jamaican girls who were starved for affection at home were vulnerable to seduction by their employers. The parents' failure to provide emotional warmth created a vacuum which impelled the daughters to violate the parents' teaching. Instead of responding to their parents' teaching, the daughters turned to alternative sources of affection, learning the "lessons" that these substitute teachers offered in the context of a more humane companionship, no matter how exploitive it might be judged by the parents or other outsiders.

Without a solid affectional base, then, parents cannot expect to succeed in socializing their children. On the other hand, warmth provides only the starting point for socialization and is not meaningful without other elements.

MODELING

I have already noted that it is difficult to distinguish between the parents' acceptance of their child (1) as a basis for socialization and (2) as an example of accepting behavior which the child may imitate. The well-known saying that "actions speak louder than words" might be the slogan for this section because children are heavily influenced by their parents' example. If parents say one thing and do another, children are more impressed by the actions than by the words. When children are too young to understand words, they still learn from what they observe. Provided only that parents and children have a positive relationship, children can be expected to follow in their parents' footsteps. During the formative years of childhood, parents are the chief example the child sees. When the proximity of that example is combined with the positive valence which parents gain by their nurturance, the parents' modeling becomes highly influential.

Sometimes parents set good examples for their children in the sense that they approve of what the children learn. In other cases, without intending it, chilidren follow in their parents' footsteps despite the fact that the parents wish they wouldn't. The difference is a matter of values, but it is useful to note the distinction because it emphasizes the potency of the parents' example whether they intend it or not.

What Winch (1952:83) called the "status-conferring function of the family" is carried on primarily by example. Most children acquire the same social status as their parents. Children of working-class parents grow up to be blue-collar workers, and children of middle-class families to be white-collar workers. From his classic study of adolescents in Elmtown, U.S.A., Hollingshead summarized the family's influence on their children's class position as follows:

> . . . the child receives the vast majority of his experiences during the pre-school years in his parental home and in the immediate neighborhood around his home. During these years essential aspects of the class culture which characterize the family are transferred through the subtle processes of informal learning from the parents to the child. What the child learns in the home is carried out of it to the neighborhood, and the child is not aware of the connection between home influence and what he does. In this way, family background goes along with the child wherever he goes, and what he has learned in the home acts as a powerful influence on his behavior in non-family social situations. (1949:441–442)

Crucial to middle-class success is occupational achievement. We have already seen that parental warmth heightens achievement motivation, and we will see later that parents make other contributions as well. Nevertheless, modeling is one way parents contribute to the development of the desire to achieve.

Some mothers set a good example for their children by going to work. Thus, Morrow and Wilson (1961) found that more mothers of high-achieveing high school boys than of low-achievers were employed outside the home (47 percent versus 37 percent).

Children absorb the defects as well as the virtues of their parents. In tracing the family origins of tension-induced duodenal ulcers, Goldberg (1958) found that patients' mothers were tense and anxious themselves. Such psychosomatic disorders as migraine headaches and skin rashes were common and two mothers even had duodenal ulcers too. Since ulcers are not genetically inherited, this is an interesting example of psychological transmission. Presumably the tenseness of the mothers was communicated to their children in nonverbal gestures like muscular rigidity and tone of voice. The mothers did not want their sons to "inherit" their tenseness, yet inherit it they did.

To be tense is not necessarily to have ulcers. Sometimes tension is directed outward in aggression against others. For Goldberg's boys, however, the pattern of turning tension in upon their own bodies followed the parents' example in yet another way. Their fathers were notably submissive, which means they were unaggressive toward others. Hence the opportunity to turn aggression outward was not presented in the repertoire of behaviors made available to the boys by their parents.

By contrast, aggressiveness was transmitted from parents to children in two studies of aggressive children. Among nursery school children, Hoffman (1960) found that children whose fathers dominated their mothers and whose mothers dominated them (the children) were more hostile and aggressive toward other children. These children exerted power over weaker children in the same way that their parents exerted power over the weaker sex and the weaker generation.

Among adolescent boys, Bandura and Walters (1959) found that aggressive boys were more apt than normal boys to have been punished physically by their parents, especially by their fathers. Nor did this use of punishment seem to be simply a reaction to the boys' own aggressiveness. Rather, many punitive fathers had been physically punished by their own fathers and were simply repeating their parents' practices. When the boys in turn were aggressive toward their peers, it seems fair to suggest that they had learned to be aggressive by observing their parents' aggression (punishment) toward them.

It seems likely that children are especially apt to learn from the way their parents behave when the parents are trying to socialize them. Insofar as parents exert leverage over the child, the child will be particularly sensitive to the parents' behavior.

A Japanese mother's typical method of influencing her child is by subtle half-hidden self-sacrificial suffering. This has a powerful emotional impact on the child which is difficult to resist just because it is so subtle. The mother uses this not consciously but subconsciously as a tool, which is more effective because it is not just an act. The child learns from her that passive suffering is proper behavior. This model makes the child more willing to accept suffering in his own life (as when his parents seek to impose an arranged marriage on him). Since children are more apt to imitate a parent of the same sex, girls are more prone than boys to accept suffering passively.

By contrast, American mothers present a model of nagging and criticism to their children which gives them a basis for dealing with problems more openly and independently. Like their mothers, they can resist openly, disagree publicly, and refuse to accept external dictation even from their parents.

Finally, parents may get their children into trouble not so much by what they do as by what they fail to do. For Myers and Roberts' neurotic patients (1959), one reason for their emotional difficulties seemed to be the parents' failure to provide a model of successful social mobility. The parents had had mobility aspirations which they successfully transmitted to their children, but the fact that they were unsuccessful themselves meant that their children could not use them as role models. The teachers and other high-status persons whom they chose as substitute models were able to meet the patients' needs for an example to imitate but not their emotional needs. Had their mobility efforts succeeded, that success would have provided an alternative source of personal satisfaction. But when their efforts failed, they were left with neither family security nor any alternative source of comfort to fall back on. Such is the risk when parents encourage their children to abandon their own model and to go out into the cold world to seek their fortune.

INSTRUCTION

For some of the situations which children face, parents are too old or too married to provide relevant models. Nevertheless they may help their child anticipate situations he will have to face alone and share with him the benefits of their wider experience. Even in areas (like achievement) where their example has considerable relevance, the child's socialization may be facilitated by instruction specifically geared to his situation. After all, the levels of achievement to be expected of 30-year-old parents and five-year-old children are quite different. The beauty of language is that it can supplement the parents' example with clues to the child's expected behavior.

The clarity and consistency with which parents set standards for the children supply key elements in the socialization lessons to be learned. But sometimes parents shy away from instructing their children. Noninstruction is nearly universal with respect to sexual behavior. Sears, Maccoby, and Levin (1957) found that New England parents relied on "information control" rather than supplying sex information to their five-year-old children. Other terms for information control might be "censorship" or "avoiding the issue." In effect, these parents postponed the sexual socialization of their children.

When parents never get around to instructing their children about sex, they leave them vulnerable to sexual exploitation. Blake (1961) found that Jamaican girls who had never been given sexual knowledge by their parents were apt to become sexually involved with the first man to come along. Chesser (1957) found conversely that English women whose parents had been their main source of sex education were less apt to engage in premarital intercourse than those whose parents gave them little or no instruction.

Setting Standards

When parents do instruct their children, their efforts will be most successful when they are nicely geared to the child's age and abilities. The difficulty of setting standards which are high enough but not too high can be seen in parental encouragement of children's efforts at school and in other competitive situations. By expecting too little, parents fail to encourage their children to develop their full potential. By expecting too much, parents discourage their children from trying at all.

McClelland's research in Germany and Japan (1961:349) showed that mothers' own needs for achievement were curvilinearly related to their sons' achievement motivation. Sons had the highest motivation when their mothers were only slightly above average in achievement motivation. Sons' motivation declined not only when mothers' motivation was below average, but also when it was high or very high. This suggests the depressing effect on children's achievement aspirations of parents who expect too much.

Lu's (1962) study of schizophrenic patients suggests that it may be even worse for children, psychologically, if they accept the aspirations of parents who expect too much. These parents expected perfection—children who were the best in school, the best in their occupation, the best in everything. By dint of conscientious hard work, the patients were able to achieve perfection as long as the competition was limited. In the "little puddle" of grade school and perhaps even in high school, they managed to graduate at the top of their class. However, once they reached college where the competition was stiffer and the standard of excellence shifted from memorization to creativity, their chances of remaining on top decreased. Had they continued to outstrip all their competitors, the schizophrenic break might have been avoided. But when they found themselves no longer best but only second-best, they could not accept the blow to their pride. Withdrawing into a world of fantasy became a way out of the dilemma posed by being trapped between excessively high standards and the breaks of life in the larger world.

Lu's findings suggest the importance of including in parental standards not only appropriateness to the child's abilities but a greater emphasis on the goal of self-fulfillment than on competitive victory. Lu's patients had normal siblings whose mental health had been safeguarded by their ability to accept realistic limits on their own capacities, to accept disappointment and frustration, to be good losers, and to adjust to changing circumstances.

Although standards for very young children must be set unilaterally by parents, the older children become, the more useful it is for standard-setting to become a joint enterprise for parents and children. By the time children reach adolescence, the unilateral imposition of standards risks a parental domination which will interfere with the child's own achievements.

In a comparative study of five nations—the U. S., Great Britain, West Germany, Italy, and Mexico—Elder (1965) found that adults whose parents had treated them democratically in adolescence went farther in school than those whose parents set too few standards or imposed them in an authoritarian manner. The differences were especially sharp in countries where traditional authoritarianism was still strong (Germany, Italy, and Mexico).

Table 15-1 shows that the inhibiting effect of authoritarian parents was not due to class differences but was visible within both the middle-class and the working-class samples. Further analyses showed that it also affected older men, both older and younger women, both rural and urban residents, and both Protestants and Catholics. In other words, the impact of the democratic or authoritarian character of parental instruction on children's educational achievements was pervasive.

TABLE 15-1 Educational Attainment, by Parent–Child Relationship and Social Class

PERCENTAGE WHO REACHED SECONDARY SCHOOL, BY SOCIAL CLASS	PARENT–CHILD RELATIONSHIP		DEMOCRATIC/ AUTHORITARIAN RATIO
	Authoritarian	Democratic	
Middle class	33%	86%	2.61X
Working class	11	24	2.18

Adapted from Elder (1965):88. Source: Representative national sample of West German men aged 18–40, excluding "lower-class" men, almost none of whom reached secondary school. Reciprocal percentages of men dropped out of school before reaching secondary school.

Contradictory Instructions   Some parents undermine their teaching efforts by giving their children contradictory instructions. Such contradictions may occur at many points: between the husband's and the wife's instructions, between what the parents put into words and what they convey nonverbally, or between the model they portray and the standards they advocate. In Elder's study, husbands and wives who treated each other democratically (in the sense of making decisions jointly) strengthened the impact of parent–child democracy on their children's educational achievement. Parents who treated each other democratically, but treated their children in an authoritarian manner, reduced or even reversed the beneficial effect of the parents' example. Apparently children resented parental authoritarianism all the more when they saw that the parents were not so rigid with each other.

Some parents encourage their children to succeed but punish them when they do. Their negative reaction to the child's fulfillment of their demands communicates contradictory messages to the child so that he doesn't know whether to do what the parents ask or to respond to their unhappiness when he succeeds. Little wonder that Lu found such contradictions had precipitated some patients' schizophrenic paralyses. To cite one of his examples:

> My father especially expected me to do well in the football field, because all through his life he had wanted to be a football coach. . . . Whenever I played football with other kids in high school, my father used to come and insist on coaching me. My friends all laughed at me on account of it. But whenever I did play real well, my father would get mad at me. He wanted to feel he was better than me. I think he competes with me. . . . (1962: 224)

This father asked his child to succeed and then punished him for doing so. With respect to anti-social behavior, parents may forbid it yet unconsciously reward the child for delinquent acts. Parents who have inner conflicts about arson, stealing, or sexual delinquency may convey their uncertainty to their children nonverbally:

> The entranced parental facial expression apparent to the child describing a stealing episode, a sexual misdemeanor, or a hostile attitude toward a teacher conveys to the child that the parent is achieving some pleasurable gratification. No amount of subsequent punishment will act as a deterrent against the recurrences of acting out. A child wishes to do the thing which

he senses gives the parent pleasure, even though he may be punished. We frequently see parents who describe the child's delinquent behavior with obvious pleasure. Suspicious questioning often conveys the parents' unconscious wish that the child comply by doing the thing verbally warned against. (Giffin, Johnson, and Litin, 1954:673)

Some parents do not respond consistently to tabooed behavior from one time to the next. If a given act is punished one day and not punished the next, the child becomes confused about what is expected of him. Such confusion increases the likelihood that the quasi-forbidden behavior will continue to be performed and produces weak internalization of the ambiguous norm. Just as Giffin, Johnson, and Litin found that children subjected to inconsistencies between what parents said and what they conveyed nonverbally developed "lacunae" or holes in their super-egoes, so Peck and Havighurst (1960) found that children subjected to discipline which fluctuated from day to day developed "amoral" personalities. For Banfield, the amoral ethos of a whole people (rural Southern Italians) was due in part to the inconsistency with which they were punished as children:

Punishment . . . is unrelated to any principle of "oughtness"; at one moment the parent kisses and at the next he cuffs. If gratification and deprivation— "good" and "bad"—depend upon the caprice of one who has power, no general principles can be internalized as conscience. (1958:161)

If contradictory instructions issue from disagreements between parents, the family itself lacks integration. The best that can be hoped for under such circumstances, is that the child will be socialized into the norms of one parent, thereby becoming integrated into a subsystem of the family even if integration into the whole family is impossible. Even so, the counter-influence of the unchosen parent is liable to weaken the influence of the chosen one.

Inconsistency may arise not only between the two parents' instructions but between messages received from the parents and from outside sources. If the parents are divided, the winner is apt to be the one whose views are supported by the larger society.

Putney and Middleton (1961) found that college students whose parents held differing religious views tended to agree with whichever parent was closer to the "modernist Christian" mode of American society generally (64 percent sided with the conventional parent and only 36 percent with the deviant parent). Nor was this simply a result of preferring a more liberal position since children with one skeptical and one modernist Christian parent tended to side with the latter. Presumably the consistency between the conventional parent and the larger society outweighed the influence of the unsupported parent. The same study found, however, that even if both parents held the same views, children were liable to be influenced away from extreme positions toward conventional views.

Table 15-2 shows that parents who shared the modal religious ideology of American society (modernist Christianity) were most successful in transmitting their views to their children. Even though majorities of both left-wing and right-wing parents also conveyed their own views to their children, they

TABLE 15-2   Child's Religious Ideology, by Parents' Ideology

| IDEOLOGY OF CHILD | PARENTAL IDEOLOGY | | |
	Skeptical	Modernist	Conservative
Skeptical (atheists, agnostics)	68%	7%	5%
Modernist Christian	30	89	18
Conservative Christian	3	3	77
Total	101%	99%	100%
Number of families	37	424	354

Adapted from Putney and Middleton (1961):129. Source: Social science students in 13 colleges and universities in the eastern United States. Eliminated were families adhering to non-Christian faiths (most of them Jewish) and families where the parents held differing ideologies.

lost larger minorities of the children to the dominant societal norm. Relatively few children, on the other hand, rebelled sufficiently from extremist parents to go all the way to the opposite extreme.

These findings about the combined or conflicting influence of parents and the larger society reflect the multiple influences to which children are subjected. Outside the family, peers are the most important influence but any institution in which the child participates is likely to have a socializing influence also. Perhaps institutions which specialize in the socialization of children are likely to be most influential—especially schools (because of the extensive time children are exposed to their influence) and, to a lesser extent, religious organizations and other agencies which serve young people in their leisure time.

We saw in Table 6-3 how the class position of parents and peers reinforce or contradict each other in determining the son's vocational ambitious-

TABLE 15-3   Vocational Ambitiousness, by Parental and Peer Influence

| PARENTAL INFLUENCES | | PEER INFLUENCE | VOCATIONALLY AMBITIOUS |
Modeling	Instruction		
+	+	+	82%
+	+	−	78
+	−	+	73
−	+	+	71
−	+	−	56
−	−	+	36
+	−	−	30
−	−	−	26

Adapted from Simpson (1962):521. Source: High school boys in two southern U. S. cities (whites only). Parental modeling was defined as positive by middle-class fathers, negative by working class fathers. Positive instructions took the form of one or both parents advising the son to enter a profession. Peer influence was positive if the boy belonged to two or more clubs or organizations and if at least one of his three best friends was from a middle-class home. Vocational ambitiousness involved enrollment in a college preparatory curriculum plus expectation of entering a high-level professional or executive occupation. Reciprocal percentages were not ambitious by one or both of these criteria.

ness. Table 15-3 presents a more detailed analysis from the same study which shows the combined effect of two types of parental teaching and of peers. At the two extremes, boys exposed to consistently positive influences were most successfully socialized and those with consistently negative influences were least apt to be ambitious. The very fact of attending school, however, presumably accounts for the fact that as many as one-fourth of the boys lacking either family influence or peer influence nevertheless managed to acquire mobility aspirations from elsewhere.

Ranking close behind the consistently positive cases were those where two out of three factors were positive. Conversely, where two out of three were negative, most boys were unambitious. The one exception to this generalization was where working-class parents actively encouraged their son to enter a profession. Even if not only the parents but all the boy's close friends were from the working class, this parental encouragement (presumably reinforced by the teacher) was able to offset the lack of middle-class models in the boy's out-of-school environment. In general, the more consistent the influences to which a child is exposed, the more effectively he will be socialized.

Reasoning

A second major aspect of instruction besides the nature of the standards themselves is the nature of the process by which they are communicated to the child. At one extreme, they are simply imposed on the child. He may be assured that they are "right" or "good for him," but if he asks "Why?", he may be told "because I said so." Such parents rely on their authority as leverage over the child. They "pull rank" on him. They ask unquestioning obedience. All the child has to do is receive and memorize the parents' instructions and he will be a "good little boy."

At the opposite extreme, parents take the time to explain every standard they advocate. They try to persuade the child that the standard is desirable, not because the parents say so but because it will benefit the child, the family, and/or the larger society. If the child is skeptical, he may challenge their assertions and precipitate a discussion of the issues.

What are the effects on children of these alternative teaching methods? Both Bandura and Walters' nonaggressive boys and Sears, Maccoby, and Levin's high-conscience children had been reasoned with more than their poorly-socialized counterparts. This suggests that reasoning is an effective element in socialization. Why?

Reasoning elicits the child's active cooperation, whereas authoritarianism treats him as a pawn. A child who is reasoned with has his mental capacities stimulated, his sympathy for others aroused as the parent describes the potential consequences of adhering to or violating the proposed norm. Reasoning penetrates to the core of the child where learning can take place, whereas parental authority is imposed externally. The very fact that reasoning takes so much time means that children who are reasoned with receive more extensive tutoring. An unreasoned-with child is almost as handicapped as a child who has gone only to grade school. When parents have the patience to "sell" their children on the standards they advocate, they are more apt to get their children to accept their product than if they say in effect, you've got to buy it whether you want to or not.

One danger with an authoritarian approach is that it may backfire. In a study of the political party affiliation of new voters, 21–24 years old, Maccoby (1954) found they were most apt to have switched parties from their parents' political affiliation if the parents had treated them either in an authoritarian, unreasoning manner or in a laissez-faire noncommunicative manner. Especially low-status parents who lacked social prestige and other resources which might have commanded their children's respect alienated their children, causing them to switch parties (in this case from the working-class Democratic Party to the higher prestige Republican Party). For young people who had been treated in a laissez-faire manner, the reason for failure in their political socialization seems to have been simple neglect on the part of their parents. When parents fail to instruct their children adequately in any way, including politically, children are open to outside influences.

Intermediate between these authoritarian and permissive extremes were parents who relied on reasoning. Their children were most apt to subscribe to the parents' political views. If such parents had a high interest in politics and therefore provided clear-cut and intensive training, political socialization was especially successful.

Standards, then, must be clearly stated, jointly stated, and persuasively stated if the child is to be effectively socialized.

ENVIRONMENTAL CONTROL

The preceding section suggests that families cannot afford to ignore alien forces in their child's environment if they wish to insure consistency in the instruction to which he is exposed. One way parents can control the environment is to select the peer groups, institutions, and other social influences to which the child is exposed, screening out those which would undermine their own teaching.

One example of environmental control was noted by Hollingshead in middle-class "Elmtown" families:

> There is continual pressure from parents . . . to avoid the lower classes.
> . . . The parents generally know the parents of the children with whom their children associate. If these friendships do not meet with their approval, they ordinarily bring pressure to bear on the child to drop the friends and activities which do not conform with parental expectation. They are not always successful, but the pressure is active. On the whole, though, children in these three classes are guided by their parents along lines approved by the class cultures with remarkable success. (1949:443)

Knowledge of the child's associates is more difficult to achieve in a large city. The smaller the community, the easier it is for parents to control their children's associates. However, community size has a paradoxical character —if it is small enough and homogeneous enough, there may be no alien influences to worry about. In many primitive tribal communities these circumstances are associated with extraordinary permissiveness by parents confident that their children can't associate with the "wrong" people because there are no wrong people. Everyone shares the same outlook and other parents will collaborate in looking after their children. In general, the smaller the community, the greater the possibility of exercising environmental control but the less the need for it. Presumably environmental control is especially appropriate for high-status families in stratified small towns like "Elmtown."

Margaret Mead's study of child-rearing in Samoa (1949) suggests that there may be unintended outcomes of the extraordinary permissiveness of an undifferentiated community. Not only was responsibility for supervising children shared throughout the Samoan village but whenever a child became dissatisfied with his own family he would move to another family which seemed more hospitable. This childhood mobility weakened the relationship between parents and children and loosened the extent to which children were integrated into the family. It seems likely that this childhood experience set a pattern for casualness in human relationships generally and for weak husband–wife ties in particular. Just as children unhappy with their parents moved away from home, so wives unhappy with their husbands "went home to mother." If one does not learn to establish close, lasting relationships in childhood, one will be poorly prepared to create or maintain them as an adult.

At the opposite extreme, families control their children's environments so strictly that the children never have an opportunity to learn how to face alien influences. Especially if parents rely on sheltering their children and fail to give them instruction, what happens when that control is finally removed and the child goes naively out to face the world? For Blake's Jamaican girls, the answer was frequently the breakdown of the gains the parents had sought:

> Authoritarian child-rearing has distinct advantages for an overburdened parent when children are young. But when they become less dependent upon adults for every need, the parent must then contend with a youngster who will act "properly" and "decently" only when under parental supervision. . . . The strictness of child-rearing . . . renders [a daughter] exceptionally vulnerable to male advances once confinement breaks down. . . . Since the girl has been "controlled" all her life, she has developed few inner controls with which to cope with freedom. Therefore, she frequently exhibits considerable abandon in her new-found status. For example, some of our respondents whose first [sexual] unions occurred after they had gone to live with a relative or employer claimed that this was the first time they had had a "chance" to associate with men. (1961:81,86)

Environmental control, then, is one means of reducing counterpressures from alien sources. Within limits, it strengthens and reinforces the instructional efforts of parents. But it is no substitute for those efforts. When environmental control is the only method used, it can succeed only if parents are perennially present to exercise it.

For some Jamaican girls, perennial control was achieved by using chaperones until daughters were "safely" married, at which point the responsibility for environmental control became the husband's. But for poor families unable to supply chaperones and for independent young people unwilling to accept chaperonage, environmental control has only supplemental value. In any case, its function is not to socialize the child positively but to prevent interference with socialization through other means.

FEEDBACK

To return to the positive aspects of socialization, it is not enough to provide the child with models to emulate and instructions to follow. Perhaps, in most cases, the parent can assume that the child will utilize those cues to proper behavior. But not always. And if the child's behavior will vary, the parents need to know how he behaves. This information may be secured in a variety of ways—by observing the child in action, by inspecting the results of his acts (in cleaning up his room or doing his homework), by asking him, and by asking others. Much of this information is conveyed spontaneously in family conversations. How it is secured matters little as long as the parents gain access to it somehow.

In discovering whether their instructions are being followed, parents learn whether their socialization efforts have been properly understood. If not, perhaps further teaching is needed to clarify their standards and the reasons for them. If the fault lies not with the child's understanding but simply with his willingness to apply that understanding, the question of discipline arises (which I will discuss in the next section).

If parents fail to inquire and fail to listen to reports of their child's behavior, this signals that they don't really care how he behaves, and their instruction loses much of its persuasiveness. In the next section we will see the negative results of punishing the child, but Table 15-4 suggests that indifference may be even worse than punitiveness.

TABLE 15-4   Self-Esteem by Mother's Reaction to Low Marks

| | *MOTHER'S REACTION TO LOW MARKS* | | | |
SELF-ESTEEM	*Indifferent*	*Punitive*	*Supportive*	*Supportive and Punitive*
High	26%	34%	44%	49%
Medium	13	25	25	25
Low	61	41	30	26
Total	100%	100%	99%	100%
Number of cases	23	228	533	178

Adapted from Rosenberg (1965):138. Source: Juniors and seniors in selected New York State public high schools. They were asked about the mother's reaction to low marks they had received on report cards in the fifth and sixth grades.

The negative impact of maternal indifference on adolescent self-esteem was paralleled by an only slightly weaker impact of indifference from fathers as well. Disinterest also damaged self-esteem when it took the form of not being interested in the child's friends or not being interested in what he had to say during mealtime conversations.

In order to be able to do a good job of socialization, parents must be interested in the child's behavior. However, parental concern with feedback can be overdone. To demand a complete account of every unobserved minute would betray a lack of trust in the child's willingness to behave. Mistrust communicates a message that the parent almost expects the child to misbehave. Even if he fails to act on that expectation, parental inquisitioning may keep too tight a rein on him. And to rein the child in is likely to stifle his creativity.

In a study of the difference between gifted students who achieved high scores on IQ tests and those who were highly creative, Getzels and Jackson (1962) found that the mothers of the high-testers were more anxious and protective. They were excessively vigilant about their children and almost constantly criticized them or tried to improve their behavior. By contrast, mothers of creative children allowed them to develop in their own ways and thereby gave them the freedom to be creative.

Feedback, then, is necessary and useful, but like most other aspects of the socialization process, it can either be overemphasized or underemphasized.

DISCIPLINE—SANCTIONS

Once information about the child's behavior has been secured, the next question is the nature of the parents' response. Depending on what the child has done and how the parents evaluate it, the parents may respond with positive or negative sanctions.

Learning theory suggests the importance of parental response. Socialized behavior sometimes brings intrinsic rewards as when a child has the satisfaction of achieving a certain goal. But achieving difficult goals often requires postponing immediate pleasures. Moreover some socialization tasks require the inhibition of spontaneous aggressive, sexual, or other anti-social behavior and are intrinsically frustrating for the child. Insofar as socialization requires the child to follow a path other than the most tempting one, what will reward him for his sacrifice? The most immediate source of potential rewards is his parents.

When good behavior is rewarded, the child's tendency to repeat that behavior in the future is reinforced. If parents fail to notice what he has done or fail to reward his good behavior, his incentive to continued self-sacrifice will evaporate.

Parents must respond appropriately if they are to reinforce selectively the behavior which they advocate and discourage the behavior they dislike. The crucial point about the use of sanctions is to relate them to the child's behavior. If all his behavior were indiscriminately rewarded, indiscriminately ignored, or indiscriminately punished, he would learn nothing. Only insofar as he receives differential sanctions for different behaviors will certain habits be strengthened and others be weakened. And, in general, the wider the range of variation in response, the more rapidly and effectively the child will learn. If the parents' response varies only slightly no matter what the child does, the child will receive correspondingly less reinforcement. But if there is a major difference in their response depending on his behavior, he will be strongly influenced.

To cite McClelland's phraseology: "motive intensity is acquired as a function of the 'amplitude of affective change' associated with the achievement situation" (1961:352). In other words, the wider the range of variation in the affective response of the parent to the child's behavior, the more intense the motivation learned (in this case, achievement motivation).

In Rosen and d'Andrade's study of boys with high achievement motivation, "Both parents typically showed keener pleasure and disappointment at the boys' success or failure than was ordinarily displayed by the parents of boys with weak achievement motivation" (1959:199). This wider range of response presumably produced the boys' greater eagerness to achieve the goals the parents set for them. Similarly, we have already seen in Table 15-4 that self-esteem was higher for adolescents whose parents responded with both support and punishment to children who received low marks. Pure punishment presumably is too discouraging and pure support too accepting, whereas parents who combine the two judiciously are varying their response according to the child's achievement.

All this assumes that parents are consistent in the standards they require the child to adhere to. Instruction is undermined if parental sanctioning is inconsistent. No matter how regularly parents may ask their child to share his toys, if they reward him sometimes and ignore him other times their teaching will be undermined. Worse yet, if they praise him for sharing one day and criticize him for "not sticking up for your own rights" the next, the inconsistent sanctioning will confuse the child about what the parents are "really" trying to teach him.

If definite sanctions are consistently applied, does it make any difference what those sanctions are? In general, the research evidence suggests that rewards are more effective than punishments and that psychological sanctions are more effective than physical sanctions.

TABLE 15-5 Conscience Development, by Type of Sanction

Type of Sanction	Correlation with Conscience Development
Praise	+.18
Withdrawal of love	+.09
Isolation	.00
Tangible rewards	−.04
Deprivation of privileges	−.07
Physical punishment	−.20

Adapted from Sears, Maccoby, and Levin (1957):386.
Source: Mothers of public school kindergarten children in two Boston suburbs.

The correlations between types of sanctions and conscience development in five-year-old children portrayed in Table 15-5 are all quite low, but the rank order of methods is consistent with the findings of other researchers.

At the two extremes are the two types of sanctions which combine most fully the reward/punishment and the psychological/physical variables which I have already mentioned. Praise is a purely psychological reward and physical punishment by definition a pure case of physical punishment. It is doubtful whether too much significance should be attached to the order of the intervening methods since they represent the mixed effects of physical rewards or of psychological punishments.

Why should rewards be more useful than punishments in motivating children to good behavior? Precisely because the task is to reinforce desired behavioral responses. I have already suggested that behavior which is rewarded tends to be repeated, both in the hope of receiving the reward again, and because the habit has been strengthened by the original reward.

But why does punishment interfere with socialization? Isn't punishment the opposite of reward and haven't I already suggested that sanctions need to vary widely if they are to assist in socialization? It is true that punishment is the opposite extreme of reward, but the research evidence suggests that sufficient variance is achieved when sanctions fluctuate over the range from maximum reward to non-reward (*i.e.,* to neutrality). Once the neutral point is passed and punishment is introduced, something seems to go wrong.

The trouble with punishment is that it tends to destroy the parent–child relationship on which socialization depends. It antagonizes and alienates the child, decreasing his sense of belonging to the family. Unless counter-balanced by extraordinary amounts of warmth and acceptance, it makes the child feel rejected and excluded from the family. The more the child is punished, the less nurturant the parent seems and the less dependent the child wants to be on such a pain-inflicting person. Punishment, then, dissipates the emotional "capital" which the parent created by nurturing the child, and it weakens the leverage that the parent has over the child. It may succeed for the moment in making the child so afraid that he will stop his immediate behavior. But it is a poor basis for the long-run task of creating a solid conscience.

The advantage of psychological rather than physical sanctions is closely allied to the advantage of reasoning over authoritarian instruction. Insofar as the goal of socialization is the internalization of norms, this is a psychological process. Verbal and emotional sanctions involve psychological processes which affect the child subjectively and internally. By contrast, physical rewards and punishments are literally external to the child and leave less of an imprint on his mind. While physical sanctions may temporarily coerce the child into conforming to family norms when the child thinks his behavior will be observed, only internalization knits the child into the family subjectively. Indeed, until the parental standards have been internalized, it is questionable whether the parents have accomplished their task. If all the child relies upon is fear of external punishment or hope of external rewards, the family has not achieved a solid integration based on socialization but only a shaky integration based on social control.

SOCIAL CONTROL: THE STRUCTURAL ORGANIZATION OF THE FAMILY

Socialization is a necessary but not a sufficient basis for integrating novitiate spouses and children into the family. No group of people, no matter how well trained, can ever function simply on the basis of the spontaneous, self-directed activity of its individual members. Always there is a need for consultation, communication, group decision-making, specialization of roles, and coordination among those roles. The collective term for these processes is "social control" which denotes the exercise of power to insure the harmonious collaboration of even the most highly socialized individuals and to coerce the collaboration of those whose socialization has not been adequate. Out of these group processes emerges a structural organization among the role incumbents—leaders, lieutenants, followers, and perhaps even a scapegoat.

The family is no exception to these organizational necessities. To be sure, people who make families seldom write constitutions or organization charts for them. Modern families like to think of themselves as "just one happy family," which implies an undifferentiated group of equals. Popular concepts like equalitarianism and togetherness discourage recognition of differences of function or, worse yet, of power. Nevertheless, such differences exist in the family as in other primary groups. Indeed, families can be expected to exhibit more differentiation than most other small groups:

1   Whereas most informal small groups consist of but one sex and a single generation, families by definition consist of both sexes and at least two generations, sometimes more.
2   Whereas most small groups last a relatively short time, families are relatively permanent organizations. The longer an organization exists, the greater the likelihood that structural differentiation will emerge.
3   Many small groups such as cliques or gangs are interested chiefly in their internal relationships, but the family is involved with outside institutions such as the occupational and educational systems. Insofar as different family members play different roles in those external systems, the internal structure of the family is correspondingly differentiated.
4   I have already noted that large nuclear families face special problems of internal coordination and therefore tend to develop more clearly-defined structural organization. Such problems are compounded when a large family consists not simply of an over-inflated nuclear unit, but of a series of interlocking units in extended or polygamous households. Such fami-

lies face all the problems which result from sheer size plus the extra complexities which result from their internal differentiation into quasi-nuclear sub-units. Consequently, structural differentiation can be expected to be most extensive in complex families.

chapter sixteen
SEXUAL DIFFERENTIATION IN THE FAMILY

The two basic ingredients for making families are sexual differentiation and age differentiation. Homosexual relationships are a pale imitation of heterosexual ones, as attested in the familiar slogan, "Vive la difference!" While that phrase has heavily biological connotations, sexual differentiation tends to produce social differentiation. Because families are composed of two sexes, it is difficult for families to remain undifferentiated wholes. Instead, roles and statuses get assigned along sex lines. And these assignments tend to be so widespread within a particular culture that they become normative elements taught each succeeding generation in the process of socialization.

The reasons for sex differentiation I will not treat extensively. They have to do with secondary consequences of biological differences—the fact that only one sex is capable of reproduction and the associated processes of menstruation, gestation, and lactation. Other significant differences involve the anatomy and physiology of sexual intercourse, the size, strength, and energy consumption of the human physique, resistance to disease and death, etc. Such physical differences mean that men and women are not identical. Societies tend to note these differences and attach social significance to them. As a result most family systems assign different roles to the two sexes. Even if they try to ignore sex distinctions, these tend to reappear whenever the society isn't looking (as we will see in the history of Israeli kibbutzim).

It would be wrong, however, to overemphasize the biological basis of sex role differentiation. Once a society settles upon differentiated roles, deviant members of the "wrong" sex can play most of them when paired with someone of the same sex. This is demonstrated by homosexual males who masquerade as women and lesbian females who act like men. Among the Nuer, a barren woman could marry another woman, playing the social role of husband/father in relation to her wife. Evans-Pritchard reported that such women frequently practiced magic and sometimes became so rich that they married several wives:

> She is their legal husband and can demand damages if they have relations with men without her consent. She is also the pater of their children, and on the marriages of their daughters she receives the . . . cattle which go to the father's side in the distribution of bridewealth. Her children are called after her, as though she were a man, and . . . address her as "father." She administers her home and herd as a man would do, being treated by her wives and children with the deference they would show to a male husband and father. (1951:108)

Thus in a sex-role differentiated family system, contrasting roles are played even in exceptional cases where the role incumbents happen to be of the same sex.

A certain measure of sex-role differentiation in the family seems inevitable. Nor are families necessarily the worse for having to cope with this division. A social structure can be built more economically out of diversified ingredients than out of homogeneous ones. Studies by Bales and Slater (1955) demonstrated that one-sex groups developed internal role differentiation over time via competition for leadership and for other roles.

Zelditch (1955) found that in family systems instrumental and expressive (or task and integrative) leadership roles were sharply differentiated along sex lines in 81 percent of his societies and weakly differentiated in an additional 14 percent, leaving only 5 percent where the leadership roles of husbands and wives were essentially identical.

Insofar as a society develops a prescribed pattern of sex-role differentiation, new families can be constructed according to that blueprint rather than having to develop their own structure by trial-and-error competing to see who will do what. On the other hand, general prescriptions handicap exceptional cases where men or women have been faultily socialized into the role of the opposite sex. They are caught between the prescriptions which social pressures attempt to force on them and the more idiosyncratic role structure which might better fit their particular personalities. With these exceptions, however, sex-role differentiation is a societal short-cut to easy family-construction.

Sex-role differentiation may be seen in several relationships: husbands and wives, fathers and mothers, sons and daughters, and brothers and sisters. For all those pairs except the first, there is the additional complication of same-sex differentiated from cross-sex relationships (*e.g.,* father and son versus father and daughter). Thus, differences of behavior according to the sex of the role-incumbent and the sex of the role-partner can be expected to color all relationships within the family.

HUSBANDS AND WIVES

The key element in nuclear families is the husband–wife relationship. The structural character of this dyadic relationship involves an organization of differentiated social roles (the role of husband versus the role of wife) which are complementary to one another and ranked into a hierarchy of higher and lower statuses. Even cases where the husband and wife share that status equally may be considered a particular form of hierarchical structure, namely one where power, prestige, and status are shared equally instead of differentially. The division of labor and the power-prestige relations between husband and wife are the crucial structural characteristics of the marital dyad.

Marital Power Structure

Power, prestige, and status are such interrelated concepts that I will treat them under a single heading. In most of the world's societies, the man's status has been higher than the woman's. Thus Queen, Habenstein, and Adams in the introduction to *The Family in Various Cultures* noted that "In most of the cultures about which we have information, women are subordinate to men" (1961:9). In reviewing the cross-cultural tendencies involved in more or less universal family customs, they found a series of masculine privileges reflecting the men's superior status: (1) the privilege of initiating divorce; (2) premarital sexual freedom; (3) freedom to marry extra wives; (4) extramarital privileges of maintaining a concubine or mistress or of resorting to a prostitute at will; and (5) even the privilege of life itself, since for societies which practice infanticide, it is limited to female babies. Conversely, most cultures assign women a series of responsibilities: (1) to be obedient and submissive to their husbands; (2) to be cloistered, confined, hobbled, veiled, or chaperoned; (3) to surrender their maiden name and family ties and move to the husband's household.

These status differentials are not universal, however. They occur more commonly and more distinctly in some kinds of societies than in others. In Chapter 1 we saw that sex differentials were particularly marked in feudal agrarian societies, most notably in the sexual aspect of marriage. For example, among Greek shepherds:

> Obedience to her husband is a moral imperative for the wife. She will not be excused by public opinion, however badly she may have been treated by the man. She cannot refuse to cohabit with him sexually. Conversely, the act of disobedience by which she damages her husband most severely is adultery. . . . Adultery attacks the moral integrity and honour of the family and makes a laughing-stock of its leader and head. [The shepherds] always insist that if a husband surprises the guilty parties in the act, he must first kill his wife and then her seducer. (Campbell, 1964:152)

Similarly it may be no accident that the sharpest power differential between tradition-oriented arranged marriages and modern-style love matches in my Tokyo study was in the greater domination by arranged-marriage husbands in the decision when to have intercourse.

Even though patriarchal authority theoretically allows the husband unlimited power over his wife, it would be a mistake to assume that the typical patriarch rules by brute force or even by issuing orders. Insofar as the wife has been successfully socialized, she has learned to anticipate his wishes and to respond to them almost before he is aware of them. The husband may appreciate these services though he is not likely to say so since his wife is only doing what is expected of her. In any case, he is not likely to reciprocate with corresponding services since deference and personal service are expected to flow unidirectionally. Nor do the wife's concessions elicit counter-concessions from the husband since they do not see themselves in a bargaining situation. Only in equalitarian marriages may concessions from one partner be expected to trigger similar concessions from the other. In patriarchal families, the ideal model is not compromise but benevolent despotism within which there is no room for overt bargaining, and influence attempts from the wife must be wielded with great subtlety if they are not to be rejected:

> . . . ultimately, the authority of the husband over the wife is absolute. A wife must show respect to her husband before strangers at all times. If they

have a walk together in the village or the town, the wife follows some two or three yards behind him. When visitors are entertained in her hut, the wife never sits and eats with her husband and the guests, but stands erect and motionless ready to attend to the needs of the squatting men. Even in the extended family household husband and wife do not eat together. The men eat first, the women of the household afterwards. No portion of a cooked dish is set aside for the women, who must satisfy themselves with whatever is left by the men; this is often very little. The act of eating together implies sharing equally in what is placed upon the one common dish from which the [shepherd people] customarily eat. It indicates in that particular context, a certain equality between those who partake. Only sometimes in the intimacy of the elementary family may the husband, wife, and children sit and eat together. (Campbell, 1964:151)

Halfway around the world in feudal Japan, the wife expressed her subordination almost identically by allowing the husband to walk ahead and to eat first (as well as take the first bath). Even in contemporary Japan, the bride is expected to invite fewer guests to her wedding than the husband in order to express her inferiority.

In India, the cloistering of women was carried to extremes in the custom of purdah which kept women behind the walls of their home for most of their married years. According to Minturn and Hitchcock, among aristocratic high-caste Rajputs:

Most men wish to keep their wives in purdah, although it is a luxury, since to do this the men must do without their help in the fields and hire servants to help them run the house. . . . The subordinate status of women is further emphasized by the custom that women must crouch on the floor and pull their saris over their faces when in the presence of their husband or any man older than their husband. This custom is so pervasive that young women usually cover their faces even in front of older low-caste serving men. This is a sign of respect for the man's status. . . . When a man has entered the house for his meal, he will quickly retire into a room or behind the wall of his hearth. The women are then free to move about their business quietly. (1963: 240)

The last sentences reflect the constraints that come with high status. Just as famous men sacrifice the freedom to move about anonymously, Rajput husbands cannot move freely about in their own homes because they would paralyze their women. If one wished to command the respect of one's women, one could not afford to exercise that power for very long or no work would get done.

Few patriarchal societies carry sex distinctions to so great an extreme. In most, the primary purpose of sex differentiation is to impress outsiders, and husband and wife can be more spontaneous in private. Among Greek shepherds, Campbell found that:

. . . there is a marked difference between the public and private behavior of a man and his wife towards each other. Publicly a husband addresses his wife in a stern severe voice. Requests are commands, barked out in sharp phrases. It is important for a man's self-regard that other men should see that he is master in his own house. In public the wife is meek and modest, silent and submissive. She does not smile at him or laugh with him before strangers. But in the seclusion of the hut matters are otherwise. She abandons the mask of expressionless humility and discusses with her husband all the affairs of the family, putting forward her own suggestions in a respectful but fearless fashion. (1964:151–152)

The phrase "petticoat government" indicates that women are not without weapons of their own even in feudal societies. The ability to appeal to the man's sympathy by crying, to appeal to the sympathy of others by complaining, or to hurt the husband by refusing sexual relations are weapons of resistance which women employ whenever their power position is weak.

Chivalry   One of the paradoxical relationships between men and women is expressed in chivalry, a code summarized in the phrase "Ladies first!" This seems to imply a higher status for women than for men. And in the early days of chivalry this may indeed have been true. Originally, chivalry was the code governing the behavior of the knight on horseback (*le cheval*) toward his mistress who was the wife of his master and his superior in status and prestige. Later the code become generalized to women in general, first by aristocratic men and later by bourgeois men though seldom by members of the proletariat. To treat women deferentially raised their status substantially higher than in societies where all the deference was supposed to go to men.

Despite the softening of male superiority which chivalry brought, it did not mean that the position of the sexes was reversed. Rather chivalry was a "gift" which still-superior men bestowed on their ladies most notably during courtship when they were trying to win their favor. Such men did not surrender power, however. They continued to make the decisions. All that changed was a series of symbolic gestures which made the ladies feel like queens even when they knew the king still wielded the royal sceptre.

One way of documenting this paradox is to note that among my Japanese married couples (Blood,1967) it was men in old-fashioned arranged marriages who were both more patriarchal in the sense of making more of the family decisions, and more chivalrous in allowing their wives to sit down when only one seat was available on a train or bus. To grant women the symbols of courtesy is not the same as giving them the reins of power. Indeed, this research suggested that equalitarianism in power is likely to bring equality in courtesy as well. Husbands and wives in truly equalitarian marriages will take turns sitting down, depending on who is most tired rather than routinely giving the wife that privilege.

Equalitarianism   Under modern economic and social conditions, patriarchalism tends to give way to a new norm of equality between husbands and wives. In contrast to patriarchy where the husband theoretically has absolute power and may issue orders which the wife dare not question (much less, resist), in equalitarian marriages ordering and obeying give way to mutual consultation and negotiation. No one may give orders, one may only make requests which may or may not be accepted. Either sex may initiate such requests and either is equally free to refuse. Indeed, the old sex distinctions supposedly become irrelevant to this new power structure, since the roles of husband and wife in decision-making are presumably identical and therefore interchangeable.

In addition to equality of status, a second feature of the modern ideal is shared power. Theoretically, equality might be achieved by separately exercising autonomous jurisdiction over two equal halves of the marriage: I will make half the decisions and you make half. But the 50/50 concept which is often applied to contemporary decision-making does not refer to unilateral decision-making by separate-but-equal partners, but to joint decision-making. Ideally all decisions are made together; 50/50 describes the amount of influence exercised by the two partners in every decision, not the number of decisions each makes separately.

There seems little doubt that this picture of a shared-equal (or "syncratic") exercise of power represents the normative power structure for the advanced countries of the world. In the United States, France, Belgium and even urban Japan, power seems to be exercised generally in this fashion (Blood, Hill, Michel, and Safilios-Rothschild, 1970). On the other hand, in such quasi-feudal south-European countries as Yugoslavia and Greece, the patriarchal tradition still survives, especially in rural areas and in families without much education (Buric and Zecevic, 1967). Moreover, even in advanced countries, the syncratic norm is not fully implemented in practice any more than are wives in feudal societies completely powerless.

How, then, does the exercise of power in advanced countries depart from the syncratic norm?

We have already seen in Chapter 13 that roles tend to become more specialized the longer a marriage is in existence. I found in my Tokyo and Detroit research that this was true for decision-making as well as for other activities. Time either with or without children consistently increased unilateral decision-making in both countries. Consequently, it seems that the syncratic norm is most effective at the beginning of marriage, but the longer a couple lives together, the more other factors intervene:

> (1) They become less interested in doing things together as their initial joy in companionship wears off. (2) Their roles are differentiated by the mother's preoccupation with her children, leaving less time for discussing issues to be decided. (3) In addition, they often discover through early joint deliberations which partner is more knowledgeable, more interested, or otherwise more competent than the other. Gradually he takes over responsibility for that area, relieving the spouse of his share of the burden. Joint decisions may be "nice" but they take time and energy. Because energies gradually dissipate with age or are gobbled up by other roles (parental and occupational), efficiency is needed and appreciated. (Blood, 1967:174)

In this paragraph it is suggested that there is an intrinsic pressure away from the syncratic norm. However, this does not mean the reemergence of a patriarchal counterrevolution. The main shift is from syncratic equality to autonomic equality, from joint to separate-but-equal decision-making. But insofar as the balance of power shifts, it leans in the wife's direction, rather than the husband's.

TABLE 16-1 Husband's Aggregate Power, by Stage in Family Life Cycle

| COUNTRY | STAGE IN FAMILY LIFE CYCLE | | | | | |
	Newly Married	Pre-School	Pre-Adolescent	Adolescent	Post-Parental	Retired
France	2.09	2.20	1.90	2.02	1.73	—
Greece	3.08	2.87	2.67	2.55	2.46	—
Japan	5.15	5.28	5.08	—	—	—
U.S.A.	5.35	5.71	5.41	5.06	4.79	4.44
U.S.A. (childless)	—	5.30	4.72	4.20	—	—

Adapted from the following sources: France (Michel, 1967:338); Greece (Safilios-Rothschild, 1967: 346); Japan (Blood, 1967:225); U.S.A. (Blood and Wolfe, 1960:42). Sources: Paris and Bordeaux, Athens, Tokyo, and Detroit, respectively. Childless couples in the U.S.A. had been married an equivalent length of time to couples with children in the same column.

Since measures were not identical in the different countries, the husband's power cannot be compared between countries but only between stages within a country.

Table 16-1 shows that families generally (with the exception of those in Athens) experienced an upsurge of the husbands' power with the birth of their first child. This however is so obviously a consequence of the increased dependence of the wives on the husbands that it should hardly be attributed to a resurgence of ideological patriarchalism. Moreover, the rise in the husbands' power is only temporary—by the time the oldest child reaches school age in most countries (and adolescence in the U.S.A.), their power has fallen below its initial level. Indeed with only one exception, it falls steadily in every country with each succeeding stage of the family life cycle after the preschool peak. And among American couples who never have children, the effect of time on the husbands' power is consistently negative.

It is impossible to say for sure why the balance of power shifts in the wives' direction. If I had not already described the initial starting point in most of these countries as equalitarian, it would be possible to assert that women who were initially timid gradually become braver as they get older and more used to their husbands. However, this reasoning is relevant only to the Greek data in Table 16-1 (which may explain why Athens is an exception to the general tendency for the husbands' power to increase with the birth of the first child). In general, what seems to happen in marriage is not that wives become more assertive but that husbands drop out of the marital power structure, leaving their wives saddled with increasingly unilateral responsibility. That this burden is not welcomed is suggested in my study by Tokyo wives' increasing dissatisfaction both with their own role in decision-making and with their husbands' interest in decision-making in the same years that the wives were gaining increased unilateral power.

Why then do husbands drop out of the power structure? Perhaps because at best they are only partly domesticated. Women even in modern marriages continue to take their domestic roles seriously. The mother–child relationship is still the core of the family. Men are fully integrated into the family only for a few years. But after the novelty wears off, they lose some of their interest and invest less of their fading energies in that direction. As a result, sexual differentiation in the marital power structure increases—with not only the husband and wife making fewer decisions jointly, but the husband making fewer decisions at all.

Even at the beginning of marriage, however, there tends to be some specialization by sex. Although modern marriages tend to be fairly equalitarian and although shared power is the ideology preferred by most couples, that ideology is carried further in some areas of marriage than others.

The data reported in Figure 16-1 were not limited to the initial "honeymoon" period when marriages conform most closely to the syncratic norm. Nevertheless they were based on couples married a relatively short time, too short to have children who had reached adolescence, and therefore before specialization had become extensive. Perhaps because most of the Tokyo couples had been married fewer years than the Detroit couples, the former shared a larger number of decisions. A majority of the Tokyo couples shared decisions about holiday outings, special gifts, choice of the children's school, and decisions about out-of-school lessons. Another caution, however, is that children of many of these couples were not yet old enough for them to have actually made the last two decisions, so they should be discounted somewhat as sometimes hypothetical. Such answers would reflect the equalitarian ideology of contemporary Tokyo wives. Indeed, young childless Tokyo wives consistently predicted that their husbands would share more actively in decisions affecting the children than was reported in actual practice by couples who already had made those decisions.

In Detroit, no questions were asked about child-oriented decisions and only two decisions were made jointly by a majority of couples: choice of vacation destination and of house or apartment. The latter is such an important decision that it is surprising to find only 59 percent of couples always made it jointly. A few other decisions were made jointly by less than half the couples but still exhibited a modal pattern of jointness: insurance decisions, choice of radio and TV programs, and choice of family doctor. But within the overall framework of shared power were some areas which were distinctly autonomous. Husbands and wives, for example, decided their own participation in the occupational system pretty much by themselves. Cars in Detroit (and presumably in most countries) were chiefly a masculine toy. Spending money for the children's allowances, for groceries, and for the wife's clothes, fell in the wife's jurisdiction.

Conspicuous about these unilateral areas is that every one of them is closely linked to role specialization in the division of labor. As we will see shortly, the wife is primarily responsible for housekeeping and child-rearing, so she makes routine decisions unilaterally in these areas. Only questions of major import such as the Japanese child's elementary school (which will affect his secondary schooling, his university entrance, and his vocational opportunities) interest the husband. Correspondingly, a man's or a woman's employment affects him or her so much more than the spouse that it is considered his own business. Most departures from the shared power norm, then, reflect the division of labor. And since the division of labor even in modern societies is sex-linked, this means that specialized facets of equalitarian power structures are sex-linked also. Theoretically, equality might allow husbands and wives to specialize in whatever areas they happen to be competent in. In practice, competence is gained by getting one's hands dirty in the division of labor. Hence, efficient decision-making adheres closely to the pattern of task-performance.

Repercussions   What difference does it make whether the power structure is patriarchal or equalitarian?

The greater the power differential between the partners, the more deferential and respectful the wife will be to the husband. This means that they are unlikely to use terms of endearment for each other and may not even call each other by their first names, using instead role terms in addressing each other (such as "Father" and "Mother"). If they do not feel close to each other, they cannot treat each other familiarly, cannot joke or play with each other.

Table 16-2 selects the patriarchal and syncratic cases from my Tokyo and Detroit samples, discarding the deviant autonomic and wife-dominant cases. The table shows that Japanese wives who were dominated by their husbands more often felt like servants and were relatively dissatisfied with the courtesy and respect they received, despite the fact that (as mentioned earlier) conservative Tokyo husbands are more chivalrous than new-style husbands. Apparently equality in decision-making is more important than etiquette in engendering a basic feeling of respect. On the other hand, the patriarch benefits (although remarkably slightly) from his superior vantage point when asked how satisfied he is with the wife's courtesy and respect toward him. The asymmetry of this satisfaction reflects the lack of reciprocity in patriarchal marriages.

Both partners, by contrast, suffered a loss of a sense of companionship in patriarchal marriages. The husband might be "top dog" in receiving the obeisance of his wife, but this did not make her close to him. Indeed, mutual alienation was characteristic of these patriarchal Japanese marriages (and presumably in the U. S. as well, although data were available only for wives).

One consequence of the closeness which shared power creates in marriage is greater accessibility for purposes of emotional relief when the individual has had a bad day. For all three groups, therapeutic utilization of the partner was greater in syncratic marriages than in patriarchal marriages (although wives of Japanese patriarchs utilized their husbands so often that there was relatively little room for improvement in equalitarian marriages). With this exception, both husbands and wives in patriarchal marriages seldom turned to each other for therapeutic relief, the husband presumably because a dependent wife was too far beneath him to play psychiatrist, the wife because the husband was too far above her to be bothered with his troubles.

Even though Japanese wives violated this concept rather extensively by "bothering" their husbands, they got essentially the same "I can't be bothered" response as wives of American patriarchs. In both countries, patriarchal husbands were more apt to dismiss the wife's troubles as inconsequential or to not bother to respond at all after the wife had recited her troubles. Syncratic husbands, by contrast, were more sympathetic (since they presumably could more easily put themselves in their wife's shoes) and more often helped her forget her troubles by such concrete measures as taking her out to a show.

FIGURE 16-1. Husband's Power and Percentage Equalitarian for Specific Decisions

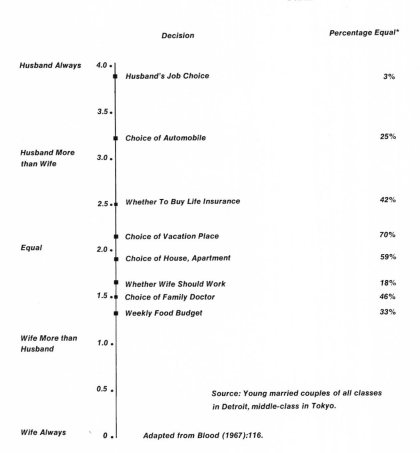

Who Decides?

Detroit

	Decision	Percentage Equal*
Husband Always 4.0 •	Husband's Job Choice	3%
3.5 •	Choice of Automobile	25%
Husband More than Wife 3.0 •		
2.5 •	Whether To Buy Life Insurance	42%
	Choice of Vacation Place	70%
Equal 2.0 •	Choice of House, Apartment	59%
	Whether Wife Should Work	18%
1.5 •	Choice of Family Doctor	46%
	Weekly Food Budget	33%
Wife More than Husband 1.0 •		
0.5 •		
Wife Always 0 •		

Source: Young married couples of all classes
in Detroit, middle-class in Tokyo.

Adapted from Blood (1967):116.

Tokyo

Decision	Percentage Equal*

4.0 •

3.5 •

3.0 •■ When To Have Sexual Intercourse — 33%

2.5 • ■ Whether To Buy Life Insurance — 31%

■ Choice of Radio, TV Program — 45%
■ Choice of Holiday Outing Place — 53%
2.0 •■ Choice of Obituary, Congratulatory Gift — 58%

■ Choice of Children's School — 72%

1.5 •■ Whether Wife Can Buy New Clothes — 31%
■ What Special Lessons for Children — 51%

1.0 •■ Amount of Children's Spending Money — 16%

0.5 •

0 •

*Percentage of couples reporting equal decision-making

TABLE 16-2   Marital Repercussions of Patriarchal and Equalitarian Power Structures

		MARITAL POWER STRUCTURE	
REPERCUSSIONS	CITY	Patriarchal	Syncratic
Wife feels like a servant	Tokyo	0.70	0.28
Satisfaction with courtesy and respect			
Husband's satisfaction	Tokyo	4.49	4.44
Wife's satisfaction	Tokyo	4.30	4.64
Satisfaction with companionship			
Husband's satisfaction	Tokyo	3.97	4.32
Wife's satisfaction	Tokyo	3.86	4.06
	Detroit	3.92	4.13
Husband tells troubles	Tokyo	2.28	2.47
Wife tells troubles	Tokyo	3.14	3.16
	Detroit	2.36	2.71
Husband's response (selected)			
Sympathy	Tokyo	3%	5%
	Detroit	31	40
Help her get away	Tokyo	4	9
	Detroit	2	6
Dismissal	Tokyo	27	18
	Detroit	10	6
Passive (no response)	Tokyo	10	6
	Detroit	20	12
Aggregate marital satisfaction			
Husband's satisfaction	Tokyo	5.79	5.80
Wife's satisfaction	Tokyo	5.55	5.83
	Detroit	4.89	5.19
Minimum number of cases	Tokyo	90	142
	Detroit	103	64

Adapted from Blood, 1967:196–197.

For wives, the combined effect of these services from syncratic husbands was to make their marriages extraordinarily satisfying. For husbands, however, satisfaction was derived almost equally from either type of marriage. The kinds of satisfaction differed, but when all were added together, it didn't matter very much quantitatively whether he got his satisfaction from ruling supreme over a servant wife or from sharing more strenuously with a companion wife. If joint satisfaction is the measure, syncratic marriages won the prize (with 45 percent of the Tokyo couples mutually satisfied, compared with 38 percent in the patriarchal marriages and even fewer in the deviant autonomic and wife-dominated marriages).

The Division of Labor

Looked at cross-culturally, the division of labor is less complicated than the power structure of marriage because it varies less. In primitive and feudal societies, men were assigned the most strenuous tasks which required their larger muscles: metal-working, stone-cutting, lumbering, killing or herding large animals, and killing men. They were also given tasks which required geographical mobility: hunting, fishing, warring, and trading away from home. Men's ability to fulfil these mobile tasks lay not so much in superior physical ability as in their exemption from the child-bearing and child care which chronically beset women in precontraceptive days. Conversely, women were given the residual tasks of keeping house and gardening or gathering food in the immediate vicinity because they could tend their babies at the same time. Women's manual dexterity with tasks involving fine muscle control contributed to their assignment to such finger tasks as sewing and weaving. Finally, primitive beliefs about the menstrual uncleanliness of women cut them off from military, religious, and political tasks such as making weapons, musical instruments, or ceremonial objects (Murdock, 1937).

In modern societies, beliefs have changed and biological factors have diminished in importance with the development of machines for manual labor and the expansion of white-collar jobs. The equalization of the sexes in equalitarian power structures has reduced masculine embarrassment in helping with formerly feminine tasks. In general, the division of labor by sex has become more flexible.

Nevertheless, the division of tasks along sex lines remains quite pronounced in most societies, and continues to follow many of the traditional lines described above. One factor which accounts for this stability is the continued monopoly of child-bearing by women. As a result, it is still more efficient for women to raise children and do the housework than for men (if the assignment is to be given to one sex alone). A second factor which has facilitated the persistence of the traditional division of labor (though it has not necessitated it) is the decreased time required for housework. Just when the equalization of the sexes might have been expected to put pressure on husbands to help out at home, prepared foods and labor-saving devices took the pressure off women by slashing the number of hours required by housework. Moreover, the rising affluence of modern societies made it possible for families to purchase goods and services which previously had had to be provided at home. So while the modernization of society makes a shared division of labor more ideologically possible, it makes it less practically necessary. Even in two-income households where (as we will see in Chapter 19) husbands do more housework, the wife still does most of it herself.

Figure 16-2 shows how few couples shared any tasks except taking the children out on Sundays (which perhaps is hardly a chore). By contrast with the considerable number of modally shared decisions in Figure 16-1, many of the tasks portrayed in this table are almost never shared. This specialization is particularly striking because the lists of tasks have been restricted in both cities to activities which theoretically either partner could do and which both could do together if they so wished. The fact that they did not is dramatized in the fact that the proportion of families in the two countries who share family decisions was almost exactly double the number who share household tasks (43 percent versus 22 percent).

Examination of the particular tasks which were performed primarily by the husband or the wife shows how traditional the division of labor in both countries was. The man's assignments were the heavy outdoor work of shoveling snow, mowing grass, and carrying heavy objects, plus the technical work of making home repairs (which in Tokyo apartment houses were less often

FIGURE 16-2. *Wife's Task Performance and Percentage of Shared Tasks for Specific Tasks*

Adapted from Blood (1967):120.   Sources: Same as preceding figure.

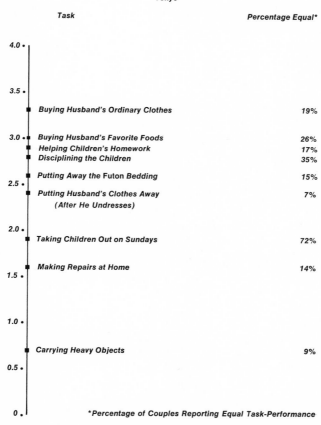

Tokyo

Task	Percentage Equal*
Buying Husband's Ordinary Clothes	19%
Buying Husband's Favorite Foods	26%
Helping Children's Homework	17%
Disciplining the Children	35%
Putting Away the Futon Bedding	15%
Putting Husband's Clothes Away (After He Undresses)	7%
Taking Children Out on Sundays	72%
Making Repairs at Home	14%
Carrying Heavy Objects	9%

*Percentage of Couples Reporting Equal Task-Performance

structural and therefore more often shared by wives than in Detroit's single-family homes). The wife's assignments involved shopping for food and clothing, cooking, cleaning house, and caring for children. One could hardly invent a more traditional allocation.

TABLE 16-3   Wife's Aggregate Task Performance, by Stage in Family Life Cycle

	STAGE IN FAMILY LIFE CYCLE					
COUNTRY	Newly Married	Pre-School	Pre-Adolescent	Adolescent	Post-Parental	Retired
Belgium	3.13	3.19	3.47	3.65	3.64	3.40
Japan	4.12	4.55	5.00	—	—	—
U.S.A.	4.55	5.14	5.58	5.53	5.47	5.50
U.S.A. (childless)	—	5.00	5.11	5.25	—	—

Adapted from the following references: Belgium (Silverman and Hill, 1967:358); Japan (Blood, 1967:225); U.S.A. (Blood and Wolfe, 1960:71). Sources: Louvain, Tokyo, Detroit respectively. Childless American couples had been married an equivalent length of time to couples with children in the same column. Since the measures were not identical in the different countries, the wife's task performance cannot be compared between countries but only between stages within each country.

Table 16-3 shows that the wife's proportion of the total housework rose steadily from the beginning of marriage but crested when children were still in the home. In the later stages of marriage, the children's departure relieves the wife of some of her responsibilities, while the husband's tasks remain essentially unchanged. Therefore the net balance shifts in the husband's direction even if he does no more work than before. In the case of childless couples in Detroit, the progressive increase in the wife's share of the work suggests that just as with decision-making, husbands drop out of housework. However, the speed of this shift in the division of labor is glacial in relation to the speed of dropping out of decision-making.

Despite the lightening of the wife's share of housework load in the later stages of the life cycle, there is no corresponding decrease in role specialization. Throughout the entire life cycle in the Detroit sample, the number of tasks performed unilaterally increased progressively. The launching of the last child brought a particularly large increase in specialization. In Belgium there was a slight decline in specialization and an even greater decline in the traditionalism of sex-role assignments in the post-parental years. Reasons for this international discrepancy are not readily apparent but the fact that specialization at the end of the life cycle is greater than at the beginning even in Belgium suggests that task specialization generally increases with length of marriage.

When they first get married, couples try out various tasks and enjoy working together. But specialization increases as work assignments become habitual. Gradually couples discover which partner has more time and more skill at each task. In most cases, because of differential socialization in childhood and because of the pressure of social norms in adulthood, couples settle into traditional sex-linked grooves. With some tasks, "practice makes perfect," so that whoever has done the task before tends to do it the next time. This widens the skill differentials between the partners over time.

The efficiency of the traditional division of labor is nowhere so apparent as in the brief history of the Israeli kibbutzim. We saw in Chapter 6 that the kibbutzim originally abolished the division of labor between the sexes and assigned both men and women to collective tasks without regard to sex. However, within the lifetime of the original settlers, the old division reasserted itself. This can be attributed to the usual forces of childbearing plus the fact that these collective communities frequently specialized in hard farm work which reintroduced the old muscular differences between the sexes. In any case, despite their devotion to an equalitarian ideology, the kibbutzniks found that sex differentiation was a practical necessity.

Because such biological factors as reproduction and body musculature affect physical tasks more than mental activities, the division of labor is more sex-linked than the power structure of modern marriage. In housework, efficiency increases with increased specialization. "Too many cooks spoil the broth" is literally relevant to many household tasks.

But in decision-making, choices must often be made between alternatives that are not equally attractive to both partners but which affect both. Therefore, both want to influence them. For example, many decisions involve the allocation of scarce resources such as money—and money spent for one thing will not be available for another. Hence every financial decision deprives the couple of the possibility of purchasing something else. Other decisions affect the time and energy of the partners—for example, where they are to spend their vacation and where they are to live.

Even though in the short run such decisions might be made more efficiently (in the sense of more quickly) by one partner alone, in the long run the greatest good of the greatest number is more apt to be served if all the affected parties participate in the decision-making. Insofar as decisions are made jointly, the outcome is more likely to take into consideration the interests and values of both partners.

Repercussions We have already seen that specialization in making decisions tends to prevent companionship between husbands and wives. The same thing happens as a result of segregation in the division of labor. Because housework is a more continuous process than decision-making, more may be lost by splitting up household tasks than by splitting decisions.

Table 16-4 divides married couples into arbitrary categories which may be loosely compared with each other. Servant wives, a small minority in each country, are those who work almost entirely unaided. Japanese servant wives probably work harder than American ones since they customarily serve as valet to their husbands, laying out his clothes in the morning and putting them away when he undresses at night. In neither country do very many "colleagues" receive equal help from their husbands. In Tokyo, most husbands work such long hours and spend so much time commuting that they are seldom home to help out even if they wanted to. Nevertheless in each country, colleague wives get more help than their compatriots.

Table 16-4 suggests that servant wives in Tokyo felt more like servants than like wives. They were conspicuously dissatisfied with the lack of help from their husbands and with their marriages as a whole. Even though the scales are not directly comparable in the two countries, the effect of the division of labor on marital satisfaction appeared to be sharper in Japan than in the States, perhaps because the transitional position of a society just emerging from its feudal past made it a more controversial issue there. Regardless of differences between countries, the impressive feature of Table 16-4 is the consistently positive effect on marriage of the husbands' helpfulness in both countries, for both sexes. Helpfulness and marital satisfaction may influence one another in a truly reciprocal fashion. Nevertheless, even in post-feudal Japan, the relevance of helping with household tasks to marital satisfaction was unmistakable.

TABLE 16-4   Marital Repercussions of the Division of Labor

| | | DIVISION OF LABOR | | |
| | | Servant | | |
REPERCUSSIONS	*CITY*	*Wives*	*Moderates*	*Colleagues*
Wife feels like a servant	Tokyo	0.86	0.46	0.26
Wife's satisfaction with husband's helpfulness	Tokyo	1.98	3.51	4.33
Aggregate marital satisfaction				
Husband's	Tokyo	5.23	5.48	6.00
Wife's	Tokyo	3.65	5.17	5.97
	Detroit	4.37	4.82	5.10
Minimum number of cases	Tokyo	44	231	158
	Detroit	26	202	143

Adapted from Blood, 1967:201. The three categories of wives divide each sample into extremes and an intermediate category which are roughly comparable proportions of each sample but not necessarily comparable in terms of the amount of housework done in the two countries.

Although segregation of the sexes in the division of labor may be "natural" and efficient, it is not consistent with the ideals of modern marriage. Love and companionship—not efficiency—are the main concerns today. If couples are to emphasize fellowship in common work, specialization in work can only be carried so far. The more specialized the husband and wife become, the greater the danger that they will lose touch with each other even though the house may be operated in a very business-like fashion. The division of labor, then, cannot consist entirely of unilaterally performed tasks, nor must it saddle the wife with too large a proportion of the load if the marriage is to satisfy modern concepts of fairness and companionship.

Under pre-modern conditions, servant wives faced an additional hazard. The larger the amount of work they did, the more easily their husbands could afford extra wives.

The work referred to in Table 16-5 is not housework, but subsistence activity—gathering and growing food or otherwise supporting the family economically. The table shows that the larger the proportion of economic activities in a society, the greater the likelihood that the society will allow men to have more than one wife. Conversely, the only two societies in the sample which allowed plural husbands required them to be almost entirely self-supporting. A polygamous household is a large and costly operation. Its expense is mitigated when the plural sex is substantially self-supporting.

Conversely, the emancipation of the single sex from some of his economic responsibilities enables him to devote more of his time to the family responsibilities he has incurred through his multiple marriages. In a polygynous household, the man is so busy being husband, father, and household administrator that he has less time for the ordinary tasks of economic production. Thus the larger economic contribution of the plural sex is balanced by a larger social contribution from the solitary sex. Conversely, in monogamous family systems the basic pattern is for the man to do most of the economic production while the wife does most of the domestic work.

TABLE 16-5   Form of Marriage, by Female Contribution to Subsistence

FORM OF MARRIAGE	FEMALE CONTRIBUTION TO SUBSISTENCE				
	0–19%	20–29%	30–39%	40–49%	50+%
Polyandry	4%	0%	0%	0%	0%
Monogamy	39	32	24	22	19
Polygyny	57	68	76	78	81
Total	100%	100%	100%	100%	100%
Number of societies	54	82	89	68	105

Adapted from Heath, 1958:79. Source: Murdock's world ethnographic sample of primitive, historical, and contemporary societies.

FATHERS AND MOTHERS

It has already become apparent that child-care in most societies is the primary responsibility of the wife. This means that mothering is more nearly a full-time role than fathering. Especially when the child is young and, as we will see, especially if it's a girl, the mother's responsibility is nearly complete. Conversely, as sons approach maturity, the role of the father becomes more important.

The vast difference between the parents in relation to infants may be illustrated in a Mexican Indian community:

> Although fathers are generally affectionate toward their infant children, it is not thought to be their duty or responsibility to care for them. The father actually spends only a small part of the daylight hours in the household, for he is generally out in the fields. In the evening, or early in the morning, the father may pick up his infant child and jounce him on his knee for a short period, but if the child is wet or cries, the mother, sister, or grandmother will immediately take the responsibility of attending to the infant's needs. In the interviews, no mother reported that her husband aided in the care of the infant. Most reported that at night or during siestas or early in the morning the husband might hold the baby for a moment or two, but nothing more.
>
> Babies spend a great deal of time in their mothers' arms, and they are generally offered the breast at every little cry. They are rocked and go to sleep with the breast in their mouths, which thus serves as a pacifier. (Romney and Romney, 1963:644)

Consequences of the Division of Labor Between Fathers and Mothers

In Chapter 15 we saw that parental nurturance produced dependency feelings which in turn were the basis for socializing children. Insofar as caretaking activities are performed by the mother, this means that dependency also is oriented primarily toward her.

Mother–Child Dependency The intensity of mother–child interaction in most societies creates closer ties between the child and his mother than with his father. This means that the mother will have more influence on her child's socialization than the father.

Putney and Middleton (1961) found that American students more often chose their mother's than their father's religious faith when the parents disagreed about religion. This is not surprising since American women tend to be more religiously active than men. But even the political socialization of children (where men might be expected to be influential) tends to be dominated by the mother if the parents differ in their party affiliation (Maccoby, 1954). Thus, one consequence of the role differentiation between fathers and mothers is to make the mother the chief agent in socializing children.

It is difficult enough for a child to have to choose between his father's and his mother's faith or politics. But it is far more difficult to have to choose between one's father and mother, as happens whenever parents get divorced. In unilineal societies, the dominant kin group automatically retains the children—the father in patrilineal societies, the mother in matrilineal societies. But in other societies, the answer is not prescribed by the larger kin group. Under optional circumstances, the children's dependence on the mother leads her to retain them after divorce, save in the most exceptional circumstances.

In Goode's sample of Detroit divorcees (1956), almost 95 percent of the mothers had exclusive custody compared to only 2 percent of the fathers. In working-class London, similarly:

> Some evidence for this closer attachment to the mother arose when people talked about divorce or separation. The children usually sided with the mother, and even when the separation took place not when the children were young or in their teens but after they were married they appeared to have little or nothing more to do with their fathers. (Townsend, 1957:83)

And in Java, Geertz found ". . . a strong feeling that after divorce, the children should remain with the mother, even though she may remarry several times, with the result grown children have considerably stronger ties to their mothers than to their fathers" (1961:45). So strong is this tendency for the mother to keep the children in bilineal societies that exceptions generally require the husband to prove to the court's satisfaction that the wife is a chronic alcoholic, a prostitute, or otherwise conspicuously incompetent to raise the children.

Rites of Passage In societies where men are superior to women and guard their military and religious secrets from contamination by the weaker sex, the intimacy between mothers and children creates a problem. How can sons when they reach maturity be retrieved from their mothers and integrated into the society of warriors?

In many primitive societies, the problem is solved by elaborate rituals which mark the transfer of pubescent boys from their mothers to the custody of their male elders. The sharper the segregation of adult males from association with women and children, the more elaborate the rites of passage. Central features of those rites are removal of the boy from his home and isolation in the wilderness. Fasting, torture, and other forms of hazing impress upon the boy the fact that he is no longer a boy but has become a man. The elaborate rituals are reminiscent of wedding ceremonies and serve an analogous function—to sever old ties and establish new ones.

Rites of passage are not universal because not all societies require boys to sever their ties with their mothers. In patrilocal extended families, the boy continues his close association with his mother into adulthood, even after marriage. For such societies, no uprooting of the old maternal dependency is necessary. But where life is split into two phases—a feminine-dependent phase and a purely masculine phase—rites of passage convey the young man from one phase to the other.

Consequences of the Division of Leadership Between Fathers and Mothers

At the beginning of the chapter, we noted that groups tend to develop differentiated leadership and that Zelditch found only 3 out of 56 societies which failed to differentiate between husbands and wives in this respect. It is time now to examine the direction of that differentiation. We have already seen that nonequalitarian power structures are almost always husband-dominated. When we add children to the family and examine the leadership roles of the parents, we would expect correlatively that the husband would most often play the role of "instrumental" leader, leaving the wife as the "expressive" leader of the family.

Before testing this hypothesis, it is necessary to define these terms. According to Zelditch, an instrumental leader "is boss–manager of the farm; leader of the hunt, etc. . . . the final court of appeals, final judge and executor of punishment, discipline, and control over the children of the family." Conversely, an expressive leader "is the mediator, conciliator, of the family; . . . soothes over disputes, resolves hostilities in the family; . . . is affectionate, solicitous, warm, emotional to the children of the family; . . . is the 'comforter,' the 'consoler,' is relatively indulgent, relatively unpunishing (1955:318).

Table 16-6 shows a strong tendency for leadership roles to be played by the expected partner. In no cases were the roles completely reversed, and in only two societies (4 percent of the sample) were they primarily reversed. Not only did a majority of the societies fit the hypothesis perfectly, but most of the rest did so in the primary role emphasis of both partners.

This means that in most societies, fathers are what Freilich labeled the high-status authority, and mothers the high-status friend, leaving children the residual role of low-status subordinate. One complication exists for mothers in patriarchal societies. If the mother's status is sufficiently inferior to her husband's it will be difficult for her to be the tension-reducer in the family since "the amount of tension reduced by a given [high-status friend] is directly proportional to the difference in status between [the high-status friend and the low-status subordinate]" (1964:538).

TABLE 16-6 Allocation of Instrumental and Expressive Leadership Roles to Fathers and Mothers

Relation to Hypothesis	Father	Mother	Percentage of Societies
Completely consistent	I	E	59%
Muted consistent	i	E	9
Both partners primarily consistent	Ie ie I IE	E E Ei EI	15
One partner consistent	Ie e	ie E	13
Both partners primarily inconsistent	Ei E	Ie Ie	4
Completely inconsistent	E	I	0
Total			100%
Number of societies			53

Adapted from Zelditch, 1955: 347–348. *I* or *E* means unambiguously instrumental or expressive. A small *i* or *e* means a subordinate role component. *IE* or *ie* (or vice versa) means both components are almost equal but the first component is judged to be possibly dominant.

In such circumstances, another male may have to be imported to be the expressive leader. The mother's brother is often recruited for this purpose, extending the mother's attempt to play this role. On the other hand, in matrilineal societies, the mother's brother wields considerable authority over his sister's children. Hence in such societies, the father's instrumental role may be considerably muted. Indeed, all the lower-case "i" or "ie" father-roles in Table 16-6 were matrilineal in nature.

The relationship between the father's instrumental role and the mother's expressive role is complementary. To be the task master is to command the fear and respect of one's children.

> The Arab boy was taught not to sit down when his father was standing, and to get up when his father approached. If he had begun smoking, he could not do so in his father's presence. . . . He could not dispute with his father in an argument. (Goode, 1963:143)

This strains the integration of the family, creating the ultimate danger that the children may run away from home to escape the father's authority. The role of the mother is to interpret the father's good will to the children, and to intercede with him when he pushes his authority too far. By serving as peacemaker and communication link within the family, she holds the family together. Yet without her husband's instrumental leadership, the family would starve. Both roles are necessary if the family is to function effectively.

The fact that fathers specialize in instrumental leadership to the neglect of expressive leadership creates hazards in the socialization process. If he pushes too hard, the child may be either alienated or crushed. Research on achievement motivation in the United States has demonstrated that if the father tries too hard to motivate his children, his pushing will boomerang. Conversely, the very fact that mothers are expressive enables them to push their children without alienating them. Rosen and d'Andrade summarize the differences in the roles of the two sexes in stimulating their sons to want to achieve as follows:

In order for high n Achievement to develop, the boy appears to need more autonomy from his father than from his mother. The father who gives the boy a relatively high degree of autonomy provides him with an opportunity to compete on his own ground, to test his skill, and to gain a sense of confidence in his own competence. The dominating father may crush his son (and in so doing destroys the boy's achievement motive), perhaps because he views the boy as a competitor and is viewed as such by his son. On the other hand, the mother who dominates the decision-making process does not seem to have the same effect on the boy, possibly because she is perceived as *imposing her standards* on the boy, while a dominating father is perceived as *imposing himself* on the son. It may be that the mother–son relations are typically more secure than those between father and son, so that the boy is better able to accept higher levels of dominance and rejection from his mother than his father without adverse effect on his need to achieve. Relatively rejecting, dominating fathers, particularly those with less than average warmth—as tended to be the case with the fathers of low n Achievement boys—seem to be a threat to the boy and a deterrent to the development of n Achievement. (1959:216–217)

The more authoritarian the father, the less autonomy he will grant his sons and the more apt he is to crush them. Authoritarianism is culturally supported in quasi-feudal countries like Turkey and Brazil (Rosen, 1962). Bradburn found that Turkish fathers were almost universally authoritarian with their families, making all decisions without consulting anyone:

Almost universally, the Turks interviewed described their fathers as stern, forbidding, remote, domineering, and autocratic. Few of them had ever argued with their fathers, and those who had had done so at the price of an open break. Several men reported that after having argued with their fathers they had not spoken to them for over 10 years. . . . One man reported that even after he was married and had his own family, he did not dare smoke or even sit with his legs crossed in his father's presence or in any way contradict him. Another man, when asked whether he had ever had any disagreement with his father, remarked that he had never had a discussion with his father on any topic, as his father had died when he was very young. It later turned out that he was 19 when his father died. (1963:192)

In such a country, the only way a boy may develop the desire to achieve for himself is to be separated from his father by the time he reaches adolescence.

TABLE 16-7 Achievement Motivation, by Father-Son Relationship

	FATHER–SON RELATIONSHIP	
SON'S ACHIEVEMENT MOTIVATION	Unbroken	Broken
High	36%	71%
Low	64	29
Total	100%	100%
Number of families	73	45

Adapted from Bradburn, 1960. Source: 47 male Turkish education students, 47 business students and 24 senior executives. The dividing line for the first group was separation from the father before age 14, for the remaining two groups before age 18. For each group taken separately, the results were essentially as portrayed in the combined table shown here.

Table 16-7 shows that Turkish men who had been separated from their fathers by 14–18 were twice as apt to have high achievement motivation as those who remained under the control of their fathers. On the other hand, McClelland (1961) noted that achievement motivation may also be impaired by losing the father so early that the mother and son develop an overdependent relationship. This can be seen in the lack of achievement motivation in polygynous societies where the father's role in the family is so marginal that the mother–child relationship is overdeveloped. In other words, the task of the father is to free the child from his mother's influence without dominating the child too much himself.

It should not be assumed, however, that the only possible role for fathers is this largely negative one. In the United States, fathers are so much less domineering than in Turkey that they may play what Bradburn called "a more encouraging role, setting high standards for the boy in encouraging him to achieve" (1963). If a boy has such a father, to lose him at any point in childhood would lower rather than raise his achievement motivation.

I have suggested that in most societies fathers tend to be more authoritarian than mothers. Within a given society, contrasting allocations of leadership between fathers and mothers have correspondingly diverse effects on children. For example, in the United States most young men report that their fathers had been their chief disciplinarian. But in exceptional cases where the mother had been, sons were correspondingly feminized. Henry (1956) found that father-disciplined boys tended to blame others whereas mother-disciplined boys often blamed themselves in conflict situations. This presumably reflects the aggressive, sadistic tendencies of males in contrast to the passive, masochistic tendencies of females. In an earlier work, Henry and Short (1954) had found that this differential direction of blame was carried to its logical conclusion when sons commit murder. Father-disciplined sons more often committed homicide and mother-disciplined sons committed suicide. Rarely has the parent provided the son with an exact example of this behavior, but the general attitude of the masculine or feminine parent has been inculcated in the child who is his or her chief disciplinary responsibility. Thus, the leadership roles played by fathers and mothers have a profound impact on their children.

SONS AND DAUGHTERS

Many of the above studies were confined to children of one sex. But parents tend to treat children of the two sexes differently. Insofar as the roles of husbands and wives—and more especially of fathers and mothers—are differentiated by sex, the modeling effects of parental behavior almost inevitably produce corresponding differences in children. As children become aware of their sexual identity, they can be expected to imitate the same-sex parent more than the opposite one.

The tendency of children to echo the parents' role differentiation is compounded by the fact that few parents treat their children uniformly. Most treat their sons differently from the way they treat their daughters, partly to train them for their sex roles, partly for other reasons. Whatever the reasons, sons and daughters are customarily treated differently by their parents and develop differently because of their differential upbringing.

Differential Treatment of Sons and Daughters

Even before they are born, sons and daughters are anticipated with differential eagerness. If a society grants males a higher status than females, male children will be preferred. In the United States, parents want children of both sexes, but slightly prefer boys to girls (Westoff, *et al.*, 1961). But in male-dominated quasi-feudal societies, parents strongly prefer sons. Landy (1959) cited a Puerto Rican man with ten daughters—which was a "cutting blow" to his pride. Among the Rajputs of India, Minturn and Hitchcock (1963) found that sons (but not daughters) were celebrated with elaborate birth ceremonies and that midwives who delivered them were paid twice as much. Worse yet, sons received better medical treatment so that 75 percent survived the hazards of infancy compared to only 59 percent of daughters. Even though Rajputs were not a poor caste by Indian standards, parents were so unhappy about girls that they failed to provide medical treatment promptly or to continue it as long as with boys. While not deliberately designed to kill off their daughters, this differential treatment is reminiscent of the tribal custom of controlling population by female infanticide.

Reasons why Rajputs preferred sons are typical of the crucial roles of males in patrilineal, patrilocal family systems:

> The family prestige depends largely on wealth and manpower; boys are potential farm hands and fighters for the family name, and, since the society is patrilineal, they are the bearers of the family continuity. Also, a son is necessary for the performance of certain funeral rites at the pyre of his father. Without a son, a man's salvation is jeopardized. A girl, on the other hand, is always a financial liability. She requires an extensive dowry at the time of marriage, and she is committed to making gifts to her husband's household when she returns to visit him for at least the first few years of their marriage. (Minturn and Hitchcock, 1963:302)

In agrarian societies because sons are expected to inherit the family land, daughters are freer to migrate to the city. From Irish farms, single women predominated among young people migrating to Dublin or to foreign countries (Humphreys, 1966). The marginal position of girls in family continuity is also reflected in carrying the family name down through the male line. In the United States, the lesser importance of girls' names to the larger family is reflected in less frequently naming girls after their parents or ancestors. Only boys, for example, are named "Junior" or given higher numerals (like John D. Rockefeller IV).

The higher status of boys in societies just emerging from feudalism is visible in the fact that they are the first sex (and for a long time the only one) to receive an education. This differential treatment of sons and daughters in turn sets boys apart from men at a time when girls and women are still indistinguishable. In medieval Europe:

> . . . boys were the first specialized children. They began going to school in large numbers as far back as the late sixteenth century. . . . The education of girls . . . developed slowly and tardily. Without a proper educational system, the girls were confused with the women at an early age just as the boys had formerly been confused with the men, and nobody thought of giving visible form, by means of dress, to a distinction which was beginning to exist in reality for the boys but which still remained futile for the girls. (Aries, 1962:58)

In general, then, the roles that sons and daughters will play in their families in the future and their roles in the larger society affect how their parents feel about them at birth and how they are treated subsequently.

Energetic Boys/Passive Girls   A second major difference between boys and girls is biological. Boys' larger muscles and higher energy level (symbolized in higher calorie consumption) produces physical restlessness, mobility, and aggressiveness. As a result, boys are harder to handle and family structure is correspondingly altered.

Among mentally retarded children, Farber (1960) found that boys caused their parents more strain than girls with equally defective intelligence. Retarded girls tended to fit into subdued and sedentary domestic roles, whereas boys tended to get into trouble by wandering away from home, picking fights, and being sexually aggressive.

Despite the fact that boys—whether retarded or normal—are harder to handle (or perhaps because of it), parents give their sons freer rein than daughters. Yet Bronfenbrenner (1961) concluded that this undersocialized boys and oversocialized girls.

Figure 16-3 shows that parental power reaches a point of diminishing returns with respect to responsibility training much sooner with girls than with boys. The same study showed that parents also depressed the responsibility of girls in several other ways: parental rejection, affection, and affiliation (doing things with children) all became excessive sooner for girls than boys. Thus the danger of oversocializing girls and undersocializing boys stems from several facets of the socialization process. As the psychologically weaker sex, girls succumb to parental discipline which boys more easily shrug off. This means that, according to the study, parents who wished to treat

FIGURE 16-3.   Sons' Versus Daughters' Responsibility, by Parental Power

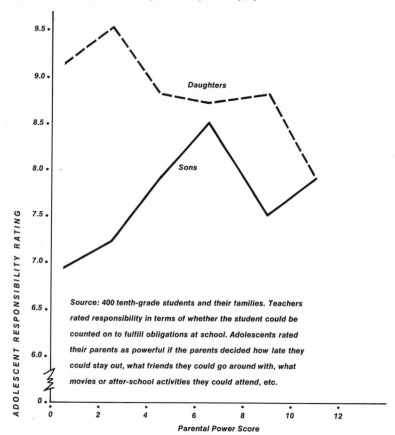

Source: 400 tenth-grade students and their families. Teachers rated responsibility in terms of whether the student could be counted on to fulfill obligations at school. Adolescents rated their parents as powerful if the parents decided how late they could stay out, what friends they could go around with, what movies or after-school activities they could attend, etc.

Adapted from Bronfenbrenner (1961):95.

their sons and daughters optimally would reverse the usual practice and give their daughters more freedom and sons less.

Same-Sex Identification

When boys come to think of themselves as members of the masculine sex, they turn to the chief sex-role model available to them—their father. Girls do the same with their mothers. Consequently boys follow in their fathers' footsteps and girls in their mothers'—other things being equal. We know from discussing the different roles of fathers and mothers, however, that other things are not ordinarily equal. Children interact so much more with their mothers than with their fathers that mothers leave more of an imprint on them. When the principles of same-sex identification and greater influence of the mother combine as in the case of girls, the influence of the mother should be doubly strong. When they diverge, as in the father–daughter relationship, parental influence should be conspicuously weak.

This can be tested by examining the differential influence of divergent parents on children of each sex. Maccoby found that parents of divergent political affiliation particularly influenced the political socialization of children of the same sex but that the mother's influence was generally stronger than the father's. Both Landis (1949) and Putney and Middleton (1961) found that mothers were more apt than fathers to win the religious affiliation of their children and that parents influenced children of the same sex more than of the opposite sex.

TABLE 16-8   Influence of Parent's Religion, by Sex of Parent and Sex of Child

		SEX OF PARENT	
		Mother	*Father*
Religious Ideology Closer to Specified Parent, by Sex of Child	Same sex	78%	69%
	Opposite sex	72%	65%
Number of cases	Same sex	82	55
	Opposite sex	74	74

Adapted from Putney and Middleton, 1961: 131. Source: Religious ideologies of students attending Eastern U.S. colleges whose parents held contradictory ideologies. The data are limited to that parent whose ideology was more consistent with the general American religious ideology (modernist Christianity). For example, if the mother's religious ideology was more conventional, 78 per cent of the daughters' and 72 per cent of sons' beliefs were closer to the mother's than to the father's beliefs. Reciprocal percentages of students held ideologies closer to the other parent.

Table 16-8 shows the combined effect of these two factors. Of the four same-sex and cross-sex combinations, the mother–daughter relationship was closest as measured by success in religious education, while the father–daughter relationship was most distant. Children, thus, are more influenced by their mothers than by their often-absent and less-interested fathers; but this paternal handicap is partially counteracted in the case of sons because both are of the same sex. These outcomes of socialization provide clues to the structure of the family—children are closer to the mother but they are also closer to the parent of the same sex.

If family structure involves special closeness between children and the same-sex parent, it necessarily involves greater distance from the other parent. In equalitarian societies, this separation may be difficult to detect, but in systems where the sexes are segregated and stratified, distance is easily observed. In such families, sex grading and age grading combine to place the father in a lofty position and the daughter in a lowly one. Prior to puberty, the father and daughter may reach across that gap, but once the daughter reaches puberty, their relationship is likely to cool. Among Campbell's Greek shepherds:

> . . . from the age of seventeen until she marries . . . a girl's deportment inside and outside the family changes considerably. She must now behave as a maiden of virtue who is acutely sensitive to shame. No longer may she show her feelings in an uninhibited way, and in her conversation and her movements a careful self-control is demanded. Her relations with her father now become less familiar. Since she left school at thirteen, a certain barrier has already arisen between them, and from that age she is expected in front of strangers to show him respect by standing when he sits and helping her mother to wait on her father and his guests. By the time a girl is seventeen there is a noticeable neutrality of tone in her conversation with her father. She is careful to avoid any reference to sexual matters or the possibility of her marriage. They are both conscious of the categorical obligations they owe to one another and the severe penalties which sanction their fulfillment. If a father does not arrange an honourable and successful marriage for his daughter, his reputation in the community is diminished. If a daughter does not preserve her virginity and her reputation for virginity, she faces death possibly; or should she avoid this fate, she must certainly endure dishonour and a dishonourable marriage to a widower or a poor man of ill repute. (1964:158–159)

BROTHERS AND SISTERS

The fact that siblings come in two sexes splits the sibling group along sex lines. This is one basis for the formation of subgroups within large families.

Insofar as boys and girls play different roles in the family, they are functionally differentiated even if their status is more or less equal. In Okinawa, the Maretzkis found that parents expected older brothers and sisters to assume similar responsibilities for their younger siblings, though "boys try to escape this duty by 'making a deal' with their sisters. Girls are therefore more frequently seen caring for younger siblings, but when there are no older girls in the family, a boy must assume this responsibility" (1963:517).

Only in a novel situation, such as the first sister of several boys, were older brothers as willing to baby-sit as girls generally were. Even when they assumed the same responsibility, boys did not treat their charges as patiently as girls. Perhaps because of the masculine aggressiveness and restlessness mentioned before, or perhaps because boys saw baby-sitting as less appropriate for them than for their sisters, they dealt more impatiently with their siblings than did girls.

The bigger the status differential between the sexes, the greater the likelihood that adult brothers will be given responsibility for their sisters. Young Greek shepherds shared with their fathers the responsibility of protecting their sisters' virginity and for marrying them off, complete with dowries. This meant that all the sisters were supposed to be married before the brothers could marry. On the other hand, the society placed so much emphasis on the division of labor between the sexes that the sex ratio within the family could not be allowed to become so unbalanced. Therefore, Campbell found, at least one sister was customarily kept at home until she could be replaced by the bride of her eldest brother.

In another Greek community, Lambiri (1965) found that girls did not always appreciate their brothers' and fathers' concern for their virginity. As new industries moved into a previously agrarian society, single girls found it difficult to persuade the male members of their families that they should be allowed to work in a factory. Whereas mothers characteristically sympathized with their daughters' desire to work, fathers were ambivalent and brothers often opposed it. In a given family, as soon as one girl overcame these male barriers, her sisters could follow suit and get jobs too. This suggests that in these Greek families, sisters (and mothers) tended to form a radical coalition seeking liberation from domination by their conservative brothers and fathers. Perhaps brothers and sisters are not ranged against each other in stable feudal societies, but once such societies begin to modernize, the feminist revolt is likely to split families into sex-linked factions.

SEX ROLES IN KIN NETWORKS

If nuclear families tend to split along sex lines, kin relations should be correspondingly differentiated. We have already seen in Chapter 7 that bilateral kinship systems tend to have a matrilateral bias. In the light of the present chapter, the differentials which began in childhood should affect parent–child and sibling relationships in adulthood.

Intergenerational Interaction   ·

Earlier in this chapter, we saw that mothers interact with their children more than fathers, and that daughters are closer to their parents than are sons. After children are launched from the home, these pre-launch ties produce continuing differentials in the frequency of interaction.

Table 16-9 shows that working-class women in East London saw their parents much more frequently than men did. Conversely, 67 percent of the same old people saw at least one daughter every day, whereas only 48 percent saw a son that often. These differences support the old British saying that "A son's a son till he gets him a wife; a daughter's a daughter all her life." From Wales, Rosser and Harris cited an old miner's comments on this saying:

Ay, ay, I've heard that before—and there's no doubt about it, it's damn true.
I've always thought the wedding ceremony in church was all wrong myself.

TABLE 16-9 Frequency of Contact with Parents, by Sons and Daughters

	SEX OF CHILDREN	
FREQUENCY OF SEEING PARENTS	Sons	Daughters
Daily	26%	45%
At least once a week	42	33
At least once a month	19	15
At least once a year	9	5
Never	4	2
Total	100%	100%
Number of individuals	314	312

Adapted from Townsend, 1957:38. Source: Living children (regardless of residence) of working-class East London men aged 65+ and women aged 60+.

Don't they say "Who giveth this woman in marriage?" And the father of the bride hops forward and says "I do." But he doesn't at all, at least if he does he's not speaking for his wife, now is he? I say it should be altered. "Who giveth this man in marriage"—that's the proper question, lad. And make the *mother* of the bridegroom say "I do." Most fathers don't give a damn either way in my experience. (1965:258)

Although daughters see their parents more than sons, mothers do not have as much of an edge over fathers. Visits are usually made by the daughter to the father and mother living together. Particularly after the father retires, he is home when the daughter arrives, so contact between both parents and the daughter occurs simultaneously. Nevertheless contact with the father is often an accidental by-product of intended contact with the mother. In East London slums:

Both sons and daughters expressed a greater affection for their mothers than for their fathers. It was chiefly Mum they visited and Mum they supported, materially and emotionally. The men indeed often accepted this. One married man, a pensioner, in talking of his children's visits to the home said, "They come up every week to see their mother." Although he was at home at the time of their visits he did not say his children visited both him and his wife. (Townsend, 157:83)

And for working-class American women, Komarovsky (1964) found that relationships with their fathers were characteristically distant and sometimes completely broken (whereas if they did not get on well with their mothers, they hated them passionately but seldom ignored them).

Insofar as women are close to their mothers, grandchildren in turn have closer relationships with maternal than with paternal grandparents. But in patrilocal family systems, women are cut off from contact with their own relatives and have nowhere to turn their affectional and affiliative capacities save to their own children. Since they lose their daughters after marriage, their strongest and longest lasting ties are with sons. And since ties with their husbands are weakened by *his* mother, their relationship to their sons frequently has an emotional and quasi-erotic tone which the husband–wife relationship lacks:

> The relation between Arab mother and son was an extremely intense one. Aside from the expected love of a mother for her son, she had some reason to find in him a major center of her being. By producing a son, the woman helped to build up her husband's house, both symbolically and in fact (since a son became part of her husband's work force). She was unlikely to be divorced if she bore a son, and he represented her primary link with her husband's line. Basing their conclusions in part on Rorschach materials from Bedouins, Miner and De Vos [1960] comment, ". . . the erotic attachment of men to their mothers and sisters is very strong . . . nor are these feelings one-sided." Although a girl baby is likely to continue nursing for as long as one or one and a half years, the boy is nursed until he is two or two and a half, and gets far more tender treatment. (Goode, 1963:143)

Insofar as Arab children had any contact with maternal relatives, that relationship was quite different from the tight, authoritarian bonds which bound them to the paternal relatives with whom they lived. Goode noted that "Since the mother was a major source of solace and tenderness for a boy, who increasingly spent most of his time with adult males, so was the relation with the mother's side of the family likely to be a warm one, uncontaminated by severe demands" (Goode, 1963:144).

In general then patrilocal extended families embed children in a close relationship with paternal relatives, but ties with maternal relatives are notably affectionate. In matrilocal systems, the consequences of patrilocalism are reversed. In nominally bilateral systems, maternal kin ties predominate. Thus in all three types of family systems, children have differentiated rather than symmetrical relationships with their relatives on the masculine and feminine "sides" of the family.

So far I have dealt chiefly with differences in sociability and feeling between relatives. Differences are exacerbated in exchanging help. Because modern women carry the main burden of household tasks both within the nuclear family and within the kin network, the help pattern has an even sharper feminine bias than the sociability pattern. Nearly all the personal and domestic services exchanged between households are performed by women. Exceptions occur mainly when men are more or less forced into providing "feminine" services because no female relative is available. Thus a grandfather may baby-sit for his grandchildren if no one else can be found, but ordinarily he would leave that responsibility to his wife or another female relative.

So strong was the tendency in Table 16-10 for women to help one another that nearby daughters even helped their mothers with tasks which a retired husband could have done himself. Some of the daughters included in the table actually lived within the home, but most were married and had their own household responsibilities. The daughter's help to her aging mother was much appreciated by the mother, but it left the husband vulnerable to criticism, especially if he was retired and had nothing else to do. The table

TABLE 16-10   Husband's Help in the Home, by Husband's
Work Status and the Availability of Daughters

PERCENTAGE OF HUSBANDS WHO HELPED, BY WORK STATUS	DAUGHTER WITHIN 5 MINUTES' WALK	
	Yes	No
Husband employed	20%	60%
Husband retired	35	67

Adapted from Townsend, 1957:73. "Help" was defined as performing at least once a week at least one domestic task, such as shopping, washing up, cleaning windows, or making the fire. Reciprocal percentages of husbands did not help that much. Source: Working-class London households of men aged 65+ or women aged 60+.

does show that a few retired husbands took over some responsibility from their daughters, but for most families, his do-nothing retirement made the burden of housework worse rather than better. One of Townsend's married women said of her retired husband:

It's different with him at home. Because he's at home he wonders what you're doing. Before that he wasn't here and you could get on with things. Now he's asking you what you're doing this for and what you're doing that for. (1957:74)

This suggests that mother–daughter collaboration tends to estrange the mother from her husband and to create tension and bitterness.

Kin networks are often split into two factions: an unhappy old man and a close-knit mother–daughter pair. Asked to compare their relationships with their husbands and with their children—

A number of women admitted greater loyalty to their married children than to their husbands. One said, "Some wives put their husbands first, but I, now, I've always been the other way. I'm all for the children, and I leave my husband to himself." Others made it clear they did not want the man's retirement to interrupt their daily routine. One woman's daughter said "*She* wouldn't want him to [retire]. She couldn't stand him here all day. She wants him out of the way." A number of other wives were scornful or critical of their husbands and sided with their children in arguments. Occasionally, a husband was ridiculed by his wife and her children even when he was present. In contrast, only one wife was ridiculed by her husband and no example was encountered of children criticising the mother publicly. (Townsend, 1957:73)

This quotation describes extreme cases from a working-class British sample. Being working-class matters because segregation between husbands and wives is more pronounced among couples with less education and in blue-collar occupations. Nevertheless, the contrast between the occasional isolation of the man from his wife and children and the generally central position of the wife in the kin network can be observed throughout the class structure in the majority of modern societies. Sex-role differentiation profoundly affects patterns of kin contact and kin help and reinforces sex-role differentiation between husband and wife in the nuclear family.

Sibling Attachments

Generally speaking, sibling relationships are less vital than intergenerational relationships (at least as long as the mother survives). Nevertheless, both before and after her death, similar patterns are visible in sibling relationships to those we have seen between parents and children—namely, the closeness of females to one another and the distance between family members of the opposite sex. Just as mother–daughter relationships tend to be especially close, we should expect a special closeness between sisters. However, it is more difficult to predict the difference between brother–brother ties and brother–sister ties since the former has the advantage of similarity of sex whereas the latter has the advantage of involving a sociable female.

TABLE 16-11　Frequency of Contact Between Siblings and Change in Closeness Since Marriage, by Sex

	SEX OF SIBLINGS		
FREQUENCY OF CONTACT	*Two Brothers*	*Opposite Sexes*	*Two Sisters*
Contact at least once a week	32%	26%	35%
Less than once a week	68	74	65
Total	100%	100%	100%
Change in relationship since marriage			
Closer	22%	22%	48%
About the same	46	29	17
Less close	32	49	35
Total	100%	100%	100%
Number of relationships	41	83	46

Adapted from Adams, 1968:102, 120. Source: Blue-collar young married men and women in Greensboro, North Carolina.

Not all studies reveal a consistent pattern, but Table 16-1 illustrates some of the factors in the working class, where the sexes are more sharply segregated. The table shows that sisters had the closest relationship, brothers next, and cross-sex siblings least. The lower half of the table shows how respondents felt their relationships had changed since they got married. Marriage brought these working-class girls into a common role which gave them something to talk about and made them feel closer to each other. For siblings of the opposite sex, marriage introduced contrasting roles and separated them even more than before. For brothers, marriage was a less significant event and therefore their relationship was less affected.

In general, then, sibling relationships resemble intergenerational relations. They are especially close when following same-sex lines but hampered when crossing sex lines. The greater the segregation and differentiation of the sexes generally in a particular segment of a society, the more these barriers between the sexes may be expected to split both the nuclear family and the kin network.

chapter seventeen

AGE DIFFERENTIATION IN THE FAMILY

The second major ingredient in family structure is age differentiation. This refers primarily to differences between generations, but secondarily to the ordering of siblings by their serial arrival.

Age differences are less a question of number of years than of the rank order of successive generations and successive siblings. Basically, families are hierarchical social structures in which older generations and older siblings hold positions of authority, prestige, and power over those who come after them. There are some exceptions, and there are differences in the degree of stratification by age. But the tendency for elders to exercise control over newer arrivals can be detected, however faintly, in family systems throughout the world.

PARENTS AND CHILDREN

The crucial vertical relationship is between parents and children. In many societies, childless couples are not considered truly married until the arrival of their first child.

After children grow up, there may be some doubt about how much inequality exists between parents and children, but with dependent infants there can be no doubt that the power differential between the generations approaches infinity.

In the last chapter, we saw a general tendency for fathers to play the role of task leaders and for mothers to be integrative leaders. Although this sex differentiation places the father in the highest position and the mother in between, from the children's standpoint both parents are their superiors. In this chapter, we will ignore the difference between fathers and mothers and concentrate on the difference between parents and children.

The Superiority of Parents

If one looks at family systems around the world, the superiority of parents to children is striking. Parents generally exercise authority over their children, and children obey that authority. Correlatively, parents treat their children "like children," whereas children treat their parents with respect.

One illustration is the difference in terms of address. Parents generally speak to their children by their personal names, frequently with the addition of diminutives and other expressions of endearment. Children, on the other hand, address their parents more formally, using titles such as "father" or "mother," or addressing them with the equivalent of "Mr." or "Sir." If the personal name is used at all, diminutives and other special suffixes are inappropriate for such an older, bigger person.

In Java, an entire language of respect has developed which goes far beyond terms of address. Children are supposed to master this special language and to use it when talking with their parents, but its very peculiarity introduces special barriers into the child–parent relationship. Geertz (1961) notes that "Many young students never write letters to their parents for fear of making an error, more obvious because in writing; they communicate, if at all, to a younger sibling in familiar language messages to be relayed [orally] to the parents" (1961:22).

The more power parents exercise over their children, the more respectfully and deferentially the children normally respond. Where children are controlled by their parents not simply in their leisure but all day long, the generation gap is widened. In agrarian societies, the boy is his father's employee, so respect for "the boss" is great. For a Greek shepherd boy, at least up to the age of twenty:

> . . . he does not smoke or drink ouzo in his father's presence. Similarly, he does not swear or make coarse remarks or jokes about sexual matters before his father. If a youth is sitting in the village coffee-shop when his father enters, he unobtrusively gets up and leaves. Drinking, smoking, and playing cards in the coffee-shop are the social activities of those equal in status, and are therefore incompatible with the respect owed by a son to his father. (Campbell, 1965:160)

Hierarchical relationships are not restricted to families where the children are involved in the family enterprise. So the reasons for the general superiority of parents must be located elsewhere. (1) I have already mentioned the dependence of the infant on his parents. This initial biological dependence becomes transformed into a social dependence which lasts indefinitely. (2) Parents by virtue of having lived longer have had more experience and therefore are wiser than their children. In societies which change slowly, and most of all in illiterate societies which depend on memory for knowledge about the proper ways of doing things, elders are in a strategic position to control children on behalf of the larger society. (3) In all societies, parents have a head start in achieving positions of power in the outside world which increases the resources which they bring to the family. Such factors strengthen their power over their children.

The lower the power of a parent, the less the gap between parent and child. After a father leaves home because of divorce or separation, his relationship with his children becomes warmer and more affectionate because he no longer exercises distance-creating discipline or authority. His children respect him less but the undercurrent of hostility and resentment normally associated with respect disappears. So paradoxically the removal of the father from the home may bring him emotionally closer to his children.

The Segregation of Children   Children have always been set apart from their parents by differences of power and status. But they have not always been separated from the life of adults.

In primitive societies operating on the edge of starvation, children were pressed into economic activity from an early age. Just as such societies could not afford the luxury of retirement (and left the old and feeble behind to starve), so they could not afford the luxury of childhood as a carefree period of play or as a prolonged preparation for adulthood. Life had to be serious and productive as early as possible. So children were inducted into full-fledged adulthood as soon as they reached puberty.

In feudal societies with extended family systems, the emphasis on economic productivity also came early in peasant families. However, extended families created a very special kind of parent–child relationship which prolonged the authority of the parent until his death or retirement. In that sense, children in feudal extended families remained "children" into middle age. Nevertheless, they were laboring children and their lives took on a "grown-up" character even though they were not independent grown-ups.

Only in the feudal aristocracy did children have a life of their own which was different from that of their elders. The segregation of the life of children from that of adults began in the upper reaches of feudal society and spread downward only in affluent modern societies. Aries described this process of segregation as "the invention of childhood." That invention he traced through analyzing the portrayal of children in European art:

> Medieval art until about the twelfth century did not know childhood [because] there was no place for childhood in the medieval world. An Ottonian miniature of the twelfth century [portrays] the scene in the Gospels in which Jesus asks that little children be allowed to come to Him. . . . the miniaturist has grouped around Jesus what are obviously eight men, without any of the characteristics of childhood; they have simply been depicted on a smaller scale.
>
> From this religious iconography of childhood, a lay iconography eventually detached itself in the fifteenth and sixteenth centuries. These . . . paintings were not as a general rule devoted to the exclusive portrayal of childhood, but in a great many cases there were children among the characters depicted. . . . This suggests [that] children mingled with adults in everyday life, and any gathering for the purpose of work, relaxation or sport brought together both children and adults. (1962:33, 37)

Aries noted that children played the same games and wore the same types of clothes as adults. They were not sheltered from the sexual jokes and sex play indulged in by their elders. All the burdens and pleasures of adult life were there as soon as they could share them:

> In medieval society the idea of childhood did not exist; this is not to suggest that children were neglected, forsaken or despised. The idea of childhood is not to be confused with affection for children: it corresponds to an awareness of the particular nature of childhood, that . . . which distinguishes the child from the adult, even the young adult. In medieval society this awareness was lacking. That is why, as soon as the child could live without the constant solicitude of his mother, his nanny or his cradle-rocker, he belonged to adult society. (Aries, 1962:128)

The invention of schools changed all that. Schools segregated children from adult society in order to prepare them for entrance into that society. Segregation in educational institutions eventually resulted in the segregation of children in other settings (for example, Sunday Schools were invented in the mid-nineteenth century—prior to that children went to church alongside their parents). Children were forbidden by child labor laws to participate in the occupational system. Political participation had never been possible for children but before the rise of democracy they were no worse off than their parents. With the granting of suffrage to adults, another wedge was driven between the generations. Eventually, the segregation of children became so extensive that they developed their own subculture, exacerbating in-group/out-group feeling, hostility, and prejudice. Although most of this segregation arose outside the family, it could not help affecting relationships within the family. So in modern societies, intergenerational relationships are colored by a psychological gap produced by the segregation of the generations.

A second characteristic of modern societies accentuates subcultural differentiation—the rapidity of social change. We saw in Chapter 8 that one consequence of rapid change is alienation of the generations. Although the speed of social change varies among modern societies, any society based on an industrial economy is inevitably and continuously changing. In contrast to illiterate societies, where the task of the young is to learn the wisdom of the old, changing societies undermine the authority of the old and make it difficult for the generations to understand each other's language, customs, and values. At worst, the relationship between generations seems as difficult as between people from different societies who do not speak the same language.

An industrial society also develops an increasingly complex division of labor which requires increasingly prolonged educational preparation. This makes segregation of the generations largely inevitable. Inevitability, however, does not relieve the difficulties created for intergenerational relationships in contemporary families.

Negotiation with Children   If families are to hold together and not fly apart in the face of these centrifugal forces, parents must make an effort to keep in touch with their children. This affects their problem of social control. Either they may impose their authority unilaterally, or they may enter into negotiations with their children—with correspondingly different effects on their relationship.

To negotiate is considered by some adults a sign of weakness and a betrayal of their superior status. They announce their orders and tolerate no back talk. If the whole society is authoritarian, children may submit to this tyranny (as in Brazil where cultural support combines with parental affection to make authority difficult to resist). But within minority subcultures in democratic societies, parents find it almost impossible to persuade children to accept a totalitarianism which others do not experience.

One minority in the United States is the Old Order Amish. Kauffman found that Amish families were significantly more authoritarian than other families in a mid-Western community—parents less often asked their children's opinion when deciding on major purchases, gave them less freedom to make their own decisions, less often gave them allowances, and seldom allowed them to keep money they earned away from home. At the same time, parents less often demonstrated affection for their children or played games with them. In general parents kept themselves aloof from their children and exercised tight control.

What were the effects of this authoritarianism? According to a "Child–Parent Relations Index," Amish families rated significantly poorer than democratic rural families of other faiths. Amish teen-agers felt their parents had been too strict in their discipline, felt deprived of affection, felt rebellious toward their parents and showed more nervous symptoms. The U.S.A. is so democratic that few American parents can maintain an authoritarian grip on their children, especially when they reach adolescence. Authoritarianism is more likely to provoke the rebelliousness that these Amish young people demonstrated.

At the opposite extreme are indifferent parents. They are hardly preferable from the child's point of view. In authoritarian homes children at least know their parents are concerned even if they don't express affection very openly. But when parents pay little or no attention to their children, their lack of caring is obvious. Rosenberg (1965) found that New York high school students with indifferent parents had the lowest self-esteem. If the mother or father knew few of the child's friends or paid little attention to the child's grades, self-esteem was conspicuously low. Even students punished for low marks had more self-esteem than those who were simply ignored.

A completely laissez-faire approach to children may involve no communication between parents and children at all. Not to be communicated with is more humiliating than to receive an unpleasant communication.

TABLE 17-1   Adolescent Difficulties, by Family Authority Pattern and by Sex

DIFFICULTY	SEX	FAMILY AUTHORITY PATTERN		AUTHORITARIAN/ DEMOCRATIC RATIO
		Authoritarian	*Democratic*	
Has trouble getting	Boys	17%	6%	2.84X
along with parents	Girls	24	8	3.00
Wants to leave home	Boys	9	2	4.50
	Girls	12	3	4.00
Number of cases	Boys	396	769	
	Girls	533	537	

Adapted from Landis and Stone, 1952:24–25. Source: High school seniors in Washington state. Reciprocal percentages did not have the specified difficulty. Democratic parents were defined as those who allowed their children to go out as many evenings as they wished, never criticized where they went on dates, were "fairly generous" with allowance money, "usually" gave reasons for requests, discussed family problems with their children, and respected their children's opinions and judgment "at least half the time."

Table 17-1 indicates the value of democratic methods in controlling American adolescents. The crucial elements in the definition of democracy were presumably the last three: giving reasons for requests, discussing family problems, and respecting the children's opinions. Each suggests a two-way communication process and a willingness on the part of the parents to negotiate with children about areas of common concern. In any case, democratic parents were more successful than authoritarian ones in achieving family integration. Both the absence of conflict within the family and the desire of children to remain as members of the family are indices of integration. Democratic families excelled on both counts.

The fact that girls showed more rebelliousness than boys may be related to the parents' lesser willingness to negotiate. A glance at the numbers of cases at the bottom of the table shows that parents were more apt to be authoritarian with girls than with boys. Perhaps the average authoritarian parents were more authoritarian and the average democratic parents less democratic with girls. If both types of parents were more restrictive with girls and less willing to reason with them, this may explain why their control efforts were less persuasive.

TABLE 17-2   Political Rebellion, by Strictness of Parental Control

| | STRICTNESS OF PARENTAL CONTROL | | |
	Permissive	*Average*	*Strict*
Rebelled from political views			
Of father	55%	36%	46%
Of mother	49%	34%	40%
Number of girls	104	315	166

Adapted from Middleton and Putney, 1963:533. Source: Women students at 16 U. S. colleges and universities. Their political views were related to their parents' control efforts in high school: "When you were in high school, did your parents (a) want to have quite a lot to say about your friends and the places you went and so on, or (b) were you pretty much on your own?" These answers were classified as strict and permissive respectively, with intermediate responses classified as average. Reciprocal percentages of students held the same views as the specified parent.

Another study showing that girls rebelled more than boys (and against fathers more than against mothers) is summarized in Table 17-2. The rebelliousness portrayed here is the converse of the successful socialization discussed in Chapter 15. It shows the tendency of high school girls to react negatively to either excessively strict or excessively weak control. The "average" parents presumably engaged in the most dialogue with their children, communicating their own concern but listening to the children's responses in return.

To negotiate with children minimizes the superiority of parents. Paradoxically in modern societies, such generosity is the most effective way parents can retain their superiority as models for their children's socialization. Conversely, those who insist on their superiority are more apt to alienate their children than to control them.

The Resourcefulness of Parents

How generous parents can be with their children depends on how many resources they have to dispense. Some resources are psychological but others are more concrete. In Chapter 2 we saw that upper-class parents control their children more effectively than poverty-stricken parents because they have more money and family prestige. When parents have little to offer, children feel resentful and have nothing to lose by rebelling.

Sometimes a whole generation of parents are caught in a situation where they have little to offer but trouble. The changing fate of a given society affects parent–child relationships correspondingly. The world-wide depression of the 1930s meant that young people faced a bleak economic future when they left school. To bring up children in such a world is to breed resentment which destroys respect for parents (Davis, 1940).

In the 1950s the world was so peaceful that parent–adolescent relations improved. Elkin and Westley (1955) found that the subcultural gap between the generations had diminished so much in a Montreal suburb that they labeled their report "The Myth of Adolescent Culture." As far as they could see, parents and teenagers shared a common affluent culture.

But in the 1960s American involvement in Vietnam split the generations apart again. Young people were concerned not only for the bleakness of their own futures, but with the injustice of the whole operation. War protest and draft resistance spilled over into protest and resistance against parental norms.

Immigrant parents from almost any country are in a weak position until they become Americanized. Studies prior to World War II showed acute conflict between the generations and widespread rejection by college students of responsibility for their parents (Dinkel, 1944). Such parents had only an obsolete pattern to offer their children and the latter were almost required to reject that pattern if they were to become Americanized.

In general, the less parents have to offer their children, the harder it is to control them. Such parents often try to compensate for their lack of resources by increased authoritarianism. Yet the less they have to offer, the greater the likelihood that authoritarianism will boomerang in rebellion. So parents in a precarious position must scale down their control efforts if the whole process is not to go wrong.

Adaptation to Growing Children

Much of the preceding discussion referred to adolescents—with good reason. Parent–child relationships begin with the dependency of infants, but they do not stay there. At the beginning the child is incapable of negotiation because he cannot talk. The parents necessarily control him 100 percent. By the time he is launched from the family, he must be capable of controlling himself 100 percent. Therefore parents must do a complete about-face in just two decades. Nor can this be a simple one-step change. From the time the child begins moving toward independence at around age two until he finishes that process at launching, a whole series of steps be taken. To grant independence at age two would be absurd. To delay it until launching would both leave the child unprepared for the sudden assumption of self-control and out-Amish the Amish in provoking rebellion. The switch from 100 percent to 0 percent family control is too enormous to be accomplished in anything less than a long series of small emancipatory steps. In a sense, the family must continuously readjust the balance of power between parents and children throughout the entire period.

To make matters even more complicated, the speed with which this relaxation of control takes place must be nicely adjusted to the growing capacities of the child and coordinated with other families in the child's peer group and in his school class.

In the preceding section, I suggested that parents may be either too permissive or too authoritarian. But that cannot be judged simply in terms of permitted acts. Whether parents are too permissive or too authoritarian depends on the age of the child. The question might more fruitfully be rephrased: Do parents relax their grip too early or too late?

TABLE 17-3   Unreasonableness of Paternal Child Rearing
Policies and Sense of Paternal Rejection,
by Family Authority Pattern

FEELING ABOUT FATHER	FAMILY AUTHORITY PATTERN					
	Autocratic	Authori-tarian	Democratic	Equali-tarian	Permissive	Laissez-faire or Ignoring
Policies unreasonable	49%	25%	15%	23%	25%	—
Father rejects me	40%	18%	8%	11%	11%	58%

Adapted from Elder, 1962:258–259. Source: Students in grades 7–12 in Ohio and North Carolina. Definitions were as follows:

Autocratic: Child not allowed to express his views.
Authoritarian: Child allowed to speak but parents make all decisions.
Democratic: Child may make decisions but they must be approved by parents.
Equalitarian: Parent and child share decision making 50/50.
Permissive: Child more influential than parents.
Laissez-faire: Child may disregard parental wishes in making his decisions.
Ignoring: Parents pay no attention to child's behavior.

Table 17-3 shows the reactions of junior high and senior high school students to varying parental control systems. They generally reacted negatively to both over-control and under-control. They responded best to relying on parental approval of their decisions (the "democratic" pattern) rather than to complete equality with their parents. Presumably at a later age complete equality comes to be preferred. Within this group a more refined analysis showed that senior-high students viewed permissive policies more positively than did junior-high students. Thus the older the students became, the more appropriate relaxed controls seemed to them.

At any one point in time, overly permissive parents have moved too fast while overly authoritarian parents have clung to their power too long. Authoritarianism is appropriate at age one, but not much longer; and complete permissiveness at twenty-one, but not much sooner.

Pacing depends on so many factors that it cannot be given any general formula. It depends on the child's increasing knowledge, his understanding of human relations, his increasing socialization and developing conscience. It also depends on the hazardousness of the environment in which he lives and the number of temptations to deviant behavior which it presents. Parents must repeatedly assess their child in relation to his environment in determining how fast they can safely relax their controls and transfer power to him.

The trouble is that the Establishment seldom surrenders gracefully. From the parents' viewpoint, the child never seems quite so mature as he seems to himself. Children mature "overnight" when parents aren't looking. Since the status quo worked well in the past, parents cling to it, not realizing it has become obsolete. Thus at any point in the process of emancipation, most children feel they deserve more freedom than their parents are prepared to grant. And in view of the tendency of all institutions to resist change and lag in adapting to changing circumstances, the children are usually right.

To illustrate the difference in perspective between the generations, compare the views of women students at Temple University in Philadelphia with the views of their mothers on two parent–child issues: (1) Suppose a daughter is in love and wants to marry a young man, but the mother strongly objects to him; 45 percent of the mothers, but only 23 percent of the daughters, thought they should break up. (2) On the question of whether the daughter should have a close girl friend to discuss things with or discuss everything with her mother; 40 percent of the mothers thought everything should be discussed with them, compared to only 22 percent of the daughters (Bell and Buerkle, 1962).

Even if children did not grow up, we might expect both generations to want more power for themselves. But the general problem is intensified by the original infinite imbalance between the parties and the steadily growing capabilities of the children. One advantage of a democratic relationship is that it allows children to communicate with their parents and to negotiate their increasing demands. Conversely, conflict in either laissez-faire or authoritarian homes is intensified by poor communication between the generations.

The consequence of lagging in the emancipation process is liable to be rebellion. But if the child is so encapsulated in the parents' affections that he is unable to rebel, he may be in an even worse predicament. He may remain a child in the family as long as his parents survive, never marrying and never achieving independence. If, however, he succumbs to social pressure and marries, he may find himself trapped between his family and his marriage. If the trap is tight enough, there may be only two ways out—suicide or schizophrenia.

In Japan, Vogel noted that children "are very close to their parents, spend little time away from home even in their late teens, participate in very few extra-curricular activities in high school, spend relatively little time at friends' houses during the high school age, and make most major decisions only on very close consultation with their parents" (1961a:19). Although Vogel and Vogel argued elsewhere (1961:166) that ". . . there are no serious personality disturbances among these children even though Japanese children do not meet the Western ideal of independence," Japan has a conspicuously high suicide rate between age 15 and 24—just the years when launching should occur. Caudill commented that suicides seem to be "connected with the difficulty that [Japanese] young people have in loosening childhood ties to their parents (and especially to the mother) at a time when they are expected to assume adult roles in college, occupation, and marriage" (1970:6). In other words, excessive integration into the family may not create mental illness in the usual sense of the term, but it may place the child in a dilemma from which suicide is the culturally approved escape.

In the United States, suicide is less popular so young people caught between family ties and other responsibilities are more apt to escape into a schizophrenic withdrawal from reality. In a study of schizophrenic married women, Towne, Messinger, and Sampson (1962) found that many had had launching difficulties. Their mothers had clung to them so fiercely that they had not been able to experience the normal emancipation. Many had never lived away from home, never dated anyone other than the spouse, and had not even dated him enough to develop much of an attachment to him. Even though they married later than usual, they were neither emotionally nor socially prepared when they did.

Marriage subjected these women to severe cross-pressures. In some cases, wife, husband, and wife's mother all lived together in an extended household ruled by the mother. Although extended family systems work well when they are culturally prescribed and socially supported, they are so deviant in American society that they made both partners uneasy and ambivalent. The husbands resented being dominated by their mothers-in-law and pressured their wives to leave their mothers. Unable to break their ties with their mothers and unable to please their husbands, the wives became mentally ill.

Suicide and schizophrenia are extreme ways out of the dilemma. But they illustrate the stresses on children when parents fail to adapt to their children's growth.

It would be a mistake to imply that all the stresses of adapting to the changing age of children fall on the child. The parent, after all, is the one who must do the adapting. At every age, children present their parents with new problems.

TABLE 17-4   Parents' Problems, by Age of Oldest Child

	AGE OF OLDEST CHILD			
PARENTS' PROBLEMS	*Under 6*	*6–12*	*13–18*	*19+*
Restrictions on freedom	19%	15%	9%	5%
Burdens	21	13	16	20
Children's illnesses	15	19	12	9
Financial problems	14	19	10	17
Worries about children	10	11	17	8
None	21	22	36	40
Total	100%	99%	100%	99%
Number of families	127	136	101	63

Adapted from Blood and Wolfe, 1960:143. Source: Representative sample of Detroit Metropolitan Area white families.

Table 17-4 shows that a majority of Detroit respondents found that children created problems at every age. When they were young they tied the parents down. In adolescence, their greater freedom brought increased worries about what they might do with that freedom. After adolescence, children who were still at home were either in college (making them a financial burden) or retarded in their development (making them a burden in other ways). Nevertheless, for an increasing minority of parents, successful socialization meant that children were no longer a problem of any kind as they grew older.

Adaptation to Aging Parents

The younger generation gradually gains power until they are launched on their own. From that point on, the two generations treat each other more or less as equals in modern societies. For many years, a relationship of mutual respect between equally competent members of the two generations is maintained. However, as parents retire from normal adult responsibilities and lose their capacities to function as independent adults, the balance of power shifts in the opposite direction. Some adults maintain their independence until they die "with their boots on," but others find it necessary to depend on their children as they grow old.

Although most aging parents prefer to maintain an independent household, this becomes less and less feasible the longer they live. Willmott and Young (1960) found that whereas only 11 percent of parents in their sixties lived with a married son or daughter, 25 percent of those in their seventies and 41 percent of those over 80 did so. Doubling up was especially common for parents who were widowed, both because to live alone was too lonely and because aged men needed feminine services. If the parent becomes senile or infirm, personal care is apt to become the responsibility of a daughter or daughter-in-law. And in poor families, parents may need financial support from their children.

In the Philippines, the financial problem is solved not by moving in with children but by adopting a grandchild:

A common method of ensuring one's old age is by taking in a grandchild (preferably the second grandson) when he is about school age and providing him with food and clothing, often in greater quantity than he could expect at home. This child gradually takes over the farming and can expect whatever property might be left at his grandparents' death to come to him. This expectation, coupled with a strong feeling of obligation for his childhood support, ensures good treatment of the grandparents at the hands of this "second son." (Nydegger and Nydegger, 1963:741)

Regardless of whether the child or the grandchild assumes such responsibility, the tendency is for the superiority of the older generation to be reversed in old age. However, this is a more variable and idiosyncratic phenomenon than the predictable changes in inter-generational relationships at the beginning of the family life cycle.

GRANDPARENTS, PARENTS, AND GRANDCHILDREN

In the next chapter, I will examine the intergenerational relationships of extended families. Here I am interested in relationships among the same three generations when they live in separate nuclear households.

One might expect that if parents are superior to children, then grandparents should be even more superior and command super-respect. In extended family systems like the classical Chinese family this was true. But in many societies, the reverse has been true—there is more affection and less age-status differentiation between grandparents and grandchildren than between parents and children.

Among the Kenyan Gusii, LeVine and LeVine noted that "sex avoidance and unilateral respect characterize the relations of adjacent generations, while less restrained behavior is possible for persons of alternate generations and those of the same generation" (1963:52). In other words, the relationships of grandparents and grandchildren were almost as informal and familiar as those among members of the same generation.

In Java, as noted earlier, children were expected to address their parents in extraordinarily respectful language. However, grandparents were an exception to the general rule that flowery language should be used with relatives:

> When, as is often the case in Java, grandparent and grandchild are linked closely by mutual affection, the child will speak familiarly to the grandparent long after he has adopted respect language in addressing his own parents. (Geertz, 1961:23)

What are the reasons for this lack of age differentiation between generations so far removed from each other? After noting that African kinship systems generally were marked by "friendly familiarity and almost . . . social equality" between alternate generations, Radcliffe-Brown pointed out that grandparents often played the role of mediator in the relations between parents and children:

> A child who feels that he is being treated with severity by his father may appeal to his father's father. The grandparents are the persons above all others who can interfere in the relations between parents and children. (1950:28)

In other words, the very fact that parents are superior to children makes grandparents potentially superior to parents and therefore a possible court of appeals for children.

Secondly, insofar as grandparents have no responsibility for controlling their grandchildren, their relationship can be familiar, whereas the disciplinary responsibility of parents creates an attitude of respect. From the standpoint of the older generation, this means that children for whom one does not have responsibility can be enjoyed as toys to play with and as sources of affectionate response. For old people who no longer have any children and for uncles and aunts who are not yet married and do not yet have any children of their own, the son's or brother's children are welcome playthings. In Greek shepherd families:

> In general, uncles and aunts . . . are notoriously indulgent towards their nephews and nieces in their childhood days. Of the father's brothers who may be living for a time in the same extended household, it is the unmarried uncles who are the favourites of the children, dangling them on the knee and buying them sweets. (Campbell, 1964:106)

Thus intergenerational relationships are characterized by respect and social distance only insofar as one generation exercises control over the other. Grandparents and uncles can establish affectional relations with their juniors insofar as they are outside the mainline of the power structure.

OLDER SIBLINGS AND YOUNGER SIBLINGS

Age differentiation between the generations is a familiar concept. That the structure of the sibling group is also differentiated is less familiar. Americans like to think children should be treated alike. But the fact that children are not all the same age makes this difficult if not impossible. Moreover, successive children enter a family which is correspondingly larger, so another source of inequality is introduced into the sibling group. The family is unusual in this respect:

> In the wider world of non-kin, friends who are precisely the same in age, sex, wealth, and so on may address each other with exactly the same degree of respect or familiarity. But among kin there can be no such equal relationships. There is no one among all his kin who is precisely equal to Ego; even his brothers are divided into those above him and those below him. (Geertz, 1961:20)

In Java, this meant that kin must be treated differentially depending on whether they were older or younger than the individual. No one within the family was an equal in the same way that friends were. They were either superiors or inferiors, never equals. In other societies, differences in age status exist but are not recognized as a basis for social discrimination. Nevertheless, even in societies which think of siblings as equal, there tend to be unrecognized status differentials.

Differential Inheritance

In modern societies, equal inheritance among sons and daughters is the ethical norm and frequently prescribed by law. But in agrarian societies where land is scarce and already subdivided into tiny plots, further subdivision may be so difficult as to make equal inheritance impossible. Moreover, the extended family systems which arise in agrarian societies require a hierarchical social structure which also discourages equal treatment of children. Such family systems are normally unilineal rather than bilineal, and this discourages inheritance by the sex which leaves the family line (*i.e.,* daughters).

Even among the group of sons, the problem of designating a successor to the family "throne" produces financial discrimination among the heirs. Since only one son can succeed his father as head of the family, that son has greater importance to the family and greater financial responsibility than the others. Although theoretically a larger proportion might be allocated to him and smaller portions to his brothers, in practice the usual custom is to give him the entire estate and let him support his brothers. To do this he uses the proceeds of the estate which the brothers work collectively under his direction. If the estate is not big enough to support all the brothers, the surplus personnel may be required to leave home and support themselves in the city or a foreign country. Aries cited a 1661 comment by the Frenchman, Varet:

> People are afraid that if they share their property equally among all their children, they will not be able to add to the glory and lustre of the family as much as they would wish. The eldest son will not be able to hold and keep the posts and offices which they are trying to obtain for him, if his brothers and sisters enjoy the same advantages as he. They must therefore be rendered incapable of challenging this right of his. They must be sent into monasteries against their will and sacrificed early in life to the interests of the one who is destined for the world and its vanity. (1962:372)

The remaining question is which son will be the chosen heir. At this point, the customary solution is to turn to birth order. Most often the first-born son is chosen and the system is called "primogeniture." This system utilizes the age superiority of the oldest son as a basis for legitimizing his leadership in the family. Because he is the oldest, he has tended to boss his younger brothers around anyway, so taking over the family when his father dies or retires simply perpetuates a leadership which he can be assumed to have exercised from early childhood.

In polygynous societies the problem is more complicated because there is not just one set of sons but separate sets for each wife. Under these circumstances, not only priority of birth among sons but priority of marriage among wives must be taken into consideration. Kuper found that among the Swazi:

> The status of the wives affects the behavior between the father and his various sons. The first-born son of the first wife is the father's confidant—he is told about the allocation of family property and who the father considers a suitable heir. The father makes special provision for the first-born during his lifetime. (1950:96)

In this case, the eldest son of the first wife may not necessarily be the eldest among the half-brothers, but his mother's priority outstrips sheer biological age in determining his superiority. Among the sisters, Kuper found that the eldest was referred to informally as "the princess" and was given an especially nice cow as a gift even though she was not legally entitled to share in the family property.

Family systems which give priority to the eldest child in inheritance also frequently marry their children off in order of birth as well. Among Greek shepherds, Campbell found that siblings of the same sex married strictly in order of seniority. This systematic rule prevented conflict within a family system where marriage was not just an individual but a family affair: "It removes from the sphere of competition a matter which, in the case of brothers, is intimately connected with status and prestige" (1964:176). Campbell also noted that ". . . since sisters . . . marry strictly in order of seniority, competition to snare a husband does not exist." (p. 178)

Conversely, in societies which do not have age priorities for determining unilateral succession but leave the choice to the judgment of the father, the family may be torn by the uncertainty of the situation. In rural Ireland, Humphreys concluded that the lack of a regular system of inheritance was dysfunctional for the family:

> . . . centrifugal factors present in the structure of the rural farm family [include]: the lack of any binding custom specifying which son will succeed to the holding; the father's tendency to conceal his selection of the heir and to postpone long into his old age the transfer of the farm; the consequent necessity for the sons to remain celibate and at the same time extremely subordinate to their father who treats them as boys and refers to them as "boys" even when they are in their thirties; and finally, a son's fear that he may sustain all this in vain if the father designates a brother as an heir.

Such a combination of circumstances constitutes a powerful motive for sons, often enough all of them, to take life in their own hands, to leave the land and its frustrations. (1966:20)

Similarly in rural Poland in the early twentieth century, Thomas and Znaniecki found that inheritance must either be equal or go to an age-determined son if it was not to cause ill feeling:

. . . trouble starts [when] fathers . . . divide their property unequally without . . . any family reasons for such a division. Neither the old standard of group welfare nor the new standard of individual justice is complied with. The result is that the sons who have received the worse shares have an unmitigated feeling of being wronged. (1958:1144)

In other words, equal inheritance and age-graded inheritance are both satisfactory systems, but to have no system at all opens the door to favoritism and sibling jealousy. Differential inheritance, then, is not necessary if families have enough wealth to divide equally among their children. If equal inheritance is not feasible, age differentials offer the most incontestable basis for discriminating between an heir and his disinherited siblings.

Differential Stimulation

Not only do first-born sons tend to inherit more than their share of the family estate, but they tend to be better trained for independent achievement. Indeed, the modern equivalent of feudal primogeniture is the outstanding achievement motivation of first-born sons.

We have already seen in Chapter 14 that first-born sons are disproportionately admitted to medical schools. *Newsweek* magazine reported on January 6, 1969, that 21 of the first 23 American astronauts were either eldest or only sons. Even the other two were hardly exceptions (one lost his elder brother early in life and the other was born thirteen years after his older brother and grew up quite separately). In reviewing the literature, Clausen (1966) found that first-born children earned higher grades in school, went farther in school, and achieved greater success in academic and intellectual careers. However, they were less successful in athletics and had difficulty getting along with their peers. This means that the achievement motivation of eldest sons is directed toward academic and intellectual achievement and away from athletic and sociable goals. In American society, achievement-oriented first-born girls have had little opportunity to fulfill their needs directly through their own achievements but they have often achieved their goals vicariously through motivating their sons to greater achievement than the sons of later-born women.

Table 17-5 was derived from a representative sample of adult U. S. men. It shows that only sons (who are a special variety of eldest sons) went farther in school than boys with siblings but that oldest sons in relatively small families went almost as far. On the other hand, the table reminds us that the advantages of being an eldest son disappear in large families where he is often forced to drop out of school to help support his siblings. Therefore the conclusion that eldest sons have high achievement motivation must be limited to relatively small families. In large families, by contrast, it is the youngest child who goes farthest in school, although no child in large families approaches even the worst one in small families.

TABLE 17-5   Education, by Birth Order and Family Size

NUMBER OF CHILDREN	BIRTH ORDER			
	Only	Oldest	Middle	Youngest
Less than five	4.98	4.90	4.62	4.82
Five or more	—	4.10	4.00	4.42

Adapted from Blau and Duncan, 1967:299. Source: Representative sample of U. S. men age 20–64. The number of respondents was 20,700. The table was controlled on father's occupation to eliminate the effect of that stratification variable. Education was weighted on a scale where 4.00 represented a high school drop-out and 5.00 a high school graduate.

The newest feature of the table is the low achievement of middle sons. Although education tends to decrease as family size increases, it is not the last-born child but the intervening children who suffer the most.

What are the reasons for the superiority of the first-born sons in small families, of last-born sons in large families, and for the inferiority of middle-sons in all sorts of families? First-born sons temporarily enjoy the advantages of only children—a two-to-one parent-child ratio and the undivided attention of both parents. Even after his younger siblings are born, the oldest child is still especially interesting to his parents because he does everything first (even though parents of large families are too busy to pay much attention any more). Surrounded by adults and given constant verbal stimulation, oldest children develop their verbal skills faster and are more oriented to the adult world than to their peer culture. Their parents, because they are novices, are nervous and anxious in handling a first-born child, and this causes a restlessness in him that tends to be converted into achievement motivation.

Last-born children also are only children when their siblings have grown up and left home. Even before that, they have a special place in the affection of their parents because they are the parents' last grip on youthfulness. In large families, where being last is advantageous, they come along at a time when their elder siblings are old enough to provide financial assistance and quasi-adult stimulation. For them the adult–child ratio improves, the larger the number of siblings who have already approached or reached adulthood.

Middle children, on the other hand, are never alone in the family and never the focus of special attention. They tend to become "lost in the shuffle," never commanding attention from either their parents or their older siblings.

Although the preceding discussion has focused on boys, eldest daughters also presumably receive more stimulation than their sisters. Kammeyer (1966) found that first-born women were more apt to agree with their parents' orientation toward the feminine role (regardless of whether that was traditional or modern). This suggests that parents interacted more with oldest daughters and socialized them more successfully than their neglected younger sisters.

Neglect, incidentally, is not always regretted by the child. Another way of describing the same phenomenon is to say that parents control their oldest children more and give younger ones more freedom. In the words of one college girl in a class taught by the author:

> With the progression of children, each of us was given privileges at an earlier age. For instance, I was allowed to go on dates in a car at an earlier age than my older sister, and my younger sister was given this privilege at still an earlier age. My parents explain their increased leniency with the feeling that, after the experience of giving the oldest daughter gradual independence and having her use it successfully, they did not fear the consequences of this change, and they were more familiar with the characteristics of this age group.

Similarly in a Japanese family consisting of two sons and two daughters, the elder son and elder daughter accepted their parents' control in arranging their marriages. The younger siblings, less closely supervised and less tightly controlled by their parents, took advantage of their freedom to marry for love.

To be an oldest child, then, is to incur both the benefits and the liabilities of being the center of attention. For adult-oriented activities this is beneficial. For peer-oriented activities, it is detrimental.

Differential Responsibility

In Chapter 14 we saw that oldest daughters in large American families were coopted into service as assistant mothers, caring for their younger siblings or helping with housework. On a worldwide basis, this responsibility for younger siblings is by no means limited to large families nor limited to girls alone. Indeed, save in societies where mothers have so many maids or so many appliances that they have plenty of time for their younger children, baby–sibling sitting is a general responsibility of older siblings. In the Philippines:

> A major chore for school children is baby tending. Once the children have changed clothes after school, busy mothers and grandmothers anxious to collect firewood or vegetables before dusk or to begin the evening meal, set babies, but not young infants, before them with a sharp: "Now take care of your [younger sibling]!" The older children put the youngster on a hip and run off to play. The younger children find this too tiring and content themselves with . . . playing in groups around or with the baby who is generally toddling or close to toddling age. The rule seems to be the older the child, the younger the sibling he cares for.
> Since baby tending is a requirement for all children and careful care is highly rewarded, children show little objection to this duty and generally are both nurturant and ingenious in thinking of games and toys to amuse their charges. A baby's laugh rewards his older sibling almost as much as it does his mother. But, admittedly, almost as rewarding is the chance of justifiably punishing the younger children who are under supervision, and schoolchildren can be severe task-masters. (Nydegger and Nydegger, 1963: 851)

The last point is echoed in the Maretzkis' account of Okinawan children whose baby brother or sister is strapped to their back:

The child on the back finds his child caretaker far less sympathetic and indulgent than mother and grandmother and more literal in applying rules of behavior. Young caretakers, under threat of severe punishment, tend to enforce stringently the rules of safety and permit a much narrower latitude with respect to obedience. (1963:517)

These accounts suggest how seriously older children take their responsibility for the welfare of their charges.

TABLE 17-6 Maternal Child-Rearing Practices, by Birth Order

MATERNAL CHILD-REARING PRACTICE	BIRTH ORDER			
	Oldest	Middle	Youngest	Only
Expects child to do chores	60%	52%	32%	25%
Punishes aggression against peers	80	67	27	50
Exhibits warmth, praises child	39	57	62	88

Adapted from Minturn and Lambert, 1964:259, 270, 277. Source: Families in six societies (except for punishment of aggression which is restricted to U. S. data only).

Table 17-6 shows that chores of all sorts were more apt to be loaded on older children than on younger ones. Responsibility loading was most differentiated for oldest and only children because in the latter case there was no one to be cared for and relatively little housework to be done because the family unit was small. Although the reference in Table 17-6 was not restricted specifically to child-rearing chores, other data from the same book show that the larger the number of younger siblings in the family, the more a child was expected to do chores around the house.

The presence of older children in the house reduced the mother's own responsibilities for child care. If an infant had no older siblings, 52 percent of mothers had primary responsibility for its care, but if there was an older sibling in the family, only 38 percent of mothers were responsible. The same general pattern held with respect to responsibility for child care in the years following infancy.

If we put these data together, they suggest that older children relieve their mothers of some of the responsibility for caring for young children and are expected to be generally useful around the house. When this is formulated in terms of the amount of time mothers spend caring for babies, Minturn and Lambert found that, in a Human Relations Area Files sample of 54 societies, the time mothers spent caring for their babies was reduced more than 30 percent by the aid of older children (the correlation between these two variables being $-.56$).

In addition to supervising their younger siblings, older children are often expected to set a good example for them. Humphreys (1966) noted that Irish parents demanded more of their older children and were more severe with them to prevent them from setting a bad example. Presumably this is one reason for Table 17-6's finding that punishment for aggression against peers declined with the birth of successive children. As with chores, middle children were only slightly less responsible for behaving themselves in the presence of impressionable younger siblings. Why then should only children be punished more than the last-born? Perhaps in this instance only children felt the effects of family size, receiving the undistracted attention of their parents, whereas youngest children experienced their parents' weariness with discipline. It should be noted, however, that these findings were limited to American families (*i.e.,* oldest children in Minturn and Lambert's five other societies were not punished more than their younger siblings for aggression).

Generally speaking, then, older children are given responsibility for their younger siblings during the years when they are growing up together. This responsibility of older siblings continues even after they leave home. More especially after the parents die, the quasi-parental role of older siblings is enhanced. In England:

> After the death of the mother the eldest sister sometimes prevented or delayed the disintegration of the sibling group. She protected its unity. Her role was of particular importance if the mother died before all the children were married or when some of them were separated from their wives, or were widowed, crippled, infirm or mentally backward. She partly assumed her mother's role and looked after the interests of the family, taking responsibility for the family problems and continuing its traditions. (Townsend, 1957:106)

The greater the age disparity between the eldest sister and her younger siblings, the greater the authority she tended to exert over them. Indeed in large families, the age gap was often great enough so that the oldest daughter could have been the mother of her youngest siblings. In such cases, the eldest might have left home before the last child was born, so her responsible role was not a continuation of an earlier relationship. Nevertheless, once the mother died, such an older sister came to be seen as the successor to the family headship just because she was nearer the mother's age.

Thus, the responsibility of older siblings for younger ones may structure not only the nuclear family but the primary kin network as well.

In extended families, the eldest son has greater responsibility than the other children because he will become the family head after his father retires. In anticipation of that day, he may be trained to exercise responsibility by delegation of certain duties from his father. If the father retires prior to the marriage of the younger sons, the oldest brother will control them paternalistically. Among Greek shepherds:

> The eldest brother, who normally acts as the executive head [of the family after the retirement of the father] implements the general decision of the group. He also acts as its treasurer and all money is controlled by him. . . . If one of his brothers wants cigarettes or requires money to play cards in the coffee-shop he comes and states his needs without embarrassment. (Campbell, 1965:72)

The fact that a younger brother would feel no embarrassment in asking his elder brother for spending money shows how thoroughly institutionalized was the latter's superiority.

Differential Dependence

The converse of the greater responsibility of older children is the greater dependence of younger ones. However, the latter depend not only on their older siblings but on their parents as well. Table 17-6 shows that mothers gave more warmth and praise to a last child or an only child than to an eldest child. This is the reverse of the greater demands on their oldest child. This affectionate relationship to younger children makes them more emotionally secure and dependent.

Displacement of the Eldest   The first-born child temporarily enjoys the security of being an only child, but with the intrusion of a second child, he loses his unchallenged position in the affection of his parents. Indeed, we have already caught suggestions that the eldest child's very prominence as the most powerful sibling disqualifies him from being as lovable as the baby. In a close parallel to the leadership differential between the parents, the eldest child tends to become the instrumental leader of the sibling group and the beloved last child becomes the expressive leader or at least the expressive focus of the group.

The difficulty of being displaced as the only child depends on how old he is (*i.e.,* on the spacing between himself and his successor). In many societies, displacement occurs so early that the child loses not only his mother's exclusive attention but her milk (he must be weaned in order that his successor may be fed). In societies which depend exclusively on breast-feeding, weaning is frequently postponed until it is necessary to redirect the flow to the newest baby. Such societies frequently have poor health and sanitary standards and high infant mortality so that the mother's milk is the safest food supply.

Because the arrival of his first sibling represents a crisis of accession for the first-born child (comparable to the impact of his own arrival on his parents), weaning is more difficult for first-born children than for later ones. In their Filipino community, the Nydeggers found that 33 percent of first-born children had been difficult to wean compared to 14–22 percent of later children (1963:832). In addition to the child's resentment of his drastic replacement, the authors suggest that weaning difficulties may be accentuated by the mother's lack of experience so that she vacillates between indulgence and punitiveness when he demands the breast.

The Nydeggers found that grandmothers, aunts, and other interested persons intervened more with the weaning of first children than with subsequent ones. Such intervention may cushion the shock of weaning from the mother if the intervener becomes a substitute source of physical and emotional nurturance. In this tightly knit Filipino community, close relatives usually served as mother-substitutes for the displaced oldest child. If the relative had already become the primary caretaker prior to weaning, the shock of weaning and the sense of having been displaced were reduced even further.

Subsequent children not only had less to lose in the sense that they never enjoyed the exclusive attention of the mother but also had elder siblings as proximate mother-substitutes. The Nydeggers gave an example:

One of our sample children, a very mature girl of 10, took over the care of her young sister who was weaned at the birth of the next child. In the mother's words: "Marina takes care of her sister now. Since she was weaned, they sleep together and when Marina went away she cried for her. She calls her 'my mother Marina.'" (1963:832)

For the last child, the usual argument for weaning is missing. With no new child needing the breast, why should it ever be denied? Stephens concluded from comparative data on many primitive societies that "When a mother has no more babies, she may nurse her last child more or less indefinitely—for four or five years, or even longer" (1963:361). The lack of a successor may account for slightly increased weaning difficulties in third and fourth children in the Nydeggers' sample, some of whom presumably were last children. In any case, if weaning was attempted during pregnancy it was more difficult than after the arrival of the successor: "It was noticeable that delivery settled a number of difficult weanings—apparently the reality of the new infant and its obvious necessity for food force the weanling to accept his changed status" (1963:832).

Although our focus has been on weaning difficulties because they so poignantly express the displacement process, other behavior problems also demonstrate the effects of displacement. In one psychological clinic in south India, Rao found that jealousy of a new sibling was an important cause of the behavior disorders of client children. Of the total children treated at the clinic, 75 percent were first-born, 10 percent intermediate children, and 15 percent last-born children, suggesting anew the intense displacement problems of eldest children (1943:210).

In general, then, first-born children suffer the greatest displacement trauma, though this may be cushioned by mother-substitutes and by awareness of the needs of the successor. Last-born children, by contrast, are never displaced and tend to be nursed longer than any of their predecessors.

Jealousy Toward the Successor Hostility toward the successor is a natural consequence of displacement even though it may be buffered by the mechanisms mentioned above. On the basis of this reasoning, resentment should be greatest in the first-born child toward the second child, but in lesser degree felt by each succeeding child toward his successor.

A secondary consequence can be derived from this. If the first child resents the second and the second resents the third, the first and third child have a common enemy. Consequently, alternate siblings should have a positive relationship to one another in a fashion reminiscent of alternate generations of grandparents and grandchildren. Investigating the Zambian Tonga, Colson found that the contrast between the negative relationship of successive children and the positive ties between alternate children was culturally recognized:

. . . proximate siblings whether of the same or opposite sex have an underlying hostility towards one another due to "milk." A child is expected to dislike its next younger sibling who robbed it of its mother's milk, and this dislike is reciprocated. It is expected to have a very close relationship with the next younger sibling, for whose care it is generally responsible. This pairing of alternate siblings is expected to continue into later life. (1958:248)

Displacement within the family structure also occurs when men marry successive wives. Alternate wives should feel closer than proximate ones in polygynous households and in the serial polygyny of men who enter successive monogamous marriages. One case does not prove an hypothesis but it is suggestive. An American first wife who had been hostile toward the woman who displaced her found herself sympathizing with the third wife when she was displaced by a fourth. Wives #1 and #3 corresponded regularly with each other and when #3 traveled abroad, #1 telegraphed flowers to her hotel room and asked an old friend of the family to look her up so she wouldn't be lonely.

Perhaps, then, negative feelings toward proximates and positive feelings toward alternates apply not only to generations and to siblings but also to spouses as well.

The Beloved Baby   We have already seen that the last child tends to be weaned later than his predecessors. We also know that he is given less responsibility training. Indeed he is pushed less with respect to all sorts of behavior. In Mexico, the Romneys found that the last child was trained later with respect to responsibility, self-reliance, succorance, obedience, and nurturance (1963:662).

Not only are weaning and child-training generally delayed, but the last child's departure from home is also delayed. Last children are apt to marry later than older children and more apt never to marry at all. After they marry, they tend to settle closer to their parents and to see their parents more often. By comparing oldest and youngest children of older people in East London, Townsend found that about half the younger children lived closer to the parents and another quarter equally close, leaving only a fourth who were farther away than their eldest siblings. In the same study, youngest children (especially youngest sons) were more apt than oldest children to see their parents every day (see Table 17-7).

Frequent contact between parents and their last child is symptomatic of strong bonds of affection between them. In some cultures, the special place of the "baby" of the family is recognized in prescribed customs. Among the

TABLE 17-7   Parental Contact with Children, by Birth Order and Sex of Children

PERCENTAGE SEEING CHILD DAILY BY SEX	BIRTH ORDER		YOUNGEST/ ELDEST RATIO
	Eldest	Youngest	
Sons	9%	31%	3.44X
Daughters	28	44	1.58

Adapted from Townsend, 1957:88. Source: Men aged 65+ and women aged 60+ living in East London and their eldest and youngest married or widowed sons and daughters. Limited to cases where two children of the same sex could be compared with each other. There were 70 pairs of sons and 71 pairs of daughters. Reciprocal percentages saw the specified child less than once a day.

African Swazi, Kuper found that affectional ties between women and their children generally were stronger than with their husbands, but the warmest tie of all was with the youngest son:

> When a girl marries, the mother's care and affection are recognized in the special beast known as the "wiper away of tears" . . . given her by the groom. This remains the mother's property and may not be taken by her husband; it is inherited by her youngest son, the accepted darling, and not by the eldest who inherits the main property of her hut. (1950:95)

In other words, the last son gets a consolation prize which symbolizes the special affection felt for him but which contrasts with the wealth and responsibility which the eldest son inherits. Money and prestige he may lack, but the last-born child remains secure in the affections of his family. Who is to say which is better?

GENERATIONAL AND SIBLING DIFFERENCE: FAMILY STRUCTURE

When all these differences are put together, the structure of the family is complete. In general from the last two chapters we should expect the top position in the family to be occupied by the father, with the mother as his lieutenant. The rank and file members of the family should be the children, ordered from oldest to youngest, though this ordering may be complicated by differences in the sex of the children.

The structure of the family resembles almost any small group except that age and sex categories largely predetermine who will occupy which position. Whereas among friends of the same sex and same generation, the structure of a group emerges out of the interaction of the members, the structure of a family is largely given by the socially-ranked age and sex categories. To be sure, there are variations between families depending on the particular resources of the individual members (as we will see in Chapter 19). But these are variations on a theme which is standardized for a given society by its evaluation of age and sex roles.

Table 17-8 gives an example of the power structure of nuclear families.

TABLE 17-8 Family Influence, by Age and Sex of Family Members, in Normal and Abnormal Families

| TYPE OF FAMILY | FAMILY POSITION | | | |
	Father	Mother	Older Child	Younger Child
Normal	13.2	13.1	12.8	11.5
Abnormal	12.3	12.3	11.8	10.7

Adapted from Ferreira and Winter, 1968:24. Source: 36 normal and 49 abnormal families in treatment in Palo Alto, California. Older children were typically in senior high school and younger children in junior high with a median age difference of 2.6 years. The numbers represent the absolute number of positive suggestions each family member made, in response to a questionnaire, that were eventually agreed with by the family as a whole. Topics: famous people they might want to meet, foods to eat, films to see, countries to live in, sports events to attend, magazines to subscribe to, and colors for their next car.

In this American sample, the differences between mothers and fathers were barely detectable, but the differences between the generations and between successive children were clear-cut. The fact that power structures were almost identical for psychiatrically normal and abnormal families adds to the stability of the finding. Unfortunately the researchers failed to specify the sex of the children. It is interesting to note that the gap between older and younger children is greater than between parents and older child, suggesting the extent of the focusing of parental interaction on the older child to the neglect of the younger one (or, to put it another way, the powerful position of the older sibling and the weakness of the younger one).

chapter eighteen

THE STRUCTURAL PROBLEMS OF COMPLEX FAMILIES

In Chapter 14, we saw that the larger the family, the greater its tendency to become differentiated into subgroups. In large nuclear units, it is difficult to predict what form those units may take. To some extent they follow sex lines and are relatively homogeneous in age. Nevertheless, it is risky to guess exactly what form the subdivisions will take on the basis of the age and sex of family members alone.

In extended and polygamous households, however, uncertainty vanishes. Such households are composed of quasi-nuclear sub-units. Indeed they are often called "composite" families because they are composed of an aggregate of nuclear sub-units. An extended family is composed of a vertical series of nuclear units, a polygamous family of a horizontal series. The only thing which keeps such families from falling apart is the fact that one or more key individuals belongs to two or more sub-units and links them together. The chief intellectual problem in understanding such families is not to be aware of their tendency to become differentiated but rather to discover what keeps them together. This is why I have labeled this chapter the structural "problems" of complex families.

The size and complexity of composite families create organizational problems which simpler families do not have to face. In complicated families, the achievement and maintenance of integration becomes a bigger problem than it would ever be in a nuclear family, no matter how large. Possibilities for conflicting loyalties and factional rivalry are built into the very structure of such families. And with this larger conflict potential, complex family systems can be expected to develop more elaborate mechanisms of social control. So if we wish to understand control mechanisms, complex families should be a good place to look.

GROUP MARRIAGE

Group marriage (combining both plural wives and plural husbands) has occurred in short-lived experimental communities but has rarely if ever been the pattern of a whole society. Murdock (1949) in classifying marriage patterns in 250 societies found no cases of group marriage and asserted that it had never been the normative pattern in any known society. Stephens (1963) disagreed, suggesting that the polygynous tendency of men led them to add extra women to polyandrous households whenever they could. Thus polyandry provided a basis for group marriage in exceptional instances. However, this is a far cry from classifying such societies as primarily practicing group marriage. Indeed, Stephens' summary statement is that the Indian Toda tribe "*had* fraternal polyandry, which *occasionally slipped* into group marriage" (1963:36, italics mine).

If group marriage has rarely or never occurred as a cultural pattern, this implies that it may be a difficult or perhaps impossible arrangement: Perhaps there is something about group marriage which makes it unlikely to be tried or which makes it break down so quickly that it cannot become an institutionalized pattern handed on from generation to generation.

Unlike polygyny which is handicapped by the more or less equal distribution of the sexes (so that there are not enough women to supply every man with two wives), group marriage between equal numbers of men and women would be consistent with the supply of potential partners. But group marriage has other handicaps which polygamy does not encounter.

The last two chapters suggested that nuclear families in most societies have a predetermined social structure provided by the age and sex categories of which they are composed. One trouble with group marriage is that the structure lacks this clarity. With two or more husbands and two or more wives, it is all very well to suggest that the first husband should boss his successors and the first wife hers, but how is the set of husbands to be related to the set of wives? Should the second husband be superior to the first wife because he is a man or subservient to her because she entered the household before he did? How about a second wife acquired before a second husband? Or if the group marriage were to be enacted all at once so that there were no time priority among either sex, then the husbands would have to contend with each other for instrumental leadership. Eventually, presumably a power structure would emerge from such contention, but the unity of the marriage might be destroyed in the process.

Secondly, group marriage creates problems of sexual jealousy. They are bad enough in polygamous marriages as we will soon see. But with multiple husbands and multiple wives, both sexes would compete among themselves for the privilege of intercourse with the most popular member of the opposite sex. To minimize such competition it would be desirable to maintain an equal balance between the sexes so that whoever lost out in the competition would have someone to sleep with even if he/she didn't get his/her first choice. Probably, however, an impersonal rotation system would be necessary to provide for a change of partners every night, every week, or at some other fixed interval to minimize sexual conflict and disappointment.

Such rules might go far to solve the problems of group marriage. Still, the complexities resulting from the larger size and shared age-and-sex statuses of group marriage would presumably make it less stable than other forms of marriage, and therefore a less satisfactory basis for a stable society.

Despite the difficulties, some segments of modern societies have begun to experiment with group marriages. A panel of Swedish sociologists convened in 1969 by the *Svenska Dagbladet* forecast a trend toward collective living which would include communal marriages, particularly in Swedish cities. Whether the forecast is correct and how those marriages will work out will be a research task for the future.

POLYGAMY

Polygamy is a collective term for marriage involving plural mates of either sex (but not usually of both). Polygyny involves plural wives married to one man; polyandry means plural husbands married to one woman. Whereas group marriage is rare, polygamy is a widespread phenomenon, even more common than exclusive monogamy if societies are taken as the unit of counting.

TABLE 18-1 Frequency Distribution of Polygamous Societies

Form of Polygamy	Percentage of All Societies
Polygyny	81%
Polyandry	1
Group marriage	0
None (monogamy only)	18
Total	100%
Number of societies	238

Adapted from Murdock, 1949:28. Source: Human Relations Area Files, primarily primitive societies but also some historic and modern civilized societies.

Table 18-1 shows that polyandry has been almost as rare as group marriage. Indeed, Murdock labeled it "an ethnological curiosity." (1949:25) Polygyny, on the other hand, occurred in so many of Murdock's societies that it could almost be labeled a universal tendency. It is important to recognize, however, that in any given society at any one time, a majority of households are not polygamous. The sex ratio is never unbalanced enough and the resources of the minority sex never ample enough to allow every man to have more than one wife. At best, a majority of men may hope to add a second wife before they die. This means that generally speaking only the rich old men can be polygynous, not the average man for the bulk of his life or perhaps even at all. Among the African Nyakyusa, Wilson found that:

> Many men have not cattle with which to marry until they are well over 25, while their fathers may be able to afford more than one wife. . . . among 3,000 men presumed to be 18 years or over, 34 percent [are] bachelors, 37 percent monogamists, and 29 percent polygynists, and . . . generally speaking it is the young men who are bachelors, and the men over 45 who are polygynists. Few commoners have more than 7 or 8 wives, but a chief may have as many as 40. (1950:112)

Most families in polygynous societies, then, are nuclear for a long time and are transformed by the addition of a second wife only tardily. To make this change after a nuclear pattern has been so long established means that the family structure is drastically altered in what must be at least as much a "crisis of accession" as the arrival of the first child in a nuclear family.

The Jealousy Problem

Plural contenders for scarce resources always tend to be jealous of one another. We have seen neurotic husbands jealous of the first child, and first-born children jealous of the second; now we must expect first wives or husbands to be jealous of their successors. (To simplify the discussion from now on, I will ordinarily speak of plural wives, but the reader should understand that polyandry usually presents the same problems with the sexes reversed.)

Descriptions of polygynous societies are replete with accounts of jealousy among wives. For example:

> Despite their desire for polygyny, Nyansongo men recognize that it brings them trouble. Dissensions among co-wives is one of the most common themes in Gusii folklore. . . . There is a special word . . . which means "hatred between co-wives." (LeVine and LeVine, 1963:41)

Among the Ashanti, "It is notorious that co-wives often show great jealousy of one another. They call each other . . . 'jealous one' " (Fortes, 1950:381). Among both the Lozi and the Zulu, Gluckman found that "jealousy between the co-wives of one man for his sexual and other favours is pronounced. It is recognized in proverb and saying and appears in charges of sorcery" (1950: 180).

In urban Lagos, the capital of Nigeria:

> Jealousies and rivalries may lead to irreconcilable quarrels. A woman may prefer to return to her own people, rather than suffer the introduction of a new wife into the household—particularly if her husband did not consult her beforehand. (Marris, 1960:203)

Among the Tonga, Colson found that women generally disliked polygyny intensely and said that "there must always be jealousy and quarrelling between wives who share one man" (1958:123). The rules of the tribe required men to secure the approval of the first wife before taking a second, but this was no guarantee that jealousy would not occur:

> Some women give their consent only after a long struggle. In one such case, the husband said, "My wife has finally agreed that I may marry again, but she has agreed only with her lips. She does not agree in her heart. Women never agree to polygyny in their hearts until after they have lived with the other wife for many years and they have learned to get along together." (1958:124)

Gluckman found:

> Men expect their wives to be jealous of one another and to quarrel over the husband's favours. It is commonly believed that co-wives resort to vari-

ous love medicines in an attempt to gain first place with the husband or that they may use sorcery against one another or one another's children to eliminate them from the scene. Sometimes the tension explodes into open accusations of dealings in sorcery, which may end in the divorce of the accused or a demand that she pay damages to her co-wife. (1950:132)

With such intense jealousy between wives, it is not surprising to discover that it extends to the children of different wives. Goode noted the prevalence of sibling rivalry in traditional Arab families and added that if the children had different mothers, "some conflict between them was expected, and Arab folk tales emphasize this hostility, just as it emphasized the hostility within the polygynous household generally" (1963:144). Thus polygynous families are typically torn by jealousy between wives and between children of those wives.

Loss of Status   Reasons for jealousy can be easily imagined. One is the loss of status which the first wife experiences when her position *vis-à-vis* the husband must be shared with another woman. As long as she is the only wife, she can negotiate with her husband as more or less an equal. Once the husband has an alternate wife, he can play the two wives off against each other to his own advantage. Thus the LeVines analyzed the extreme opposition of many Gusii wives to the addition of other wives:

Women realize that monogamy gives them much greater power in the family, and some of them are determined to retain that power. The wife of a monogamous husband can punish him by refusing herself to him sexually or by refusing to work in home and garden. She most often does this by going to live with her parents for a week or more. When the precipitating quarrel has concerned the husband's taking a second wife, he may be sufficiently cowed by her desertion to give up the idea. On the other hand, though, he may become convinced that a second wife is needed to free him from exclusive dependence on her. Once he has a second wife, the situation is reversed; *he* is the one who can punish by abandoning one or the other, and they become dependent on his favor. (1963:41)

After a husband has taken a second wife, the only way the wives can restore their status to equality with the husband is by joining forces against him. The normal jealousy between wives makes this difficult, but if the wives resent the husband more than they resent each other, a conspiracy may succeed in nullifying his divide-and-conquer policy. Among the Tonga, Colson found that:

Sometimes . . . co-wives form a common front against their husband, abetting one another in their love affairs, going off in companionable couples to beer drinks and funerals while he is left at home to shift for himself, siding with one another in any quarrels which may arise. In one notable instance, they clubbed together to finance the purchase of a powerful medicine with which to dispose of the husband under the expectation that they would then all be free to marry their lovers. (1958:133)

This is hardly a solution to the family's structural problem though it may have given the wives an emotionally satisfying revenge!

Competition Among Wives   The first wife feels the loss of status most acutely, but all wives tend to compete with each other. I have already mentioned their practice of competing for scarce resources such as the husband's attention, affection, and sexual companionship. In this sense, competition among wives for the husband's favors directly parallels rivalry among siblings for their parents' favors. But just as sibling rivalry is quite capable of detaching itself from the goal of parental favor, so jealous wives learn to compete for status, prestige, and more tangible measures of success, quite apart from the husband's recognition.

One of the major activities of women in polygynous households is bearing children. The LeVines found that for women in one African community, "Childbearing is a matter of invidious distinction among co-wives in a polygynous family, and they are sensitive to any inequalities in the distribution of living children" (1963:130).

Similarly, women may be expected to compete for their fair share of the family income. If wives had no children, it would be easy for the husband to allocate his money evenly among them. But when wives have different numbers of children of various ages and sexes, it would take a computer to discover how best to divide up the family's funds. In Lagos, Marris found this a major source of difficulty in polygynous families:

> The marriage may break down when money problems . . . press upon it, especially in a polygamous household. When a man has to share his income amongst several wives, the place of any one of them is less secure. (1960: 203)

Discriminatory Treatment by the Husband   The preceding section suggests that even if husbands were scrupulously fair in dealing with their wives, the latter would be liable to feel competitive. Some husbands don't try to be even-handed but favor one wife over another—usually the latest acquisition. She is younger than her predecessors and has fewer wrinkles in societies where the hard work expected of polygynous wives ages them prematurely. More importantly, however, she is new and therefore more fascinating than the predecessors who have belonged to the household longer:

> Each wife tends to be the husband's darling when she is the latest and to maintain that position until he marries again. A Gusii proverb admonishes . . . that the older wives should not be neglected, but polygynists are said to . . . prefer younger wives . . . as they get older. This tendency in itself causes jealousy among the wives. In addition, any inequality in the distribution of gifts or money, or in the number of children born and died, or in the amount of education received by the children, adds to the jealousy and hatred. A woman who becomes barren or whose children die almost always believes that her co-wife has achieved this through witchcraft or poisoning. She may then attempt retaliation. (LeVine and LeVine, 1963:42)

Wilson similarly noted that "Often the latest bride ousts a former favourite and there is bitter antagonism between them—accusations of witchcraft against co-wives are frequent" (1950:113).

The tendency of the newest wife to displace the others as the center of attraction is a natural one—just as natural as the displacement of an older child by his successor in his mother's attention. A new wife does not require her husband's attention to survive the way a new infant does, but she excites his interest more than his accustomed partners. The naturalness of these tendencies, however, does not make them any easier for displaced wives than for displaced children. So if sibling rivalry is a natural component of the relationship between successive children, jealousy is equally natural to the relationship between successive wives.

For these causes of jealousy there are corresponding cultural solutions. They may not always resolve the problem completely, but insofar as they are applied, they reduce the tension and conflict within the family. If enough of them are used, the conflict may be reduced to manageable proportions. Essentially these solutions are social control mechanisms which individual families have invented and which have been enshrined in the folk wisdom of particular cultures as ways of making it possible for polygamous households to live together in comparative harmony despite their inherent strains.

Hierarchical Ordering Among Wives

To cushion the displacement of the first wife from her monogamous throne, most polygynous societies accord her a superior status within the group of wives. The title of "first wife" carries greater dignity than any subsequent number. Among the Nyakyusa, she was called "great wife," given precedence in family and social rituals, and accorded respect by her co-wives. Her eldest son succeeded to the family headship in the next generation and inherited the major share of the family property (Wilson 1950:113). Among the Tonga, similarly, her title was "chief wife" and Colson gave examples of the ritual statuses which she held:

> It is her house which is identified with the ancestors of the husband's paternal line. The husband should sleep in her house before he departs on a journey and immediately after his return. When the homestead is moved, he should sleep with her before he cohabits with the other wives on the new site. She should be consulted in advance of the other wives, and her voice should carry the greatest weight with the husband. When the husband sells his crop or livestock he should bring the money to her house. She is likely to be extremely jealous of these prerogatives, especially where the second marriage is of recent date. (1958:130)

We have seen before that in extended families the new bride tends to be treated as a maid-servant to her mother-in-law. In polygynous families, similarly, Murdock reported that "Another common solution [to the problem of jealousy] is to give one wife, usually the one first married, a superior social status and to delegate to her general supervisory authority over the feminine tasks of the household" (1949:30). If the first wife's loss of status *vis-à-vis* the husband is offset by gaining a servant whom she can order around, her frustration will be diminished. If enough wives are added to the household, she may be able to retire from housework altogether and spend her time as foreman of the crew of wives.

We have already seen that among the Nyakyusa, the eldest son of the first wife is the most important child of a polygynous family. Wilson also reported that he held the most important position in matters of ritual: ". . . although in minor matters the eldest of each group of brothers may officiate as priest, whenever serious trouble comes the prayers of the senior brother must be sought on behalf of all his junior half-brothers . . ." (1950: 120). Nor is this superiority limited to the eldest son of the first wife. Among the Kaffir, Radcliffe-Brown and Forde pointed out that "a son of a wife of inferior rank will apply to all the sons of the great wife (his half-brothers) the term used for 'elder brother' even when they are younger than himself" (1950:24). For this reason, within polygynous families some anthropologists use the term senior brother and junior brother to refer to the status of half-brothers of successive wives. Thus the status hierarchy among multiple wives applies not only to the women themselves but to their respective children.

Sororal Polygyny   One way of insuring the superiority of the first wife is to marry women who are inferior to her. This may be achieved by recruiting secondary wives from lower-status families. I have already mentioned that subsequent wives are universally drawn from lower-age grades because to marry an older woman than the first wife would set age-grading and wife-grading at cross purposes.

The best way to guarantee a clear-cut hierarchical arrangement is to marry women who have already established a "pecking order" among themselves. This is a virtue in marrying sisters. Murdock found that 14 percent of his societies with general polygyny allowed only younger sisters as secondary spouses while another 29 percent recommended sisters although other sources were allowed. One evidence of the relative lack of conflict in sororal polygyny is that in 86 percent of Murdock's societies with exclusively sororal polygyny, the wives lived together in the same house, compared to only 49 percent of the societies where wives were usually unrelated.

Gluckman compared two polygynous African societies, the Zulu, with relatively stable marriages, and the Lozi, with highly unstable marriages. He found contrasting attitudes toward sororal polygyny associated with these contrasting divorce rates:

> The Zulu approve of marriage to two sisters. Often a woman will urge her husband to marry her younger sister, who will become subordinate to her, so that she may have a "companion" who will share her labours and her loving care for her children without the jealousy of a stranger co-wife. "The love of sisters overcomes the jealousy of polygyny." The husband cannot marry his wife's senior sister . . . because she cannot be a subordinate wife to her own junior. Among the Lozi it is considered very bad to marry even a classificatory sister of your wife while the later is alive. . . . Lozi say, "The jealousy of polygyny spoils the love of sisters. It will break up their family." They must not be put in the position of competing for a man's favours or their children in the position of competing for their inheritances in both their lines. Among the Zulu their inheritances and relative status would be fixed.
>
> Among the Lozi, each marriage is potentially so unstable that a sister co-wife would very likely get involved in trouble with her husband arising

from a quarrel with her sister, and their competition is likely to lead to the divorce of one or other. . . . among the Lozi a woman's main tie remains with her kin, and is not with her husband's: "The love of sisters" must not be endangered. (1950:180–182)

When the sexes are reversed, Radcliffe-Brown and Forde noted that the most common form of polyandry was fraternal polyandry with the woman married to two or more brothers (1950:64).

These societies have found that the socialization of new marriage partners is simpler if they are recruited from a common family of orientation where the parents have already taught the younger sibling to respect and obey the elder sibling. Sibling polygamy reproduces in marriage a social structure which has already been created in childhood. Since there is never any question which wife is superior, jockeying for position among wives is eliminated.

If the first wife has no sister or if the husband wants to marry a non-related woman, perhaps the only way to prevent jealousy would be for the husband to persuade the first wife of the desirability of adding a second one and for the first wife to join the husband in courting her until positive feelings have had an opportunity to develop among the entire triangle. If the second wife's introduction into the family were delayed until all three parties felt ready and eager for it, the outcome might be happier. But triangular relationships being what they are, this is almost as far-fetched as expecting a first child to want to be displaced by a little brother or sister. It might happen in exceptional circumstances, but it could hardly be expected to become a general practice for non-sororal polygyny. Were it the rule, that form of polygyny would most likely disappear for want of first-wife participants.

Sub-Unit Decentralization

We have already seen that unless co-wives are sisters, they are more apt to live separately than together. Usually this involves a separate hut for each wife and her children, sometimes clustered around a single courtyard, sometimes separated by each wife's field or garden plot. In other societies, wives have separate apartments or at least separate rooms within a larger building. Physical separation gives each nuclear sub-unit a distinct geographical identity and reduces the friction which would be created if all were crowded indiscriminately into the same space.

The separation of sub-families applies to more than just sleeping space. Polygynous families tend to be subdivided in their consumption activities as well. Instead of having a common kitchen and dining-room, each mother–child unit tends to cook and eat separately. Even in Nyakyusa long-houses where wives only had separate alcoves for themselves, each wife had her own cooking fire in her own alcove, supplied her own water and firewood, and ate there with her daughters and pre-adolescent sons (Wilson, 1950:112).

Even the productive activities of polygynous households tend to be decentralized. We saw in Chapter 16 that polygyny is correlated with major economic activity assigned to women. In many polygynous societies, each wife largely supports herself and her children by her own labors. Among the Nyakyusa, for example:

Each wife in a compound family has her own fields in which she works with her unmarried daughters. Unmarried sons hoe with their fathers, working in some households only in the fields of their own mothers, while in others they work as a group with their fathers, hoeing each woman's plot in turn. Often a boy brings his friends—usually only two or three, but sometimes as many as ten—to work in his mother's fields, and he in turn will assist these friends. Those who have been working together always eat food prepared by the woman whose field they have been hoeing, for the produce of a woman's fields is used to provide food for her husband, her own children, herself, and any others who have been working in her fields for the day on which they have worked. . . . no co-wife has any rights over another's food. (Wilson, 1950:116)

Decentralization of economic activity prevents wives from fighting over whether each woman has worked as hard as she should to contribute toward a common fund. If a woman is lazy, she damages only herself and her children, not her co-wives and their children.

Decentralization of a polygynous family means that siblings with the same mother are closer to one another than to their half-siblings who live and work elsewhere (even if elsewhere is only a few meters away). Wilson reported that:

Good relations between half-brothers . . . are valued, but quarrels leading to legal separation occur. By contrast, quarrels between full brothers seem rarely to be serious and never to go to the length of a lawsuit; the unity of a group of full brothers is in fact maintained by their distinction from, and in some situations by their opposition to, their half-brothers." (1950:119)

The Isolation of the Husband   If the family is decentralized into nuclear subunits, this poses a problem for the father. Where should he live? Theoretically he might live with the first wife as one perquisite of her superior status. But if he were to do this, his departure to visit his other wives would be particularly noticeable, intensifying the first wife's resentment of his extra women.

Most decentralized family systems assign the husband to separate living quarters from which he sallies forth to visit his wives but never to live with any one for very long. For instance, among the African Yako, Forde found that most men provided themselves with "a separate man's house, usually a small and simpler dwelling than a woman's, in which they keep their personal belongings, meet their friends, and often sleep" (1950:291). The man's house could be smaller because it housed fewer people than a mother-plus-children group. Usually the man lived alone, sometimes with adolescent sons who were not yet married or who were married to wives with whom they didn't live either. His house could also be simpler because it didn't need cooking facilities

At meal times in a decentralized household, a man frequently ate alone or in company with other similarly isolated men, the food being provided by their several wives either simultaneously or in rotation. Among the Nyakyusa, Wilson reported that "The husband eats alone or with neighbors of his own age, his wives each sending him a dish or taking turns to cook the whole meal" (1950:112). Among the Gusii, similarly, the LeVines found that "Every wife has to bring the husband a basket of porridge at least once a day, and although he cannot consume all that is brought, he eats at least a mouthful from the basket brought by each wife. The rest of the food is then taken back to be eaten by the children" (1963:39).

If a man is isolated from his wives and children much of the time, the normal difference between father–child and mother–child ties is sharpened. Ties between fathers and children are weaker and between mothers and children stronger than in nuclear families. Only when boys leave their mothers at puberty to come under the father's care does he have a consistent relationship to them, but by then their tie to the mother has become very strong. And for daughters in a decentralized household, the father never has much contact.

From the mother's standpoint, having to share her husband with other women means that she cannot depend on him for emotional support and affection. To meet her own needs, she relies on her children and especially on her sons. Goode noted "the high emotional significance of the son–mother relationship" as a major pattern in African family life and attributed much of this to the structure of polygynous households.

> . . . the tie is in part an outgrowth of the impact of polygyny on the son–mother tie: the son was emotionally dependent on his own mother whose uniqueness was emphasized by the existence of other mothers and other sons in the same family. Thus, to affirm his own existence the son had to invest the relationship with great meaning. At the same time, however, the mother could not be merely an "expressive" figure, acting mainly as a source of solace, a mediator of conflicts, and an emotional support. Because of the great social distance between father and son she had also to act to some extent as "instrumental" leader, advising, analyzing, teaching techniques, and so on. (1963:167)

Thus in decentralized households extensively (but to some extent even in undecentralized ones), the mother–child tie became extraordinarily close and the father–child tie more diluted than usual. The father's structural isolation made him a shadowy figure who drifted in and out of the lives of his women and of his children.

Non-Discriminatory Treatment by the Husband

Even if the husband was a shadowy figure, this did not make him unimportant. The very fragmentation of his resources made the capture of her fair share by each wife all the more important. We have seen that insofar as husbands discriminate among wives, this was a potent source of jealousy. The best way for husbands to remove this source would be to stop discriminating. Some husbands learned this the hard way. Many polygynous societies recognized the value of strict equality and imposed rules on men designed to prevent discrimination. Some rules referred to economic and other mundane matters, but the most widespread rules governed sexual matters and reproduction where the toughest problems arose.

Tongan culture prescribed that husbands must treat their wives with scrupulous fairness:

All wives have equal rights to maintenance and should fare similarly in sharing items of food provided by the husband, obtaining equivalent clothing for themselves and their children, and having an equal share in the husband's attention. He should divide his personal possessions among the huts of his wives, or move them with him as he alternates his time among them. Each is entitled to his company for an equal number of nights, and this incidentally means the whole of the night. If he comes to her only for intercourse and then leaves to spend the rest of the night at the house of another wife, he is treating her like a mistress and she is entitled to a divorce. (Colson, 1958:128)

Murdock commented from his cross-cultural analysis that this widespread custom of compulsory rotation saved wives from public humiliation which would accentuate their loss of status:

He may not actually have intercourse with an old or unattractive wife, or with one whom he has come to dislike, but he sleeps in their huts on the nights when their turns come around, and they are spared the mortification of public rejection. (1949:30)

Among the Gusii, there was less pressure for husbands to engage in equal intercourse except when a wife wanted to bear a child. Then "he is supposed to honor each woman's desire to have children at regular intervals, regardless of his preference" (LeVine and LeVine, 1963:40). Such rules oblige the husband to treat all his wives dispassionately rather than according to his passions.

The Sexual Problems of Polygynous Husbands   Because most men cannot afford to marry extra wives until they are middle-aged, they acquire extra sex partners when their sexual powers have decreased. This means that the demands of older wives for equal sexual treatment may not be easily met, and that such husbands have a biological reason for wishing to concentrate their attention on their newest wife. The allocation of sexual services may be not only a source of jealousy among co-wives but a supply problem for the husband. Presumably the weaker the demand from wives, the greater the likelihood that the husband's supply of sexual energy will go around and that he will be spared the humiliation of seeming to be sexually inadequate.

TABLE 18-2   Sexual Restriction of Girls in Polygynous and Non-Polygynous Societies

Premarital Intercourse for Girls	Strongly Polygynous	Not Strongly Polygynous
Prohibited	47%	6%
Permitted	53	94
Total	100%	100%
Number of societies	17	18

Adapted from d'Andrade, 1966:188. Source: Analysis of 35 primitive societies by Ford and Beach (1951).

Table 18-2 suggests a social mechanism which some polygynous societies have developed to reduce indirectly the wives' demands. In this sample of primitive societies, strongly polygynous societies were more apt to prohibit girls from having premarital intercourse. This prohibition prevented the wife from having previous sexual partners with whom the husband might be invidiously compared. It brought each wife to marriage sexually uninitiated and therefore relatively dormant. (Kinsey's American research [1953] demonstrated that premarital intercourse awakened the woman's capacity to experience orgasm and therefore made intercourse more enjoyable for her.) It would seem therefore that a polygynous husband is in a safer position married to virgin brides. In d'Andrade's words, "Perhaps restrictiveness is needed because strong female sexuality on the part of adult women poses too great a threat for the husband of many wives" (1966:188).

The problem is exacerbated if the husband becomes sterile or impotent before his wives have borne as many children as they wish. The fact that his latest wives may never have been married before and need children to keep them company in their separate huts makes childbearing more urgent than in a monogamous marriage between an old man and a young bride who might keep each other company. In at least one polygynous society, husbands tacitly allowed other men to supply the sperm they could not furnish themselves:

> The sterility or impotence of a husband is likely to result in the dissolution of the marriage. When a man becomes sterile or impotent later in life, the need for his wives to have more children may be honored by a clandestine breach of their obligation to remain faithful to their husband. Although it is regarded as shameful, the impotent man may allow his wives to have sexual relations with other men of their own choosing. Nowadays such a husband often takes employment outside the district so as not to be at home while his wives are being impregnated by other men. The adult children of such women may not accept this practice; they have been known to insult and even stone the men who are thus serving their father's wives. Children born of these unions are legally children of their mothers' legal husbands and have no relationship with their physiological fathers. (LeVine and LeVine, 1963:130)

This practice is parallel to the modern practice of artificial insemination except that the latter's anonymity saves the donor from the hazards of insults and stoning. The existence of those hazards demonstrates that this solution to male infertility was hardly socially acceptable. Nevertheless the invention of a socially disapproved solution to the young wife's problem demonstrates the seriousness of the problem not only to her but to her husband who must otherwise cope with her reproductive frustration.

That such stratagems fail to solve the problems of the low ratio of men to women and the imbalance in the ages of husbands and wives in polygynous families is shown by Muhsam's finding that the fertility of first and second wives of polygynous husbands was one third less than for wives in monogamous marriages (1956). Muhsam believed that possible causes for the fertility differential included the age differential, a longer post-partum sex taboo, and long visits home by polygynous wives. Presumably the longer period of sexual abstinence after intercourse was made possible by the existence of other wives to meet the husband's sexual needs (indeed many husbands gave the wife's unavailability as an argument for acquiring an extra wife). Conversely some husbands welcomed customary restrictions on the new mother's sexual availability because it was another way of limiting the sexual demands of their wives. Long visits home were more possible in polygynous households where the husband could be fed by a wife who stayed behind. Psychologically they were more necessary for segregated wives with a relatively weak relationship with their fractional husband. Presumably the wives were lonelier for adult companionship than monogamous wives and missed their mothers more.

I have not attempted to give a balanced picture of the advantages of polygyny. Rather I have focused on the organizational problems created by the complexities of uniting more than one nuclear family together through a spouse shared in common. We have seen that polygynous societies have developed structural mechanisms for solving these problems, the effect of which is to impose restrictions on where extra spouses may be recruited and how they must be treated after they are acquired. Even so, with the best of rules, polygyny does not succeed very generally in solving its intrinsic problems of social control.

SERIAL POLYGAMY

Cynical commentators have suggested that monogamous societies which allow divorce and remarriage have substituted serial polygamy for the traditional form. When couples have no children, substituting one spouse for another creates few structural problems. But when children are involved, acquiring a substitute parent creates problems which in some ways resemble those of polygynous families.

Because children normally stay with the mother after divorce, I will focus on a plurality of husbands passing through the family (a modern form of polyandry). Unlike ordinary polygamy, the original monogamous marriage is discontinued (whether via divorce or death) some time before the second marriage is undertaken. This means that the structure of the family changes from full monogamy to a broken home to monogamy again. The longer the broken-home interval, the stronger the mother–child tie becomes, only to be challenged when the next husband moves in. We have already seen an overdevelopment of mother–child ties in the sub-units of polygynous families and we will see a similar development in broken nuclear families in a later chapter. This suggests that from the standpoint of the children, serial polygyny presents more difficult problems than ordinary polygyny. In the latter, the problem is the displacement of the first wife by her successors and jealousy focuses between co-wives. In the former, the problem is the displacement of the children by the new father in the affection of the mother, and we should expect hostility between stepfather and stepchildren.

First let me present an American case I observed:

> While my brother was in the process of getting a divorce from his wife, he met a recently divorced woman with two children and they began dating. She worked at his company so they saw each other frequently. Within two months after his divorce was final, they were married.

Her children were Mary, age thirteen, and Tom, age nine. My brother had a definite disadvantage as he was considered an outsider in his new home situation. One reason was that the children were older and definitely preferred their mother. Also, during the courtship, the children had not been involved in activities, so that my brother had not become acquainted with Mary or Tom.

Tom continued to identify with his real father. As my brother stated, "He seems to resent me very much. He acts as though he were blaming me for the separation of his parents." My brother probably provoked this reaction by not spending much time with the boy. He did not attempt to play with Tom. He was spending most of his time working to build up his business. During this period Mary remained very quiet and withdrawn. When I would visit in the home, both the children would leave the room.

Within a year after their marriage, a daughter was born, which delighted my brother. He devoted all his valuable leisure time to his new baby. I am certain the other children felt they were being discriminated against, which in effect they were.

This case illustrates the hypothesized difficulty between stepfather and stepchildren and adds a new element in suggesting the further displacement of children with the subsequent arrival of half-siblings to whom the stepfather is likely to be more attached.

TABLE 18-3 Children's Affection for Parents in First Marriages and Remarriages

PERCENTAGE HIGHLY AFFECTIONATE BY SEX OF PARENT	FIRST MARRIAGES Own Parent	REMARRIAGES Own Parent	Stepparent
Mother/Stepmother	47%	43%	20%
Father/Stepfather	34	39	18

Adapted from Bowerman and Irish, 1962:116. Source: Seventh to twelfth grade white boys and girls in Ohio and North Carolina high schools. Reciprocal percentages of children had only moderate or little affection for the specified parent. The total number of cases was 17,738 first marriages, 1,115 remarriages involving a stepfather, and 254 involving a stepmother.

Table 18-3 shows that both stepfathers and stepmothers had weaker relationships with their stepchildren than the real parents who had always lived with them. This should occasion no surprise, but it is a useful reminder of the importance of the dependency relationships which originate in infancy and can rarely be equalled by any later adoptive relationship.

Thomas and Znaniecki discovered that Polish–American stepfathers frequently had sexual relations with their stepdaughters and suggested that this "tends to prove that the steprelation ceases to be felt as a family relation" (1958:1747). In Japan, where the ordinary mother–child tie is unusually intense, Vogel observed that stepchildren frequently felt neglected by their stepmothers:

No matter how much the stepmother tries to be fair, it is someone else's child whom she is caring for, and feelings of fondness are not ordinarily as deep as those between the mother and her true children. . . . The public wrath against [step-mothers] expressed occasionally in newspapers, TV "home dramas," and "movies" suggests the extent to which everyone has strong feelings about the evils of inadequate mothering. (1963:241)

Table 18-3 also shows that despite the presumed upsurge in affection for the mother during the broken home interval, children feel even less affectionate to remarried mothers than to mothers whom they have always shared with fathers. This implies resentment toward the mother for having remarried. Curiously this was not the case when fathers remarried (with the exception of sons in grades 10–12). Junior high boys and girls of all ages felt more affectionate toward fathers who had remarried than to fathers under ordinary circumstances. Perhaps loss of the mother had thrown ordinarily uninvolved fathers into such a central position in the family that the father–child tie was strengthened enough to survive even the trauma of the father's remarriage. Further analysis showed, incidentally, that remarriages following the death of a parent were far more traumatic than after losing a parent through divorce. Presumably divorced parents had such a poor relationship to the child that they were not greatly missed, but the replacement of a beloved deceased parent seemed like a betrayal of his or her memory.

TABLE 18-4 Self-Esteem and Psychosomatic Health of Children in First Marriages, Broken Homes, and Remarriages

| | MARITAL STATUS | | |
ADOLESCENT CHILD HAS	First Marriages	Broken Homes	Remarriages
High self-esteem	46%	40%	32%
Few psychosomatic symptoms	52%	41%	33%
Minimum number of families	2,439	49	86

Adapted from Rosenberg, 1965:99. Source: Juniors and seniors enrolled in selected public high schools in New York State. Reciprocal percentages of students had low self-esteem or more than two psychosomatic symptoms (e.g. headaches, tics, dizziness). In all broken homes and remarriages, the children were with the mother following divorce.

The data in Table 18-4 excludes cases caused by death and those where children remained with the father. It shows the impact on the child of the remarriage of a divorced mother to a strange man. How much of the loss of self-esteem and how many of the psychosomatic symptoms may be attributed to the poor relationship between stepchild and stepfather and how much to feeling betrayed by the mother cannot be differentiated. But which adult is to blame is not the point. The point is that for children who have already suffered the loss of the natural father, life is made even more difficult by the introduction of a new father.

Further analyses by Rosenberg showed a similar loss in the child's self-esteem if a widowed parent remarried (but hardly any if the parent remained single). Transferring loyalty to a stepparent was more difficult for older children than for younger ones. The older the child when he lost a parent, the higher his self-esteem if that parent was not replaced and the greater the loss if he was replaced.

In general, the less attached the child was to the missing parent and the less inflated his attachment to the remaining parent, the easier it should be for him to share his last surviving parent with an adult competitor. Presumably if the new parent were to woo the children as successfully as he wooed the parent, the children might see him as a gain rather than a loss. Unfortunately, no research has tested this hypothesis.

Half-Siblings Research is also inadequate on the complications introduced into a split-level family by adding half-siblings or step-siblings. I assume that these create more than the usual sibling rivalry. This was suggested by the case cited earlier and by the following ethnological report from Java:

> Women who have stepchildren are very conscious of the fact that they must show no sign of favoritism to their own children for fear that the stepchildren or the husband will be resentful. . . . children never consider their stepmother in the same way they consider their own mother. They are more disobedient to the stepmother than they would be to their own mother. If the wife and the stepchildren quarrel, they end with not speaking to each other, but a real mother would never cease to speak to her own children. She would always make up with them soon after a quarrel. It is much easier . . . if the children are those of the wife and the husband is their stepfather, because a woman is with the children all the time, while the father is in the house only occasionally. If her own children are naughty, the mother can keep the father from knowing and can tell him only their good side; but if she has stepchildren, she not only does not hide the children's bad side but also complains to the father about them, and there is always fighting in the house. (Geertz, 1961:41, 44)

The emphasis on the need for the woman to treat her own children and her stepchildren equally is reminiscent of the need for polygynous husbands to treat their wives equally. Presumably impartial treatment prevents rivalry between step-siblings and half-siblings as effectively as impartial treatment of wives reduces jealousy among them. It may also be that other mechanisms of social control which we discovered in polygamous households, such as decentralization of sub-units and hierarchical ordering among the sets of children would be useful in serial polygamy as well. However, without multiple mothers in the household, decentralization could not be as thorough. Hence, serial polygamy presents some problems which are more difficult to solve than true polygamy.

FRATERNAL FAMILIES

As serial polygamy is a deviant form of monogamy, fraternal families are a transitional stage in extended family life. When brothers and their wives and children live together, this is usually a temporary state following the retirement or death of the father and prior to the establishment of new three-generation households with the addition of children and grandchildren.

Hsu has suggested that fraternal families present difficult structural problems. Whereas nuclear families centered around a husband–wife axis can be differentiated on the basis of sex, and father–son or mother–son centered extended families are differentiated on the basis of generations, differentiation among brothers offers the mildest and therefore the weakest barrier to competition within the family:

> . . . the feature which distinguishes the brother–brother relationship from all other axes . . . is its inherent competitiveness. Where there is acknowledged unequalness between the parties of a relationship, there is little potential source of competitiveness. This is the situation of the father–son and mother–son axes. The father and the son or the mother and the son are not equal. In the husband–wife axis the relationship may be equal in conception but never really equal in reality, for men and women are different and they are bound to perform different roles, however such differences are minimized by other factors. The brother–brother axis is one in which the parties to the relationship are more equal and more similar than the parties to any of the other three axes and, therefore, more competitive with each other. (1961:438)

In comparison to either nuclear or extended families, fraternal families may be expected to have tougher problems of social control. However, the previous chapter suggested that birth order may be a basis for differentiating among siblings, so the eldest brother should become the head of the family without much question. Moreover, fraternal families have the advantage of being organized around a childhood bond among the brothers; hence they may experience some of the stability which comes from sororal polygyny or fraternal polyandry.

On the other hand, polygamous families are held together by a central figure in the minority spouse. Similarly in extended families, the husband is simultaneously son to his parents, and head of his own nuclear family so he links the nuclear families of succeeding generations. Fraternal families, unlike any other complex families, are composed of discrete nuclear units which have no common member. Each husband and wife, plus their children, could form a separate nuclear family without stealing anyone from the other nuclear units. We will see shortly that this is precisely what happens eventually to most fraternal families. Indeed, such families stay together only under two conditions: Either the living pattern must be sufficiently decentralized to allow the nuclear pattern to predominate, or the loyalty of the brothers to each other must be stronger than their loyalty to their wives and children.

In any case, even if brothers have grown up together, their wives have not (unless they happen to be sisters). So the same difficulties of trying to get strange women to live together which afflict non-sororal polygyny create problems for fraternal families.

Decentralized Fraternalism

One Mexican Indian tribe offers an example of decentralized fraternalism:

> Ideally, a group of siblings, together with their wives and families, will occupy separate dwelling units surrounding a common courtyard. Each nuclear family typically maintains separate sleeping and cooking facilities and eats apart from the others while it shares the courtyard and engages in a

number of common activities with the other families. (Romney and Romney, 1963:556)

This is a borderline case. Indeed the researchers were not sure whether it should be classified as separate nuclear families living in close proximity or as a loosely-structured complex family. While they decided to label it the latter, it was so loosely structured that wives could associate or not as they saw fit. Because of this voluntary element in the residential decentralization of the larger family, and because neither wives nor children necessarily depended on anyone outside that nuclear household, jealousy and friction among wives could be avoided simply by withdrawal. The researchers felt that this arrangement offered a particularly happy balance between the excessive isolation of nuclear families and the excessive proximity of undecentralized composite families.

Undecentralized Fraternalism

Greek shepherd families customarily passed through a series of phases beginning with a nuclear family which developed into a patrilocal extended family and then into a fraternal family before splitting up into nuclear units. The fact that men married late in life (in their thirties) meant that the rigors of sheepherding often forced them to retire at about the age their eldest son was old enough to marry. Since retirement meant handing over the leadership of the family business, the eldest son often became the head of a fraternal family which persisted at least until all his siblings were married and perhaps longer.

Solidarity Among the Brothers   Brothers who had grown up in the same family and who had cooperated in herding their flock of sheep approached marriage with a fraternal solidarity which placed a new bride in a marginal and subordinate position in the household:

> Her behaviour is extremely modest. She speaks only if she is addressed, and then her replies are made with the utmost show of respect. She addresses her husband's brothers as "master," and his sisters as "mistress." She follows her husband in his modes of address to all senior relatives. . . . The family and kinsmen address the newcomer as simply "bride." In the first months the bride will rise to her feet and remain standing when a man of the family comes into the hut and will not sit down unless specifically requested to do so. (Campbell, 1964:64)

During the early months of marriage, the husband tends to side with his brothers against his wife, holding her at a distance or hiding his contacts with her from his brothers so he will not seem disloyal to the group:

> During the early months of the marriage the young husband gives the minimum of overt public attention to his bride. He may, in stern, almost harsh, tones, make some . . . request of her for food and drink or dry clothes, but he does not make conversation. For her part, a bride will never address her husband before other members of the family. If she requires anything she arranges it through her husband's brother. There is not, during this period,

the slightest inclination on the part of the husband to champion his wife in any dispute which she may have with the other women of the family. Nor does he show the least annoyance when a brother, in his presence, gives his wife some peremptory order. The husband's obligations and affections are still entirely contained within his own family of origin. Indeed his behaviour reflects an almost compulsive assertion that "this is how it will always be." (Campbell, 1964:65)

Although the husband avoided his wife in front of other members of his family, this did not mean that he had no sexual access to her. But how could he exercise this right without disturbing his solidarity with his brothers? Only during the honeymoon week was he granted unrestrained access to his wife in a temporary hut built for the purpose. Once the honeymoon was over, husband and wife moved back into the family hut where it was difficult to have enough privacy for intercourse, much less to keep it secret. Nevertheless valiant attempts were made. Whereas unmarried men returned from the sheep pastures to the family homestead every three weeks, married men returned every two weeks without criticism. But since this was hardly enough to satisfy a relatively young man with a new bride, he supplemented these public visits with secret ones:

> The bride sleeps near the door, a cold and draughty part of the hut. . . . The groom arrives at the hut some time after midnight when the family is asleep, slips into the hut, remains with his young wife for an hour or so and then, well before dawn, is already on his way back to the sheep which may be two or three hours' walking distance away. Naturally the family are aware that these visits occur. Stories are told about grooms who tripped over milk cans as they entered the pitch dark hut or failed to convince the dogs of their true identity. They are considered to be hysterically funny; perhaps an indication of the ambivalent feelings which this conflict of loyalties provokes. (Campbell, 1964:68)

These maneuvers designed to maintain the public fiction of solidarity with the brothers are reminiscent of the severe restrictions on intercourse within the Oneida community (which we saw in Chapter 6 were designed to minimize dyadic withdrawal within that utopian community).

The extraordinary priority given to fraternal solidarity over marital solidarity was manifested most strikingly during the honeymoon when the special hut for the Greek couple did not protect them from verbal intrusion. Nor was it the unmarried brothers who were the intruders. Rather the groom himself, caught in an ambivalent position between his loyalty to his brothers and the task of coping with his new wife volunteered to report back to his brothers on his efforts with her:

> In this first sexual communion the entire family identifies itself with the young husband. There is no question at this stage of his having any affection for his bride. This may emerge later partly as a result of the intimacies now initiated. It is something of an ordeal and a matter of considerable anxiety for all Sarakatsan bridegrooms that they should be able to effect a techni- cally successful assault upon this strange woman and uphold their reputa-

tion for manliness in its most literal sense, a reputation which affects the prestige of the entire family. The stress on physical and moral manliness in the stereotype of the ideal man encourages in the Sarakatsani a deep-seated fear of sexual impotence on this critical occasion which is, indeed, almost a public ceremony of initiation. In the morning success or failure on the previous night is discussed with brothers in embarrassed monosyllables and, if there has been difficulty, they try to give advice and encouragement. (Campbell, 1964:66)

Thus the fraternal collectivity preserve their solidarity *vis-à-vis* the invading woman by guaranteeing that she is put in her place and kept there.

Conflict Among Wives   As long as there is only one wife and all the brothers are arrayed against her, it is relatively easy to keep the family under control. A household consisting of one married couple and unmarried siblings is not much different from a nuclear family with unmarried children. But the larger the number of wives, the more the situation resembles a polygynous family. Bringing unrelated women so close together has the usual results—trouble:

The Sarakatsani claim that brothers would undoubtedly live together all their lives were it not for the quarrels of their wives. The Sarakatsani expect the wives of brothers to quarrel and on the whole they are not disappointed. (Campbell, 1964:71)

One reason for quarreling among wives is the difficulty of insuring that all the women will work equally hard. Unlike the Mexican women whose decentralized fraternalism involved separate hearths or the customary arrangement in so many polygynous families where each wife has her own hut, the Sarakatsani women worked together preparing common meals and caring for the baby lambs. Campbell reported that this "partnership works smoothly so long as each wife is thought to be pulling her weight. . . . This clearly may often be a matter rather of opinion than obvious fact. And while the brothers are usually careful not to express any displeasure they may feel for one another, wives are only too ready to criticize one another in public" (p. 76). The willingness of the wives to violate the norm of public solidarity contrasted sharply with the behavior of the brothers. They had come as strangers from diverse families into a situation of extreme interdependence where the negligence of one hurt everyone else.

A second source of difficulty between wives was discriminatory treatment by the head of the family. Shepherd families were not wealthy and therefore wives quarreled over the allocation of funds and the purchase of goods for the family. Under these financial circumstances, "what is given to one wife is by definition not given to the other." Insofar as wives had differing needs, "inevitably each believes that the other is the better treated." Campbell reported that no method of allocating funds seemed to work under these circumstances:

An elder brother often makes a conscious effort to treat his younger brother's wife with particular consideration and tact, supplying from the family purse without debate the money required for all her children's needs. . . . This may merely infuriate the elder brother's wife who sees herself and her children sacrificed to her husband's wish to maintain intact the relationship with his brother. On the other hand, the younger brother's wife is seldom grateful. She may not believe that she is being favourably treated and, at best, she will still resent the fact that she must apply to her husband's brother for the requirements of her children. (Campbell, 1964:73)

While wives often quarreled about their individual rights, once they had children there were larger questions at stake in the competition among nuclear units. Not only did wives fight for the rights of their children, but husbands who had relatively little interest in their wives as long as they were childless came to their defense as soon as they were mothers because the men were interested in the welfare of their own children:

Each wife/mother is in herself a symbol of the kinship distance which separates her children from their paternal cousins, and therefore her husband from his siblings. The worst quarrels between wives are about their children. And such quarrels are particularly dangerous to the unity of the brothers. Two married brothers frequently stand together and verbally or even physically chastise their wives who make trouble in the family by quarrels over personal differences; but when the issue between the wives concerns their children (however trivial its origin may be) the two sibling/fathers, out of loyalty to and identification with their children, are inevitably committed to the support of their wives. (Campbell, 1964:78)

From India comes an almost identical report of conflict among wives in fraternal households:

. . . in spite of the great solidarity among brothers, many forces tend to break the joint family into separate hearths after the father's death. Individually, wives are likely to feel that their own husbands contribute more than they receive, that their own children do not receive a fair share, and that they, themselves, must adjust to too many ways and personalities." (Goode, 1963:241)

Collapse of the Family   The larger the family grows with the addition of wives and children, the more difficult it becomes to live together in the same hut. Eventually the level of conflict and noise becomes unbearable:

[There is] increasing difficulty of maintaining discipline in a joint household without causing offence to the constituent elementary families. When Theodoros . . . shook a worried head and said "We are eighteen individuals in this house," this was the cause of his anxiety. As head of the house he could directly discipline only his own wife and children. He would not verbally reprimand a brother's wife in her husband's presence, unless she was a newly married bride or without children; . . . he could not interfere in her relations with her children. No brother would ever strike another brother's wife. Even the control of the mother-in-law over her sons' wives, though it is still considerable, becomes less complete after three or four years of marriage. In this household there are eight young children and babies playing, fighting, and screaming. Except in the early evening when a sleep of exhaustion stills their activities, the scene is one of constant tumult. (Campbell, 1964:78–79)

This case portrays the internal strains on a large complex family. It also shows that the attempt to decentralize the family by giving each brother responsibility for his own wife and children did not prevent the elder brother from having to live with the tensions of his younger brothers' failure to keep their families under control. Indeed it is questionable whether eighteen people, many of them unsocialized youngsters, could ever live harmoniously in a single hut, no matter what control mechanisms were employed.

Eventually undecentralized fraternal families got so big and complicated that they collapsed of their own weight. Campbell hinted at the critical size which could not be exceeded when he pointed out that "In groups of four or more brothers, it is generally not possible to wait until all the brothers are married before some division occurs" and that "after the first two or three brothers have contracted out of the extended family, the remaining two or three younger brothers hold together until the youngest is married and established before a further and final division is made" (Campbell, 1964:81–82). These sentences suggest that three brothers plus their wives and children was the maximum number who could live in a single hut, sharing all things in common. Even this was a relatively short-lived arrangement, seldom lasting more than a decade. Eventually even for a relatively small fraternal family, the number of children got so large, the children got so old, and the wives became so antagonistic that the system collapsed into nuclear families with separate huts.

After the family split up, brothers continued to cooperate in their sheep-herding until their own sons became old enough to do men's work. But once the fraternal household had been subdivided, economic cooperation became more difficult: "Sheep must then be branded, accounts kept, and in different ways the possibility of friction between the associated brothers is greater than when the flock is undivided" (Campbell, 1964:57). For wives now at their longed-for goal of having a hut of their own, the dissolution of the compound family brought a welcome release from years of tension: "Brothers often point out . . . the relative peace and goodwill which prevails between their wives and children after the division of the extended family household" (p. 86).

In summary, an undecentralized fraternal family seems capable of surviving only for a limited time. The larger its constituent nuclear units become, the greater the urgency of giving each unit a home of its own so that the boundaries of the nuclear family can be respected. Undecentralized familism contains intrinsic strains which make it at best a transitory phenomenon.

EXTENDED FAMILIES

In Murdock's cross-cultural sample (1949), almost half the societies possessed some form of extended family either instead of or in addition to polygamy. The extended pattern has been practiced in roughly twice as many societies as restricted themselves to nuclear families alone. Moreover, in comparison to polygamy, which was practiced most extensively among the relatively small tribes of Africa, extended families were characteristic of such large and powerful empires as China, Japan, and India. Therefore, the number of people living under extended family systems was very large and this was the background out of which modern nuclear family systems directly evolved.

With polygamy, there were a number of reasons why the majority of people at any one time were unlikely to live in multiple-spouse households even though they might have looked forward to the time when additional spouses could be added. The same discrepancy between ideal and actuality often existed in societies supposedly governed by extended family norms. The ideal might have taken either of two forms—a stem family in which one member of each succeeding generation remained in the home with his spouse and children or a fully extended family in which all the children of one sex stayed home. For the sake of simplicity I will refer to the latter simply as an extended family and with respect to both extended and stem families I will ordinarily assume that the male offspring stay home to establish a patrilocally extended family.

The larger the number of sons and the smaller the family's resources, the less possible it is for all sons to remain together. We saw in the preceding section that the larger a complex family became, the more it tended to fall apart because of its internal tensions and conflicts. In a settled agrarian economy such as sustained most extended family systems, psychological and social problems were overshadowed by the difficulty of supporting an increasingly large family on the family estate. This was one reason for the development of the stem family system which made it possible for one son (usually the eldest) to be guaranteed a place in an extended family, but which conversely required all the other sons to found new families which by definition would be nuclear for a whole generation.

In a stem family society, the proportion of the total population living in extended families depends on the ratio of eldest sons to other sons. Only if the average family had one son apiece would stem-families predominate. Since extended family systems normally had high birth rates, the average family had surplus sons for export.

In ordinary extended family systems, wealthy families might be able to accommodate all their sons for a generation or two. But even if their financial resources were unlimited, such families could not proliferate indefinitely without becoming unmanageable. And since most families do not have unlimited resources, their ability to adhere to the ideal of indefinite proliferation is accordingly limited. In most extended family systems, three generations are the maximum who live under one roof. Once the fourth generation arrives, subdivision has usually already occurred. To say that three generations live together does not mean that all related persons in each generation are together but rather that the patriarch lives with all his sons and their nuclear families. Once the patriarch dies or retires from "office" as head of the family, the sons tend to split up as heads of new three-generation households since by that time their own children are likely to be marrying and bearing children. For the poorer people in such a society, even this is too costly. For them, a stem family may be the best they can manage even though it is not the societal ideal.

In China, for example, Levy (1949) found that the cultural ideal of six generations living together could not be attained even by the gentry (who seldom lived together for more than three or four generations), much less by the peasantry. The average Chinese lived in a stem family averaging only about six members, from which younger sons were forced out because of lack of funds. Since the peasants in most agrarian economies made up the bulk of the population, the number of people who could fulfill the extended family ideal even for as short a time as three generations was likely to be a small minority.

In discussing extended family systems, therefore, it should be remembered that this refers to the normative pattern of a society and to those relatively few actual cases in which more than one generation of nuclear families live together. The fact that this is not a universal pattern attests to the difficulties, again, of managing any complex family system.

The Jealousy Problem

We have seen that polygyny creates jealousy between wives. For extended families, similar conflicts arise between the mother and her son's wife. To be sure, they do not compete for the son's sexual favors, but they do compete for his affection. Prior to the son's marriage, the mother enjoyed his exclusive affection. In a nuclear family this might not have been so close a tie since nuclear wives normally rely on their husbands as their chief affectional resource. But since husband–wife ties are weak in extended family systems, mothers rely on their sons for affectional gratification. The significance of this tie to the mother can be seen in Campbell's report that Greek shepherd mothers mourned a son's death for five years (whereas fathers did so for only one year):

> Each morning at dawn, each evening at dusk, during these long years she sings her dirges and lamentations again. Even when the period of mourning is completed, she will never again dance at a festival, or sing a ballad, during the remaining years of her life. (1964:168)

When a son married, this threatened the mother's source of affection and made her fear displacement by the young bride. For classical China, Levy (1949) summarized the mother's approach to her daughter-in-law thus:

> The mother-in-law's treatment of her . . . daughter-in-law was likely to be unfeeling and domineering and was quite frequently harsh, vindictive, and unjust. . . . Often harsh treatment was further reinforced by extreme jealousy on the part of the mother-in-law. She had warm relations with her son, and she was likely to react sharply to the entrance of another woman in his life, especially if the son were unusually attentive to his wife. (1949:109–110)

The unhappiness of such wives could be seen in the extraordinary number who committed suicide or who attempted it.

With the arrival of children, the young bride turned to them to relieve her sense of isolation and oppression in the extended family. But even there her mother-in-law might intervene, creating a new source of conflict. We have already seen in Chapter 17 that grandparents tend to be soft on their grandchildren, which means that grandmothers and mothers are liable to disagree about the discipline of the children, and that children may side with the grandmother against the mother in open rebellion. In Okinawan extended families, the Maretzkis reported thus:

> Mothers in extended households complained that grandparents often intervened on behalf of the child and made disciplining very difficult. The kindergarten teacher remarked on the differences between children who have grandparents and those who do not. "Those who do not have grandparents are much easier to handle, they don't cry so easily and do many things for themselves. My child always runs to grandfather whenever I scold her . . . and we mothers end up by being scolded by the old folks."
> It is not an uncommon sight to see a child crying and running to his grandmother on being reprimanded by his mother. With carrying, hugging, and venting anger against the mother, the old woman comforts the child. Children soon learn that if no one else complies with their demands, grandmother or grandfather will grant them satisfaction. (1963:477–478)

Such conflict between the mother and grandmother produces resentment in the mother at interference with her disciplinary responsibility and resentment in the grandmother at her daughter-in-law's punitiveness toward her beloved grandchild.

In Rajput Indian families, Minturn and Hitchcock (1963) reported a similar touchiness with respect to interference by other women in disciplining a woman's own children. Even though theoretically the Hindu joint family gave the matriarch the right to discipline any children she wished to, in practice the mother was expected to discipline her own children if she was present and had seen the misbehavior. The harsher another woman's intervention (with severe scoldings or especially physical punishment) the more the mother resented it. Indeed, only if two women were on extraordinarily good terms would one scold the other's child.

In extended families with more than one wife in the same generation, possibilities for conflict correspondingly multiplied. In Rajput Indian families, the problems of close proximity were compounded by the custom of purdah which prohibited women from escaping from the home they had to share:

> The women are more openly quarrelsome than the men. Tempers have no chance to "cool off" in the close quarters of the courtyard. A woman . . . said that if they could take a walk for an hour, most of the quarrels would not occur. Quarrels often begin over some minor matter. Two women may disagree over the cooking or the children, and the bickering begins. In an extended family, the other women usually take sides, and eventually all the women are lined up against each other. . . . in some houses the women fight daily, in some once a week, and in some not for months at a time. (Minturn and Hitchcock, 1963:261)

In general, conflict among women in an extended patrilocal family was an intrinsic hazard. The larger the number of women involved, the greater the potentialities for conflict. As with other types of complex families, these problems in social control required the development of conflict-preventing mechanisms such as we have seen before.

Hierarchical Ordering of the Generations

The extended family was organized on the basis of age differentiation: priority of generations and priority of birth order within each generation. Applied to the problem of jealousy of women, this meant that the matriarch's position was protected against disturbance by the newcomer and that the latter had to wait a generation or two to have her turn as head of the female hierarchy.

The mother's power was exercised even before marriage in selecting her daughter-in-law. This minimized the threat to her position by allowing her to choose a bride whom she thought she could get along with. After marriage, there was not the slightest doubt about her authority to treat the bride as her servant (whereas in polygynous households the lesser age gap between wives left some variation in this respect).

When additional sons married and brought their wives into the household, it was the mother's responsibility to control disputes among her daughters-in-law. In the Greek shepherd family, as long as the mother remained alive, conflict was suppressed, but once she passed away, her successor (the wife of the eldest brother) found it difficult to exercise authority successfully. Since she had less age superiority and less influence over her brothers-in-law, she could not long hold together the fraternal family derived from the previous extended family:

> The mother acts as the diplomat and peacemaker between the dissident wives. Despite the ambivalence of attitude between mother and daughter-in-law, wives work amicably enough under the instructions of their husband's mother. They do not work amicably under the wife of the eldest brother and it is noticeable that extended families, where the mother of the brothers is dead, do not survive long. In such cases there is lacking a social personality that symbolizes and mediates the mutual attachment of the various [nuclear] families within the extended group. (Campbell, 1964:165)

Against her mother-in-law, a bride had almost no effective means of protest. Extended families were authoritarian institutions which expected unquestioning obedience from the subordinates. In China we have already seen that unhappy brides sometimes attempted suicide and Levy believed that this desperate measure was almost the only means of protest available. In India, Rajput wives discovered another way of ameliorating their situation. Indicative of the weakness of their power position, the method involved an indirect subterfuge, namely pretending to be possessed by evil spirits:

> In general, women are more susceptible to possession by ghosts than men. . . . Girls on the eve of their marriage are sometimes possessed, but even more frequently young daughters-in-law residing for the first time in a strange household become possessed by some hostile spirit. Such possession makes these young brides temporarily the center of concern and attention despite their low status. The ghost is feared, and his demands, spoken through the patient, must be obeyed. (Minturn and Hitchcock, 1963:281)

With these exceptions, young women were expected to suffer in silence, taking orders from their mothers-in-law, waiting until they became mothers-in-law themselves and could take revenge on their sons' brides.

Patriarchal Authority   For males in an extended family, the problem of conflict was lessened. After all, the son had been subject to his father longer than he could remember. In adulthood he simply was expected to continue the same obedience he had always given his father. In China, filial piety was erected by Confucianism into the central concept of an entire ethical system, and in most extended family systems, obedience to parents as representatives of the ancestors was the cardinal virtue.

The difference in power structure between extended families and nuclear families is highlighted in Gore's inquiry into decision-making about children's schooling, selection of mates and choice of occupation in Indian families. Parents made such decisions in less than 20 percent of extended families, but they did so in more than 80 percent of nuclear families (1961:233). Thus patriarchal men not only controlled their grandchildren in most extended families, but even wielded power over some living in supposedly independent households.

In Greece, the patriarch's power continued to some extent even after the formal transfer of authority to his son:

> . . . even after a father's retirement a son continues to owe filial respect to him as long as this does not interfere with his full control of the extended family's affairs. A father must give his consent to the arrangement of a daughter's or son's marriage if this is made after his retirement. And at the celebration of a wedding he always acts as the formal head of the family. (Campbell, 1964:164)

In rural Ireland, Humphreys found a filial piety that was remarkably Confucian in tone:

> The uniquely advanced age at which parents marry and accede to control of the farm, and in turn relinquish it to their successors, has profound and singular effects upon the obligations of filial piety. It makes for a pronounced glorification and veneration of the aged, especially of the authority of the father and devotion of the mother. And this . . . leads to the sanctioned expectation of prolonged celibacy, subordination to parental control and, in special circumstances, of the sacrifice of individual achievement through occupation and through marriage in the interests of family welfare. This has resulted in the creation of a process of socialization of the children which instills in them a deep sense of inferiority, of submissiveness and many other notable juvenile traits. (1966:22–23)

This picture suggests the extraordinary success of the Irish extended family in solving its structural problem by socializing its sons into docile acceptance of the parents' superiority.

In extended families the contending male parties have had a life-long hierarchical relationship. Father and son are like sisters in sororal polygyny except that intergenerational differentiation is sharper and more powerful than inter-sibling differentiation. Moreover, the authority of the elders in extended families is doubly powerful because both father and mother have claims over the son.

As long as the father is the head of an extended family there is no question about the son's responsibility to obey him. But some extended families have trouble deciding when the father should retire and the heir take over. The more prescribed retirement is on the basis of age or the marriage of the son or any other definite criterion, the less room there is for conflict. Among Greek shepherds, the signal for retirement was the birth of the eldest son's first child, but this rule was not followed rigidly enough to prevent anxiety about when the father would surrender control:

> A father cannot in accordance with customary right long delay his retirement beyond the time when his eldest son has his first child, for it is an important value of this community that a man who is married and a parent should be the "master" in his own household. But after the son's marriage and before the birth of the first child the father insists that he should continue to control the affairs of the extended family while the son is learning under his guidance the elements of his future role. Until the pregnancy of his wife is well established, the irritating uncertainty about the transfer of power, which will confer on him the status and prestige of a family leader in the community, sometimes tempts the son to show a lack of respect to his father which previously he would not have dared to express so freely. (Campbell, 1964:68)

Thus one of the potential points of conflict in extended families centered around the timing of the transition in authority from one family head to his successor. So powerful was the family head, that there was very little the successor could do but wait until the father was ready to retire. Irritability and lack of respect from the son were not likely to impress the father with his readiness to assume so heavy a responsibility.

One other conflict for the son was between his loyalties to his parents and to his wife, but we have already seen that the claims of the parents had priority. The relative importance of these conflicting claims was perhaps nowhere more graphically symbolized than in the contrasts between the length of time a Chinese man was expected to mourn the death of a parent or of his wife—13 months versus 3.

Role Segregation

We have seen that the young man's role of son to his parents was accorded higher priority than the role of husband to his wife. Concretely this meant that many roles performed by wives for their husbands in nuclear families continued to be performed by mothers for their sons in extended families. In the Rajput Indian joint family, Minturn and Hitchcock (1963) found that mothers continued to cook for their sons even after the latter married and indeed that sisters came next in order, so that wives cooked for their husbands only when no female blood relative was available in the household.

Reciprocally, parents exercised many functions on behalf of the daughter-in-law which would also be performed by the husband in a nuclear family. The same researchers found that:

> A husband is not supposed to show any open concern for his wife's welfare; this is the responsibility of his parents. If the wife is sick, the mother-in-law

and father-in-law see that she goes to a doctor; if they do not, neither she nor her husband should complain. (1963:241)

These are additional examples of the priority of vertical relationships over horizontal relationships in extended families.

But husbands could not ignore their wives altogether. They had to have sexual relations in order to enable them to perform their child-bearing duty on behalf of his family. Out of this sexual relationship at least a minimal affection for the wife tended to develop. Yet it was precisely these sexual and affectional relationships which were dynamite for the extended family. To protect the family against an explosion of jealousy, the normal solution was secrecy:

> Ideally a man and his wife are not allowed to talk to each other in front of the older members of the family. Since the [Rajput] mother-in-law is virtually always present in the courtyard and the young wife cannot leave the courtyard, this means in effect that the young couple may converse only surreptitiously at night. (Minturn and Hitchcock, 1963:241)

> The [Indian] husband and wife are not supposed to show affection toward one another in public, and have limited opportunities to be alone together, even at night. In traditional households, the men eat first, separate from the women. Although there are traditional rationalizations for all these rules, as a by-product the rules reduce the intimacy between husband and wife, and thus the likelihood that the small conjugal family will break off from the joint unit. (Goode, 1963:240)

By hiding the role of companion to his wife, the son minimized the extent to which the first woman in the family felt displaced by the second. Thus the son could play conflicting roles within the family even though his role of husband suffered considerably.

In Indian families, even the role of son was inhibited by the segregation of women. We have already seen that this threw the women into proximity with each other where their jealousy could be expressed in open conflict. But insofar as it kept the women at a distance from their men, it reduced the occasions when jealousy might be provoked. They were so cut off from contact with any supportive members of their family of marriage that they retained strong ties with their families of origin. By no means customary in all extended family systems, but indicative of the sequestering of women in the Hindu joint family, was the continued strength of these childhood ties:

> A young bride usually returns home for a protracted visit after the first months or weeks of marriage and spends about half of the first eight years of her married life in her mother's home, sometimes visiting for a year or more at a time. . . . The emotional ties of women to their parental homes are so strong that they persist throughout life, no matter how happy the adjustment to the husband's village may be. (Minturn and Hitchcock, 1963: 235)

These prolonged visits home are reminiscent of the absence of polygynous wives for the same reason. In both cases the husband–wife tie is weak; in both another woman (in this case the mother) is available to substitute for the missing wife in performing the normal household tasks; in both, the effect of the visits is to prolong the ties with the family of origin and to inhibit the development of ties with the new family.

Symbolic also of the priority of ties to the family of origin is the fact that Rajput women were closer to their siblings and cousins than to their spouses:

> The relationship between a brother and his sister or female cousins also seems warmer and less restrained than the marital one and is considered sacred. A sister, even after marriage, may sit with her face uncovered and converse freely with her male relatives. (Minturn and Hitchcock, 1963:242)

In general, then, extended families safeguarded the original family against disruption by the bride. This left the bride's primary loyalties with her own family until she rose to the top of her husband's family either because of the death or retirement of his mother or because the subdivision of his family made her mistress of her own house even sooner. In the meantime, both she and her husband were low-status children, subordinated to the rule of his parents and forced to hide their own nascent relationship from public view. Only when that older public was removed from the scene was it safe for the couple to emerge from hiding:

> After the death of the mother-in-law, a woman can talk to her husband in the presence of her sisters-in-law. When her sons marry, she assumes a new and prestigeful role. She is now in charge of the young women and is released by virtue of her relative age from many of the restrictions of purdah. Age in the courtyard brings respect, and every bride can look forward to the day when she assumes this role. There are some women who in spite of purdah and the status inferiority of women become very powerful. In many ways it would seem as if in her young years a woman's relation to her husband is primarily sexual and procreative, and that with age and the death of his mother it may become more one of a companion or even an advisor. (Minturn and Hitchcock, 1963:241)

The husband–wife relationship which was so thoroughly inhibited at the beginning of marriage to avoid offending the husband's parents could bloom at last when the inhibiting influence of the parents was gone. Paradoxically, the emphasis on marital companionship which flourishes most in nuclear families during the "honeymoon" period, could grow in extended families only in the last stage of the family life cycle. Only when couples had no one above them to answer to any more, could they treat each other as they wished.

This is not to say that the marital bond for old couples in extended families was identical with that for families which had been nuclear and neolocal from the very beginning. The long decades of suppression of the marital bond forced the couple to direct so much attention upward to their parents, laterally to their siblings, and downward to their children that they became accustomed to orienting their attention in other directions. Moreover, once the husband's parents were removed from the scene, the husband and wife assumed heavy new responsibilities for the family extending downward beneath them. This meant that they must be deeply engrossed in exercising their authoritarian responsibilities and in receiving the filial adulation of their children and grandchildren. This is far different from the undisrupted mutual absorption of nuclear couples prior to the arrival of children and after their departure. Only in comparison with the prior inhibition of the marital bond could the patriarchal and matriarchal rulers of the extended family be said to have achieved a more nearly nuclear type of relationship.

Division of the Family

I have already pointed out that stem families by definition sloughed off their extra members in every generation and that families which tried to retain all their sons in each succeeding generation soon became overpopulated. This presented overextended families with the problem of how and when to divide the family. The stronger the devotion of the society to an ideal of an indefinitely proliferating family, the more painful this process became and the more families tried to put it off as long as they could.

One Japanese community (Shirakawa-mura) attempted to compromise between the hardheartedness of the stem-family solution and the impossibility of giving all sons equal shares in a dwindling resource base. This compromise consisted of a stem-family system of legalized marriage for the eldest son combined with allowing the younger sons and all the daughters to stay home unmarried. Although some feudal societies might have enforced celibacy on these unmarried children, they were permitted to engage in nonmarital intercourse and the daughters raised their illegitimate children within the extended family household. This arrangement allowed the extended family to utilize their common land for generation after generation without the splitting which would have been necessary if younger sons could have legally married.

This compromise produced its own strains, however, and eventually the system broke down. Watanabe (1968) reported that the younger sons and the daughters were dissatisfied with their inferior status and felt like slaves to the head of the family, exploited without getting a fair return. They preferred to form nuclear family units, bringing man, woman, and children together in a home of their own with their own property and the power of governing their own lives. The Shirakawa compromise preserved the extended family only at the expense of destroying most of the nuclear family units of which extended families are normally composed. The cost was too great for the non-stem members to accept. As soon as alternative economic opportunities became available with the industrialization of Japan, the unmarried sons and daughters did what younger siblings in stem families have done everywhere. They left.

The Shirakawa compromise was labeled "an irregular cohabitant complex family with the husbands of collateral women lacking" by Ariga (1965: 99). It postponed, but did not prevent, the ultimate dissolution of the large family system. Without it, the division of the extended families would have come sooner.

By division is not meant the abandonment of an extended family system, but rather the splitting of given extended families into smaller units which initially are smaller extended units or even nuclear units, but which eventually grow back into large extended families once more. Just as animal cells divide and divide again, so extended families with many sons must divide and divide again every generation or two. The fact that division is necessary, however, does not make it any less painful for family members who cherish the ideal of remaining together. In India:

> . . . the joint family as a system has no clear institutionalized point at which a division into nuclear families should take place. It is likely to take place when the parental couple dies, or when all the younger siblings of the brother's generation are grown up and taken care of. Nevertheless, the division makes Hindus uncomfortable and requires some sort of explanation or rationalization. (Goode, 1963:241)

For Rajput families, Minturn and Hitchcock reported similarly that "It is a weakness of the ideal extended family that fractionating is inevitable but not accepted emotionally." (1963:232) These authors pointed out that family division was frequently a multi-stage process of response to the strains of living in an ever-expanding family:

> The first break in the pattern usually comes when a man and his wife decide to have a separate hearth. This step . . . may be rationalized on the basis of convenience. More frequently, however, . . . it results from tension and quarrels among the women. (Minturn and Hitchcock, 1963:232)

That first step in decentralization was relatively modest, less clearcut for example than the separate huts favored in polygynous families:

> . . . separate hearths are no real threat to the extended family, for basic patterns of authority and of property allocation and economic cooperation are not broken. The older women still have charge of giving out the daily ration of food. The father runs the farm. Further division, however, is a threat to basic patterns. The division of the courtyard into two sections by building a wall, or the setting up of a new household, entails the division of property: the milk cattle, furniture and food. Now the mother-in-law no longer has to be approached for the daily ration, and the young wife has a source of pocket money, for she can sell amounts of grain at the store and spend the money for bangles without permission of her mother-in-law. (Ibid.)

At that point, the division of the extended family had proceeded roughly to the equivalent of a decentralized polygynous household.

> Further divisions may be more drastic. The land may be divided up among brothers, or brothers and cousins, at the death of the older generation, thus setting up separate joint farm families. The men may still share a dwelling and their wives a courtyard, but the economy of each family is now distinct. (Ibid.)

Even this third-stage division was not the ultimate one. If men still lived together even after the land had been parcelled out, it is apparent how extraordinarily reluctant the members of extended families were to separate completely.

Eventually however population growth required completely separate living arrangements. Only then had the extended family become completely divided. This suggests that the extended family was likely to resist decentralization as a solution to the conflicts among its female members and that its cohesive forces were likely to be stronger than the centrifugal forces until the burdens carried by the family became extraordinarily heavy. Only then, and reluctantly at that, would an overextended family dissolve into fragments each of which became the nucleus for a new extended family. Only when the social control problems of an extended family became so complex that the control mechanisms broke down completely, did the family subdivide into manageable units, only to repeat the cycle of growing stress and subdivision.

The only type of extended family which had systematically solved the problem of division was the stem family which retained only one son in each generation. For such families, not only was the problem of division solved, but the problem of conflict also was minimized because there were no near-equals in any one generation to compete for the family's resources. In general stem families had relatively few structural problems in comparison with broadly extended families or polygamous families.

COMPLEX AND SIMPLE FAMILIES

We have seen that complex families have their greatest difficulties in the relationships among competing women and among competing children. To meet these problems, complex families repress the expression of affection and insist on conformity and obedience from children. The isolation of nuclear families should cause stress between the mother and her children since she must cope with her children unaided all day long. Thus nuclear families have their own strains, particularly when children are small. But the foci of strain and the means of coping with them differ from those in complex families.

Control of Conflict

In studying large nuclear families, we saw that the larger the family, the greater the reliance on rules and on parental authority to keep the family members under control. In studying extended families we have also seen that the authority of the elders is a characteristic feature. Therefore we should expect complex families to control family members in general and children in particular more severely than ordinary nuclear families.

Children in complex families present two problems. Until they are properly socialized into the virtues of filial piety and unquestioning obedience, they are liable to challenge the power structure of the family. I therefore expect more emphasis on obedience training in complex families and heavier punishment for disobedience. One index of the latter would be the degree to which the mother punishes aggression against herself. Presumably in complex families, such aggression should be less tolerable because a child who gets away with such aggression is liable to disobey other elders within the household as well.

A second problem which children create in complex families is the threat of chaos among the large number of half-siblings, step-siblings, and cousins within the family. If problems of jealousy among adult women are bad enough in such families, the possibilities for sibling rivalry are even more numerous. Therefore I expect heavier punishment in complex families for aggression against the superabundant and all-too-proximate peers. By contrast, the smaller the nuclear family and the more independent its residence from other families, the less dangerous and more tolerable aggression against the few siblings and the remote unrelated peers.

TABLE 18-5   Maternal Punishment of Children's Aggression in Nuclear and Stem Families

MOTHER PUNISHES AGGRESSION	FAMILY TYPE	
	Nuclear	Stem
Against herself	40%	76%
Against peers	44%	69%
Number of families	50	25

Adapted from Minturn and Lambert, 1964:272, 276. Source: Sample families in a local community in each of five countries: India, Kenya, Mexico, Okinawa, and the Philippines. Reciprocal percentages of mothers did not prohibit or punish aggression toward the specified target.

Table 18-5 shows that mothers in stem families punished children more for aggression than did mothers in nuclear families in the same societies. The difference between these two types of families was greater for aggression against superiors than for aggression against peers, perhaps because stem families are extended only vertically, not horizontally.

Minturn and Lambert found that the larger the number of adults in the household (especially the larger the number of women, since they were around more than men), the more apt the mother was to punish aggression against herself. However, punishment of aggression against peers was affected relatively little by the number of adults within the household and even less by the number of relatives living nearby. The biggest source of variation in punishment of aggression against peers was the number of siblings in the household (41 percent when the number was small, 68 percent when it was large). Thus, aggression within complex families seems to have been generally repressed, but control was applied most rigorously at the points of greatest strain where trouble was liable to erupt.

When the unit of comparison is whole societies instead of variance between families in the same societies, the differential emphasis on preventing aggression is even greater. Whiting (1959) found that 92 percent of societies with extended family systems had severe aggression training for children compared with only 25 percent of societies with nuclear family systems. Thus the type of family system advocated by the society sets the tone for socialization of children's aggression.

Excluded from Table 18-5 was the United States because no within-society comparison between nuclear and stem families was possible. For punishment of mother-directed direction, the New England town was typical of nuclear families in the other five countries. For peer-directed aggression, however, New England mothers were extraordinarily permissive, only 8 percent generally prohibiting aggression against peers and punishing retaliation against peers. Minturn and Lambert believed that this extraordinary permissiveness resulted from the residential isolation of those families:

> The New England families are the only group whose members are not living next door to their relatives and whose livelihood does not depend upon the support of their neighbors. Their insistence that their children stand up for themselves may be seen both as a lack of concern with maintaining constant friendships, "If you can't get along with them, play with somebody else; there are lots of people in this world," and a reluctance to complain to their neighbors on behalf of their children, "You couldn't go to the parents and tell them." These two situations are peculiar to the United States sample. In all the other samples there are a limited number of friends available to children, but mothers can complain to other mothers and expect some cooperation if these friendships are disrupted. (1964:161)

Where families live close to their relatives, even nuclear families must control fighting among children although their need for control is not as great as when families live together in the same great house. But the farther away families live from their relatives or even from their friends, the more they can tolerate fighting since it doesn't go on under their noses. In the small New England town, most families had few relatives within the same community, much less next door, so the need to control aggression toward peers was almost nonexistent.

Inhibition of Affect

The effect of family composition on the expression of feeling toward children is more complicated than the control of aggression. In stem families like those portrayed in Table 18-5, Minturn and Lambert found that 68 percent of mothers expressed warmth and praised their children frequently, whereas this was true of only 48 percent of mothers in nuclear families. This shows that affect was hardly inhibited toward children in stem families. Presumably the presence of grandparents within the household produced warmer treatment of the child. We already know that grandparents generally express warmth toward grandchildren. When there are no cousins around to object, there is no reason why either grandparents or parents should inhibit affection toward children. Children in a stem family are in a quite different situation from the adult women who compete with each other and toward whom the son/husband must inhibit expression of affection. Precisely because affection cannot be expressed toward the spouse, it is redirected toward children. On the other hand, in nuclear families, the opportunity for expressing affection spontaneously between husband and wife decreases the emphasis on it in mother–child relations.

When we move from stem families to larger extended families, new complications arise. The wife is still motivated to turn her affection to her children. But the presence of so many children in a large complex household creates a barrier to the free flow of warmth or of any other emotional expression. Table 18-6 shows less expression of either positive or negative emotion in complex households than in simple ones where "outside" children were not involved. At the same time, women in complex households were less apt to reward or punish their children than in simple households. Perhaps the larger number of adults in complex households shared responsibility for the children and relied on social pressure to control them.

TABLE 18-6   Maternal Exhibition of Affect in Simple and Complex Households

MATERNAL EXHIBITION OF AFFECT	HOUSEHOLD TYPE	
	Simple	Complex
Exhibits warmth	74%	59%
Exhibits hostility	48	37
Praises child	63	57
Punishes physically	53	39

Adapted from Minturn and Lambert, 1964:168. Source: 76 societies drawn from the Human Relations Area Files. Reciprocal percentages of societies were low on the specified maternal practices. Simple families included nuclear families and decentralized polygynous families where each mother occupied a separate dwelling. Complex families consisted of centralized polygynous families and extended families.

The effect of household complexity on maternal behavior may not be straightforward but curvilinear. Minturn and Lambert summarized this relationship as follows:

. . . the presence of grandparents in a house, particularly a grandmother, reduces the isolation of mothers in nuclear families, provides an alternate caretaker, and therefore allows the mother to express more warmth to the children than when she is their sole custodian. But . . . the presence of sisters-in-law or co-wives, often unrelated to the mother and with children of their own to care for, provides a fertile field for bickering and leads to a mating of affects to avoid such strife. In such houses grandmothers must also be wary of showing favoritism which might incite jealousies among their daughters-in-law. (1964:260)

A paradoxical feature of the relationship between family size and maternal warmth is that warmth increases with the number of adults but decreases with the number of cousins. Perhaps this reflects the ratio of adults to children. The larger the ratio, the more affection can be showered on children. The lower the ratio, the more competitive the situation becomes.

Supplementary Control Agents

The previous discussion suggests that complex families not only have additional problems of social control, but also under certain circumstances supply mothers of young children with additional agents of social control.

We have seen that the best system of easing the burden on mothers is the stem family whose extra adults supply no competing children of their own but assist the mother wholeheartedly with the children who are their own grandchildren.

TABLE 18-7 Maternal Responsibility and Instability in Nuclear and Stem Families

| | *FAMILY TYPE* | |
MOTHER'S BEHAVIOR	*Nuclear*	*Stem*
Exclusively responsible for child care	54%	38%
Fluctuates in warmth, hostility	56%	44%
Number of families	50	25

Adapted from Minturn and Lambert, 1964:263,267. Source: Sample families in one local community in India, Mexico, Okinawa, and the Philippines. Reciprocal percentages of mothers did not exhibit the specified behavior.

Table 18-7 shows that stem families in four different societies provided assistance which nuclear mothers could less easily obtain. Only a minority of mothers in stem families had to bear the full responsibility of caring for their children because the grandparents were unwilling to help out. By contrast, most mothers in nuclear families had full responsibility for their children. The strain created by sole responsibility is evidenced in the nuclear mothers' tendency to emotional instability, fluctuating between positive and negative feelings toward the child.

A direct test of this relationship showed that the less the mother had exclusive responsibility for her children, the less her moods fluctuated in dealing with them. This suggests that mothers in nuclear families and perhaps in mother–child units experience stress because the very simplicity of their family structure affords them no relief from responsibility.

Some relief comes from having extra men around. Minturn and Lambert found that women in households with two or more men present exhibited less emotional instability toward children than those with only one man. Extra women are more directly useful as caretakers, however, especially for infants. The larger the number of women in the household, the less apt mothers were to carry the burden of infant care alone (and to a lesser extent to care for older children alone).

When Minturn and Lambert examined particular societies, the United States headed the list in the proportion of time that children were in the hands of their mothers. Babies were cared for primarily by their mothers in 79 percent of the New England homes, and older children (age 3 to 10) in 92 percent of those homes (in contrast to an average of 54 percent of nuclear families in the societies portrayed in Table 18-7). This heavy responsibility of American mothers was commented on by the researchers:

The mothers of Orchard Town, living as they do in nuclear family households isolated from their kinsmen, spend more of their time in charge of their children than the mothers of any other group. This isolation from a kin group not only means that other women are not around to help with baby care, but that the number of older children who may help is also less, since child caretakers may be cousins as well as siblings. This isolation of the New England mothers is enhanced by the fact that their older children are in school and their husbands work away from home. (1964:100)

Another study gives an inkling of the chief sources from which New England mothers get any help at all. Table 18-8 shows that when middle-class American mothers got any outside help, they relied most on employed mother substitutes. Working class families, lacking the financial resources to hire such care, relied on voluntary help. In the lower-lower class Puerto Rican families, that help was perhaps more compulsory than voluntary, as older siblings were pressed into baby-sitting.

TABLE 18-8   Supplementary Child-Care Agents, by Social Class

NON-PARENTAL CHILD-CARE AGENTS	SOCIAL CLASS		
	Lower-Lower*	Upper-Lower**	Upper-Middle**
Older sibling	65%	7%	2%
Grandmother	12	61	35
Other relatives	17	20	5
Maid, sitter, friend	6	12	58
Total	100%	100%	100%
Number of families	18	174	198

Adapted from Landy, 1959:210. Sources: Rural Puerto Rican families with incomes under $800 per year. U. S. data from a study in Greater Boston by Maccoby *et al.* which has been reported elsewhere in different form (1954).
* Puerto Rico
** U. S.

The reliance of Puerto Rican mothers on their older children to care for their babies is reminiscent of the only one of Minturn and Lambert's six societies in which a majority of babies were cared for by older children, namely Kenya. There, polygyny forced mothers to work to support their own subfamilies, and made it difficult to care for their infants without commandeering the help of their older children. A few years later the same mothers bore heavy responsibility for the care of their older children (almost as much as the New England mothers) because by the time their children reached primary school age, the children were needed to assist their mothers with the field work as well as with the care of the latest baby.

Although New England mothers carried the heaviest child-rearing responsibilities, the polygynous mothers of Kenya had the heaviest domestic responsibilities as a whole. Presumably this explains why Kenyan mothers far exceeded even the second-place Americans in the unpredictability of the warmth and hostility they directed toward their children:

These mothers not only have almost complete responsibility of the care of children, but must, with the help of their children, farm the gardens and care for the herds allocated to them by their husbands. They are, as a group, the busiest and most harassed of all the mothers in our study. This harassment is evidently reflected in their temperamental instability. Suspicious of their hostile co-wives, whom they often view as witches, and their husbands' relatives, who may be their own families' enemies, overburdened with work in their fields, which they do without their husband's help, plagued with the responsibility of keeping their own children out of trouble with their neighbors and with the necessity of being hypocritically friendly with people they may hate, these mothers are extremely irritable and unpredictable with their children. They frequently cane children, particularly the younger ones; they expect instant obedience but may ignore disobedience if their children absent themselves until their anger is abated. (Minturn and Lambert, 1964:89)

The rank order of societies in terms of the mother's instability is neatly correlated with the parent–child ratio:

Kenya (polygynous)	100% unstable
New England (nuclear)	58%
Mexico (fraternal)	55%
India (cloistered extended)	46%
Okinawa (extended)	21%
Philippines (extended)	17%

In polygynous Kenya the wife must cope with her children unaided by even a husband. In nuclear New England, husband and wife together managed the children. In fraternal Mexico, the nuclear families were loosely associated around the courtyard, but the father and mother again were primarily responsible for the children. In joint-family India, the older generation was present to help but the cloistering of women placed them under emotional tension from which they could not escape. Only in Okinawa and the Philippines did mothers have the regular assistance of the husband's parents and at the same time the opportunity to leave home freely. They experienced the full benefits of the extra adults in extended families.

In the Philippines, the field researchers remarked on the lightness of the care-taking burden for mothers of pre-school children:

The preschooler's caretakers are many, and, in effect, all the children of the housing group belong to all the households. A child desiring a drink of water, assistance in fixing a plaything, or a little sympathy over a skinned knee may go home for it or to a grandmother or to any of a variety of "aunties." . . . In the same way, any of the group of adults will chastise any child observed misbehaving: "We all help to raise our children" is a recurrent statement from mothers and fathers who clearly find this a satisfying system. No mother need worry overmuch if her child does stray a bit far from home, for she knows that any adult seeing him headed for possible trouble will prevent it, scold him for his irresponsibility, and send him home, thus reinforcing her own warnings. (Nydegger and Nydegger, 1963:834)

Thus, the larger the number of adults who share in meeting the children's needs and controlling their behavior, the less the strain on the mother.

Stem families give mothers the most help; decentralized polygynous families, the least. Paradoxically, then, the very decentralization which relieves tension between women in polygynous families increases the mother's isolation. Conversely the subordination of a young mother to her mother-in-law in an extended family embeds her in a structure of assistance in raising her children. Indeed, from the standpoint of the extended family, those children are not just hers but the property and responsibility of the whole family headed by the grandparents.

chapter nineteen

THE STRUCTURAL CONSEQUENCES OF DIFFERENTIAL EXTERNAL INVOLVEMENTS

Having examined the structural problems of complex families, I turn now to structural variations within simple families. The ordinary structure of marriage in nuclear families is equalitarian. However, around the equalitarian norm there is a wide range of variation in the structure of particular families. Variations have numerous causes, some too psychological to concern us, some too idiosyncratic to be generalizable. But much of the variation in the structure of marriage results from variance in the participation of the members of the family in external social systems.

The most important facet of the structure of marriage is the power structure. The chief determinant of the balance of power between husband and wife is the resources which they bring to marriage. Those resources are derived from participation in external social systems. Some of that participation occurs prior to marriage and some during marriage. In either case, the resources of money, information, self-confidence, etc., which the partners bring to the bargaining table determine whether they will be equals or whether one partner will dominate.

Although my main focus will be on industrial societies, the resource theory of power is relevant to other societies as well. In agrarian societies, the patriarchal position of the man derived from the wife's insulation from the outside world. With the man as the sole link between the family and society, he naturally dominated the crucial decisions, especially those involving transactions between the family and the external system.

Although feudal women generally had a weak bargaining position, even such societies allowed some variation. In describing husband–wife relationships in feudal Japan, Goode noted some sources of variance between families:

> The subordination of the wife to her husband or his family is a function of the bargaining position allotted to her by her individual qualities and the social structure. Strong-willed women, wise women, beautiful women, are not easy to dominate in any society or in any period. The bargaining position of any given segment of women, leaving aside their individual differences, is determined by the extent to which the society gives them opportunities for production, decision, and action outside the control of their

men. Their wishes must be respected more, because husbands and families wish to continue receiving the benefits of this outside activity, whether it is money, power, or prestige. (1963:346)

Although I will focus on the structure of husband–wife relationships, I will occasionally refer to variation in relations between parents and children which result from the children's participation in external systems. Although the intergenerational balance has been less thoroughly studied than the marital balance, the same basic theory applies throughout the family: External participation increases the individual's resources and thereby increases the leverage which he exerts in interpersonal situations. To be more precise, the increasing involvement of children in external systems as they grow older provides a basis for gradual emancipation from parental authority and for gradually equalizing their position *vis-à-vis* their parents. As they grow older, they gain in experience, knowledge and wisdom which gives them a basis for challenging their parents' dictates. The longer they go to school, the better educated they become until eventually their education may eclipse their parents', undermining or even overturning their parents' authority. When they move out from under the father's roof, they become independent of parental authority. When they join peer groups and formal organizations, they acquire bases for challenging the father's authority. When they get married, they enter an external relationship which is expected to take priority over their residual loyalty to their parents. When they take jobs working for others, they acquire financial resources and no longer must depend on "the hand that feeds them"—they can start "biting" it if they choose.

In such tangible ways, children gain power over against their parents, wives against husbands, and husbands against wives. The final balance of power between any two sets of family members depends on the balance of resources which family members derive from participation in external systems. Although to some extent the power structure of a family can be predicted simply from knowing how much a single family member (such as the wife) participates outside the family, the best predictions can be derived by comparing the relative rates of participation of all persons whose balance of power is being assessed. Thus the comparative participation of husband and wife or of parents and children most directly indicates who is likely to dominate the relationship. In general, whoever participates more actively in the external system can be expected to dominate the family.

PRIOR INVOLVEMENTS

Simply for convenience, I will discuss outside involvements in chronological order. The earliest involvements are conferred on the child by his parents and affect not only the structure of marriage but the structure of the premarital dyad. The latter in turn sets a precedent for marital interaction patterns.

Differential Birth Order

Perhaps the logical place to begin is at birth. We saw in Chapter 17 that the sibling group tends to be structured by the order of birth. This means that children begin to be shaped into domineering or submissive marriage partners from the moment of birth. Their childhood participation in their family of origin gives them major resources if they are first-born and meagre resources if they are middle-born. I assume that if a first-born son or daughter marries a middle-born child, the balance of power will favor the first-born child.

Unfortunately the effect of the comparative birth order of the husband and wife on the power structure of marriage has not been studied. However, my Tokyo research compared the marriages of eldest sons with the marriages of younger sons (disregarding variation in the birth order of their wives). Japanese society traditionally emphasized the distinction between elder sons as potential heads of the stem family and younger sons. As recently as 1958, Dore described in the present tense:

> . . . the general tendency to give precedence to the eldest son in all matters of daily life. He is early given a sense of his own importance as heir designate; he has the use of the family bath before his brothers; he is given the most tasty part of the fish; he is generally indulged more than his younger brothers . . . ; if money for education is scarce, he would have a superior claim. (p. 124)

Given such an inflated role in life from childhood, elder sons should be more domineering than their younger brothers.

TABLE 19-1   The Structural Consequences of the Husband's Birth Order

	HUSBAND'S BIRTH ORDER	
	First-born	Other
Husband's power	5.30	5.12
Wife's task performance	4.69	4.33
Wife feels like a servant	0.50	0.39
Wife tells troubles to her husband	3.07	3.00
Husband tells troubles to his wife	2.26	2.32
Minimum number of cases	198	244

Adapted from Blood, 1967:147. Source: Middle-class young Tokyo married couples.

Table 19-1 shows that eldest sons tended to dominate their wives in family decision-making and to help their wives less with the housework. As a result, their wives were more apt to feel like servants than wives of younger sons. However, there was some compensation in being married to a superior husband. He offered a stronger shoulder to weep on, as evidenced by the greater tendency of wives to tell their troubles to eldest-son husbands. Conversely, those superior beings told their troubles less to their servant wives.

In general, then, husbands who have participated in the superior status of eldest son in their childhood families tend to dominate their own families just as they dominated their younger siblings. Presumably eldest sons married to junior daughters are even more domineering than those challenged by eldest-daughter wives who have becomed accustomed to positions of responsibility in their own sibling group.

Differential Age

It follows logically from all we know about the dominance of younger generations by older generations and of younger siblings by their elders that a younger spouse should be dominated by an older spouse. To live longer is to gain more experience and wisdom. Therefore an older man with a young wife should have a father–daughter relationship and an older woman seems likely to mother a young husband. In childhood, differences of as little as a year matter greatly, especially when they involve a difference in grade in school. Once adulthood is reached, however, age differences become less visible unless they are wide. Therefore I do not expect age differences to have much effect on husband–wife relationships unless the gap is fairly sizable.

TABLE 19-2   Husband's Power by Comparative Age of Husband and Wife

| | COMPARATIVE AGE | | | | | | |
| | HUSBAND OLDER | | | | EQUAL | WIFE OLDER | |
	11+	7–10	4–6	1–3	EQUAL	1–3	4+ years
Husband's Power							
Detroit	6.09	5.80	5.43	5.21	4.97	4.78	5.00
Tokyo	—	5.10	5.23	5.21	5.30	4.92	—
Number of cases							
Detroit	23	42	85	147	36	37	11
Tokyo	—	53	125	148	47	24	—

Adapted from Blood, 1967:144. Source: Young Detroit couples of all social classes and Tokyo middle-class couples. The extreme categories for Tokyo have been combined because of the small numbers of cases so they should read "husband older by seven or more years" and "wife older by one or more years."

Table 19-2 shows for Detroit that with a single exception, the greater the husband's age exceeded the wife's, the more he tended to dominate the relationship. The exception is peculiar, however, because wives who were four or more years older should have been conspicuously powerful. Why they were not may be an artifact of the small number of cases involved. However, my Tokyo findings were even less regular, exhibiting a curvilinearity which does not fit my resource theory. Therefore, for the time being at least, generalizations about the effect of comparative age on marital power structure must be viewed skeptically. Perhaps when differences are more sizable than the range represented in the table, the effect on marriage would be more predictable. But within the relatively narrow range represented in this analysis, length of participation in life must be considered a weak and unreliable supplier of resources affecting the structure of marriage.

Premarital Relationships   In Jamaica, Blake found that older women made heavier demands on men than young girls as a price for entering into quasi-marital liaisons. The reason for their greater demands was not simply that they had gained independence by living longer but that they had gained encumbrances:

> . . . since available older women usually have a number of illegitimate children to support (and hence are seeking both conjugal stability and financial aid), a relationship with a young girl has distinct advantages for a man and very few penalties. . . . to a young lower-class girl as distinct from an older one, a man's ability to give even a pittance makes him appear both powerful and attractive—a fact that makes young girls ideal casual partners. (1961:89)

In other words, young Jamaican girls were easily impressed and therefore could be obtained cheaply. In the United States, Kanin (1957) found that high school girls were more apt to be exploited sexually by men appreciably older than themselves than by boys the same age. In a total sample of relationships involving equal numbers of sexually aggressive and nonaggressive males, only 37 percent of same-aged boys were aggressive but 67 percent of 3–5 years older ones and 81 percent of six-or-more years older men offended their dating partners (1957:199). Presumably this higher frequency of sexual aggressiveness reflected both the greater sexual experience of the older men and their tendency to dominate younger and weaker girls.

Perhaps age differences affect these premarital relationships more consistently than marital relationships because a few years make so much difference in maturity for girls of high-school age. Perhaps differences in age between husbands and wives have an initial impact on their relationship but tend to be eclipsed by more active contemporary involvements later in marriage. In any case, age differences are at best a crude indicator of differential prior involvement in the world at large.

Differential Inheritance

Since many of the crucial decisions in marriage have to do with the allocation of money, whichever partner has contributed more wealth to the family exchequer should have a special say in deciding how it is to be used.

Many feudal societies did not allow women to inherit wealth or own property. But in Muslim law, the woman could own property. Goode reported that even though her husband usually managed whatever property she brought into the marriage, "she did have a certain independence of at least a small sort" which derived from her financial contribution. (1963:139)

Theoretically a Muslim woman was entitled to half as large a share in the family estate as a brother. Even though most women did not actually claim that share, this gave them further leverage over their husbands because it gave them a basis for claiming support from the brother who held the inheritance in trust. For Goode, this created "the possibility of at least a mild rebellion" against the husband (Ibid). Such rebelliousness was unthinkable in societies where women were excluded from inheritance and ownership of property.

In Muslim Java, Geertz implied that inheritance might substantially alter the structure of marriage:

A woman can own in her own name property that was hers before the marriage or that was settled on her in inheritance from her kindred. Such property—a rice field, a house, jewelry, a horse cart, a supply of cloths for sale —may even be the principal source of family income, which, in turn, is hers to dispose of as she sees fit. The property of the man, too, from outside the marriage is strictly his own. (1961:125)

Two factors were involved here: which partner received an inheritance and whether that partner had the right to spend that inheritance irrespective of the wishes of the spouse. In Java, the ability of wives not only to inherit wealth but to spend it as they saw fit made them potentially powerful.

TABLE 19-3 Husband's Power by Inheritance of Farm by Husband or Wife, by Size of Farm

HUSBAND'S POWER BY SIZE OF FARM	HEIR		WIFE/HUSBAND DIRECTION
	Husband	Wife	
Small (under 5 hectares)	5.01	4.56	—
Medium (5 to 20 hectares)	5.99	4.25	—
Large (20+ hectares)	6.81	4.62	—

Adapted from Lupri, 1969:142. Source: Representative sample of farm families in West Germany. The total number of inheriting husbands was 406, of inheriting wives 339.

In West Germany, almost half of the representative sample of farms studied by Lupri were inherited from the wife's family. Table 19-3 shows that husbands were far less powerful when they married into the wife's family than when the wife came to live on his farm. In the latter case, the larger the farm, the more powerful the husband (as would be expected from our study of stratification in Chapter 2). The effect of the size of the wife's inheritance on the balance of power was less clear. We might say that with one reversal, the larger the wife's inheritance, the more powerful she was, too, but differences were neither as large nor as regular. One reason for the ambiguity of the effect of the wife's inheritance was that the husband became the farm manager and thereby acquired power to offset the wife's inherited resources. The wife turned her inheritance over to her husband and thereby placed some power in his hands.

In general, I conclude that whichever partner inherits the most wealth from his parents tends to dominate the marriage, especially if custom allows him to dispose of that wealth autonomously.

Differential Class Background

Closely related to inheritance of property are other less tangible resources conferred by the family upon their children. Self-confidence, knowledge, and skill in human relations are some of the benefits which children acquire from high-status families and which place them in a powerful position in dealing with the opposite sex, both premaritally and maritally.

We have already seen that older men were more apt to commit sexual aggression against high-school students. Table 19-4 shows that college men

TABLE 19-4   Maximum Premarital Intimacy, by Comparative Social Class of Partners

MAXIMUM PREMARITAL INTIMACY	COMPARATIVE SOCIAL CLASS			GIRL/BOY DIRECTION
	Boy Higher	Equal	Girl Higher	
Holding hands	6%	6%	20%	+
Necking, light petting	13	39	47	+
Heavy petting	16	26	16	=
Sexual intercourse	66	30	18	−
Total	101%	101%	101%	
Number of relationships	154	531	107	

Adapted from Ehrmann (1959):147. Source: 531 male students at the University of Florida (Gainesville) enrolled in a course on preparation for marriage, reporting their experience in dating various partners. Of the 531 men in the study, 338 had dated only at their own class level; 86 dated both equals and lower girls; 39, both equals and superior girls; and 68, at all three levels. Necking and light petting included kissing, hugging, and fondling the girl's clothed breasts. Social class was measured in terms of father's occupation.

were more intimate with lower-status girls and less intimate with girls from higher-status backgrounds. The latter finding is interesting because college men from lower-class backgrounds originated in a social context characterized by intense sexual involvement. However, we saw earlier that Kinsey found upwardly mobile men even more conservative sexually than men born into higher-class positions. Now perhaps we have a reason for their conservative behavior. If a college man from a lower-class family dates a girl from a middle-class family, he feels more timid and pushes her less far (or the girl resists him more). Their relationship tends to be dominated by the girl.

Conversely, Ehrmann found that when a Florida man went home and dated a "townie," he was more apt to have intercourse than when he dated his fellow coeds. Partly this may have been "exploitation" of vulnerable, impressionable girls; partly a willingness of non-college girls to go all the way with college men in hope of trapping them in marriage. In either case, the man dominated the situation when the girl was not only from a lower-class background but was not a college student herself and seemed destined to remain permanently in a lower status (unless she succeeded in marrying her superior dating partner).

Presumably when interclass marriages occur, the partner from the higher class background again dominates the relationship. The same attitudes which influenced the premarital relationship presumably continue to hold sway. Moreover, a differential flow of help from the two sets of kin would provide an imbalance in the couple's family-supplied resources (i.e., the family with the higher standing seems likely to give more gifts than the poorer family, strengthening the power position of the superior partner). At the same time, the superior partner is likely to participate more effectively in external systems because of his childhood advantages, further strengthening his position in the marriage.

Komarovsky found that blue-collar husbands married to wives of higher class backgrounds were conspicuously unhappy. Any inter-class marriage is liable to create a clash of cultures between the partners, but if the wife has the higher status, this conflicts with the "natural" superiority of men discussed in Chapter 16. The result is apt to be a power struggle between an aggressive wife and a resistant husband:

> A characteristic conflict of such a marriage concerns social life—especially as regards recreational activities without the children. "He likes us all to be together all the time and I'd like to leave the children home and have us do things by ourselves sometimes," said a mother of four children, a high school graduate who married "down." "Sometimes I think it's because he didn't have any education and he has nothing else to do or to think about than just relaxing at home with the TV." The couple disagree about baby-sitters. The husband shares the frequently held attitude of low blue-collar families: "I wouldn't leave my children with a stranger." The wife on the other hand would prefer to pay a stranger instead of depending upon services given by relatives that she would have to repay. Social life is a bone of contention in still another way. The husband expects relatives to join in all the social entertaining, but the wife considers personal congeniality on social occasions to take precedence over ties to kin. Education is another subject of disagreements in this family. The husband resents the money spent by his wife on the *Reader's Digest* and its series of abridged books. He does help the young children with their homework but frequently feels that chores around the house are more important than school work, while his wife emphasizes the latter. The yearning for a more romantic approach to love-making was expressed by one 34-year-old high school graduate who married a rough, less educated but benevolent patriarch. "I'd be happy if we'd just go along the road and park somewhere sometimes," she said. "What do you think you're doing?" he is likely to say. "We're too old for that kind of stuff." This is a restless, energetic woman with an inquiring mind, married to a good provider who likes his home and wants to be left alone to enjoy his comfort. She tries to stimulate and to rouse him but succeeds only in evoking a stubborn defensiveness. (1964:333–334)

These cases suggest the unwillingness of wives from superior family backgrounds to submit to the husband's life pattern. When the husband is superior, we may similarly expect him to dominate the marriage but with less stress and less resistance from the wife.

Differential Education

While all the preceding factors are beyond the individual's control, education depends more on the individual's initiative and therefore should be more closely related to the role played in marriage. I assume that the more actively and successfully one participates in activities outside the home, the more actively and successfully one will participate in the decision-making process at home.

Education is one component in stratification. Whereas in the preceding section the individual's family background determined his class position, now the question is the individual's own education. Since the child's education (and class position) may differ from his family's this provides a more direct measure of the individual's resources.

The specific hypothesis is that whichever partner has more education will dominate the relationship. The resources include knowledge and communication skills relevant to decision-making and also preparation for more effective participation in the outside world. Thus the educated person is not only more skillful in dealing directly with his partner but more skillful in bringing home various kinds of intangible as well as tangible "bacon."

TABLE 19-5   Husband's Power by Comparative Education of Husband and Wife

| HUSBAND'S POWER BY | | COMPARATIVE EDUCATION | | | WIFE/HUSBAND |
Country	Location	Husband More	Equal	Wife More	DIRECTION
France	Paris–Bordeaux	2.07	1.99	1.85	—
Germany	Urban	5.27	4.75	4.81	—
	Farm	6.01	5.42	5.05	—
Greece	Athens	2.67	2.80	2.67	=
Japan	Tokyo middle-class	5.25	5.07	4.88	—
U.S.A.	Detroit	5.45	5.22	4.91	—
Yugoslavia	Kragujevac auto workers	2.37	2.05	1.90	—

Adapted from Michel (1967):341; Lupri (1969):143; Safilios-Rothschild (1967):349; Blood (1967):154; Blood and Wolfe (1960):38; and Buric and Zecevic (1967):329 respectively.

Table 19-5 shows that with only two reversals out of 14 paired comparisons, the partner with more education dominated the marital decision-making while equally-educated partners fell in between. The fact that this finding was supported in six different countries on three continents and in both urban and rural samples in the case of Germany makes this one of the most thoroughly tested generalizations in family sociology. More detailed analysis showed that this relationship held up even when controlled by social class in the United States and by size of farm in West Germany. Therefore, this finding is not simply a result of the fact that better-educated husbands tend to be located in the middle class and inferior-educated husbands in the working class. Similarly the restriction of the Tokyo sample to middle-class couples again suggests that the difference in education was directly responsible for differences in the balance of power.

Komarovsky found that high-school-educated wives of drop-out husbands exercised their superior position in marriage to resist their husbands' sexual advances and were often described by their husbands as sexually frigid. The same wives criticized their husbands for selfishly spending their leisure away from home, coming and going as they pleased, and giving no help with the housework. Wives who hadn't finished high school were not happy about these characteristics but were less apt to criticize the husband overtly.

Komarovsky also found that educationally inferior husbands got along conspicuously badly with their mothers-in-law, presumably because the latter were critical and domineering like their daughters. In general, then, superior-educated wives tend to be disappointed with their husbands and express that disappointment both to the husband and to their mothers.

In feudal India, Goode pointed out that the husband's traditional authority "was based to a considerable extent on the fact that the bride was not only very young but uneducated, and had little opportunity to taste the experience of the outside world" (1963:259). He added that Indian men with superior educations often had acquired an equalitarian ideology but their inferior wives were neither willing nor able to claim the rights their husbands were prepared to grant them.

This suggests that the balance of power in marriage is not likely to change just because one partner thinks it should, but only if the balance of resources is changed. If men want their wives to share power with them, women must be given educational or other external resources which will enable them to do so. Once women acquire as much education as their men, they will seize power whether their husbands want them to or not.

CONTEMPORARY INVOLVEMENTS

Although education is ordinarily completed prior to marriage, some societies provide opportunities for further education after marriage. If an equalitarian husband really wanted his less-educated wife to catch up with him, he could send her to school. By furthering her education, she would raise her power position both immediately and for the longer run. While she was attending school, the opportunity to get away from home and to secure the independent authority of her teachers and books would emancipate her from depending on her husband. Even after she quit school, the memory of that independence and the knowledge and skills she had gained would continue to bolster her self-confidence.

Postmarital formal education is relatively rare in comparison to other forms of external participation. Instead of the school system, adults participate in the occupational system and in other formal organizations and informal groups. The occupational system is important because of the tangibility of the financial resources which it provides. But all external activities tend to bolster the mental and emotional resources of the active spouse, regardless of whether more visible benefits may be earned.

Differential Occupational Participation

One reason for the subordination of elite women in feudal societies was their retirement from productive work. Peasant women in the same societies and most wives in primitive societies had a more equalitarian relationship because they shared the responsibility for keeping their family alive. The farm work of peasant women and the fishing and gathering of wild fruits and berries by primitive women were indispensable to the physical welfare of their families and earned them the respect and gratitude of their husbands and children.

In industrial societies, economic activity for the wife is more optional. We can expect to find major differences in the structure of marriage depending on whether or not the wife works. Moreover, her work should affect her relationship not only with her husband but with her children and the relationship of sons and daughters with each other. Therefore the consequences of the wife's employment will need to be examined not simply for the structure of marriage but for the structure of the whole family. (Theoretically this could be done for other forms of external participation, but the research literature is most adequate here.) Finally, I will examine the consequences for parent–child relationships of the employment of children themselves outside the home.

The Wife's Employment and the Balance of Power in Marriage   First let me document some of the assertions I have made about the effect of the economic contribution of women in premodern societies. Goode noted that in Japanese fishing villages where the men were away most of the time, farming fell by default to the women. Nor was this their only responsibility:

> They also helped prepare for the fishing expedition and later took part in processing the catch. In some coastal areas, women were also divers. In mountain villages devoted to forestry, again the women did much of the farming and helped the men in their work. Where silk culture was important, before the industry moved to the cities, women did much of that work. Indeed, Koyama comments on the strong position of the woman, "Only fifty years ago, the wife who was gainfully employed in the early stage of the silk textile industry was known for her . . . petticoat government." (1963:346)

Thus even in a country noted for its patriarchal tradition, women who engaged in productive activity had a powerful voice in family affairs. Presumably it was chiefly in elite families whose women did not dirty their hands that the patriarchal tradition flourished.

In Java, Geertz noted that the position of women was generally "very strong" and attributed this to the fact that women could not only own land and supervise its cultivation but could enter most occupations. This meant that "a woman has no difficulty supporting herself and her children, should she want to" (1961:45).

The ability to be self-supporting gives the wife in any society leverage *vis-à-vis* her husband. If she doesn't like something he is doing, she can threaten to leave. In this sense, the wife's ability to go to work is perhaps the most powerful lever she could possibly have, her ultimate weapon to be used if all else fails. Other resources may be useful in bargaining with the husband, but the possibility of quitting the marriage altogether requires economic resources. If those resources are not available from anywhere else (such as from relatives), the ability to be self-supporting gives the wife a base of economic security and makes it impossible for the husband to wield his authority over her unchallenged.

Table 19-6 shows that without exception, the balance of power in marriage in six different countries reflected the comparative employment status of husbands and wives. Cases in which only the wife is employed have seldom been studied in cross-section samples, mostly because such cases are so rare in the general population that they must be located by special methods. The finding from the U.S.A. suggests that the balance of power shifts more drastically when the wife becomes the sole supporter of the family than when she is just a supplementary supporter.

Additional findings from the studies represented in Table 19-6 give more details about the effect of the wife's employment on the balance of power. (1) Wives who worked full-time gained more power than those who worked only part-time (Germany). (2) The more years the wife worked after marriage, the more powerful she became (U.S.A.). (3) In a detailed analysis of my Detroit data, I found that working wives had more influence over major economic decisions (what car to buy, what house to choose, whether to buy insurance, and whether the wife should work) but their influence decreased over internal household decisions such as what doctor to call when someone is sick (Blood, 1963:292). This suggests that an outside occupation increases the wife's influence over decisions governing the allocation of economic resources but that this increase in power may be partially offset by decreased power in areas related to her traditional child-rearing role.

TABLE 19-6 Husband's Power by Comparative Employment Status of Husband and Wife

| | EMPLOYMENT STATUS | | |
COUNTRY	Husband Only Employed	Both Employed	Wife Only Employed
France	2.03	1.90	—
Germany (urban)	5.40	4.52	—
Greece	2.78	2.33	—
Japan	5.40	4.92	—
U.S.A.	5.44	4.48	2.67
Yugoslavia	2.79	1.94	—

Adapted from Michel, 1967:339; Lupri, 1969:140; Safilios-Rothschild, 1967:347; Blood, 1967:163; Blood and Wolfe, 1960:40; and Buric and Zecevic, 1967:328 respectively. Samples were the same as in Table 19-5 except for omission of the German farm families. The effect of employment status on the balance of power in the urban German sample held when controlled by the husband's income and occupational status.

Closely related to the decreased involvement of working wives in decisions affecting their children is a tendency of the same wives to reduce or eliminate having children at all. To be sure, wives sometimes work because they are unable to have children. But the evidence is reasonably clear that many wives reduce their childbearing because they are already employed or wish to work in the future.

Potts (1967) reported that in certain Eastern European countries, legal abortions were three times as common among working wives as among full-time housewives. Freedman et al. (1959) found that a larger proportion of working wives in the United States used contraception than in the case of non-working wives. Such data suggest that working wives are not only more independent of their husbands but assert their independence of the claims of potential children who might interfere with their continued employment. Thus working wives wield their power in a variety of nontraditional ways.

The Wife's Employment and the Division of Labor in Marriage   As soon as the wife leaves home to work elsewhere, the family time budget is drastically altered. Generally speaking, the hours she is away are subtracted from the hours she is at home. Consequently she is less available to engage in her usual domestic activities. Either she must sleep less, play less, or work less around the house—or perhaps curtail all three.

TABLE 19-7   Wife's Working Hours by Employment Status and Number of Children

| Employed outside home? | NUMBER OF CHILDREN | | | | | | | |
| | None | | One | | Two | | Three+ | |
	No	Yes	No	Yes	No	Yes	No	Yes
Hours/week devoted to:								
Housework	55	27	53	32	56	36	55	39
Child-rearing	0	0	17	8	19	11	23	11
Employment, commuting	0	51	0	45	0	37	0	34
Total	55	78	70	84	75	84	78	84

Adapted from Girard, 1958:606–607. Source: 1,020 urban French wives under age 47. Excluded from the table were time spent in eating, sleeping, personal care, entertainment and rest in and outside the home, religious activity, and helping the husband with his work.

Table 19-7 does not give direct information on sleep, or recreation, but the longer work-week totals for working wives must necessarily be deducted from non-work activities. That employed mothers were approaching the limits of human capacity is suggested by the fact that no matter how many children they had, their total work week failed to rise beyond an 84-hour maximum. Apparently twelve hours a day, seven days a week, is about as many working hours as the average wife can squeeze out of other activities. The limits to human capacity are also suggested by the fact that the larger the number of children, the fewer hours the wife worked outside the home. Because extra children require more care and more supporting household activities, such wives could less easily spare the time for full-time employment. But if we remember that the reason why most wives work is primarily economic and that larger families have greater financial need, we can sense the pressure on working mothers.

In working-wife families, time devoted both to child care and to housework is sharply curtailed. Children suffer the biggest percentage decline and housework the biggest absolute loss. Betty Friedan (1963) would claim that most of these losses reflected increased efficiency rather than reduced performance. But the fact that the third and subsequent children required four more hours of work from nonemployed wives but got no more care from employed mothers throws this interpretation in doubt.

The best test of this question is whether working mothers require the assistance of their husbands and children in getting the housework done. If so, this indicates that increased efficiency does not solve the problem completely.

Table 19-8 shows that in three countries, the balance of housework shifted inversely with the balance of external employment. Whether husbands helped their wives voluntarily or were drafted into housework cannot be ascertained, but the average working wife's husband helped more around the house.

If marriage were really a 50/50 proposition, we might expect the division of housework to become 50/50 when both partners hold outside jobs.

TABLE 19-8 Husband's Task Performance by Comparative
Employment Status of Husband and Wife

Husband's Task Performance	Husband Only Employed	Both Employed	Wife Only Employed	Both/Husband Direction
Belgium	1.47	1.84	—	+
Japan	5.23	6.15	—	+
U.S.A.	3.32	5.02	6.67	+

Adapted from Silverman and Hill, 1967:356; Blood, 1967:163; Blood and Wolfe, 1960:62.
The Belgian sample was representative of the Louvain metropolitan area.

Husbands are not generally that helpful, however. In one American study, the number of hours devoted to household tasks by husbands increased only from 15 percent to 25 percent of the total (Blood and Hamblin, 1958). Thus, the main burden of responsibility for housework continued to rest on the wives' shoulders even when they had full-time jobs elsewhere. Husbands carried an increased share of that burden but rarely an equal share.

My 1963 analysis showed that Detroit husbands of working wives were more apt to do all the lawn-mowing and snow-shoveling since their wives were too busy to do such outside work. They helped their wives more with such traditional feminine tasks as getting their own breakfasts, doing the evening dishes, and straightening up the living room when company was coming. They also took over a larger share of household repairs and grocery-shopping. Only one task continued to be done by working wives as much as before—keeping track of the money and bills. But this is not a routine chore; it is so closely related to decision-making about the allocation of funds that the working wife's increased involvement in money matters offsets her decreased time, leaving her as active as ever in this critical area.

Although husbands did more housework when their wives worked outside the home, the above shifts meant that they shared some tasks less with their wives (the traditional masculine ones) while they shared feminine tasks more. The trend was therefore mixed as far as sex-linked role assignments were concerned—more traditionally masculine and less traditionally feminine. Both shifts symbolize the strain on couples when wives take outside employment.

The shift into traditional feminine fields is a better indicator of stress than the assumption of masculine tasks. Ordinarily, American men avoid feminine tasks no matter how much time they have on their hands. Ballweg (1967) found that retired husbands with nothing else to do spent more time on masculine tasks like burning trash and repairing furniture but scrupulously avoided the laundry, cleaning, and bed-making. As long as the wife has enough time to do these, most men are content to let her do them alone. Only when dual employment creates a crisis are men willing to cross the traditional boundary line and come to the wife's rescue.

The Mother's Employment and the Structure of the Group of Siblings The English language contains no word for the collectivity of children in a given family and sociology has no concept for the structure of that group. Nevertheless I assume that any group of people who interact with one another for as many years as children growing up in the same home will develop a group structure.

We have already seen that in many societies this group develops a differentiated structure on the basis of sex—the boys higher, the girls lower. Now the question is whether an altered balance of power and division of labor between the parents affects their children. The female parent becomes more powerful and less domesticated as a result of her external employment. Insofar as children identify with the parent of the same sex, daughters might be expected to become more assertive and less domesticated like their mothers. Insofar as the mother's exodus creates a crisis in the division of labor, children of both sexes, like their fathers, may be pressed into domestic service. Predictions must be ambiguous about the daughter's role in the division of labor but we can more confidently predict that daughters will become assertive in imitation of their mothers.

TABLE 19-9   Sons' and Daughters' Domestic and External Employment by Mother's Employment Status

| | MOTHER'S EMPLOYMENT STATUS | | EMPLOYED/NOT RATIO |
	Not Employed	Employed	
Median Domestic Chores			
Sons	9.4	11.1	1.18X
Daughters	24.7	25.3	1.02
Percentage Employed Outside the Home			
Sons	46%	29%	0.63X
Daughters	16	36	2.25

Adapted from Roy, 1961:343. Source: Rural high school students in Stevens County, Washington. Urban students were analyzed separately and showed the same pattern.

The mother's employment affects sons and daughters more complexly and less consistently than the relationship between husband and wife. Table 19-9 presents a few selected findings which are suggestive but not conclusive. Children of both sexes were pressed into domestic service, like their fathers. Since this finding occurs in many studies, we can be fairly confident that all members of the family tend to be recruited into sharing the household chores which the mother abandons when she goes to work.

The bottom half of the table presents a finding which is not supported consistently by other research: girls followed their mothers into outside employment, but boys were more apt to stay home. The researcher thought the boys' lesser employment might result from the increased work they had to do at home. Their sisters apparently were more influenced by their mothers' example than handicapped by their extra burden at home. In any case, daughters of working mothers assumed more responsibility both at home and away from home. Differences were especially marked for rural girls perhaps because it is more difficult for either a rural mother or a rural daughter to secure employment than for a town girl,

A similar example of the role of mothers in "breaking the ice" for their daughters by their own outside employment comes from rural Greece. Lambiri (1965) found that two thirds of the mothers of girls working in the first factory in a previously nonindustrialized community had been employed on other people's land in their own youth whereas only one third of the mothers of girls who declined to go to work in the factory had had such independent employment experience.

Differences in the impact of the mother's employment on children of the two sexes appeared in a carefully matched study of the behavioral characteristics of kindergarten children in two California suburbs. Siegel and her associates (1959) found that maternal employment made daughters more aggressive, self-reliant, and sociable and less obedient. For every variable, the effect on sons was the opposite. These findings suggest that even at age five, daughters sense and respond positively to the more powerful position and assertive behavior of their mothers, whereas sons reflect the lowered power position of their fathers and become somewhat withdrawn and demoralized.

In general, the shift in the balance of power between fathers and mothers is apparently echoed in a corresponding shift in the morale of sons and daughters. Just as working wives become more independent of their husbands, their daughters become more independent of their parents (and vice versa for husbands and sons).

In primitive societies, women cannot secure outside employment, but they may be able to contribute to their family's subsistence by gardening, gathering, fishing and similar activities. Minturn and Lambert found in an analysis of 68 societies in the Human Relations Area Files that the more women engaged in subsistence activities, the more likely they were to expect both sons and daughters to do chores. Again busy mothers kept their children busy.

TABLE 19-10   Direction of Nuptial Economic Flow, by Female Contribution to Subsistence

DIRECTION OF ECONOMIC FLOW AT MARRIAGE	FEMALE CONTRIBUTION TO SUBSISTENCE				
	0–19%	20–29%	30–39%	40–49%	50+%
From wife's side	9%	5%	11%	3%	0%
No payment or mutual exchange	43	51	35	21	29
From husband's side	48	44	54	76	71
Total	100%	100%	100%	100%	100%
Number of societies	56	73	83	68	106

Adapted from Heath, 1958:79. Source: Human Relations Area Files. Contributions from the husband's side included bride-service, bride-price, and sister exchange.

The higher status of economically productive women in primitive societies is suggested in Table 19-10. Although the table contains several reversals, in general the greater the economic value of the woman, the greater the likelihood that her family received some tangible consideration when she was betrothed. To be more precise, the greater the loss the woman was to her family and the bigger the gain to her husband, the higher the price she commanded in the marriage market. Presumably this also meant that she had correspondingly more bargaining power with her husband after marriage.

Thus in both primitive and modern societies, the mother's economic activity places increased responsibility on both sons and daughters, but in the case of daughters this raises their status *vis-à-vis* the opposite sex whether among their brothers or their future husbands.

The Employment of Parents and Children and the Intergenerational Balance
We have already seen that working mothers demand more work of their children. They also demand more of their children in general.

Minturn and Lambert found that women engaged in subsistence activity were less permissive with their children and more punitive for aggression directed against them. This suggests that such mothers exerted more influence over their children in a fashion analogous to the greater influence they exercised over their husbands. In other words, working mothers became powerful women and exercised that power in all directions within the family—both vertically and horizontally.

When the younger generation secure outside employment, their power to defy their parents increases. Goode reported the effects of industrial employment on South African children's relationships to their parents:

> Complaints were widespread . . . that children were not so hard working or obedient as they used to be. The wages now earned by the young were of more monetary value than was the produce of the land and thus the father loses the economic hold over the child and cannot compel him to turn over his wages, or demand support from him in his old age. When the sons wish to establish their own homestead, instead of turning to the older generation for assistance, they can obtain the support of their wives who have some migrant wage earnings before marriage and do not wish to submit to a mother-in-law. (1963:196)

Similarly in Dublin, one of Humphrey's informants talked about the extraordinary independence of girls in terms that could as easily (though perhaps less remarkably) be applied to boys once they secured their first job:

> Once the girls start working, even if they are only fifteen or sixteen years old, they demand a good deal of independence and in nine cases out of ten they get it. That is because they are contributing to the income of the household and because they are supported in their demands by the fact that all the other girls who work also have that independence.
>
> I think that the reason why it was so different when I was a boy is that any claim to independence a boy or a girl might make then, they simply could not back up because they were not bringing in the money they are today. (1966:173)

In general, the external employment of any member of the family—father, mother, or child—is likely to raise his status *vis-à-vis* the other members. Thus the structure of the whole family is influenced by the relative involvement of the various members in the economic system.

Differential Income

Participation in the economic system presumably supplies the husband or wife with a variety of resources, but the most tangible one is money. This is crucial partly because the allocation of money is a crucial test of family power structure and partly because high income signifies successful participation in the economic system. A person with a low income may be working only part-time and/or may have a low-status job and/or may be performing poorly on the job. Any of these reasons for low income would lessen the resources derived from such marginal participation in the economic system. Therefore, the comparative income earned by the two partners when both are employed should alter the balance of power from the more-or-less equalitarian structure which we expect where both the husband and wife are employed outside the home.

TABLE 19-11 Husband's Power by Comparative Income
of Husband and Wife in Dual Income Households

| | COMPARATIVE INCOME | | | WIFE/HUSBAND |
HUSBAND'S POWER	Husband More	Equal	Wife More	DIRECTION
France	1.95	1.92	1.64	—
Germany	5.70	4.34	4.07	—

Adapted from Michel, 1967:341, and Lupri, 1969:143. Source: Paris and Bordeaux, France and national sample of West German cities of 5,000+ population.

Table 19-11 shows that in both France and Germany, whichever partner earned more income held the balance of power. Although this aspect of comparative external participation has been tested in relatively few countries, it seems safe to assume that further research will confirm these findings.

In discussing the impact of children's employment on parent–child relationships, I have already suggested that their ability to be self-supporting undermines their dependence on their parents. Goode noted that traditional Chinese families forbade earning outside income because they suspected it would undermine the elders' authority in the extended family:

> Implicitly, the Chinese always recognized that if the young lived apart from the older generation and had independent incomes, the authority of the elders would be undermined. From the T'ang through the Ch'ing Dynasties, living apart from parents and possessing property of one's own was considered unfilial behavior for which punishment was prescribed. (1963:275)

Independent income, then, raises the status of whoever earns it, whether marriage partners *vis-à-vis* each other or children *vis-à-vis* their parents.

Differential Organizational Participation

To hold a job is not only to earn money and prestige but to participate in an outside organization (an economic organization). In Chapter 5, I suggested that children's participation in the school system gave them an independent base of operation which undermined the unquestioned authority of parents. In Chapter 6 the same phenomenon appeared with reference to children's participation in peer groups. Now the time has come to recognize that this is a general phenomenon which applies to the participation of any member of the family in any kind of organization.

The effect of organizational participation presumably varies with the nature of the organization (economic organizations being most important). Clearly it varies with the extent of participation—whether brief or extensive, marginal or responsible. The higher the position the person holds within the organization, the greater the resources of knowledge and skill he should bring back to his family. In any case, insofar as any two members of the family participated differentially in outside organizations, the relationship between them should be correspondingly altered.

Formal Organizations   Participation in formal organizations is primarily a middle-class phenomenon and is more extensive in the United States than in most countries. Komarovsky found that only a few of her better-educated blue-collar wives were active in organizations. If the husband was less well-educated than the wife, he usually participated less actively or was less of a leader than his wife.

> . . . a few of the more educated wives enjoy wider contacts and a higher status outside the home than their husbands. Thus two wives are PTA presidents while neither of their husbands occupies a position of such eminence. The husbands go to the meetings at which their wives preside. The telephone messages and the correspondence received by these families are largely for the wives. (1964:228)

My guess is that wives who wield such leadership outside the home are also likely to be leaders within the home.

Table 19-12   Husband's Power by Comparative Participation of Husband and Wife in Formal Organizations

FORM OF PARTICIPATION		COMPARATIVE ORGANIZATIONAL PARTICIPATION			WIFE/ HUSBAND DIRECTION
		Husband More	*Equal*	*Wife More*	
Number of organizational memberships	U.S.A.	5.36	5.14	5.05	—
Frequency of church attendance	U.S.A.	5.70	5.21	4.72	—
	Germany	5.10	4.90	4.60	—

Adapted from Blood and Wolfe, 1960:39 and Lupri, 1969:143. Source: Representative samples of Detroit Metropolitan Area and of West German cities. Organizational memberships referred to the number of types of organizations to which the individual belonged (e.g., labor organizations or fraternal organizations).

No information is available about the marital power wielded by organizational leaders, but Table 9-12 does show the impact on the power structure of sheer organizational membership. The fact that this correlates so nicely with marital power is all the more striking because most Detroiters belonged to few organizations and attended meetings infrequently. Moreover, only *types* of organizations were counted, so multiple memberships within the same category were not enumerated. Presumably a direct count of the number of specific organizations, frequency of attendance, and especially leadership positions would even more powerfully predict the structure of marriage.

The remainder of the table shows the effect of the comparative frequency of attending only one type of organization and one type of program —religious services. Comparing the two American indices shows that frequency of church attendance is a more powerful predictor of marital power than simply belonging to formal organizations. Since religious services allow little room for laymen to exercise leadership, at least part of the reason for its influence may be because it offers an entree into church-related organizations where active leadership is possible. Nevertheless, even going to church takes the individual out of the home and exposes him to new ideas. Therefore it is reasonable to assume that church attendance in itself has some bearing on the partners' status in marriage. The fact that this finding is confirmed in Germany increases the likelihood that almost any form of organizational participation has some influence on the marital power structure.

Informal Organizations   Save that they are usually less stratified and therefore offer less differentiated leadership opportunities, informal organizations may provide many of the same resource potentials as formal organizations.

Suttles (1971) has suggested that for slum dwellers, adult peer groups served some of the functions that formal organizations perform for suburbanites. By defending the neighborhood against outside predators, providing connections for getting jobs and know-how about survival in the urban environment, male peer groups provided many of the resources which come through more formal channels for white-collar workers. Thus it seems likely that lower-class men gain resources relevant to their power position within the home from participating in gangs on the street corner or in the neighborhood tavern or poolroom.

Another informal source of resources is the network of kin. Farber hypothesized that differential kin contacts affect the structure of marriage:

> Identity and a great amount of contact with one set of kindred rather than the other provides emotional support and reinforcement within the nuclear family for the parent who is a member of that kindred. . . . Therefore the kindred with whom there is a higher involvement and participation would provide one parent with support and sustenance for maintaining a relatively more powerful position in nuclear family relations. (1966:71)

The influence of unilateral kin may be illustrated by the balance of power in those exceptional marriages in patrilocal societies where the man is recruited into a son-less household to marry the daughter and take over the family name and fortune. Among Greek shepherds:

> After the elder daughters have been married off in the normal manner, the youngest girl marries a man who "goes as bridegroom" into the home of

his wife. . . . Materially, the bridegroom may do very well out of this trans-action, since eventually he becomes the trustee of the whole of his father-in-law's flock. Yet it is difficult to find a man from a family of good standing and moderate wealth to take this step. Particularly in the earlier years [of marriage] a man loses his self-respect and manliness in a situation where he is at the beck and call of his wife's parents, who feel entitled, without embarrassment, to exploit his labour in return for the eventual inheritance of the wife's patrimony. . . . [The Greek shepherds] say of such a bride-groom that his fate is "worse than that of a skinned fox." (Campbell, 1964: 144–5)

Such a husband's loss of self-respect is a subjective reflection of the low power position in which he is placed in dealing with the combined forces of his wife and her family. The wife's kin-reinforced position is improved by the prospective inheritance which the couple will receive through her family line.

Perhaps personal friends and confidantes outside of marriage similarly affect the husband–wife relationship. In the next chapter we will see how such outside relationships cause conflict in marriage—something which may reflect greater independence of the spouse. Insofar as an individual begins to depend on an outside person for emotional support, the jealous reaction of the other partner may reflect a sense of losing control as the partner's power position rises. It seems legitimate to suggest that personal friendships affect the structure of marriage in much the same way as participation in larger social groups.

In short, any personal involvement outside of marriage tends to raise the status of that person inside the marriage. This does not mean that the marriage partner necessarily likes it—indeed more often than not the partner will dislike it since it means a corresponding loss of power for himself. But my concern is not with the subjective evaluation of the change, simply with the fact that external participation alters the structure of marriage.

Separate Residence

We have already seen that in feudal China, not only a separate income but a separate residence was considered an unfilial betrayal of the extended family. To live separately is hardly to participate in an external social system. Rather this is an ecological or geographical factor. In Chapter 9 we saw that geo-graphical mobility strains relationships between separated family members and weakens those relationships. One consequence is a weakening of the hold of the residual family members over the migrating member. Thus the Chinese disapproved of separate residence for children because it would weaken the power of the older generation and correspondingly increase the power of the young to determine their own affairs.

Does migration increase the power of the migrating member *over* the family he has left behind? If the base family wishes to persuade the departing member to return, concessions will have to be made to meet the demands of the absent one. For example, if a husband leaves home, his wife will have to give in to his wishes if he is to be persuaded to return. After a temporary departure at least, the absent one gains power over those whom he has deserted. Waller (1938) labeled this the "principle of least interest," meaning that whichever partner was least interested in maintaining a relationship controlled the behavior of the more interested partner. Indeed, it is not necessary for the least interested one actually to leave—merely to threaten to do so is sufficient to gain the desired ends, provided the other partner wishes to maintain the relationship.

In Arab countries, Goode noted that the ability of the wife to go home made her more powerful than women in countries like Japan or China who could not exert this leverage over the husband:

> . . . the wife typically had insurance in the fact that nowhere in the Arab world did she completely sever her ties with her own family; she never became part of her husband's lineage. This has several structural ramifications. Essentially, it meant that if the wife found life in her new household too difficult, she could always return home. This was not morally scandalous, and she could set conditions for her return to her husband, who would always need her services more than she needed his. . . . the woman's lot was often bettered in her home situation by virtue of this right. (1963:140)

Presumably children who threaten to run away from home or whose relatives or neighbors are willing to take them in gain similar leverage over their parents. Thus, any member of the family may gain power not only by participating in external social systems but simply by going out the door.

ORGANIZATIONAL CRISES

Most families in most societies pass through the processes of family formation and family growth reasonably smoothly and establish family structures which prevent serious conflict among family members. But the crises which afflict some families enable us to understand family structure and functioning even though they are comparatively rare. Some crises result from external invasions (Chapter 20). More result from internal frictions (Chapter 21). Regardless of the causes, crises divide the family into warring camps, undermine the leadership functions of the parents, or shatter the family completely (Chapters 22 and 23).

chapter twenty

EXTERNAL THREATS: INVASION FROM WITHOUT

External involvements may disrupt the family either by luring a member away from the family or by bringing intruders in. It matters little whether the intruders are invited by the whole family or barge in at their own initiative—the violation of the integrity of the family when nonmembers move into the household almost inevitably causes stress.

DOUBLING UP

The most common invaders are primary relatives: parents coming to live with their children, children bringing a spouse home to live with parents, or divorced or widowed children returning home. Frequently invasions are intended to resolve financial stringency since two families can live together more cheaply than apart. For aging parents, the need may be less financial than personal as their capacities weaken and they need personal care. In any case, doubling up most often means a reunion between one or both parents and a child with or without a spouse and with children of the next generation. It creates a kind of extended family but in societies where this is not the standard pattern and when families merge together after an extended period of separation there are dual reasons that doubling up is more stressful than institutionalized extended family arrangements.

Stress was reported by Komarovsky (1964) from a majority of her blue-collar American families who doubled up with relatives. In a London suburb, Willmott and Young reported that for parents who moved in with a child "Tension is almost inevitable. The parent is whirled off into someone else's house. The someone else is not strange, but the house is, the daily round is, the relationship is, of being subordinate rather than mistress" (1960: 45). German old people who lived with their children found that their relationship to their children worsened as a result. Whereas 80 percent of those living separately were on good terms with their children, only 61 percent of those living doubled up reported good relations (Tartler, 1961:65). Such research findings indicate that doubling up in modern societies tends to strain both the invaded family, the invading unit, and their interrelationship.

Doubling up is not always equally stressful, however. What are the conditions under which stress is lessened? Such conditions may resemble the solutions which earlier societies invented for the problems of institutionalized composite families.

Matrilineal Doubling Up

We saw in Chapter 7 a tendency for modern kin interaction to center around the mother–daughter relationship. The same reasons which lead mothers and daughters to see a lot of each other when they live in separate houses apply with compelling force when they must share the same house. The more intimate the relationship, the greater the advantage of involving the wife's mother instead of her mother-in-law. To express it more technically, matrilineal doubling up should be more satisfactory for both generations than patrilineal mergers.

Many studies in modern societies show that parents and married daughters are more apt to live together than parents and sons. In Wales, Rosser and Harris found three times as many matrilineal as patrilineal composite households. They reported that "the tensions of 'doubling-up' are less when it is a case of mother and married daughter sharing one kitchen rather than mother-in-law and daughter-in-law" (1965:151).

We have seen that in polygynous societies a customary solution to the problem of competition among wives was sororal polygyny which linked women from the same family of origin. Moreover, centralized households where wives lived together occurred almost exclusively among wives who were sisters. Doubling up, by definition, means living in the same house and is therefore relatively centralized. In modern societies the division of labor takes men away from home but leaves women at home most of the time. Therefore even when doubling up brings two couples together, it is primarily the women who are thrown together. From this perspective, the problems of doubling up are analogous to those of polygyny. Matrilineal doubling up is analogous to sororal polygyny. In both cases women who are primary relatives can live together more happily than women who are unrelated except by marriage.

Thus, both on theoretical grounds and from empirical evidence, I conclude that matrilineal doubling is less stressful than patrilineal doubling up.

Decentralized Doubling Up

Another customary solution to the problems of composite households is decentralization. Even though doubled-up families live under the same roof, a variety of living arrangements is possible. If a house contains separate apartments, a nuclear family may be hardly more disturbed than if the other family lived next door. (Komarovsky's blue-collar families found separate apartments in the same house far less stressful than joint households.) Especially if each family has its own entrance, they may be able to operate quite independently of each other.

Most houses are not well-equipped for independent living, so doubling up can seldom be thoroughly decentralized. Townsend (1957) found in London's Bethnal Green that most married couples ate separately from their children and grandchildren and that "almost invariably they had separate kitchens" (1957:41). But suburban zoning laws seldom allow separate kitchens in single-family dwellings. Townsend also reported that parents in their sixties continued to maintain some evening activities of their own. However, the older parents became, the more apt they were to lose their capacity for independent activity and so the greater the invasion of the children's privacy tended to become. Particularly after one parent died, separate living became too lonely for the survivor, and any merger with the junior family became more extensive.

The closer the merging, the greater the stress. Komarovsky reported that where the boundary line was to be drawn between the integrity of the nuclear family and the activities of the invader was the most difficult problem of living together:

> The right of the married pair to some privacy is generally acknowledged, but there is also a large undefined area. What rights, for example, does a parent living with the married couple have in the living room when the family is home alone or when friends are visiting?
>
> One [high school] educated wife, sharing an apartment with her parents, longs for a home for her and her husband. With her parents in the same apartment, she and her husband cannot begin to make love in a spontaneous way—they have to get into bed, and this "takes the surprise out of it" for her. (1964:276–277)

The existence of "a large undefined area" is one consequence of doubling up in a society where this is an uncommon practice to which normative solutions have not yet been developed.

I have suggested that decentralization reduces stress. The relationship can be turned around the other way—the greater the actual or anticipated stress, the more likely families are to decentralize. Since mergers are more stressful, it is correspondingly more valuable to decentralize such households. Townsend (1957) found that this occurred among his British families: "Married sons and their wives, when living in the home, maintained more of a separate establishment than married daughters" (1957:41).

Internal decentralization, therefore, minimizes the threat to the integrity of the nuclear family when relatives move into the home. Without decentralization, the disruption of a family who open their arms to even close relatives is likely to be substantial.

Useful Doubling Up

Even if invading relatives are disruptive, they may offset some of the stress by servicing the family. If they contribute enough to the division of labor in the home, they may relieve the physical burden on the wife even while they remain a psychological burden. If they pay their own way out of retirement pensions or welfare payments, they may help the husband with mortgage payments or other indebtedness he may have been carrying alone.

How helpful parents may be depends on the resources they have to offer. If they are old and feeble, they may have nothing to offer, only needs which must be met:

> "Occasionally I long to escape," said one daughter. "It gets a bit of a strain. I can never go out." The [adult] children's resentment is understandable if they have to act nurse as well as companion to old people who cannot go upstairs except on all fours, who are always up in the middle of the night clattering about in the kitchen making cups of tea, or who imagine that their children are plotting to starve them. (Willmott and Young, 1960:43)

Under such circumstances, aged parents are like a crippled child, requiring the whole family to respond to their dependency requirements. The only difference is that feeble parents seldom live as long as crippled children, so the invasion may be more transitory.

Even parents with considerable resources may not be put to much use if their children have few opportunities to use their services. In a tiny urban apartment, there may be little an old woman could do and even less for an old man. On a farm, however, there are tasks for all ages and both sexes and more than enough for everyone. Similarly, the usefulness of elderly parents expands when there are young children in the home.

Townsend found that grandparents felt useful and were appreciated more by their children when there were small grandchildren to be dressed, fed, and supervised. Grandparents as built-in baby-sitters may enable the mother to tackle a full-time job or enable the husband and wife to spend more leisure in a way which strengthens their relationship. Grandparents might even rescue the family from the crisis of accession. However, they are rarely seen as a net gain. Usually they are taken in for quite practical reasons or out of kindness. Rarely is the relationship mutually advantageous. The services they perform may ease the strain but seldom obliterate it altogether (much less leave the family better off than they were before).

Submissive Doubling Up

In extended family systems, the structure of the family follows the order of generations: the oldest at the top, the youngest at the bottom. When children double up with parents in the latter's home, the same structural arrangement emerges. But when elders become so infirm that they can no longer exercise power, they are forced to retire, yielding control to their children.

In many modern families, doubling up means that parents move in with their children. If parents are still vigorous, this creates a conflict of interest. Parents used to bossing their children can't easily accept the child's authority as head of his own house, nor can the child surrender easily to his parents:

> A crucial question is, who is in command? However hard the children try to compromise, they are bound to expect their parents to adjust to the ways of the household, to accept its customs, rather than the other way around. No wonder a parent complains. From being head of her own home, she (or he) is now lodger in someone else's. (Willmott and Young, 1960:44)

The only dependable solution to the problem of intergenerational dominance is for doubling up to occur in the home of the grandparents as long as they are functionally fit. Even that doesn't work as well in modern societies used to neolocal living as in feudal societies where extended families are the norm. Modern children are not trained for the obedience and filial piety necessary to accept the domination of their parents easily even in the latter's home. Perhaps a give-and-take democracy would be an appropriate relationship between parents and their grown children, since they are all adults, regardless of whose house it is. But such democracy takes more energy to operate than more dictatorial arrangements. Presumably, in the long run, everyone would be happier if decisions were made mutually after consultation and discussion. But the complexity of a doubled-up household would make such decision-making processes arduous and time-consuming at best.

We have already seen that patrilineal households are more apt to be decentralized than matrilineal ones. A corollary is that in those exceptional cases where a wife is willing to accommodate her husband's mother at all, she is less apt to be willing to surrender the management of her own home than where her own mother was involved:

> . . . examples of widows sharing a home with married sons, although comparatively rare, suggested that the mother's authority was delegated to the younger woman and her role sometimes became that of a subordinate housekeeper. She tended to be divested of domestic power and her responsibilities were much more consciously (and narrowly) defined. Only in this way was harmony preserved and the rights and responsibilities of a wife honoured. This shows some of the difficulties to be contemplated by some old people not able to live alone. (Townsend, 1957:43)

Townsend's last remark suggests that although submitting to the daughter-in-law's rule may be nice for the junior family, it is likely to be difficult for the mother-in-law. This illustrates the potential power struggle in composite families built out of what ideally would be nuclear families in modern societies. Again, perhaps, only some kind of compromise will be mutually satisfactory, but a compromise likely to be skewed in favor of whichever generation owned and operated the house before the invader moved in. A truly 50/50 compromise could perhaps be expected only if both families moved into new quarters. Only then would they be on an equal footing in their new home.

Such strategies presumably would alleviate the stress caused both generations by doubling up. Nevertheless, even under ideal circumstances, it seems likely that each nuclear family would continue to view the other as an intruder, disturbing the peace and privacy they enjoyed as long as each family had a shell of its own.

STRANGERS IN THE HOUSE

If parents and children have trouble living together, it is easy to imagine the difficulties when unrelated strangers invade the home. We have already seen problems created by remarriages which pit the stepfather on one side against the children on the other with the wife/mother somewhere in between. New husbands, however, are hardly complete strangers even to the children, much less to a wife who has been successfully courted. So we must turn to unromantic, commercialized relationships if we wish to examine the effect of genuine strangers.

Roomers and boarders are the best examples. They invade poverty-stricken families everywhere. The host family needs the income and the boarder needs the cheaper rates of a private home compared to a public hotel. Besides, the boarder frequently prefers the comforts of a home to the impersonality of an institution.

But there's the rub. If the boarder remained a stranger, the relationship might be a reasonable bargain. But boarders have traditionally been males seeking their fortune in the big city or in a far-off land. They are lonely and there are rarely enough unattached women to go around. Insofar as migration has skewed the sex ratio of the entire community (or at least of the migrant's ethnic and socioeconomic subsection of the community), the "hostess" may be one of the few sources of love and sex available to him. Moreover, her propinquity makes her highly accessible, save for the fact that she is married.

The other side of the coin is that the same poverty-stricken families which most urgently need the income can least cope with the temptations involved. The poorer the family, the weaker the marriage is likely to be. Indeed the husband–wife relationship may have become so embittered after years of quarreling over money that almost any new man would be a welcome relief.

With both the boarder and the wife emotionally vulnerable, no wonder the history of boarding is replete with love affairs! Among immigrant Poles in American cities prior to World War I, Thomas and Znaniecki (1958) found that many wives had sexual relations with their male boarders. Among blacks migrating from the rural South to Northern cities, Frazier (1937) found the same phenomenon, compounded in this case by the crowded quarters which housing discrimination forced on black families.

It may seem contradictory to suggest that the same centralization which makes two women get on each other's nerves makes a boarder and his landlady get sexually involved. Yet the lack of privacy in overcrowded living quarters makes it difficult to preserve the boundary line between the nuclear family and the outsider. Regardless of whether living close to an invader produces conflict with an enemy or sex with a lover, the nuclear family suffers.

Strangers Down the Hall

If housing is crowded enough, the stranger doesn't have to invade the apartment in order to become a menace. When poor families crowd into old tenements or chopped-up mansions, they often share common facilities. Common toilets, baths, or water taps require men and women to use the halls day and night and wait for one another to take turns. Just as Campbell's Greek shepherds believed that public wells were dangerous because seductions originated there, so shared urban facilities create risks of extramarital affairs. Presumably shared facilities which bring only one sex together (such as laundries) are less hazardous.

In any case, one problem for poor families is achieving and maintaining group identity amid a welter of outside stimuli. Perhaps it is remarkable that so many families survive rather than that so many fall apart in such difficult environments.

CONFIDANTES

Same-sex friends don't necessarily intrude upon a marriage relationship. Indeed, Locke (1951) found that happily married couples had more friends of both sexes than subsequently divorced couples. Nevertheless, under certain circumstances both same-sex friends and especially opposite-sex friends do threaten the relationship. In this section I will refer primarily to best friends of the same sex (and secondarily to psychotherapists, regardless of sex), leaving cross-sex affairs for the last section of the chapter.

Women more often have a girl-friend than men a pal with whom they share their secrets. A possessive partner may be jealous of any friendship which competes with the spouse's exclusive devotion, but friendships do not generally threaten marital solidarity. The crucial turning point seems to be when the wife (to focus on her) tells her marriage troubles to her girl friend and the friend allies herself with the wife against the husband. If the husband discovers this, he resents the wife's having shared family secrets with an outsider and even more the meddling of the friend. Even if he does not discover the confidante's involvement, the wife may be encouraged to adopt a hard line in dealing with him which makes reconciliation difficult.

Confidantes differ in their response to the wife's marital problems. We saw in Chapter 7 that middle-class confidantes often encouraged wives to understand the husband's viewpoint. Even mothers who might be expected to side with their daughters against the son-in-law were especially helpful in interpreting the husband to the wife.

Such breadth of vision depends on an enlightened attitude toward marriage which only well-educated adults usually achieve. It also requires a happy marriage for the confidante herself. If her marriage is bad, too, confidante and wife are likely to commiserate that all men are stinkers and encourage each other to retaliate rather than solve their problems.

Since marriages are less happy in the lower classes, confidantes are more apt to play a negative role there. In her study of blue-collar marriages, Komarovsky found that unhappy wives were more apt to have confidantes than happy wives (77 percent versus 57 percent). It is understandable that a wife who cannot rely on her husband for sympathy needs to turn to a girlfriend instead. But in meeting her personal emotional need, the wife compounds her marital difficulties. Komarovsky noted that "Her disclosure may in turn cause further estrangement between the spouses" and "In some cases the very existence of a confidante was in itself so resented by the husband that it caused conflict" (1964:218).

The fact that a majority of Komarovsky's happy wives had confidantes, too, suggests that the relationship is not necessarily threatening to the marriage. Only when the confidante invades the marriage by showing greater concern for the wife as an individual than for the couple as a pair does she become destructive. It is not so much confidantes in themselves as meddling confidantes who are a threat. Sometimes it is difficult to know whether a confidante caused trouble by meddling or whether the wife enlisted her confidante's support in existing struggles with her husband. In any case, the coalition between one partner and her friend against the other partner intensifies the conflict by escalating the number of parties involved.

In studying the kin relations of harmonious and conflicted families, Bell (1962) found that the latter lined up their relatives on each side of the battle line. Not only the wife but the husband turned to relatives for support in the battle with the partner. Conversely each counterattacked the other's allies, condemning their interference. Some relatives independently intensified the conflict by saying or doing the wrong thing. For example:

> Mrs. McGinnis' mother gave her grandson gifts of money just at the times when Mr. McGinnis was berating his son for his failure to earn his own spending money. The money mitigated the economic problem, but increased father–son conflict and eventually the whole family was at odds. (1962:182)

Some marriage partners displaced hostile feelings for each other onto the in-laws as "safer" targets. This may not have produced as much tension between the partners as a direct attack, but it consolidated each partner's external alliance by forcing him to come to the defense of his maligned relatives. Thus disturbed families tended to be sucked into external alliances which waged war on each other at the expense of the marriage.

Therapists as Intruders

One might think professional therapists would know how to intervene in the life of a married client without wrecking the marriage. Indeed, clients often seek therapy because their marriages are in trouble. Nevertheless, a growing body of evidence suggests that if the therapist deals with only one spouse, his effect may be just as disastrous as any girlfriend's—and for some of the same reasons.

If the therapist hears only one side of the story, he tends to sympathize with that partner's point of view and to look upon the unseen spouse as a disturber of the patient's peace. Spiegel confessed as much when he reported that each of his staff therapists assigned to a different member of the family came to identify with his own patient and to side with him against the other family members and their therapists:

> Implicitly or explicitly, the helper is asked to judge, referee, or take sides. The [therapeutic] interviewers seeing our families are inevitably pitted against each other in a semicoalition with the particular member of the family they are seeing. (1957:562)

Discovering that these coalitions tended to "get out of hand" and cause trouble in the family relationships, Spiegel sought to minimize the difficulties by asking the therapists working with the same family to meet together regularly to neutralize their competitive relationship and learn to see things from the standpoint of the other therapists (and indirectly of the other family members). The members of the family never had an organized opportunity to resolve their problems together. I assume that their involvement with separate therapists created coalitions which may have exacerbated the already existing tensions within the family. Even if the therapists by meeting together were able to keep their own feelings under control, the family members were likely to perceive each other's therapists as enemies arrayed against them.

Multilateral therapy has the virtue of giving each partner his own confidant to bolster his position against the other, making it better than unilateral therapy where only one partner gets outside help, altering the balance of power in marriage. The individual in treatment gains added resources from his coalition with his therapist which puts the nonsupported partner at a disadvantage. Aided and abetted by the therapist, the patient is likely to pressure his spouse into changing the marriage to the patient's advantage. The partner tends to react to this pressure by becoming defensive and counterattacking, making matters worse. At this point, both patient and therapist are likely to become disgusted with the alienated partner and come to the conclusion that the only way to save the patient's mental health is to sue for divorce. Removing the recalcitrant spouse from the scene would be good not only for the patient but for the therapist (by removing a threat to his success in healing the patient). Thus the involvement of the patient and the therapist with each other leaves the untreated spouse feeling not only left out but threatened by a hostile coalition. The coalition in turn feels threatened by the partner's negative reactions.

So far I have analyzed unilateral therapy chiefly in power terms. The problem is complicated by both sexual and affectional overtones. If therapist and patient are of opposite sexes, they are apt to be attracted to each other. The worse the marital relationship, the worse the spouse is likely to look in comparison to the sympathetically listening therapist. The therapist, to be sure, is supposed to be professionally trained to keep from becoming overinvolved with his patients, but he is human, and cannot help reciprocating in some degree the positive sentiments of his patients.

Even if the patient is of the same sex, the development of positive sentiment with the therapist is likely to worsen any negative relationship with the spouse.

Hurvitz (1967) suggested that the transference relationship which is encouraged between patient and therapist is not only likely to complicate the general relationship between the spouses but more specifically to complicate or create sexual problems. The therapist may come to be seen as not only a meddling confidant but worse yet as an extramarital lover.

Hurvitz also believed that unilateral therapy encourages the patient to discuss her marriage problems with the therapist but discourages her from tackling them with the spouse. The spouse in turn feels left out, useless—which hardly encourages him to tackle the problem constructively either. This shift in the focus of interaction away from the marital dyad to the patient–therapist dyad lowers the integration of the alienated spouse in the marriage, moving him to a marginal position where he more easily leaves home altogether.

Insofar as the husband and wife have been neurotically interdependent, any success in curing the patient's neurosis threatens the spouse's need for her to remain neurotic. If the husband is neurotically sadistic and was attracted to his wife because of her masochistic need to be mistreated, the husband's emotional equilibrium will be disturbed if the wife is cured of her masochism. Because husbands and wives often are interdependent, improvement in the patient often produces pathological reactions in the partner (Kohl, 1962). The alienated partner may fight back in a variety of ways or leave the marriage in disgust (if the patient has not already left him). In either case, the net result of the therapist's intervention in the life of the patient is frequently to destroy the marriage.

In Chapter 24, I will suggest how joint treatment of family members may avoid or at least resolve the problems caused by unilateral treatment or by multilateral treatment by separate therapists. Therapists who see only one partner do not inevitably destroy a marriage, but the structure of the situation makes them hazardous confidants for people whose marriages are already shaky.

LOVERS

We have already seen how marital crises are created when wives (or husbands) fall in love with their boarders or their therapists. Most extramarital affairs are less institutionalized than either of these arrangements. Like love affairs before marriage, they originate out of ordinary friendships rather than from commercialized transactions.

Of all the threats to marriage, lovers are both the most common and the most disastrous. Confidantes are almost universal, but they seldom are a threat unless the marriage is already in trouble. Lovers, on the other hand, invade even good marriages and threaten the relationship even if they do not always destroy it.

Perhaps lovers need to be defined. First, I assume that extramarital intercourse belongs in this category. Second, deeply affectionate relationships short of intercourse may threaten the marriage but their effect is more variable. The more one-sided the relationship, the more apt the spouse is to feel left out. Conversely, if the other woman maintains a close relationship with both the husband and his wife, she can more easily be perceived as a mutual friend than as a threat.

Because extramarital intercourse is a more clear-cut phenomenon, evidence of its incidence and consequences is more abundant. Kinsey (1953) estimated that half of all American husbands and one fourth of all wives committed adultery sometime while they were married. The larger proportion of men reflects the fact that some of their partners were not married but single or divorced women, and also the fact that some of the women (whether married or not) who engaged in nonmarital intercourse were extraordinarily promiscuous.

Even in primitive societies, extramarital intercourse is rarely viewed with equanimity. In striking contrast to the 70 percent of Murdock's societies which permitted premarital intercourse only 2 percent permitted extramarital intercourse. Murdock commented that the rarity of this cultural permission "suggests that the ideal of marital fidelity . . . has a strong practical utility" and went on to explain what he meant:

> Extramarital affairs are peculiarly likely to generate jealousy and discord between spouses which will interfere with their cooperative performance of the family's essential functions, so that most societies have found it necessary to forbid them. The experience of mankind thus warns us to resist the development of a permissive attitude toward adultery, such as is said to characterize certain so-called "emancipated circles" in our own society. Marital fidelity is far from being an outmoded superstition. On the contrary, it is one of the main buttresses of any social structure. (1950:4)

The striking difference between the widespread tolerance of premarital intercourse and the almost universal prohibition of extramarital intercourse in Murdock's societies reflects the fact that the latter threatens the stability of marriage more directly than the former. I have already shown that premarital intercourse tends to weaken the boundaries of marriage, but adultery shatters those boundaries. Premarital intercourse involves two people who may eventually marry each other. If both partners are unattached to anyone else, it breaks no commitment to any third party. Adultery by definition breaks the marital commitment. It doesn't necessarily mean that the individual wishes to abandon his partner altogether, but it violates the assumption of sexual fidelity on which marriage rests.

Even if there were not cultural, religious, or moral norms requiring sexual faithfulness, the triangular nature of adultery would make it difficult. The nonparticipating spouse tends to react negatively to the partner's involvement with another person because this seems like rejection. No matter how much the unfaithful spouse asserts that his involvement supplemented rather than supplanted his marriage the partner is likely to wonder "What did I do wrong?"

Male and Female Affairs

The feminine ego is particularly vulnerable to feeling hurt by the partner's extramarital involvements since the female role in marriage depends on being sexually attractive and desirable. Spiro (1956) found that middle-aged wives in an Israeli kibbutz worried about the potential unfaithfulness of their husbands not because they had shown any noticeable interest in other women but because the wives' physical charms were fading in an environment which demanded hard work and offered few feminine frills. Nonworking wives in other societies depend on their husbands more for emotional support than vice versa because the men have occupational and other external sources of accomplishment to support their egos.

Despite the greater vulnerability of the feminine ego, the double standard in patriarchal societies allowed extramarital freedom to the husband but denied it to the wife. (Murdock's permissive 2 percent were the only societies giving freedom to both sexes.) Sexual freedom for the man was consistent with his general freedom outside the home and was less of a threat to marriage because it did not introduce additional heirs into the family as unfaithfulness by the wife might have done in a pre-contraceptive era.

The greater the status differential between the sexes, the more the husband expected to exercise his sexual freedom with impunity. Patriarchal societies traditionally expected wives not to be jealous of the husband's extramarital affairs but to be apathetic, having no opinions of their own. Girls raised from childhood to expect their future husbands to be unfaithful were socialized into accepting the inevitable. This did not mean, however, they preferred things that way if given a choice. To be sure, ladies of refinement in many societies were also taught not to enjoy sex themselves. Such wives may have preferred that their husbands have intercourse with their girl friends instead of "bothering" them. But this was not the same as accepting competition with equanimity.

As long as the mistress was defined by the wife as a kind of prostitute, they were not competing in the same game. But insofar as the husband preferred his mistress as a human being over his wife, loved her more and gave her more affection and sympathy, even an aristocratic wife was likely to feel hurt. So even though male adultery in patriarchal societies did not destroy many marriages legally, it often estranged the wife emotionally.

Limited Freedom

Table 20-1 shows that young people in modern societies likewise were rather less worried about casual sexual affairs than about serious love affairs. The more casual the affair, the more the partner could dismiss it as primarily biological in motivation.

TABLE 20-1 Approval of Adultery in Varying Circumstances by Danish and American Students

PERCENTAGE WHO APPROVE OF ADULTERY, BY CIRCUMSTANCE	UNIVERSITY	
	Copenhagen	Purdue
If he or she feels the need for sexual release (with prostitutes or others) during periods of long absence from the spouse	39%	9%
If he or she has fallen in love with an unmarried person	34	6
If he or she has fallen in love with another married person	28	5

Adapted from Christensen, 1962:130. Reciprocal percentages of students disapproved of marital infidelity under the specified circumstances.

This is not just a rationalization. One argument for polygyny is that it enables the man to satisfy his sexual needs within the family when another wife is pregnant or otherwise unavailable. Masters and Johnson (1966) found among the college-educated husbands in their American sample that almost one fourth had resorted to extramarital intercourse during the months just before and after childbirth when their wives were unavailable. In Komarovsky's working-class sample, one husband reported that extramarital resources were regularly utilized under these circumstances:

> . . . Mr. D. reported that the doctor told him "to lay off when my wife was six months pregnant the first time, so I got myself another woman." He did it again during the second pregnancy. He said his friends knew about it and the married ones did the same thing. No, he "didn't tell her. . . . No use making trouble." (1964:104)

Presumably these cases were mostly motivated by biological forces and the husbands may have been happy to return to their wives as soon as they were available again.

When extramarital relationships are organized on a group basis, taboos on affectional involvement frequently develop. Slater noted that ". . . the higher the incidence of extramarital affairs in a given collectivity, the greater will be the societal intrusion upon such affairs, especially with regard to sexual choice" (1963:357). In many of the primitive societies which allowed extramarital relationships most freely, he noted that potential lovers were most rigidly prescribed. Societies which permitted sororal polygyny often gave men sexual access to the sisters-in-law who were their potential secondary wives. But this "pre-remarital" permissiveness is quite different from complete freedom of choice of extramarital partners. Presumably the more both husband and wife knew in advance who the extramarital partner might be, the less hurt the wife would be when she discovered that her husband had taken advantage of the societal permission.

In monogamous societies, the culture cannot designate extramarital partners, so it places its heaviest ban on affectional involvements which might lead the lovers to wish to abandon their marriage partners for the sake of a new marriage. Among the middle-aged businessmen and lower–middle-class girls who used the cocktail lounge of the leading hotel in a West Coast American city as a meeting place for sexual liaisons, strict informal rules had developed which minimized the threat to the men's marriages from their sexual involvements. The most important rule was that "They did not permit themselves or the young women with whom they consorted to become emotionally involved" (Roebuck and Spray, 1967:393). By limiting the relationship to sex, this quasi-institutionalized system of adultery reduced the likelihood that the men would want to abandon their wives in favor of their sex partners.

How the wives felt about their husbands' expenditure of so much time and money on these young women was not ascertained, but the fact that two thirds of the men were active Catholics provided an additional guarantee that their extramarital escapades would not lead to the divorces they claimed not to believe in and not to want. Even though these men lived in a modern society, they expressed a consistently double-standard philosophy, claiming that they could be good husbands and good fathers at home "where they were loved and loved in return" at the same time that they carried on these non-love affairs outside. The very fact that their sex partners could not be labeled "lovers" saved them from threatening the men's marriages as seriously as they otherwise might have.

Marital Repercussions

A variety of research data suggests that the more extensively husbands and wives become involved with external sex partners, the greater the demoralization of their internal relationship. In World War II, Hill (1949) found that marriages suffered most both during the period of separation and on the husband's return when both partners adopted a policy of sexual freedom for the "duration" of their separation. Next worst was a policy of freedom for only one partner, *i.e.,* a double standard giving the man freedom for new relationships while he was away.

Among the Zambian Tonga, the threat to marriage from adultery also varied with the extent of the partners' participation in it. The larger the number of external liaisons a husband contracted, the less his wife was willing to overlook it:

> The Tonga have no respect for promiscuity. [But] occasional adultery is another matter. It does not strike at the existence of the household. The sexual tie is only one among the many that exist between husband and wife as they work together in the interest of their household and family. Laziness, quarrelsomeness, or inefficiency are far greater dangers to the well-being of a household than a casual liaison or two. (Colson, 1958:174)

The greater the stress placed by the family on the husband's role as breadwinner, the less significantly adultery threatens that role unless the husband lavishes presents on his partners. Conversely, the more stress the society places on the husband as companion, sex partner, and lover to his wife, the more directly adultery seems to involve the abandonment of his marital commitment.

In some societies it is not adultery itself but public knowledge of it which humiliates the wife and forces her to retaliate. Geertz found this emphasis on external appearances in Java:

> Since Javanese living quarters are usually rather crowded, and any adulterous liaison is likely to involve a number of accomplices, there results a typical Javanese pattern for dealing with such deviance. Nearly everyone except the injured spouse knows about it, but no one cares enough to interfere and to risk the anger of all sides. Moreover, the wife herself may be aware of what is going on, but she does not have to act to protect her self-respect as long as it is not apparent to others that she knows. Only when the affair becomes public knowledge should she force her husband either to divorce her or to give up the other woman. (1961:130)

Presumably public knowledge of the affair pitted the wife and the other woman openly against each other and forced the wife to assert her claims to priority over the husband or else she would suffer a humiliation too hard to bear in front of friends and relatives. Hiding the affair from the public and the spouse is like decentralization in polygynous households—enabling the man to be involved with two women simultaneously with a minimum of jealousy between them.

No matter how much a society may discount extramarital affairs in and of themselves, they divert resources away from the marriage and therefore undermine it to some degree.

The fact that the other woman does not "belong" to the man means that she must either be paid for her services or courted in much the same way the wife was originally. The man is likely to invest more time and money in her than in the wife he has already secured. The same man who turned to another woman whenever his wife became pregnant reported that "The woman cost me a lot of money because she wanted all kinds of presents" (Komarovsky, 1964:104).

For Liebow's black men, the chief problem in trying to cope with two women simultaneously was sexual. Just as we saw that multiple wives created sexual problems for polygynous husbands, so extra women created similar problems for monogamous husbands with women on the side:

> In attempting to sustain simultaneous relationships with one's wife and one or more other women, it frequently happens that one such relationship compromises the other. . . . The marriage relationship, in particular, may suffer sexual damage. . . . the men talk about coming home from an engagement with another woman and being unable or unwilling to meet the sexual demands of their wives or women they are living with. Each man has a characteristic way of dealing with this predicament: feigning illness, or staying up to watch the late show on TV until the wife has gone to sleep; or precipitating an argument in order to have an excuse not to sleep in the same bed with the woman; or feigning drunkenness or tiredness from the job; or not coming home until the wife is asleep. The damage inflicted on marriage by such avoidance behavior tends to be assessed one way by men, another by women. The man tends to look at the problem in simple terms. . . . True, he has violated the marriage, but only in this one narrow area of sexual fidelity.
>
> In fact, the damage is much wider and deeper, as suggested by the wife in one of the streetcorner marriages that was falling apart. In bitterness mixed with resignation, she told of how her husband had been running around with other women and avoiding her sexually. She could live with this, she said, but what made the situation intolerable was his determination to find fault with everything she did, such as the way she cared for the children or cleaned the room. What started out as a transparent attempt to create arguments as an excuse for avoiding sex with her had gotten out of hand. The result . . . was that all areas of their life, not only the sexual, were being poisoned. (1967:123–125)

Presumably the primary problem in this case was not the adultery as such, but the husband's unwillingness to continue to meet his wife's sexual needs. Had he imitated polygynous husbands by rotating evenly among his women, he would have angered his wife less. The trouble with this marriage was that the husband openly rejected his first wife in favor of the new women. Had he made positive efforts to maintain the marital relationship, the situation wouldn't have been so bad. His avoidance techniques intensified the rejection which the wife already felt by virtue of the adultery itself. This case reveals not only the direct effects of unfaithfulness but the indirect effects of the husband's defensive reactions to the crisis which his infidelity created.

In Kinsey's female sample, 40 percent of the unfaithful wives believed that they had successfully hidden their affairs from their husbands. Presumably even these cases had some negative repercussions on the relationship.

Where adultery became known to the spouse, negative consequences were more visible. 42 percent of those wives reported serious difficulties when the husband learned of their unfaithfulness and another 16 percent reported minor difficulties (1953:434). The fact that the remaining 42 percent claimed no difficulties must be viewed skeptically in the absence of information directly from the husband.

TABLE 20-2 Extramarital Intercourse as a Cause of Divorce, as Reported by Adulterous and Innocent Husbands and Wives

SIGNIFICANCE IN CAUSING DIVORCE	ADULTEROUS PARTY		INNOCENT PARTY	
	Men	Women	Men	Women
Major	18%	14%	51%	27%
Moderate	9	15	32	49
Minor	12	10	17	24
None	61	61	0	0
Total	100%	100%	100%	100%
Number of cases	181	234	82	181

Adapted from Kinsey, 1953:445. Source: Divorced men and women. In the first two columns, all respondents were divorced and had engaged in extramarital intercourse but this was not known by the spouse in all cases. In the last two columns, all individuals knew that the partner had committed adultery.

When individuals whose partners had committed adultery and who divorced those partners were asked how much the adultery had caused the divorce, they gave the answers shown in Table 20-2. True to the double standard, men blamed their wives' unfaithfulness more often than vice versa. Note that no one of either sex claimed that the spouse's known adultery had not contributed to the break-up of the marriage.

On the other hand, when Kinsey's divorced respondents who had committed adultery which was not necessarily known to the partner were asked how much their own unfaithfulness had contributed to their divorce, the table shows that a majority felt it had not contributed at all. This emphasizes the importance of the partner's discovery of adultery in creating negative repercussions, but does not guarantee that claims of lack of effect are to be taken at face value even where unfaithfulness is not known by the spouse.

The Kinsey data fail to show what happens to marriages generally when confronted with adultery since they focused on couples who had already secured divorces.

Table 20-3 shows how divorced couples compared with happily married couples in the proportion of each group who had ever engaged in extramarital intercourse. The table shows that affairs were more common for husbands than for wives but that for both sexes they were more common among divorced couples.

TABLE 20-3 Extramarital Intercourse in Marriages of
Happily Married and Subsequently Divorced Couples

| NUMBER OF EXTRAMARITAL PARTNERS | SEX AND MARITAL STATUS | | | |
| | MEN | | WOMEN | |
	Happy	Divorced	Happy	Divorced
None	83%	53%	99%	95%
One or more	17	47	1	5
Total	100%	100%	100%	100%
Number of cases	200	251	200	274

Adapted from Locke, 1953:149. Source: 200 happily married couples and 201 divorced couples plus some divorced individuals in an Indiana county.

It is difficult to unravel cause and effect in such a table. Presumably the affairs of the happily married couples neither resulted from nor caused major difficulty in marriage—or if they did, the couples were able to surmount the difficulty. For the divorced couples, some individuals seem likely to have turned to other lovers only after being "turned off" by the unhappiness of their marriages.

The table demonstrates that adultery does not inevitably destroy or even undermine marriages. Nevertheless the fact that five times as many wives and almost three times as many husbands committed adultery in divorcing marriages as in happy marriages illustrates the correlations between extramarital affairs and marital difficulty. I conclude from this that lovers inevitably compete with spouses even though the spouse may eventually win.

chapter twenty-one

INTERNAL CONFLICTS: COALITION FORMATION

The previous chapter described the destructive effect of alliances between individual members of the family and outside parties. The present chapter focuses on the disintegration of the family into hostile subgroups. We have seen before that internal decentralization occurs when families grow excessively large or complicated. Such decentralization frequently prevents or reduces internal conflict. When members of a family begin to fight one another, however, a different kind of decentralization occurs. If, for example, the husband and wife declare war on each other, each is likely to solicit the children's assistance. Coalitions are established between parents and children, the primary purpose of which is to wage civil war. In other families, generations line up against each other for the same purpose.

TABLE 21-1 Disagreements, by Stage in Family Life Cycle

Disagreement	Honey-moon	Preschool	Pre-adolescent	Adolescent	Post-adolescent	Post-parental
Money	10%	28%	24%	23%	23%	21%
Children	—	13	29	32	20	10
Recreation	30	17	13	16	3	17
Personality defects	20	14	16	11	23	14
In-laws	15	8	5	2	3	2
Marriage roles	0	5	4	4	5	4
Religion-politics-sex	10	4	3	3	2	5
None	15	11	7	10	22	26
Total	100%	100%	100%	101%	101%	99%
Number of families	20	130	140	101	65	97

Adapted from Blood and Wolfe, 1960:247. Source: Cross-section sample of Detroit Metropolitan Area white families. "Honeymoon" = childless couples married less than four years. The child-rearing stages were defined by age of oldest child still living at home: under 6, 6–12, 13–18, and 19+ respectively.

Table 21-1 suggests one reason why children become embroiled in their parents' conflicts—because they are what the parents are fighting about. Children between the ages of 6 and 18 were the most important single area of controversy between their parents. How they should behave, how they should be punished when they misbehave, how much freedom they should be granted —such questions offer endless opportunities for parents to disagree. And when they do, the chances are that the child in question will line up with whichever parent is closer to his point of view. If this temporary alignment is repeated time and again, the makings of a parent–child coalition against the other parent are in the works.

VERTICAL COALITIONS

Some children are adept at playing their parents off against each other to their own advantage. However, that does not require establishing long-term coalitions but quite the opposite—remaining aloof from an alliance with either parent.

Coalition formation is generally initiated by parents, often when children are so young they don't know what is happening. The basic process is the development of differential relations between the two parents and one or more children. In a family where the husband and wife get along badly, the fact that the wife is devoted to a particular child may be enough to make the husband resent that child. Given this negative feeling, it is easy for him to overpunish the child as a pseudo-legitimate way of hurting his wife. Liebow's black men had discovered the effectiveness of this tactic:

Women are especially resentful of men's instrumental use of children, their use of children as tools for punishment or control in the man–woman relationship. The mother–child relationship, generally conceded to be far closer than the bond between father and children, renders the mother especially vulnerable to such tactics. One woman dreads a fight with her husband because the children will suffer for it. She knows and he knows that he can "get" her by slapping the children around. (1967:95)

This punitiveness alienates the children, driving them more securely into the arms of the mother, and leaving the man even more marginal than he might have been in the first place.

Liebow discovered that the chief image most ghetto children have of their fathers was of an enemy:

> . . . from the child's point of view . . . the father is the man who ran out on his mother, his brother and sisters and himself; who had, perhaps, to be taken to court to force him to pay a few dollars toward the support of his wife and children; and who, even when he was home, is perhaps best remembered with a switch or belt in his hand. (*Ibid.*:98)

Frozen-Out Partners The conventionally differentiated roles of men and women in the family make it easy for mother–child coalitions to form against the father. Insofar as the father is the instrumental leader and the mother the integrative leader, the mother has a softer, more attractive role. Children feel that she understands and sympathizes with them whereas the father is a hard taskmaster.

In normal families, the collaboration of these two leaders is required if the group is to stay united. The integrative leader is supposed to integrate the children not with herself but with the instrumental leader in spite of his harshness. Her job is to interpret the father to the children, to help them appreciate him, and persuade them to accept his leadership.

In families in conflict, the collaborative relationship between the father and mother gives way to antagonism. The father's attempts at task-leadership are rebuffed by the wife and children, leaving him ineffective and isolated. Deprived of the buffering services of his wife, he is apt to intensify his pressure tactics, alienating the rest of the family still further. Eventually, if he is deprived of any ally within the family, he may find sympathy in an outside lover and leave the family altogether.

Although the man is more apt to be isolated and excluded from the family, women are not entirely immune to this fate. Sampson *et al.* (1962) found that schizophrenic women were often frozen out of their families. This exclusion characteristically occurred in two stages. During the first, the wife remained at home but was largely ignored by the husband as she was in a disengaged state of equilibrium. However, if anything traumatic happened to disturb this equilibrium, the husband arranged for her to be hospitalized. During her absence, the husband and children developed an even more solid coalition from which she was necessarily omitted.

If the wife was allowed to return at all, she was accepted by the coalition of "normal" members only on a marginal basis. They were apt to stigmatize her as an ex-mental patient and treat her as a disturbed child needing the special care of *her* mother since no one in the family was prepared to give her that much care.

Needless to say, the coalition of the rest of the family against the wife tended to intensify her illness, undermining any progress she might have made while she was institutionalized. The coalition protected the rest of the family against the wife's bizarre behavior, but paradoxically their very success in sealing themselves off from the wife/mother prolonged her illness. Thus, the excluded one became the victim as well as the cause of the conspiracy of the rest of the family against her.

Children as Pawns

Once an excluded partner is expelled from the family, conflict ceases. But as long as both partners remain in the family, children tend to be caught in the middle. Even if the mother is likely eventually to win the loyalty of most of her children, the father may not surrender easily. He is apt to fight back with pressure and inducements to win the children to his side. As long as the children are not firmly aligned on one side, they are subjected to cross-pressures from both parents.

It is not easy for children to choose one parent and reject the other (save on a very specific issue). Children prefer to have two parents and want those parents to get along with each other. They sense that siding with one will antagonize the other, threatening the relationship they would like to maintain with both.

As long as children feel loyal to both parents and waver between joining the mother's faction or the father's, they feel torn apart. Wanting to side with both parents but forced to choose sides, they are faced with an acute dilemma. With mixed feelings toward both parents, they don't know which direction to go.

One "solution" to the dilemma is to withdraw into schizophrenia. A child who is biologically vulnerable may break under the stress of being courted by both parents into hostile coalitions. Although it is difficult to start from a family in conflict and predict which children will crack up, it is easier to trace the role of parental stresses in schizophrenic patients.

Lidz and his associates noted that the family background of schizophrenic patients had been characterized by marital "schisms" and "skews." Half of their patients came from schismatic families split into vertical coalitions:

> A particularly malignant feature in these marriages is the chronic "undercutting" of the worth of one partner to the children by the other. The tendency to compete for the children's loyalty and affection is prominent; at times to gain a substitute to replace the affection missing from the spouse, but at times perhaps simply to hurt and spite the marital partner. (1957:244)

Coalition formation in the family of a schizophrenic child is nicely illustrated by one of their cases:

> Mr. Reading, a forceful and successful but paranoidally suspicious man, sought to control his wife's behavior from the start of the marriage. He was infuriated and disillusioned when she joined a church group against his orders to remain aloof from any organizations. He was dependent upon his mother,

who lived in the home for many years, following her advice in household matters in opposition to his wife's, whom he considered incompetent to furnish the house. Marked strife began with the birth of the elder of two daughters, for he was clearly jealous of the attention the wife paid the child. He disapproved of everything she did in raising the child, often with good reason, but he competed rather than supported. Mrs. Reading was obviously overprotective of the children, whereas her husband wished to inure them to the hard knocks of life. Violent scenes, filled with Mr. Reading's dire threats and marred by occasional violence, were commonplace. The marriage further disintegrated into a hostile battleground after Mrs. Reading discovered that her husband was having an affair, which she reported to her mother-in-law to gain an ally her husband feared. Mr. Reading never forgave his wife for this betrayal and, apparently to spite her, sold their home in the best section of the city to move into a two-family house in an undesirable neighborhood. Thus, he struck a foul blow at Mrs. Reading's major preoccupations—her social aspirations and her insistence that her daughters associate with only "proper" companions. The family, previously split into two groups, now united against Mr. Reading and refused to eat meals with him. (1957:245)

Little wonder a child might become schizophrenic in so tense a home. Not only was this family split into hostile coalitions competing for control of the children, but in addition the husband's mother invaded the home and the husband established an external alliance with another woman. Perhaps if he had been frozen out of the family earlier and more completely, the children would have suffered less. But by the time the family united against the father to exclude him from the dinner table, the emotional damage had been done.

"Skewed" families in the same study were less overtly split into factions. Nevertheless, below the surface appearance of peace and harmony lay buried resentments and antagonisms between the parents which sometimes were even more difficult for children to cope with than open schisms.

It is all very well to discover conflict in the family background of schizophrenic patients, but is there any evidence that normal individuals come from families which are any different? Gerard and Siegel (1950) found that 87 percent of schizophrenic men came from families marred by open discord, whereas only 13 percent of a matched control group of non-schizophrenic men came from families as severely conflicted. The fact that the percentages were not 100 and 0 reminds us that some children emerge relatively unscathed even when they have been used as pawns and that factors other than family conflict may also cause children to go awry. Nevertheless, the sharp difference between the two statistics suggests the impact of parental conflict on children caught in the crossfire.

In a controlled experimental study of families with and without a member (usually a child) in therapy, Ferreira and Winter compared the length of time required for families to reach consensus on decisions. Abnormal families required almost 30 percent longer than normal families did to make their decisions. Moreover, conflicts did not focus on the identified patients but were scattered throughout the abnormal families (1968:23). When family life bogs down in prolonged arguments and decisions can be made only with difficulty, the mental health of the children (and presumably of everyone else) suffers.

Children as Lovers

So far I have stressed the strain produced by involvement in battles between parents. But children suffer in another way from that conflict. Because the father and mother are estranged from each other, neither partner can obtain the emotional support and sexual gratification which are normally supplied to one another. The more the marriage degenerates, the more frustrated the partners become. Angry, hurt, and lonely they turn elsewhere to satisfy their need.

We have seen that some adults regress to depending on their parents for emotional support. Having received love and affection (particularly from their mothers) for so many years, it is natural to "go home" psychologically when the marriage fails. The mother's ability to respond to her son or daughter depends on her availability. The longer the marriage lasts, the smaller the proportion of men and women who still have parents alive. Moreover, long-distance sympathy isn't nearly so gratifying as face-to-face sympathy. So the mother needs to be geographically propinquitous as well as simply alive. Finally, the man is especially apt to feel deprived not just of sympathy but of sex. If the warring wife is boycotting him sexually, a sympathetic mother will solve only one of his frustrations.

To recruit a new lover by having an affair is a second alternative. This, too, is a familiar experience since it reproduces the courtship which the husband or wife conducted in recruiting the present partner. However, ability to recruit a new partner depends on two factors: (1) ability to meet potential partners, and (2) ability to interest them. Many women are handicapped in finding opportunities to meet other men. The more children they have, the more likely they are to be so tied down that few opportunities for extramarital adventures will arise. Men have more opportunities to meet other women, so their main problem is to find the resources to attract them. For men with little money, self-confidence, or savoir-faire, it may not be easy to attract women. Men with poor social and psychological resources are more apt to resort to prostitutes, but if they lack money, even that avenue may be closed.

Parents of either sex who find adults of the opposite sex unavailable may turn to their children as a last resort. For mothers, to derive affectional gratification from children may not be a new experience. No matter how much satisfaction a women derives from a loving husband, child-rearing offers additional emotional rewards. Masters and Johnson (1965) found that breast-feeding was so sexually stimulating that some women experienced orgasm from it. The reduction of tension in the breast by the infant's feeding was also indirectly pleasurable.

As a child grows older, his companionship becomes increasingly meaningful to his mother. Because mother–child relationships are close to start with, they offer a natural resource to be exploited more fully if the mother has the misfortune to lose the affection of her husband. Perhaps, then, only for fathers can children be said to be a last-resort source of substitute gratification.

Mothers and Sons Sons are not the only children to whom mothers turn for emotional response. We have had many occasions to see that mothers are normally closer to daughters than to sons. However, it is precisely the normalcy of mother–daughter bonds which makes them relatively harmless to the daughter. If a girl grows up to resemble her mother, that is only to be expected. If a mother holds onto her daughter so much that the daughter can't grow up, the effects may be serious, but they are less bizarre than if she treats a son the same way. To be sure, a mother–daughter coalition may turn the daughter against the opposite sex so thoroughly that she may not wish to marry anyone, but at least she is less likely than a son to become "married" to the mother.

The sexual overtones of mother–son combinations are a distinctive feature of these relationships which make it appropriate to call them "love affairs." Because the mother has lost the man in her life, she needs another person of that sex to fulfill her need for heterosexual interaction. This rarely means a need for heterosexual intercourse, partly because such women have frequently been "turned off" by unpleasant sexual experiences with the husband, partly because mother–son intercourse reverses the usual combination of age and sex roles (male older, female younger).

The absence of intercourse does not mean the absence of sexual feelings, however. Heterosexual relationships normally have a different emotional quality than relations between members of the same sex. In normal families, these overtones are played out overtly in the relationship between husband and wife but suppressed in the relationships between parents and their opposite-sexed children. In families rent with conflict, the pent-up desires to flirt with and attract the opposite sex tend to be diverted into vertical coalitions.

One form of mother–son affair is maternal overprotection. Levy's classic study of overprotected children found they were more apt to be sons than daughters. One element in the mother's behavior was "excessive physical contact." Thirty percent of the mothers slept with their sons, sometimes well into their teens. In particular cases he found such sexual elements as "excessive social contact, much fondling and kissing, and sleeping with the mother during the father's absences from home on account of business." One ten-year-old boy "embraced and kissed his mother while she lay on a couch and then proposed they do to each other 'what dogs do,' illustrating with body movements" (1966:43). That the mother had indirectly stimulated this sexual invitation is suggested by the fact that she constantly tried to bathe him and when he refused to allow it stayed outside the bathroom door and gave him directions.

What, then, were the sexual relationships of these seductive mothers with their husbands? For three-fourths of the mothers they were either poor or nonexistent, varying from passive conformity with the husband's demands to active refusal. A comparative analysis by Martha P. Lewenberg of overprotective and non-overprotective cases from the files of the same Institute of Child Guidance rated 87 percent of the overprotective mothers as sexually maladjusted, in contrast with 46 percent of the non-overprotective mothers.

Sex was not the primary element in Levy's overprotective cases, nor was sexual deprivation the only complaint the mothers made about their husbands. Most of the mothers had been outgoing and sociable before marriage, but their husbands allowed them few outside social contacts after marriage. They turned to their sons as substitute companions, attempting to monopolize them by discouraging them from making friends with other children. Lewenberg's comparative figures suggest how impoverished the mothers' social lives were: 88 percent of the overprotective mothers had socially maladjusted marriages, compared to 38 percent of the non-overprotective mothers.

Sexual and social incompatibility might suffice to turn mothers to their children for substitute satisfaction. In Levy's cases, however, the mothers' need for affection was compounded by the fact that most of them had had unsatisfactory relationships with their own parents in childhood. They had been so emotionally starved for their entire lives that they had an extraordinarily great need to find in their children the love which they had not received from their husbands.

A second possible consequence of intensive relationships between mothers and sons is that the son may become a homosexual. Although this did not happen to any of Levy's overprotected boys, Bieber's study of male homosexuals indicated that involvement with mothers was a common causal factor.

TABLE 21-2 Family Backgrounds of Heterosexual and Homosexual Men

Family Relationship	Heterosexuals	Homosexuals	Homosexual/ Heterosexual Ratio
Father–Mother Alienation			
Mother spent little time with father	37%	59%	1.60X
Mother's and father's interests diverged	61	82	1.34
Mother was sexually frigid	47	64	1.36
Mother tried to ally with son against father	40	62	1.55
Mother openly preferred son to father	38	58	1.52
Mother–Son Coalition			
Son was mother's favorite child	50%	66%	1.32X
Mother was more intimate with patient than with his brothers	29	56	1.93
Mother and son spent much time together	27	56	2.07
Son was mother's confidant	36	52	1.44
Mother–Son Jealousy			
Mother demanded to be center of son's attention	36%	61%	1.69X
Mother interfered with son's girl friends	35	58	1.66
Number of cases	96	96	

Adapted from Bieber, 1962:45, 145. Source: Homosexual and heterosexual men in psychoanalytic treatment in New York City.

Table 21-2 suggests that families of homosexual men were apt to be split into hostile coalitions. The father and mother were typically estranged from each other and the mother turned to her son as a husband-substitute.

If there was more than one son, she was particularly intimate with the one who became homosexual. That outcome was partly due to her interference with any interest he might have shown in girls, but also due to the feminizing effect of being locked in such a tight maternal embrace. Having grown up in a feminine environment, the son absorbed so much of a feminine sexual identity that he became uncomfortable with the masculine role in heterosexual relationships. The mother felt her love affair with the son less threatened by friendship with other boys than with girls who might steal him away from her.

When Bieber classified the mothers of homosexual men in terms of their overall characteristics, 69 percent were labeled "close-binding intimate." These mothers used their sons as sources of affection:

> The outstanding characteristic of these mothers was an extraordinary intimacy with their [homosexual] sons. Pathological sexual attitudes and behavior were frequently expressed, covertly or subtly, and constituted central aspects of the relationship. The [close-binding-intimate] mother exerted a binding influence on her son through preferential treatment and seductiveness on the one hand, and inhibiting, over-controlling attitudes on the other. In many instances, the son was the most significant individual in her life and *the husband was usually replaced by the son as her love object.* (1962:47, my emphasis)

Homosexuality is an extreme outcome of mother–son coalitions. The fact that it is not inevitable is evidenced by the fact that 32 percent of the heterosexual patients in Bieber's study also had close-binding-intimate mothers. My main concern is not so much to discover the effect of the vertical coalition on the child as to describe the intensity of that coalition in families where the marriage relationship becomes sour. The worse the marriage, the greater the likelihood that the partners will turn elsewhere for substitute gratification. And if there are children of the opposite sex in the home, the greater the chances that they will be exploited by the frustrated parent.

Father and Daughters I suggested earlier that fathers are more apt to turn to other women than to their daughters as wife-substitutes. Particularly when the motive is sexual gratification, adult women are normally preferred over young daughters. Some men, however, are such poor lovers that they cannot secure extramarital sex partners. They find it easier to befriend their daughters in incestuous relationships. Since incest represents the most full-blown of father–daughter affairs, it reveals most graphically the kind of family situations in which parent–child coalitions are established.

In a study of father–daughter incest in Boston, Kaufman, Peck and Tagiuri (1954) found that the marriages of the parents were universally bad. The mothers had "deserted" their husbands sexually and one mother went home to her mother every night, leaving her daughter to play the role of substitute wife in more ways than one. The researchers reported that "Incest usually began when the father and daughter felt the mother had abandoned them, either by giving birth to a new sibling, turning to the maternal grandmother, or developing some new interest outside the home" (1954:275).

Significantly, the love that developed between father and daughter met the needs of both parties because both felt lonely and starved for affection.

Why didn't the fathers turn to adultery instead? The answer lies in their severe personal inadequacies. They were school drop-outs who had been raised in unhappy homes where they received little affection from their parents. As adults, they had been occupational failures, either unemployed for long periods of time or drifting in and out of low-status jobs. Most had taken refuge from their sense of personal failure in alcoholism. In a larger study by Weinberg (1955) of 159 cases of incest in Illinois, the fathers had completed only five years of schooling on the average and a majority were rated either dull-normal or subnormal in intelligence. Thus the men lacked the resources necessary for extramarital adventures.

How was it possible for them to breach the incest taboo and carry their affairs with their daughters all the way to intercourse? Whatever rudimentary inhibitions Kaufman's men might have had in spite of their inadequate childhood socialization presumably dissolved in the alcohol which they characteristically consumed prior to their incestuous episodes. The daughters manifested no guilt about their sexual experience and felt deprived when their sexual relationship to the father was terminated by outside intervention. Weinberg found that incestuous relationships lasted longer with mentally deficient daughters than with more intelligent girls. The duller the girl, the more dependent and compliant she was. Indeed both father and daughter often relied on each other because they found it difficult to cope with the outside world.

Even though mothers were hostile to their husbands, they generally tolerated incestuous affairs, partly to relieve their own guilt about not meeting their husbands' needs. The mothers did not give their permission openly but tacitly conveyed either permission or even encouragement to the father and the daughter:

> The mother did this, not only by being absent, but more actively by setting up a situation where this could occur. An example of this was one mother who felt very guilty over the incest, but when asked to discuss the circumstances said she could not tolerate her husband's snoring and went to sleep in another room. Then out of concern that he would be lonely she put the daughter in her place in bed with her husband. (Kaufman *et al.*, 1954:276)

Thus these father–daughter affairs developed in families where both parties had been betrayed by the mother and fell in love "on the rebound." That these cases should not be interpreted as simple sexual exploitation of the child by the father but as genuinely loving relationships is suggested by an interview with an eleven-year-old girl whose father had been sent to prison for five years:

> She said that she had wanted to do what was best for her father but she was very sorry now that she had told anyone about it. She didn't know that he would be put in prison. . . . She was always her father's favorite and felt she could talk to him and never to her mother. She hated her eight-year-old sister, but loved [her baby sister]. She wanted to live with her father

and the baby because this baby seemed like her own child. She added that she wanted to be everything to her father because he had no one. (1954:273)

Paralleling the father–daughter coalitions in most of these families were mother–son coalitions. The researchers described the mothers as rejecting their daughters but "pampering" their sons. Presumably the mother–son coalitions both gratified the mothers' emotional needs and provided a suggestive model which their husbands imitated in allying themselves with their daughters.

Because both father–daughter and mother–son coalitions resulted from failure of the normal husband–wife coalitions, perhaps we can assume that whenever unhappy parents have children of both sexes each parent will tend to form a cross-sex parent–child coalition. However, if men are more apt to turn to other women than to their daughters, perhaps it would be more conservative to predict dual parent–child coalitions chiefly in families where the father is forced to restrict himself to intrafamilial resources.

In any case, vertical coalitions may be expected not only to appease the parents' needs for love and affection but to divide the family into even more firmly entrenched competitive subdivisions. Insofar as a man loses not only his wife but his son, or a woman not only her husband but her daughter, each parent has suffered a double loss and now has dual enemies. Thus the parent–child coalition creates a cozy dyad for the participants but exacerbates the civil war within the family.

HORIZONTAL PSEUDO-COALITIONS

For families riddled with tension, some solution must be found if the family members are not to go crazy or the family itself to crumble to pieces. Some families achieve a cease fire by a stalemate between coalitions. For example, if evenly balanced cross-sex coalitions have formed, each may say to the other, "We'll leave you alone if you leave us alone." By accentuating the positive satisfactions gained within their sub-unit, they may deemphasize the warfare between sub-units.

Some families, however, cannot tolerate such an open split. Their need to believe that they are a "successful" family may be so great that they must somehow patch over their divisions.

This may be done in either of two ways—either the parents may divert their hostilities toward a common enemy, or they may suppress them altogether and pretend they don't exist. The first of these deviant "solutions" to marital conflict I will call horizontal pseudo-coalitions, the second global pseudo-harmony.

By a horizontal pseudo-coalition I mean a coalition between the husband and wife against a common enemy outside their dyad. A genuine coalition between husband and wife as task and integrative leaders respectively is an essential feature of the structure of normal families. That coalition is based on love and respect between the partners and has for its purpose the successful rearing of the children as individual human beings with their own independent integrity. The coalition exists not to fight anyone, much less to destroy anyone, and certainly not to exploit the children as pawns for the sake of the parents.

A pseudo-coalition has a false foundation. For husbands and wives who basically mistrust and resent each other but who are afraid to do so openly, fabricating a pseudo-coalition is a way of denying to themselves and to each other the hostility which they covertly feel. But since hostile feelings are constantly generated in the course of living together, the husband and wife must drain off those feelings if they are to maintain the pretense that they do not exist. The easiest way to do this is to find a common enemy. Then they can mask their hatred for each other in open vituperation of the external foe.

"External" in this context means any object outside the husband–wife dyad. It might be an inanimate foe such as an encroaching desert or poison ivy, a social enemy such as a Communist conspiracy or the Black Power movement, or a personal enemy such as a despised neighbor or relative. From the standpoint of coalition formation within the family, the most relevant object is a member of the family. In doubled-up families this might be an intruding grandparent. In nuclear families, it is necessarily a child. Because the latter is more common, I will concentrate on children as the basis for pseudo-coalitions.

The Child as Enemy

A young child is a very suitable choice for a family scapegoat. The fact that he is a member of the family means that he is always available to be punished. The fact that he is the common responsibility of the parents enables them to join forces in persecuting him. The fact that he is young means that he is easily exploited and cannot fight back as fiercely as an older target might. It also means that he is incompletely socialized and has plenty of defects which can be seized upon as focal points for attack.

Vogel and Bell discovered that children could even learn defective behavior in order to serve as family scapegoats:

> Because the child's personality is still very flexible, he can be molded to adopt the particular role which the family assigns to him. When the child does take on many of the characteristics which the parents dislike in themselves and each other, he becomes a symbolically appropriate object on which to focus their own anxieties. (1960:386)

Nor can the child escape being scapegoated just by failing to become what the parents need him to be. If they need a scapegoat badly enough, they may pretend he is "bad" even if he is not:

> For example, in one family which was very concerned about the problems of achievement, the focus of the family's problems was the eldest son. Although he was receiving passing grades in school, whereas the parents had had very poor school records, the parents were very critical of his school performance. Because of this pressure, the child worked hard and was able to get somewhat better marks on his next report card. However, the mother stoutly maintained that her son didn't deserve those grades, that he must have cheated, and she continued to criticize him for his school performance. (*Ibid.*:389)

If the reader concludes from this case that the scapegoat "can't win," he is right. No matter what the child does, the parents' need for him to fail may be so great that he can never satisfy them.

Vogel and Bell found that in families with more than one child, one scapegoat was enough. The other children frequently joined the parents in ostracizing him. Although most of Vogel and Bell's families had a rather rigid scapegoating pattern, Ackerman (1964) reported from clinical observation that the role of scapegoat sometimes changes hands. Presumably a disturbed family requires not so much that any particular person be the scapegoat, but rather that some target be available to deflect the venom which the father and mother might otherwise direct to each other. The larger the number of children in the family, the larger the number of potential targets who may at one time or another be used by the parents to maintain their pseudo-coalition.

GLOBAL PSEUDO-HARMONY

If the parents need not only to pretend that nothing is wrong with their marriage but also that nothing is wrong with their children, they cannot rely on scapegoating a child to solve their family problem. If their need to believe that everything is perfect is sufficiently strong, they will have to patch over the split between husband and wife and keep the lid on all tensions within the family, no matter how much anger may be seething underneath. Every quarrel, every hostile or hurt feeling, will have to be suppressed or repressed so fast that the members of the family will be able to claim, however desperately, that everyone is happy. This means adopting a pose of global harmony within the family to hide their conflicts from public view and from personal awareness even more thoroughly than scapegoating could.

Wynne and his associates found such pseudo-harmony in the family backgrounds of many schizophrenic patients. For example, the mother of one patient insisted on the normalcy of her entire family:

> We are all peaceful. I like peace even if I have to kill someone to get it. . . . A more normal, happy kid would be hard to find. I was pleased with my child! I was pleased with my husband! I was pleased with my life! I have *always* been pleased! We have had 25 years of the happiest married life and of being a father and mother. (1958:211)

The desperation of this mother is symbolized in the dramatic and repetitive nature of her assertions. Their falseness was given away by the blunt fact that her "normal, happy kid" was at that very moment hospitalized with a psychosis.

Wynne noted that the need for harmony in such families was so acute that they not only avoided open conflict but even forbade their children to develop normal independence and individuality. Presumably the precariousness of their attempt to hide from their own awareness the tension in their families made even the slightest independence appallingly dangerous. As an added protection, Wynne's families created "a pervasive familial subculture of myths, legends, and ideology which stress[ed] the catastrophic consequences of openly recognized divergence from the fixed family role structure" (*Ibid.*). Thus, intellectually as well as practically the families mobilized their resources to insist to one another and to the outside world that all was well.

That vulnerable children should develop schizophrenia under circumstances involving such rigidly disguised conflict is not surprising. However, the psychotic breakdown of a vulnerable child was an unintended consequence of the family strategy (unlike the symptom formation of scapegoats which is unconsciously intended by the parents). To have a child "go crazy" threatened the pretense of normalcy in pseudo-harmonious families. Such families went to extraordinary lengths to try to ignore or explain away the difficulties which their pseudo-harmony had precipitated. Negative behavior in the child might be blamed on forces beyond his control rather than accepted as evidence of his hostility against them. For example, one of Wynne's hospitalized patients rebelled against his parents by destroying a clock, radio, magazines, and food parcels that his parents brought, but they felt that his behavior had nothing to do with them because they had left the gifts with nurses who in turn had transmitted them to the son.

Ultimately, the intervention of outside agents who label the child deviant, his forced removal from the home to the hospital (despite the parents' protestations that nothing is wrong with him), and the acting out of the child once he is away from the confines of his family, make it impossible for the family to maintain its illusion of solidarity any longer.

At that point, the family might alter its defensive maneuvers from global pseudo-harmony to a horizontal pseudo-coalition against the psychotic child. By converting him into a scapegoat, the family could defuse the child's threat to their equilibrium as they try desperately to salvage their sense that their little world is still safe and not about to collapse about them.

STRUCTURAL RIGIDITY

Regardless of their form, the hard-won and precariously maintained deviant equilibria that families achieve as the solution to their internal conflicts are maintained with extraordinary tenacity. Sensing that chaos may break loose if anything is done to destroy their defenses and force them to confront their problems, families cling to their contrivances and resist all threats to them.

In an experimental demonstration of this rigidity, Miller and Westman (1966) tested 15 normal families and an equal number of deviant families in which nonreading sons of normal intelligence and normal vision served as scapegoats for their parents' pseudo-coalitions. In a laboratory experimental game, the researchers first discovered who the dominant family member was and then systematically manipulated the game so that every subsequent choice by that person was wrong. One third of the normal families noticed that something had gone wrong and transferred leadership to another family member so the family began to win again, but not a single problem family altered their leadership.

In real life, Wynne noted that his pseudo-harmonious families also exhibited "a persistent sameness of the role structure of the family, despite physical and situational alterations in the life circumstances of the family members, and despite changes in what [was] going on and being experienced in family life" (1958:209). Specifically these families found it almost impossible to adapt to the growing capacities of their children and to grant them increasing independence with adolescence.

Is there any evidence that the structural rigidity of these families "worked"? Were their fears of impending catastrophe justified? Would trouble really arise if they were to tinker with the carefully wrought structures they had created to hold their families together?

The answer to these questions all too often is "Yes." When a family has created a deviant equilibrium to defend itself against internal conflict, any change will produce defensive maneuvers or else the family is likely to collapse completely.

As soon as the nurses in Wynne's case refused to be intermediaries, forcing the parents to give their presents directly to their son, the parents could no longer ignore his rejection of them. The mother's blood pressure rose so alarmingly that her doctor forbade her to visit the hospital. This physiologic maneuver saved the mother from having to face her son's rejection. Thus the family's pseudo-harmony was preserved a while longer.

Among Vogel and Bell's scapegoated children, successful therapy for the children reduced their usefulness as scapegoats and "blew the lid off" the family tensions: "In the two families with the most severely disturbed children, when the scapegoating of the child eased up during therapy, the explosions between parents became so severe that there was serious fear that the family might break up" (1960:395). Miller and Westman similarly noted that "in some instances the child may improve his reading at the cost of breaking up the family or inducing psychosis in a parent" (1966:59). Thus the evidence seems clear that removing the behavior for which a child has been scapegoated is liable to make the family collapse like a pile of jack straws.

Resistance to Therapy

Families which have solved their problems to their own satisfaction are extraordinarily resistant to therapeutic intervention. We have already seen how they deny that anything is wrong with their family in general or with a scapegoated child in particular. The latter maneuver is more difficult because by definition there is something wrong with him which they have organized to attack. Nevertheless, the goal of maintaining the status quo can be achieved by asserting that his behavior is hopeless and would not yield to therapy.

Such families rarely take the initiative in taking their child into therapy. Ordinarily, outside forces (most often the school system) impose therapy on the child despite the family's reluctance to allow him to become involved in such a "dangerous" undertaking.

If, despite their efforts to the contrary, the child is hospitalized or inveigled into out-patient treatment, the patient and rest of the family may conspire to prevent the treatment from destroying their carefully built barricades. Miller and Westman (1966) found it practically impossible for highly skilled therapists to teach boys to read when their illiteracy was necessary to the family's horizontal coalition. Even though the boy as scapegoat had been excluded from that coalition, he unconsciously felt responsible for holding his family together. So he resisted abandoning his role as scapegoat as much as the rest of the family dreaded the loss of that role.

Miller and Westman discovered a variety of ways in which these families defeated the therapeutic intervention. The families frequently behaved like a closely coordinated team:

> At times, when interviewed together, they all feel persecuted, or they all become confused, or they all find it hard to think of anything to say, or they all are preoccupied with and silent about the same secret, or they all agree on a fabricated version of a touchy incident, or they all start arguing with one another and then blame the therapist for upsetting them. (1966:57)

I suggested earlier that scapegoats are in a can't-win situation *vis-à-vis* their families. Now it is apparent that defensive conspiracies put therapists too in a can't-win situation *vis-à-vis* the whole family. The purpose of this conspiracy is to protect and maintain the structural status quo. In order to achieve that end it is necessary to maintain the symptom which enabled the family to scapegoat the son:

> The average family with a retarded reader convinced their son that he was doing as well as might be expected in view of his presumed limitation in intelligence. They denied clinical reports that his intelligence was normal, or disparaged the validity of the tests. Some mothers [continued to coach] their sons in reading [even] after being told that the boring drills would kill their son's budding motivation to learn. Some parents set such high standards that their sons were bound to think they failed no matter how well they performed. Some parents were so punitive when their sons got poor grades that the boys retaliated by failing even more. (*Ibid.*:58)

A third defensive maneuver involved hiding family secrets from the therapist. Those secrets concerned controversial matters which might have been the key to unlocking the family's protective armor. By keeping their secrets the family preserved the status quo and prevented the therapist from gaining a strategic victory over the family. If one family member inadvertently started to give away the secret, the rest of the family introduced distracting topics into the conversation. If he couldn't be distracted, they tried to talk him out of his opinion more directly. More often than not, however, the whole family collaborated in keeping secrets so that even these abortive disclosures were not risked.

In a few of Miller and Westman's cases, despite all these defensive tactics, a child began to read. This presented the family with the ultimate danger and forced them to utilize their ultimate weapon—to terminate therapy:

> They missed appointments and offered carefully reasoned excuses; they . . . accused [the therapists] of using ineffectual methods or of persecution; they punished the boys for other faults and seemed indifferent to the improvement; they even changed their hours of work or their jobs, which meant a cessation of psychotherapy. (*Ibid.*)

Ultimately if a family needs to maintain a child's pathology badly enough, a therapist cannot win as long as the child remains a part of the family. Only by destroying the family, could the child be salvaged. If the child were removed from his family, the parents' pseudo-coalition would probably fall apart unless a new foe could be found. Severing the parent–child relationship by removing the child would presumably be echoed by a relapsing of the husband–wife dyad into open conflict which they could not tolerate. So ultimately the marriage would be destroyed, too.

This is not to say that destroying the family or the marriage would necessarily be undesirable from the standpoint of the individual members. We will see in Chapter 23 that it may be advantageous for the tensions to be ended by the ultimate in decentralization. The point here is simply that insofar as a family threatened with dissolution staves off that fate by devising a defensive internal substructure, dismantling that structure is likely to lead to the collapse of the whole family.

chapter twenty-two

LEADERSHIP IMPAIRMENT

So far I have discussed the structural organization and crises of the family under fairly normal conditions with both parents living together and functioning in their normal roles—the husband as chief bread-winner and the wife as chief housekeeper. What happens to families when one parent (or both) is unable to play his usual role effectively, either because his functional efficiency is impaired or because he is temporarily or permanently absent or lost from the family?

The loss of a child has little structural impact on a family. Most children are mere consumers and dependents on the family, so few if any services are lost when they leave. If they are incapacitated, the burden on the family is increased (as we saw in Chapter 14), but our concern in this chapter is not with the effects of increased dependency but with the effects of lost services. Thus we may ignore the consequences for the family of any tragedy which may befall children.

Parents are another story. Family life centers around them. The division of labor and the family power structure primarily embrace them. They supply the chief or only financial resources on which the family depends for subsistence and they allocate those resources in consumable form among the family members. The socialization of children is almost exclusively their responsibility and they supply the love on which the emotional well-being of everyone else depends. I have referred to the father and mother as the instrumental and integrative leaders of the family as a decision-making group, but they are also the leaders of the family in almost every activity. Just as all organizations are critically endangered when something happens to their leaders, the family's severest crises result from parental failure and parental absence.

THE AMBIGUITIES OF ROLE IMPAIRMENT

I will reserve for the next chapter the permanent loss of a parent through desertion, divorce, or death. In this chapter I am concerned with the impairment of parental functioning (as through alcoholism or unemployment) and with the temporary absence of a parent.

In some ways these leadership impairments are more difficult for families to cope with than the complete loss of a parent. If the father is still present but unable to play his usual roles because he has lost his job or is sick, it is difficult for others to take over his roles because they resent doing his work for him.

Unpredictability of Outcome

If the impaired partner's disability were sure to remain chronic or worsen, the family could take over his functions more gracefully. But if he might resume them sometime in the future, the family will be reluctant to "freeze him out" of those functions by taking them over.

Some role impairments have the added problem that their prognosis is uncertain. It may be difficult to predict whether the future will be better or worse. The individual's condition may fluctuate wildly so that one day he functions reasonably normally, building up hopes that all is well, only to dash those hopes the next day with a relapse.

Jackson (1954) noted that such fluctuations were characteristic of alcoholics. One day a husband will be roaring drunk and the next completely sober. If he wants to "kick the habit," he may promise repeatedly to stay sober but just as repeatedly give way to temptation. If he performs his roles rather well when he is sober, the family is reluctant to take them over completely. If it attempts to do so, the husband is likely to feel insulted and protest his ability to perform them better than his role-substitute can. Such a family cannot establish a stable re-equilibrium short of total exclusion of the husband from the family or total abstinence by the husband. All intermediate measures must be subject to revision as the husband's behavior changes.

Thus families with a malfunctioning parent may find it next to impossible to establish a stable new equilibrium as broken families can.

Unpredictability of Duration

Sometimes the duration of a parent's absence is unknown. This raises the dilemma whether to concentrate on getting along without him (which will make his return more difficult) or to leave his roles open for him (which will make his absence more difficult). Sometimes only in retrospect does the family discover whether the absence was temporary or permanent, since whether the missing parent will ever return may also be uncertain.

In any case, the unpredictability of so many partial role impairments and temporary absences is their worst feature.

The Dual Crises of Impairment and Recovery

For every parent who leaves and subsequently returns, there must be a double adjustment—one to his departure and one to his return. While the latter seems to involve simply returning to the status quo, the longer the parent is away, the greater the likelihood that that status quo will have been rendered obsolete by intervening events. Indeed, the more successful the adjustment to the parent's absence, the more difficult it will be for the prodigal to find his way back into a family which has closed ranks behind him.

THE CAUSES OF ROLE IMPAIRMENT

The causes of role impairment may be either external or internal to the family.

External Causes

Troubles which originate outside the family are generally perceived as involuntary. For example, the drafting of the husband into the armed forces is almost always beyond his control. Illness is blamed on germs and political persecution on the government (unless the family feel their man stuck his neck out farther than he should have). If someone or something outside the family can be blamed, the crisis may draw the family members together in emotional solidarity and win the sympathy of others. Even though the loss of a parent's services upsets the organization of the family, psychologically they may become more cohesive.

TABLE 22-1 Effect of Political Repression on Family Solidarity

| | POLITICAL REPRESSION | |
| | None or Mild | Serious |
FAMILY SOLIDARITY	Repressions	Repressions
Increased	48%	64%
Unchanged	30	21
Decreased	22	15
Total	100%	100%
Number of families	213	227

Adapted from Geiger, 1955:65–66. Source: Russian refugees living in Germany, Austria, and New York City. Serious repressions included imprisonment for a year or more, exile, execution, or the disappearance of a member of the family (presumably by action of the secret police). Respondents had not personally experienced serious repression but were reporting on the experience of their family of childhood or family of marriage.

Table 22-1 shows the effect on family cohesiveness of political persecution. These anti-Soviet families tended to grow closer together in the face of the threat of political oppression, but when that threat materialized, solidarity increased still more. Specifically, "The members of the . . . family drew closer during the Soviet regime. They spoke freely among themselves about things that they could not talk about with other people, and the children drew closer to their parents since they only felt secure at home" (Geiger, 1955:59). To lose a member of the family during Stalin's reign of terror was a severe crisis, but the family's common resentment of that terror brought them closer to each other. It is difficult to say what the effect of removing a family member may have been on the relationship between the persecuted one and the residual family. There can be little doubt however that those left behind cowered more closely together the fiercer the persecution became.

In addition to persecution by the secret police, Geiger's refugee families had been ostracized by their neighbors. One schoolboy reported that after his father was arrested his teachers and fellow students viewed him with suspicion as a disloyal member of the Communist state. Classified by the whole community as "socially undesirables," family members were forced even more to rely on one another.

Internal Causes

When the cause of the difficulty lies within the family, the reaction of the family is less likely to be sympathetic.

Mutual Recrimination If no outsider can be blamed, there is often disagreement over whether the impaired individual or the rest of the family is to blame. For example, the family may blame mental illness or alcoholism on the "weakness" of the individual, but the patient blames the hostility of the family.

Who is to blame for unemployment or low income? If everyone or almost everyone is laid off by a strike or a general depression, the husband can hardly be blamed. But if the husband is unemployed while others are working or the husband is poor while others are getting ahead, his difficulties may seem due to not trying hard enough to find a job or get a raise. During the 1930s, the Soviet Union offered widespread opportunities for upward mobility. As a result, men who earned less than average were often blamed by their families. At the same time, the men felt frustrated in their economic aspirations. Geiger reported that "in many cases such frustrations led to mutual recriminations and interpersonal hostility among family members" (1955:64). Geiger's refugee families were more apt to suffer from decreased solidarity if their living conditions were worse than average for their social group. Thus, when a man fails to function as well as might be expected in comparison with his peers, he is vulnerable to attack by his family. Such attacks tend to develop into endless recriminations which exacerbate the individual's problems and unsettle the family relationships.

Delinquent Individuals If blame is pinned on the impaired individual and he accepts that blame, relations between him and the rest of the family may be less tense but more distant. If everyone agrees that the husband was sent to prison because he committed a crime when he shouldn't have or bungled it when he might have gotten away with it, the husband may be frozen out of the family as they establish a coalition against him.

Among wives of British prisoners, the freezing-out process was symbolized by the fact that ten times as many wives went home to their own families as stayed with the husband's family (an extraordinarily matrilateral tendency). Moreover, the more often the husband went to prison, the more matrilateral this doubling up became, increasing from 88 percent among wives of first offenders to 93 percent for doubled-up wives of recidivists (Morris, 1965).

TABLE 22-2   Effect of Repeated Imprisonment on Wife's
Attitude Toward Marriage

WIFE'S ATTITUDE TOWARD MARRIAGE	FREQUENCY OF IMPRISONMENT	
	Once	More Than Once
Stronger than ever, miss him a lot	26%	17%
Quite happy about it	51	39
Occasionally regret it	7	17
Often regret it	16	27
Total	100%	100%
Number of wives	236	179

Adapted from Morris, 1965:102. Source: Representative samples of prisoners in England and Wales.

Progressive alienation of these wives from their husbands is also visible in Table 22-2. The more often the husband was imprisoned, the more the wife regretted her marriage. Perhaps he could be forgiven for landing in prison once, but the more he got himself in that fix, the more likely he was to be perceived as a bad husband.

Recidivists apparently failed their families not only while they were in prison but while they were out. More than half again as many wives of recidivists reported conflicts with their husbands about poor work records, inadequate income, involvement with other women, and excessive drinking. How much this may have been due to more deviant behavior by the husbands and how much to an increasingly critical attitude by the wives is impossible to ascertain. In either case, the complaints reflect increasing estrangement between the partners. Indeed, the few areas where wives of recidivists reported *fewer* conflicts also reflected progressive alienation—fewer conflicts over sex, over children, and over in-laws probably meant that the husbands were less involved in their marriages so there was less opportunity for these issues to arise.

If a delinquent husband has been enough of a trouble-maker, the family may feel relieved to have him gone. It would be wrong to assume that a husband's departure always creates a crisis. Sometimes it resolves a crisis that the husband has created by abusive behavior.

One soldier's participation in World War II was a relief to his family:

Mr. A was a very prosperous lawyer who was able to provide well for his wife and three children, but the marriage relationship had turned from one of love to a cold business partnership. Mr. A would not divorce his wife because of the damage to his reputation that would ensue, but delighted to practice refined mental torture on her. She bore this because there was no other way of providing for the children, and her husband's departure for the service meant a blessed respite from his cruelty. (Hill, 1949:59)

The more delinquent the husband, the less severe the crisis and the greater the benefits created by his absence.

In other cases, the departure of a husband makes little difference one way or another. If the husband's role in the family has already become marginal, there may be few role functions to be missed if he leaves altogether. He may still be blamed, but the more extensive his role impairment has been, the less noticeable will be his physical departure.

Delinquent Families   Only if the family blame themselves for their troubles is an emotional split likely to be avoided. The willingness of the family to do this depends not so much on the nature of the problem, but on their lack of defensiveness and their sympathy for their impaired member.

Sometimes a crisis forces the family to realize that something is wrong, to take stock of their own involvement, and to discover their responsibility for the vulnerable member's difficulties. In Morris' study of prisoners and their families, dominant wives of passive husbands were forced by the husband's imprisonment to recognize that they had driven their husbands to crime by undermining their feelings of adequacy so that they turned to drink, gambling, and other women as escapes. While the husband was in prison, these wives had ample opportunity to reflect on their behavior, to apologize, and to resolve to be better wives in the future. Husbands characteristically responded to these overtures by reassuring their wives that they were not so bad after all, forgiving them, and joining in resolving to improve the marriage upon release. Such couples frequently symbolized their new solidarity by conceiving another child.

Although a family's admission of responsibility for the delinquent may avoid a split within the family, it may precipitate a split between the family and the community. If the family feel embarrassed by what they have done to their member, they may shun contact with others which might reveal their secret sin. If the community is so tightly knit that their responsibility cannot be kept secret, they may be subjected to social ostracism, complementing their own withdrawal. A split between the family and the community may increase the cohesiveness of the family by sharpening its boundary line, but at the same time it may deprive the family of the support which outsiders give when troubles are seen as beyond their control.

Although deviant families may shy away from association with normal families, other deviant families can offer a supportive neocommunity. Wives of alcoholics find support in Al-Anon, wives of prisoners in wives' associations, and couples with marriage problems in therapy groups with similar couples. However, these alternative resources are formally organized and not universally available. Families which do not have the good fortune to have such special groups available may have to suffer alone the humiliation of having a damaged spouse.

THE CONSEQUENCES OF LEADERSHIP IMPAIRMENT

Farber (1964) suggested that families which encounter a role impairment first try to ignore the problem. Families, like other organizations, tend to be conservative and resist change if they can possibly avoid it. As long as the members of the family wear the proverbial rose-colored glasses, the fiction of normality may be long maintained. Optimistic people like to avoid the psychological strain of admitting that something has gone wrong with their family, of having to face the unpleasant reality that a spouse has let them down, and of having to reorganize their family. It is psychologically more "economical" to pretend that a problem does not exist and hope that it will go away.

From the standpoint of the family as an organization, it is also more economical to retain the old pattern as long as possible. Reorganization is a complex and difficult procedure. Jackson found that families of alcoholic men initially denied that any problem existed. This collective denial was possible because of the gradual onset of the disease. It was reinforced by the husband's denial that he was "hooked" on alcohol. He characteristically asserted "the sacredness of drinking behavior to the male" whenever the wife tried to deprive him of access to alcohol. Moreover Jackson found that friends generally minimized the seriousness of the problem when the wife consulted them, thus reinforcing the tendency to deny that the problem existed (1956: 365).

The ability of a family to sustain this pose depends on the importance of the roles which have been neglected. If the mother has a nervous breakdown, so many family functions suffer so soon that the family is forced to come to grips with its difficulties very fast. If the father loses his job and there is money in the bank, the family may be able to ignore his problem for awhile. Eventually, however, the fiction of normalcy collapses for every family faced with any appreciable impairment of a leadership role.

Demotion of the Impaired Parent

Every family faced with an impaired parent must do two things. The abandoned roles must be taken over by someone else and the impaired parent must be given a new role consistent with his reduced capacities. I have referred before to the expulsion of deviant members from the family. This is not the most common fate of impaired family members, however. By contrast with the economic system which fires any employee as soon as he fails to do his job, many families continue to shelter deviant members no matter how great the burden becomes. One reason families do this is that their normal role structure includes dependent roles. They are used to caring for children who are financial burdens and who need nurture and discipline. Thus they know what to do with persons who lose their competence and become dependent—they simply treat them like a child. Moreover, the fact that the impaired parent himself was a child once makes it easier for him to regress to childish dependence than if he had never played that role in life. Freezing-out may be necessary as a last resort if an impaired parent becomes unmanageable and exacts too great a toll of the family's emotional resources. But expulsion is not necessarily the expected fate of a damaged parent (even though it may happen more often than with damaged children for whom parents feel responsible).

The demotion of an impaired parent relieves the family's frustration and disappointment over his inability to perform his usual services. By no longer expecting him to act like a parent, they will no longer be disappointed when he fails to do so. Not only does this relieve the psychological strain on the family, but it relieves the strain on the malfunctioning spouse. Instead of resenting his nonperformance of his duties, the family can even feel sorry for his sufferings. This redefinition of the malfunctioning spouse's status in the family is facilitated by reallocating his functions to the unimpaired spouse. For example, Jackson found that after the wife took over her husband's roles in action, "the alcoholic husband is ignored or is assigned the status of a recalcitrant child by the wife and children" (1956:366). This new status meant that as the husband becomes less disruptive to the on-going family organization and function, hostility toward him diminishes and feelings of pity and protectiveness arise.

For a demoted parent, however, the loss of status may be painful. For men whose occupational prestige and income are slashed by retirement, the chief basis of self-worth may be lost. If the family adds insult to injury by demoting him within the home, his ego problem will be worsened. Even to find another job at lower pay may not salvage the situation if the family is unsympathetic. Yet because any member's status within the home depends on the resources he contributes to the family, demotion is an expected consequence of downward mobility in the occupational system.

Townsend found that external demotion was followed by internal demotion among many of his elderly working-class London men:

> Accepting a lower-status job had two important consequences. First, the man's wage fell. Second, the man's position in the home and family became less secure. While the mother was continually renewing her bonds with her children through seeing them frequently, advising and helping in the rearing of their babies and receiving, in her turn, help with the household chores, for his position the father relied mainly on his traditional authority in the home, derived largely from his role as breadwinner, and from his experiences in his occupation and in his outside sporting and social activities. This position was weakened if he was forced to take a job with lower pay and status. I remember in particular the laughter of a wife and her married daughter when they said the husband had become a messenger boy in his old age. (1957:140–141)

Townsend found that the chief insurance against such painful demotion was a pension sufficient to provide the husband with his accustomed amount of spending money. If retirement brought the loss of even the little pocket money a blue-collar man had been used to, the last vestiges of freedom and independence were lost and the man felt that he became a "poor relation" who could not hold his head up among the children on whom he depended.

Perhaps only when a parent is genuinely incapacitated by illness is demotion to a dependent role a comfortable regression. To find oneself demoted simply because one has reached age 60 or 65 is a painful experience for men who have always relied on their income as their main contribution to the family. If at the same time their internal demotion imposes extra burdens on the rest of the family, the pain is not merely personal and is harder to bear.

Regardless of the emotional consequences, an incapacitated parent must expect to be demoted. The less useful and more burdensome he becomes, the more his status must be redefined from that of a responsible parent to that of a dependent child.

Reallocation of Neglected Roles

The functions which the incapacitated parent abandons must be performed by someone else if the family is not to suffer. Most families find substitute role-performers as best they can, although like substitute teachers they may not do as well as the original person did when he was up to par. Still, a substitute parent is better than no parent at all and improvisation is mothered by necessity.

Substitute parents may be recruited either from inside or outside the family. The simplest substitution is impossible, however, for families with an impaired parent—recruiting a new one. Only after an impaired parent dies or has been divorced is the residual parent free to court a new partner.

Overloading the Residual Parent   The most accessible parent-substitute is the remaining parent. If the husband is incapacitated, the wife is the only other adult in a nuclear family. She is grown up enough to perform her husband's tasks better than her children could and physically present enough to do them more consistently than outsiders.

Morris (1965) found that a prisoner's place in the family was more effectively reserved for him if the wife took over the prisoner's functions rather than install someone else to take his place. The very fact that this overloaded the wife made her ready to return the tasks to the husband when he returned from prison. By contrast, if the wife moved in with her parents, the husband was more likely to find himself frozen out of the reconstituted family. A truncated nuclear family needs the husband back to restore it to normal, but a reestablished childhood family views the returning errant spouse as intruding in the new-old happy family.

The key roles which the wife must take over involve procuring external resources for the family's subsistence and the instrumental leadership of the family. If the sexes are reversed, the husband must take over the housekeeping and child-rearing.

When a husband is handicapped in earning money, the wife needs to go to work. During the Great American Depression, men were laid off by the millions but feminine services in restaurants and offices were still needed. Many families shifted their economic dependence from the husband to the wife. Under these circumstances the husband might be expected to take over the housekeeping. Bakke (1940) found, however, that as long as the husband remained in the labor market, actively searching for work each day, he helped very little at home. To be sure, an unemployed man is likely to be able to carry his normal tasks in the division of labor at home, but he is reluctant to "freeze himself out" of the labor market and take over the primary housekeeping responsibility, no matter how overloaded this may leave his wife.

If the husband is unable to do even his normal tasks around the house, the wife may have to mow the lawn, shovel snow, juggle storm windows and screens and generally strain her physical capacities. Household repairs she may bungle, producing minor catastrophes. The more arduous the burdens, the greater her resentment is likely to become and the more guilty the husband is likely to feel. Reallocating tasks within the family may get the work done but it has the disadvantage of "rubbing in" the impaired parent's incapacity since the new task-performers are persons he formerly supported himself.

A functionally impaired spouse may continue to offer his opinions in family decision-making but those opinions are likely to be less influential than when he was a more "resourceful" person. An absent spouse necessarily drops out of the family power structure as long as he is out of communication with his home base. This absence promotes wives to top position in the family, no matter how subordinate they might have been before.

Queen, Habenstein, and Adams (1961) attributed the change in the Roman family from a patriarchal to an equalitarian structure to the increased power of wives who were used to ruling the home while their husbands were away in the Roman army or the imperial administration. In modern Algeria, women who had previously been considered ignorant and helpless gained respect by governing their families while their husbands fought in the revolution (Goode, 1963). In sub-Saharan Africa, the prolonged absence of men engaged in industrial labor away from home produced increased feelings of independence among the self-governing women left behind. Perhaps of all the responsibilities which men may abandon, decision-making responsibility is taken over by wives with the greatest enthusiasm because it gives them the feeling of importance which the man loses when he is demoted from the top position.

Child-rearing is normally a maternal function anyway, so the absence of the husband is less crucial. However, insofar as the family system assigns the husband the responsibility for discipline, that task has to be taken over by the wife. Grönseth (1964) reported that Norwegian sailors were absent from home for months and years at a time. Their wives became so used to disciplining their children in the husband's absence that even during his shore leaves they continued to be the chief disciplinarian. Moreover, they adopted a more masculine style of discipline than that used by wives in intact families. They were more controlled and less impulsive in meting out discipline.

Wives, thus, take over many functions abandoned by their absent or incapacitated husbands. In so doing, they are liable to become overloaded with responsibility. In most of the world's families, it takes two parents to carry the burdens of family life. In decentralized polygynous families we might say that the role of husband is systematically impaired since there is only a fractional husband available per wife. We have already seen in Chapter 18 that this leaves each wife saddled with heavy economic and child-rearing responsibilities. That she is overloaded by these burdens is suggested by the frequency with which polygynous wives punish their children when they are angry or aggressive toward the mother. In the six societies studied by Minturn and Lambert (1964) polygynous mothers were more punitive toward their children than mothers in societies with one-to-one husband–wife ratios.

In nuclear families, the more completely an incapacitated parent's services are lost, the heavier the overload on the residual parent becomes. Whether the wife collapses under that overload depends both on how heavy the family burden is and how strong the wife is. Morris (1965) found signs of both variables among her prisoners' wives: (1) The larger the number of children, the worse the family's adjustment to the crisis of imprisonment because of the financial and child-rearing responsibilities involved; and (2) wives who had previously depended on dominant husbands felt quite lost without them and sometimes became so thoroughly demoralized that they could not even manage to visit them in prison, thus depriving themselves of the moral support which visits might have provided. By contrast, stronger wives bore similar burdens with less stress or in some cases even thrived on the emancipation from control by their husbands.

Promoting a Child   If the burden is too heavy for the mother to bear by herself, the overload must be transferred to other shoulders. I have already suggested that in becoming head of the family, a wife is promoted to a position of responsibility previously held by the husband. If she asks her children to share that responsibility, this means they too are promoted. In some cases, the child may be promoted all the way to the top, in other cases to a position of equality with the wife. In either one he has been elevated from the status of child to the status of substitute husband. Lesser promotions may be to a newly created post of assistant parent.

Perhaps in most families, the demotion of the father is accompanied by a compensatory rise in the status of one or more children. Just as co-parents with too many children draft the older ones into auxiliary service, so a residual parent is likely to respond to his overload in the same way. The difference is that whereas co-parents in large families need help simply with the financial, housekeeping, and child-rearing burdens of too many children, a partially bereaved wife needs the replacement of her husband's marital functions as well. Thus the range of services demanded of children in truncated families is greater than in overexpanded families.

In Bakke's unemployed families, children were pressed into housework especially when the mother went to work while the father was still actively seeking employment. If the children themselves helped support the family, they gained dual reasons for appreciation from the parents and for higher status within the family. As substitute housekeepers they had been promoted to a maternal role and as supplementary wage-earners to a paternal role.

Emotionally dependent wives in Morris' sample missed their imprisoned husbands most and turned to their children as husband-substitutes. To replace the husband's emotional support, they poured out their worries to their children. One mother frequently kept her fourteen-year-old boy home from school in order that he could keep her company.

One way of replacing the husband's companionship is to develop a mother–son coalition. Table 22-3 shows how much longer wives of men who were away at sea nurtured their children than wives in an adjacent village whose husbands brought their boats ashore every day. Wives stranded ashore apparently derived from their children some of the affection and companionship which they otherwise would have obtained from their husbands. Like Morris' prisoners' wives, they apparently missed their husbands most at night, as shown by the late age (almost to the child's adolescence) to which they continued sleeping beside the child on the tatami matting.

TABLE 22-3 Mother–Child Closeness by Occupational Roles of Father and Mother

MOTHER'S NURTURANT ACTIVITY	OCCUPATIONAL ROLES OF FATHER AND MOTHER			
	FATHER AWAY (Deep-sea Fishing)	NORMAL (Off-shore Fishing)	(White-Collar Work)	MOTHER BUSY (Shopkeeping)
Breast-feeds child	32 months	21 months	16 months	12 months
Carries child on back	44	30	23	18
Sleeps with child	130	56	45	35

Adapted from Vogel, 1963:230. Source: Japanese deep-sea and off-shore fishing villages in the same prefecture and families of company employees and small shop-keepers in the same Tokyo suburb. Approximately 60 families were involved in each community.

Conversely, the shopkeepers' wives portrayed in the table were so busy helping their husbands out in the family business (in the front rooms of the family home) that they had to curtail their nurturant activities earlier than usual. This maternal role impairment presumably could not be replaced by anyone else, so the child not only suffered the loss of maternal care but had no compensatory coalition to make up for it. Such children were not promoted affectionally, because busy as the father and mother may have been, they still found companionship in working together in the shop.

The age and sex of the children determine the ease with which they may be promoted. The older the child the better he can perform the required tasks. And if the child is of the impaired parent's sex, he is an especially suitable candidate. If there are several children in the family, the eldest of the proper sex has priority for promotion. If the father is unemployed, the eldest son goes to work. If the mother cannot do the cooking, the eldest daughter takes over. If the mother is starved for affection, a son is a more suitable husband-substitute than a daughter.

Thus leadership roles which are normally divided between the parents are reallocated among the remaining parent and one or more children. This means that the whole structure of the family tends to be reorganized, with one parent demoted to the status of "child" and one or more children becoming "parents."

Falling Back on Grandparents   Sometimes the reallocation of functions extends beyond the limits of the nuclear family. If the family's resources are limited (the wife weak, the children young), the overload must be transferred elsewhere. The logical candidates are the maternal grandparents on whom the wife depended when she was a child and who are a familiar resource in time of trouble. To regress to an earlier pattern of dependence is easier than devising a new one. So going back home or soliciting the help of nearby grandparents is a useful way of filling the vacuum created by role impairment within the home.

Going home is easiest when the spouse is absent. The more prolonged the absence, the more likely the residual family is to return home. If the impaired spouse is still living at home, living with in-laws would only aggravate the bad feeling which his impairment is likely to have created already. But if the husband is away in the wars or in prison, there is nothing to prevent the wife from returning to her childhood nest, taking her children with her.

The absence of the husband weakens the wife's involvement with him and enables her to give more attention to her parents. This may explain why one effect of the husband's imprisonment on Morris' wives was to improve their relationship with their parents. Similarly Hill (1949) found that for wives who moved in with their parents, the hardship of war separation was reduced more effectively than by any other stratagem.

We have already seen, however, that going home is not the best preparation for re-establishing the nuclear family. This reversion to an earlier family group is easier on the wife, pleasing to the parents, but threatens the husband's residual status within the family.

Recruiting a Quasi-Spouse   Even though recruiting a new spouse is impossible as long as the old spouse is attached to the family, a quasi-spouse in the form of a lover may be possible. Just as going home to grandparents is difficult with an impaired spouse physically present, recruiting a quasi-spouse is even more difficult. But if the spouse is absent, a temporary love affair is more feasible. Indeed, in the case of absent husbands, both partners lack sexual companionship and both may turn to substitute lovers.

In Africa, Goode (1963) noted that adultery was frowned upon as long as family patterns were stable but became tolerated in societies where husband-absence was chronic. If the husband's family had paid cattle to acquire rights to whatever children the wife might bear, the husband and his kin group might even look with favor on putting her reproductive capacity to use when the husband was unable to function as genitor. In Swaziland such a wife

> . . . is said "to hit birds" for her husband who has the right to the adulterine children. This recent tolerance of adultery under present conditions, when large numbers of men are away from their homes for long periods working for Europeans, appears to be a defense technique of the husband and his group anxious to benefit by the fertility of the woman for whom they gave the marriage-cattle. (Kuper, 1950:92)

In modern societies, neither married women nor their absent husbands view adulterous conceptions so positively, and unwanted extramarital pregnancies are likely to be terminated by abortions. The sexual relationships out of which those conceptions spring are viewed more positively however by the lonely individual (if not by the spouse). The chief difficulty in recruiting a quasi-spouse, however, is that the same force which removed the real spouse may have removed most potential quasi-spouses. In wartime most men may be at the front while wives remain behind, and in African mining camps or Western frontier communities, men may have to share the few women who can sell their services at high prices while their wives remain in a home village or home country populated by women and children but few men.

For such reasons, quasi-spouses do not often become an institutionalized solution to the problem of role reallocation. At best they are a deviant solution to the problem of loneliness and sexual frustration.

Among the Nuer, Evans-Pritchard found a special type of marriage between women. If a woman was sterile and therefore incapable of acquiring a man as a marriage partner, she could marry a woman and play the social role of father or "pater" to her wife's children. Since she could not be the biological father of those children, she had to recruit a quasi-spouse for that purpose:

> When the marriage rites have been completed the husband gets a male kins-man or friend or neighbor, sometimes a poor [foreigner] to beget children by her wife and to assist, regularly or when assistance is particularly required, in those tasks of the home for the carrying out of which a man is neces-sary. (1951:108)

This quasi-spouse performed those functions which only a male can in the biological and social division of functions between the sexes.

Unallocated Residuals Precisely those sexual and affectional functions a quasi-spouse is intended to serve are most likely to remain unmet by any new resource when the true spouse abandons them. The sexual function of mar-riage is the most difficult to replace in view of the incest taboo on using children or parents for this purpose and the intolerance of adultery. Second only to the shortage of money, wives of first offenders found the loneliness and sexual frustration of doing without their imprisoned husbands the most difficult:

> Most wives who mentioned loneliness said that they missed their husband in the evenings and at nights, . . . "I miss him like. I was in bed with my sister the other night and I was asleep like, and I forgot, and I said 'move over Jimmy,' and he wasn't there." (Morris, 1965:91)

Even wives whose husbands had never been good companions to them missed them when they were gone. Men might have been out with the boys almost every night in the week, yet they came home eventually. Once a man went to prison, however, his wife had no one even to wait up for. Some wives felt a bad husband was better than no husband at all. They even missed the husband "knocking them about" because "they were used to it, it was part of home and family life" (*Ibid.*). To miss being beaten up attests poignantly to the desperate loneliness of a wife who must do without her husband for months or years.

If the wife is mentally ill or is otherwise handicapped and the husband departs, the family is doubly deprived. With no third parent available within the family and no normal residual parent to recruit alternative resources from outside the family, missing functions may not be reallocated to anyone.

One example of dual impairment was uncovered by Pedersen (1966) in studying the effect of father-absence on adolescent sons of American soldiers. Most of the boys had been born after World War II had ended and had been separated from their fathers relatively short periods of time. In contrast with Norwegian sailors who left for two-year whaling trips and returned only briefly before leaving again, the average soldier had been separated from his children only 18 months spread over almost as many years. This 10 percent absence was too little to make much difference in the life of sons provided the mother was competent to run the family in her husband's absence.

However, within an emotionally disturbed group of sons, Pedersen found that the longer the father had been away, the more severe the disturbance. Those whose fathers had been away relatively long periods of time were more given to daydreaming and got along poorly with their peers and family. The explanation appeared to be that their mothers were themselves emotionally disturbed, being more hysterical, schizoid, paranoid, hypochondriacal, and depressive as measured by the Minnesota Multiphasic Personality Inventory.

Since the fathers of the disturbed boys were no different from the fathers of the normals, the researcher believed that the absence of the father removed the "buffering effect" which he exerted when he was present. In other words, the mother's impaired ability to rear her children was normally offset by the father. But when he abandoned his family for active military duty, no one took over the functions which he normally performed. So the son was exposed to the deleterious effects of his mother's emotional problems. And the longer the father was gone, the worse her impact on the son.

Perhaps the U. S. regulation that last-surviving sons may not be drafted into military service should be paralleled by a ruling that residual normal parents should not be separated from their families, either. In any case, Pedersen's findings suggest that limited absence of the father may be adequately compensated for by reallocation of roles provided that the remaining parent is reasonably competent. On the other hand, when impairment of one parent is matched by absence of the other, the children will suffer.

Family Disintegration

Despite the best efforts of a family to reorganize itself by taking unfulfilled functions away from the impaired member and reassigning them to other members, the new organization is seldom as strong as the family was before its troubles began and especially not as strong as a normal family which never confronted such troubles.

Change itself creates disorganization. One of the most disorganizing factors which can hit a family is to have the husband assigned to shift work—working the evening shift, the "graveyard" shift or worse yet the "swing" shift (which means that every week his working hours change from the week before). Mott and his colleagues found that this chaotic work schedule made it next to impossible for the man to perform any of the usual roles of husband and father save the basic one of bringing home his wages.

> [Shift work] increases the difficulty of performing the husband and father roles. The shift worker cannot provide companionship for his wife during the normal evening hours, and, if he is an afternoon shift worker, he seldom sees his children, except on his days off. Since he cannot fulfill the normal male role in family activities, serious problems of coordinating family activities develop. Among the families of afternoon and night shift workers, functional integration is lower and conflict among the members is more prevalent than it is among day shift workers. (1965:301)

Worse yet, the need for the husband to sleep at odd hours imposes extra strains on the family in addition to his role impairment: "The wife must make many more meals each day, and she must do her housework at unusual times when her husband and children are not sleeping." (*Ibid.*) The children, similarly, must restrain their play when the husband is sleeping.

Where parental malfunctioning results from socially deviant behavior, adverse effects on the family are even more to be expected. Earlier I cited Morris' finding that the husband's imprisonment shocked some wives into realizing they could improve their marriages. Even in those cases, the improvement was relatively short-lived. Second honeymoons gave way to reassertion of old destructive patterns of wife-dominance and husband-escape. Foreshadowing renewed trouble was the fact that even wives who thought things were going to be better experienced headaches and other psychosomatic symptoms of tension as the husband's return approached. When all marriages are considered together, twice as many deteriorated as improved. Improvements were confined almost exclusively to first imprisonments; repeated imprisonment almost always affected marriages negatively, if at all.

Worse than outside crime is deviant behavior within the home. Alcoholism and mental illness not only impair the husband's ability to perform his usual functions but turn him into a menace to the rest of the family. Drunken husbands are notoriously violent toward their wives and even children may not be exempt from abuse. Such husbands mistreat their families so badly that it is difficult to keep the family from disintegrating completely—*i.e.,* from throwing him out. Indeed, as we will see in the next chapter, expulsion from the family is often the denouement of such abusiveness.

Defensive Efforts If family disintegration is threatened by role impairment, can a family do anything to defend itself against that fate? The necessary steps depend on the nature of the problem. If the problem is the husband's absence, communication efforts are needed to bridge the distance. If the problem is deviant behavior, alienation of the children may be reduced by hiding that deviance from them.

For more than a third of Morris' families, the children had no idea that their father was in prison. Mothers often "explained" that he was in a hospital. When the children went to visit their fathers, they were puzzled by the guards' uniforms and keys, but their "awkward" questions were handled by simple denials and evasions. This strategy works with preschool children but becomes increasingly difficult as children become more perceptive. The longer the fiction of behavioral normalcy can be maintained, however, the less the strain on the family's integration.

Maintaining contact with imprisoned husbands was handicapped by British prison policy in Morris' study. Visits were forbidden during the first two months of incarceration and limited to one a month thereafter. Prisoners were frequently transferred from nearby prisons to remote ones because of overcrowding of prisons in populated areas, so visiting became more difficult or impossible. Letters were limited to one a week per prisoner, which placed wives in competition with mothers and other relatives to see who would get to write. Even when visits materialized, husband and wife were kept at arm's length by cages and screens which made the visit so frustrating that wives and especially children were discouraged from returning. Such institutional policies were not intended to destroy family integration, but they had that effect.

Insofar as wives managed to take advantage of even these limited opportunities for maintaining contact, they helped keep the family intact.

For soldiers, similarly, visits from the wife or furloughs home have a beneficial effect. Hill (1949) found that the larger the number of days spent back home, the better the family's adjustment to the crisis of war separation (despite the pain of parting when each furlough ended). Letters kept husband and wife in touch with each other: The larger the number of letters and number of topics covered in them, and the higher the quality of communication conveyed by them, the less difficult the crisis for the family. "If the wife could pour out her affection and troubles into her letters, she obtained a release from her household worries and tensions, and, if in turn his letters were loving and affectionate, she obtained great satisfaction from them" (1949:141).

A couple's ability to carry on high-quality communication depended on having a reasonably good marriage in the first place and on communication skill. For couples with bad marriages, letters might only make matters worse. One of Hill's husbands answered a letter by urging his wife, "Let me fight one war at a time!" For Slater and Woodside's working-class British couples communicating in writing was painfully difficult:

> Men and women, unaccustomed to writing, had somehow to get their feelings on to paper. This in itself was a source of misunderstandings. When one husband in the Middle East tried to expound his philosophy of life, his wife thought he was going "mental." Another wife who had heard nothing for months, decided her husband had ceased to care, and embarked on adventures "to forget." (1951:218)

On the other hand, some of their working-class couples had had such poor oral communication before the war separation that the effort to communicate in writing enabled them to understand each other better than ever before. Such dramatic reversals of the usually deleterious effect of separation testify to the integrative value of communication.

CRISES OF RECOVERY

After this emphasis on the difficulties created by role impairments, it may be surprising to suggest that the return or recovery of the impaired parent sometimes creates new problems. For some families, the prodigal spouse returns to open arms and the family blissfully returns to normal. Potentially, however, new adjustments may be necessary which justify the use of the term "crises of recovery."

The worse the impaired parent treated his family, the greater the likelihood that it will not be his loss but his return which provokes the chief crisis. This was particularly the case for women so alienated from criminal husbands that they had separated from them prior to the husband's imprisonment. Morris (1965) found that 39 percent of these separated wives were afraid the husband would return home and physically injure them after release from prison. That release therefore created a crisis for them.

Second Courtship

If the partner never leaves home, the spouse will be able to keep abreast of changes in his personality so there will be no need to become reacquainted when he returns to normal. But if the spouse has been away, he may return a stranger. The longer the separation and the greater the contrast in the experiences of the two partners, the more likely they are to have grown apart by a process of differential socialization.

Slater and Woodside described such estrangement for their communication-handicapped war-separated couples:

> Readjustment was needed, even when the marriage had been untroubled. A few said they were able to take things up where they had left off, without any feeling of estrangement. In the majority there were difficulties of one or another kind. Some of them were sexual. . . . In other cases they were the psychological results of the differing paths of development that had been followed by husband and wife in the intervening period. The outlook of a wife might seem narrow and restricted to a husband who had been broadened by life in the Army, travel in other countries, perhaps the responsibility of rank, and education in both the Army sense and a more liberal one. Other husbands, less secure, disliked or disapproved of their wives' new friends and interests, acquired during their absence. Several women complained of the unfairness that expected everything would be just the same after all those years away: "they've been around, they've seen the world." (1951:223)

Morris found that prisoners came home worried about the sexual side of marriage and that wives had similar anxieties about that most intimate side of marriage after prolonged separation: "Closely associated with these fears of sexuality, there is often the feeling that they will be like strangers to each other" (1965:121).

Strangers are precisely what separated couples do become, to a greater or lesser degree. Insofar as they do, it would be as inappropriate for them to go straight to bed as for any strangers. They need to become reacquainted, to court each other over again, and to rebuild the love whose foundation has been eroded by their separation. For couples who recognize this necessity, reunion may be a delightful opportunity for a second courtship. For those who by-pass it, reunion can be almost like rape.

Role Reallocation

The hard work of shifting responsibilities away from the impaired parent must be reversed when he returns to normal. Families assume that they can return automatically to the role structure which existed prior to the deviance. Family members who have been saddled with the deviant parent's responsibilities may be glad to get rid of them. But changing the role structure of the family has so many repercussions that restoring the status quo ante may no longer be either possible or appropriate. Obstacles may lie in the path of every stage in the reversion process.

Reinstating the Impaired Parent   The return of an absent spouse signals the time for establishing a normalized arrangement. But if the partner has been ill, cures are seldom so dramatic that they remove all doubt about his readiness for reinstatement. With either mental illness or alcoholism, the problem has fluctuated so much and the evidences of normalcy are so subtle and ambiguous that the family is liable to resist or at least feel anxious about the patient's resumption of full responsibility. It may be easier to allow him to resume tangible roles such as employment (which has the added advantage of taking place away from home) than to readmit him to the emotional confidence of the family. Thus in the case of alcoholics:

> Mother has for years managed the family, and now father wishes to be reinstated in his former roles. Usually the first role reestablished is that of breadwinner. . . . With the resumption of this role, the husband feels that the family should reinstate him immediately in all his former roles. . . .
>
> The wife, who finds it difficult to conceive of her husband as permanently sober, feels an unwillingness to relinquish control, even though she believes that reinstatement of her husband in his family roles is necessary to his sobriety. She remembers events in the past when his failure to handle his responsibilities was catastrophic to the family. (Jackson, 1956:368)

For Sampson's women who had been committed to mental hospitals, reintegration into the family was even more difficult. Returning to the role they played immediately prior to hospitalization would not have meant functioning normally but resuming the role of impaired parent. They needed to revert to behavior prior to both hospitalization and the illness which precipitated it. Yet the fact that illness developed out of that supposedly normal situation suggests that the wife needed not to be reinstated in an old role, but to find a new one which would be more satisfying. To do that would require the reorganization of the family along lines they had never experienced before. Few families possess that much creativity unaided. Sampson found that most couples achieved only "a limited and transient reorganization of the surface of marital life" (1961:151). However the professional personnel who treated the mental patient might theoretically assist families in reorganizing more thoroughly (see Chapter 24).

Even if the parent has only been absent and always functioned well when he was home, reinstatement may encounter resistance. Insofar as reinstatement demotes the wife and children or severs ties with grandparents or lovers, there are vested interests to be overcome. The changes which took place during the parent's absence may have involved gains as well as losses. In any case, change always means "you can't go home again" to a situation just the way it was before. Reinstatement requires giving the returning parent significant roles but those roles must be tailored to the new family situation which was created by his abandonment of his old roles.

Usually a returning father wishes to become a responsible family member again. In exceptional cases, however, the man may have enjoyed freedom from responsibility and be reluctant to go back to "work." Almost 10 percent of Hill's veterans found it hard to settle down after being in the army where they were taken care of and had little responsibility. Although they rarely admitted it openly to their wives, the latter could tell from the husband's restlessness and moodiness at home and from his impatience with the children that he was hardly ready to resume a normal family life. In these cases, reinstatement met with resistance even from the husband himself.

Demoting the Wife   For wives who have managed a family all by themselves, the return of the husband inevitably means demotion. She may not return to the subordinate position she held before, but even sharing power equally is quite a come-down from wielding it all by oneself.

Hill (1949) found that the return of soldiers from World War II created a "crisis of reunion" for wives who had grown so independent during the husband's absence that they were unwilling to play second-fiddle again. If the husband tried to reassert his old dominance, a power struggle was precipitated which had to be resolved if the family was not to split up. The extraordinarily large number of divorces in the immediate post-war years suggests that some couples were unable to resolve their conflicts.

For Slater and Woodside's British couples this problem seems to have been widespread: "Men generally did not welcome the increased independence of women which had been brought by the war, by responsibilities personally shouldered, by an independent income and out-of-home contacts" (1951: 223). Regardless of whether men welcomed their wives' new stature or not, I assume from Chapter 19's examination of the effect of increased resources on the balance of power, that the post-return balance shifts in the wife's direction from what it was before the separation. Wives were not generally demoted all the way to their earlier position but were given a new intermediate status commensurate with their experience.

The greatest resistance to demotion may be expected from women who felt better off during the husband's absence than before. Eight percent of Morris' respondents felt better while their husbands were in prison because they were free to have social contacts which the husbands had previously forbidden. After the husband's return, such women would not easily surrender the freedom to go out more than they had before his imprisonment. Some compromise might be possible between the husband's wishes to keep his wife at home and her wish to go out, but a genuine compromise would necessarily be different from anything the couple had known before.

In general, then, the return of an impaired spouse threatens the privileges and powers which the residual spouse has exercised and creates a potential conflict requiring an accommodation between the partners. Although in some cases, the wife may be able to maintain her interim status unimpaired, in general the return of her husband means she must surrender at least part of the higher status which she has gained. Thus at least partial demotion for the wife is almost inevitable when the husband returns.

Demoting the Child   Restoration of the status quo is particularly inappropriate with children since the sheer lapse of time changes them more than the parents. Normal families must loosen the reins on their children as they get older. The fact that children age during the father's absence means that he tends to be behind the times in recognizing how much they have grown up and how much more freedom they deserve. If he tries to treat them the way he did before, his methods will have become so obsolescent that they will rebel.

The problem caused by the sheer lapse of time is exacerbated by whatever promotion the child received in the reallocation of the father's abandoned roles. If the child acted as a husband-substitute, it is doubly inappropriate to be reduced to a little child again. To be demoted is difficult enough for a wife, but for a child struggling for increased freedom, to be put back in jail is particularly offensive.

If mother and child have developed a loving coalition to substitute for the missing husband, the return of the father is like the intrusion of a stepfather in a mother–child household. Not only does the father come in as a stranger half-remembered or not remembered at all, but he robs the child of the mother with whom he has become intimate. Jealousy, resentment, and rebellion against the attempts of this strange man to reassert control over the child are to be expected. The younger the child when the father left, the longer he was gone, the closer the attachment between mother and child, and the faster the father tries to resume control, the more negative the reaction.

Fifteen percent of Hill's fathers returned from the war to find that their children had grown so close to their wives or other relatives that they were resented rather than welcomed. Such children generally refused to accept the father's discipline although they might begrudgingly accept him back into the family as a companion. They resisted demotion and were prepared to reinstate the father only in a lower status than before.

In a study of children born during World War II, Stolz (1954) found such reactions were widespread because the children were so young that the father came home as a complete stranger. (The typical child was born four months after the father left for the front and was 18 months old when he returned.)

Most of the fathers resented the closeness between mother and child, feeling so jealous and excluded that the expected second honeymoon was spoiled. All of the couples quarreled over methods of child-rearing. Fathers felt that both the mother and the maternal relatives were too kind to the child and had spoiled him by overindulgence.

Despite these quarrels, a third of the fathers were able to accept the child, but half were ambivalent and the remainder showed no interest or rejected the child. The children responded with shyness, aloofness, or indifference to this strange man's advances. They cried, rebuffed his demonstrations of affection, refused to let him do things for them, and even expressed fear. The harder the father pushed the child, the stronger the resistance. Men who waited patiently for the child to warm up to them fared better. Both generations needed time for a leisurely courtship if they were to fall in love with each other.

One reason children feared the returning father was the harshness of his disciplinary methods. Stolz compared returning fathers with a matched group of never-separated fathers and found that the former punished their children more frequently and more severely. More than half the war veterans spanked the child so hard that it hurt, shook him roughly, yelled at him, or fought him. Stolz felt that the men wanted to hurt or frighten the child, though they rationalized their severity as needed to overcome the child's spoiled behavior.

This rough treatment further alienated the child and drove him back into his mother's arms, cementing their coalition and creating a vicious cycle. Instead of father and child drawing closer as the years went by, they frequently drove each other farther and farther apart.

Fathers and children fought over every conceivable issue. They battled over food, the child refusing to eat and the father trying to force-feed him. They battled over toilet-training accidents and over the child's unwillingness to go to bed. Fathers retaliated against the child by taking away his toys or favorite blanket and refusing to allow the mother to rock him to sleep. These tactics only made it more difficult for the child to go to sleep.

The father's behavior perpetuated the close relationship between the mother and the oldest child. But when the next child was born, the father felt particularly close to it and established a father–second child coalition to match the mother–first child tie.

TABLE 22-4 Differential Closeness of First- and Second-Born Children to Their Parents, by War Experience of Father

| | *WAR EXPERIENCE OF FATHER* | |
	Not Separated	*Separated*
Closeness of first-born child:		
Closer to mother	26%	89%
Equally close to both parents	58	5
Closer to father	16	5
Total	100%	100%
Number of families	19	19
Closeness of father, by birth order:		
Closer to first-born child	31%	0%
Equally close to both children	44	12
Closer to second-born child	25	88
Total	100%	100%
Number of families	16	16

Adapted from Stolz, 1954:70. Source: Married student families at Stanford University.

Table 22-4 shows that normal families were fairly evenly balanced. First-born children felt equally close to both parents, and fathers felt equally close to their first and second children. Moreover, in those exceptional cases where equal closeness did not occur, the chances were almost 50/50 as to which way the relationships would veer. In war-separated families, however, relationships were almost never evenly balanced and almost always skewed in the direction of a mother–child coalition for the first child and a father–child coalition for the second. Thus separation in the early months of a child's life profoundly distorted not only that child's relationship to his parents but the next child's, too. Despite their criticism of the wife for spoiling the first child, fathers spoiled their own ally just as much and then defended him vindictively against the older child's jealousy.

The war-separated children's personality development involved what Stolz labelled a "legion of problems." However, in trying to pinpoint the origin of those problems, Stolz discovered that they had not manifested themselves while the father was away but only after his return. She concluded that "Their allotment of difficulties seem[ed] to be the legacy of the fathers' return" (1954:148). In other words, it was the crisis of recovery rather than the removal of the father which precipitated the disturbed development of these children. Apparently these children resisted demotion indefinitely and never allowed their fathers back into their lives in a normal capacity.

In Norwegian sailor families, Grönseth found that periodic visits home allowed the sailor to play only a quasi-paternal role. Since these sailors never settled down ashore they never were candidates for normalization:

> The sailor family adapts to the sailor's short stays at home somewhat as if making room for a dear guest, with the sailor taking the corresponding role which, towards the children, is typically that of a "kind uncle." (1964:307)

If children have been mistreated by their father in the past, they are reluctant to accept demotion. Jackson found that children were often unable or unwilling to allow their alcoholic fathers to resume jurisdiction over them. Faced with resistance, fathers often tried too hard "to manage this change overnight, and the very pressure put upon the children toward this end defeats him" (1956:368). Morris found that children feared most the return of fathers who had abused them sexually. These fathers apparently had not seduced their daughters but more nearly raped them against their will. The daughters did not want to be exposed to attack again.

In a variety of ways, then, children resist the reimposition of authority by the father after he has relinquished it. They resent displacement by the father in the mother's bed or at least in her heart after he has "deserted" her. For the mother, demotion is partially compensated by the husband's renewed companionship. For the child, however, it means simply being shoved out of the especially cozy nest the mother has built. Unless the father is extraordinarily sensitive and loving, demotion seems all loss and no gain to the child.

Leaving Grandparents   Grandparents are in much the same position as children. The return of the son-in-law threatens to destroy the happy family which they have reconstituted. Therefore grandparents are likely to resist the return of the son-in-law and he in turn to resent his wife's closeness to her parents.

For Stolz's war veterans, clashes with the wife's family were almost as universal (84 percent) as clashes over children. For immature wives who had gone home to live with their parents during the husband's imprisonment Morris found that his release posed a crisis: "Should the wife leave home to go back to live with him again?" Most wives did go back, but their ambivalence indicates the problem.

Abandoning Lovers   The return of the husband normally means that both partners have left their interim lovers physically, but that is not the same as leaving them psychologically.

Table 22-5 shows that husbands who had been involved with a single lover during the war were most apt to have difficulty resuming sexual relations

TABLE 22-5 Affectional and Sexual Readjustment of Husband and Wife by Sex Experience of Husband During Separation

| | HUSBAND'S SEX EXPERIENCE DURING SEPARATION | | | |
	One Lover	Played Around	No Chance	No Interest
Love/sex problems	3	0	2	1
No problems	0	2	5	5
Total husbands	3	2	7	6

Adapted from Stolz, 1954:32. Source: War-separated couples at Stanford.

with their wives. By contrast, men who played around without becoming seriously involved or who were not involved with other women were more apt to resume the marital relationship without difficulty. Thus lovers who had taken the place of the spouse during the separation stood in the way psychologically of a resumption of loving relationships between husband and wife.

chapter twenty-three
ORGANIZATIONAL DISSOLUTION: BROKEN FAMILIES

The last chapter dealt with the earlier stages of family dissolution—the impairment of parental functioning and the temporary departure of one parent. The present chapter carries this process of organizational dissolution to its ultimate conclusion in the permanent departure of one or both parents. The mode of departure varies from informal desertion to formal divorce, with or without continuing contact with the departed parent, and on to the bereavement which is the ultimate fate of every marriage. Our primary focus will be on the consequences of losing the parent(s) for the remaining members of the particular family and for the family system in general.

VOLUNTARY FAMILY DISSOLUTION AS A MODE OF CONFLICT RESOLUTION

In the preceding chapters, we have seen how conflicts between husband and wife create tensions within the family and divide the family into hostile camps. We have seen the toll which tension and division exact of the members of the family, and more especially of children torn between the parents or used as scapegoats to hold the family together. We have seen that salvaging such children may require the destruction of the family. This raises the question of whether children or the residual parent are generally better off after the expulsion of one parent than in the presence of two parents who cannot get along with each other.

Table 23-1 suggests that terminating the marriage may benefit children who otherwise would have been subjected to continuing tension. Since many divorced parents in Nye's study had remarried by the time of his study, it is not entirely clear whether the improvements shown were due to the divorce or to the remarriage. In an earlier chapter, however, we found that remarriage was usually a negative experience for children. Therefore, I assume that most if not all of the benefits portrayed in the table resulted from the cease-fire between the parents made possible by breaking up the marriage. The ratios show that children still living in unhappy homes had anywhere from 20 percent to 81 percent more personal and family problems than those whose parents had terminated their unhappy marriages. This suggests that if conflict is sufficiently severe, it is in the children's interest to expel one of the warring partners for the sake of peace.

TABLE 23-1   Effect on Children of Parental Unhappiness or Divorce

CHILD'S CHARACTERISTIC	MARITAL STATUS OF PARENTS		UNHAPPY/ DIVORCED RATIO
	Unhappy	Divorced or Separated	
Disagrees with mother about values	47%	26%	1.81X
Feels rejected by father	69	40	1.73
Psychosomatic illness	50	31	1.61
Disagrees with father about values	53	34	1.56
Rejects father	55	37	1.49
Feels rejected by mother	55	44	1.25
Delinquency	48	39	1.23
Rejects mother	42	35	1.20
Number of cases	112	115	

Adapted from Nye, 1957:359. Source: Ninth- to twelfth-grade boys and girls in three Washington State high schools. One sixth of all homes were broken by divorce but most parents had remarried by the time of the study. A similar number of unhappy homes were selected for comparison on the basis of self-rated marital unhappiness, quarreling and arguing between the parents, attempted domination of each other, and lack of mutual activities or interests. Reciprocal percentages of adolescents did not exhibit the specified characteristics.

For Morris' prisoners' wives, separating from the husband prior to his imprisonment cushioned the damage which he could do to the family by his actions when he was present or by his absence when he was imprisoned. Wives already separated from the husband had already experienced the "crisis" of losing him and so were less affected by his imprisonment than those who lost the husband directly. Moreover, so bad was the relationship between most of the men and their families that the typical wife felt relieved to have him behind bars where she could be sure that he would not bother her or the children.

In a manner reminiscent of Nye's findings, Morris found that there was less delinquency among the children of broken marriages than among children who had lived with both parents up to the time of the father's imprisonment. Perhaps the dissolution of these families had not only resolved the tension of an unhappy home but removed the delinquent example of the father. Since children of criminals tend to follow in their father's footsteps, terminating marriage to such a man might be expected to be doubly beneficial.

The previous studies did not report which spouse took the initiative in breaking up the marriage. Usually the man leaves home, but that may be either his own idea or the result of expulsion by the rest of the family. The more deviant the husband's behavior, the greater the need for the wife to protect her children by divorcing him. But in protecting the children she may at the same time destroy the husband. What if the husband threatens suicide or is liable to relapse into an alcoholic binge?

Jackson reported that wives of alcoholics found it very difficult to decide whether they should separate from their husbands: "The mental conflict about deserting a sick man must be resolved, as well as the wife's feelings of responsibility for his alcoholism" (1956:367). To separate may mean losing what little money the alcoholic husband contributed to the family in his sober moments. Moreover, once the wife's departure seems imminent, the husband is liable to go on the wagon in an effort to induce her to stay. Wives most frequently were convinced by physical violence that they should separate. Yet this hazard may not be entirely removed by separation. Many wives feared that the husbands might respond violently to their desertion and abuse them and/or the children still further.

After the divorce crisis is navigated and the marriage has been legally terminated, relations are decentralized enough to reduce overt conflict almost to zero. The children's use as pawns becomes attenuated by virtue of the fact that the parents have custody of them alternately rather than simultaneously. Conflict may not disappear completely, but it cools off remarkably once the parents are out of each other's way.

RESTRUCTURING THE RESIDUAL FAMILY

The departure of the husband does not solve all the family's problems. Most husbands were good for something even if they did more harm than good. So their loss spells the loss of whatever services they still performed. It creates problems at the same time that it solves them. In case of bereavement, losses are greater, especially if the partner died suddenly in the prime of life when he was fully performing his roles.

Many of the problems created by the loss of the husband are the same as those which we have already seen when a parent is partially incapacitated. But once a family is broken, the partner's total absence makes restructuring the family correspondingly drastic. With destruction of the marital coalition, the surviving parent must establish new coalitions with substitute companions inside or outside the family.

Internal Coalition Formation

Even though a divorced woman no longer needs allies in fighting her husband, she still needs the fellowship she found by forming a vertical coalition after her relationship with her husband deteriorated. Therefore, a woman who has lost her husband may be expected to be particularly close to her children.

Table 23-2 suggests that solo mothers had even closer relations with their adolescent children than happily married women. The latter presumably invested in their husbands some of the affection that solo mothers devoted to their children.

For the children, that may have been too much of a good thing. Adolescence is normally the time for children to achieve a considerable amount of independence. But children of solo mothers feel so obliged to keep their

TABLE 23-2   Mother–Child Relationships in Happy and Unbroken Homes

MOTHER–CHILD RELATIONSHIP	MARITAL STATUS OF MOTHER		BROKEN/ UNBROKEN RATIO
	Happily Married	Solo Mother	
Child feels rejected by mother	31%	27%	0.87X
Child rejects mother	31	17	0.55
Child disagrees with mother's values	23	17	0.74

Adapted from Nye, 1957:359. Source: Ninth- to twelfth-grade boys and girls in three Washington State high schools. Solo mothers had lost their husbands either through death or divorce and had not remarried.

mothers company that it is more difficult for them to rebel. The result is likely to be overprotection and delayed maturity.

One effect of overprotection is a lower need for achievement in sons of solo mothers. McClelland (1961) noted that boys who lost their father from an early age rarely benefited from the lack of paternal dominance so much as they suffered from clinging to their mothers. This seems to explain the weak achievement motivation of American children of widowed and divorced women, of lower-class black boys generally, and of children in decentralized polygynous mother–son households in Africa. Boys in these fragmented families are held so close to their mothers that they are reluctant to venture forth into independent external achievement.

Not only does the loss of the father intensify the immediate tie between mother and children, but this coalition generally persists throughout the mother's remaining years. Insofar as mother and children are "married" to each other, the children are less likely to marry anyone else and less quick to enter into competing relationships.

TABLE 23-3   Age of Marriage of Sons and Daughters by Marital Status of Mother

AVERAGE AGE AT MARRIAGE BY SEX OF CHILD	MARITAL STATUS OF MOTHER		DIFFERENCE
	Married	Widowed	
Sons	25.3	27.6	+2.3
Daughters	23.2	25.0	+1.8

Adapted from Townsend, 1957:82. Source: Children of men and women of retirement age living in an East London slum. Excluded were cases in which the child did not marry at all.

Table 23-3 shows that for children who married at all, sons and daughters of widows married a couple of years later than young people who were not responsible for their mothers. While the averages represented all marriages of these children, differences were especially marked for the last one or two unmarried children at home. The longer such children delayed marriage, the greater the chances were they might never marry. For example, "two unmarried daughters caring for an infirm mother said they could have married but did not because they were so fond of their mother" (*Ibid.*:80).

After marriage, Adams (1968) found that American men and women from intact families felt closer to their parents than before, perhaps because they had taken on the same roles as their parents and faced similar problems.

Children of widows, by contrast, felt alienated from their mothers (the difference being especially great in the case of sons who had replaced their mothers with wives). To counteract their guilt about this alienation, married children of widowed mothers felt an *obligation* to keep in touch with them, whereas the usual reason for keeping in touch with married parents was simply mutual enjoyment.

TABLE 23-4 Mother–Daughter Activities of Married Women by Marital Status of Mother

MOTHER–DAUGHTER ACTIVITY	MARITAL STATUS OF MOTHER			DIVORCED/ MARRIED RATIO
	Married	*Widowed*	*Divorced*	
Home visits	78%	83%	95%	1.22X
Joint activities elsewhere	44	54	52	1.18
Joint rituals	51	56	76	1.49
Aid to mother	38	60	67	1.76
Number of cases	257	109	21	

Adapted from Adams, 1968:85. Source: Young married women in Greensboro, North Carolina. Reciprocal percentages of women engaged in the specified activities with their mothers less than three times a year.

Table 23-4 shows that despite the fact that daughters of widows felt farther apart from their mothers than they had before marriage, they still maintained closer relations with them than did daughters of both-surviving parents. Table 23-4 offers an opportunity to compare the strength of mother–daughter coalitions after bereavement and after divorce. With one exception, the tie between a married woman and a divorced mother was even closer than with a widow. Perhaps this reflects the early development of mother–daughter coalitions during the period of warfare with the husband and the greater emotional needs of women whose memories of marriage are unpleasant. In general it seems that the greater the need of the mother, the stronger the coalition with the daughter.

Contact with the External Husband/Father

Paralleling the internal coalitions are new external coalitions, but since they do not involve reorganization of the existing family I will postpone discussing them until a later section of this chapter.

The other parent from the old family is the husband/father. Following separation and divorce he is relegated to a position outside the family, but this rarely means that contact is completely lost. In modern societies he is guaranteed at least occasional access to his children and he may have intermittent contact with his ex-wife. In both relationships, new patterns of interaction must be established to replace those which existed when he lived at home.

Wife–Husband Contact The more bitterly the husband and wife fought prior to the collapse of their relationship, the less they want to have to do with each other. Nevertheless, if the wife depends on the husband for financial support, she may have to dun him to collect the money. For Liebow's black men, "contacts between the men and their separated families were almost always initiated by the mothers, usually for the purpose of getting money for the children" (1967:76). Since the financial needs of the residual family and of the man conflicted, these contacts often reactivated the old hostilities between partners.

Separation (and even divorce) need not necessarily end all positive relations between husband and wife, however. In a substantial minority of cases, divorce suits are withdrawn between the time they are filed and the time they come to trial. For couples who have not initiated divorce proceedings but have merely separated, chances of reconciliation are even better. More than half of Morris' previously separated wives corresponded with their husbands while they were in prison and almost a fourth visited occasionally. Many of those who went to the trouble of visiting ended the separation when the husband was discharged. Just as communication during any absence sustains relationships for normal couples, the greater the communication between separated couples, the greater the chances are that the gap may be closed.

Child–Father Contact   Insofar as parents fight over the child before divorce, they compete for his loyalty and affection. Nor is it simply a matter of hoping to win a positive response for oneself. To win a child for oneself is to rob the partner in a zero-sum game.

Terminating the marriage attenuates but does not end this competition. Husband and wife no longer fight face to face but find new ways. They are no longer evenly matched. After divorce, one partner has major custody of the children while the other has hardly more than visiting rights. In most modern societies, the mother customarily wins the children, while the husband is reduced to marginal contact.

This imbalance in post-divorce roles alters the relationship of both parents with the children. The custodian becomes the disciplinarian and child-rearer. This means that along with indulgent affection the mother must exercise whatever discipline the child will henceforth receive. The father, on the other hand, is relieved of disciplinary responsibility and can afford to be purely ingratiating. The net result is that most fathers woo their children with gifts and good times like indulgent grandparents.

Liebow graphically described this paternal indulgence for lower-class black men separated from their children:

> The men who do not live with their own children seem to express more affection for their children and treat them more tenderly than those who do live with them. . . .
>
> Fathers who live with their children, for example, seem to take no pleasure in their children and give them little of their time and attention. They seldom mention their children in casual conversation and are never seen sitting or playing with them on the steps or in the street. The fathers do not take their children to tag along while they lounge on the streetcorner or in the Carry-out, nor do they promenade with them on Easter Sunday or take them for walks on any other Sunday or holiday. When the father walks into the home, the child may not even look up from what he is doing and

the father, for his part, takes no more notice than he receives. If their eyes happen to catch one another's glances, father and child seem to look without seeing until one or the other looks elsewhere.

Compared with fathers who live with their children, separated fathers who remain in touch with their children speak about them more often and show them more warmth when father and child are together. For separated fathers, the short, intermittent contacts with their children are occasions for public display of paternal tenderness and affection. (1967:79,81)

The base-line of normal father–child relations in those poverty-stricken, unstable families was unusually weak. But at any class level we might expect the same difference between the chronic behavior of steady fathers and the superb behavior of intermittent fathers. Just as married couples can never sustain the fervor which they felt when they first fell in love, fathers could not be expected to be as effusive toward their children all year round as separated fathers can manage on weekends. As Liebow put it: "Since his meetings with the child are widely spaced, he comes to them fresh and rested; since the meetings are brief, he can give freely of himself, secure in the knowledge he will soon go back to his own child-free routine" (*Ibid*:83).

The contrast between separated fathers and resident fathers sets them apart from resident mothers saddled with continual responsibility for their children. The following personally observed case nicely portrays a reversal of these roles when custody of a child shifted from one parent to the other:

When I was four years old, my parents were divorced. At that time, my mother obtained custody of my sister and me although our father also wanted us. While we were living with our mother, she was afraid of being too strict and therefore placed little pressure on us. She was consistent, though, and punished and rewarded us at the expected times without being rigid. But our father, hoping to win our favor and perhaps alienate us against our mother told us many times we didn't have to do what she said or gave us huge presents for no reason while she had been saving for months to get us the same present as a reward for some special behavior.

When we were 10, we went to live with our father and there was an abrupt reversal of his policy. He put forth rules which were to be strictly followed while our mother started overlooking noncompliance and made few demands. In Mary Ann's case, the results have not been good. While she was Mom's responsibility, Dad encouraged her to rebuke that control and was on her side, but now Mom is on her side against Dad. Mom claims that Dad treated her the same way and Mary Ann sympathizes with her but doesn't have actual respect for her. In fact, Mary Ann right now is unable to have any real respect for anyone. At times she admires various people but always loses faith in them.

Thus the resident parent exercises authority over the child, but the nonresident parent plays a seductive role which undermines that authority. The child is caught between dependence on the caretaking parent and occasional romantic flings with the irresponsible parent.

For the responsible parent, the seductive behavior of the ex-partner is infuriating because it undermines the disciplinary efforts and social control policies which she is struggling to maintain. Since she cannot compete with the ex-husband on his own generous terms, her most frequent defense is to malign the husband's character during the many hours she has the ear of her child. Whatever faults the husband manifested during marriage can be "taught" the child in the hope of nullifying his seeming niceness.

Morris' British prisoners were particularly vulnerable in this regard, because they had committed socially recognized crimes. Whereas nonseparated wives tried to hide knowledge of those crimes from the children in order to protect the father–child relationship, wives whose marriages had broken up prior to the husband's imprisonment often deliberately told their children that their father was in prison (rather than in a hospital) and why. This turned children against their fathers and helped to cement the mother–child coalition.

In general, expelling the father from the family brings the mother and children closer together and attenuates both the marital and the father–child relationships. However, the father frequently tries to compensate by being extra nice to his children when he sees them. This places the children in an ambiguous position not unlike the pawns they became when the parents were together, and creates tension between the father and the mother. However, the very fact that the parents live apart reduces tensions substantially below what they were when they lived together in the same house.

REALLOCATION OF NEGLECTED ROLES

The loss of a parent creates the same problems of role reallocation as we have already seen in the case of partial impairment. There is a difference of degree since whatever marginal functions an impaired parent may have performed are lost completely. One asset, however, is that after the old partner has left, it is possible to recruit a new one to take his place—or at least to try. With those exceptions, the patterns of role reallocation reinforce the generalizations which we have already derived from studying parental impairment.

Overloading the Residual Parent

Although the evidence in Table 23-5 is rather indirect, it suggests that if the mother is divorced when she is too young to bear the strain, her children suffer from reduced self-esteem.

TABLE 23-5 Child's Self-Esteem by Age of Mother at Divorce

	AGE OF MOTHER AT DIVORCE		
SELF-ESTEEM	*23 or Under*	*24–31*	*32 or Over*
High	23%	39%	43%
Medium	29	22	27
Low	48	39	29
Total	100%	100%	99%
Number of cases	31	111	106

Adapted from Rosenberg, 1965:91. Source: Juniors and seniors in selected New York State public high schools.

Rosenberg found the same relationship between early loss of the spouse and damage to the child's self-esteem among children of widows as well. For both young widows and young divorcees loss of the spouse means that the mother is saddled with a young child who is all burden and no help. We saw before that early marriage and early child-bearing overload parents even when the marriage remains intact. Young mothers are generally cold and rejecting. If immature mothers are overloaded despite the aid of husbands, how much more may this be expected for those with no husband to assist them or to support them financially and emotionally!

One of the greatest stresses for spouse-less women is the necessity of supporting themselves financially. In Aberdeen, Scotland, Illsley and Thompson noted that widowed mothers faced hard times financially:

> For the most part they lived precariously. In times of unemployment, with no special skills, limited time and heavy family responsibilities, their earnings were small and often irregular. Casual jobs, part-time jobs and those without rigid time-tables were more suitable than factory jobs and so they usually worked as cleaners, domestics, cooks and waitresses. (1961:33)

Needless to say, the kinds of jobs these women were able to dovetail with their child-rearing responsibilities were the lowest paid ones on the labor market.

Most Scottish widows suffered a severe cut in their standard of living after the husband died. The only exceptions were wives of men whose illness had been so prolonged and so expensive that bereavement relieved the family of the burdens of medical expenses and home nursing care. Such wives had more time to seek outside employment, meager as the return from working might be.

Divorced men are theoretically expected to assume financial responsibility for their children but in the United States support payments are seldom high enough to cover the actual costs of raising children. Despite the fact that men are legally bound to make these payments, the obligation is widely evaded. As a result, a mother who gains custody of her children usually carries a heavy financial burden as well as the other responsibilities which go with heading a family alone. As for widows, few American husbands carry enough insurance to support their wives and children for more than a few years. If the husband dies while the children are young, the insurance money runs out long before the children are able to become self-supporting. The death of the husband is typically a major tragedy for his wife and children and places a heavy burden on the wife's shoulders unless she is able to remarry.

Whereas the death of the father places a financial burden on his widow, the death of the mother deprives the family of housekeeping and child-rearing services. Few fathers of small children can manage alone. So overloaded are they that they must either recruit a new partner or surrender their children to relatives or institutions.

Table 23-6 shows a sharp difference between widows and widowers in their ability to care for young children. Most widows were able to manage even with preschool children (though not without difficulty). Widowers, on

TABLE 23-6 Custody of Daughter Following Death of
Father or Mother, by Age at Bereavement

CHILD-REARING AGENT	AGE OF DAUGHTER AT BEREAVEMENT		
	0–4	5–9	10–13
After death of father			
Solo parent	53%	81%	84%
Residual parent and step-parent	36	16	13
Other relatives	5	1	0
Institution, foster-parents, etc.	5	1	3
Total	99%	99%	100%
Number of daughters	73	69	74
After death of mother			
Solo parent	9%	34%	84%
Residual parent and step-parent	31	34	3
Other relatives	50	26	9
Institution, foster-parents, etc.	10	5	3
Total	100%	99%	99%
Number of daughters	58	38	32

Adapted from Illsley and Thompson, 1961:32. Source: Family backgrounds of women who
bore their first child in Aberdeen, Scotland, in 1952–54.

the other hand, often turned their children over to relatives unless they found
a new marriage partner.

For both sexes, the older the daughter at bereavement, the greater the
ability of the surviving parent to care for her and/or for her to care for herself. By the time daughters reached their teens, they presumably became assets
for their unmarried fathers, able to keep house and help care for their younger
siblings. Particularly striking in the table is the fact that just as many daughters
beyond age 9 stayed with their solo fathers as with solo mothers. It was, then,
widowers with preadolescent children who were least able to carry the burden
of dependent children unaided and who either got assistance or sloughed the
burden off onto others.

Promoting a Child

The loss of the father encourages the promotion of children as husband-
substitutes even more than the impairment of a father still tied to the family.
The more authoritarian the father, the more his removal benefits the child.

We saw in an earlier chapter that the death of the father enabled Turkish
boys to develop achievement motivation which might otherwise have been
suppressed. If emancipation benefits sons in patriarchal societies, it should be
even more beneficial to daughters who suffer the double disabilities of youthfulness and femininity in feudal societies.

In rural Greece, Lambiri (1965) found that the death of the father
benefited girls in two ways. It allowed them to go to work in the new factory
(29 percent of the working girls versus 17 percent of the nonworking girls
had lost their fathers). And among the factory girls, it allowed them to feel

more independent as a result of their work. Living fathers maintained such strict control over their daughters that the chances were only 50/50 that such a girl would feel more independent after going to work in the factory. A feudal father's death thus removes the main barrier to the emancipation of children of both sexes and especially of the weaker sex. In modern societies, we may expect the loss of the father to have similar effects, but differences between children with and without fathers should be less striking because modern fathers are less domineering.

Falling Back on Grandparents

The loss of the husband frees the wife from conflicts of loyalty to her husband and her parents, enabling her to move back to her childhood home with a clear conscience. In Vienna, Rosenmayr and Köckeis (1963) found that 27 percent of all widows and divorcees under age 50 were living with their parents (compared with only 8 percent of married women the same age). In Britain, Morris (1965) found that 40 percent of the previously separated wives of prisoners were living with their parents, compared to only 21 percent of those who were living with their husbands prior to sentencing. Morris felt that the availability of parents often made separation possible as a way out of marital stress:

> We have reason to believe that where wives do *not* have relatives able and willing to take them in, this fact plays an important part in preventing the physical break-up of the marriage, since particularly if they have young children, the wives often have nowhere else to go. (1965:125)

By moving in with their parents, wives could live more comfortably. The parents' homes, to be sure, were a bit crowded after the wife and children had moved in, but their furnishings were generally better than the impoverished homes the wives would have established if they had tried to go it alone. The grandparents also babysat with the children while the mother went to work, thereby easing her financial situation. Alternatively, the mother cared for the home, releasing the grandmother to go to work. Either way, by joining forces with the grandparents, women who had separated from their husbands secured two adult colleagues where they had had only one before. Since the husband had often been a parasite, dunning his wife for funds when he wasn't in prison, sympathetic parents were often more useful than the husband had ever been. The more deficient the husband, the greater the gain to the family in shifting to grandparents for economic and social security.

In extended family systems, economic and social security are built into the family itself so the loss of one man is cushioned and nobody has to move in order to secure the services of relatives. Since an extended family consists of two or more married couples, there is always another adult male or female to fill the hole left by the death or expulsion of a parent. Kingsley Davis described the classical Chinese family in terms of the benefits to the child but it might as easily have been described from the standpoint of the surviving spouse:

> . . . if one parent is lost through death or divorce, the child's domestic environment is not seriously disturbed. He tends to remain in the same household, among the same intimate relatives, feeling just as secure and loved as ever. Also, what might be called the principle of kinship substitution usually operates—the principle that if one kinsman is lost, another is available to take his place. . . . The principle means that the child is seldom left without some relative to function as a parent for him. . . . Actually, so far as daily behavior is concerned, the child may have drawn little distinction between his parents and the other adults in the household anyway. It is therefore easy for him to make the adjustment when a parent is lost. Things remain for him pretty much as they were before. (1944:705)

Extended families offer the smoothest role reallocation of any family system. For nuclear families, falling back on grandparents is the nearest equivalent. The mother simply regresses to childhood dependency. The grandchildren turn to persons whom they already know and love.

Recruiting a New Spouse

Freedom to remarry is the greatest advantage in losing a spouse completely instead of just for a certain period of time. In modern societies, most of those who lose a spouse hope to remarry. The younger the individual, the better the chances for remarriage. The unhappier the first marriage, the greater the motivation for trying again to grasp what was missed on the first round. For such reasons, a majority of divorced Americans remarry. Since bereavement usually occurs later and leaves pleasant memories as a barrier to remarriage, this solution is less widely utilized by widows and widowers than by divorced persons.

At first glance, remarriage seems the simplest method of reallocating roles. Broken marriages then are reclassified as unbroken. The family seems restored to normal with a full complement of role incumbents—one man, one woman, the children. The basic roles of bread-winner and housekeeper seem taken care of. This depends, however, on the residual parent's success in recruiting a competent spouse. In Great Britain between the World Wars, eligible men were so scarce that widowed mothers often faced a choice between remaining unmarried or marrying a man who might be an ambiguous asset or even a liability:

> To obtain a husband a widow often had to lower her standards; in many cases the step-father was himself a chronic invalid or a casual or unemployed laborer and remarriage usually brought with it the chance of further children. (Illsley and Thompson, 1961:34)

Such a new husband increased the overload on the wife by his economic and physical dependency and by generating additional children, leaving her worse off than before.

Even if the new recruit is a competent individual and further reproduction is prevented, a new husband does not necessarily replace his predecessor. We have seen before that new husbands seldom share fully in rearing their stepchildren. The children resist his discipline and rebuff his affection while he feels alienated by their resistance. Therefore, remarriage only partially relieves the wife of the overload imposed by loss of the original father, while it may cause the children more problems than it solves.

Even though a new partner may not solve problems too well, most broken families find some kind of outside help useful. Wives who separated from their husbands prior to imprisonment were not free to remarry but often acquired a "man friend" to live in the home and contribute financially to its upkeep (Morris, 1965). Similarly, broken families in Parisian furnished hotels recruited substitute family members from nonrelatives if they could not find them in the kin network. Michel cited a deserted woman and a divorced woman who teamed up as quasi-spouses for each other.

> The first, Nadia, is a metal-worker by profession, whose husband deserted her and their three-year-old child. She is currently unemployed since her health does not permit her to continue her previous, overly-strenuous job as a spray-gun painter. The second, Simone, also a metal-worker, is a young divorcee whose child is with a foster mother. . . . Nadia takes care of the two rooms, does the shopping, and prepares the evening meal. Simone works all day in a factory. She furnishes Nadia with the money needed to run what can be called the household of the two young women. The dinners are prepared and served in Nadia's room. Their spare time in the evenings is spent together in playing cards and talking. (1960:290)

Other solo mothers in those hotels relied on neighbors to supervise their children or to provide extra beds. Thus broken families unable to recruit new parents or rely on old kin may recruit quasi-kin to serve the same functions.

Forming a Quasi-Family

All my assumptions so far have been that only one parent was impaired or lost. But what if both parents go? Then some kind of family must be constructed out of new ingredients if the children are to survive. A wide range of quasi-families may be fashioned. The closest resemblance to the original family is adoption into another family. Next is care in a foster home without the security of adoption. That lack of security often means lack of continuity—many foster children move from family to family so fast that meaningful relationships with foster parents cannot be established.

Similar to foster homes are quasi-families improvised to care for abandoned children. In central Europe these often consist of children of both sexes and mixed ages presided over by a single woman who mothers them on a 24-hour-a-day basis just as if they were her own children. By devoting her life to her "children" she gives them the love, security, and continuous mothering which they need.

Least family-like is institutional care. Children's "homes" generally are more like institutions than homes. Their staff turns over so rapidly (due to low pay and poor working conditions) that most children go through a whole series of house-parents during their childhood. If the working hours of staff members are "normal," the children must change parents with every shift. Continuity and consistency in parent–child relations are minimal.

Most institutions cannot afford a low ratio of children to staff. In Spitz's classic study of children's institutions, the ratio was 7 to 1 (1946). This puts institutions in the same category with large families whom we have already seen overburdened and unable to perform their child-rearing functions effectively. Institutions are holding operations at best, hopefully (but not necessarily) keeping their charges alive until they can be placed in more familistic settings.

Unallocated Residuals

Some broken families are unable to utilize any of these external resources—new mates, old relatives, or friends. And even if they do establish such relationships, they may not fill the gap in the family completely. But especially for those who do not succeed in getting any outside help, the residual loss is likely to be appreciable.

Bereaved Spouses   Hardest hit of all are widows and widowers whose children have left home and who are left alone on the death of the spouse. With no children at home, it is impossible to establish an internal coalition to make up for the spouse. The older the survivor, the less the possibility of remarriage or of expanding friendships. Loneliness, therefore, is to be expected for those who lived all their adult lives with a built-in companion and suddenly find themselves bereft.

Studies in three countries (Denmark, Britain, and the U.S.) by Shanas and her associates (1968) showed that loneliness was felt most acutely after a crisis of departure. Those who had just lost the spouse felt lonelier than those whose bereavement occurred in earlier years and who had gradually become accustomed to living alone.

Figure 23-1 suggests that feelings of loneliness are practically universal immediately following the death of the spouse but tend to disappear as the survivor adjusts to being single again. Widowers were hit harder than widows, perhaps because old women gained more substitute satisfaction from association with their married children than did unsociable old men. Insofar as kin ties in modern societies are primarily matrilineal, kin are more accessible to women for purposes of role reallocation. Moreover, for the very practical tasks of everyday living in the retirement years, the loss of a man deprives the wife of few practical services, but a man who loses his wife has no one to cook and care for him. Nevertheless, even the women in Townsend's study missed the spouse badly in the early years of bereavement, though their recuperative powers were generally greater than those of widowers.

Earlier in life, another unallocated residual appears. Loss of the spouse interferes with the ability of the surviving parent to have children. If remarriage occurs soon enough the deficiency may be made up in the next marriage. But in societies with unlimited child-bearing, fertility is depressed by any severing of the husband–wife relationship. In many African countries Goode (1963) found that high divorce rates depressed the number of children born, and in Jamaica, Blake found that the instability of consensual unions had a similar effect:

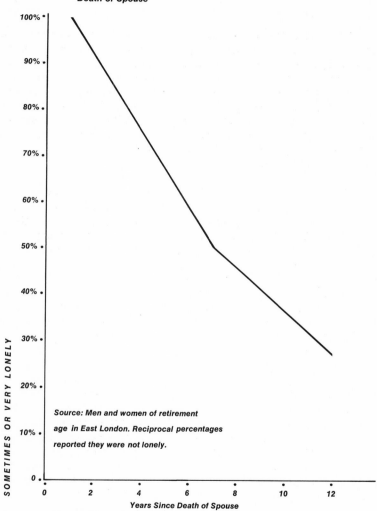

FIGURE 23-1. *Loneliness of Widows and Widowers by Interval Since Death of Spouse*

Source: Men and women of retirement age in East London. Reciprocal percentages reported they were not lonely.

Years Since Death of Spouse

SOMETIMES OR VERY LONELY

Adapted from Townsend (1957):175.

. . . if most unions are unstable, each woman will normally have more than one union. Since she cannot, or may prefer not, to jump immediately from one union into another, the probability is high that she will spend a greater part of her reproductive span unexposed to the risk of pregnancy than would have been the case had she been in a stable union from the first. (1961: 18)

In modern societies, the effect of family instability on fertility depends on the rate of remarriage. If chances of remarriage are low, losing the spouse early in marriage may prevent the wife from having her full complement of children in much the same way as in premodern societies. In Aberdeen, Illsley and Thompson found that women from broken homes were more apt to be only children and less apt to be from families of four or more children than women who had grown up in complete families. This reflects the fact that remarriage rates in Scotland during the interval between the two world wars were so low that only a small minority of parents who lost a spouse ever secured a replacement.

Orphaned Children   The loss of parents generally leaves children scarred in some degree. The larger the number of parents taken from the child, the greater the loss. The greater the trauma preceding their departure, the greater the effect (so that children who lose a parent or two via divorce are worse off than those whose parents drop out of a happy family through death). For children who lose only one parent, the loss of the mother is generally more painful than of the father. Losing a parent affects children of the same sex more than children of the opposite sex who still have a role model to identify with. Except when children are too young to notice, in general the younger the child when the loss occurs, the greater the impact since the parent's services are missed over a correspondingly long span of formative years.

The impact on the child depends on the resources of the residual or alternative caretakers. If the child continues to live with a residual parent, the higher the social status of the parent (better education, financial resources, etc.), the better equipped the parent is to manage alone and the less damage to the child. Conversely the very poverty stricken families who are most apt to experience desertion, divorce, and early bereavement are least equipped to deal with them. Where both parents are lost, the fate of the child depends on whatever substitute family or quasi-family he acquires instead.

Table 23-7 illustrates the trauma for children who lost one or more parents and were brought up by the residual parent or by persons or agencies other than parents. For both sons and daughters, the larger the number of parents lost, the worse the socialization outcome for the child. Thus for children either partially or fully deprived of their parents, the alternative arrangements are less satisfactory than a home which was never broken.

The effect of the age of the child when he is separated from his parents can be seen in Maas' study (1963) of children who had been evacuated from the London slums to the country during World War II. Nineteen years later, he found that children who were taken away from their parents under the age of one fared worst whereas those who were four or more years old were relatively normal. The latter survived the three-year separation well enough so that returning to their parents for the remainder of their childhood salvaged their lives. The younger the child, when the three-year separation occurred, the greater the damage to his emotional life (less vitality and spontaneity), his inner controls (more impulsiveness), his ability to achieve good personal relationships, his performance of key social roles (either performed badly or not at all), and his intellectual functioning (either consistently below par or fluctuating and unstable). The value of a quasi-family to replace the real one is suggested in the fact that children who were removed to the country *as a group* fared better than those who were placed with strangers. In general, then, the younger the child the greater the damage is in losing parents and quasi-parents either temporarily or permanently.

TABLE 23-7   Sons' Educational Attainment and Daughters' Premarital Reproductive Experience, by Number of Parental Caretakers

	NUMBER OF PARENTAL CARETAKERS		
	Two	*One*	*None*
Educational attainment of sons	4.48	4.22	4.18
Premarital experience of daughters			
Illegitimate births	5%	9%	12%
Premarital conceptions	23%	27%	38%

Adapted from Blau and Duncan, 1967:336, and from Illsley and Thompson, 1961:44. Sources: Representative sample of American men aged 20–64, and all women bearing their first child 1952–54 in Aberdeen, Scotland.

For children who lose both parents permanently and wind up in institutions, the unallocated residuals are most disastrous. Spitz found that children institutionalized in infancy developed "hospitalism," an illness marked by passivity, susceptibility to contagious disease, and high mortality rate. Infants wasted away psychologically and physically from the lack of maternal stimulation and love in a sanitary but unstimulating environment. They were not fondled enough, held enough, or talked to enough to stimulate their mental development or to maintain the morale necessary for the will to live. They died of neglect.

Goldfarb (1945) compared children who had always lived in foster homes with children who had spent their first three years in orphanages. In follow-up studies, he found deficiencies in the personalities of the previously institutionalized children which are reminiscent of Maas' findings of the effects of temporary separation from parents at the same early age. The children who had been institutionalized scored poorly on IQ tests and did poorly in school. They were less able to think clearly, to grasp basic concepts of time and space, to remember the past, and to learn. They lacked self-control and were highly distractible. Although they indiscriminately demanded the affection they lacked in infancy, they could not establish close relationships with people. Thus children who passed through institutions were retarded in their mental and emotional development and undersocialized in comparison to normal children. Apparently they were scarred for life by being robbed of family security and affection in their earliest years.

FAMILY INSTABILITY AS A SOURCE OF FAMILY INSTABILITY: THE DOMINO EFFECT

In societies with high rates of family dissolution, newly married couples hardly expect their marriages to survive. They protect themselves against disappointment in ways which unintentionally increase the likelihood that their marriages will fail. Failure in such societies becomes a self-fulfilling prophecy.

In Java, Geertz found that "No one builds a new house for a pair of newly-weds; the risk is too great that they will be divorced within the year" (1961:75). As a result, newly married couples move in with whichever set of parents has room to spare, thereby imposing on the fragile marriage the burdens of living doubled up. Presumably if couples were provided with their own living quarters from the very beginning, the 50 percent Javanese divorce rate would be reduced.

If divorce is widespread, both husband–wife and parent–child relations are altered. The husband–wife relationship becomes tenuous and the mother–child relationship stronger in anticipation of the husband's possible departure. In Islamic countries, Goode (1963) noted that easy divorce gave men the ability to threaten their wives with a conform-or-else approach. This threat has two possible consequences. If the wife wishes to maintain the marriage, it weakens her bargaining position. If she does not, it weakens the marriage because the threat is likely to be fulfilled.

A similar fragility in husband–wife relationships was observed by Rainwater, Coleman, and Handel in their study of working-class American wives:

> It is hard, these women feel, to get a husband to do what they want or to change his ways. Men go their own ways and as often as not the wife feels she has little influence. She seems unable to free herself altogether from the view that men are quite independent and can easily leave. (1959:71)

This feeling of insecurity reflects the fact that working-class divorce rates are higher than for the middle-class.

Fearing that the husband/father may leave at any time, the mother and children turn toward each other, anticipating the coalition which so often forms as a result of his departure. If the mother and children feel they can depend on each other but not on the man, this freezes him out of the family psychologically and structurally. Thus his actual departure is speeded by fear of that departure.

Children who grow up in such an atmosphere conclude that marital ties are undependable and blood ties the only ones which can be depended upon. Children learn to depend not only on their mothers but on each other more heavily than in societies where children can look forward to leaving home to establish stable homes of their own. In Nigeria, Marris found strong reliance on the sibling group in polygynous subfamilies:

> To protect themselves against the rivalries of a polygamous household, and the instability of the relationship between their parents, the children of the same mother tend to be drawn together with an enduring affection. As children grow up, therefore, it is natural for them to place their strongest affections and loyalties in the family group, rather than in a relationship with one man or woman. (1960:125)

If children grow up with the idea that only siblings can be trusted and not one's spouse, they are not likely to invest sufficient energy in their marriages to enable them to survive the expected crises.

Besides weakening ties between the husband/father and his immediate family, high rates of dissolution weaken his involvement with in-laws. If a man is not to be trusted in his relations with his wife, he can hardly be expected to be trusted with her family. Insofar as high rates of dissolution are associated with high rates of extramarital intercourse, a man cannot be trusted sexually with the the feminine members of his wife's family. Gluckman found that high divorce rates among the African Lozi affected relations between men and their in-laws quite differently from low rates among the Zulu:

> [Lozi] men are often afraid to work gardens for, or help, the wives of their brothers who are labour migrants, lest their brothers charge them with being lovers of their sisters-in-law. [Among the Zulu] as marriage is far more stable. . . . suspicions of adultery do not arise so easily. For example, men always help their absent brothers' wives.
>
> Lozi trust and confide in their mothers and sisters, with whom their ties are enduring, rather than in their wives, with whom their ties are ephemeral. (1950:179)

High divorce rates thus undermine both relations within the family and relations with affinal kin. In such societies, only mother–child ties and brother–sister ties have lasting significance. These attitudes contribute to the domino effect of family instability in undermining other families.

Family instability even weakens the mother–child relationship in at least one way. In Java, Geertz found that second marriages were usually love matches, whereas first marriages were normally arranged by parents. This means that the mother's control over her children's mate-selection was also decreased by marital instability. From the child's point of view, this meant a desirable freedom. But from the standpoint of family structure, this weakened the relationship between the mother and her once-married children. Although instability drove mother and children together while the children were young, it weakened their relationship once they had entered the marriage market and had begun to play it for their own purposes. Ultimately, then, family instability undermines almost all family relationships—with the possible exception of ties among siblings.

chapter twenty-four
THE PREVENTION AND CURE OF FAMILY CRISES

Some families manage unaided to find their way out of crisis back to normal. Relatively little is known about these processes of collective recovery. In recent years, however, various professions have become increasingly skillful in aiding families in resolving their problems. Nor is professional help limited simply to restoring a status quo ante of pre-crisis family living. Both family therapists and family educators are increasingly concerned with helping families achieve higher-than-normal levels of functioning. Such programs go far beyond preventing divorce or preventing crises. Their objective is to improve the quality of family life. By analyzing such experimental programs we may understand both how families function "in sickness and in health" and how family life may change from the former to the latter.

THERAPY FOR TROUBLED FAMILIES

Once families get in trouble, how can outsiders rescue them? Chapter 20 suggested that outside agents sometimes make things worse by creating divisive alliances with one or more family members against the rest. In this chapter, my concern will be with interventions which avoid such divisiveness —essentially by dealing with the family as a total unit.

Intervention in Family Crises

Some families take the initiative in turning to agencies for help, but some do not recognize their troubles. If they have established a pseudo-coalition, they will be afraid to recognize that their "solution" to their marriage problems is no solution at all from the standpoint of the scapegoated child.

Even families who recognize that they are in trouble may hesitate to turn to professional agencies from sheer embarrassment. It may seem more comfortable to continue fighting behind closed doors than to let anyone know that their family life is less than perfect. To call for help would be too humiliating an admission of failure. Koos found this attitude prevalent among middle-class families. When they had crises, less than 10 percent turned anywhere for help: "For most there is even shame in turning to the home-and-school counselor, to the school psychologist, to the minister, for to do so is to admit failure in the family" (1950:78).

These twin resistances—to recognizing the existence of a problem and to seeking help with a recognized problem—mean that a total program for family therapy cannot rely completely on self-referral. Agencies must sometimes be willing to intervene forcefully for the sake of the children in particular and hopefully of the family as a whole.

In Western civilization, outside intervention has a long and honorable history. Christian theologians taught that parents did not have unlimited power over their children but held power in trust from God and the Church. If they failed to safeguard the welfare of their children, the priest could intervene on the children's behalf or even take the children away. In the latter instance, the children might be raised in orphanages by monks and nuns of the Church.

After the Protestant Reformation, this supervisory responsibility was secularized with the transfer of authority from ecclesiastical courts to civil courts. Although the agency changed, the tradition of intervening on behalf of children continued uninterrupted.

In the Orient, no such tradition existed. Many oriental philosophies had a less clearly defined concept of God as an external force so they gave more authority to the family. As recently as 1967, Kiyomi Morioka told me that no concept of social responsibility for children existed in Japan. It was still taken for granted that children would be cared for by their parents and that society had no right to interfere. If children were orphaned, relatives were expected to care for them. That some orphans might lack relatives or that some relatives might shirk this responsibility did not cross the mind of the Japanese government. As a result, orphans whose relatives failed them sometimes had to fend for themselves in "parentless" households, the older children forced to go to work prematurely to support their "family" of siblings. Social machinery to cope with these crises had not been invented because the society failed to recognize that the problem existed and that it could solve the problem—even when the problem came to public view.

In Western societies, the intervening agencies are of many different kinds. The participation of children in schools gives teachers widespread opportunities to observe family-originated stress. Pediatricians detect children who have been "battered" by their parents. Public health officials and private doctors become aware of premarital pregnancies. Truant officers, juvenile police officers, and other guardians of law and order encounter other results of family crises.

Symptoms of family stress most often appear in the problem behavior of children. But wives and even husbands sometimes bear visible scars. Police, clergymen, case workers, and public health nurses are some of those who may detect family troubles in such ways. When they do, their intervention helps move families into the treatment which in turn may help resolve their problems.

All that is necessary to get some families into treatment is to suggest that they need it and help them make contact with the appropriate agency. In resistant cases, greater pressure may need to be applied or they may have to be forced into treatment by court order. Although force often doubles resistance and makes treatment more difficult, it does not necessarily prevent it from having any value at all.

Family Therapy

Once contact has been established between a disturbed family and a professional agency, what kind of treatment will be most helpful? The basic criterion is that whichever family members are involved in conflict with each other must be treated together if that conflict is to be resolved. Since conflict has a way of involving most family members, this means that treatment needs to involve correspondingly many people. For childless couples or for parents who have not involved their children in their squabbles, the marital dyad may be the appropriate unit. But when children are involved in family troubles, they and their parents need to join forces in approaching their common problem.

When a married couple is the unit of treatment, the procedure is frequently labeled "marriage counseling." When parents and one or more children are involved, the usual designation is "family therapy." The same professional person may offer both types of services in which case they will differ less in method than in the number of people involved and therefore in the complexity of the processes at work.

Marriage counseling and family therapy are two forms of joint treatment. Whenever family members are seen jointly, the therapist demonstrates his interest in the relationships among the family members. This encourages reciprocal concessions among the family members. The therapist's presence encourages the family members to discuss possible improvements in their ways of relating to each other. It also guarantees that whatever concessions are made by one family member will be reciprocated by another.

Joint treatment does not prevent competition for the therapist's affection. But with competition occurring openly, the therapist can deal with it equally openly and help the family members shift their focus toward utilizing each other rather than himself as their main source of gratification. By supporting, encouraging, and protecting all the members of the family, the therapist helps them build positive relationships with each other.

Joint treatment is generally quicker and more conclusive than work with isolated individuals or partial fragments of the total family. It is quicker because it works on all the interacting family members simultaneously, requiring them to make coordinated changes. It is more conclusive for the same reason. Whereas an individually treated person may revert to his pathology as soon as he returns to his old environment, a total family which has worked out a new pattern has presumably achieved an equilibrium which will persist because all the parts are in balance with each other.

Joint treatment is also superior to individual treatment because the therapist can observe the family in interaction rather than being forced to rely upon verbal accounts of what happens in family crises. Regardless of what the family talks about in the therapy room, the way they interact with each other verbally and non-verbally gives the therapist innumerable opportunities to gain first-hand information about family interaction patterns.

Ability to observe the family in interaction benefits not only the therapist but the family members as well. By feeding his observations back to the family, the therapist helps them recognize where they go awry and also recognize their strengths. When patterns are pointed out to them immediately, they can be understood more easily and convincingly than when past events are recalled, subject to all the distortions which affect memory.

Carry-over from joint therapy into the "real world" is facilitated by the fact that the same group who practice in the office live together at home. Sundberg and Tyler (1962) suggested that understandings achieved in joint sessions were more apt to carry over into extra-therapy hours because the context in which the understanding was achieved was the same in which the individuals lived. For both the therapist and the family, the fact that the same people are involved in treatment and in applying the results of that treatment assures maximum continuity between office and home.

Home Treatment   One way of increasing coordination between home and office is to move the treatment site into the home. This may be necessary if a key family member is unwilling to leave the house because of fear, shyness, and withdrawal from social interaction. But even if all family members were willing to come to the office, treatment in the home enhances the values of joint treatment. Within the home, the therapist gets a truer picture of the family's behavior. And within the home, the family is more likely to continue its new behavior patterns after the therapist leaves.

In visiting a family with a schizophrenic daughter, Friedman discovered that a cat and dog were also important "members of the family":

> . . . the family dog and family cat both were revealed to have the same phobia that the primary patient had. They rarely went out of the house voluntarily, and they trembled in fear when they were taken near the door.
> In [another] family, it was observed that whenever the father became particularly anxious or tense during a session, he would reach over for the female family dog and begin to stroke her rather intensely. It was later revealed in the therapy that the tragedy of this father's life was that he had lost a daughter to whom he was most attached when she died at five years of age. He was able to talk about how he had transferred this feeling and attachment to the dog after the girl's death. (1962:135,136)

In addition to enlarging the number of family members in treatment, therapy within the home enlarges the range of family behavior which may be observed and thereby involved in the treatment process. Friedman found that issues of cleanliness, dress, eating, drinking, bathroom and bedroom behavior all could be observed in the home whereas they tended to be hidden from view in the office. At home the "identified patient" might show up half dressed and other family members might seek to escape from crucial issues under discussion by excusing themselves to raid the refrigerator or use the bathroom. Such evasions could then be confronted and used as material for gaining insight into sensitive areas of family relations.

If such benefits can be gained from brief visits in the home devoted to therapy, they should be enlarged by extensive visits when the therapist could observe the family's daily round of behavior. One social worker (Hansen, 1968) spent an entire week living with a family of two parents and six children ranging in age from 6 to 14. Although she originally planned to limit her therapeutic interventions to a daily evening session, Hansen found herself drawn increasingly into full-time therapy with the family:

> So many issues emerged during the day . . . that we could not possibly consider them all in one [therapy] session. Further, it became clear that if some issues were not dealt with immediately, they could enlarge and create new issues. I decided that one major advantage of living-in was the opportunity to work on the spot, to prevent the build-up of disappointments and quarrels. Moreover, acting as a therapist during the day allowed me to deal with individuals' thoughts and feelings as they naturally emerged, without the distortion that results through the passage of time. Thus, my role gradually changed to that of a full time therapist. (1968:71)

Hansen found this role exhausting but she felt it benefited the family more than an extensive series of office visits. Presumably living-in is especially appropriate for families whose problems are severe and whose verbal skills are weak so that they cannot communicate to the therapist what takes place at home.

Outpatient Treatment   In recent years, mental health practitioners have discovered that hospitalization cuts patients off from the outside world and makes their reentry into the community more difficult. Hospitalization has increasingly been seen as a drastic measure to be avoided as long as possible in favor of outpatient treatment which does not tear the patient loose from his roots in the community.

From the standpoint of the individual's membership in his family, outpatient treatment is especially valuable. In the words of Langsley and his associates,

> The removal of an individual from his family to a hospital is more likely to complicate than aid the situation. It removes one member from a family, permits extrusion and scapegoating and avoids the family problem which may have precipitated the crisis. The action denies that the family can be helped to solve its own problems. (1968:146)

Outpatient treatment allows the family structure to remain intact while the impaired family member is working through his personal problems in relation to the web of family ties which nurtured those problems and which his pathology affected. Even if mental hospitals invited families to come to the hospital for therapy sessions with their hospitalized family member, removal of the patient from the home cuts him off from ordinary family activities and undermines the purpose of family therapy—to help families attack their problems as a group.

Langsley experimented with outpatient "crisis therapy" for a randomly selected 50 percent of families who had requested hospitalization for a mentally ill family member, comparing the results with hospitalization of the remaining 50 percent. Outpatient treatment consisted of about five office sessions of family therapy, one home visit, and a few telephone calls spread over three weeks. Inpatient treatment lasted an average of 26 days and included individual and group therapy focused on the patient. The rest of the family (with the patient apparently excluded) were seen by a different therapist, so the experiment contrasted the dual effects of inpatient individual therapy with outpatient family therapy.

TABLE 24-1 Days Lost from Family Role Functioning as Breadwinner or Housekeeper for Men and Women Receiving Inpatient Versus Outpatient Treatment for Mental Illness

DAYS LOST FROM ROLE FUNCTION	*TREATMENT*		*INPATIENT/ OUTPATIENT RATIO*
	Inpatient	*Outpatient*	
During acute treatment	24.3	8.1	3.00X
During six months after termination	48.2	16.9	2.85X
Total days lost	72.5	25.0	2.90X
Number of patients	75	75	

Adapted from Langsley, Pittman, Machotka, and Flomenhaft, 1968:153. Source: Random sampling of families all of whom originally sought inpatient treatment at the Colorado Psychiatric Hospital. The numbers indicate the average number of days lost by men from employment and by women from housekeeping responsibilities.

Table 24-1 shows that out patient treatment was three times as effecttive as hospitalization in restoring patients to their normal role functioning. Since all the patients held crucial role positions as father or mother, this correspondingly reduced the crises their families experienced in having to reallocate their role functions. From a financial point of view not only were men able to resume earning money sooner but the cost of treatment to the families of both men and women was sliced from $1,300 to $200 by avoiding hospitalization.

In a scale measuring improvement in the patients' social and family relations, outpatients improved almost four times as much as inpatients. Some notion of the process by which the outpatient approach improved the family's functioning can be deduced from Langsley's description of his therapeutic methods:

> The treatment process begins at the time the patient and family come for help. Though the initial request was for hospitalization, the family are seen at once by a member of the clinical team and are promised immediate help. Absent family members are called in from home, school or work and significant others in the family are included. The history of events leading up to the crisis is obtained and the interactional aspects of the crisis are stressed. Efforts to avoid the family crisis by scapegoating one member and labeling him a "mental patient" are blocked. Regression is discouraged. Tension is reduced with active reassurance, support, and specific advice. Drugs are used for symptom relief in any member of the family. Tasks are assigned for resolving the crisis and returning each member to functioning. With this directive and supportive approach, symptomatic relief occurs very quickly (in hours or days). Conflicts in role assignments and performance can then be negotiated. (1968:147)

This outpatient family therapy stressed immediate resolution of the family crisis which had precipitated the identified patient's emotional state. By assisting the family in finding a mutually satisfactory solution to its group problem, the "patient's" symptoms rapidly subsided and he was able to resume his normal role functioning within a reorganized family.

When hospitalization proves necessary, the disruptive effects of separating the individual from his family might be minimized by scheduling family therapy sessions in the hospital, encouraging visits and correspondence with the patient in the hospital, encouraging progressively longer visits home by the patient, and continuing family therapy after the patient's discharge until a satisfactory new family pattern has been achieved.

Involvement of Extra-Familial Personnel If a nuclear family is heavily involved with relatives or nonrelated persons who contribute to their pathology or resist their treatment, some therapists have found it useful to expand the participating group to include these "significant others." Speck (1967) found family therapy blocked in different cases by a lawyer, a priest, and a brother-in-law on whom families depended and who felt threatened by the families' counter-dependence on the therapist. Each of these authority figures refused to join in the family therapy and wrecked what Speck attempted to accomplish with the families. In another case he extended his treatment to the entire social network of a schizophrenic 54-year-old woman and her 20-year-old son. In group meetings of 12 to 35 relatives and friends of the original patients, Speck was able to relieve tensions not only between mother and son but in many of the other nuclear family units in the network. Although the focus of such extensive therapy may be on the benefit to the initial family, all those involved may find their own family behavior improved thereby.

Multiple-Family Therapy

It is a short step from involving extra-familial personnel whose lives are entwined with each other to involving families with similar problems who do not know each other in advance.

Groups of married couples or groups of total families assembled to work on similar problems have several advantages. A family may recognize its own problems more easily by observing another family than when it has only its own behavior to observe. Other families may assist the therapist in analyzing a given family's behavior, giving added weight to his observations. By commenting on another family's behavior, individuals may gain courage in coping with their own family's problem.

The last advantage was particularly therapeutic for schizophrenic boys who had withdrawn in the face of severe conflict between their parents. When Barcai got three sons and their six parents together for multiple-family therapy, the larger setting allowed the sons to express themselves more freely than if each had been locked in with his parents exclusively. When the therapist legitimated self-expression for the boys by placing each one in turn in charge of the group session, the other parents joined with the therapist in criticizing the belittling behavior of the parents of the presiding boy:

> The group was silent for the first several minutes after Mike became chairman. The parent subgroup then started to joke about it while the sons remained quiet. Mike seemed confused. When his parents continued to belittle him, the therapist . . . [stated] rather forcefully that he thought the group was not cooperative and that they were not paying due respect to their new leader. He proceeded then in a friendly peer fashion to encourage Mike to assert his authority. A triumphant gleam appeared in Mike's eyes. For the first time he experienced the ability to speak to both parents directly, telling them that he had been made the boss although he would still remain their son after the meeting. The two other schizophrenic boys shared in the vicarious pleasure of one of their kind being the leader and supported him. The adults in the other two families jokingly and hesitantly followed suit. By sheer volume and number, Mike's parents were coerced to stop their belittling attitude. (1967:189)

When each set of parents in turn behaved the way Mike's had, it became apparent to everyone that this contributed to each son's passivity. Although this had already been apparent to the therapist, only when the families acted out their problem in front of each other and pressured each other in support of the therapist did the therapeutic breakthrough finally occur.

If such therapeutic progress can be achieved by bringing families together for an hour or two in an office, even more extensive benefits should be possible when families can interact with the therapist over a longer period of time. Just as home visits enable a therapist to become involved in a wider range of the behavior of an individual family, a residential multi-family weekend or more extended sojourn provides the same benefits on a multi-family scale.

Landes and Winter (1966) experimented with a residential weekend for four families with aggressive or self-destructive teenage boys. They included their own families and those of three other nonprofessional staff members. This enabled the abnormal families to learn from observing normal families. The residential feature of the weekend enabled the families to engage in collective recreation (volleyball) and work (constructing, painting and erecting a large sign) as well as in multiple-family therapy. Working and playing together provided grist for the mill of the therapy sessions, making them livelier and more meaningful than ordinary office sessions.

Although Landes and Winter gave no tangible evidence of long term benefits to the families, each of the abnormal families felt they had benefited from observing how the other three families were "sicker" than they. Parents in the patient families felt drawn together by their common problems and accepted advice from each other more readily than from the therapists. At the same time, they learned more from observing the therapists' behavior with their own families than from the merely verbal communication which the therapists usually relied upon. In general, then, the residential weekend offered a rich mix of family interaction which had many educational values in addition to contributing to the formal therapy sessions. Landes and Winter concluded that the experiment had been so beneficial for the weekend that it deserved to be extended to a two-week summer vacation.

The opportunity to observe normal families in interaction may be imported into the therapy office by utilizing husband–wife teams or at least male–female teams of therapists. John Sonne and Geraldine Lincoln (a psychiatrist and psychologist respectively) reported that their own interaction provided models for patient families to observe:

> It seemed false to expect the family to communicate directly with one another on a feeling level without holding up the same standards for ourselves. In experiencing the stress of the indirect communication of the family and seeking for more honest and direct communication, we found it impossible to tolerate any vagueness in our relationship. We expected no difficulties to remain unresolved. When we were appreciative of each other we said so. When we didn't like something the other had said or done, we said so. We allowed little time lag before eliminating any static, and each of us felt free to take the initiative. (1965:184–185)

Such a model of communicative behavior could have been provided by cotherapists of the same sex, suggesting that any paired therapists may have more modeling value than solo therapists. But Sonne and Lincoln found there were values in cross-sex pairing which a same-sex team would not have experienced. Whenever the two therapists reacted to their patients the same way, they reinforced one another more dramatically because they held similar views despite their difference in sex. But they often reacted differently because of their sex difference. These contrasting reactions helped the therapists understand their patients better than they could have otherwise. Discussing the discrepancies produced more creative insights than would have occurred to either therapist alone. By openly resolving male/female differences in their own "marriage," the therapists demonstrated for the patient family the possibility of fruitful conflict between the sexes. Co-therapist teams therefore offer an additional way in which disturbed families may learn from normal families or healthy pseudo-families.

The point of all this is not to suggest that families must necessarily be treated with normal families but that the more familistic and realistic the therapy situation becomes, the greater the likelihood of involving the real problems of the family in the therapeutic process and of applying the insights gained in therapy to everyday living.

EDUCATION FOR FAMILY LIVING

In the United States, education for family living has become a large scale enterprise. Kerckhoff (1964) estimated that one-and-one-half million high school students were enrolled in courses in family-life education each year, and Landis (1959) estimated enrollment in college courses on preparation for marriage at more than 60,000 students per year out of a total of more than 100,000 in various kinds of courses on the family. These figures contrast with the situation in most countries where functional courses in preparation for family living are rarely if ever offered.

The goals of family life education are two-fold: to prevent family crises and to improve family functioning. Although numerous studies summarized by Duvall (1965) have demonstrated that such courses increase students' factual knowledge and change their attitudes, few have attempted to measure their effects on family life.

Clark Ellzey reported that 31 percent of the women students enrolled in a Stephens College course "changed their plans" in one way or another during the semester and 41 percent said the course had "influenced their decision regarding when to marry" (Duvall, 1965:180). However, such verbal statements need to be followed up to see whether they are carried out in broken engagements, postponed marriages, and other concrete effects of classroom study.

Table 24-2 shows the results of a five-years-later follow-up study of alumni of a university course in preparation for marriage. The table suggests that the course reduced unhappy marriages and increased very happy ones (although it is impossible to tell for certain whether electing such a course indicated greater motivation for success in marriage which in itself produced these results). Until someone assigns students randomly to such courses from a pool of applicants, possible selective factors will not have been controlled. In the meantime, I assume that education for marriage does produce marriages which are more satisfactory to the participants.

Such courses may also benefit parent–child relationships. Dyer (1963) found that 75 percent of couples who had never taken a family living course in high school or college found the birth of their first child an extensive or severe crisis. By contrast, if either the husband or wife had had such a course, the proportion reacting to the advent of the first child as a crisis fell to 31 percent. The magnitude of the difference suggests that courses in family living cushion the transition from marriage to parenthood.

TABLE 24-2 Marital Happiness of Men and Women, by Education for Marriage

	EDUCATION FOR MARRIAGE	
MARITAL HAPPINESS	None	Some
Very happy	74%	84%
Happy	16	14
Less than happy	10	2
Total	100%	100%
Number of cases	111	593

Adapted from Dyer, 1959:232. Source: Married alumni of a University of Minnesota course in preparation for marriage compared with a control group of married students who had not taken this course, matched by year in school, major, and sex. Marital happiness was self-rated by the respondents.

Schvaneveldt (1964) found that mothers who had taken a course in child development and/or family relations were less apt to overprotect their children than mothers who had not taken such a course.

Such findings suggest that generalized courses in preparation for marriage benefit those who take them in a variety of ways.

Education for Family Planning

In addition to education for family life in general, some educational programs concentrate on specific goals. In a number of underdeveloped countries, population control programs have undertaken experimental field research programs to discover how families can be most effectively informed about new methods of contraception and persuaded to use them.

Major experiments were conducted in Puerto Rico by Hill, Stycos, and Back (1959) and in Jamaica by Stycos and Back (1964). In neither case was the experimental program introduced in a contraceptive vacuum. On both islands a minority of the population already practiced birth control prior to the experiment. In Jamaica, a family planning clinic had been established in 1939 in the capital city of Kingston but its services were handicapped by the fact that the average client did not approach the clinic until she already had 4.5 pregnancies (more than the national average for women of completed fertility). The clinic thus served excessively large families more than it reduced the general birth rate of the community.

In Puerto Rico the researchers found that clinics and other professional sources were relatively unimportant in comparison to informal influences. Relatives most often persuaded people that they had had enough children while friends and neighbors were the chief stimulus for using birth control and the chief source of information about methods in common use. Only when couples sought more effective methods than the ones they first tried did professional sources become more important (and even then only for a third of those who tried a new method).

TABLE 24-3 Persistence and Success in Birth Control by
Chief Source of Influence and Information

BIRTH CONTROL EXPERIENCE	CHIEF SOURCE OF INFLUENCE AND INFORMATION				
	Relatives	*Friends*	*Self*	*Husband*	*Clinic*
Long-term regular use	13%	19%	15%	33%	28%
Short-term irregular use	40%	34%	36%	32%	26%
Median failures per year	.62	.62	.56	.50	.46
Number of cases	104	117	121	92	81

Adapted from Hill, Stycos and Back, 1959:362. Source: Puerto Rican women with less than seventh-grade education, married 5 to 20 years, with one or more children. This table is restricted to those who had ever used any method of birth control. Residual percentages used no method. Failures represent the median number of unplanned pregnancies per year for each group after couples began to practice contraception.

Table 24-3 shows that clinics were the most effective source of contraceptive information in the sense of reducing the number of unwanted pregnancies. This resulted primarily from the greater technical effectiveness of the methods provided by clinics in contrast to the frequent advocacy by other sources of unreliable "natural" methods such as rhythm and withdrawal. On the other hand, the table also shows that husbands outstripped clinics in influencing long-term regular use of birth control. This reflects the fact that when husbands and wives cooperate with each other, family planning is likely to be more regularly and persistently practiced.

Hill and his colleagues found that where both husband and wife believed in joint responsibility for birth control, 58 percent made long-term use of birth control methods, whereas only 43 percent of those believing the husband should take primary responsibility and 37 percent of those saying the wife should do so kept it up for very long (*Ibid.*:316). They also found that the more often husbands and wives talked about problems of family size and of birth control, the more apt they were to practice birth control at all or to use it for a long time.

The husband's cooperation was especially important in Puerto Rico because of the role of the male in a still-patriarchal society. The value of husband–wife teamwork in effective contraceptive practice suggests that educational programs should be directed toward husband–wife pairs (like joint treatment in family therapy). However, most contraceptive education programs have focused chiefly or exclusively on wives because their cooperation could be obtained more easily than that of husbands.

Educational Methods   The Puerto Rican experiment found that public meetings were more effective than pamphlets in influencing the long-term behavior of those who were reached, but that getting any rural working-class people to come to meetings was extraordinarily difficult. By scheduling meetings on weekends, inviting families personally, and providing transportation to those who lived some distance away, Hill and his associates were able to persuade

59 percent of the women and 40 percent of the men to attend one of a series of three meetings—but only 16 percent of the women and 8 percent of the men attended all three. This contrasts with 100 percent readership of pamphlets distributed in the similar Jamaican experiment. Moreover the Puerto Rican researchers found that a larger percentage of nonusers began birth control after reading pamphlets (42 percent) than after attending meetings (31 percent) even though the meetings had longer-lasting effects. This suggests that pamphlets reach a wider audience than meetings but that a combined approach may be even more effective than one method alone in reaching an entire community.

The Jamaican project also used pamphlets and meetings but added home visits by caseworkers and combined all three methods to assess the cumulative persuasiveness of a multifaceted approach. Table 24-4 shows that the triple-barrelled approach was the most effective as assessed by a variety of criteria.

TABLE 24-4 Effects of Various Methods of Education for Family Planning on Women Without Previous Family Planning Experience

| | *EDUCATIONAL METHOD* | | | | |
BIRTH CONTROL EXPERIENCE	*None*	*Pamphlets*	*Visits*	*Meetings*	*Combined*
Talked to husband about program	—	53%	58%	62%	78%
Went to a clinic or doctor					
Rural	3%	14%	18%	7%	—
Urban	9%	14%	23%	20%	43%
Used any method of birth control					
Rural	21%	17%	24%	16%	—
Urban	19%	34%	38%	45%	55%
Number of cases					
Rural	87	86	121	31	—
Urban	32	98	64	20	40

Adapted from Stycos and Back, 1964:230,259. Source: Lower-class Jamaican women who had had a child within the past five years and who had never used any method of family planning prior to the experimental program. Visits were by caseworkers to women in their own homes. The combined program consisted of meetings followed by pamphlet distribution and subsequently by a caseworker's visit.

Table 24-4 shows that even a control group exposed to no educational program tended to try family planning. In the rural area, paradoxically, family planning was tried by more women in the control group than by those either invited to meetings or given pamphlets. With those exceptions, all the educational programs increased family planning behavior. Thus many kinds of family planning education are likely to have at least some effect.

Although pamphlets were the least effective method, they were also the cheapest. Had the people been totally illiterate, pamphlets would have been less effective, although cartoons might still have had some value. Most of the Jamaican respondents could read and the few who could not asked others to read the pamphlets to them. Pamphlets were especially effective in stimulating actual use of contraception among women who had completed elementary school rather than among those who had dropped out. The researchers were struck not only by the universal readership (aided perhaps by the relatively small amount of printed material available in these poverty-stricken homes), but by the fact that women who went to clinics took the pamphlets with them and asked the doctors for more information about what they had read. As much as three years later, many women reported that they still had the pamphlets and continued to refer to them from time to time.

Meetings and home visits were about equally effective, depending on the criterion used for effectiveness. On the crucial measure of adopting family planning, meetings were more effective with better educated women whereas home visits were needed to get poorly educated women to do anything.

It is important to remember that Table 24-4 shows only the effect of meetings on those who actually attended—a select group most likely to be influenced by an educational program. Casework visits on the other hand were useful in hostile communities where group meetings could not be arranged. Individual suspicion could be overcome by a skillful worker in the privacy of the home. Casework was therefore more effective in reaching "hard core" resisters to family planning.

In general, individual visits were the most expensive method in terms of the amount of staff time required. If an educational program has limited funds, pamphlets or meetings seem preferable. But if funds are plentiful, Table 24-4 shows that a multipronged approach will reach more women than any single method.

In addition to family planning, specific educational programs in the U.S.A. deal with sex education, education for childbirth, and education for child-rearing (*i.e.,* parent education for those who already have children). In each case, the purposes of these programs is both to prevent family malfunctioning and to improve the quality of family life.

Workshops for Improved Family Functioning

In recent years, experimentation has begun with workshops for married couples and whole families, the purpose of which is to enable normal families to achieve richer levels of family living. The methods used in these evening, weekend or vacation workshops resemble those in multiple-family therapy. The difference is that families participate not because they are falling apart but because they want to achieve new depths of family relationships by joining with other families in exploring their potentialities.

By role-playing their own parts or reversing roles (the husband playing the part of the wife and vice versa), by games and exercises derived from encounter groups and sensitivity training labs, by learning body massage and communication skills, such programs hope to enable married couples to express their love to each other and to offset the apathy which affects most couples with the passing years.

Although the effectiveness of such workshop programs has yet to be measured, it seems likely that they will play a growing role in societies blessed with affluence, education and leisure. Just as humanistic psychology developed a concern to increase the capacity of individuals to reach what Maslow

(1964) called "peak experiences," the marriage and family workshop movement should increase the capacity of families to attain collective peak experiences. In so doing, professional assistance moves beyond prevention and cure of family crises to positive goals for family living.

REFERENCES

Ackerman, Charles. "Affiliations: Structural Determinants of Differential Divorce Rates," *American Journal of Sociology* 69 (1963):13–20.

Ackerman, Nathan W. "Prejudicial Scapegoating and Neutralizing Forces in the Family Group, with Special Reference to the Role of 'Family Healer,' " *International Journal of Social Psychiatry* 2 (1964):90–96.

Adams, Bert N. "Interaction Theory and the Social Network," *Sociometry* 30 (1967):64–78. [Referred to as 1967a.]

————. "Occupational Position, Mobility, and the Kin of Orientation," *American Sociological Review* 32 (1967):364–376. [Referred to as 1967b.]

————. *Kinship in an Urban Setting.* Chicago: Markham, 1968.

Aldous, Joan, and Reuben Hill. "Social Cohesion, Lineage Type, and Intergenerational Transmission," *Social Forces* 43 (1965):471–482.

Anderson, Nels, editor. *Studies of the Family.* Vol. I, Tubingen: J. C. B. Mohr, 1956. Vol. II, Gottingen: Vandenhoeck & Ruprecht, 1957. Vol. III, *ibid.,* 1958. [Also published as *Schriftenreihe des Unesco-Instituts für Sozial Wissenschaften* (Cologne), volumes 3, 5 and 7.]

Anshen, Ruth Nanda, editor. *The Family: Its Function and Destiny.* New York: Harper, 1959.

Aries, Philippe. *Centuries of Childhood: A Social History of Family Life.* New York: Vintage, 1962.

Ariga, Kizaemon. "Daikazoku Seido to Nago Seido" (Large Family System and 'Nago' System), in *Ariga Kizaemon Chosaku-shu* (Collected Works of Kizaemon Ariga), volume III. Tokyo: Mirai-sha, 1967. [Cited by Aiko Inouye in an unpublished term paper at International Christian University, 1968.]

————. *Nihon no Kazoku* (Families in Japan). Tokyo: Sibundo, 1965. [Cited by Watanabe (1968).]

Baber, Ray E. *Youth Looks at Marriage and the Family.* Tokyo: International Christian University, 1958.

Bakke, E. Wight. *Citizens Without Work.* New Haven: Yale University Press, 1940. [Abridged in Bell and Vogel (1960):112–125.]

Bales, Robert F., Paul A. Hare, and Edgar F. Borgatta. "Structure and Dynamics of Small Groups; A Review of Four Variables," in Joseph B. Gittler, ed., *Review of Sociology.* New York: Wiley, 1957.

Bales, Robert F., and Philip E. Slater. "Role Differentiation in Small Decision-Making Groups," in Parson and Bales (1955):259–306.

Ballweg, John A. "Resolution of Conjugal Role Adjustment After Retirement," *Journal of Marriage and the Family* 29 (1967):277–281.

Baltzell, E. Digby. "Social Mobility and Fertility within an Elite Group," *Milbank Memorial Fund Quarterly* 31 (1953):411–420.

Bandura, Albert, and Richard H. Walters. *Adolescent Aggression: A Study of the Influence of Child-Training Practices and Family Interrelations.* New York: Ronald, 1959.

Banfield, Edward C. *The Moral Basis of a Backward Society.* Glencoe, Illinois: The Free Press, 1958.

Barber, Elinor C. *The Bourgeoisie in 18th Century France.* Princeton: Princeton University Press, 1955. [Excerpted in Goode (1964b):65–67.]

Barcai, Avner. "An Adventure in Multiple Family Therapy," *Family Process* 6 (1967):185–192.

Barry, Herbert, III, Irvin L. Child, and Margaret K. Bacon. "Relation of Child Training to Subsistence Economy," *American Anthropologist* 61 (1959):51–63.

Bates, Alan. "Parental Roles in Courtship," *Social Forces* 20 (1942):483–486.

Beardsley, Richard K., John W. Hall, and Robert E. Ward. *Village Japan*. Chicago: University of Chicago Press, 1959.

Bell, Norman W. "Extended Family Relations of Disturbed and Well Families," *Family Process* 1 (1962):179–193.

———, and Ezra F. Vogel, editors. *A Modern Introduction to the Family*. Glencoe, Illinois: The Free Press, 1960; revised edition, New York: The Free Press, 1968.

Bell, Robert R., and Jack V. Buerkle. "The Daughter's Role During the 'Launching Stage'," *Marriage and Family Living* 24 (1962):384–388.

Bieber, Irving, assisted by Harvey J. Dain, Paul R. Dince, Marvin G. Drellich, Henry G. Grand, Ralph H. Gundlach, Malvina W. Kremer, Alfred H. Rifkin, Cornelia B. Wilbur, and Toby B. Bieber. *Homosexuality: A Psychoanalytic Study*. New York: Basic Books, 1962.

Blake, Judith. *Family Structure in Jamaica: The Social Context of Reproduction*. New York: The Free Press, 1961.

Blau, Peter M., and Otis Dudley Duncan. *The American Occupational Structure*. New York: Wiley, 1967.

Blood, Robert O., Jr. "Romance and Premarital Intercourse—Incompatibles?" *Marriage and Family Living* 14 (1952):105–108.

———. "The Division of Labor in City and Farm Families," *Marriage and Family Living* 20 (1958):170–174.

———. "Social Class and Family Control of Television Viewing," *Merrill-Palmer Quarterly* 7 (1961):205–222.

———. "The Husband-Wife Relationship," in Nye and Hoffman (1963):282–305.

———. *Love Match and Arranged Marriage: A Tokyo–Detroit Comparison*. New York: The Free Press, 1967.

———. "Kinship Interaction and Marital Solidarity," *Merrill-Palmer Quarterly* 15 (1969):171–183. [Referred to as 1969a.]

———. *Marriage*. New York: The Free Press, 1969. [1969b.]

———. "Social Change and Kinship Patterns," in Hill and König (1970):189–201.

———, and Robert L. Hamblin. "The Effect of the Wife's Employment on the Family Power Structure," *Social Forces* 36 (1958):347–352.

———, Reuben Hill, Andrée Michel, and Constantina Safilios-Rothschild. "Comparative Analysis of Family Power Structure: Problems of Measurement and Interpretation," in Hill and König (1970):525–535.

———, and Donald M. Wolfe. *Husbands and Wives: The Dynamics of Married Living*. Glencoe, Illinois: The Free Press, 1960.

———. "Negro-White Differences in Blue-Collar Marriages in a Northern Metropolis," *Social Forces* 48 (1969):59–64.

Bossard, James H. S. "Family Table Talk: An Area for Sociological Study," *American Sociological Review* 8 (1943):295–301.

———, and Eleanor S. Boll. *Ritual in Family Living*. Philadelphia: University of Pennsylvania Press, 1950.

———. *The Large Family System*. Philadelphia: University of Pennsylvania Press, 1956.

Bott, Elizabeth. *Family and Social Network*. London: Tavistock Institute of Human Relations, 1957.

Bowerman, Charles E., and Donald P. Irish. "Some Relationships of Stepchildren to Their Parents," *Marriage and Family Living* 24 (1962):113–121.

Bradburn, Norman M. "Achievement and Father Dominance in Turkey," *Journal of Abnormal and Social Psychology* 67 (1963):464–468. [Reprinted in Geiger (1968): 191–198.]

Bradburn, N. M. "The Managerial Role in Turkey: a psychological study." Unpublished doctoral dissertation. Harvard University, 1960. [Cited by McClelland (1961):375.]

Brav, Stanley. *Jewish Family Solidarity*. Vicksburg: Nogales Press, 1940.

Bresler, Jack B. "The Relation of Population Fertility Levels to Ethnic Group Backgrounds," *Eugenics Quarterly* 8 (1961):12–22.

Broderick, Carlfred B., and Stanley E. Fowler. "New Patterns of Relationships Between the Sexes Among Preadolescents," *Marriage and Family Living* 23 (1961):27–30.

Bronfenbrenner, Urie. "Toward a Theoretical Model for the Analysis of Parent-Child Relationships in a Social Context," in John C. Glidewell, editor, *Parental Attitudes and Child Behavior*. Springfield, Illinois: Thomas (1961):90–109.

Brown, Julia S. "A Comparative Study of Deviations from Sexual Mores," *American Sociological Review* 17 (1952):135–146.

Burchinal, Lee R. "Research on Young Marriage: Implications for Family Life Education," *The Family Life Coordinator* 9 (1960):6–24.

———, and Loren E. Chancellor. "Ages at Marriage, Occupations of Grooms and Interreligious Marriage Rates," *Social Forces* 40 (1962):348–354.

———. "Survival Rates Among Religiously Homogamous and Interreligious Marriages," *Social Forces* 41 (1963):353–362.

Bureau of the Census. "Annual Report of the Labor Force, 1958," *Current Population Reports, Labor Force*. Washington, D. C.: U. S. Government Printing Office, 1959. [Cited in Nye and Hoffman, (1963):15.]

Burgess, Ernest W., and Leonard S. Cottrell, Jr. *Predicting Success or Failure in Marriage*. New York: Prentice-Hall, 1939.

Burgess, Ernest W. and Paul Wallin. *Engagement and Marriage*. Chicago: Lippincott, 1953.

Buric, Olivera and Andjelka Zecevic. "Family Authority, Marital Satisfaction, and the Social Network in Yugoslavia," *Journal of Marriage and the Family* 29 (1967):325–336.

Campbell, J. K. *Honour, Family and Patronage: A Study of Institutions and Moral Values in a Greek Mountain Community*. Oxford: Clarendon, 1964.

Campisi, Paul J. "Ethnic Family Patterns: The Italian Family in the United States," *The American Journal of Sociology* 53 (1948):443–449.

Caudill, William. "Consequences for Children of Varying Family Patterns" in Hill and König (1970):3–11.

Chen, Theodore Hsi-En. "The Marxist Remolding of Chinese Society," *American Journal of Sociology* 58 (1953):340–346.

Chesser, Eustace. *The Sexual, Marital and Family Relationships of the English Woman*. New York: Roy, 1957.

Christensen, Harold T. "Cultural Relativism and Premarital Sex Norms," *American Sociological Review* 25 (1960):31–39.

———. "A Cross-Cultural Comparison of Attitudes Toward Marital Infidelity," *International Journal of Comparative Sociology* 3 (1962):124–137.

————, editor. *Handbook of Marriage and the Family.* Chicago: Rand, McNally, 1964.

————. "Scandinavian and American Sex Norms," *Journal of Social Issues* 22 (1966):60–75.

————, Robert Andrews, and Sophie Freiser. "Falsification of Age at Marriage," *Marriage and Family Living* 15 (1953):301–304.

————, and Hanna H. Meissner. "Studies in Child Spacing: III. Premarital Pregnancy as a Factor in Divorce," *American Sociological Review* 18 (1953):641–644.

Christenson, Reo M. "A New Attack on Poverty," *The Progressive,* January 1969:35–38.

Clausen, John A. "Family Structure, Socialization and Personality," in Hoffman and Hoffman (1966):1–53.

Cobb, Sidney and John R. P. French, Jr. "Birth Order Among Medical Students," *Journal of the American Medical Association* 195 (1966):172–173.

Cohen, Albert K. *Delinquent Boys: The Culture of the Gang.* Glencoe, Illinois: The Free Press, 1955.

Colson, Elizabeth. *Marriage and the Family Among the Plateau Tonga.* Manchester: Manchester University Press, 1958.

Cumming, Elaine and William E. Henry. *Growing Old: The Process of Disengagement.* New York: Basic Books, 1961.

Cumming, Elaine and David M. Schneider. "Sibling Solidarity: A Property of American Kinship," *American Anthropologist* 63 (1961):498–507.

Cutler, Beverly R. and William G. Dyer. "Initial Adjustment Processes in Young Married Couples," *Social Forces* 44 (1965):195–201.

d'Andrade, Roy G. "Sex Differences and Cultural Institutions," in Eleanor Maccoby, editor, *The Development of Sex Differences.* Palo Alto: Stanford University Press, 1966:174–202.

Davis, Fred. *Passage through Crisis: Polio Victims and Their Families.* Indianapolis: Bobbs-Merrill, 1963.

Davis, Kingsley. "The Sociology of Parent-Youth Conflict," *American Sociological Review* 4 (1940):523–535.

————. "Children of Divorce," *Law and Contemporary Problems* 10 (1944):700–710. [Reprinted in Landis and Landis (1952):351–359.]

Deutsch, Martin and Bert Brown. "Social Influences in Negro-White Intelligence Differences," *Journal of Social Issues* 20 (1964):24–35.

Deutscher, Irwin. *Married Life in the Middle Years: A Study of the Middle Class Urban Postparental Couple.* Kansas City, Missouri: Community Studies, Inc., 1959.

Dinkel, Robert M. "Attitudes of Children toward Supporting Aged Parents," *American Sociological Review* 9 (1944):370–379.

Dore, R. P. *City Life in Japan: a Study of a Tokyo Ward.* London: Routledge and Kegan Paul, 1958.

Douvan, Elizabeth, and Joseph Adelson. *The Adolescent Experience.* New York: Wiley, 1966.

Duvall, Evelyn Millis. "How Effective Are Marriage Courses?" *Journal of Marriage and the Family* 27 (1965):176–184.

Dyer, Dorothy. "A Comparative Study Relating Marital Happiness to University Courses Helpful in Marital Adjustment," *Marriage and Family Living* 21 (1959):230–232.

Dyer, Everett D. "Parenthood as Crisis: A Re-Study," *Marriage and Family Living* 25 (1963):196–201.

Ehrmann, Winston W. *Premarital Dating Behavior.* New York: Holt, 1959.

Elder, Glen H., Jr. "Structural Variations in the Child Rearing Relationship," *Sociometry* 25 (1962):241–262.

———. "Family Structure and Educational Attainment: A Cross-National Analysis," *American Sociological Review* 30 (1965):81–96.

———, and Charles E. Bowerman. "Family Structure and Child-Rearing Patterns: The Effect of Family Size and Sex Composition," *American Sociological Review* 28 (1963):891–905.

Elkin, Frederick, and William A. Westley. "The Myth of Adolescent Culture," *American Sociological Review* 20 (1955):680–684.

Epstein, Ralph. "Social Class Membership and Early Childhood Memories," *Child Development* 34 (1963):503–508.

Evans-Pritchard, E. E. *Kinship and Marriage Among the Nuer.* Oxford: Clarendon, 1951.

Farber, Bernard. "Family Organization and Crisis: Maintenance of Integration in Families with a Severely Mentally Retarded Child," *Monographs of the Society for Research in Child Development* 75 (1960).

———. "Interaction with Retarded Siblings and Life Goals of Children," *Marriage and Family Living* 25 (1963):96–98.

———. *Family: Organization and Interaction.* San Francisco: Chandler Publishing Company, 1964.

———, ed. *Kinship and Family Organization.* New York: Wiley, 1966. [1966a]

———. "Kinship Laterality and the Emotionally Disturbed Child," in Farber (1966a): 69–78. [1966b]

Ferreira, Antonio J. and William D. Winter. "Decision-Making in Normal and Abnormal Two-Child Families," *Family Process* 7 (1968):17–36.

Fischer, John L., and Ann Fischer. "The New Englanders of Orchard Town, U.S.A.," in Whiting (1963):869–1010.

Flexner, Eleanor. *Century of Struggle: The Women's Rights Movement in the United States.* Cambridge, Mass.: Belknap Press, 1959.

Foote, Nelson. "Matching of Husband and Wife in Phases of Development," in *Transactions of the Third World Congress of Sociology* 4 (1956):24–34. London: International Sociological Association.

Ford, Clellan S. and Frank A. Beach. *Patterns of Sexual Behavior.* New York: Harper, 1951.

Forde, Daryll. "Double Descent Among the Yako," in Radcliffe-Brown and Forde (1950):285–332.

Fortes, Meyer. "Kinship and Marriage Among the Ashanti," in Radcliffe-Brown and Forde (1950):252–284.

Frazier, E. Franklin. "The Impact of Urban Civilization upon Negro Family Life," *American Sociological Review* 2 (1937):609–618. [Reprinted in Bell and Vogel (1960):101–111.]

Freedman, Deborah S. "The Relation of Economic Status to Fertility," *American Economic Review* 53 (1963):414–426.

Freedman, Ronald. "Norms for Family Size in Underdeveloped Areas," *Proceedings of the Royal Society* 159 (1963):220–245.

———, Pascal K. Whelpton, and Arthur A. Campbell. *Family Planning, Sterility, and Population Growth.* New York: McGraw-Hill, 1959.

Freedman, Maurice. "The Family in China, Past and Present," *Pacific Affairs* 34 (1961–62):323–336. [Reprinted in Geiger (1968):12–26.]

Freilich, Morris. "The Natural Triad in Kinship and Complex Systems," *American Sociological Review* 29 (1964):529–540.

Friedan, Betty. *The Feminine Mystique*. New York: Norton, 1963.

Friedman, Alfred S. "Family Therapy as Conducted in the Home," *Family Process* 1 (1962):132–140.

Fromm, Erich. *The Art of Loving*. New York: Harper, 1956.

Fueto, Toshio. "The Discrepancy between Marriage Law and Mores in Japan," *The American Journal of Comparative Law* 5 (1956):256–267.

Fukutake, Tadashi. *Nihon Noson no Shakaiteki Seikaku* (Social Characteristics of the Japanese Agricultural Community). Tokyo: Tokyo Daigaku Shuppan-kai, 1952. [Cited by Aiko Inouye in an unpublished term paper at International Christian University, 1968.]

Gebhard, Paul H., Wardell B. Pomeroy, Clyde E. Martin, and Cornelia V. Christenson. *Pregnancy, Birth, and Abortion*. New York: Hoeber, 1958.

Geertz, Hildred. *The Javanese Family*. New York: The Free Press, 1961.

Geiger, H. Kent. "Deprivation and Solidarity in the Soviet Urban Family," *American Sociological Review* 20 (1955):57–68.

———. "Changing Political Attitudes in Totalitarian Society: A Case Study of the Role of the Family," *World Politics* 8 (1956):187–205. [Reprinted in Bell and Vogel (1968):219–234.]

———. "The Soviet Family," in Nimkoff (1965):301–328.

———. *Comparative Perspectives on Marriage and the Family*. Boston: Little, Brown, 1968. [Referred to as 1968a.]

———. "The Fate of the Family in Soviet Russia: 1917–1944," in Bell and Vogel (1968):48–67. [Referred to as 1968b.]

Gerard, D. L., and J. Siegel. "The Family Background of Schizophrenia," *Psychiatric Quarterly* 24 (1950):47–73. [Cited by Lidz *et al.* (1957).]

Getzels, Jacob W., and Philip W. Jackson. *Creativity and Intelligence: Explorations with Gifted Students*. New York: Wiley, 1962.

Giffin, Mary E., Adelaide M. Johnson, and Edward M. Litin. "Specific Factors Determining Antisocial Acting Out," *American Journal of Orthopsychiatry* 24 (1954):668–684. [Reprinted in Bell and Vogel (1968):670–682.]

Gilbreth, Frank B., and Ernestine G. Gilbreth. *Cheaper by the Dozen*. New York: Crowell, 1949.

Girard, Alain. "Le Budget-temps de la Femme Mariée dans les Agglomerations Urbaines," *Population* 13 (1958):591–618. [Cited in Wilensky (1961):54.]

Glick, Paul C. *American Families*. New York: Wiley, 1957.

Gold, Martin. *Status Forces in Delinquent Boys*. Ann Arbor, Michigan: Institute for Social Research, 1963.

Gluckman, Max. "Kinship and Marriage Among the Lozi of Northern Rhodesia and the Zulu of Natal," in Radcliffe-Brown and Forde (1950):166–206.

Goldberg, David. "Another Look at the Indianapolis Fertility Data," *Milbank Memorial Fund Quarterly* 38 (1960):23–36.

Goldberg, E. M. *Family Influences and Psychosomatic Illness: An Inquiry Into the Social and Psychological Background of Duodenal Ulcer*. London: Tavistock, 1958.

Golden, Joseph. "Patterns of Negro–White Intermarriage," *American Sociological Review* 19 (1954):144–147.

Goldfarb, William. "Psychological Privation in Infancy and Subsequent Adjustment," *American Journal of Orthopsychiatry* 15 (1945):247–255. [Reprinted in Martin and Stendler (1954):397–403.]

Goldstein, Sidney, and Calvin Goldscheider. "Social and Demographic Aspects of Jewish Intermarriages," *Social Problems* 13 (1966):386–399.

Goode, William J. *After Divorce.* Glencoe: The Free Press, 1956.

————. "The Theoretical Importance of Love," *American Sociological Review* 24 (1959):38–47.

————. "Illegitimacy, Anomie, and Cultural Penetration," *American Sociological Review* 26 (1961):910–925.

————. *World Revolution and Family Patterns.* New York: The Free Press, 1963.

————. *The Family.* Englewood Cliffs: Prentice-Hall, 1964a.

————. *Readings on the Family and Society.* Englewood Cliffs: Prentice-Hall, 1964b.

————. "Achievement, Aspiration, and Family Structure," *Research Forum,* New York: Institute of Life Insurance, 1964: 25–39. [Referred to as 1964c.]

Gore, Madhav S. *The Impact of Industrialization and Urbanization on the Aggarwal Family in Delhi Area.* Unpublished Ph.D. dissertation. New York: Columbia University, 1961. [Cited in Goode (1963):240–265.]

————. "The Traditional Indian Family," in Nimkoff (1965):209–231.

Grabill, Wilson H. and Robert Parke, Jr. "Marriage, Fertility, and Childspacing: August 1959," *Current Population Reports,* Series P-20, #108 (1961).

Green, Arnold. "The 'Cult of Personality' and Sexual Relations," *Psychiatry* 4 (1941): 343–348. [Reprinted in Bell and Vogel (1960):608–615.]

Greenfield, Sidney M. "Industrialization and the Family in Sociological Theory," *American Journal of Sociology* 67 (1961):312–322.

Grönseth, Erik. "Research on Socialization in Norway," *Family Process* 3 (1964):302–322.

Gurin, Gerald, Joseph Veroff, and Sheila Feld. *Americans View Their Mental Health.* New York: Basic Books, 1960.

Habakkuk, H. J. "Family Structure and Economic Change in Nineteenth-Century Europe," *The Journal of Economic History* 15 (1955):1–12. [Reprinted in Bell and Vogel (1968):140–149.]

Hansen, Constance Collinge. "An Extended Home Visit with Conjoint Family Therapy," *Family Process* 7 (1968):67–87.

Harlow, M. K., and H. F. Harlow. "Affection in Primates," *Discovery,* January, 1966.

Hartshorne, Hugh, and Mark A. May. *Testing the Knowledge of Right and Wrong.* Chicago: Religious Education Association, 1927.

Heath, Dwight B. "Sexual Division of Labor and Cross-Cultural Research," *Social Forces* 37 (1958):77–79.

Heer, David M. "The Marital Status of Second-Generation Americans," *American Sociological Review* 26 (1961):233–240.

————. "Negro-White Intermarriage in the United States," *Journal of Marriage and the Family* 28 (1966):262–273.

Henry, Andrew F. "Family Role Structure and Self-Blame," *Social Forces* 25 (1956):34–38.

————, and James F. Short, Jr. *Suicide and Homicide.* Glencoe: The Free Press, 1954.

Herman, Robert D. "The 'Going Steady' Complex: a Re-examination," *Marriage and Family Living* 17 (1955):36–40.

Hill, Reuben. *Families Under Stress: Adjustment to the Crises of War Separation and Reunion.* New York: Harper, 1949.

――――. "Courtship in Puerto Rico: An Institution in Transition," *Marriage and Family Living* 17 (1955):26–35.

――――, and René König, eds. *Families in East and West: Socialization process and kinship ties.* The Hague: Mouton, 1970.

――――, J. Mayone Stycos and Kurt W. Back. *The Family and Population Control: A Puerto Rican Experiment in Social Change.* Chapel Hill: University of North Carolina Press, 1959.

Hillman, Christine H. "An Advice Column's Challenge for Family-Life Education," *Marriage and Family Living* 16 (1954):51–54.

Hillman, Karen G. "Marital Dissolution and Its Relation to Education, Income and Occupation." Unpublished master's thesis, Northwestern University, 1960. [Cited in Winch and Greer, 1964.]

Hindus, Maurice. "The Family in Russia," in Anshen (1949).

Hoffman, Lois Wladis and Martin L. Hoffman. *Review of Child Development Research.* New York: Russell Sage, Vol. 2, 1966.

Hoffman, Martin L. "Power Assertion by the Parent and Its Impact on the Child," *Child Development* 31 (1960):129–143.

Hollingshead, August B. *Elmtown's Youth.* New York: Wiley, 1949.

――――. "Cultural Factors in the Selection of Marriage Mates," *American Sociological Review* 15 (1950):619–627.

――――. "Marital Status and Wedding Behavior," *Marriage and Family Living* 14 (1952):308–311.

Homans, George C. *The Human Group.* New York: Harcourt, Brace and World, 1950.

Hsu, Francis L. K., editor. *Psychological Anthropology: Approaches to Culture and Personality.* Homewood: Dorsey, 1961.

Huang, Lucy Jen. "Some Changing Patterns in the Communist Chinese Family," *Marriage and Family Living* 23 (1961):137–145.

Humphreys, Alexander J. *New Dubliners: Urbanization and the Irish Family.* New York: Fordham University Press, 1966.

Hunt, Chester L. and Richard W. Coller. "Intermarriage and Cultural Change: A Study of Philippine-American Marriages," *Social Forces* 35 (1957):223–230.

Hurvitz, N. "Marital Problems Following Psychotherapy with One Spouse," *Journal of Consulting Psychology* 31 (1967):38–47.

Illsley, Raymond, and Barbara Thompson. "Women from Broken Homes," *Sociological Review* 9 (1961):27–54.

Inselberg, Rachel M. "Marital Problems and Satisfaction in High School Marriages," *Marriage and Family Living* 24 (1962):74–76.

Jackson, Joan K. "The Adjustment of the Family to the Crisis of Alcoholism," *Quarterly Journal of Studies on Alcohol* 15 (1954):562–586.

――――. "The Adjustment of the Family to Alcoholism," *Marriage and Family Living,* 18 (1956):361–369.

James, John. "A Preliminary Study of the Size Determinant in Small Group Interaction," *American Sociological Review* 16 (1951):474–477.

Jeffery, Arthur. "The Family in Islam," in Anshen (1959):201–232.

Jeffery, C. Ray. "Social Class and Adoption Petitioners," *Social Problems* 9 (1962):354–358.

Kammeyer, Kenneth. "Birth Order and the Feminine Sex Role Among College Women," *American Sociological Review* 31 (1966):508–515.

Kanin, Eugene J. "Male Aggression in Dating-Courtship Relations," *American Journal of Sociology* 63 (1957):197–204.

———. "Premarital Sex Adjustments, Social Class, and Associated Behaviors," *Marriage and Family Living* 22 (1960):258–262.

———, and David H. Howard. "Postmarital Consequences of Premarital Sex Adjustments," *American Sociological Review* 23 (1958):556–562.

Kantner, John F., and Clyde V. Kiser. "The Interrelation of Fertility, Fertility Planning and Intergenerational Social Mobility," *Milbank Memorial Fund Quarterly* 32 (1954): 969–1003.

Kapadia, E. M. *Marriage and Family in India*. London: Oxford University Press, 1958.

Katz, Alvin, and Reuben Hill. "Residential Propinquity and Marital Selection," *Marriage and Family Living* 20 (1958):27–35.

Kaufman, Irving, Alice L. Peck, and Consuelo K. Tagiuri. "The Family Constellation and Overt Incestuous Relations between Father and Daughter," *American Journal of Orthopsychiatry* 24 (1954):266–277. Reprinted in Bell and Vogel (1960):544–554.

Kauffman, J. Howard. "Family Structure and Interpersonal Relationships In Old Order Amish Families," an unpublished paper written in 1965.

Kelly, E. Lowell. "Consistency of the Adult Personality," *American Psychologist* 10 (1955):659–681.

Kennedy, Ruby Jo Reeves. "Premarital Residential Propinquity and Ethnic Endogamy," *American Journal of Sociology* 48 (1943):580–584.

———. "Single or Triple Melting Pots: Intermarriage in New Haven, 1870–1950," *American Journal of Sociology* 58 (1952):56–59.

Kephart, William M. "The Duration of Marriage," *American Sociological Review* 19 (1954):287–295. [Referred to as 1954a.]

———. "Some Variables in Cases of Reported Sexual Maladjustment," *Marriage and Family Living* 16 (1954):241–243. [Referred to as 1954b.]

———. "Occupational Levels and Marital Disruption," *American Sociological Review* 20 (1955):456–465.

———. "Experimental Family Organization: An Historico-Cultural Report on the Oneida Community," *Marriage and Family Living* 25 (1963):261–271.

———. *The Family, Society, and the Individual*. Boston: Houghton Mifflin, second edition, 1966.

Kerckhoff, Alan C. "Patterns of Homogamy and the Field of Eligibles," *Social Forces* 42 (1964):289–297.

Kerckhoff, Richard. "Family Life Education in America," in Christensen (1964):881–911.

Kinsey, Alfred C., Wardell B. Pomeroy, and Clyde E. Martin. *Sexual Behavior in the Human Male*. Philadelphia: Saunders, 1948.

———, and Paul H. Gebhard. *Sexual Behavior in the Human Female*. Philadelphia: Saunders, 1953.

Kirkendall, Lester A. *Premarital Intercourse and Interpersonal Relationships*. New York: Julian, 1961.

Kloskowska, Antonina. "Changing Family Models in the Popular Magazines in Poland," in Anderson (1958):159–182.

Kohl, R. N. "Pathologic Reactions of Marital Partners to Improvement of Patients," *American Journal of Psychiatry* 118 (1962):1036–1041.

Kohn, Melvin L. "Social Class and Parent-Child Relationships," *American Journal of Sociology* 68 (1963):471–480.

Komarovsky, Mirra. *Blue-Collar Marriage.* New York: Random House, 1964.

Koos, Earl L. "Class Differences in Family Reactions to Crisis," *Marriage and Family Living* 12 (1950):77–78, 99.

Kuper, Hilda. "Kinship Among the Swazi," in Radcliffe-Brown and Forde (1950):86–110.

Lahey, Edwin A. "Cuban Family Life Purified by Exile," *Detroit News,* March 8, 1967.

Lambiri, Ioanna. *Social Change in a Greek Country Town: The Impact of Factory Work on the Position of Women.* Athens: Center of Planning and Economic Research, 1965.

Landes, Judah and William Winter. "A New Strategy for Treating Disintegrating Families," *Family Process* 5 (1966):1–20.

Landis, Judson T. "Marriages of Mixed and Non-Mixed Religious Faith," *American Sociological Review* 14 (1949):401–407.

———. "The Teaching of Marriage and Family Courses in Colleges," *Marriage and Family Living* 21 (1959):36–40.

———, and Mary G. Landis. *Readings in Marriage and the Family.* Englewood Cliffs: Prentice-Hall, 1952.

Landis, Paul H. "Sequential Marriage," *Journal of Home Economics* 42 (1950):625–628.

———, and Carol L. Stone. *The Relationship of Parental Authority Patterns to Teenage Adjustments.* Pullman: Washington Agricultural Experiment Station, 1952.

Landy, David. *Tropical Childhood: Cultural Transmission and Learning in a Rural Puerto Rican Village.* Chapel Hill: University of North Carolina Press, 1959.

Lang, Olga. *Chinese Family and Society.* New Haven: Yale University Press, 1946.

Langsley, Donald G., Frank S. Pittman III, Pavel Machotka, and Kalman Flomenhaft. "Family Crisis Therapy—Results and Implications," *Family Process* 7 (1968):145–158.

LeMasters, Ersel E. "Social Class Mobility and Family Integration," *Marriage and Family Living* 16 (1954):226–232.

———. "Parenthood as Crisis," *Marriage and Family Living* 19 (1957):352–355.

LeVine, Robert A., and Barbara B. LeVine. "Nyansongo: A Gusii Community in Kenya," in Whiting (1963):15–202.

Levinger, George. "Marital Cohesiveness and Dissolution: An Integrative Review," *Journal of Marriage and the Family* 27 (1965):19–28.

Levy, David M. *Maternal Overprotection.* New York: Norton, 1966.

Levy, Marion J., Jr. *The Family Revolution in Modern China.* Cambridge: Harvard University Press, 1949.

Lewenberg, Martha P. "A Study of the Marital Relationships of Overprotecting and Non-overprotecting Mothers." [Cited in Levy (1966):120, 126.]

Lewis, Oscar. *Life in a Mexican Village: Tepoztlan Revisited.* Urbana: University of Illinois Press, 1951. [Cited in Stephens (1963):365.]

———. *Tepoztlan: Village in Mexico.* New York: Holt, Rinehart and Winston, 1962.

Lidz, Theodore, Alice R. Cornelison, Stephen Fleck, and Dorothy Terry. "The Intrafamilial Environment of Schizophrenic Patients: II. Marital Schism and Marital Skew," *The American Journal of Psychiatry* 114 (1957):241–248. [Reprinted in Bell and Vogel (1968):650–662.]

Liebow, Elliot. *Tally's Corner: A Study of Negro Streetcorner Men.* Boston: Little, Brown, 1967.

Lifton, Robert Jay, ed. *The Woman in America*. Boston: Houghton Mifflin, 1965.

Linton, Ralph. *The Study of Man*. New York: Appleton-Century-Crofts, 1936.

Lipset, Seymour M., and Reinhard Bendix. *Social Mobility in Industrial Society*. Berkeley: University of California Press, 1962.

Litwak, Eugene. "Geographical Mobility and Extended Family Cohesion," *American Sociological Review* 25 (1960a):385–394.

———. "Occupational Mobility and Extended Family Cohesion," *American Sociological Review* 25 (1960b):9–21.

Locke, Harvey J. *Predicting Adjustment in Marriage: A Comparison of a Divorced and a Happily Married Group*. New York: Holt, 1953.

———, Georges Sabagh, and Mary Margaret Thomes. "Interfaith Marriages," *Social Problems* 4 (1957):329–333.

Longmore, Laura. *The Dispossessed: A Study of the Sex-Life of Bantu Women In and Around Johannesburg*. London: Jonathan Cape, 1959.

Lu, Yi-Chuang. "Contradictory Parental Expectations in Schizophrenia: Dependence and Responsibility," *Archives of General Psychiatry* 6 (1962):219–234.

Lupri, Eugen. "Contemporary Authority Patterns in the West German Family: A Study in Cross-National Validation," *Journal of Marriage and the Family* 31 (1969): 134–144.

Maas, Henry S. "Long-Term Effects of Early Childhood Separation and Group Care," *Vita Humana* 6 (1963):34–56.

Maccoby, Eleanor E. "The Family and the Political Behavior of Youth," *Public Opinion Quarterly* 18 (1954):23–34.

———, Patricia K. Gibbs and the Staff of the Laboratory of Human Development, Harvard University. "Methods of Child-Rearing in Two Social Classes," in Martin and Stendler (1954):380–396.

MacDonald, John S., and Leatrice D. MacDonald. "Chain Migration, Ethnic Neighborhood Formation and Social Networks," *Milbank Memorial Fund Quarterly* 42 (1964):82–97.

Mace, David R. "Marriage Breakdown or Matrimonial Offense: A Clinical or Legal Approach to Divorce?" *The American University Law Review* 14 (1965):178 ff.

———, and Vera Mace. *The Soviet Family*. Garden City, New York: Doubleday, 1963.

Maretzki, Thomas W., and Hatsumi Maretzki. "Taira: An Okinawan Village," in Whiting (1963):363–540.

Marris, Peter. "Slum Clearance and Family Life in Lagos," *Human Organization* 19 (1960):123–128. [Reprinted in Geiger (1968):199–212.]

Martin, William E. and Celia Burns Stendler. *Readings in Child Development*. New York: Harcourt, Brace, 1954.

Martinson, Floyd M. "Ego Deficiency as a Factor in Marriage," *American Sociological Review* 20 (1955):161–164.

Maslow, Abraham H. *Religions, Values, and Peak Experiences*. Columbus: Ohio State University Press, 1964.

Masters, William H., and Virginia E. Johnson. *Human Sexual Response*. Boston: Little, Brown, 1966.

Mayer, John E. "Jewish-Gentile Intermarriage Patterns: A Hypothesis," *Sociology and Social Research* 45 (1961):188–195.

———. *The Disclosure of Marital Problems*. New York: Community Service Society of New York, 1966. [1966a]

————. *Other People's Marital Problems: The "Knowledgeability" of Lower and Middle Class Wives.* New York: Community Service Society of New York, 1966. [1966b]

McClelland, David C. *The Achieving Society.* Princeton: Van Nostrand, 1961.

McGuire, Carson. "Conforming, Mobile, and Divergent Families," *Marriage and Family Living* 14 (1952):109–115.

Mead, Margaret. *Coming of Age in Samoa.* New York: Mentor, 1949.

Merton, Robert K. "Intermarriage and the Social Structure: Fact and Theory," *Psychiatry* 4 (1941):361–364, 370–374. Reprinted in Goode (1964b):56–64.

Michel, Andrée Vieille. "Kinship Relations and Relationships of Proximity in French Working-Class Households," in Bell and Vogel (1960):287–294.

————. "Comparative Data Concerning the Interaction in French and American Families," *Journal of Marriage and the Family* 29 (1967):337–344.

Middleton, Russell. "Brother–Sister and Father–Daughter Marriage in Ancient Egypt," *American Sociological Review* 27 (1962):603–611.

————, and Snell Putney. "Political Expression of Adolescent Rebellion," *American Journal of Sociology* 68 (1963):527–535.

Miller, Daniel R. and Jack C. Westman. "Family Teamwork and Psychotherapy," *Family Process* 5 (1966):49–59.

Miller, Walter B. "The Corner Gang Boys Get Married," *Trans-Action* 1 (1963):10–12.

Miner, Horace M. and George De Vos. *Oasis and Casbah: Algerian Culture and Personality in Change.* Ann Arbor: University of Michigan Press, 1960. [Cited in Goode (1963):142.]

Minturn, Leigh, and John T. Hitchcock. "The Rajputs of Khalapur, India," in Whiting (1963):203–362.

Minturn, Leigh, and William W. Lambert. *Mothers of Six Cultures: Antecedents of Child Rearing.* New York: Wiley, 1964.

Monahan, Thomas P. "How Stable Are Remarriages?" *American Journal of Sociology* 58 (1952):280–288.

————. "Does Age at Marriage Matter in Divorce?" *Social Forces* 32 (1953): 81–87.

Morgan, James N., Martin H. David, Wilbur J. Cohen, and Harvey E. Brazer. *Income and Welfare in the United States.* New York: McGraw-Hill, 1962.

Morris, Pauline. *Prisoners and Their Families.* New York: Hart, 1965.

Morrow, William R., and Robert C. Wilson. "Family Relations of Bright High-Achieving and Under-Achieving High School Boys," *Child Development* 32 (1961):501–510.

Moss, J. Joel, and Ruby Gingles. "The Relationship of Personality to the Incidence of Early Marriage," *Marriage and Family Living* 21 (1959):373–377.

Mott, Paul E. *The Organization of Society.* Englewood Cliffs: Prentice-Hall, 1965.

————, Floyd C. Mann, Quinn McLoughlin, and Donald R. Warwick. *Shift Work: The Social, Psychological, and Physical Consequences.* Ann Arbor: University of Michigan Press, 1965.

Moynihan, Daniel P. *The Negro Family: The Case for National Action.* Washington, D. C.: U. S. Government Printing Office, 1965.

Muhsam, H. V. "Fertility of Polygamous Marriages," *Population Studies* 10 (1956):3–16. Cited in Goode (1963):183.

Murdock, George P. "Comparative Data on the Division of Labor by Sex," *Social Forces* 15 (1937):551–553.

————. *Social Structure.* New York: Macmillan, 1949.

————, Luther E. Woodward, and Frederick Bolman. "Sexual Behavior, What is Acceptable?" *Journal of Social Hygiene* 36 (1950):1–31. [Excerpted in Landis and Landis (1952):403–418.]

Myers, Jerome K. and Bertram H. Roberts. *Family and Class Dynamics in Mental Illness.* New York: Wiley, 1959.

Narain, D. "Growing Up in India," *Family Process* 3 (1964):127–154.

National Office of Vital Statistics. "Socioeconomic Characteristics of Persons Who Married Between January 1947 and June 1954: United States," *Vital Statistics—Special Reports* 45 (1957):337.

Nimkoff, M. F., ed. *Comparative Family Systems.* Boston: Houghton Mifflin, 1965.

————, and Russell Middleton. "Types of Family and Types of Economy," *American Journal of Sociology* 66 (1960):215–225.

Nizarali, Mamdani. "Marriage and Courtship Among the Ismailis." Unpublished term paper, International Christian University, Tokyo, 1968.

Nydegger, William F., and Corinne Nydegger. "Tarong: An Ilocos Barrio in the Philippines," in Whiting (1963):693–868.

Nye, F. Ivan. "Child Adjustment in Broken and in Unhappy Unbroken Homes," *Marriage and Family Living* 19 (1957):356–361.

————, and Lois W. Hoffman, eds. *The Employed Mother in America.* Chicago: Rand McNally, 1963.

Ogburn, William F. "The Changing Family," *The Family* 19 (1938):139–143. Reprinted in Winch and Goodman (1968):58–63.

Osmond, Marie. "Toward Monogamy: A Cross-Cultural Study of Correlates of Types of Marriage, *Social Forces* 44 (1965):8–16.

Parsons, Talcott. "Age and Sex in the Social Structure of the United States," *American Sociological Review* 7 (1942):604–616.

————, and Robert F. Bales. *Family, Socialization and Interaction Process.* Glencoe, Illinois: The Free Press, 1955.

Patai, Raphael. *Sex and Family in the Bible and the Middle East.* New York: Doubleday, 1959. [Cited in Stephens (1963):225.]

Pavela, Todd H. "An Exploratory Study of Negro-White Intermarriage in Indiana," *Journal of Marriage and the Family* 26 (1964):209–211.

Pearlin, Leonard I., and Melvin L. Kohn. "Social Class, Occupation, and Parental Values: a Cross-National Study," *American Sociological Review* 31 (1966):466–479.

Peck, Robert F., and Robert J. Havighurst. *The Psychology of Character Development.* New York: Wiley, 1960.

Pedersen, Frank A. "Relationships Between Father-Absence and Emotional Disturbance in Male Military Dependents," *Merrill-Palmer Quarterly* 12 (1966):321–331.

Peterson, Esther. "Working Women," in Lifton (1965):144–172.

Pinard, Maurice. "Marriage and Divorce Decisions and the Larger Social System: A Case Study in Social Change," *Social Forces* 44 (1966): 341–355.

Plath, David W. "Where the Family of God Is the Family: The Role of the Dead in Japanese Households," *American Anthropologist* 66 (1964):300–317. [Reprinted in Geiger (1968):27–47.]

Potts, Malcolm. "Legal Abortion in Eastern Europe," *The Eugenics Review* 59 (1967): 232–250.

Powdermaker, Hortense. *Life in Lesu.* New York: Norton, 1933. Cited in Stephens (1963):349–350.

Pratt, Lois. "Changing Patterns of Family Life in Relation to Suburban Economic Development," a paper presented to the joint meeting of the National Council on Family Relations and the International Union of Family Organizations, August 24, 1960.

Putney, Snell, and Russell Middleton. "Rebellion, Conformity and Parental Religious Ideologies," *Sociometry* 24 (1961):125–135.

Queen, Stuart A., Robert W. Habenstein, and John B. Adams. *The Family in Various Cultures.* Chicago: Lippincott, 1961.

Radcliffe-Brown, A. R., and Daryll Forde, editors. *African Systems of Kinship and Marriage.* New York: Oxford, 1950.

Rainwater, Lee. "Social Status Differences in the Family Relationships of German Men," *Marriage and Family Living* 24 (1962):12–17.

———. "Marital Sexuality in Four Cultures of Poverty," *Journal of Marriage and the Family* 26 (1964):457–466.

———. *Family Design: Marital Sexuality, Family Size and Contraception.* Chicago: Aldine, 1965.

———. "Some Aspects of Lower Class Sexual Behavior," *Journal of Social Issues* 22 (1966):96–108.

———, Richard P. Coleman, and Gerald Handel. *Workingman's Wife: Her Personality, World and Life Style.* New York: Oceana, 1959.

Rao, C. K. U. "A Study of Behavior Disorders in Children," *Indian Journal of Social Work* 4 (1943). [Cited in Narain (1964):134.]

Rapoport, Rhona, and Robert N. Rapoport. "New Light on the Honeymoon," *Human Relations* 17 (1964):33–56.

Read, Grantley Dick. *Childbirth without Fear.* New York: Harper, 1944.

Reiss, Ira L. *Premarital Sexual Standards in America.* New York: The Free Press, 1960.

———. *The Social Context of Premarital Sexual Permissiveness.* New York: Holt, Rinehart and Winston, 1967.

Ribble, Margaret A. *The Rights of Infants: Early Psychological Needs and Their Satisfaction.* New York: Columbia University Press, 1943.

Richards, A. I. "Some Types of Family Structure Amongst the Central Bantu," in Radcliffe-Brown and Forde (1950):207–251.

Riesman, David. *The Lonely Crowd.* Garden City, New York: Doubleday Anchor, 1954.

Rodman, Hyman. "Marital Relationships in a Trinidad Village," *Marriage and Family Living* 23 (1961):166–170.

Roebuck, Julian and S. Lee Spray. "The Cocktail Lounge: A Study of Heterosexual Relations in a Public Organization," *American Journal of Sociology* 72 (1967):388–395.

Rogers, Candace L., and Hope J. Leichter. "Laterality and Conflict in Kinship Ties," in Goode (1964):213–218.

Romney, Kimball, and Romaine Romney. "The Mixtecans of Juxtlahuaca, Mexico," in Whiting (1963):541–692.

Rosen, Bernard C. "Family Structure and Achievement Motivation," *American Sociological Review* 26 (1961):574–584.

———. "Socialization and Achievement Motivation in Brazil," *American Sociological Review* 27 (1962):612–624.

———, and Roy d'Andrade. "The Psychosocial Origins of Achievement Motivation," *Sociometry* 22 (1959):185–218.

Rosenberg, Bernard, and Joseph Bensman. "Sexual Patterns in Three Ethnic Subcultures of an American Underclass," *The Annals of the American Academy of Political and Social Science* 376 (1968):61–75.

Rosenberg, Morris. "The Dissonant Religious Context and Emotional Disturbance," *American Journal of Sociology* 68 (1962):1–10. Also published in Rosenberg (1965): 64–81.

————. *Society and the Adolescent Self-Image.* Princeton: Princeton University Press, 1965.

Rosenfeld, Henry. "Processes of Structural Change Within the Arab Village Extended Family," *American Anthropologist* 60 (1958):1127–1139. [Cited in Goode (1963): 128.]

Rosenmayr, Leopold, and Eva Köckeis. "Propositions for a Sociological Theory of Aging and the Family," *International Social Science Journal* 15 (1963):410–426.

Rosenthal, Erich. "Studies of Jewish Intermarriage in the United States," reprinted from the *American Jewish Yearbook* 64 (1963).

Rosser, Colin, and Christopher Harris. *The Family and Social Change: A Study of Family and Kinship in a South Wales Town.* London: Routledge and Kegan Paul, 1965.

Rossi, Alice S. "Naming Children in Middle-Class Families," *American Sociological Review* 39 (1965):499–513.

Roth, Julius, and Robert F. Peck. "Social Class and Social Mobility Factors Related to Marital Adjustment," *American Sociological Review* 16 (1951):478–487.

Roy, Prodipto. "Maternal Employment and Adolescent Roles: Rural-Urban Differentials," *Marriage and Family Living* 23 (1961):340–349.

Royal Commission on Population. *Report of the Royal Commission on Population.* London: Her Majesty's Stationery Office, 1949. [Cited in Rosser and Harris (1965).]

Safilios-Rothschild, Constantina. "A Comparison of Power Structure and Marital Satisfaction in Urban Greek and French Families," *Journal of Marriage and the Family* 29 (1967):345–352.

————. "Good and Bad Girls in Modern Greek Movies," *Journal of Marriage and the Family* 30 (1968):527–531.

Sampson, Harold, Sheldon L. Messinger, Robert D. Towne and David Ross, Florine Livson, Mary-Dee Bowers, Lester Cohen, Kate S. Dorst. "The Mental Hospital and Marital Family Ties," *Social Problems* 9 (1961):141–155.

Sampson, Harold, Sheldon L. Messinger, and Robert D. Towne. "Family Processes and Becoming a Mental Patient," *American Journal of Sociology* 68 (1962):88–96.

Schneider, David M. and George C. Homans. "Kinship Terminology and the American Kinship System," *American Anthropologist* 57 (1955):1194–1208.

Schorr, Alvin L. "Problems in the ADC Program," *Social Work* (1960):3–15.

Schvaneveldt, Jay D. "The Development of a Film Test for the Measurement of Perceptions toward Maternal Overprotection." Unpublished Ph.D. dissertation, University of Michigan, 1964. [Cited by Duvall (1965):181.]

Scott, John Finley. "The American College Sorority: Its Role in Class and Ethnic Endogamy," *American Sociological Review* 30 (1965): 514–527.

Sears, Robert R., Eleanor E. Maccoby, and Harry Levin. *Patterns of Child Rearing.* Evanston: Row, Peterson, 1957.

Seggar, John F. and Harry K. Schwarzweller. "Kinship Involvement and Social Psychological Adjustment of Rural Kentucky Migrants to the Ohio Valley," *Ohio Valley Sociologist,* ca. 1964:26–27.

Shanas, Ethel, Peter Townsend, Dorothy Wedderburn, Henning Friis, Poul Milhoj, and Jan Stehouwer. *Old People in Three Industrial Societies.* New York: Atherton, 1968.

Shuttleworth, Frank K. "A Biosocial and Developmental Theory of Male and Female Sexuality," *Marriage and Family Living* 21 (1959):163–170.

Siddiqui, H. R. "Patterns of Help at the Time of Crisis," unpublished paper analyzing data from the Detroit Area Study under Professors Ronald Freedman and David Goldberg. Ann Arbor: University of Michigan Department of Sociology, 1962.

Siegel, Alberta E., Lois M. Stolz, Ethel A. Hitchcock, and Jean Adamson. "Dependence and Independence in the Children of Working Mothers," *Child Development* 30 (1959):533–546.

Silverman, William and Reuben Hill. "Task Allocation in Marriage in the United States and Belgium," *Journal of Marriage and the Family* 29 (1967):353–359.

Simpson, Richard L. "Parental Influence, Anticipatory Socialization and Social Mobility," *American Sociological Review* 27 (1962):517–522.

Slater, Eliot, and Moya Woodside. *Patterns of Marriage: A Study of Marriage Relationships in the Urban Working Classes.* London: Cassell, 1951.

Slater, Philip E. "On Social Regression," *American Sociological Review* 28 (1963): 339–364.

Smith, Charles E. "Negro–White Intermarriage: Forbidden Sexual Union," *Journal of Sex Research* 2 (1966):169–177.

Sonne, John C. and Geraldine Lincoln. "Heterosexual Co-Therapy Team Experiences During Family Therapy," *Family Process* 4 (1965):177–197.

Speck, Ross V. "Psychotherapy of the Social Network of a Schizophrenic Family," *Family Process* 6 (1967):208–214.

Spiegel, John P. "The Resolution of Role Conflict within the Family," in Milton Greenblatt, Daniel J. Levinson, and Richard H. Williams, editors, *The Patient and the Mental Hospital,* Glencoe, Illinois: The Free Press (1957):545–564. [Reprinted in Bell and Vogel (1968):391–411.]

Spiro, Melford E. *Kibbutz: Venture in Utopia.* Cambridge: Harvard University Press, 1956.

Spitz, Rene A. "Hospitalism: A Follow-up Report," in Otto Fenichel, editor, *The Psycho-Analytic Study of the Child* 2 (1946):113–117. New York: International Universities Press.

Spock, Benjamin. *The Pocket Book of Baby and Child Care.* New York: Pocket Books, 1947.

Stendler, Celia B. "Sixty Years of Child Training Practices," *Journal of Pediatrics* 36 (1950):122–134. [Cited in Vincent (1951):204.]

Stephens, William N. *The Family in Cross-Cultural Perspective.* New York: Holt, Rinehart and Winston, 1963.

Stolz, Lois M. *Father Relations of War-Born Children.* Stanford: Stanford University Press, 1954.

Straus, Murray. "Work Roles and Financial Responsibility in the Socialization of Farm, Fringe, and Town Boys," *Rural Sociology* 27 (1962):257–274.

Strauss, Anselm. "Strain and Harmony in American-Japanese War-Bride Marriages," *Marriage and Family Living* 16 (1954):99–106.

Streib, Gordon F., and Wayne E. Thompson. "The Older Person in a Family Context," in Clark Tibbitt, ed. *The Social Gerontology Handbook.* Chicago: University of Chicago Press, 1960:447–488.

Stycos, J. Mayone. *Family and Fertility in Puerto Rico: A Study of the Lower Income Group.* New York: Columbia University Press, 1955.

————, and Kurt W. Back. *The Control of Human Fertility in Jamaica.* Ithaca: Cornell University Press, 1964.

Sundberg, N. D., and L. E. Tyler. *Clinical Psychology.* New York: Appleton-Century-Crofts, 1962.

Sussman, Marvin B. "The Help Pattern in the Middle-Class Family," *American Sociological Review* 18 (1953):22–28. [Referred to as 1953a.]

————. "Parental Participation in Mate Selection and Its Effect upon Family Continuity," *Social Forces* 32 (1953):76–81. [Referred to as 1953b.]

————. "The Isolated Nuclear Family: Fact or Fiction," *Social Problems* 6 (1959): 333–340.

Suttles, Gerald D. "Vigilante Peer Groups and the Defended Neighborhood," in Suttles' book entitled *Cultural and Structural Issues in the Study of Territoriality.* Chicago: University of Chicago Press, 1971.

Talmon, Yonina. "Social Change and Family Structure," *International Social Science Journal* 14 (1962):468–487.

————. "Mate Selection in Collective Settlements," *American Sociological Review* 29 (1964):491–508.

————. "The Family in a Revolutionary Movement—The Case of the Kibbutz in Israel," in Nimkoff (1965):259–286. [Referred to as 1965a.]

————. "Sex-Role Differentiation in an Equalitarian Society," in Thomas E. Lasswell, John H. Burma, and Sidney H. Aronson, eds., *Life in Society.* Chicago: Scott, Foresman, 1965:144–155. [Referred to as 1965b.]

Tamaki, Hajime. *Nihon ni okeru Daikazoku no Hokai* (The Destruction of Large Families in Japan). Tokyo: Toko Soin, 1959. [Cited by Watanabe, 1968.]

Tartler, Rudolf. *Das Alter in der modernen Gesellschaft.* Stuttgart, 1961. [Cited by Rosenmayr and Köckeis (1963):417–418.]

Thomas, John L. *The American Catholic Family.* Englewood Cliffs: Prentice-Hall, 1956.

Thomas, William I., and Florian Znaniecki. *The Polish Peasant in Europe and America.* New York: Dover, 1958.

Thorpe, Alice C., and Irma H. Gross. *How Homes Are Used on Farms and in Small Cities.* East Lansing: Michigan State University Agricultural Experiment Station, 1955.

Tien, H. Yuan. "The Social Mobility/Fertility Hypothesis Reconsidered: An Empirical Study," *American Sociological Review* 26 (1961): 247–257.

Tiller, Per Olav. "Father Absence in Sailor Families," in Anderson (1957), vol. 2:115–137.

Timasheff, Nicholas S. "The Attempt to Abolish the Family in Russia," in *The Great Retreat.* New York: Dutton, 1946:192–203. [Reprinted in Bell and Vogel (1960): 55–63.]

Towne, Robert D., Sheldon L. Messinger, and Harold Sampson. "Schizophrenia and the Marital Family: Accommodations to Symbiosis," *Family Process* 1 (1962):304–318.

Townsend, Peter. *The Family Life of Old People: An Inquiry in East London.* Glencoe: The Free Press, 1957.

Udry, J. Richard. "Marital Instability by Race, Sex, Education, and Occupation Using 1960 Census Data," *American Journal of Sociology* 72 (1966):203–209.

Vincent, Clark E. "Trends in Infant Care Ideas," *Child Development* 22 (1951):199–209.

————. *Unmarried Mothers.* New York: The Free Press of Glencoe, 1961.

Vogel, Ezra F. "The Democratization of Family Relations in Japanese Urban Society," *Asian Survey* 1 (1961). Cited in Goode (1963). [Referred to as 1961a.]

———. "The Go-Between in a Developing Society: The Case of the Japanese Marriage Arranger," *Human Organization* 20 (1961):112–120. [Referred to as 1961b.]

———. *Japan's New Middle Class: The Salary Man and His Family in a Tokyo Suburb.* Berkeley: University of California Press, 1963.

———, and Norman W. Bell. "The Emotionally Disturbed Child as the Family Scapegoat," in Bell and Vogel (1960):382–397.

———, and Suzanne H. Vogel. "Family Security, Personal Immaturity, and Emotional Health in a Japanese Sample," *Marriage and Family Living* 23 (1961):161–166.

Waller, Willard. "The Rating and Dating Complex," *American Sociological Review* 2 (1937):727–734.

———. *The Family: A Dynamic Interpretation.* New York: Cordon, 1938.

Watanabe, Eimi. "The Large Family System in Shirakawa-Mura," unpublished paper. Mitaka: International Christian University, 1968.

Waters, Elinor, and Vaughn J. Crandall. "Social Class and Observed Maternal Behavior from 1940 to 1960," *Child Development* 35 (1964):1021–1032.

Watson, John B. *Psychological Care of Infant and Child.* New York: Norton, 1928.

Weinberg, S. Kirson. *Incest Behavior.* New York: Citadel Press, 1955.

Westoff, Charles F., Robert G. Potter, Jr., and Philip C. Sagi. *The Third Child: A Study in the Prediction of Fertility.* Princeton: Princeton University Press, 1963.

———, and Elliot G. Mishler. *Family Growth in Metropolitan America.* Princeton: Princeton University Press, 1961.

Whelpton, Pascal K., Arthur A. Campbell, and John E. Patterson. *Fertility and Family Planning in the United States.* Princeton: Princeton University Press, 1966.

Whiting, Beatrice B. *Six Cultures: Studies of Child Rearing.* New York: Wiley, 1963.

Whiting, John W. M. "Cultural and Sociological Influences on Development," in *Growth and Development of the Child in His Setting.* Maryland: Maryland Child Growth and Development Institute, 1959. [Cited in Minturn and Lambert (1964):169.]

Whyte, William Foote. "A Slum Sex Code," *American Journal of Sociology* 44 (1943): 24–31.

Whyte, William H., Jr. "The Wife Problem," *Life,* January 7, 1952:32–48. [Reprinted in Winch, McGinnis and Barringer (1962):111–124.]

———. *The Organization Man.* Garden City, Long Island: Doubleday Anchor, 1957.

Wiegand, Elizabeth. *Use of Time by Full-time and Part-time Home-makers in Relation to Home Management.* Ithaca: Cornell University Agricultural Experiment Station, 1954.

Wilensky, Harold L. "The Uneven Distribution of Leisure: The Impact of Economic Growth on 'Free Time'," *Social Problems* 9 (1961):32–56.

Willmott, Peter, and Michael Young. *Family and Class in a London Suburb.* London: Routledge and Kegan Paul, 1960.

Wilson, Monica. "Nyakyusa Kinship," in Radcliffe-Brown and Forde (1950):111–139.

Winch, Robert F. *The Modern Family.* New York: Holt, Rinehart and Winston, 1952.

———, and Louis Wolf Goodman. *Selected Studies in Marriage and the Family.* New York: Holt, Rinehart and Winston, 1968, third edition.

———, and Scott A. Greer. "The Uncertain Relation between Early Marriage and Marital Stability: a Quest for Relevant Data," *Acta Sociologica* 8 (1964):83–97.

———. "Urbanism, Ethnicity, and Extended Familism," *Journal of Marriage and the Family* 30 (1968):40–45.

Winch, Robert F., Robert McGinnis, and Herbert R. Barringer. *Selected Studies in Marriage and the Family.* New York: Holt, Rinehart and Winston, 1962.

Work, Henry H. An unpublished paper on adoptive families presented to the American Academy of Pediatrics, summarized by Ursula Vils in *The Japan Times,* January 25, 1968, under the headline "Adopted Children Said More Likely to Wind Up in Psychiatrist's Office."

Wynne, Lyman C., Irving M. Ryckoff, Juliana Day, and Stanley I. Hirsch. "Pseudo-Mutuality in the Family Relations of Schizophrenics," *Psychiatry* 21 (1958):205–220.

Yaukey, David. *Fertility Differences in a Modernizing Country.* Princeton: Princeton University Press, 1961. [Cited in Goode (1963):113.]

Young, Michael, and Peter Willmott. *Family and Kinship in East London.* Glencoe, Illinois: The Free Press, 1957.

Zelditch, Morris, Jr. "Role Differentiation in the Nuclear Family: A Comparative Study," in Parsons and Bales (1955):307–351.

Zimmerman, Carle C. and Lucius F. Cervantes. *Successful American Families.* New York: Pageant, 1960.

AUTHOR INDEX

649

SUBJECT INDEX

Abortion
  availability of, 97
    legality, 97, 374
    revolutions and, 226, 229
  contraception failure and, 374
  economic resources and, 87
  family growth and, 374
  as family-planning method, 374
  legalization of, 97, 374
  for Negro women, 87
  occupational status and, 53
  parental control of, 221
  as population growth control, 97
  premarital pregnancy and, 87
  as public health service, 97
  religious attitudes on, 115
  social change and, 221
  taboos against, 115
  for white women, 87
Acculturation
  colonization and, 237–38
  See also Migration; Social change
Achievement motivation
  age roles and, 471–72
  birth order and, 393, 471–72
  divorce and, 600
  family size and, 391–92, 393
  occupational status and, 71, 443–46
    parental warmth and, 407
    in polygyny, 446
    punishment and, 412
    range of parental response and, 419–20
    working mothers, 408
  parent-child relationship and, 407–12,
      443–46
    authoritarianism and, 411, 412, 445
    divorce and, 600
    maternal need for, 411
    modeling and, 408
  peer groups and, 149
  sibling relationships and, 471–72
  socialization and, 407
  See also Social mobility
Adolescence
  military conscription creation of, 92
  occupational status and, 71, 119
  parental expectations and, 411
  rebellion in, 221, 229, 230–31
  sexual drives in, 340
  See also Children; Parent-child relation-
      ships; Premarital behavior; Sociali-
      zation of children
Adoption, 374–77
  in agricultural societies, 6, 376–77
  in apprenticeship system, 120
  in blue-collar families, 65
  by boyless couples, 376–77

by childless couples, 375–77
child's age and, 377
child's welfare and, 374–75
economic resources and, 42–43, 401
into extended families, 42–43, 375
in family expansion, 374–77
farming out children as quasi-, 377
by grandparents, 375, 467
of illegitimate children, 375
incest taboos and, 298
infertility and, 375–76
inheritance and, 6
within kinship system, 65, 216, 375, 377,
    399–401
occupational status and, 65
of orphans, 375, 609
parent-child relationships and, 375–76,
    377
psychiatric problems in, 376
revolution and, 228
social pressure for, 148
of surplus children, 377, 378
of unwanted children, 375
in utopian communities, 154
in white-collar families, 65
Adultery, see Extramarital affairs; Pre-
    marital intercourse
"Adversary" system of divorce, 99–100
Advice columns, 62
Affection
  in cousin relationships, 215
  in grandparent-grandchild relationship,
      467, 468
  kinship system interaction patterns and,
      189–90
    in industrial society, 189, 190
    migration and, 251, 252
    practical help and, 193–94
    primitive societies, 183–84
  nurturance and, 406–407
  in parent-child relationship, 189, 190, 406
  See also Mate selection
Affluence, 32–35
  child-rearing and, 10, 34
  dating and, 319
  family formation and, 33
  family growth and, 33–34
  family stability and, 34–35
  leisure activities and, 141
  polygyny and, 42
  sexual division of labor and, 435
  sexual freedom and, 33
  women's status and, 34, 41, 435
  See also Economic resources; Poverty
Age roles, 15–17, 457–80
  in agricultural societies, 15
  descent groups and, 16–17

Deviant behavior
  corporate intervention and, 32
  family friends homogeneity and, 151
  kinship system social control of, 202,
    205–206
  state interest in, 93
  See also Role impairment *and specific
    forms of deviant behavior*
Discipline, 419–21
  of adopted children, 376
  in blue-collar families, 66–69
    autocratic nature of, 69
    emotional rejection, 67, 69
    masturbation taboos, 68
    obedience training, 66–67, 69
    parental erraticism in, 69
    parental socialization, 69
    physical coercion, 66, 69
  consistency in, 420
  economic resources and, 40, 398–99
  in extended families, 504–505, 516
  family size and, 398–99
  in fraternal families, 501, 502
  in nuclear families, 513–15
  occupation status and, 66, 69
    control policies in, 69, 71–72
    parental consistency in, 69
    parental socialization and, 69
    physical coercion, 66, 69
    punishment, 66
    reasoning, 66, 69
    rebellion in, 70, 71–72
  positive sanctions in, 419, 420–21
  physical punishment, 66, 69, 409, 420–
    21
  poverty and, 40
  range of parental response in, 419–20,
    421
  reasoning in, 66, 69, 420–21
  as reinforcement, 419, 421
  in white-collar families, 66–69
    equalitarian nature of, 69
    parental consistency, 69
    parental socialization, 69
    permissiveness in, 68
    psychological methods of, 66, 69
  See also Child-rearing; Punishment; So-
    cialization of children
Displacement trauma, 476–77, 483–86
  of first born child, 476–77
  in polygyny, 483, 484–85, 486
Division of labor
  biological factors in, 434–35
  in double-couple living, 543, 544, 545
  family decision making and, 430–31
  family size and, 393, 394
  first child accession crisis and, 378,
    380–81
  in hunting and gathering societies, 167
  in industrial society, 7
  on kibbutzim, 158
  marital role socialization and, 354, 361,
    362
  mate selection and, 284, 285
  See also Sexual roles *and specific types
    of families*
Divorce, 597–615

affluence and, 35
alcoholism and, 599
alternatives to, 116–17, 221
anomie and, 137–39
betrothal financial transactions and, 332
betrothal termination vs. 334–35
in blue collar families, 59, 65
child-bearing and, 159, 160, 383, 384
as conflict resolution mode, 597–99
of cross-cousin marriages, 182–83
economic resources for, 35, 59, 83, 137,
  159, 234
of educational dropouts, 79–80
excommunication and, 116
extramarital affairs and, 346–47, 557–58
family friends and, 151, 153
family instability expectations and, 614–
  15
family restructuring after, 599–604
  father-child contact, 458, 602–604
  husband-wife contact in, 601–602,
    603–604
  internal coalition formation, 599
  mother-child relationship, 599–601
of graduate school students, 80
in inter-caste mixed marriages, 303
in Islam, 107, 108, 116
kibbutzim social control of, 159, 160
kinship systems and, 186, 210
levirate and, 182
masculine privlege of, 425
modernization and, 224
mother-in-law/daughter-in-law   conflict
  and, 363
of newlyweds, 355
occupational status and, 59, 65
premarital intercourse and, 346
premarital pregnancy and, 383
premature marriage and, 325
racial differences in, 83
reconciliation in, 100, 101, 602
remarriage and, 313–14
revolution and, 224, 228–29, 231
role impairment recovery and, 593
role reallocation in, 604–13
  child promotion, 606–607
  to grandparents, 607–608
  new spouse recruitment, 608–609
  quasi-families in, 609–610
  remarriage in, 608
  resident parent overloading, 605–606,
    609
secular wedding and, 336
serial polygamy and, 495
social change and, 221
social collapse and, 234
social control of, 159, 160
social mobility and, 274
social taboo on, 137, 139
sororal polygyny and, 487–88
state control of, 94, 98–101
  "adversary" system, 99–100
  annulments, 98
  child support payments, 101
  compulsory waiting periods in, 100
  grounds for, 98–99, 100, 101
  remarriage and, 98, 101

housekeeping, 532–33, 534
sexual specialization of, 533
wife's employment and, 531–33
economic resources of, 43
educational systems emancipation of, 124–25
in fraternal families, 497–98, 502
friends as quasi-kin in, 217
in hunting and gathering socities, 17
in-law conflicts in, 209–10
in industrial society, 19–20
intergenerational conflict in, 536
neolocality and, 171, 249
nomadic, 242–43
parent-child relationship in, 515–18
affection in, 515
emancipation and, 521
employment of children and, 536
independence in, 536
maternal warmth, 515
mother-substitutes in, 518
supplementary control agents in, 517–18
parent death and, 165
pre-polygynous family as, 482–83
sibling relationships in, 514, 515, 518
social collapse and, 234, 235
social mobility of, 273
urban environment emancipation of, 138
See also Marital power structure; Migration *and specific nuclear families and relationships*
Nurturance, *see* Children; Parent-child relationship

Obedience training
occupational status and, 66–67, 69
social control and, 513
Occupational mobility, *see* Achievement motivation; Occupational status; Social mobility
Occupational status, 51–72
abortion and, 53
achievement motivation of children and, 71, 119
adolescence and, 119
adoption and, 65
child-bearing and, 64–65
child rearing and, 66–70
academic expectations, 68
control policies, 69
emotional rejection, 67, 69
masturbation taboos, 68
maternal anxiety, 68
modesty training, 68
obedience training, 66–67, 69
parental consistency, 69
parental socialization and, 69
physical coercion in, 66, 69
psychological methods of, 66, 69
punishment, 66
self-control training, 66–67, 69
television-consumption, 68–69
toilet-training, 68
weaning, 69
confidantes and, 62, 64

contraception and, 53
discipline and, 66, 69
control policies, 69, 71–72
parental consistency in, 69
parental socialization and, 69
physical coercion, 66, 69
punishment, 66
reasoning, 66, 69
rebellion and, 70, 71–72
divorce and, 59
engagement period and, 53
family crises and, 59–64
communication in, 64
marital dissolution, 59
newspaper advice columns, 62
physical nature of, 60, 61
psychological, 60, 61
response to, 61–64
social service agencies in, 61
type of, 60–61
wife's confidantes in, 62, 64
father-child relationship, 71–72, 86
achievement motivation, 71–72
childhood memories, 71
juvenile delinquency, 71–72
mate-selection and, 304
incest and, 56
on kibbutzim, 158
kinship system interaction and, 199–200
migration and, 249, 252
practical help, 192, 193
psychological help, 199–200
marital dissolution and, 59
marital interaction patterns and, 20–21, 53–58
emotional support, 57
extramarital intercourse, 55
"informative companionship," 57
premarital peer groups and, 56
sexual roles and, 56–57
sexual satisfaction, 54–56
sexual segregation, 56–57, 455
marital power structure and, 57–58
marital satisfaction and, 54–56, 306
marital segregation and, 56–57, 455
masturbation and, 51, 68
mate selection and, 53, 304
migration and, 245, 246, 249, 252
mixed mariages by, 305–306, 526–27
inter-faith, 307–308
marital power structure in, 305, 306, 526–527
marital satisfaction, 306
nomadism and, 242, 243
parent-child relationship and, 60–61, 70–72
achievement motivation, 71
childhood memories, 71
communication in, 70, 72
control policies in, 69
discipline method and, 66, 69
educational expectations, 68
emotional closeness, 71
forms of address in, 70–71
juvenile delinquency and, 71–72
maternal rejection in, 68
parental control in, 69, 71–72